FOURTH EDITION

UNDERSTANDING CONTEMPORARY CHINA

EDITED BY
ROBERT E. GAMER

LYNNE RIENNER PUBLISHERS
BOULDER
LONDON

Published in the United States of America in 2012 by
Lynne Rienner Publishers, Inc.
1800 30th Street, Boulder, Colorado 80301
www.rienner.com

and in the United Kingdom by
Lynne Rienner Publishers, Inc.
3 Henrietta Street, Covent Garden, London WC2E 8LU

Library of Congress Cataloging-in-Publication Data
Understanding contemporary China / edited by Robert E. Gamer. — 4th ed.
p. cm. — (Understanding: Introductions to the States and Regions of the Contemporary World)
Includes bibliographical references and index.
ISBN 978-1-58826-844-0 (alk. paper)
1. China. I. Gamer, Robert E., 1938–
DS706.U47 2012
951—dc23
2011052684

British Cataloguing in Publication Data
A Cataloguing in Publication record for this book
is available from the British Library.

Printed and bound in the United States of America

The paper used in this publication meets the requirements of the American National Standard for Permanence of Paper for Printed Library Materials Z39.48-1992.

5 4 3 2 1

UNDERSTANDING

Introductions to the States and Regions of the Contemporary World
Donald L. Gordon, series editor

Understanding Contemporary Africa, 5th edition
edited by April A. Gordon and Donald L. Gordon

Understanding Contemporary Asia Pacific
edited by Katherine Palmer Kaup

Understanding the Contemporary Caribbean, 2nd edition
edited by Richard S. Hillman and Thomas J. D'Agostino

Understanding Contemporary China, 4th edition
edited by Robert E. Gamer

Understanding Contemporary India, 2nd edition
edited by Neil DeVotta

Understanding Contemporary Latin America, 4th edition
edited by Richard S. Hillman

Understanding the Contemporary Middle East, 3rd edition
edited by Jillian Schwedler and Deborah J. Gerner

Understanding Contemporary Russia
edited by Michael L. Bressler

Contents

Illustrations

Maps

Tables

Figures

Photographs

Preface

China is about superlatives. It has the largest population, the fastest growing economy, and the most cell phones, Internet users, new car sales, and air pollution of any country in the world. It is producing high-speed trains, freeways, urban sprawl, supercomputers, foreign aid projects, treasury surpluses, and much else at stunning speed; and the gap between rich and poor is growing every day. In China, landscapes and lifestyles can change almost overnight. But other aspects have endured for millennia. So staying abreast of "contemporary" requires both perspective and agility. For this fourth edition of *Understanding Contemporary China*, this has meant a lot of new data to gather and new books and articles to cite, along with thoughtful assessment of what endures amid all this rapidly accelerating change within a fragile world economy. When we began this project in 1996, we were well aware that creating a coherent, readable introduction to contemporary China that stays contemporary would require a combination of talents. That is why we sought out distinguished scholars from a variety of disciplines with strong publication records who go to China frequently or live there, and who teach undergraduate courses. Those scholars have created a single text with readable chapters that introduce China from the perspectives of a number of disciplines. In each edition they have been sure-footed about tracking the most important current issues and identifying what has changed and what has not.

As teachers, our authors also recognize the importance of paying attention to the needs of our readers, especially in introductory courses. In this book, we begin by assuming our readers want to know about China in some depth, but that they likely are not familiar with the people, places, and events being discussed. Each of us also knows that many of our readers are not familiar with our own particular disciplines, so we avoid or explain jargon. And we have taken great care to make sure that each of our chapters blends with the others to form a coherent whole. Because the chapters are designed to be complete in themselves, they can be assigned individually. But although they focus on different topics, they are tied to complementary themes, which are introduced in Chapter 1. This makes the book useful for courses offering broad multidisciplinary coverage of China, as well as courses that approach it from the perspective of a particular discipline. For the latter, it offers a convenient introduction to aspects of China beyond the focus of the course.

The chapters are highlighted with facts, narratives, experiences, and observations derived from the authors' close personal contacts with China; we share an interest in the lives of ordinary people. Each chapter also contains a bibliography of books and articles that we believe are important contributions. The many new sources in this fourth edition make the bibliographies especially useful for students and instructors who want to look further into particular topics. It lets one home in immediately on a great deal of current, authoritative source material.

Some of the topics covered—geography, history, politics, economy, family and kinship, religion, literature, and international relations—are essential components of any introduction to China. Others—such as the environment, the roles and problems of women, popular culture, sexuality, demographics, and urbanization—are important topics that are often ignored in introductory works. All chapters give historical overviews along with discussions of the most current events and the problems and prospects facing China in the future.

Chapter 1 introduces several traditions, both within China and in the West, whose interactions are responsible both for China's progress and for many of its problems. And it presents several challenges that China faces as it becomes increasingly absorbed into the global community. These are all deliberated in subsequent chapters. The next two chapters introduce China's geography and long history. Readers will find some useful reference points here to which they can return when reading later chapters of the book: the table on how to pronounce Chinese terms in Chapter 1, the maps in Chapters 2 and 3, and the dynastic chart in Chapter 3.

The rest of the book covers topics of major interest regarding China today. Chapters 4 and 5 discuss the evolution of China's political institutions and entrepreneurial traditions and how they interface with current reforms. Chapter 6 covers four topics of special concern to China: Hong Kong, Taiwan, Tibet, and the large number of overseas Chinese. Chapter 7 gives an overview of China's foreign policy. The rapid political and economic changes in today's China have contributed to and been affected by population growth, urbanization, and environmental problems—the topics of Chapters 8 and 9.

Then we turn to an examination of China's society. Chapter 10 looks at China's family structure and the rapid changes taking place in sexual behavior and family relations, especially in urban China. Far more than in most countries, thanks to Confucianism, the family plays a central role in economic relations and political ideology, which makes these changes especially consequential. Chapter 11 focuses on how women are involved and affected, both positively and negatively, as the economy grows. Chapter 12 provides a historical overview of how China's indigenous religions and those of nearby neighbors shaped Chinese society and how these traditions are being challenged by Christianity, communism, and consumerism. Chapter 13 discusses how China's literature and performance art have always had their roots in popular culture and explores what people are reading, watching on television and at the movies, and exploring on the Internet today. This chapter also elucidates the rapid changes taking place in contemporary China's social and family life.

The closing chapter, on trends and prospects, returns to the challenges introduced in Chapter 1 and points briefly to how they have been discussed throughout the book and how they may play out in the near future. It gives alternative scenarios of where China's reforms may lead and also indicates some outcomes that are unlikely to occur.

* * *

First and foremost, I wish to thank my eleven coauthors for their four rounds of writing, rewriting, and editing. They come from both sides of the Pacific and from a variety of disciplines. Yet from the beginning they have been symbiotic in analyzing trends; in this edition, those include the proliferation of high-speed trains, superhighways, cars, and motorcycles; the vast westward-moving public works and speculative real estate projects; urban sprawl and migration to cities; the new entrepreneurs; growing gaps in income, benefits, education, gender balance, and wealth; labor unrest; unemployment, housing, and other middle-class anxieties; the Internet and cell phones enabling greater independence and public protest; fears of a hard landing for the booming highly leveraged economy; mounting environmental challenges; rising Chinese tourism; deepening connections with Taiwan; competition over the South China Sea and oil; China's growing presence in Africa, Latin America, and the Middle East; nationalism, heightened public security, and military modernization; "new left" ideology; and the moves to increase domestic consumption and make China more competitive in changeable global markets. Those of us who do not live in China visit it frequently for our research; we are hands-on China watchers. Donald and April Gordon created the format for this series with their *Understanding Contemporary Africa*. It has worked out well.

It is easy to see changes in Shanghai and Beijing and Hong Kong. To see change in the interior provinces of China takes more effort. Before each new edition of this book, I have made visits to parts of China that are on the outer reaches of modernization. In 2007, for the third edition, my wife and I traveled long stretches of the former Silk Road—from Kaifeng in Shanxi province to Kashgar in the far west and then around southern Tibet, returning to Beijing on the world's highest stretch of railway, exactly a year after the day it opened. For this fourth edition, we traveled to a number of Dong, Miao, Zhuang, Yao, Gao, and She ethnic minority villages in Guangxi, Guizhou, and Fujian provinces. That required travel on local buses, in vans, and on the backs of motorcycles along rutted mud roadbeds merging into the amazing new networks of toll superhighways and high-speed trains (including the Wenzhou overpass where two trains crashed three months later) that were just arriving to challenge traditional ways of life. I wish to thank the many people from all walks of life we met on these trips. For this latest trip, Winnie Lu, Ivan Cheung Hoi Fung, David Liao De Ming, Billy Zhang, Grace Hui Li, Michael de Golyer, Odalia Wong, Simon-Hoey HaoRan Lee, Jerry Wang Ke Zhong, Jiang Yinghan, Chen Xuding, and Shang Zehua offered special assistance and hospitality. They help keep the book focused on how life affects everyday people.

My interest in the other side of the Pacific, in scholarship, and in independent travel began early. In 1926, my parents sailed around the world for seven and a half months on the Ryndam, as faculty on the first university afloat. That pioneer voyage stopped in Cuba, Japan, China, Siam, Singapore, Java, Ceylon, India, Ethiopia, Egypt, Palestine, Turkey, Malta, Greece, Italy, Algeria, Spain, Norway, Sweden, Scotland, and England. Word spread of its itinerary. At every stop this unusual boatload of 500 US students with their faculty of forty-five (including luminaries like the former governor of Kansas Henry J. Allen editing the ship's newspaper and the national president of Phi Beta Kappa) was greeted and hosted by high dignitaries. They arrived in Shanghai in November 1926, at the height of Chiang Kai-shek's Northern Offensive. My father was in the crowd at Le Bourget airport in May 1927 to watch Charles Lindbergh land *The Spirit of St. Louis*. My parents' tales about this adventurous voyage fascinated me. I read with excitement and envy Richard Henry Dana's *Two Years Before the Mast*, Thor Heyerdahl's *Kon Tiki*, James Hilton's *Lost Horizon*, and Charles Lindbergh's *We*.

My father was a political science professor who received his PhD at the University of Illinois, and my aunt was head of the Romance Language division at the University of Chicago. They and their academic friends—among them Mulford Q. Sibley, Hans Morgenthau, Quincy Wright, and A. J. Muste—traveled widely, had classical educations that broke through the narrowing disciplinary boundaries of the twentieth century, had historical perspective and cultural sensitivity, and were passionate about addressing the great moral issues of the day.

During my freshman year in college, I had my own first independent travel adventure, crossing the Atlantic on Holland America Line's *Waterman* to spend the summer living with a family in Torino and journeying around Italy with the President's Scholarship of the Experiment in International Living.

During my junior Washington Semester at American University, I had another adventure, working in the office of Senator Kenneth Keating of New York. Then three summers as an interpretive park ranger in Mesa Verde National Park during the Wetherill Mesa excavations gave me the chance to closely engage archaeologists as they analyzed their finds. And I studied at Monmouth College with Samuel P. Thompson, Charles Speel, and Madge Sanmann. All this helped me develop a broad curiosity, which Brown University's innovative approach let me indulge while in their PhD program. Under the guidance of Lea Williams, Whitney Trow Perkins, and Guy Howard Dodge, I was introduced to China from the perspectives of history, international relations, and political theory. C. Peter Magrath and Elmer Cornwell were valued teachers and mentors.

I became the first US lecturer at the University of Singapore—the predecessor to the National University of Singapore—during the time of Singapore's expulsion from Malaysia and Konfrontasi with Indonesia, at the height of China's Cultural Revolution and the war in Vietnam. My four years in their Political Science Department allowed me to interact frequently with individuals at every level of government, the diplomatic corps, business, and education and to host many foreign visitors sent to campus by government ministries or the US Embassy. Teaching rounds of a shared course on political development with David Gibbons and Joseph P. L. Chiang provided much intellectual stimulation. For my research I had unfettered access to the files of the Housing and Development Board. My students, colleagues, neighbors, friends, and everyone else around me were primarily Chinese. I was also fortunate to marry a Singaporean, May Lim Tay, who has been a fellow sojourner, interpreter, and good companion on adventures ever since. This immersion into Singapore and its neighboring countries let me begin to fathom—and cherish—the cuisines, culture, languages, economy, and politics of the Chinese diaspora. I was blessed with a unique vantage point.

My thinking about China has benefited from reading, knowing, and hearing many academics, journalists, and observers who study it; the bibliographies and references in this book indicate who many of them are. Numerous trips to and around China, and to academic conferences, have allowed me to listen to and converse with many individuals in academia, journalism, government, and commerce. Grants, stipends, and subsidies from the University of Missouri–Kansas City, the Carter Center, and the Ministry of Civil Affairs of the People's Republic of China (PRC), People to People International, San Francisco State University, the Taipei Economic and Cultural Representative Office in Washington, DC, and the Danish Ministry of Foreign Affairs have helped pay for some of this travel. So have visiting lectureships at Hangzhou and Shanghai Universities. Chinese are much more candid in discussing controversial topics than Americans tend to imagine. For example, immediately after the bloody crackdown at Tiananmen Square I found myself in very open and frank discussions about it with a provincial party chief, a minister of education, a high-ranking general, and a number of other high-ranking party members. Subsequent conversations with Huang Hua, former translator for Mao and foreign minister; Gao Shangquan, minister of the State Commission for Restructuring the Economy; Yu Keping, adviser to Hu Jintao; Jason Hu, then director of the Kuomintang's Department of Cultural Affairs; and Lt. Gen. Feng Shih-kuan of the Office of DCGS/Intel in Taiwan's Ministry of National Defense have been similarly forthright. This broad exposure within and beyond academia has given me diverse views of China. I am grateful for all of these opportunities.

My students at the University of Missouri–Kansas City—undergraduate, graduate, and in my several Carolyn Benton Cockefair Chair courses—have helped me hone the craft of teaching about China. I learned a lot from Shou Huisheng and Yan Liang in the process of helping with their recent master's thesis and dissertation, respectively. Cheng De and Jane Cheng helped ensure consistent transliteration. Bambi Shen has offered useful assistance in translating. Thanks to Robbyn Abbitt, GIS coordinator, Department of Geography, Miami University, for the maps. Our department's administrative assistant, Ann Hubbard, makes life easier on a daily basis with her words of wisdom and rapid response to any task thrown her way. My colleagues on the board of the Edgar Snow Memorial Foundation are a constant inspiration, with E. Grey Dimond and Henry Mitchell leading the way.

—Robert E. Gamer

UNDERSTANDING CONTEMPORARY CHINA

1

Introduction

Robert E. Gamer

One morning in March 2011, my wife and I were taking a public bus from the traditional village of Zhaoxing to the modern town of Congjiang, in Guizhou, one of the poorest provinces of China, located in China's southwest region (see Map 2.2). The bus was filled with rural dwellers. It stopped frequently at the entrance to small villages along the way so peasants could get on and off, toting plastic bags filled with farm produce or goods they had purchased. The bus, like the others frequenting these roads, was clean, modern, and comfortable, once the extra passengers jammed into the center aisle had disembarked. Stretches of the road were only mud, while other portions were graveled or black-topped. It took us two hours to traverse the sixty miles (100 kilometers).

A decade earlier, according to backpackers' blogs, this road was almost entirely deeply rutted mud. Instead of its current graded roadbed, it followed a circuitous path through the contours of the land, along the edge of rivers and over the many hills. Buses had to limp through the muck in wet weather. Peasants in adjoining villages could walk to nearby villages to sell their animals and produce and buy small household goods at weekly outdoor markets. But going farther to a town on a bus was hard to accomplish. They were isolated from the modern world. Watching these peasants get on and off this bus with such ease reminded me of those days and someone I had met in that era.

In 2002, two friends and I were climbing the Simatai section of the Great Wall of China, a less-frequented section high atop the craggy and sparsely populated mountain range northwest of Beijing. From its highest tower you can see Beijing. The young woman who followed us to sell a souvenir guidebook loved taking in that view. To her it was almost a mirage; she had never been to Beijing. And she had visited the township capital, a modern town with tall buildings and a new park and shopping strip about ten miles away, only twice in her life—on her wedding day and one afternoon to window-shop with her son.

In 2002, change had hit China's peasants, but they were trapped in a time warp. Only ten years before that, in 1992, Deng Xiaoping had given a speech in which he said, "It doesn't matter whether the cat is black or white, so long as it can catch mice." That was the signal that economic reforms that had before been limited to special zones along China's coast would now be allowed throughout China. Immediately, coastal cities were building soaring modern buildings, office and industrial complexes, apartments and condominiums, highways, and shopping centers filled with a vast array of goods. Businesses were freed to fire many workers and offer fewer benefits like housing, health care, and pensions. For this young woman, it meant that the school in her village had closed, and she had to pay tuition and bus fares for her son to attend grade school in another town. Meanwhile, her village's agricultural production had declined, and she had to eke out an income selling these guidebooks. The contrast between life in the booming cities and that in rural villages like hers, or like Zhaoxing, had become stark.

Now, a decade later, that contrast is rapidly being reduced. Reforms have expanded into every corner of the nation. During our Guizhou bus ride we were observing that change. Between 1988 and 2010, China built or improved over 1.9 million miles (3 million kilometers) of roads. There are now over 10 million tractors, 100 million motorcycles, and 120 million electric bicycles. Though many of China's 1 million villages do not yet have a graveled or black-topped road adjoining them, all over China hundreds of millions of peasants once isolated in the back country have gained access to modern urban commerce through the road improvement program. And there are even more landscape-transforming public works projects, one of which we would experience during the last legs of this bus journey. Between 1988 and 2010, China built 40,400 miles (65,000 kilometers) of toll expressways, connecting towns and cities throughout China. The road on the next leg of our trip, between Congjiang and the county of Rongjiang, was largely graveled or black-topped. But all the way from Zhaoxing we had been watching on the horizon a six-lane toll expressway rising above the valleys on its tall concrete pillars. Starting in Rongjiang on to the city of Kaili and then to the capital of Guizhou province, Guiyang, we joined the finished portion of that expressway, where our buses sailed along smoothly, averaging 50 miles (80 kilometers) or more an hour. The portion we had been watching earlier was due to open by summer.

The arrival of these expressways gives easy access to vehicles carrying all manner of materials and equipment needed for manufacturing and major building projects, as well as consumer goods. Since 2008, Rongjiang, Kaili, and Guiyang have all built long rows of high-rise condominiums, largely sitting vacant and unsold at the time of our trip. Urbanites live in buildings with modern plumbing, and nearby shops have large selections of food, clothing, household goods, vehicles, and mechanized farm equipment. They displace buildings built in traditional styles and traditional clothing, habits, and customs. As Chapters 8 and 10 discuss, China has fifty-five ethnic minorities, and many of them live in Guizhou. Millions of Chinese now go on tours, and ethnic minority villages are popular destinations. Zhaoxing, the largest village of the Dong minority, is famous as a colorful example of a minority village that looks and acts much as it has for centuries. When the new roads and two new airports nearby make it possible for tour buses to easily reach Zhaoxing, there will be the infrastructure and incentives to build new hotels, shops, and other facilities—boosting the economy and sanitation and other services, but hastening the decline of traditional culture and family and community life. Many Chinese, while proud of these accomplishments, nonetheless ask: Is all this happening too fast?

Many other programs are raising that same question. In 1990, China had 1 million cars; by 2010, it had 85 million and was producing 18 million new cars a year in its factories (versus 11 million in the United States), adding to both mobility and pollution. In 2010, 13.5 million cars were sold in China, versus 11.6 million in the United States. In addition, over 440 airports have paved runways, and most cities have new terminals. China has opened 53,000 miles (85,000 kilometers) of railway line, with 75,000 miles (120,000 kilometers) projected by 2015. By 2011, high-speed bullet trains going 120 to 220 miles per hour (195–360 kilometers per hour), which went into service in 2007, were operating on 6,000 miles (9,700 kilometers) of track, radically shrinking travel time. The government planned to quadruple that length by 2020, but the crash of two bullet trains in 2011, which killed forty and injured more than 200, brought the attention of bloggers to concerns over safety, low ridership, high energy consumption, and low profitability. These concerns have slowed down expansion of the network. Japan has had bullet trains since 1964, without a single death from a moving train, and the Chinese bloggers want more attention to safety for China's new bullet trains and other spectacular showcase construction projects like the 26.7 mile (43 kilometer) long Jiaozhou Bay Bridge, the world's longest cross sea bridge, built in only four years over miles of water that freezes heavily in winter.

More than 900 million Chinese have a cell phone (not to mention 375 million conventional telephones). More than 500 million Chinese are online with the Internet (with over 15 million Chinese websites). Over half of them tweet, blog, and chat on Sina Weibo, QQ, and other sites. China's eBay equivalent, Alibaba's Taobao, has 370 million registered users; together with Alipay, the Chinese version of PayPal, China is making a wide array of consumer goods, sold on Taobao Mall by thousands of resourceful young entrepreneurs with start-up online companies, available even to rural villagers.

Popular talk radio shows discuss sex and relationships. Young people wear the latest fashions, eat fast food, and dance to rock music late at night in discos. Engineering projects transform entire valleys and islands from swamp or desert into metropolises. All this helps China achieve the dubious distinction of being among the world's greatest purveyors of air and water pollution, with one-thirtieth the world average of water resources per person. But its economy is now second to the United States—US$10.1 trillion versus US$14.7 trillion in 2010—in gross domestic product (GDP) calculated in purchasing power parity (PPP) (i.e., what the money will actually buy at home). Its real GDP, in actual current dollars, is two-fifths the size of US GDP.

China has more than four times the population of the United States, so its economic output is less than a sixth of ours on a per capita basis, ranking it only 126th in the world in 2010. The United States is the world's largest consumer of petroleum, using over 18.7 million barrels a day. China is now the world's second-largest consumer, using over 8.2 million barrels a day. China's real growth in GDP (10.5 percent versus 1.7 percent between 2000 and 2009), has been much greater than that of the United States. Though China's growth is slowing, its real GDP is likely to surpass that of the United States between 2020 and 2030. Even then, its per capita GDP will still be a fourth to a fifth as large as that of the United States.

So today China has the world's fastest-growing economy, a fifth of the world's population, and escalating trade and travel through its borders. It has a highly motivated populace spreading to all corners of the world, a modern-

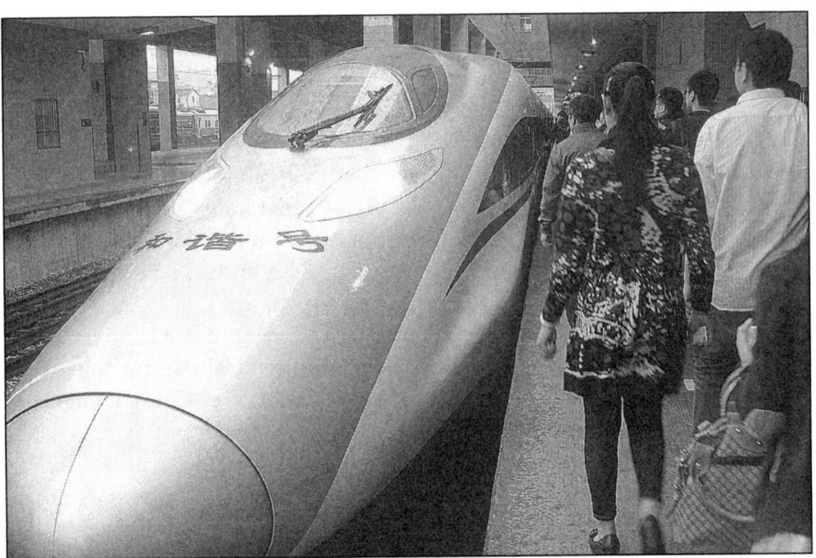

Robert E. Gamer

These bullet trains began operation in 2007.

ized army, world-class moviemakers, and competitive Olympic teams. It is a major market for Coke, Pepsi, Boeing, Avon, Cisco, Ford and General Motors, Sprint, Black and Veatch, Warner Brothers, and a host of other Western companies. Its goods line the racks in US stores.

China is ubiquitous—its clothes, electronics, food, people, and even air (its dust storms can indeed reach the western United States) are ever present in all places. Check the labels next time you go shopping. And this presence has another unique element: China still regards the more than 65 million Chinese living overseas as part of China. Although many of those overseas Chinese have become loyal citizens of other countries, they are often tied to China's 1.34 billion inhabitants by custom, family, and tradition. The richest of those families in Hong Kong (now part of China), Taiwan, Southeast Asia, Australia, and North America control very large amounts of investment capital; much of that money is invested directly or indirectly in China and in the Pacific Rim, including the coast of North America. This investment constitutes a major bond linking China to the Americas, the Middle East, Africa, and Southeast Asia. Some 23 million of these overseas Chinese live in Taiwan. China still claims Taiwan as part of its own territory, while many in Taiwan want to declare independence. China's prosperity has depended upon the investment of overseas Chinese; their prosperity, in turn, depends upon China's prosperity. Such interdependency explains a lot about how the communist nation of China can be as immersed in free markets as it is; those markets are embedded in the social structure of this widely dispersed Chinese community. The dispersed community shares some attitudes and habits, and some amazing economic achievements, passed from generation to generation for thousands of years. It is also quite diverse. As you read *Understanding Contemporary China,* you will see these attitudes and habits, along with social divisions, showing up in many ways. The rest of this chapter will give you an overview of those attitudes, habits, and divisions. But first I should say a bit about something that can be confusing without a brief introduction: Chinese words.

China has no alphabet. Its written language, which is thousands of years old, consists of single characters that represent entire words. Often these began as a simple stick drawing of a man, the sun, or another object that gradually became more complex and stylized over time. People had to memorize the individual characters for thousands of words. Only the educated scholar-officials and families of merchants in cities were in positions to devote the time it took to memorize these characters and learn to create them with careful brush strokes. After the communists came to power, they created about 2,200 simplified characters that could be taught to schoolchildren and used in newspapers, so as to spread literacy. But when Westerners arrived in China during the nineteenth century, they needed to transliterate the sounds of Chinese words into their Roman alphabet (Romanize them). Two English sinologists, Sir Thomas Wade and Hubert A. Giles, devised a system (Wade-Giles) to do that. For geographical names, some other Romanizations fell into common usage. During the 1930s, a new system, *pinyin,* came closer to replicating the sounds of the words as they are pronounced in the Mandarin (literary) Chinese used around China's capital, Beijing. In 1958, this system was adopted by the People's Republic of China for its official publications, and in 1979, Xinhua (the China News Agency) began using *pinyin* for all dispatches. The *New York Times* and many other newspapers and scholarly publications now use *pinyin;* we use it throughout this book, except for a few words still commonly transliterated in other spellings (e.g., Yangtze, Sun Yat-sen, Kuomintang) and when referring to people and movements in Taiwan, where Wade-Giles (or often-careless variations on it) is still in vogue. Some fields like history still use a lot of Wade-Giles, and it is used often in transliterating literature. So you will encounter it in some books. Table 1.1 compares the *pinyin* names of some provinces and cities with transliteration common on older maps and the names of dynasties and some other words in *pinyin* and Wade-Giles. It includes many of the Chinese words used in this book.

It is common for Chinese words to have only one or two syllables; when there are two, they are given equal emphasis in pronunciation. Words with similar sounds (and identical transliterations) may be differentiated by inflection of the voice—up, down, down-up, or flat—as each syllable is pronounced; each would have a different character in written Chinese script. When looking at names, Chinese give their family name first and then their personal name; Mao Zedong's family name was Mao, and his personal name was Zedong.

On another practical note, you will notice at the end of each chapter a bibliography; and within each chapter, parentheses call attention to books and articles where you can learn more about topics being discussed.

Creative Tensions

A rubber band's ability to stretch helps it hold things together; its elasticity actually lets it wrap tightly around objects. China has many traditions that combine those traits, pulling apart while unifying. Chapters in *Understanding Contemporary China* highlight many tensions between

- Confucianism and both petty and modern capitalism
- Confucianism, Christianity, and communism
- Popular culture and formal traditions
- Regions and the capital city
- Cities and the rural hinterland
- The heartland and its global outreach

Put another way, China's political system, economic system, social system, religions, popular culture, and geographic regions all have both a symbi-

Table 1.1 Romanization of Chinese Terms

Pinyin	Older Geographical Transliteration	Pronunciation
Provinces		
Fujian	Fukian	foo jian
Gansu	Kansu	gahn soon
Guangdong	Kwangtung	gwong doong
Guizhou	Kweichow	gway joe
Hainan	Hainan	hi! nanh
Hebei	Hopeh	hü bay
Hubei	Hupeh	hoo bay
Jilin	Kirin	gee lin
Shaanxi	Shensi	shahn shee
Shanxi	Shansi	shehn shee
Sichuan	Szechwan	sü chwahn
Xinjiang	Sinkiang	sheen jyang
Zhejiang	Chekiang	juh jyang
Cities		
Beijing	Peking	bay jing
Chengdu	Chengtu	chung doo
Chongqing	Chungking	chawng ching
Hangzhou	Hangchow	hong joe
Nanjing	Nanking	nahn jing
Qingdao	Tsingtao	ching daow
Tianjin	Tientsin	tien jin
Xi'an	Sian	shee ahn

Pinyin	Wade-Giles	Pronunciation
Dynasties		
Han	Han	hahn
Qidan	Ch'i-tan	chee don
Qin	Ch'in	chin
Qing	Ch'ing	ching
Song	Sung	soohng
Tang	T'ang	tahng
Xia	Hsia	shah
Names		
Deng Xiaoping	Teng Hsiao-p'ing	dung sheeaow ping
Jiang Zemin	Chiang Tse-min	jyang dze min
Mao Zedong	Mao Tse-Tung	maow dze doong
Zheng He	Cheng Ho	jung huh
Zhang Xueliang	Chang Hsüeh-liang	jang shuey lyahng
Zhou Enlai	Chou En-lai	joe un lie
Zhuang-zi	Chuang-Tzu	jwong dz
Other terms		
baojia	pao-chia	bough dja
danwei	tanwei	don weigh
Dao	Tao	dow
guanxi	kuan-hsi	gwahn shee
Guomindang	Kuomintang	gwaw min dahng
Tiananmen	T'ienanmen	tien ahn mun
Xinhua	Hsin-hua	sheen hwa
Zhong guo	Chung-kuo	djohng gwaw

otic and adversarial relationship with one another. The same is true of China's relationship with the economic systems, religions, and ideologies of the Western world. But rather than phrase this so formally, let's sit back and approach it all through the narrative that follows.

China is slightly larger than the United States but has more than four times the number of people. Its rivers cross high, dry plateaus to connect the world's highest mountains with enormous floodplains. Its eastern provinces are among the world's most populous, its western provinces among the world's least inhabited. It first became a unified nation 200 years before the birth of Christ, with the north conquering the south; that unity has waxed and waned ever since. At the time of Christ, China was abandoning feudal states and starting to adopt both petty capitalist trade among family-run enterprises (often associated with the south) and a Confucian ethic (coming from the north). Since that ethic emphasizes family loyalty and hard work on the one hand and interfering government bureaucracy and unquestioned loyalty to northern-based leaders on the other, it both benefits and interferes with capitalism. Daoism (deriving from folk culture) and Buddhism (from India) helped individuals cultivate their inner personal lives while conforming to the rigid social conventions associated with Confucianism and family enterprises. So did popular forms of entertainment, which at the same time provided inspiration for China's highly refined art and literature. China developed some of the world's earliest large cities, which sent Chinese to ports and oases in distant parts of Asia to establish a lively trade. In 1400, nine of the world's twenty-five largest cities were in China, and its output of manufactured goods was world's highest. In 1700, it still produced a third of the world's manufacturing output.

By the late eighteenth century, these cities were in contact with the emerging capitalism and the Industrial Revolution of Western Europe, which increasingly competed with China's petty capitalist enterprises. These foreigners also brought with them Christianity and Western ideas about human freedom and progress, which competed for favor with China's established religious traditions. As large factories and cities began to widen the divide between city and countryside and among social classes, communist ideology began to compete with Christianity and capitalism for favor among workers, urban intellectuals, and peasants. Like many previous movements, those ideologies developed some Confucian traits as they adapted to China, especially those associated with strong rule emanating from the north. Today, as China strengthens its ties with international capitalism and capitalist nations, weakens its actual and ideological ties to international communism, and experiences rapid social change, traditions of both Confucianism and popular culture help fill its spiritual void. And overseas Chinese help fill its investment coffers.

Thus, China blends many traits and traditions, which seem to both pull people apart and bring them together. People are expected to give their highest loyalty to their families and to friends with whom they have special *guanxi* (relationships); yet the same traditions simultaneously bid them to follow the directives of the nation's top leaders. For thousands of years, China has both encouraged and strictly controlled small manufacturers and traders, who worked closely with local officials. China's regions have held closely to their own traditions while sharing in a common Chinese culture. That culture viewed itself as civilized and the outside world as barbarian, yet continuously absorbed civilization from the barbarians. Today China has dazzlingly modern cities short distances from peasants tilling fields with animal and hand labor to supply those cities with food; both may be watching the same television shows and talking on their cell phones. Families driving Toyotas visit their horse-back-riding cousins who live in yurts lit by solar panels.

These diverse traits and traditions have come to support one another. Their distinctions and competition create tensions but do not hold back progress. That has not always been so. Between the 1839 arrival of the Christian West in the first Opium War and the introduction of communism after World War II, and during the cataclysms of the Great Leap Forward and the Great Proletarian Cultural Revolution, many millions lost their lives in conflict among contending social forces. But China has learned to use conflict as a means of adapting to change. It has a disciplined social core, weakened but still strong despite television, the Internet, cell phones, consumerism, tourism, crime, and other assaults of modern culture. Its families have shown an ability to control their size, save, work hard, engage in creative entrepreneurship, and divide labor between the sexes. China's civilization has focused on an attachment to the land that has survived amid many centuries of urbanization. People who have migrated to China's cities are welcome to return to their home regions, keeping alive rural social bonds and safety nets even as people move out to the ends of the earth. When the Central Pacific Railway found its European immigrant laborers fleeing the arduous task of building a transcontinental railway across the United States in the 1860s, it turned to Chinese laborers, who arrived already organized into disciplined work units under their own foremen. For millennia, China has used this labor and considerable scientific skills to channel its vast amounts of water, mine rich seams of coal, build tunnels, enclose its cities and borders with walls and towers, and manufacture a variety of goods prized for their excellence around the planet. Even when divided by ideology or temporary political division or separated by vast distances after migration, families and clans deriving from the same villages have habits of cooperation to further such enterprises by sharing capital, labor, markets, and special connections. They hold together tightly even while stretching to take on global challenges.

As a result, China can contribute to global capitalism without being absorbed by it. These traits that help make it a great producer also make it a great consumer; its enormous population produces ever-increasing amounts of goods not only for world markets but also for itself. Extensive use of low-skilled labor holds down the cost of manufacturing while providing millions of people with income to buy these new goods. Unlike many third world countries, China has developed huge budget surpluses stemming from a favorable balance of trade. Yet China's form of capitalism holds back many of the processes (e.g., impartial civil and criminal law, bureaucratic independence, investigative reporting) required for modern capitalism to thrive. If it wishes to sustain its current rates of growth, it must find new ways to adapt to global capitalism by increasing the technical skills of its workforce, raising wages to expand domestic consumption, increasing efficiency, reducing corruption, enforcing business contracts, and cooperating with other nations on efforts to reduce worldwide economic and political instability. Global capitalism, in turn, must adjust to the needs of China's dynamic sector of the world economy, recognizing some of its unique obligations at home and in the region.

New Challenges

China still has great challenges ahead. Like many third world countries, China's traditions offer little support for democracy. With its focus on obeying family and community leaders, China has suppressed individual expression. It has never allowed independent interest groups to form. Although it has long had laws, it has no tradition of rule of law. Competing political parties clash with Chinese traditions of harmony and unquestioning obedience to authority. This clash lets all elements of Chinese society support movements rejecting foreign influences even as they adapt to world technology, trade, and popular culture; yet this balancing act is becoming increasingly harder to maintain.

China's development has resulted in major problems. Deforestation, removal of ground cover and wetlands, water and air pollution, and giant engineering projects pose serious threats to China's food and water supplies, health, and standard of living. Despite the "one-child" policy, a growing population increasingly moving to cities is a growing strain on resources. The growing economy widens the gap between rich and poor individuals and regions (even with the new programs to extend greater prosperity to the countryside) and brings new opportunities for corruption; capital that should go into development ends up in personal bank accounts and shoddy construction. And many new blocks of flats and toll roads built to stimulate the economy remain empty and underused, leaving the banking system loaded with unrepaid loans. This inefficiency, fast economic growth, and reduction in central planning have caused severe inflation and severe deflation, overbuilding, unemployment, declines in social services, dangerous products and deadly accidents, and social discontent.

These problems are amplified by an unpredictable legal system that leaves business contracts and individual liberties unprotected and makes both foreign investors and educated Chinese uneasy. In addition, China has put inadequate resources into educating a workforce with skills to run all the new enterprises; it is rapidly working to rectify that deficiency, but it still has a long way to go. Hong Kong and Taiwan, both critical to China's economic future, are especially sensitive to these concerns. Military threats to Taiwan or offshore islands and crackdowns on dissidents and ethnic minorities periodically threaten to upset the peace. These problems challenge China as it strives to retain its fast-paced economic growth. Its leaders are sensitive to all these problems and have devised an array of programs—minimum wage, living allowances, health and unemployment insurance, pensions, tax relief and school subsidies for poor farmers, environmental projects and regulations, and many more—to address them. Their desire to do so derives from the long tradition of the Mandate of Heaven, explained in Chapter 4. They recognize that their legitimacy and grip on power depend on continuing economic growth that prevents poverty and social disorder from increasing. But they are also hesitant to make moves that affect their own personal fortunes and do not hesitate to use the public security apparatus to crack down on some of the same phenomena (e.g., blogging, election campaigning, formation of interest groups, educational reform, judicial independence) that are needed to make such programs a success. Will they spend the large amount of money and political capital needed to make those programs work? Can they work without democratic reforms? What is the potential for such reforms to occur?

Young people who marched in the 1989 demonstrations and elders who once fought for a workers' revolution are preoccupied with making money and enjoying consumer goods. Many younger Chinese also revel in newfound freedoms to express themselves in music, dress, sexuality, and other nonpolitical ways. Many of them are buying new condominiums, and all those cars and iPhones. Meanwhile, the security of guaranteed jobs, housing, and social services provided by work units during the Maoist years fades away. Increasing numbers of people cannot find full-time work and cannot afford to rent or buy housing, much less a car. They are using their computers and cell phones to blog complaints about their situation, official corruption, government cover-ups, and much more. And it is becoming more difficult for the government to stop them from spreading this "harmful information." Both citizens and leaders are profoundly torn by whether to follow traditional Chinese ways or, rather, trends from the outside world. They want to solve the many problems accompanying the rapid change without destroying the fabric that has held China together as a great nation over millennia. Many of them are studying and traveling abroad and lining up at Pizza Hut and McDonalds. But they want other countries to respect their sovereignty and their accomplishments. One of the greatest challenges in this regard is sorting out the relationship between China and Taiwan. A growing number of younger, and many older, people in Taiwan would like it to declare full independence from China and go its own way; in contrast, many young and old citizens of China are fiercely nationalistic and believe Taiwan must be a part of China. Will China find creative or destructive ways to deal with these tensions?

During the past decade, China's central government has become increasingly attentive to a threat that has been made worse by its rapid degradation of the environment: water shortages. China's productivity over the centuries has depended on its prolific supply of water from the Himalayas and other high ranges nearby. In recent years, the western part of China has experienced declining rainfall. Its 46,298 glaciers (in 2006) are melting at two to four times the rate they were forty years ago. They feed the headwaters of the Yellow, Yangtze, West, Brahmaputra, Mekong, Ganges, Salween, Irrawaddy, and Indus Rivers. If this rate of melt continues, by many estimates they will all be gone by the end of the twenty-first century or much earlier. In addition, most of the revival of agricultural production in the north of China depends on irrigation supplied by groundwater. Water tables there decline at a rate, in many places, of 4 feet a year. Without these water sources, large portions of China could turn to desert. Is this a real possibility? And are China's new environmental and water management policies appropriate and sufficient to supply China with the water it needs?

We explore all this in the pages ahead.

2

China: A Geographic Preface

Stanley W. Toops

China is moving onto our horizon. Though most of us know little about it, we are increasingly aware that somehow it is going to be a big factor in our lives. With over 1.3 billion people, China has more than a fifth of the world's population (Donald and Benewick, 2005; National Geographic Society, 2008). Just slightly larger than the United States, covering 3.7 million square miles, it is territorially the world's third-largest country. China's economy is the second largest in the world after the United States; with its 10 percent annual growth, its overall economic output could surpass our own (CIA World Factbook, 2011; China Development Gateway, 2011). Once isolated from the outside world, China's goods, people, and culture are rapidly penetrating all corners of the globe and heavily affecting our own economy and society. The next few pages will quickly introduce you to how China connects with its neighbors, how it is inhabited, and what its natural environment is like. These facts will prepare you for an overview of its history in Chapter 3 and give you a convenient reference point when geographic places and features are mentioned in later chapters.

We start by looking at China's location on the map and its historical connections with neighboring states. Historically, China's culture and imperial power strongly influenced its closest neighbors—Korea, Japan, and the countries of Southeast Asia; in modern times, neighboring Russia, Japan, and Southeast Asia have had a powerful effect on China's political and economic development. Then we look at China's internal divisions, north and south, and east and west. Those regions have starkly different histories, and the differences persist. Finally, we examine China's natural landscape, which contains the world's highest mountains, huge deserts, and major rivers emptying into the world's most abundant floodplains. China encompasses a great diversity of cultures and physical features. It consists of much more than peasants tilling rice fields. China atlases

Robert E. Gamer

A new highway in Xinjiang.

provide great detail on the geography of the country (Benewick and Donald, 2009; Geelan and Twitchett, 1974; Institute of Geography, 1994, 2000; Ma, 2002; Cooke, 2010; National Geographic Society, 2008).

In simplest terms, we're talking about space, region, and landscape (Veeck et al., 2011; Cannon, 2000; Lu and Hsieh, 2004; Tregear, 2007; Tuan, 2008; Weightman, 2011). Geographers have examined the impact of China's development on regions (Cannon, 2000; Li and Tang, 2000; Wei, 2000; Fan, 2008), especially South China (Cartier, 2001), the Yangtze Delta (Marton, 2000), and West China (Yeung and Shen, 2004; Toops, 2004; Yeh, 2009). Cultural landscape (Knapp, 1992, 1998; Kong, 2010; Oakes, 2002), tourism (Lew et al., 2002; Su and Wall, 2009), land issues (Lin, 2009; Lin and Ho, 2005), and urban development (Chan, 2009; Gaubatz, 1996; Hsing, 2010) are also topics geographers study. Alexander Murphy (2010) and Clifton Pannell (2007) profile the great geographical issues facing China today. Harm de Blij (2005) considers the geographical factors behind China's rise. What space do China and its neighbors occupy on the map? How do its regions vary? How does China's natural landscape affect the way its people live?

Space

Where is this place, and how is it linked to its neighbors? China is located on the eastern end of Eurasia, the planet's largest continent (see Map 2.1), but its

Map 2.1 Regional Map of Asia

Geographic Information Systems Lab, Miami University, 1997 M.A

land connections on that continent have consisted of poor roads over harsh terrain. To the west are expanses of Central Asian dry lands and to the north is the cold steppe of Russia (see Map 2.4). To the south are the high mountains of the Himalayas, and to the east is the Pacific Ocean. In traditional times, China occupied an area not easily accessible to European travelers and traders. The distances are far and the physical barriers were formidable.

Since the early 1990s, that has changed rapidly as China has entered into a major initiative to expand and improve its nearly 1,900,000 miles (3,000,000 kilometers) of paved roads, including 40,000 miles (65,000 kilometers) of expressways and paved highways linking Beijing with Tibet and the far northwest (CIA World Factbook, 2011). Today over 350 airports with paved runways long enough to serve 747s offer travelers same-day connections to cities throughout China. Fifty-three thousand miles (85,000 kilometers) of railroad, over a third constructed during the last decade, move passengers and freight long distances every day; 8,100 miles (13,000 kilometers) of that track serves, or will soon serve, the new high-speed trains. The new rail line into Tibet and the high-speed rail links from Shanghai to Beijing are but two examples of the expansion. The July 2011 crash of two trains in Zhejiang will certainly require further emphasis on safety (see Chapter 4), but China will continue its high-speed rail expansion (McColl, 2011; Su and Wall, 2009; Johnson, 2011). As with highways, those networks are expanding rapidly. Spatial linkages (by road, rail, and air) are critical to China today.

China's closest cultural and physical connections are with Japan and Korea. No high mountains, deserts, or long stretches of ocean separate these three countries. Together they constitute East Asia. Sometimes Westerners call this the Far East, but that term only refers to the distance from Europe. East Asia is a better term for this region, describing its location at the eastern end of Eurasia: it is only far from places that are far from there. Southeast Asia (from Vietnam down to Indonesia) is situated to the southeast (Kolb, 1971).

To situate China, look at the country in an East Asian context. China, Japan, and Korea have very distinct cultures, histories, and natural experiences. Their religions are quite different. Unlike China, Korea is located on a peninsula, whereas Japan occupies a series of islands. But all three have been heavily influenced by Confucianism, a philosophy that began in China and has guided its ruling elite for centuries (you will read much more about this in Chapters 3, 4, and 12), and by Chinese art. Though their spoken languages are radically different, both Japan and Korea used Chinese characters to write words before they developed their own alphabets; the Japanese still use Chinese characters blended with words written in their alphabet, and many Koreans use Chinese characters for scholarly writing. This diffusion of philosophical ideas, artistic expression, and writing practices connects the people of East Asia (Borthwick, 2007; Kolb, 1971).

The connections to China's other neighbors are not as strong, but these linkages are not insignificant for China. The Buddhist religion began in India and came to China via the "Silk Roads" (see Map 2.1 and Chapter 12), which also brought China's silks and other luxury goods to other parts of the continent. Confucianism influenced bordering countries in Southeast Asia, which in turn developed the technology of wet-rice agriculture (planting seedlings in wet paddy fields) that spread throughout south China. Islam, born in the Middle East, has a stronghold in western China. From the north came historically powerful external threats: the Mongol and the Manchu (Boulnois, 2004; Cooke, 2010).

The Middle Kingdom

China's name has historical and geographical significance (Cannon and Jenkins, 1990). The Chinese call their country *Zhong guo*. The first character (*zhong*) means middle or central. Notice how it looks like a box or cake cut through the middle. The second character (*guo*) means country or kingdom. The outside square is the wall of defense for the country. So China is the Middle Kingdom, the kingdom located at the most central position.

The very name of the country imparts an idea of centrality. China has seen itself as central to the world, both in terms of looking up and looking out. The Chinese worldview placed the emperor at the connection between heaven and earth. The emperor resided in the capital, at the center of the world, so it was natural that this should be the prime connecting place between land and sky. Around this center, other countries or dominions were far away in the periphery. Those faraway people were barbarians (Veeck et al., 2011).

The name *China* comes from the first dynasty to unify China. The Qin (pronounced "chin") dynasty unified the country in 221 B.C.E. The Chinese people of that time called their country after that dynasty (Borthwick, 2007). The ancient Greeks knew of China as Seres, the land of silk. Silk was part of the trade across the vastness of Eurasia on the Silk Roads. Another name for China is Cathay. This comes from Khitai, an ethnic group that occupied northern China in the eleventh century. Marco Polo wrote about Cathay. People in Slavic-speaking areas still call China Khitai.

The Chinese people call themselves Han, after the Han dynasty that immediately succeeded the Qin, and adopted Confucian policies as its base. The Han are the dominant group in China. Although they loosely share some common physical features, their looks and average height vary from region to region, and they come from many distinct lineages. They are united by their common acceptance of the Confucian cultural norms that emerged during the Han dynasty (Veeck et al., 2011). Chapters 3 and 12 discuss this further.

According to Confucius, you should look carefully at the name of a person to understand what that person's role is (see the rectification of names discussed in Chapter 4). The same can be said for the name of a country. China or *Zhong guo,* Qin dynasty or Middle Kingdom, these two names describe a country that is unified and located at the center of civilization. Its people, the Han, grant the country loyalty on the basis of traditional values.

Challenging the Middle Kingdom

China and its view of itself were both fundamentally challenged when the Pacific Ocean was opened to the fleets of Europe. China itself had sent ships as far as the Indian Ocean. But once European ships entered the Pacific in numbers, China became vulnerable militarily, culturally, and economically (Sivin, 1988). Chapters 3, 6, and 7 all have much more to say about this. When China found it could not resist those onslaughts, many in China began to question whether they were any longer the names they had been calling themselves, the people of Han traditions living in the center of the civilized world. Their space had been invaded.

Regions

China is a land of enormous internal contrasts. It is slightly larger than the United States (Lu and Hsieh, 2004). If a map of China were superimposed on one of Europe, China would stretch from the North Sea south to the southern edge of the Sahara, east from Portugal to as far as the Ural Mountains. As the United States or Europe vary regionally, so does China. It is easy to approach this subject by focusing on two major divisions, east-west and north-south.

East and West

A historical division exists between China Proper and the Frontier. This is a distinction between the east and the west. China Proper is east of a line from Yunnan in the southwest looping around Beijing and Hebei to the sea (see Map 2.2). As Map 2.3 helps you quickly comprehend, this region has the heaviest population densities; 90 percent of the country's population lives here (China Development Gateway, 2011). Most of those people are Han and live in a Confucian society. Much of this area is suitable for agriculture in river basins,

Map 2.2 Provincial Map of China

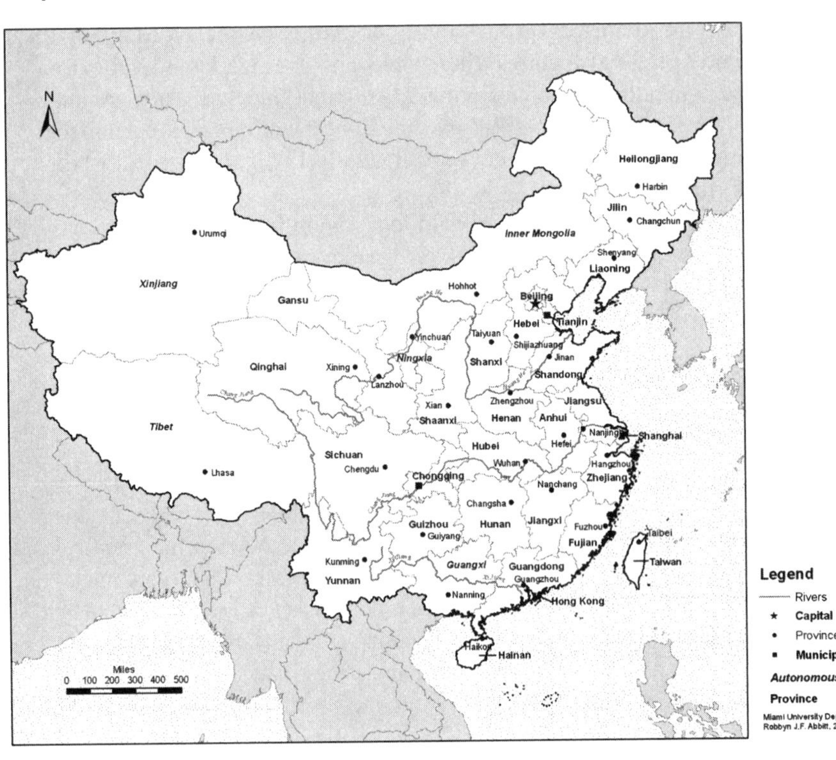

and China also focused its industrial might here. The people who live within China Proper consider themselves the center of China's civilization.

The Frontier is west of that line bisecting the country. Western China includes Inner Mongolia, Heilongjiang, Jilin, Liaoning, Ningxia, Gansu, western Sichuan, Tibet, Qinghai, and Xinjiang (see Map 2.2). Western China has far fewer people. Much of the population—including Mongols, Tibetans, Hui, and Uyghur—does not consider itself Han. Tibetans and Mongols adhere to Lama Buddhism, while Hui and Uyghur follow Islam. This region consists of mountains and deserts and has low rainfall. Traditionally, people were nomadic herders or farmed in oases. There is still very little industry here, even though this is one of China's richest sources for oil and coal (Veeck et al., 2011; Yeung and Shen, 2004).

Northeast and Southeast

Another regional difference exists within China Proper. A line following just north of the Yangtze River separates the northern and southern portions of China Proper (Borthwick, 2007). The Yellow River waters northern China (see Map 2.4). This is the cultural heart of China. Rainfall is adequate for agricul-

Map 2.3 Population Map of China

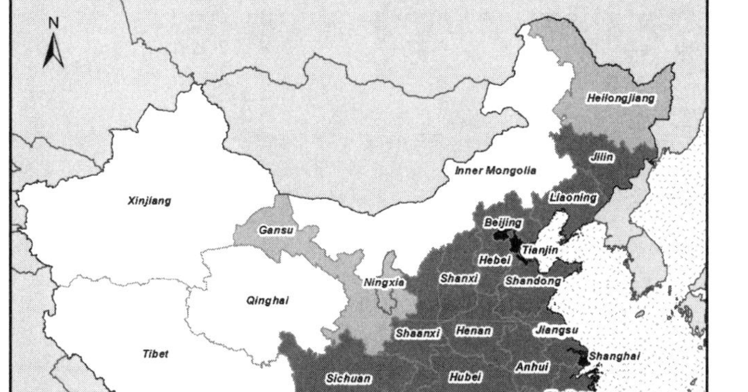

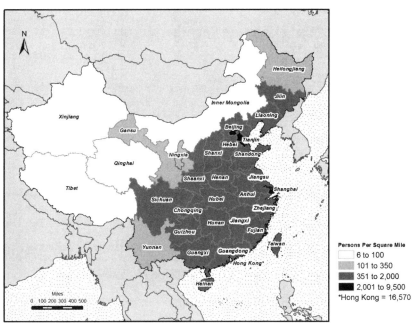

Miami University Dept of Geography, Robbyn J.F. Abbitt, 2011

ture. People raise wheat, which they eat in the form of noodles or steamed bread. Much of China's heavy industry is in the north because of the coal and oil here. The northern Mandarin dialect is the basis for the standard language.

The Yangtze River and West River are the lifelines of the southern region (Map 2.4). Southern China is lush compared with the north. Paddy (wet-field) agriculture is practiced here, and rice is the main food crop. Tea is grown in the hillsides (Hoh and Mair, 2009). The south focuses on light industry such as textiles; it has few fuel resources. Southern dialects of the standard language, such as Cantonese, are spoken here.

Part of this regionalization is expressed in the food styles of China. Cantonese style in the Guangdong province has a delicate flavor and sensibility, a more subtle approach. Sichuan food is spicy hot and mouth numbing because of the combination of peppercorns used in its preparation. Food from Hunan, Mao's home province, is the spiciest. Shanghai style makes liberal use of seafood and is slightly sweet. Northern China style is plainer, using onions, garlic, and cabbage but few other vegetables. Beijing style is exceptional because of the imperial dishes like Beijing duck. In the north, noodles are the staple food for people, whereas rice is the staple in the south. Except in Muslim areas, pork is the main meat all over China. In northwestern China, rice pilaf, spicy noodles, and lamb kebabs are common. In Tibet, roasted bar-

Map 2.4 Physical Features of China

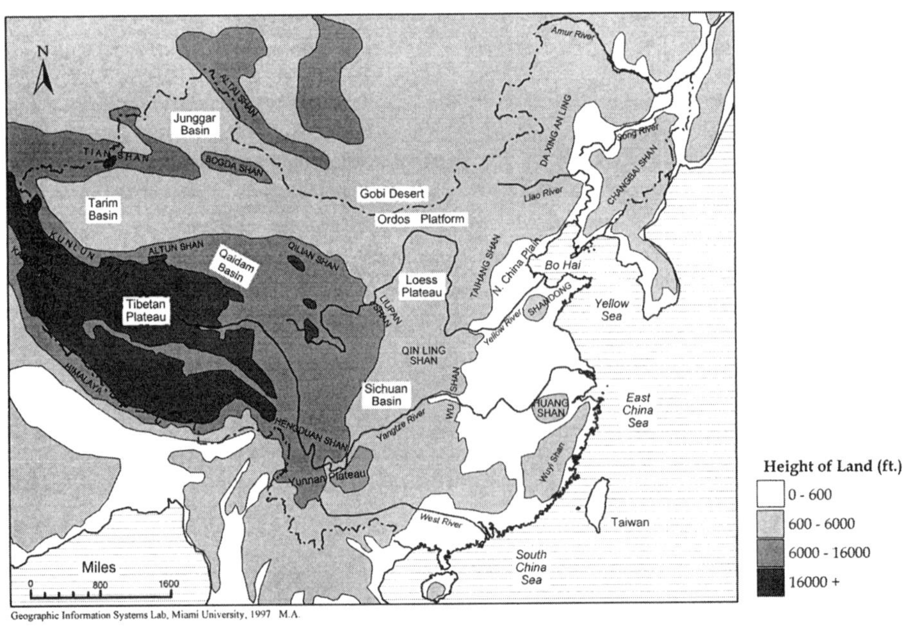

Geographic Information Systems Lab, Miami University, 1997 M.A.

ley flour is the staple, supplemented by some yak meat. All over China, tea is the preferred beverage. Chinese love food and savor the specialties of their regions.

How different are the dialects? They are as different as the foods of China. *I love you* is expressed in three characters: the first character means "I," the second "love," and the third "you." Anyone who can read Chinese characters knows this. But the pronunciation of the words varies. Although the Chinese use these same characters everywhere, in the north people say *wo ai ni* in Mandarin dialect. Cantonese living in Guangdong province to the south say *ngoh oi lei* in Cantonese dialect—quite a difference. Eventually, people have to write love notes to understand each other. A Cantonese writing these three characters to a lover in the north would immediately convey the meaning on paper, even though the words sound entirely different when spoken (Ledderose, 2000). In Uyghur, a Turkic language spoken in northwest China, *men sizni yahxi koremen* means "I love you"—quite different indeed. But since Uyghur has its own script based on Arabic, communication with outsiders becomes more complicated than it is among literate Chinese who can read the same characters but speak different dialects.

我爱你

The regions of China are different in climate, culture, topography, agriculture, and industry (Toops and Andrus, 1993). Not only regional differences but regional identities are important. When you meet other people in China, you ask where they are from. In this fashion, identity is set up: "I am a Beijing person." "I am a Sichuan person." Regional identities are strong (Veeck et al., 2011; Oakes, 2002).

The Natural Landscape

China's regional differences have their roots in physical geography. China is a land of extremes, of diverse topographies and varied landscapes. The highest point, Mt. Everest (Qomolangma) at 29,029 feet (8,848 meters), is on the border of Tibet and Nepal. The lowest point, the Turpan Depression at 505 feet (154 meters) below sea level, is in the far west of China (Geelan and Twitchett, 1974). The Chinese people have been working this land for 4,000 years, constantly shaping and forming it. The terraces and waterworks are a good example of this. The Chinese have sculpted the landscape, but they are not masters of it. Floods and droughts still plague China. The Chinese have not transformed fierce and austere mountains and deserts into fields of grain, though irrigation and the tree-planting program discussed in Chapter 9 have allowed oases filled with grapes and other crops to dot the landscape.

The Chinese have a phrase, "vast in territory and rich in resources" (*di da wu bo*). One perception of China is of unlimited land and resources. Another perspective of Chinese reality is that "the land is scarce and the people are many" (*di shao ren zhong*). Ten percent of China's vast territory is cultivated; 90 percent of its 1.3 billion people live on terrain about the size of the United States to the east of the Mississippi River (Zhao, 1994).

Three Tiers

It is easiest to approach China's physical geography by visualizing the country in three parts. As Map 2.4 shows, nature orders this landscape in three tiers, ranging from mountains to floodplains (Zhao, 1994:15). Powerful rivers have their origins high in the mountains of western China and then flow east to the sea. The rivers run through several tiers of mountains, hills, and then basins. Over two-thirds of China is mountainous, hilly, or high plateaus. This mountainous nature is a major constraint on human use of the land (Veeck et al., 2011).

The highest tier is the mountains, shown on Map 2.4; the two darkest gradations of shading represent land ranging from 6,000 to 29,029 feet (1,829 to 8,848 meters) in elevation. Tibet lies in the heart of this region, but it also extends into Qinghai, Xinjiang, Sichuan, Gansu, and Guizhou provinces (see Map 2.2). The Himalaya range, at the southern end of this system, contains the world's highest mountains, Everest and K2. *Shan* means "mountain." You will notice several other ranges on Map 2.4 that are less familiar to you. The intermediate shading represents altitudes from 6,000 to 16,000 feet (1,829 to 4,877 meters); keep in mind that (except for 20,320-foot Mt. McKinley) the highest mountains of North America are less than 15,000 feet. All the major rivers of China have their origins in these regions, as do the Brahmaputra, Mekong, Ganges, Irrawaddy, and Indus. Altitude is a major constraint on the habitation of people, plants, and animals (Cannon and Jenkins, 1990; Yeh, 2009; Yeung and Shen, 2004).

The middle tier is the hilly area, represented in the lightest shading—a broad expanse of basins, hills, and plateaus between 600 and 6,000 feet (183 and 1,829 meters). To the north are the Tarim and Junggar Basins and the Ordos Platform (Mongolian Plateau). Population in the northern portions of this tier (Tarim and Mongolia) is quite sparse because it is so dry. The deserts and the mountains combine to form effective barriers to the outside. Below them is the Loess Plateau, and east of Tibet are the Sichuan Basin and the Yunnan Plateau (south of the Hengduan Shan). Here there is more rainfall. The southern portion of this tier (Sichuan and Yunnan) has a dense population. Along the coast rise four ranges of hills—Changbai, Shandong, Huang, and Wuyi. Hainan Island to the south contains another range (Zhao, 1994).

The lowest tier (without shading), with floodplains and lowlands, is both the smallest and most populous. Notice from comparing Maps 2.3 and 2.4 how this portion of China supports the highest population densities—the land is scarce and the people are many. This segment following the coast lies lower than 600 feet (183 meters). The North China Plain follows the path of the Yellow River, while the Yangtze River and the combined paths of the Liao and Song

Rivers form plains to the south and north. These densely populated plains are the agricultural and industrial heart of China. The North China Plain has less water, and the plain formed by the Liao and Song Rivers is quite cold in winter; as one moves south toward the delta of the West River the warm, wet, fertile plains provide the principal basis for China's rich agricultural output (Veeck et al., 2011).

The two highest tiers are the result of tectonic activity, the moving of the earth's plates. The Himalayas are still growing; earthquakes strike China regularly. Basins are usually not vulnerable, but the tectonic boundaries (fault lines) between plateaus and the mountain ranges have earthquakes fairly often. The most disastrous earthquakes have been those in populated areas. In 1976, an earthquake in Tianjin, near Beijing, killed more than 250,000 people (Cannon and Jenkins, 1990). The 2008 Sichuan earthquake killed more than 80,000 people. Many were crushed in poorly constructed schools, and more than 350,000 were injured (Elegant, 2008).

The Rivers Linking China

The mountains and deserts may divide China, but the river basins link it together. The natural landscape of China sometimes is summed up as Huang He Chang Jiang, the names for the two largest rivers, the Yellow and the Yangtze. These river systems connect the three physiographic tiers we just discussed. Over long spans of time, the rivers flowed through the mountains and plateaus carrying eroded material that washed into the sea to form and then build up the lowlands; they still break through dams and dikes during flood seasons to lay down more silt from upstream, contributing to the fertility of the soils in eastern China (Lu and Hsieh, 2004).

The river of greatest historical importance is the Yellow River, since imperial China had its origins along its banks and those of its tributaries (see Chapter 3). As Map 2.4 shows, the Yellow River (Huang He) starts in the high mountain areas, runs north, cuts south through the Loess Plateau, and flows into the Bo Sea (Bo Hai) and out to the Yellow Sea (Huang Hai). The Yellow River and Yellow Sea gained their names from the fine fertile loess (yellow-brown soil) the river carries in its muddy waters. When the Chinese speak of "the River," it is this one. The Yellow River is also called "China's Sorrow." According to Chinese historical records, it has changed its course twenty-six times in the past 4,000 years. Since the North China Plain is very flat, people have built dikes and then more dikes to control it. Over the years, it has deposited much silt on its bottom, raising the riverbed. People in turn raised the dikes to hold up the banks. Now the riverbed is higher than the surrounding plain. When dikes break, the flood carries for miles. This is the sorrow. The river also brings joy by irrigating fields along its floodplain. When the ancient Chinese organized to build the dikes and irrigation channels, their agricultural surplus increased, and Chinese civilization developed. Over 200 million people live in the valley of the Yellow River (Veeck et al., 2011).

The longest river in China and the third longest in the world is the Long River (Chang Jiang). This river is also known as the Yangtze (Yangzi in *pinyin*); technically, this refers only to the estuary (mouth) of the river, but Europeans and Americans who were introduced to it when arriving from the ocean adopted that name—which we use in this book—to describe the whole river. As you can see on Map 2.4, the Yangtze starts in the high mountain areas not far from the headwaters of the Yellow River, but the rivers take different paths to the sea. Out of Tibet, the Yangtze passes through Sichuan and then goes through the narrow Three Gorges in Wu Shan before coming out into the Yangtze Plain. Unlike the Yellow River, this river is very important for transportation, linking the interior to the East China Sea. More than 400 million live in the valley of the Yangtze River (Zhao, 1994).

The Yangtze is also prone to flooding that affects millions of people, especially since this area gets plenty of rainfall. The government has built large dams and reservoirs to lessen flood damage and to generate hydroelectricity. The government has completed the Three Gorges Dam, the world's largest dam. The reservoir fills much of the spectacular Three Gorges (Cannon, 2000; Heggelund, 2004; Veeck et al., 2011), and many people are concerned about the impact of such a dam on the environment (see Chapter 9).

The West River (Xi Jiang) drains southern China. As you can see from Map 2.4, this river rises out of the Yunnan Plateau and cuts through the South China Hills before it reaches the South China Sea. The Pearl River Delta, the estuary of the West River, has been an important economic area for China. Hong Kong is located there. The area is hilly, but peasants have built terraces over the years for paddy (wet-field) agriculture. This southern section of China has more than adequate moisture for wet-rice fields, and the hillsides are also good for tea. More than 100 million people live in the valleys of the Xi Jiang and its tributaries (Veeck et al., 2011).

The Chinese have a saying, "When you drink water, think of the source" (*yin shui si yuan*). These rivers are very important for China. Without water, the land is worth little. Plans are now under way to divert water from the Yangtze north to the valleys of the Yellow River. The goal of the South to North Water Diversion Project is to bring water to the dry north to use in its farms, cities, and industries. The scale of this engineering project dwarfs that of the Three Gorges Dam; its environmental impact will also be very great (Cannon, 2000; Veeck et al., 2011; Zhang et al., 2009). As Chapter 9 discusses, lengthy periods of drought in western China are rapidly shrinking the glaciers there and imperiling that source for all these rivers.

Climate, Soil, and Vegetation

The monsoon controls China's climate. The winter monsoon blows dry, cold air out of the northern Siberian steppe, bringing no moisture. The summer monsoon blows in hot and humid air masses from the South and East China

Seas (see Map 2.4); by the time these air masses reach the interior, they have rained themselves out but are still hot. This north-south monsoon mechanism drives the climate process in China. It keeps south China warm and wet, whereas the north is cold and dry—relieved only by the Yellow River flowing from the south and winds from the East China Sea and Sea of Japan (Geelan and Twitchett, 1974).

The Chinese designate their soils by color. Red soil is in the southeast, and the marshy areas of the south are blue. The loess of the north is yellow-brown, and the northeast has black soil. The deserts of the west have white soil. No soils anywhere in the world have fed so many people for so many generations (Tuan, 2008). Because of China's size and diversity, it helps to examine each region of the country to understand the linkage among climate, soils, and vegetation (Zhao, 1994).

The southeast, the wettest part of China, receives over 60 inches (152.4 centimeters)—sometimes nearly 80 inches—of rain, most in the summer. The southeast portion of the United States, by comparison, has a similar climate but receives 40–60 inches (101.6–152.4 centimeters) of rain. China's southeast is subject to typhoons in the summer. Summers are extremely hot and sticky, and winters are cool and damp. In much of this part of China, people do not have heating, so the winter feels cold. Since the growing season is quite long, it is common to cultivate two crops of rice a year. On Hainan (see Map 2.2), a tropical island, three crops are possible.

Soils in the southeast are thick and sticky. Broadleaf evergreen forests originally covered this area. Now much of the region grows rice, on fields immersed in water to nourish the young paddy shoots, and the sticky soils hold the roots firmly. They have been farmed for a long time and leached of much of their nutrients, but the farmers add night soil (human waste from outhouses and buckets) to provide humus. The greatest competition to farmland is the ever-expanding urban centers that subsume cropland (Veeck et al., 2011).

North of the Yangtze, the climate begins to change. The North China Plain (see Map 2.4) gains enough precipitation for crops. The yearly variability of precipitation is marked; some years may not reach 20 inches (50.8 centimeters), whereas others get closer to 40 inches. Wheat, rather than rice, dominates. Water is at a premium; Chapter 9 discusses the new project to divert part of the Yangtze's flow northward. Summers are hot and winters are quite cold. In the winter, dust storms sometimes come off the Gobi Desert, blanketing Beijing with a fine dust. Heilongjiang and Jilin (see Map 2.2) are cold indeed, especially in the long winter. Summers are short but warm, with enough moisture for crops such as corn and soybeans. Most of China's great cities are located in the East and are expanding into agricultural areas along the Yellow, Yangtze, and West Rivers (Veeck et al., 2011).

The sediment left by river flooding in the North China Plain is quite fertile, though dry. This area was originally covered by forest, although now fields of wheat are most common. Some of the soils have been irrigated so much that they have become salty. Because wet-field paddy cannot be formed in the dry fields of the north, less rice can be grown here. Heilongjiang, Jilin, and Liaoning (see Map 2.2) have poor soils except in the floodplains of the Song and Liao Rivers. Conifer forests still cover much of the mountain region.

Aridity (lack of rainfall) begins to increase in the interior of the country; half of China's territory gets less than 20 inches of rainfall a year (Lu and Hsieh, 2004). The Loess Plateau and Mongolian Plateau (Ordos Platform), shown on Map 2.4, are part of the 20 percent of China that is semiarid, with 10–20 inches (25.4–50.8 centimeters) of rainfall a year. Wheat and some corn and millet are grown here with irrigation from the Yellow River. Summers are very warm and dry, and winters are quite cold and dry. The loess (the brownish-yellow soil that gives the Loess Plateau its name) is very deep and fertile, but erosion is a major problem in this area. The original vegetation was grassland and shrub; cattle have overgrazed much of the remaining vegetation, and most has been plowed into fields. When the rains come, they fall hard and fast. Much of the surface loess ends up in the Yellow River (Veeck et al., 2011).

Over 30 percent of China is almost completely arid, with less than 10 inches of rainfall a year (Lu and Hsieh, 2004). The Takla Makan Desert in the Tarim Basin (Map 2.4) is the most extreme case, with less than 1 inch (2.54 centimeters) of rain per year. Turpan has recorded temperatures up to 118 degrees Fahrenheit (48 degrees Celsius). In this dry stretch of land, only the snowmelt from the mountains can give any water for sustenance. Ürümqi gets its water from the glaciers in the Tian Shan. With global warming, these water sources are receding. Even though the temperature is high, it is not humid, so the summers are bearable. Because Siberia, the source of the winter monsoons, is immediately to the north, winters are severely cold. The many oases make the desert livable; they are highly productive, growing specialty crops such as melons, grapes, and cotton. In the northern portions of this arid area, steppe grasslands afford livestock grazing. The mountains have conifer forests (Veeck et al., 2011; Starr, 2004; Yeung and Shen, 2004).

The Tibetan Plateau (Map 2.4) has a unique and harsh climate. Altitude and location on a continent's interior combine for a dry, cold climate, much like the polar extremes. Every month has temperatures below freezing. The area's interior receives less than 4 inches (10.16 centimeters) of precipitation per year. The summer is quite short, but if you stay in the sun it is warm. Soils are poor in Tibet because there is not much plant life to decay into humus. Barley is grown in the south. The yaks, sheep, goats, and *dzo* (a cross between a yak and an ox) are the only livestock in this harsh climate. The yaks provide meat, milk, and hides for the Tibetans (Geelan and Twitchett, 1974; Yeung and Shen, 2004; Yeh, 2009). They also keep donkeys and horses, and wild asses roam the countryside.

China's 1.34 billion people have many challenges. Only 10 percent of the land will grow crops. Deserts and mountains make up much of western China. Northern China does not have enough water. Only the southeast has a climate that provides an abundance of food. Raising the economic well-being of the people will require careful management of the natural resources.

Economic Resources

When Marco Polo came to China, he found the Chinese burning "black rocks"; the abundance of coal and other fuel has long contributed to China's high economic output. China has several sources of energy. In the rural areas, the energy of the sun and of plants is the major source for most peasants. The burning of coal and oil provides energy for most urban areas. In areas with great rivers, hydroelectric power contributes increasing amounts of electricity.

Peasants use minimal amounts of oil. Coal is the fuel in the north, and people also burn rice straw, wheat straw, cornstalks, and cotton stalks to cook food and boil water; increasingly, they are heating water with solar panels as well. It takes a lot of straw to boil water. Since this material is burned, it is not plowed back into the ground to enrich the soil. Peasants scour the countryside looking for sticks, twigs, bark, and grass to use as fuel because so much of the natural landscape is overcut. This causes the hill slopes to erode without their natural cover. Manure piles are often used to generate methane gas for cooking and light. Small-scale hydroelectric power plants provide enough electricity for lighting in many homes (Smil, 2004; Veeck et al., 2011).

In the city a different pattern emerges. Coal supplies much energy, both for industrial and for residential use. China has the world's largest coal reserves, located mainly in northern China. Coal is processed into charcoal for cooking in urban households (many of which are now switching to gas or electricity), and China's heavy industry relies largely on coal. China's rapid modernization has created the need for increasing numbers of electric power plants, 80 percent of which operate on coal. Output from these plants increases by about 20 percent a year. Because northern China has water shortages, much of the coal is unwashed and thus burns less efficiently. Shipment of coal to other areas is a major difficulty for China. As China's industrialization and modernization increases, it will burn more coal, adding to air and water pollution (Veeck et al., 2011). See Chapter 9 for a discussion of these problems.

China is a major producer of oil but can supply only half of what it consumes. Much of the oil is in northeastern China; newer sites include the Bo Hai region in the northeast (Map 2.4) and Hainan Island in the southeast (Map 2.2). The biggest potential lies in the Tarim Basin of the northwest. Exploration of this desert area has been a major focus. These sites are far from industrial areas, however, so transporting the oil is a problem. A pipeline from Xinjiang to Shanghai has been built. As China increases its use of cars, and more industries and railroads convert to oil, the demand for oil imports will also increase. China has built oil pipelines from Russia and Kazakhstan to China (Lu and Hsieh, 2004).

Eighteen percent of China's electricity derives from hydroelectric power. Strong potential (now threatened by global warming) exists for electricity production on rivers of the south such as the Yangtze. Here the problems lie in moving people and in flooding large farmland areas (Veeck et al., 2011; Heggelund, 2004). In 2011, China had fourteen nuclear power plants in operation and more than twenty-five under construction—mostly located along the eastern coast—with plans to quadruple the amount of nuclear-generated power in each of the next two decades. The nuclear disaster in northern Japan after the March 2011 earthquake has given Chinese authorities pause, but of the world's nuclear plants under construction, China still has half (World Nuclear Association, 2011; Huus, 2011).

China's iron ore reserves lie mostly to the north and northeast. The Chinese have mined iron for thousands of years, and many mining operations are small-scale and locally run. The reserves should be adequate in coming years if used more efficiently. China is looking for more minerals in western regions. Many of them are in out-of-the-way places to the north and west, so roads to the heavy industry located in the north are being built and improved at a rapid rate.

With better soils, water supplies, transportation, and terrain, the eastern portion of China has been more hospitable for living and economic production than the west. The northeast is well suited for heavy industry, and the southeast is ideal for agricultural production. Hence, the economy of China Proper to the east has far surpassed that of Frontier China to the west.

In Chapter 3, we observe that this disparity goes far back in time, and in Chapters 4 and 5, we discuss efforts to reduce it. The Yangtze River, along with new railroads, can play a pivotal role in helping move economic growth westward. The Chinese like to view the coast as a bow and the Yangtze River as an arrow that can shoot industry and economic reforms into China's interior. As discussed in the next chapter, it was the Yellow River that shot China's imperial civilization out to the coast (Veeck et al., 2011). Recent popular books have examined the rise of this economic powerhouse (Kristof and WuDunn, 1995, 2000; Gifford, 2007; Hessler, 2006, 2010; Becker, 2006; Jacques, 2009; Wasserstrom, 2010).

Bibliography

Becker, Jasper. 2006. *Dragon Rising: An Inside Look at China Today*. Washington, DC: National Geographic Society.

Benewick, Robert, and Stephanie Donald. 2009. *The State of China Atlas: Mapping the World's Fastest-growing Economy*. Berkeley: University of California Press.

Blum, Susan Debra, and Lionel M. Jensen (eds.). 2002. *China Off Center: Mapping the Margins of the Middle Kingdom*. Honolulu: University of Hawaii Press.

Borthwick, Mark. 2007. *Pacific Century: The Emergence of Modern Pacific Asia.* 3rd ed. Boulder: Westview Press.
Boulnois, Luce. 2004. *Silk Road: Monks, Warriors and Merchants on the Silk Road.* New York: Norton.
Cannon, Terry (ed.). 2000. *China's Economic Growth: The Impact on Regions, Migration, and the Environment.* New York: St. Martin's Press.
Cannon, Terry, and Alan Jenkins (eds.). 1990. *The Geography of Contemporary China: The Impact of Deng Xiaoping's Decade.* London: Routledge.
Cartier, Carolyn, 2001. *Globalizing South China.* Oxford: Blackwell.
Chan, Kam Wing. 2009. "The Chinese Hukou System at 50." *Eurasian Geography and Economics* 50(2): 197–221.
China Development Gateway. 2011. www.chinagate.com.cn/english/index.htm.
CIA World Factbook. 2011. www.cia.gov/library/publications/the-world-factbook/index.html.
Cooke, Tim. 2010. *The New Cultural Atlas of China.* Tarrytown, NY: Marshall Cavendish Corp.
de Blij, Harm. 2005. *Why Geography Matters. Three Challenges Facing America: Climate Change, the Rise of China, and Global Terrorism.* Oxford: Oxford University Press.
Donald, Stephanie, and Robert Benewick. 2005. *The State of China Atlas.* 2nd ed. Berkeley: University of California Press.
Elegant, Simon, 2008. "China's Quake Damage Control." *Time.* May 13, 2008. www.time.com.
Fan, C. Cindy. 2008."Regional Inequality in China, 1978–2006." *Eurasian Geography and Economics* 49(1): 1–20
Gaubatz, Piper. 1996. *Beyond the Great Wall: Urban Form and Transformation on the Chinese Frontiers.* Stanford, CA: Stanford University Press.
Geelan, Peter J. M., and Denis C. Twitchett (eds.). 1974. *The Times Atlas of China.* London: Times.
Gifford, Rob. 2007. *China Road: A Journey into the Future of a Rising Power.* New York: Random House.
Heggelund, Gørild. 2004. *Environment and Resettlement Politics in China: The Three Gorges Project.* Burlington, VT: Ashgate.
Hessler, Peter. 2006. *Oracle Bones: A Journey Between China's Past and Present.* New York: HarperCollins.
———. 2010. *Country Driving: A Journey Through China from Farm to Factory.* New York: Harper.
Hoh, Erling, and Victor H. Mair. 2009. *The True History of Tea.* London: Thames and Hudson.
Hsing, You-Tien. 2010. *The Great Urban Transformation: Politics of Land and Property in China.* Oxford: Oxford University Press.
Huus, Kari. 2011. "China's Nuclear Energy Policy: 'Build, baby, build.'" *MSNBC*, March 24, 2011. www.msnbc.msn.com
Institute of Geography, Chinese Academy of Sciences. 1994. *The National Economic Atlas of China.* Oxford: Oxford University Press.
———. 2000. *The Atlas of Population, Environment, and Sustainable Development of China.* Beijing; New York: Science Press.
Jacques, Martin. 2009. *When China Rules the World: The End of the Western World and the Birth of a New Global Order.* New York: Penguin Press.
Johnson, Ian. 2011. "At Least 35 Killed and 210 Hurt in Crash of 2 Trains in China." *New York Times*, July 23, 2011. www.nytimes.com.

Knapp, Ronald. 1992. *Chinese Landscapes: The Village as Place*. Honolulu: University of Hawaii Press.

———. 1998. *China's Old Dwellings*. Honolulu: University of Hawaii Press.

Kolb, Albert. 1971. *East Asia: Geography of a Cultural Region*. London: Methuen.

Kong, Lily. 2010. "China and Geography in the 21st Century: A Cultural (Geographical) Revolution?" *Eurasian Geography and Economics* 51(5): 600–618.

Kristof, Nicholas, and Sheryl WuDunn. 1995. *China Wakes: The Struggle for the Soul of a Rising Power.* New York: Vintage Books.

———. 2000. *Thunder from the East: Portrait of a Rising Asia*. New York: Knopf.

Ledderose, Lothar. 2000. *Ten Thousand Things: Module and Mass Production in Chinese Art*. Princeton, NJ: Princeton University Press.

Lew, Alan A., Lawrence Yu, John Ap, and Zhang Guangrui (eds.). 2002. *Tourism in China*. New York: Haworth Hospitality Press.

Li, Si-ming, and Wing-shing Tang (eds.). 2000. *China's Regions, Polity, and Economy.* Hong Kong: Chinese University Press.

Lin, George C. S. 2009. *Developing China: Land, Politics, and Social Conditions*. London: Routledge.

Lin, George C. S., and S. Ho. 2005. "The State, Land System, and Land Development Processes in Contemporary China," *Annals of Association of American Geographers* 95(2): 411–436.

Lu, Max, and Chiao-min Hsieh (eds.). 2004. *Changing China: A Geographic Appraisal*. Boulder: Westview Press.

Ma, Lifang (ed.). 2002. *Geological Atlas of China*. Beijing: Geological Publishing House.

Marton, Andrew. 2000. *China's Spatial Economic Development: Restless Landscapes in the Lower Yangzi Delta*. London: Routledge.

McColl, Robert. 2011. "The Rise of Eastern China." *Education About Asia* 16(1): 123–126.

Murphy, Alexander. 2010. "Reassessing Human Geography in the Wake of China's Rise." *Eurasian Geography and Economics* 51(5): 563–568.

National Geographic Society. 2008. *Atlas of China*. Washington, DC: National Geographic Society.

Oakes, Tim. 2002. "China's Provincial Identities: Reviving Regionalism and Reinventing 'Chineseness.'" *Journal of Asian Studies* 59(3): 667–692.

Pannell, Clifton W. 2007. "The China Challenge: Observations on the Outlook for the 21st Century." *Eurasian Geography and Economics* 48(1): 3–15.

———. 2011. "China Gazes West: Xinjiang's Growing Rendezvous with Central Asia." *Eurasian Geography and Economics* 52(1): 105–118.

Selya, Roger Mark (ed.). 1992. *The Geography of China, 1975–1991: An Annotated Bibliography.* East Lansing: Asian Studies Center, Michigan State University.

———. 2005. *The Geography of China: An Annotated Bibliography of Pre-1974 English-Language Journal Literature*. Ann Arbor, MI: Association for Asian Studies.

Sivin, Nathan (ed.). 1988. *The Contemporary Atlas of China*. London: Weidenfeld and Nicolson.

Smil, Vaclav. 2004. *China's Past, China's Future: Energy, Food, Environment*. New York: Routledge.

Starr, S. Frederick. 2004. *Xinjiang: China's Muslim Borderland.* Armonk, NY: M. E. Sharpe.

Su, Ming Ming, and Geoffrey Wall. 2009. "The Qinghai-Tibet Railway and Tibetan Tourism: Travelers' Perspectives." *Tourism Management* 30: 650–657.

Toops, Stanley. 2004. "Demographics and Development in Xinjiang After 1949." East-West Center Washington Working Papers, No. 1, May.

Toops, Stanley W., and Simone Andrus. 1993. "Social Intelligence in China." *Journal of Economic & Social Intelligence* 3(1): 3–20.

Tregear, T. R. 2007. *A Geography of China.* Piscataway, NJ: Aldine Transaction.

Tuan, Yi-fu. 2008. *A Historical Geography of China.* Piscataway, NJ: Aldine Transaction.

Veeck, Gregory (ed.). 1991. *The Uneven Landscape: Geographical Studies in Post-Reform China.* Baton Rouge: Louisiana State University.

Veeck, Gregory, Clifton W. Pannell, Christopher J. Smith, and Youqin Huang. 2011. *China's Geography: Globalization and the Dynamics of Political, Economic, and Social Change.* 2nd ed. Lanham, MD: Rowan and Littlefield.

Wasserstrom, Jeffrey N. 2010. *China in the 21st Century: What Everyone Needs to Know.* New York: Oxford University Press.

Wei, Yehua. 2000. *Regional Development in China.* London: Routledge.

Weightman, Barbara A. 2011. *Dragons and Tigers: A Geography of South, East, and Southeast Asia.* 3rd ed. New York: John Wiley.

World Nuclear Association. 2011. "Nuclear Power in China." www.world-nuclear.org.

Yeh, Emily T. 2009. "From Wasteland to Wetland? Nature and Nation in China's Tibet." *Environmental History* 14(1): 103–137.

Yeung Y. M., and Shen Jianfa (eds.). 2004. *Developing China's West: A Critical Path to Balanced National Development.* Hong Kong: Chinese University Press.

Zhang, Q. F., et al. 2009. "The Han River Watershed Management Initiative for the South-to-North Water Transfer Project of China." *Environmental Monitoring and Assessment* 148: 369–377.

Zhao, Songqiao. 1994. *Geography of China: Environment, Resources, Population, and Development.* New York: John Wiley.

3

The Historical Context

Rhoads Murphey

In Chapter 2, Stanley Toops showed how China is situated within Asia and how its people blend into the three tiers of its natural landscape. He also introduced some of the cultural diversity that has resulted from the blending. In this chapter, I, too, will emphasize how nature both limits and encourages human occupancy of the land, but now the focus is on the history of human settlement, conquest, and government in China. As we begin half a million years ago and move forward to the present, another kind of blending becomes evident: China's isolation from much of the rest of the planet allowed it to develop a unique culture that contributed extensively to civilizations elsewhere. At the same time, this culture was able to absorb conquests, technology, migrations, and religions from outside without losing its own identity. Even periods of disunity and conquests by Europeans and Japanese during the past two centuries have left China's unique culture and institutions fundamentally intact.

Chapter 2 introduced you to the distinction between Frontier China and China Proper and between southeastern and northeastern China. As we review the histories of China's imperial dynasties in this chapter, it will quickly become evident that China's imperial civilization began in Frontier China (see Map 3.1) but has its base in the valley and floodplain of the Yellow River (see Map 2.4). Periodically, parts of northern China have been conquered by groups of invaders coming in from the Frontier, and the Mongols (briefly) and the Manchus (more enduringly) conquered the whole country. Yet those invaders also soon adopted the habits and institutions of China Proper. And China Proper itself has a long historical division; southeastern China's culture is as old and solid as that of the northeast. Those in the northeast conquered those in the southeast. That conquest has not been forgotten.

This chapter introduces a number of other themes that, like those in the prior two paragraphs, are treated more fully in subsequent chapters. China experienced feudalism and developed a centralized state long before those social and political processes came to Europe. It developed some unique relationships between government officials and merchants that often pitted south against north and region against region yet encouraged agriculture, commerce, and the early growth of cities. It repeatedly tried to conquer and control people in adjoining territories. It has sometimes welcomed traders from around the world and sometimes kept them more at arm's length. The early parts of new dynasties often brought exciting growth and innovation; the latter parts often brought decline and stagnation. When European powers first tested the empire with the 1839 Opium War, the empire was in a period of decline (Lovell, 2011). That war exposed China's technological backwardness and resistance to change and opened up a century of conquest and humiliation by outside powers. Yet China has once again found the strength to rebound as it seeks to bring its technology to world levels.

The Peopling of China

Early Inhabitants

Remains of great apes walking on two legs (hominidae, the biological family within which our genus [*Homo*] and our species [*Homo sapiens*] falls) have been found in Africa, dating as far back as 7 million years BCE. These are *Sahelanthropus tcahadensis* and *Orrorin tugenensis*. The remains of another African hominid, *Australopithecus,* date as far back as 4 million years BCE. There is no evidence that any of these lived in China. The same is true of *Homo habilis* and *Homo neanderthalensis,* who are members of our genus. Remains of another member of our genus, *Homo erectus,* have been found in many parts of China dated as far back as 700,000 years. Remains found in caves near Beijing, popularly known as Peking Man, are the best known of these finds; Chinese schoolchildren are taught that this is their ancestor (Hooker, 2006; Sautman, 2001; Schmalzer, 2008; Ropp, 2010:1–19).

Paleoanthropologists are divided on the question of whether *Homo erectus* and *Homo sapiens,* though identified as part of the same genus, ever interbred. Recent DNA testing is gathering evidence that modern humans largely may have evolved from a few *Homo sapiens* who originated in Africa less than 300,000 years ago and migrated out of Africa about 50,000 years ago to populate the planet. They would have entered China via Southeast Asia. A 1998 genetic study of twenty-eight groups from all over China, including a number of the minorities discussed in Chapter 8, did not include many Han but concluded that most modern members of these groups descend from Africans participating in that migration, who probably had offspring with some of the *Homo sapiens* who already resided in China (Chu et al., 1998). *Homo sapien* remains

Map 3.1 Historical Boundaries of China

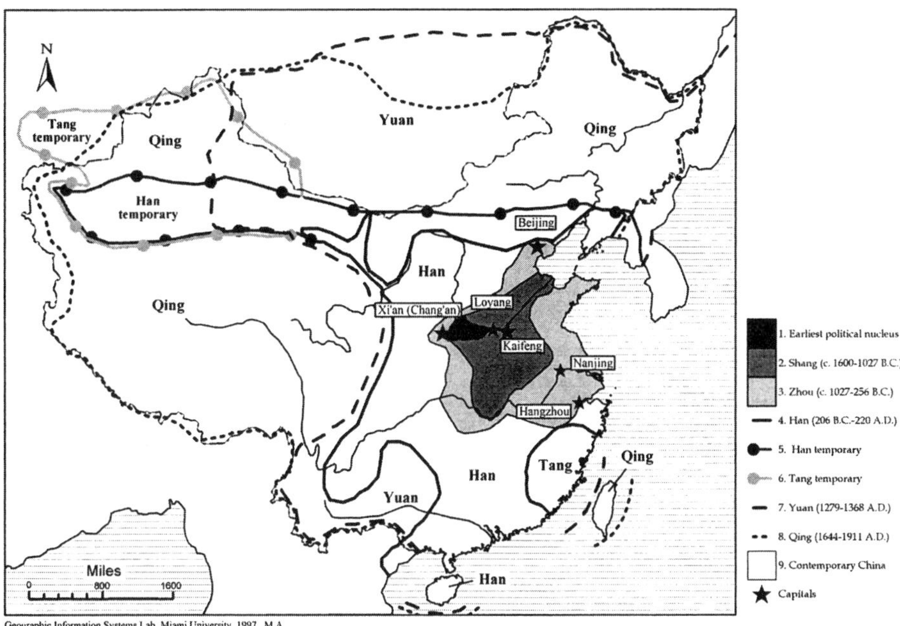

Geographic Information Systems Lab, Miami University, 1997 M.A.

found in China—which date back in their premodern form as far as 300,000 years—differ in some characteristics from African *Homo sapiens* (see Shang et al., 2007). By about 100,000 BCE, *Homo erectus* died out in China, while characteristics of *Homo sapiens* continued to evolve. By 30,000 BCE, *Homo sapiens* there began to take on the facial and body build characteristics of modern northern and southern Chinese (Sautman, 2001; Chu et al., 1998).

The question of whether Chinese developed independently from *Homo sapiens* elsewhere flows into another debate, about an archaeological site in Henan province called Erlitou (Allan, 2007, 2002; Liu, 2005; Liu and Chen, 2003; Sit, 2010). Many Chinese archaeologists and historians say this may have been a capital city of the Xia empire, ruled by the Yellow Emperor, described as the founding ancestor of all Chinese by Sima Qian in his *Records of the Grand Historian,* written during the first century BCE (Qian and Watson, 1996; Loewe and Shaughnessy, 1999:65–73; Hardy, 1999). That notion bolsters national identity of China as the Middle Kingdom, distinct from all others, discussed in Chapter 2 (Sautman, 2001). Dating between 2000 and 1500 BCE, there is no writing on the site to confirm this one way or another. The city (with large palaces and grand paved avenues) contained bronze ritual bowls that relate to the later Shang dynasty, and pottery and pottery wheels similar to those found in the Longshan sites in Shandong dating back to around 3000 BCE (Liu, 2005; Kwang Chih Chang, 1983). Those sites were cities with rammed earth walls. Earlier sites of villages date to around 7000 BCE, with evidence of rice cultivation going back that far (Loewe and Shaughnessy, 1999:42–54).

The Chinese have always been very conscious and proud of their long and glorious past. That consciousness and pride remain true today, and one really cannot understand contemporary China without considerable knowledge of its history.

North and South

China covers a huge area, larger than the United States if one includes Tibet, Xinjiang, Inner Mongolia, and Manchuria (Heilongjiang, Jilin, and Liaoning), where cultures and physical types remain different from those of China Proper (Loewe and Shaughnessy, 1999; Giersch, 2006; Allan, 2002; Bulog, 2002). Even the provinces within China Proper (which itself originally contained a wide but closely related variety of cultures and physical types) cover territory large enough to hold most of the countries of Western Europe (Loewe and Shaughnessy, 1999:54–63). In the third century BCE, with the creation of empire under the Qin dynasty (221 BCE), the people and culture of northern China conquered the central and southern regions of China Proper. Soon they were spreading their culture and then themselves southward (Ropp, 2010:20–36).

From the time of the Han dynasty (202 BCE–220 CE) and its consolidation of empire, the inhabitants called themselves "people of Han." Map 3.1 shows you how the Han dynasty moved into territory farther south and west than previous dynasties. The southernmost people conquered by the Han were distantly related to but distinct from them. Qin and Han expansion also took place at the expense of the several more closely related but distinct peoples and cultures of central and southern China. Some of these southerners had almost certainly created what we may call "civilization"—settled agriculture, metals, writing, and cities—at least as early as or earlier than these developments in the north, where in the dry climate the evidence is better preserved (Liu, 2005). Such early developments in the south would be a logical result of its proximity to the original sources of cultivated rice, pigs, chickens, water buffalo, and early making of bronze (Linduff, Han, and Sun, 2000), all in adjacent Southeast Asia (northern Vietnam and northern Thailand), probably well before they appeared in what is now China. Transmittal was easy, and there was probably also some movement of peoples. Before the Qin conquest forcibly united all Chinese into a single empire, the Guangdong area (see Map 2.2) was joined in a single state with what is now northern Vietnam, the state of Yueh, which spoke a common language (Meacham, 1983). But it is hard to imagine historical China without even one of the key elements derived from

Robert E. Gamer

These rice terraces in Ping'an, Guangxi, were built during the Yuan dynasty by the Zhuang minority.

Southeast Asia—buffalo for plowing the soil, rice and pigs as staples in the diet (Te-Tzu Chang, 1983:70–77), and bronze for casting (Barnard, 1983; Allan, 2007; Thorp, 2006). In time, these presumably spread into central and northern China, but the north was generally too dry for rice and buffalo and only marginally hospitable for pigs and chickens.

In the course of the Qin and Han conquests, a single written language was imposed as well as a common spoken language—the ancestor of modern standard spoken Chinese—for the officials who administered the empire (Connery, 1999). Originally, northern culture overlaid the widely different cultures of the south. With the fall of the Han dynasty in 220 CE, the long migration of northerners southward over some 2,000 years began, which added further pressures toward a national mode, in addition to the northern troops and administrators who had been operating in the south since the third century BCE. Distinct traces of different regional cultures and speech patterns remain among Han Chinese in the south, including differences in diet and cuisine as well as strong provincial identity amounting almost to clannishness. But the southward wave of Han Chinese conquest and settlement has taken all of the good agricultural land and greatly reduced the original non-Han population, who now live only in mountainous areas mainly unfit for agriculture, where they have been driven by Han pressures. In a few subprovincial areas of this sort they constitute a majority, yet their numbers are small, and they are divided among themselves by cultural and linguistic differences. In the southwest provinces of Yunnan, Guizhou, and Guangxi, the Zhuang, Miao, Dong, Yi, and Yao fought frequently with the Han and were used by the Han to fight other frontiersmen. Some 91 percent of China's people are Han, with the remainder widely scattered and fragmented. As Chapter 8 explains, these percentages are somewhat inaccurate because many Han in recent years have married non-Han or asserted non-Han identity to avoid the one-child policy of the government, which does not apply to non-Han. Over the centuries since the Qin and Han conquest of the south, there has been widespread intermarriage as well as pressures for cultural conformity, so that the many originally quite separate and distinct cultures of central and southern China have been overlaid by a common imperial stamp. Traces of the originally wide variety of physical types, as well as aspects of local or regional culture, continue to be apparent beneath that stamp.

Since the late nineteenth century, Inner Mongolia, along the steppe frontier, was heavily occupied by Han Chinese, mainly as farmers dependent on new irrigation and road and rail lines (Bulog, 2002; Elverskog, 2006; Sneath, 2000). The northeast provinces of Heilongjiang, Liaoning, and Jilin have been overwhelmed by mass Han Chinese migration that has almost obliterated the original Tungusic, Manchu, and Mongol population as the northeast received refugees from overcrowded and drought-ridden northern China and developed its own surplus agricultural system and the largest heavy industrial complex in East Asia, thanks to its major resources of coal, iron, oil, and water (hydropower).

To the west, in Xinjiang, Tibet, and Qinghai, other dynamics were at work, which is discussed later in this chapter and in the section on Tibet in Chapter 6.

Political Patterns of the Past

Feudalism

China's recorded history begins with the Shang dynasty (ca. 1600–1027 BCE; see Map 3.1 and Table 3.1), whose authenticity was questioned by Western scholars until excavations in the 1920s uncovered the remains of the last Shang capital, Anyang, and a great number of inscriptions giving the names of Shang kings. Later excavations (Allan, 2002; Hansen, 2000:15–54; Thorp, 2006; Liu and Chen, 2003; Hessler, 2007:142–147, 352–357) rounded out the picture of the Shang as being dependent on slaves captured in chronic wars with surrounding groups, already referred to as "barbarians," and as managing a productive agricultural system on the fertile loess (wind-laid, yellow-brown soil) of northern China. The chief Shang crop was millet, probably native to northern China, slowly supplemented by rice as rice moved northward. The major technological achievement of the Shang was in the working of bronze, from which they produced objects whose technical perfection has never been equaled (Linduff, Han, and Sun, 2000; Ebrey, 2010:10–37). Excavations in central and southern China, where high temperatures and humidity have tended to obliterate much of the evidence, have nevertheless made it clear, as hinted at earlier, that Shang achievements were paralleled, perhaps even preceded, farther south, where writing, bronze, and a surplus-producing agriculture based mainly on rice were used (Te-Tzu Chang, 1983; Gernet, 1996:40–50; Hsu, 1995:1–32).

The Shang built large and ornate palaces whose remains can tell us a good deal about the wealth generated by agricultural surpluses, including the richly decorated chariots that were buried in the royal tombs with their horses and large numbers of followers or slaves. Writing, clearly the ancestor of modern written Chinese, slowly evolved and expanded to include abstractions; many of the characters can still be read, and the system was inherited by the next dynasty, the Zhou (Te-Tzu Chang, 1983:81–94; Chun-shu Chang, 2007; Gascoigne, 2003:7–26; Li, 1985:442–459; Loewe and Shaughnessy, 1999; Ebrey, 2010:10–59; Tanner, 2010:33–83). The Zhou's successor, the Qin dynasty, would impose this northern script on all of China, replacing the different scripts already in use farther south.

In about 1027 BCE, a great slave revolt was joined by one of the Shang feudal vassals, the Zhou who guarded the western frontiers (Hsu, 1995:33–67). Originally a "barbarian" group, the Zhou had acquired most of Shang culture and technology and used what became the traditional Chinese justification for rebellion, citing the injustices and oppression of the Shang rulers and declaring that "heaven commands us to destroy it" (Kwang Chih Chang, 1983:44–55; Hsu, 1995:68–111). The last Shang king, alleged to have been a monster of depravity, died in the flames of his palace.

The Shang had ruled from successive capitals, which were frequently moved, in the central Yellow River valley, including the site of modern Zhengzhou, capital of Henan province (see Map 2.2). This was the heartland of early agriculture, but the Zhou established their new capital near modern Xi'an (see Map 3.1 and Shaanxi province on Map 2.2), their old base. Warfare continued with other groups around the fringes of the Zhou domains and periodically with groups to the south, all still called barbarians.

The Zhou adopted the feudal solution used by the Shang, a network of supposed vassals owing loyalty to the Zhou king (Gascoigne, 2003:27–54; Gernet, 1996:51–61; Hansen, 2000:55–96; Li, 1985:460–476; Hsu, 1995: 112–157; Liu and Chen, 2003; Tanner, 2010:34–58). This resembled the system in medieval Europe, where a central state with pretensions to wider power (but without the means to enforce them) made alliances with local and regional groups, symbolized by ritual homage, provision of troops, and periodic gifts, in exchange for their control over their regional lands as fiefs granted by the king. For perhaps the first two or three centuries of Zhou rule, this system

Table 3.1 China's Imperial Dynasties and Beyond

Dynasty	In China	In the Rest of the World
Xia 2100–1600 BCE (?)	Chinese characters developed	2700 BCE Egyptians build Great Pyramid
Shang 1600–1027 BCE (?)	Advanced bronze casting	1250 BCE Moses and the exodus from Egypt 1200 BCE Trojan War
Zhou 1027–211 BCE Western Zhou 1027–771 BCE Eastern Zhou 771–221 BCE	Feudalism Emperors called "Sons of Heaven" Spring and Autumn Period 771–476 BCE Confucius 551–479 BCE Warring States Period 476–221 BCE	753 BCE Rome founded 560–483 BCE Buddha in India 399 BCE Death of Socrates 336–323 BCE Alexander the Great
Qin 221–206 BCE	China unified Great Wall unified	
Han 202 BCE–220 CE Western Han 206 BCE–9 CE Eastern Han 25 BCE–CE 220	Confucianism adopted Silk Road opens Buddhism to China Paper invented	54 BCE Caesar invades Britain
Three Kingdoms 220–280	Period of disunity	
Eight Dynasties 265–589	Invasion and more division	451 Attila the Hun defeated 476 Fall of Rome
Sui 589–618	Grand Canal built	

continues

Dynasty	In China	In the Rest of the World
Tang 618–907	Expanding trade First printed book	Dark Ages in Europe 742–814 Charlemagne
Five Dynasties 907–960	Period of disunity	
Qidan 936–1122	Rule northern China	1096 First Crusade
Jin 1115–1234		
Song 960–1279 Northern Song 960–1126 Southern Song 1127–1279	Rule southern China Capital in Kaifeng Capitals in Nanjing, Hangzhou	Medieval Europe 1215 Magna Carta
Yuan 1279–1368	Genghis and Kublai Khan invade from Mongolia	1300 Renaissance 1347–1351 Black Death
Ming 1368–1644	Return to rule by Chinese	1450 Printing in Europe 1492 Columbus reaches the "New World" 1517 Reformation 1637 First British trade with Canton
Qing 1644–1911	Manchu rulers	1776 American Revolution 1789 French Revolution
Republic 1912–1949	KMT Nationalist rule	1917 Russia's communist revolution 1939–1945 World War II
People's Republic 1949–	Communist rule	

seemed to work reasonably well (Chun-shu Chang, 2007). But China was changing as regional vassals increased their power and ambitions beyond the ability of the central state to control.

The Decline of Feudalism

More basically, the spread of iron tools greatly increased farm production, hastened the clearing of remaining forests with iron axes as well as with fire, expedited new irrigation systems, and, taken together, supported a major increase in population, from perhaps 5 or 10 million under the late Shang to perhaps 20 million by mid-Zhou, spurred by rising food output, which also provided surpluses to be exchanged in trade. Towns and cities began to dot the plain and the Yangtze valley, and a merchant class of some size emerged.

As in medieval Europe, none of this fit well with the feudal system based on fixed serfdom and the dominance of a hereditary aristocracy. Serfs could escape to the new towns and begin a new life. We don't know much about the life of the common people in the first few centuries of Zhou rule, but it may be revealing that the arrangement mentioned by Mencius much later (third century BCE), which he called the "well field system," included a checkerboard plan with a well in the central plot. Serfs were supposed to give priority to irrigating and cultivating that plot, which belonged to the feudal lord, and only after that could work on the outer plots assigned to them. Serfs were bound to the lord and to his land for life, and on the lord's death could not leave but became serfs to his heir. As the economy altered and agricultural surpluses offered new opportunities for merchants and town dwellers to live and make money, such a system became increasingly hard to maintain (Li, 1985:477–490; Li, 2006).

By this time, most writing was done with brush and ink, as in all subsequent centuries, on silk or on strips of bamboo. It was thus that the main body of the Chinese classics was originally written under the mid-Zhou: the *I-ching,* or *Classic of Change* (*Yijing*—a cryptic handbook for diviners), the *Book of Songs,* the *Book of Rituals,* and collections of historical documents (see Chapters 12 and 13).

New agricultural productivity freed increasing numbers from farm labor to serve as artisans, scribes, transport workers, soldiers, officials, scholars, and merchants. Towns and cities became more important as trade centers than as centers of feudal control. At the same time, many of the original Zhou vassals were evolving toward separate statedom, as in late medieval Europe, each with its own distinctive culture. After some four centuries of Zhou rule, the political, economic, and social structure began to show strains, and eventually it disintegrated.

In 771 BCE (the first authenticated date in Chinese history), the Zhou capital, near Xi'an, was sacked by rebels, and though it was rebuilt, the capital was moved to Loyang (shown on Map 3.1) in the central Yellow River valley so as to better control the Zhou domains (Li, 2006). It was a vain hope, as the feudal structure continued to break up and vassals, now emerging states, increasingly ignored Zhou authority and fought each other for dominance (Di Cosmo, 2004). The old Zhou base in the Wei valley near modern Xi'an was given as a fief to a supposedly loyal noble of the Qin clan, the new guardians of the frontier. Five centuries later, the Qin swept away the crumbling remnants of Zhou pretension to found the first all-China empire (Li, 2006).

Toward a Centralized State

The Qin were, in fact, the smallest and weakest of the major contenders among the former Zhou vassals, at least to begin with (Lewis, 2007; Li, 1985:222–239). The other rivals were various northern and central states as well as the state of Qu in the Yangtze valley and Yueh in the far south. It is still too early to speak of any of them, or of the Zhou, as "China"; each was culturally, linguistically, and politically distinct, and for some time there were also minor racial differences (Li, 1985:59–188). The 500 final years of feudalism over which they presided are known as the Spring and Autumn Period and the Warring States Period. Though they shared technology, no one state dominated until the Qin conquest in 221 BCE (Gernet, 1996:62–82; Hsu, 1995:258–287). The state of Qu provides a good example of the differences, in that its base along the central portion of the Yangtze River led to rapid development of trade, towns, and cities. But Qu was ultimately defeated by a coalition of northern states in 632 BCE and again in 301 BCE. This may have been one of those contests that changes the course of history, giving the future to a peasant-based authoritarian empire, beginning with the Qin, rather than to a state where trade and merchants were prominent.

Increasing food production made it possible to field large armies of men who could be spared from farming for at least parts of the year and could be fed on surpluses. Warfare became larger in scale and more ruthless, no longer the earlier chivalric contests between aristocrats but efforts at wholesale conquest and fights for survival. The crossbow with a trigger mechanism, developed by or before this time, greatly increased firepower, range, and accuracy, and by the fourth century BCE foot soldiers were supported by armed cavalry. All this undermined the earlier dominance of hereditary aristocrats, their chariots, and their personal retinues. Bronze and copper coins were minted by each state, standing armies proliferated, and bureaucracies began to appear. These changes offered a new range of opportunities for able commoners (Falkenhausen, 2006). For many it was a positive and welcome change, but for others the passing of the old order and the disruptions of warfare offered only chaos and moral confusion. Confucius, who lived in the Spring and Autumn Period (see Table 3.1), made it clear that his prescriptions were an effort to reestablish order and what he referred to as "harmony," following the values of an earlier "golden age." As fighting continued, the Qin exterminated the remnant of Zhou power in 256 BCE, with no ceremony, and went on a generation later to overwhelm all the other states in a series of lightning campaigns ending in 221 BCE. China derives its name from the word *Qin* (*Ch'in* in Wade-Giles transliteration).

The chaos of the Warring States Period led to the growth of formulas for restoring order, like that of Confucius (551–479 BCE) and his later disciple Mencius (372–289 BCE), which stressed the need for order within a social hierarchy (de Bary and Lufrano, 1999; Gernet, 1996:83–100; Waley, 1939). The most important of these, after Confucianism, was Daoism, which through its cryptic text, the *Dao de jing,* or "Classic of the Way," represented a different approach to the troubles of the time (de Bary, Bloom, and Adler, 2000). The supposed author, Laozi, whose name means simply "the old one," is a shadowy figure who was a contemporary of Confucius. Where Confucius emphasized the importance of rules for human behavior and gave advice to rulers, Daoism urged believers to relax, go with the flow, and use nature as the pattern, especially water, which flows around obstructions and seeks the lowest places. Whatever exists is natural and therefore good. In practice, both Confucianism and Daoism had an appeal for most Chinese, who tended to follow both at different times: Daoism in retirement or when things went badly, and Confucianism when in office; or, as has been said, they were workday Confucians and weekend Daoists. Other later philosophical schools, especially under the Qin, adopted the doctrines called Legalism, which emphasized harsh laws to control behavior instead of Confucianism's dependence on morality (de Bary, Bloom, and Adler, 2000; Hansen, 2000:97–112). Chapter 12 discusses these thinkers in greater depth.

The Qin conquest in 221 BCE imposed stern measures to ensure conformity within the new empire. Primogeniture, whereby the eldest son inherits all of his father's property and status, was abolished, as a possible basis for power that might threaten the state. Land was now privately owned and freely bought and sold, which completed the end of the former feudal system. Walls had been built before to discourage raids along the northern steppe border, but these were consolidated and rebuilt under the Qin. These walls, often made of mud and stone, have become known as the Great Wall, which runs east and west approximately along a line between areas to the south where normal rainfall is enough for farming and those to the north that are too dry. The Great Wall and the system of imperial roads and canals were built by forced labor, levied as part of taxes (corvée), which caused much suffering (Hessler, 2010:10–43, 77–121; Lovell, 2006; Yamashita and Lindesay, 2007; Lindesay, 2008; Man, 2009; Rojas, 2010). Those who asked questions, the intellectuals, were suppressed by the new totalitarian state. Empire building is a rough business anywhere, but for all its excesses the Qin laid the groundwork for the dynasties that followed and for the modern state (Ebrey, 2010:60–85; Loewe and Wilson, 2005, 2006; Lewis, 2007; Twitchett, 1986). These moves were doubtless popular, but the oppressively heavy set of state controls led to revolts that toppled the Qin in only fifteen years and burned the emperor's magnificent palace as rebels occupied the capital near modern-day Xi'an in 206 BCE (Lewis, 2007).

By 202 BCE, a new rebel leader emerged out of the civil war, Liu Bang, who founded a new dynasty, which he called Han. He placed his capital on the site of modern-day Xi'an (see Maps 2.2 and 3.1), which he named Chang'An (Long Peace). The harsher aspects of Qin rule were softened by the more humane morality of Confucianism, but many of the empire-building systems of the Qin were retained (Loewe and Wilson, 2006). The new dynasty emphasized the Confucian precept that government exists to serve the people and that unjust rulers must forfeit the support of the ruled (de Bary, Bloom, and Adler, 2000; Hansen, 2000:112–150; Loewe, 1994; Tanner, 2010:83–134; and see Chapter 4).

What remains of the glory of the Qin was rediscovered near Xi'an in the 1970s as excavations were begun at the massive tomb of the Qin emperor, Qin Shihuang, revealing a terra cotta (pottery) army, each of the thousands of life-size figures individually portrayed and set to guard the tomb's entrance (Yang, 2004). The idea of empire is contagious, and the Han extended their boundaries still farther (Gernet, 1996:103–170). In 111 BCE, the emperor Han Wudi reclaimed the Qin conquests of Guangdong and into northern Vietnam and added southern Manchuria and northern Korea to the empire in 109–108 BCE (see Maps 2.2 and 3.1). Earlier he had conquered the desert of Xinjiang, mainly to guard the Silk Roads westward (Map 2.1), and built watchtowers and garrison posts along it while mounting several successful campaigns against the ancestors of the Mongols in Inner Mongolia (Lattimore, 1997; Kuzmina, 2008; Wood, 2004; Millward, 2007; Boulnois, 2008; Beckwith, 2009; Liu, 2010; Standen, 2007; Whitfield, 2001).

Silk caravans crossed the desert of Xinjiang by any one of three main routes and then handed over the silk to a series of Central Asian groups who carried it to the shores of the Mediterranean, where it went by ship to Rome, the biggest market, which paid for it in gold, since the Romans had nothing to offer in exchange that the Chinese wanted. Tibet remained outside the empire. Wudi's endless campaigns and the burdens they imposed nearly caused a revolt, but following the advice of the imperial censors, he issued a famous penitential edict promising to be a better and less oppressive ruler. Han rule was briefly broken by a palace coup in 9 CE when the empress's nephew Wang Mang declared himself emperor of a new dynasty, but he was overthrown in 23 CE and the Han reestablished itself in 25 CE, now as the Eastern Han, with its capital at Loyang (Map 3.1), where most of the dynasty's former grandeur was continued (Tanner, 2010:109–135). But no political order lasts forever, and in the face of rebellion, the last Han ruler abdicated in 220 CE.

The Move South

There followed a confused and confusing period sometimes called the Six Dynasties, when originally barbarian groups ruled most of the north, while the south was contested among a number of Chinese rivals. Buddhism had come in from India during the Han, and now, in this "time of troubles," it spread widely and for a time eclipsed Confucianism while at the folk level merging with Daoism (Ebrey, 2010:86–107; Gernet, 1996:174–228; Hansen, 2000: 151–190). But the model of a unified empire established by the Han remained in people's minds, and after three and a half centuries of fragmentation, a new all-China dynasty, the Sui, re-created the empire of the Han (Xiong, 2006; Ropp, 2010:50–66). The fall of the Han dynasty had stimulated a mass movement southward of Chinese fleeing trouble in the north, a major new wave in the Han people's occupation of the south, driving most of the original non-Han inhabitants up into the mountains as the Han took the good agricultural land (Lewis, 2009). This process was to continue cumulatively over the next 1,500 years or more and included the incorporation of Fujian both within the Chinese sphere and into the empires of Sui and Tang. Fujian is mountainous, and its easiest communications are by sea from the coast; its people were among the first to develop trade with Taiwan and Southeast Asia. The language of Fujian people remains different from standard Chinese but essentially the same as Taiwanese, since most of the people of Taiwan migrated from coastal Fujian beginning after 1600 CE (see Chapter 6).

The move south meant a series of adjustments to a very different environment from that in the north, where most Han had previously lived. New tools suited to wet-rice agriculture were developed, including the endless chain of paddles driven by two men pushing pedals on a crank, designed to move water efficiently from one paddy level to another (Needham, 1956–1986; Ronan, 1995; Winchester, 2008). Rice, the dominant crop, was now transplanted from seedbeds to irrigated fields, and, in the warmer and wetter southern climate, yields greatly increased as a result, and two or even three crops a year became possible. Irrigation, intensive cultivation, and the creation of more or less level paddies by terracing on slopes required huge amounts of labor, provided by a growing population sustained by increased food output. In this period also began the use of human manure, or "night soil," to build the nitrogen levels that boosted yields and increased in supply as the population grew. Perhaps the clearest and most potentially destructive impact of the rising southern population was, however, the removal of most of the original forest cover to clear land for farming. As the population continued to rise, steeper and steeper slopes were invaded by terraces, and the area covered by trees was greatly reduced, producing, as in the north where deforestation was much older, erosion, siltation of stream and irrigation channels, and flooding. But forests harbored wild beasts such as tigers and offered refuge for bandits, reasons used by peasants for destroying them, often by fire.

By about the eighth century CE, half or more of the population lived in the south, which also provided most of the imperial revenue and the food supply to feed the capital (still retained in the north because of tradition) and to guard the threatened area of the northern and northwestern frontier. But the north, the cradle of empire, had become a marginal area economically, or at least agriculturally, as the progressive removal of the forest since before Shang times led to massive erosion, siltation of streams and irrigation systems, and consequent severe and chronic flooding, especially of the silt-laden Yellow River, but also of all the other streams in the north. Irrigated and cultivated land shrank disastrously, and much of the north could no longer feed itself and had to depend on southern imports of rice. The Grand Canal was built to link the north with the south for such transport.

In the south, the wetter and warmer climate meant that forest or second growth could more easily reestablish itself, especially if it was left alone, but as the population continued to increase, that became less and less common and large areas reverted to grass and brush, much less effective in retarding erosion. The growing population not only cleared more land to farm but cut from all hillsides twigs and grass for use as fuel or as fodder for penned animals. Trade, along both rivers and the seacoast, flourished in the south and supported a growing number of cities. Most places could be reached by cheap water transport, sometimes in no other way, whereas in the north most streams (including the heavily silted Yellow River) were not navigable, and goods had to be transported by pack animal, cart, and human porters at far greater cost.

The south also benefited from overseas trade in far greater volume than before, and port cities, especially along the coast from the mouth of the Yangtze River south, multiplied and prospered on the trade with Taiwan and Southeast Asia. Permanent colonies of Chinese merchants were established in the Philippines, Vietnam, Java, and elsewhere, and there was a great advance in shipbuilding, drawing its wood from near-coastal southern forests, especially in mountainous Fujian. Such developments tended to reemphasize the cultural differences of Cantonese and Fujianese from the main body of Chinese, and such differences remain. Canton (Guangzhou) and ports north of it such as Swatow (Shantou) and Amoy (Xiamen) joined Fuzhou and other Fujianese ports in generating a maritime, mercantile, seagoing world that contrasted with the inward-centered and agricultural world of the rest of China, with its imperial capital far inland and its revenue heavily dependent on the land tax (Cohen, 2001; Wellington, 2006; Fan, 2007; Ptak, 2004; Gernet, 1996: 300–347). The Cantonese and Fujianese (Min) spoken languages remain distinct from standard Chinese, not mutually intelligible with it, and there is a prejudice among most other Chinese against the Cantonese, especially as wily traders communicating with each other in their own spoken language and practicing clannishness and sharp dealing (Faure, 2007; Hansen, 1995). Even their food and other customs are different. The Cantonese return the compliment by stereotyping northerners as slow-witted peasants or interfering bureaucrats (Lee, 2005). But there was a growing north-south trade as well, especially in tea, which had been adopted as the national drink during the Tang dynasty and was grown mainly in the misty hills of the south, in the mountains south of the Yangtze River, where it did not compete with rice for land and profited from the ample rainfall (Evans, 1992; Ling, 2010; Rose, 2010). To serve both domestic and overseas trade, the Chinese developed instruments of long-distance credit called "flying money" and, finally in the tenth century, paper money.

Rebellion, Radiance, and More Rebellion

The Sui dynasty, which reunified China in 589 CE, did so by harsh methods and hence is often compared with the Qin (Graff, 2001; Xiong, 2006; Tanner, 2010:167–200). The Sui rebuilt the Great Wall and constructed the first Grand Canal, all with corvée labor. Rebellion soon spread, as in the last years of the Qin, and out of the fighting emerged a new dynasty, the Tang, which presided over an even greater empire than the Han. The Tang is considered by most Chinese the high point of their history (Ebrey, 2010:108–135; Gascoigne, 2003:85–114; Gernet, 1996:233–291; Hansen, 2000:191–220; Morton and Lewis, 2004:81–97; Tanner, 2010:167–200). Elite culture flourished, and poetry achieved new richness, especially in the work of Li Bai and Du Fu, still thought to be China's greatest poets (see Chapter 13). The Tang capital, Chang'an, was again in the Wei valley on the site of modern Xi'an (see Map 3.1), which carried the aura of a great tradition because the first capital of the Han dynasty had been located there and named that. It was a highly cosmopolitan place to which merchants and travelers came from as far as the eastern Roman Empire and from most of Asia in between: Nestorian Christians (see Chapter 12), Jews (Goldstein, 2000), Muslims (Lipman, 1998), Turks, Indians, Persians, and others thronged the streets of the capital. Tang conquests reached far into Central Asia, where they acquired horses for the imperial stables. Perhaps the best-known aspect of Tang art is their mass production of glazed porcelain figures and paintings of their beloved horses. Under Tang rule, the development of the south continued apace as more land was cleared for farming by northern migrants and as trade flourished. Renewed contacts westward revealed, as in Han times, no other civilization that could rival the Celestial Empire, and Tang China was clearly the zenith of power and sophistication (Benn, 2004; Clark, 2007; Lewis, 2008). Did not all other people the Chinese encountered acknowledge this, by tribute, praise, and imitation of Chinese culture, and is that not the sincerest form of flattery?

Like the Han, Tang rule was briefly broken by rebellion in the mid-eighth century, and although the imperial order was restored, regional commanders continued to build their power, while rich landed families managed to slip off the tax rolls (Peterson, 1979:464–560). The civil service system begun under the Han was reestablished and strengthened, but was increasingly undermined by the rich and powerful. In the mid-ninth century, the state moved against the Buddhist establishment (Weinstein, 1987) as a potential rival, confiscating the extensive temple and monastery lands and their wealth, but this was not enough to turn the tide (Wang, 2007; Hansen, 2000:221–258). Total revenues fell by the end of the century, accompanied by spreading rebellion. In 907, one of the rebels usurped the throne and declared the Tang at an end, but fighting continued until 960, when one of the contending generals announced a new dynasty, the Song (Hansen, 2000:259–288; Ropp, 2010:67–84; Tanner, 2010: 201–238). The Song have been criticized by Chinese scholars because they gave up the wasteful and unprofitable building of empire and were ultimately overwhelmed by the hated Mongols. But the Song decision to avoid the endless wars of empire was wise and concentrated the state's energies on the provinces south of the Great Wall and east of the deserts and mountains of the west, the most productive and profitable area (Gascoigne, 2003:115–136). The chronic struggle to hold Vietnam, Korea, Mongolia, Tibet, and Xinjiang was abandoned; these conquests had never even begun to pay their way, and the state now controlled the richest land and enterprises.

Southern Strategies

The Song capital was fixed at Kaifeng at the easternmost end of the Silk Roads, on the great bend of the Yellow River (see Map 3.1), where the rebuilt Grand Canal could bring to it the rice surpluses of the Yangtze valley and where it could better administer the south, now the heart of the economy. Kaifeng became a major industrial center with a greater production of iron than the whole of Europe would have in the eighteenth century and used coal as metallurgical fuel and for heating houses seven centuries before the West. China's total population passed 100 million for the first time, and Kaifeng contained over 1 million people. The carved wooden blocks used since the Han dynasty for printing were supplemented by movable type, which was pressed onto paper, also invented in the Han dynasty, to produce books. Literacy grew, and popular literature boomed. Paper currency issued by the state served the needs of an expanded commerce (Ebrey, 2010:136–165). Government officials distributed printed pamphlets to promote improved agricultural techniques; there were also ingenious new metal tools and protomachines and new, improved crop strains. It was an age of good government, with the rich landed families and regional commanders under central control and revenues correspondingly healthy.

An important reason for the Song success was the re-creation of the civil service and its heightened strengthening (Kuhn and Brook, 2009). Most officials were selected from among those who passed the imperial examinations (whose history is discussed in Chapter 4); imperial relatives, a plague in the past, were barred from taking those exams. Once in power, officials were regularly rated for merit and promoted or passed over accordingly. Lists of successful candidates from this time include nearly half from families who had never before produced an official—a remarkable degree of mobility and opportunity whatever one's birth. This largely civilian government tended to have a low opinion of the military, and the army did not match the efficiency of the civil service. Soldiers were recruited largely from the poorer classes, and they faced formidable opponents in the mounted warriors from the steppe, who progressively detached much of the northwest and the northeastern borderland—marginal areas to be sure, but traditionally part of the empire. There were efforts at reforming and beefing up the military, but these failed due to the rigid opposition of conservatives at the capital (Ji, 2005).

The price was high: the siege and capture of Kaifeng in 1126 by a mounted nomad group originally from Manchuria, the ancestors of the Manchus (Hansen, 2000:299–334; Mote, 1999; Lorge, 2005:39–57; Tanner, 2010: 201–238). The Song army regrouped and pushed the nomads north of the Yangtze but were obliged to shift their capital south to Nanjing for four years, and then to Hangzhou (see Map 3.1), where they presided over continued flourishing in the arts and technology, building on advances in the Kaifeng period, now known as Northern Song (the Hangzhou period is called Southern Song). This is thought to be the greatest period of Chinese landscape and nature painting, which, together with vernacular literature and drama, blossomed in the rich urban culture of Hangzhou. Hangzhou was dominated by the growing merchant group but increasingly shared with city dwellers there and in many other large southern cities (Gernet, 1962; Hansen, 2000:289–298). Cut off from normal trade routes through the northwest, the Song turned in earnest to developing more sea routes to Southeast Asia and India. Ports on the southeast coast flourished and became home to large numbers of resident foreign merchants, mostly Arabs. Foreign accounts agree that these were the world's largest port cities of the time.

There was a striking advance in the size and design of oceangoing ships, some of which could carry over 600 people as well as cargo, far larger than those of any other country until modern times. The earlier Chinese invention of the compass was a vital navigational aid, and these ships used multiple masts, separate watertight compartments (not known elsewhere until much later), and the sternpost rudder. In all of this, Song ships predated modern ships by many centuries. Ironically, they helped make it possible for Europeans to later, after they adopted much of Chinese ship technology, make the sea voyage to Asia, also using the gunpowder invented in China to subdue those they visited (Buchanan, 2001; Needham, 1956, 1976, 1981). Hangzhou itself had a population over 1.5 million, but there were some six large cities within 300 miles and a network of smaller ones, depending like Hangzhou on the intricate system of waterways that crisscrossed the Yangtze Delta and adjacent areas. Marco Polo, who actually saw Hangzhou only later under Mongol rule, marveled at its size and wealth and called it the greatest city in the world, a judgment confirmed by several other Western travelers of his period (Gernet, 1962; Polo, 2008). Chapter 8 discusses China's urban history in greater depth.

The Southern Song was also an exciting time of technological innovation and even of what seem like early steps toward the emergence of modern science. Confucian scholars like Zhu Xi pursued what they called "the investigation of things" (de Bary, Bloom, and Adler, 2000), and in agriculture, manufacturing, and transport a variety of new machines and tools were developed—cultivators and threshers, pumps for lifting water, machines to card and spin and weave textile fibers, windlasses, inclined planes, canal locks, water clocks, and water-powered mills (Needham, 1956–1986; Temple, 2007). It all looked like eighteenth-century Europe, with commercialization, urbanization, a widening market (including overseas), rising demand, and hence both the incentive and the capital to pursue mechanical invention and other measures to increase production (Kuhn and Brook, 2009). Would these developments have led to a true industrial revolution in thirteenth-century China, with all its profound consequences? We will never know, because the final Mongol onslaught cut them off, and later dynasties failed to replicate the details of the Song pattern. But it is tempting to think that if the Song had had just a little more time, China might have continued to lead the world, and the rise of modern Europe might not have happened as it did.

The Southern Song dynasty was far wealthier than the Northern Song and had a booming economy (Kuhn and Brook, 2009). Unfortunately, this did not make it immune to the administrative and financial problems it inherited, but it kept functioning reasonably well until the end. Overseas trade, now a major source of revenue, was far larger than in Europe as late as the nineteenth century. Porcelain, perfected under the Tang, joined silk and lacquer as exports; and the finest pieces, called celadon, mostly made for the imperial court, have never been equaled, with their subtle bluish green or shades of white and gray glazes, exquisitely shaped. Government and private schools multiplied, to educate both the sons of the rich and the able sons of the less well-to-do (Chaffee, 1995). The explosion of printing and publication led to the spread of libraries and bookshops and the appearance of anthologies and encyclopedias, as well as maps of the empire based on a grid of coordinates. Chapter 12 discusses dynamic resurgence of philosophical and religious thinking under the Song. Mathematics was further developed, including the appearance of algebra and the use of the zero. With such a level of dynamism, why did the Song succumb?

The Song were overrun in the end because the Mongols were formidable fighters who had already conquered the world's largest empire, extending even into Europe, and because of some drastic Song errors (Hansen, 2000:335–368). In 1222, the Song foolishly made an alliance with the Mongols, and within two years reoccupied Kaifeng, but a year later they were desperately defending their gains. For forty years the fighting raged in the north, where the heavily fortified Chinese cities were both defended and attacked with the help of explosive weapons, including cannons, which the Mongols had learned about from their great neighbor (Lorge, 2005:58–77). This was the first use of cannon in warfare. Song naval ships on the Yangtze mounted cannons and mortars and helped to hold back the Mongol tide, all before this devastating new technology spread to Europe, where it was quickly copied. But the Song were chronically weakened by factionalism at court, divided counsels, and inconsistent, often faulty, strategy (Murphey, 2009:113–122; Ebrey, 2010:164–189; Gernet, 1996:350–384).

Unity and Cultural Continuity

By 1273, the Mongols had triumphed in the north and soon poured south, where Hangzhou surrendered in 1276. One false move against an opponent like the Mongols was usually all it took. But the Song put up a longer and more effective resistance to them than any of their other opponents—and the Mongols could never have won without the help of Chinese technicians, artillery experts, and siege engineers (de Hartog, 2000; Ratchnevsky, 1993; Weatherford, 2004; Lorge, 2005:78–97; May, 2007). Mongol rule in China, to which they gave the dynastic title of Yuan (see Map 3.1), lasted much less than a century and depended on many thousands of Chinese collaborators to administer the empire (Hoang, 2001; Bulog, 2002; de Francis, 1993; de Hartog, 2000: Brook, 2010; Tanner, 2010:239–280). They also employed many foreigners, including Marco Polo, who served as a minor Yuan official from 1275 to 1292. His account of his experience has been dismissed by many, but on his deathbed he told his confessor, "I have not told the half of what I saw." Marco Polo (2008), John Larner (2000), Stephen Haw (2005), and Laurence Bergreen (2008) provide readable accounts of his travels; Frances Wood (1998) disputes his tale, but Jonathan Spence (1996b) points out reasons to believe it.

Kublai Khan, the Mongol ruler whom Marco Polo served, fixed his new capital at Beijing and became almost entirely Chinese culturally, though the welcome he extended to travelers and innovations from all over the world and the many rewards he gave to his fellow Mongols disturbed his subjects (Rossabi, 1988). His successors were far less able, and the empire began to fall apart soon after Kublai's death in 1294, torn by rivalries among Mongol commanders and by widespread revolts among the Chinese against the exploitative Mongol rule (Murphey, 2009:12–122; Gascoigne, 2003:137–152; Morton and Lewis, 2004:115–122). By the end of the 1330s, most of China was in rebellion, and by 1350 control of the vital Yangtze valley was lost. A peasant rebel leader welded together Chinese forces, chased the remaining Mongols back into the steppe north of the Great Wall, and founded a new dynasty, the Ming, which was to restore Chinese pride and grandeur, from a new capital first at Nanjing and then at Beijing (Andrew and Rapp, 2000; Lorge, 2005:98–118).

The imperial capital thus moved progressively eastward, from the Wei valley and Chang'an where the Zhou, Han, Sui, and Tang had ruled, to Loyang in the later Han and Tang, to Kaifeng and Hangzhou under the Song, and finally north to Beijing (see Map 3.1). This migration reflected the eastward movement of the main area of threat to the imperial frontiers, from the nomads of the northwestern steppe in the Han to the Turkish tribes in the Tang to those who harried the Northern Song, then to the Mongols, and finally to the Manchus of Manchuria and their predecessors. But these northern capitals were increasingly unable to feed themselves as the north declined ecologically and economically; hence the Grand Canal was extended to Beijing by the Mongols to bring food up from the south. Putting the capital on the exposed frontier (Beijing is only some 40 miles from the borders of Inner Mongolia) made less sense economically than establishing one in the growing southern heart of the country, such as Nanjing. The imperial tradition of locating the capital close to frontier threats exerted too strong a pull, however, and even obliged the Ming to move to Beijing from Nanjing.

Chinese history readily divides into dynastic periods and into what is called the dynastic cycle. Most post-Qin dynasties (but not the Yuan) lasted about three centuries, sometimes preceded by a brief whirlwind period of empire building such as the Qin or the Sui. The first century of a new dynasty would be one of vigor, expansion, and efficiency; the second would build on or consolidate what the first had achieved; and, in the third, vigor and efficiency would wane, corruption would mount, banditry and rebellion would multiply, and the dynasty would ultimately fall. A new group coming to power (again with the exception of the Mongols) would rarely attempt to change the system, only its management. Culture was continuous even during interdynastic periods of chaos. By Tang times, most of the elements of modern Chinese culture were present. Irrigated rice was supplemented or replaced in the more arid parts of the north by wheat noodles (said to have been brought to Europe by Marco Polo or others along the Silk Roads as the origin of spaghetti) and steamed bread, or for poorer people by millet and *gaoliang* (a sorghum introduced from Central Asia and, like millet, tolerant of drought).

Food was eaten with chopsticks since at least the Zhou dynasty, a model adopted early by Korea, Vietnam, and Japan, although the rest of the world ate with fingers. The Chinese cuisine is justly famous, including as it does such a wide variety of ingredients (the Chinese have few dietary inhibitions), flavors, and sauces. What went on the rice—vegetable or animal—was sliced small so that its flavors were maximized and distributed and also so it could cook quickly over a hot but brief fire. There was an increasing shortage of fuel as the rising population cut down the forests and people were reduced to twigs, leaves, and dried grasses for cooking. The universal cooking utensil was the thin cast-iron saucer-shaped pot (*wok* in Cantonese, the dialect of Guangzhou) still in use, which heats quickly but holds the heat and distributes it evenly, the technique we now call "stir-frying." Not only Cantonese words like *wok* but much of the Chinese food served in restaurants in the United States and elsewhere betray their Cantonese origins, since Cantonese are the great majority of all overseas Chinese and, like many other immigrant groups, have used their native cuisine as a means of livelihood.

The Chinese landscape became converted more and more into an artificial one of irrigated and terraced rice paddies, fish and duck ponds, villages, and market towns where the peasants sold their surplus products or exchanged them for salt (Flad, 2011), cloth, tools, or other necessities not produced in all villages. Teahouses became the common centers for socializing, relaxation, and gossip, and for the negotiation of business or marriage contracts (Evans, 1992). Fortune-tellers, scribes, booksellers, itinerant peddlers, actors or jugglers, and storytellers enlivened the market towns and cities and the periodic markets held on a smaller scale in most villages at regular intervals (see Chapter 13). All this made it less necessary for people to travel far from their native places, and most never went beyond the nearest market town. Beyond it they would have found for the most part only more villages and towns like those they knew, except for the provincial capital and, of course, the imperial capital. In the dry north and the mountains of the south, many goods moved by human porter. The wheelbarrow and the flexible bamboo carrying pole were early Chinese inventions that greatly enhanced the ability to transport heavy weights, balanced as they were by each design (wheelbarrows had their single wheel in the middle, more efficient than the Western copy) and hence enabling porters to wheel or trot all day with loads far exceeding their unaided capacity. Most of these and many other aspects of Chinese culture have remained essentially unchanged today, as has the deep Chinese sense of history and of the great tradition to which they are heir (Fei, 1992; Harrison, 2005).

The Rise and Fall of Ming

The Ming dynasty, officially founded in 1368, fit the dynastic pattern of a first century of vigor and expansion, a second of complacency, and a third of decline and fall. Probably the most spectacular aspect of the first century was the expeditionary voyages of Admiral Zheng He, seven altogether between 1405 and 1433, from ports on the southeast coast with fleets of up to sixty ships each (Levathes, 1997; Hansen, 2000:369–408; Mote and Twitchett, 1988; Marks, 2006:46–48; Dreyer, 2006; Yamashita, 2006). They toured most of Southeast Asia, the east and west coasts of India (where Vasco da Gama ninety years later was to make his first Asian landfall), Ceylon (now Sri Lanka), the Persian Gulf, Aden, Jidda (from where seven Chinese went to Mecca), and on to eastern Africa. Some of his 1,681 ships may have gone as far as the Cape of Good Hope, or even perhaps around it (Menzies, 2004,

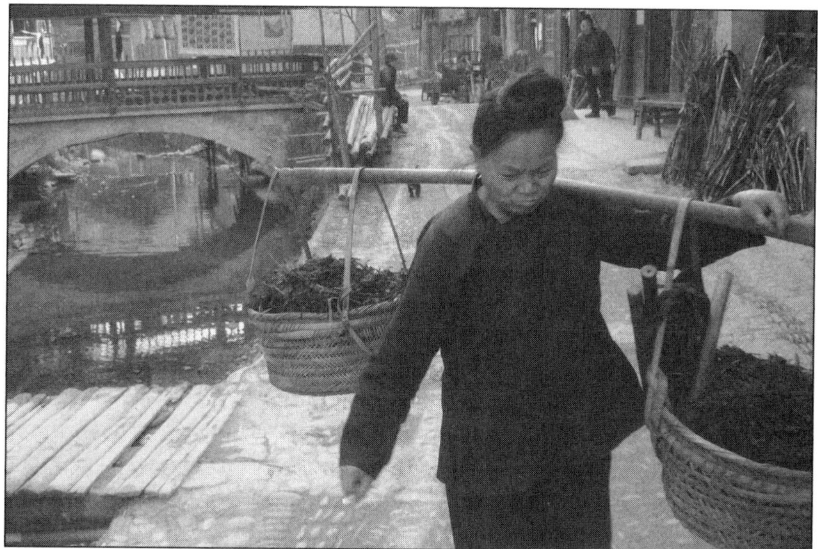
Robert E. Gamer

An early Chinese invention, the carrying pole is still commonly used in China, as shown here by a woman in Zhaoxing, Guizhou, a Dong minority town, in 2011.

2009). They brought back giraffes, zebras, and ostriches to amaze the court, and tributary agreements from a host of newly contacted states. The ships carried export goods, mainly silks and porcelains, and brought back foreign luxuries such as spices and tropical woods. The economic motive for these huge ventures may have been important, but the chief aim was probably political—to show the flag and command respect for the empire.

Despite their size (the largest of them 400 feet long and 160 feet wide, with four decks, large crews, and large cargo capacities), Zheng He's ships were faster than the far smaller (less than a fourth that size) Spanish galleons or Portuguese caravels of a century or two later. Their rig was designed to take advantage of the monsoonal wind patterns; properly timed voyages could count on sailing with the wind for about half the year as far as Africa and returning with the opposite monsoon in the other half. Like Song ships, they were built with separate watertight compartments, and despite their many encounters with storms, few were ever lost. Such exploits of seamanship and exploration were unprecedented in the world. Their grand scale was an expression of new imperial pride, but they contributed little to the Ming economy and made no lasting impression on the minds of Chinese, who continued to think of theirs as the only civilized empire and had little curiosity about foreign places. The expeditions were very expensive and, perhaps mainly for that reason, were stopped after 1433. The emperor may have felt he had made his imperial point, and it seems unlikely that trade profits even began to cover the costs. Another factor was the decision to move the capital from Nanjing to Beijing in 1421 to better command the chronically troubled northern frontier, where there was an attempted revival of Mongol power.

But the abandonment of the expeditions, like the move to Beijing, was a symptom of the Ming's basic conservatism and traditionalism. China's relations by sea had always been given a far lower priority than its land frontiers. Zheng He's explorations and contacts were not followed up. The Ming turned inward, rebuilt the Great Wall in the form we see today—of brick, with high guard towers—in the few parts near Beijing that have been restored, and reasserted the Chinese style in everything, partly as a reaction against the hated Mongol conquest (Waldron, 1990). They devoted their energies to the development of their home base, which since Shang times they had called the Middle Kingdom, meaning not only the center of the world but one that combined the advantages of a golden mean, avoiding the extremes of desert, jungle, mountains, or cold around its borders. In whatever direction one went from China, the physical environment worsened: north (too cold), south (too hot and jungly), west (too mountainous and dry), or east into a vast and, in cultural or economic terms, empty ocean. The Chinese attributed the lack of civilization they noted in all barbarians to their far less favorable environment as well as to their distance from the only center of enlightenment. China was indeed the most productive area of comparable size anywhere in the world, bigger than all of Europe, more populous, and with a far greater volume of trade, domestic and foreign. The Chinese saw their interests as best served by further embellishing their home base rather than by pursuing less rewarding foreign contacts.

For some time this worked well. Prosperity increased, and with it population, trade, and cities, continuing the developments under the Song (Brook, 1998, 2010; Dardess, 1997; Eastman, 1988; Tanner, 2010:281–309). Rice yields rose with the introduction of more productive and earlier-ripening varieties introduced from Vietnam and actively promoted by the state. In the sixteenth century, new crops from the New World, most importantly maize (corn), potatoes, and peanuts, came in via the Spanish connection in the Philippines. New irrigation and better application of manure swelled total output further, and there was a boom in silk production as well as in cotton (introduced from India and soon the basic material of clothing for all but the rich, who often wore silk). New supplies of Mexican silver came in to pay for the exports of silk, tea, porcelain, lacquerware, and other goods, and more and more of the economy was commercialized. Merchant guilds acquired new, though unofficial, power in the growing cities and followed the luxurious lifestyle of the elite. Right through the last century of the Ming, despite political decay, technological innovation continued on Song foundations, including the development of mechanical looms. Popular literature and drama flourished (Schneewind, 2006), and fine porcelains, including the famous Ming blue-

Robert E. Gamer

The Great Wall at Simitai, northwest of Beijing.

Robert E. Gamer

and-white pattern, spread beyond the court and were found in many merchant houses. Beijing was rebuilt on its Mongol foundations and filled with gorgeous palaces (Li, Dray, and Kong, 2008). The civil service system inherited from the Song also worked well until the final collapse. It was a confident and prosperous time (Mote and Twitchett, 1988, 1998; Ebrey, 2010:190–219;

Feng, 2007; Gascoigne, 2003:153–178; Gernet, 1996:387–462; Robinson, 2008; Clunas, 2007).

But by the end of the sixteenth century, there was a clear decline in administrative effectiveness, made worse by a succession of weak emperors and the rise of palace eunuchs to power (see Chapter 4). Banditry and piracy multiplied as government efficiency declined and poorer areas suffered increasing distress (Robinson, 2001; Huang, 1982; Ropp, 2010:85–101; Tanner, 2010: 310–339). Increased population, probably by now about 130 million, was not accompanied by a commensurate increase in the number of officials; existing officials were thus overworked and less effective, as well as prone to bribery to maintain their incomes. Famine and rebellion spread, and the Manchus, waiting on the northeastern border, took their opportunity to establish their own dynasty, the Qing, in 1644 (Spence, 1999:7–48; Chang and Chang, 1998; Crossley, 2002; Di Cosmo, 2006).

The Rise and Fall of Qing

Unlike the Mongols, the Qing successfully reproduced the Chinese pattern in all ways, and their control rested on widespread Chinese collaboration; Chinese filled about 90 percent of all official posts (Crossley, 2000). The dynasty was fortunate in producing three successive able emperors, who presided over the reconquest of all of the empire (Spence, 1999:49–137; Ebrey, 2010:220–261; Gascoigne, 2003:179–204; Gernet, 1996:465–533; Crossley, Sui, and Sutton, 2006; Giersch, 2006; Rowe, 2009; Tanner, 2010:340–381). The barbarian invaders on the steppe to the west were finally crushed for good, and Taiwan was conquered and added to the empire (Chang, 2007; Waley-Cohen, 2006). The peace and order provided by the Qing and its efficient administration led to new heights of prosperity, trade, and urbanization, far beyond Ming levels, and also to a population that probably tripled between 1620 and the dynasty's end in 1911, gained another 100 million by 1950, and doubled again between 1950 and 1983 to over 1 billion (Chao, 1987:41). Chapter 8 discusses that growth. By the end of the eighteenth century, production was no longer keeping pace, and in the course of the nineteenth century, China fell gradually into poverty and rebellion, as Europe and the United States rode a wave of new prosperity and technological/industrial revolution. Chinese technology had long been superior, but now it fell disastrously behind, to its great loss. Yet until as late as 1850, foreigners described China as prosperous, orderly, and admirable for its Confucian-based civil service that was open to any young man with the skill to pass the imperial examinations (Antony and Leonard, 2002).

We know more about China at this period than at any before it, not only from the voluminous Chinese records but also from the numerous foreign accounts, which are generally highly positive and, among other things, noted that China's foreign trade as late as the 1830s was probably larger than

England's, and its domestic trade was many times larger. Portuguese traders had arrived at Guangzhou (Canton) early in the sixteenth century, and Jesuit missionaries were shortly thereafter at work even in Beijing. By the eighteenth century, the British became the dominant traders with China, buying silk and tea that they paid for in silver, accompanied by French, Dutch, and other European merchants and finally by Americans. From the mid-eighteenth century, all foreign traders were restricted to Guangzhou, the chief port for foreign trade, a condition they found increasingly irritating as British and European power grew while their merchants at Guangzhou continued to be treated like minor barbarians (Weng, 1997). A party sent by King George in 1793 to request wider trade privileges and diplomatic representation at Beijing was haughtily rebuffed (see Chapter 7), as was a subsequent mission in 1816.

But despite the grand exterior, all was not well domestically, as population continued to outrun production in the absence of major technological change. As under the Ming, the number of administrator-officials rose by only 20 percent while the population rapidly expanded, and both efficiency and honesty suffered. China continued to protect itself against the disruptions of institutional and technological change, looking backward to its great tradition rather than forward, and was especially opposed to any ideas or innovations of foreign origin (Kuhn, 2002). As China declined in the nineteenth century and was wracked by increasing rebellions (Perry, 1980; Fairbank and Goldman, 2006; Ropp, 2010:102–118), the Qing had entered its third century. There might have been a different response from a new and vigorous administration, but the Qing were now old, rigid, fearful of change, and, as alien conquerors originally, anxious not to depart in any way from their role as guardians of the ancient Chinese way. The emperor Qianlong, who reigned from 1735 to 1799, was a great patron of art and rebuilt or refurbished the imperial capital inherited from the Ming in essentially the same form one can see today (Elliot, 2009). There he and other emperors received "tribute missions" from "barbarian chieftains," who knelt abjectly before the throne. China was slow to recognize that external threat now came from the "sea barbarians" instead of from its landward frontiers and looked down on them as inferior, despite their clear technological and military superiority.

Matters came to a head in 1839 over opium, which the British and Americans had begun to export from India and Persia to China in exchange for silver (Bello, 2005; Gernet, 1996:534–545; Brook and Wakabayashi, 2000; Hanes and Sanello, 2004; Dikotter, Laamann, and Xun, 2004; Grasso, Corrin, and Kort, 2009; Trocki, 1999). The resulting drain of silver from China was worrying, and in any case the opium trade had been declared illegal (Zheng, 2005). Chinese efforts to destroy the opium stored at Guangzhou led to war in which the Chinese army and navy were totally humiliated by modern British weapons (Marks, 2006; Waley, 1958). See Chapter 6 for more on this. The Treaty of Nanjing, signed in 1842, granted the access the foreigners had long sought and the right to reside and trade at several coastal ports, the "treaty ports" (Fairbank, 1978; Spence, 1999:145–166; Wang, 2005).

Such humiliations were destined to continue and grow in scope for more than a century. A war in 1858–1860 extended foreign privileges further and opened the interior to missionaries and the rivers to foreign shipping (Hevia, 2003:29–118). The empire had the help of volunteer foreign troops to put down the Taiping (see Spence, 1996a; Chin, 2000; Gernet, 1996:547–559) and Nian rebellions that took over extensive territory in southern China (Elleman, 2001; Atwill, 2006; Jenks, 1994). The Taiping rebels ruled much of Jiangsu, Anhui, and Zhejiang provinces (see Map 2.2) for eleven years. The fighting and radical social experiments (see Chapters 11 and 12) left well over 20 million casualties and formerly lush fields as barren wasteland. The Qing emperor found himself at the mercy of the foreigners and regional warlords who helped squelch the rebellions; his treasury was depleted. Foreign Christian missionaries sought converts without the traditional supervision always imposed on such activities in the past. Powerful landlords raised their own armies and collected their own taxes. In an effort to catch up, mathematics, science, and foreign languages were made part of school curricula, and sons of prominent Chinese were sent abroad for study (Gernet, 1996:566–625). Still, China suffered humiliating defeat in the Sino-Japanese War of 1894–1895. Reform efforts in 1898 to improve the navy, railroads, banking, agriculture, and industry were cut short when the young emperor who endorsed them was arrested by his aunt, Cixi, who took over as empress dowager (Seagrave, 1993; Min, 2005, 2007; Sa, 2007). Chapters 6 and 7 discuss these matters further.

But China's decline into poverty was primarily the result of its own internal problems, as summarized earlier, and indeed one can argue that the foreign traders helped China, by widening the market and introducing railways, telegraph lines, and other aspects of "modernization," much more than they harmed it, although the psychological hurt to Chinese pride was deep (Rawski, 1996, 1998).

Beyond the Dynasties

The dynasty toppled in 1911; a republic was inaugurated under Sun Yat-sen, the Nationalist leader (see Chapter 4), but China was soon torn by fighting among regional warlords and was partially unified only in 1927 under Chiang Kai-shek, with its new capital at Nanjing (Fairbank, 1987; Murdoch, 2007; Rowe, 2007; Rummel, 2007; Zarrow, 2005; Lary, 2007). There was some progress in the short decade before the Japanese attacked, burning Nanjing in 1937; killing unarmed men, women, and children; and raping and torturing women (Chang, 1997; Zhang, 2000). The full toll in human tragedy from that assault remains a topic of bitter contention between China and Japan even today (Wakabayashi, 2007; Katsuichi, 1999; Fogel and Maier, 2000; Minoru,

2006; Yoshida, 2006). The long war against Japan that followed, from a refugee capital in Chongqing in Sichuan, exhausted Chiang's Nationalist (Kuomintang, or KMT) government while it built the strength of the Chinese communists, who waged a guerrilla war in the north and captured the leadership of Chinese nationalism (Lary and MacKennan, 2002). Resumed civil war after the defeat of Japan ended in a total communist victory in 1949, and Chiang and his government fled to Taiwan. Beijing was again made the capital to realign the country with imperial tradition. Chapter 4 discusses this whole period in greater detail.

Hong Kong, ceded to Britain in 1841, joined the treaty ports as a major center of foreign trade and an entrepôt for trade with the rest of China; it remained a British colony until its return to China in 1997. Cut off from its hinterland in 1949, it built a profitable new structure of light industry and banking and successfully housed and employed the stream of refugees from the rest of China. Hong Kong's example of economic development was important to China as it pursued its own development, discussed in the next chapters.

China's Preparation for Modernity

For some 2,000 years China led the world in technology and in the art of government, in power as well as in sophistication. Still, in 1800, as it had for over four centuries, China produced a third of the world's manufactured goods (Kennedy, 1989:149; Marks, 2006; Pomeranz, 2002; Pomeranz and Topik, 2005; Gordon, 2009). But by then the Industrial Revolution and the Age of Enlightenment had begun in Europe. Soon Europeans were building giant metal-hulled ships and trains powered by steam engines, mechanized looms that mass-produced fabrics, machine guns, and aircraft, while scientists began to explore how to cure diseases and harness electricity; businesses and governments put these discoveries to use. China's long list of inventions was impressive. Most had been invented by artisans. The largest of them were designed to control the flow of water. Unfortunately for later centuries, these discoveries or innovations were not followed up by thoughts about how to put them to new practical uses outside the confines of hydrology and low-technology agriculture. Chinese intellectuals generally did not speculate about how changes in technology might affect society and commerce and the natural environment or devise experiments to observe the workings of the forces of nature—a key factor in the much later Western successes during the scientific revolution. They preferred to observe and speculate about human behavior and values. The general mindset of the Confucian power-holders against change as disruptive doubtless also retarded the kind of scientific inquiry that led to the Industrial Revolution in Europe (Lloyd and Sivin, 2003).

China did develop astronomy very early, noting and recording eclipses and sunspots in Zhou times and devising an accurate calendar. Early achievements in mathematics, mechanics, physics, and biology tended to lapse in later centuries, as did the development of instruments for predicting earthquakes, remarkable in their time. Some intellectuals in the Southern Song dynasty revived a brief interest in science, and under the Mongol Yuan dynasty, Chinese scientists resumed work in mathematics and also built a large array of instruments and structures for astronomical observations. But by the time the Jesuits, carriers of the latest scientific advances in Europe, arrived at the Ming court with great curiosity about these Yuan instruments, the Chinese said they had forgotten how to use them and the mathematics that went with them (Elman, 2005, 2009). The response of the court astronomers to their realization that the ancient calculations predicting the movement of the heavenly bodies no longer fit observable reality was not that the theory needed revision but that "the heavens are out of order." Such a response could never have happened in Europe after 1600; those scientists would have sought to revise the theory so it would accord with empirical reality (Mungello, 2005).

As Chapter 8 explains further, China has long produced more cities, and larger ones, than the rest of the world, and its urban experience is rich. European observers were impressed by it and by the huge streams of trade flowing along all China's rivers, lakes, and canals as well as in and out of its coastal ports. And it developed national identity and unity long before Europe and other parts of the world. For all its growing technological backwardness as the nineteenth century wore on, China remained vibrantly alive. And, after all the humiliations experienced by China since the Opium Wars (see also Chapters 4 and 13 on this), Chinese were determined to regain the national pride they had long enjoyed. Since the 1950s and the death of Mao in 1976, with his irrational utopian ideas that cost heavily in retarding economic progress as well as in lives lost, that vibrancy has reemerged. China has concentrated on maximizing its economic development and rapidly raising its technological levels toward world standards. Freed to once again pursue trade, China's government and business leaders seek to harness technology to their objective of achieving national power and wealth in the modern age. This endeavor has led to severe degradation of the environment (as discussed in Chapters 4, 5, and 9), suppression of personal liberties (see Chapters 4 and 10), and gaps in income. Meanwhile, China is the fastest growing economy in the world, with modernity spreading everywhere and touching virtually everyone.

As for that elusive quality we call happiness, who really knows? But China's rich literature (discussed in Chapter 13) certainly gives a picture of a generally contented populace with a strong sense of humor and a love of life. Indeed, the Chinese still value long life as the greatest of all goals, some testimony to their enjoyment of living and its pleasures. Family, together with food, remain the leading values, as they have been for thousands of years.

Bibliography

Allan, Sarah (ed.). 2002. *The Formation of Chinese Civilization: An Archaeological Perspective*. New Haven, CT: Yale University Press.

———. 2007. "Erlitou and the Formation of Chinese Civilization: Toward a New Paradigm." *Journal of Asian Studies* 66 (May): 481–496.

Andrew, Anita M., and John A. Rapp. 2000. *Autocracy and China's Rebel Founding Emperors: Comparing Chairman Mao and Ming Taizu*. Lanham, MD: Rowman and Littlefield.

Antony, Robert J., and Jane Kate Leonard. 2002. *Dragons, Tigers, and Dogs: Qing Crisis Management and the Boundaries of State Power in Late Imperial China*. Ithaca, NY: Cornell University Press.

Atwill, David G. 2006. *The Chinese Sultanate: Islam, Ethnicity, and the Ponthay Rebellion in Southern China, 1856–1873*. Stanford, CA: Stanford University Press.

Barnard, Noel. 1983. "Further Evidence to Support the Hypothesis of Indigenous Origins of Metallurgy in Ancient China." In *The Origins of Chinese Civilization*, edited by David N. Keightley, 237–277. Berkeley: University of California Press.

Beckwith, Christopher I. 2009. *Empires of the Silk Road: A History of Central Eurasia from the Bronze Age to the Present*. Princeton, NJ: Princeton University Press.

Bello, David Anthony. 2005. *Opium and the Limits of Empire: Drug Prohibition in the Chinese Interior, 1729–1850*. Cambridge, MA: Harvard University Asia Center.

Benn, Charles. 2004. *China's Golden Age: Everyday Life in the Tang Dynasty*. Oxford: Oxford University Press.

Bergreen, Laurence. 2008. *Marco Polo: From Venice to Zanadu*. New York: Vintage.

Boulnois, Luce. 2008. *Silk Road: Monks, Warriers, and Merchants*. Trans. Helen Loveday. Hong Kong: Airphoto International Ltd.

Brook, Timothy. 1998. *The Confusions of Pleasure: Commerce and Culture in Ming China*. Berkeley: University of California Press.

———. 2010. *The Troubled Empire: China in the Yuan and Ming Dynasties*. Cambridge, MA: Belknap Press of Harvard University Press.

Brook, Timothy, and Bob Tadashi Wakabayashi (eds.). 2000. *Opium Regimes: China, Britain, and Japan, 1839–1952*. Berkeley: University of California Press.

Buchanan, Brenda J. (ed.). 2001. *Gunpowder, Explosives, and the State: A Technological History*. Burlington, VT: Ashgate.

Bulog, Uradyn E. 2002. *The Mongols at China's Edge: History and Politics of National Unity*. Lanham, MD: Rowman and Littlefield.

Chaffee, John W. 1995. *The Thorny Gates of Learning: Examinations in Sung China*. Albany: State University of New York Press.

Chang, Chun-shu. 2007. *The Rise of the Chinese Empire: Nation, State, and Imperialism in Early China, ca. 1600 B.C. to A.D. 8*. Ann Arbor: University of Michigan Press.

Chang, Chun-shu, and Shelley Hsueh-lun Chang. 1998. *Crisis and Transformation in Seventeenth Century China: Society, Culture, and Modernity in Li Yu's World*. Ann Arbor: University of Michigan Press.

Chang, Iris. 1997. *The Rape of Nanking: The Forgotten Holocaust of World War II*. New York: HarperCollins.

Chang, Kwang Chih. 1983. *Art, Myth, and Ritual: The Path to Political Authority in Ancient China*. Cambridge, MA: Harvard University Press.

Chang, Michael G. 2007. *A Court on Horseback: Imperial Touring and the Construction of Qing Rule, 1680–1785*. Cambridge, MA: Harvard University Asia Center.

Chang, Te-Tzu. 1983. "The Origins of Early Cultures of the Cereal Grains and Food

Legumes." In *The Origins of Chinese Civilization,* edited by David N. Keightley, 65–94. Berkeley: University of California Press.

Chao, Kang. 1987. *Man and Land in Chinese History: An Economic Analysis.* Stanford, CA: Stanford University Press.

Chin, Shunshin. 2000. *The Taiping Rebellion.* Trans. Joshua A. Fogel. Armonk, NY: M. E. Sharpe.

Chu, J. Y., et al. 1998. "Genetic Relationship of Populations in China." *Proceedings of the National Academy of Sciences in the United States of America* 95(20): 11763–11768.

Clark, Hugh Roberts. 2007. *Portrait of a Community: Society, Culture, and the Structure of Kinship in the Mulan River Valley (Fujian) from the Late Tang Through the Song.* Hong Kong: Chinese University Press.

Clunas, Craig. 2007. *Empire of Great Brightness: Visual and Material Cultures of Ming China, 1368–1644.* Honolulu: University of Hawaii Press.

Cohen, Warren I. 2001. *East Asia at the Center: Four Thousand Years of Engagement with the World.* New York: Columbia University Press.

Connery, Christopher Leigh. 1999. *The Empire of the Text: Writing and Authority in Early Imperial China.* Lanham, MD: Rowman and Littlefield.

Crossley, Pamela Kyle. 2000. *A Translucent Mirror: History and Identity in Qing Imperial Ideology.* Berkeley: University of California Press.

———. 2002. *The Manchus.* London: Blackwell.

Crossley, Pamela Kyle, Helen Sui, and Donald S. Sutton (eds.). 2006. *Empire at the Margins: Culture, Ethnicity, and Frontier in Early Modern China.* Berkeley: University of California Press.

Dardess, John W. 1997. *A Ming Society: Tiai-ho County, Kiangsi, Fourteenth to Seventeenth Centuries.* Berkeley: University of California Press.

de Bary, William Theodore, Irene Bloom, and Joseph Adler (eds.). 2000. *Sources of Chinese Tradition: From Earliest Times to 1600.* 2nd ed., vol. 1. New York: Columbia University Press.

de Bary, William Theodore, and Richard Lufrano. 1999. *Sources of Chinese Tradition: 1600 Through the Twentieth Century.* 2nd ed., vol. 2. New York: Columbia University Press.

de Francis, John. 1993. *In the Footsteps of Genghis Khan.* Honolulu: University of Hawaii Press.

de Hartog, Leo. 2000. *Genghis Khan: Conqueror of the World.* New York: I. B. Tauris.

Di Cosmo, Nicola. 2004. *Ancient China and Its Enemies: The Rise of Nomadic Power in East Asian History.* Cambridge: Cambridge University Press.

———. 2006. *The Diary of a Manchu Soldier in Seventeenth-Century China: My Service in the Army, By Dzengseo.* London: Routledge.

Dikotter, Frank, Lars Laamann, and Zhou Xun. 2004. *Narcotic Culture: A History of Drugs in China.* Chicago: University of Chicago Press.

Dreyer, Edward L. 2006. *Zheng He: China and the Oceans in the Early Ming Dynasty, 1405–1433.* London: Longman.

Eastman, Lloyd E. 1988. *Family, Fields, and Ancestors: Constancy and Change in China's Social History, 1550–1949.* New York: Oxford University Press.

Ebrey, Patricia Buckley. 2010. *The Cambridge Illustrated History of China.* 2nd ed. Cambridge: Cambridge University Press.

Elleman, Bruce. 2001. *Modern Chinese Warfare.* London: Routledge.

Elliot, Mark. 2009. *Emperor Qianlong: Son of Heaven, Man of the World.* London: Longman.

Elman, Benjamin A. 2005. *On Their Own Terms: Science in China, 1550–1900*. Cambridge, MA: Harvard University Press.
———. 2009. *A Cultural History of Modern Science in China*. Cambridge, MA: Harvard University Press.
Elverskog, Johan. 2006. *Our Great Qing: The Mongols, Buddhism, and the State in Late Imperial China*. Honolulu: University of Hawaii Press.
Evans, John C. 1992. *Tea in China: The History of China's National Drink*. New York: Greenwood.
Fairbank, John King. 1978. "The Creation of the Treaty System." In *The Cambridge History of China: Late Ching 1800–1911*, vol. 10, pt. 1, edited by John King Fairbank, 213–263. Cambridge: Cambridge University Press.
———. 1987. *The Great Chinese Revolution, 1800–1985*. New York: Perennial.
Fairbank, John King, and Merle Goldman. 2006. *China: A New History*. 2nd enlarged ed. Cambridge, MA: Belknap Press of Harvard University Press.
Falkenhausen, Lothar Von. 2006. *Chinese Society in the Age of Confucius (1000–250 B.C.): The Archaeological Evidence*. Los Angeles: Cotsen Institute of Archaeology.
Fan, Chengda. 2007. *The River Road Home: A Complete and Annotated Translation of Fan Chengda's (1126–1193) Travel Diary Record of a Boat Trip to Wu (Wuchuanlu)*. Trans. James M. Hargett. Hong Kong: Chinese University Press.
Faure, David. 2007. *Emperor and Ancestor: State and Lineage in South China*. Stanford, CA: Stanford University Press.
Fei, Xiaotong. 1992. *From the Soil: The Foundations of Chinese Society*. Berkeley: University of California Press.
Fenby, Jonathan. 2008. *Modern China: The Fall and Rise of a Great Power, 1850 to the Present*. New York: HarperCollins.
Feng, Menglong. 2007. *Stories to Caution the World: A Ming Dynasty Collection*. Trans. Shuhui Yang and Yunqin Yang. Seattle: University of Washington Press.
Flad, Rowan K. 2011. *Salt Production and Social Hierarchy in Ancient China: An Archaeological Investigation of Specialization in China's Three Gorges*. Cambridge: Cambridge University Press.
Fogel, Joshua A., and Charles S. Maier (eds.). 2000. *The Nanjing Massacre in History and Historiography*. Berkeley: University of California Press.
Gascoigne, Bamber. 2003. *The Dynasties of China: A History*. New York: Carroll and Graf.
Gernet, Jacques. 1962. *Daily Life in China on the Eve of the Mongol Invasion, 1250–1276*. London: Macmillan.
———. 1996. *A History of Chinese Civilization*. 2nd ed. Trans. John R. Foster. Cambridge: Cambridge University Press.
Giersch, C. Patterson. 2006. *Asian Borderlands: The Transformation of Qing China's Yunnan Frontier*. Cambridge, MA: Harvard University Press.
Goldstein, Jonathan (ed.). 2000. *The Jews in China*. Armonk, NY: M. E. Sharpe.
Gordon, Stewart. 2009. *When Asia Was the World: Traveling Merchants, Scholars, Warriers, and Monks Who Created "The Riches of the East."* Cambridge, MA: Da Capo Press.
Graff, David A. 2001. *Medieval Chinese Warfare, 300–900*. London: Routledge.
Grasso, June, Jay Corrin, and Michael Kort. 2009. *Modernization and Revolution in China: From the Opium Wars to the Olympics*. 4th ed. Armonk, NY: M. E. Sharpe.
Grousset, René. 1995. *The Rise and Splendour of the Chinese Empire*. New York: Barnes and Noble.
Hanes, W. Travis, and Frank Sanello. 2004. *The Opium Wars: The Addiction of One Empire and the Corruption of Another*. Naperville, IL: Sourcebooks.

Hansen, Valerie. 1995. *Negotiating Daily Life in Traditional China: How Ordinary People Used Contracts, 600–1400*. New Haven: Yale University Press.

———. 2000. *The Open Empire: A History of China to 1600*. 6th ed. New York: W. W. Norton.

Hardy, Grant. 1999. *Worlds of Bronze and Bamboo: Sima Qian's Conquest of History*. New York: Columbia University Press.

Harrison, Henrietta. 2005. *The Man Awakened from Dreams: One Man's Life in a North China Village, 1857–1942*. Stanford, CA: Stanford University Press.

Haw, Stephen. 2005. *Marco Polo's China: A Venetian in the Realm of Kubilai Khan*. London: Routledge.

Hessler, Peter. 2007. *Oracle Bones: A Journey Through Time in China*. New York: Harper Perennial.

———. 2010. *Country Driving: A Journey Through China from Farm to Factory*. New York: HarperCollins.

Hevia, James L. 2003. *English Lessons: The Pedagogy of Imperialism in Nineteenth Century China*. Durham, NC: Duke University Press.

Hoang, Michel. 2001. *Genghis Khan*. New York: Palgrave.

Hooker, Jake. 2006. "The Search for Peking Man." *Archaeology* 59(2): 59–66.

Hsu, Immanuel Cho Yun. 1995. *The Rise of Modern China*. 6th ed. Oxford: Oxford University Press.

Huang, Ray. 1982. *1587, A Year of No Significance: The Ming Dynasty in Decline*. New Haven, CT: Yale University Press.

Isett, Christopher M. 2007. *State, Peasant, and Merchant in Qing Manchuria, 1644–1862*. Stanford, CA: Stanford University Press.

Jenks, Robert D. 1994. *Insurgency and Social Disorder in Guizhou: The "Miao" Rebellion, 1854–1873*. Honolulu: University of Hawaii Press.

Ji, Xiao-bin. 2005. *Politics and Conservatism in Northern Song China: The Career and Thought of Sima Guang (1019–1086)*. New York: Columbia University Press.

Katsuichi, Honda. 1999. *The Nanjing Massacre: A Japanese Journalist Confronts Japan's National Shame*. Edited by Frank Gibney. Trans. Karen Sandness. Armonk, NY: M. E. Sharpe.

Kennedy, Paul. 1989. *The Rise and Fall of Great Powers*. New York: Vintage.

Kuhn, Dieter, and Timothy Brook. 2009. *The Age of Confucian Rule: The Song Transformation of China*. Cambridge, MA: Belknap Press of Harvard University Press.

Kuhn, Philip A. 2002. *Origins of the Modern Chinese State*. Stanford, CA: Stanford University Press.

Kuzmina, E. E. 2008. *The Prehistory of the Silk Road*. Philadelphia: University of Pennsylvania Press.

Larner, John. 2000. *Marco Polo: Discoverer of the World*. New Haven, CT: Yale University Press.

Lary, Diana. 2007. *China's Republic*. Cambridge: Cambridge University Press.

Lary, Diana, and Stephen MacKennan (eds.). 2002. *Scars of War: The Impact of Warfare on Modern China*. Vancouver: University of British Columbia.

Lattimore, Owen. 1997. *The Desert Road to Turkestan*. New York: Kodansha Globe.

Lee, Khoon Choy. 2005. *Pioneers of Modern China: Understanding the Inscrutable Chinese*. Singapore: World Scientific.

Levathes, Louise. 1997. *When China Ruled the Seas: The Treasure Fleet of the Dragon Throne, 1405–1433*. New York: Oxford University Press.

Lewis, Mark Edward. 2007. *The Early Chinese Empires: Qin and Han*. Cambridge, MA: Belknap Press of Harvard University Press.

———. 2008. *China's Cosmopolitan Empire: The Tang Dynasty.* Cambridge, MA: Belknap Press of Harvard University Press.
———. 2009. *China Between Empires: The Northern and Southern Dynasties.* Cambridge, MA: Belknap Press of Harvard University Press.
Li, Feng. 2006. *Landscape and Power in Early China: The Crisis and Fall of the Western Zhou.* Cambridge: Cambridge University Press.
Li, Lillian, Alison Dray, and Haili Kong. 2008. *Beijing: From Imperial Capital to Olympic City.* New York: Palgrave Macmillan.
Li, Xueqin. 1985. *Eastern Zhou and Qin Civilizations.* New Haven, CT: Yale University Press.
Lindesay, William. 2008. *The Great Wall Revisited: From the Jade Gate to Old Dragon's Head.* Cambridge, MA: Harvard University Press.
Linduff, Katheryn M., Han Rubin, and Sun Shuyun (eds.). 2000. *The Beginnings of Metallurgy in China.* Lewiston, NY: Edwin Mellen.
Ling, Yun. 2010. *Chinese Tea.* Shanghai: Better Link Press.
Lipman, Jonathan N. 1998. *Familiar Strangers: A History of Muslims in Northwest China.* Seattle: University of Washington Press.
Liu, Li. 2005. *The Chinese Neolithic: Trajectories to Early States.* Cambridge: Cambridge University Press.
Liu, Li, and Xingcan Chen. 2003. *State Formation in Early China.* London: Duckworth.
Liu, Xinru. 2010. *The Silk Road in World History.* New York: Oxford University Press.
Lloyd, Geoffrey, and Nathan Sivin. 2003. *The Way and the Word: Science and Medicine in Early China and Greece.* New Haven, CT: Yale University Press.
Loewe, Michael. 1994. *Divination, Mythology, and Monarchy in Han China.* New York: Cambridge University Press.
Loewe, Michael, and Edward L. Shaughnessy (eds.). 1999. *The Cambridge History of Ancient China: From the Origins of Civilization to 221 B.C.* Cambridge: Cambridge University Press.
Loewe, Michael, and Eva Wilson. 2005. *Everyday Life in Early Imperial China: The Han Period 202 B.C. to 220 A.D.* Indianapolis: Hackett.
———. 2006. *The Government of the Qin and Han Empires: 221 B.C.E.–220 C.E.* Indianapolis: Hackett.
Lorge, Peter. 2005. *War, Politics, and Society in Early Modern China.* New York: Routledge.
Lovell, Julia. 2006. *The Great Wall: China Against the World, 1000 B.C.–A.D. 2000.* New York: Grove Press.
———. 2011. *The Opium War: Drugs, Dreams, and the Making of China.* New York: Picador.
Man, John. 2009. *The Great Wall: The Extraordinary Story of China's Wonder of the World.* Cambridge, MA: Da Capo Press.
Marks, Robert B. 2006. *The Origins of the Modern World: A Global and Ecological Narrative from the Fifteenth to the Twenty-first Century.* 2nd ed. Lanham, MD: Rowman and Littlefield.
May, Timothy. 2007. *The Mongol Art of War.* Yardley, PA: Westholme Publishing.
Meacham, William. 1983. "Origins and Development of Yüeh Coastal Neolithic: A Microcosm of Culture Change in the Mainland of East Asia." In *The Origins of Chinese Civilization,* edited by David N. Keightley, 147–175. Berkeley: University of California Press.
Menzies, Gavin. 2004. *1421: The Year China Discovered America.* New York: Harper.

———. 2009. *1434: The Year a Magnificent Chinese Fleet Sailed to Italy and Ignited the Renaissance*. New York: Harper.
Millward, James A. 2007. *Eurasian Crossroads: A History of Xinjiang*. New York: Columbia University Press.
Min, Anchee. 2005. *Empress Orchid*. New York: Mariner Books.
———. 2007. *The Last Empress*. New York: Houghton Mifflin.
Minoru, Kitamura. 2006. *The Politics of Nanjing: An Impartial Investigation*. Trans. Hal Gold. Lanham, MD: University Press of America.
Morton, W. Scott, and Charlton M. Lewis. 2004. *China: Its History and Culture*. 4th ed. New York: McGraw Hill.
Mote, Frederick W. 1999. *Imperial China 900–1800*. Cambridge, MA: Harvard University Press.
Mote, Frederick W., and Denis Twitchett (eds.). 1988 and 1998. *The Cambridge History of China: The Ming Dynasty 1368–1644*. Vol. 7, pts. 1–2. Cambridge: Cambridge University Press.
Mungello, D. E. 2005. *The Great Encounter of China and the West, 1500–1800*. 2nd ed. Lanham, MD: Rowman and Littlefield.
Murdoch, Michael G. 2007. *Disarming the Allies of Imperialism: The State, Agitation, and Manipulation During China's Nationalist Revolution, 1922–1929*. Ithaca, NY: Cornell University Press.
Murphey, Rhoads. 2008. *A History of Asia*. 6th ed. Englewood Cliffs, NJ: Prentice Hall.
———. 2009. *East Asia: A New History*. 5th ed. New York: Longman.
Naquin, Susan, and Evelyn S. Rawski. 1989. *Chinese Society in the Eighteenth Century*. New Haven, CT: Yale University Press.
Needham, Joseph. 1956–1986. *Science and Civilisation in China*. 6 vols. Cambridge: Cambridge University Press.
———. 1981. *Science in Traditional China*. Cambridge: Cambridge University Press.
O'Brien, Kevin J., and Lianjiang Li. 2006. *Rightful Resistance in Rural China*. Cambridge: Cambridge University Press.
Perdue, Peter C. 2005. *China Marches West: The Qing Conquest of Central Eurasia*. Cambridge, MA: Belknap Press.
Perry, Elizabeth J. 1980. *Rebels and Revolutionaries in North China, 1845–1945*. Stanford, CA: Stanford University Press.
Peterson, C. A. 1979. "Court and Province in Mid and Late T'ang." In *The Cambridge History of China: Sui and T'ang China, 589–906*, vol. 3, edited by Denis Twitchett, 464–560. Cambridge: Cambridge University Press.
Polo, Marco. 2008. *The Travels of Marco Polo:* Edited by Peter Harris. New York: Everyman's Library.
Pomeranz, Kenneth. 2002. *The Great Divergence: China, Europe, and the Making of the Modern World Economy*. Princeton, NJ: Princeton University Press.
Pomeranz, Kenneth, and Steven Topik. 2005. *The World That Trade Created: Society, Culture, and the World Economy, 1400 to the Present*. Armonk, NY: M. E. Sharpe.
Ptak, Roderich. 2004. *China, the Portuguese, and the Nanyang: Oceans and Routes, Regions and Trade (c. 1000–1600)*. Burlington, VT: Ashgate.
Qian, Sima, and Burton Watson. 1996. *Records of the Grand Historian: Qin Dynasty*. 3rd ed. New York: Columbia University Press.
Ratchnevsky, Paul. 1993. *Genghis Khan: His Life and Legacy*. New York: Blackwell.
Rawski, Evelyn S. 1996. "Reenvisioning the Qing: The Significance of the Qing Period in Chinese History." *Journal of Asian Studies* 55(4) (November): 829–850.
———. 1998. *The Last Emperors: A Social History of Qing Imperial Institutions*. Berkeley: University of California Press.

Robinson, David M. 2001. *Bandits, Eunuchs, and the Son of Heaven: Rebellion and the Economy of Violence in Mid-Ming China*. Honolulu: University of Hawaii Press.

———. (ed.). 2008. *Culture, Courtiers, and Competition: The Ming Court (1368–1644)*. Cambridge, MA: Harvard East Asian Monographs.

Rojas, Carlos. 2010. *The Great Wall: A Cultural History*. Cambridge, MA: Harvard University Press.

Ronan, Colin A. 1995. *The Shorter Science and Civilisation in China*. Vol 5. Cambridge: Cambridge University Press.

Ropp, Paul S. 2010. *China in World History*. Oxford: Oxford University Press.

Rose, Sarah. 2010. *For All the Tea in China: How England Stole the World's Favorite Drink and Changed History*. New York: Viking Press.

Rossabi, Morris. 1988. *Khubilai Khan: His Life and Times*. Berkeley: University of California Press.

Rowe, William T. 2007. *Crimson Rain: Seven Centuries of Violence in a Chinese County*. Stanford, CA: Stanford University Press.

———. 2009. *China's Last Empire: The Great Qing*. Cambridge, MA: Belknap Press of Harvard University Press.

Rummel, R. J. 2007. *China's Bloody Century: Genocide and Mass Murder Since 1900*. New Brunswick, NJ: Transaction Publications.

Sa, Shana. 2007. *Empress: A Novel*. New York: Harper.

Sautman, Barry. 2001. "Peking Man and the Politics of Paleoanthropological Nationalism in China." *Journal of Asian Studies* 60(1): 95–124.

Schmalzer, Sigrid. 2008. *The People's Peking Man: Popular Science and Human Identity in Twentieth Century China*. Chicago: University of Chicago Press.

Schneewind, Sarah. 2006. *Community Schools and the State in Ming China*. Stanford, CA: Stanford University Press.

Seagrave, Sterling. 1993. *Dragon Lady: The Life and Legend of the Last Empress of China*. New York: Vintage.

Shang, Hong, et al. 2007. "An Early Modern Human From Tianyuan Cave, Zhoukoudian, China." *Proceedings of the National Academy of Sciences of the United States of America* 104(16): 6573–6578.

Sit, Victor F. S. 2010. *Chinese City and Urbanism: Evolution and Development*. Singapore: World Scientific Publishing.

Sneath, David. 2000. *Changing Inner Mongolia: Pastoral Mongolian Society and the Chinese State*. New York: Oxford University Press.

Spence, Jonathan. 1996a. *God's Chinese Son: The Taiping Heavenly Kingdom of Hong Xiuquan*. New York: W. W. Norton.

———. 1996b. "Marco Polo: Did He Go to China?" *Far Eastern Economic Review* 159 (August 22): 37–45.

———. 1999. *The Search for Modern China*. 2nd ed. New York: W. W. Norton.

Standen, Naomi. 2007. *Unbounded Loyalty: Frontier Crossings in Liao China*. Honolulu: University of Hawaii Press.

Swope, Kenneth (ed.). 2005. *Warfare in China Since 1600*. Burlington, VT: Ashgate.

Tanner, Harold Miles. 2010. *China, A History: From Neolithic Cultures Through the Great Qing Empire (10,000 BCE–1799 CE)*. Vol. 1. Indianapolis: Hackett.

Temple, Robert. 2007. *The Genius of China: 3000 Years of Science, Discovery, and Invention*. New York: Inner Traditions.

Thorp, Robert L. 2006. *China in the Early Bronze Age: Shang Civilization*. Philadelphia: University of Pennsylvania Press.

Trocki, Carl A. 1999. *Opium, Empire, and the Global Political Economy*. London: Routledge.

Twitchett, Denis (ed.). 1986. *The Cambridge History of China.* Vol. 1: *Ch'in and Han.* Cambridge: Cambridge University Press.

Tyler, Christian. 2004. *Wild West China: The Taming of Xinjiang.* Piscataway, NJ: Rutgers University Press.

Wakabayashi, Bob Tadashi (ed.). 2007. *The Nanking Atrocity, 1937–1938: Complicating the Picture.* New York: Berghahn Books.

Waldron, Arthur. 1990. *The Great Wall of China: From History to Myth.* Cambridge: Cambridge University Press.

Waley, Arthur. 1939. *Three Ways of Thought in Ancient China.* Stanford, CA: Stanford University Press.

———. 1958. *The Opium War Through Chinese Eyes.* Stanford, CA: Stanford University Press.

Waley-Cohen, Joanna. 2006. *The Culture of War in China: Empire and the Military Under the Qing Dynasty.* London: I. B. Tauris.

Wang, Doug. 2005. *China's Unequal Treaties: Narrating National History.* Lanham, MD: Rowman and Littlefield.

Wang, Gungwu. 2007. *Divided China: Preparing for Reunification 883–947.* Singapore: World Scientific.

Weatherford, Jack. 2004. *Genghis Khan and the Making of the Modern World.* New York: Three Rivers Press.

Weinstein, Stanley. 1987. *Buddhism Under the T'ang.* Cambridge: Cambridge University Press.

Wellington, Donald C. 2006. *French East India Companies: An Historical Account and Record of Trade.* Lanham, MD: University Press of America.

Weng, Eang Cheong. 1997. *The Hong Merchants of Canton: Chinese Merchants in Sino-Western Trade, 1684–1798.* London: Curzon Press.

Whitfield, Susan. 2001. *Life Along the Silk Road.* Berkeley: University of California Press.

Winchester, Simon. 2008. *The Man Who Loved China: The Fantastic Story of the Eccentric Scientist Who Unlocked the Mysteries of the Middle Kingdom.* New York: HarperCollins.

Womach, Brantly (ed.). 2010. *China's Rise in Historical Perspective.* Lanham, MD: Rowman and Littlefield.

Wood, Frances. 1998. *Did Marco Polo Go to China?* Boulder: Westview Press.

———. 2004. *The Silk Road: Two Thousand Years in the Heart of Asia.* Berkeley: University of California Press.

Xiong, Victor Cunrui. 2006. *Emperor Yang of the Sui Dynasty: His Life, Times, and Legacy.* Albany: State University of New York Press.

Yamashita, Michael. 2006. *Zheng He.* Vercelli, Italy: White Star.

Yamashita, Michael, and William Lindesay. 2007. *The Great Wall: From Beginning to End.* New York: Sterling.

Yang, Xiaoneng (ed.). 2004. *New Perspectives on China's Past: Chinese Archaeology in the Twentieth Century.* 2 vols. New Haven, CT: Yale University Press.

Yoshida, Takashi. 2006. *The Making of the "Rape of Nanjing": History and Memory in Japan, China, and the United States.* New York: Oxford University Press.

Zarrow, Peter. 2005. *China in War and Revolution, 1895–1949.* New York: Routledge.

Zhang, Kaiyuan (ed.). 2000. *Eyewitnesses to Massacre: American Missionaries Bear Witness to Japanese Atrocities in Nanjing.* Armonk, NY: M. E. Sharpe.

Zheng, Yangwen. 2005. *The Social Life of Opium in China.* Cambridge: Cambridge University Press.

4

Chinese Politics

Robert E. Gamer

China has the world's oldest political system. As Rhoads Murphey explained in Chapter 3, its cultural dominance of the regions it now occupies began during the third century BCE. Its habits of governance extend to that period as well. For two millennia, those habits helped it ward off or absorb invasions from the societies that occupied Central Asia. They proved vulnerable, however, when challenged during the past two centuries by the technology and institutions of Europe and a modernizing Japan.

What are China's political traditions? What has it absorbed from communism and the West? How much must China's political system change to remain unified and sustain economic growth? Can it achieve those goals? These are the questions dealt with in this chapter.

First, we will briefly examine some of China's political and economic traditions. In the second section, we will look at the changes that took place in China's politics between the 1839 Opium War and World War II. Third, we will examine how and why the communists took over China. Their consolidation of power was followed by three periods of major economic and political change; in the fourth section we will try to sort out the changes that worked from those that did not. Next, we will look at the principal challenges facing China's contemporary leaders and their chances of surmounting them. In the last two sections, we will explore further adaptations that China is likely to absorb.

A Legacy of Unity and Economic Achievement

In Chapter 3, Rhoads Murphey explained how the Qin first unified China in 221 BCE and how the subsequent Han dynasty consolidated that conquest (see also Fu, 1996). One of the most significant and enduring achievements of the

Han was the adoption of Confucianism, a philosophy also discussed in Chapters 3 and 12. Confucian traditions would have a strong influence on China's subsequent ability to maintain unity and prosperity.

Confucius contended that stable governance derives from the proper performance of social obligations. The most fundamental obligation, called filial piety, is obedience of sons to fathers. Likewise, wives obey husbands, younger brothers defer to their older brothers, and subjects obey rulers. In turn, those being obeyed are to treat their cohorts with sincerity, affection, or respect, demonstrated through rituals of speech and behavior. Individuals who fail to carry out these mutual obligations disgrace themselves and those to whom they owe these obligations and destroy the foundations of the state. Citizens cannot expect to live in a stable country when they themselves fail to carry out their most basic social obligations within their families. When individual freedom or political theories conflict with one's obligation to one's family and state authorities, they must be rejected. Expressing an opinion or taking an action that shows disrespect for these mutual obligations and rituals actually destroys your own essence; you must rectify this by apologizing and changing your behavior, in order to restore your good name and come to grips with who you really are. To be true to yourself you must carry out your ritual obligations to others; to do so bonds state and society.

Furthermore, in Confucian philosophy, society is divided into greater and lesser orders. The emperor and his assistants hold the highest position, yet the social hierarchy limits both them and those with wealth. Directly below the emperor in this hierarchy are the peasants and artisans who produce the goods and whose families cleared the land and created the farms that set apart Chinese civilization from the "barbarian" cultures of wandering hunters and herders. Merchants, who produce nothing yet profit from the toil of others, occupy the lowest rung on the social order of Chinese civilization. All this creates a harmonious society (notice General Secretary Hu Jintao's use of that concept later in this chapter), with emperors naturally chosen to rule and even wealthy subjects predisposed to obey. That obedience ends only when peace and prosperity are supplanted by war, bad harvests, and natural disasters, proving that Heaven's Mandate to the emperor to govern has been withdrawn (see more about this Mandate of Heaven in Chapter 12). Then a challenger may rouse popular support to overthrow the emperor. The Han dynasty itself was founded by a peasant who led such a revolt against the excesses of the Qin dynasty.

Four other customs evolved that also helped to keep the emperor and those with wealth in line while still investing them with the power to rule and engage in business:

1. The system of choosing emperors and their wives. To reduce the role of the noble families that had dominated before the Qin dynasty, the sons of emperors married daughters of peasants, who were taken away from their families when they were very young. These heirs to the throne might take several wives. Sons of the first wife were thought to have more right to the throne, but emperors had some choice in designating a successor. During most dynasties, when the emperor died, his wives and their other children would return to an obscure existence, rather than become titled nobility. Although this reduced the prestige and power of those related to the emperor, it made the stakes surrounding succession into an all-or-nothing game. That created much intrigue around the court. Many an emperor or designated heir was murdered by the mother of another heir, who might rule as an empress dowager while her young son grew up (see Fu, 1994).

2. *Eunuchs.* To ensure loyalty and see to it that only the emperor had sexual access to his wives, males working within the compound of the palace were recruited at a young age from villages, removed from their families, and castrated. These eunuchs ran the compound and took care of the emperor, his wives, and their children. The eunuchs were often involved in the murders and intrigues. Public officials had to access the emperor through the eunuchs. The number and power of eunuchs grew greatly during the Ming dynasty; the Qing dynasty sought to limit their power, but it continued. (For more on their role, see Mitamura, 1970; Tsai, 1995.)

3. *The system of choosing public officials and regulating commerce.* To choose its top officials, the empire held regular competitive examinations open to all boys. These exams tested the candidates' ability to write Chinese characters and their knowledge of the Confucian classics. Those who passed became "literati," or Confucian scholar-officials. They were selected and transferred as needed by the emperor to preside over justice and administration in all the regions of China. Most who passed these exams, which required extensive education and preparation, were the sons of scholar-officials, larger landowners, or wealthy merchants. But the system moving them from post to post ensured that control of administration and of a region could not automatically stay within the hands of the same local notables, as had been the case under feudalism. Sometimes a village or lineage group would help one of their brightest children prepare for these exams, allowing him to rise from the family of a humble peasant into the highest realms of the state. Ichisada Miyazaki (1981) gives an extensive introduction to this unique—and often terrifying—system for selecting public officials.

These officials had the power to regulate commerce. They sought to ensure that agriculture remained prosperous by keeping the complex system of waterways and irrigation canals working, maintaining marketplaces where goods could be bartered, and protecting private property. They also collected taxes and presided over the civil and criminal courts and local administrators.

During the twelfth century, in the Southern Song dynasty (see Chapters 3 and 5), foreign and domestic trade began to flourish. Large numbers of people engaged in the manufacture of porcelain, textiles, alcoholic beverages, ships, and other goods. Because Confucian philosophy sees agriculture as the provider of food and the supporter of the family units on which Chinese civilization is built, the scholar-officials had always encouraged invention, trade, the buying and selling of land, and other commercial pursuits that supported agriculture. These new trends disturbed them. Young people were leaving their families to seek work in the towns and cities. People were making large amounts of money creating frivolous luxuries that competed with cloth and handicrafts once produced on the farms. The richest of them could travel between regions to escape the jurisdiction of individual literati. Scholar-officials had often used their power and income to buy large amounts of land and thus ensure their high social and economic stature. Now people without land or official status, who ranked at the bottom of the Confucian social hierarchy, were in a position to become the richest in the realm.

Song Confucian philosophers thought hard about these problems. Their neo-Confucianism (see Chapter 12) created checks on the power of merchant acquisition by placing new emphasis on the extended family (Wood, 1995). Clans should stick together in the same villages, whose property would remain under the control of their leaders. People should be punished for moving away to set up independent households. To prevent monopolies, officials should regulate the number of looms or production facilities one person could own as well as the market prices. And the state would manufacture or distribute some important goods and resources. This would slow down investment in capitalist production and discourage the creation of an independent middle class. It would also encourage community leaders to assist those less fortunate in their communities (for an insightful overview, see Gates, 1996:42–61).

4. The five Confucian relationships, guanxi. As in the past, however, these new powers for officials were softened by *guanxi* (King, 1991; Yang, 1994; Yan, 1996; Kipnis, 1997). In Confucian thinking, a man's most important relationships are as father and son, as husband, as brother, as subject of the ruler, and with certain selected neighbors, kinsmen, classmates, or other associates with whom he chooses to have special long-term relationships. These individuals exchange special favors and gifts, called *renqing* (literally, benevolence that two people owe each other; more about this in Chapter 12). This exchange affirms that these individuals have "connections." Literati and merchants had always created such connections with one another; that is how many literati had acquired land. As commerce grew, these relationships helped merchants escape from overregulation and receive clearance to engage in new business activities. Connections helped individuals make money, while ensuring that it circulated back to the community. They also continued to divert investment capital into unproductive gifts. These practices persist (Sun, 2004; Gold, 2002).

As China approached the nineteenth century, it looked back on a long tradition of political and cultural unification combined with a vibrant market economy. It was presided over by a government that both encouraged and limited capitalist enterprise and that was itself limited by the expectations of its people that its reign bring social order and bountiful agriculture. The chief restraints on governments and citizenry lay in the expectation that people should live up to their social obligations. Communities placed limits on their own members; entrepreneurs were expected to adapt to the needs of the community. International capitalism wants social peace, but it also resists social and political restraints that hold back individual initiative. The stage was set for conflict.

A Century of Turmoil

The year 1839 ushered in a century of profound challenge to these Chinese traditions (Table 4.1). In retaliation against Chinese efforts to regulate the trade in opium, British forces invaded China and forced the government to sign a treaty, which was soon followed by many others (discussed in Chapters 3, 6, and 7). Foreigners gained the right to establish settlements and businesses partially free from Chinese regulation. Workers in their factories operated outside traditional associations (Perry, 2007), and their goods competed with those manufactured in Chinese workshops. Foreigners were entitled to bypass established Chinese business groups when making deals and built railways to link their coastal commerce with inland regions. Their commerce was hard for Chinese officials or local clan leaders to regulate.

In 1894, a Guangzhou native named Sun Yat-sen, who had studied in Japan and Hawaii, founded the Revive China Society (Wei, Myers, and Gillin, 1994; Bergère, 2000; Gordon, 2009; Schiffrin, 2010). It advocated constitutional government for China, as did a commission created by the empress dowager (see Chapter 3). Following her death in 1908, under urging from Sun Yat-sen's movement, the imperial leaders let the provinces elect assemblies. After a series of army mutinies in 1911, China held elections for a new premier. Sun, the winner, returned to China from abroad to assume this post. He soon was nudged aside by Yuan Shikai, a regional leader in Beijing who had once advised the empress dowager. Sun's National People's Party, also called the Nationalist Party or Kuomintang (KMT), won the elections Yuan promised in 1913, but their victorious candidate, Song Jiaoren, was killed as he waited to board a train to Beijing. Yuan would not step down. His troops battled KMT troops, and Sun returned to exile. After Yuan's death in 1916, his successor called back Sun and the assemblies. But Yuan's successor was soon overthrown by a military coup, and Beijing's power collapsed. China fell under the control of regional warlords (for case studies, see Duara, 1988; Jowett, 2010). Because the examination system was now abolished, the old literati were no

Table 4.1 Important Dates in Modern Chinese History

1839	Beginning of first Opium War
1911	Founding of republic
1919	Founding of May Fourth Movement
1921	Founding of Communist Party
1927	KMT-Communist split
1932	Japan occupies Manchuria
1934	Long March
1936	KMT-Communist United Front
1937	Japan attacks China
1945	End of World War II
1949	Founding of People's Republic
1950	Collectivization of agriculture
1953	Start of First Five-Year Plan
1957	Hundred Flowers
1958	Great Leap Forward
1963	Socialist education campaign
1966	Start of Cultural Revolution
1976	Arrest of "Gang of Four"
1978	Deng Xiaoping starts four modernizations
1989	Bloody recapture of Tiananmen Square
1992	Deng calls for expanded economic liberalization
2000	Zhu Rongji begins China's western development program
2002	Jiang Zemin passes leadership to Hu Jintao
2008	Beijing Olympics
2009	China microblog, Sina Weibo (weibo.com), launched
2012	Hu Jintao passes leadership to Xi Jinping

longer around to help maintain the civil bureaucracy. To make matters even worse, the 1919 Versailles Conference awarded part of the Shandong peninsula (see Map 2.2 and Chapter 7) to Japan, as a reward for its support of the Allies in World War I. That began the May Fourth Movement (Mitter, 2005), which Charles Laughlin introduces colorfully in Chapter 13.

In 1921, Sun met with representatives of Russia's new government, the Soviet Union, to procure help in reuniting China. That same year a small group of men (including Mao Zedong and Zhou Enlai) founded the Chinese Communist Party (CCP). While they were organizing miners and textile workers into unions, Sun was using aid from the Soviet Union (which was asking the KMT and Communists to form a united front) to create a military academy at Whampoa, just below Guangzhou (see Map 2.2). He sent his associate Chiang Kai-shek (see Fenby, 2004; Taylor, 2009) to Moscow for training, while Zhou Enlai (see Barnouin and Yu, 2006; Gao, 2007) took over as Whampoa's director. Meanwhile, Mao Zedong led KMT/Communist efforts to organize peasants.

After Sun's death in 1925, this cozy alliance dissolved. He left leadership of the KMT to Chiang Kai-shek. After defeating warlords who controlled the region around Guangzhou, Chiang recruited their troops to help attack other warlords. Soon the KMT controlled the territory of seven provinces. But now the Communists and Kuomintang disagreed on strategy for the next move. Chiang wanted to turn the offensive along the Yangtze River and up the coast to converge on Shanghai. The Communist leaders preferred to head farther north, making alliances with warlords friendly to them there. After that they would join forces against the two most powerful warlords of the north. By then, Chiang might be pushed from leadership of the movement. The Russian advisers sided with the Communists. In addition, many of Chiang's supporters were landlords and industrialists who feared communist demands for peasant and worker rights. Communists led powerful worker organizations in Guangzhou, Shanghai, and Wuhan (see Map 2.2; Perry, 1993; Honig, 1986). In the spring of 1927, Chiang (now leading the KMT and about to marry the sister of Sun's widow—see Seagrave, 1987; Li, 2006; Pakula, 2009) made a secret deal with Zhang Zuolin, one of the northern warlords the Communists planned to attack. Early on the morning of April 12, Chiang's men began killing all the Communists they could find in Shanghai (Dong, 2001:154–193; Stranahan, 1998). Meanwhile, Zhang carried out a similar mission in Beijing. By year's end, the Communists in Wuhan and Guangzhou had been defeated as well, but the price was heavy for the Kuomintang. Warlord forces defeated some of their troops. Out of money, Chiang used triad society (organized crime) gangs to extort money from merchants in the foreign concession areas of Shanghai (Wakeman, 1996, 2002).

The following year, Chiang Kai-shek broke his alliance with Zhang and headed north to defeat Zhang's armies around Beijing. The Japanese, occupying the Shandong peninsula just south of Beijing, also had designs on Zhang's territory. They blew up a train he was riding on, killing him, and he was succeeded by his son, Zhang Xueliang, who retained control of Manchuria but ceded Beijing to Chiang's KMT Nationalists. By 1931, this position had been reversed; the Japanese controlled Manchuria (Duara, 2004), and Zhang Xueliang operated from Beijing as an ally of the Nationalists. Meanwhile, Mao Zedong was organizing peasants in rural areas to the north of Guangzhou, experimenting with policies, strategies, and institutions that would improve living standards and attract followers. Having consolidated his position in the cities, Chiang sent his troops to wipe out this last remaining communist stronghold. In 1934, these Communists began their Long March on foot to escape Chiang's forces; 370 days, numerous pitched battles, and 6,000 miles later, 8,000 of them (they started out with 80,000) arrived at a new base area in the hills to the north of Xi'an. Some had been members—often with little military training—of the Red Army, while others were civilian members of the Communist Party. Now, in this adversity, those lines were blurred, fitting Mao's notion that the army should be the masses directly serving the masses.

Mao used the organizational methods he had pioneered farther south to help his troops aid peasants in taking control of their region, setting up farming, and patrolling the perimeters (Hinton, 1970; Averill, Esterich, and Perry, 2005; Snow, 1994; Thomas, 1996; Hamilton, 2003, on Snow). By this time, Zhang controlled Xi'an, and the Japanese in Manchuria were threatening further hostilities. Chiang Kai-shek urged Zhang to wipe out Mao's new stronghold, but Zhang was convinced that the time had come for the KMT Nationalists and the Communists to make a truce and unite against the Japanese. When Chiang flew to Xi'an in 1936, he was in for a surprise. Zhang arrested him and demanded he declare a united front with the communists. Chiang did so. Six months later, Japan attacked China.

The war against Japan was long and bloody. The Japanese troops swept from Beijing almost to Guangzhou and pushed Chiang Kai-shek's headquarters inland to Chongqing, behind the Three Gorges on the Yangtze River (MacKinnon, 2008; Coble, 2003; Brook, 2007). Mao's forces gradually expanded their hold over the territory to the west of the Yellow River. Life was horrendous in all three areas:

- Though they refused to go along with the racial extermination policies of their ally Hitler and estimates by experts vary widely, the Japanese may have killed as many as 35 million Chinese by war's end (see, for example, figures in Spence, 1999:422–425, 439, 452–453; Chang, 1997; Honda, 1999; Henriot and Yeh, 2003; Wasserstein, 1999; Wakeman, 2002; Young, 1999; Lary, 2010; and the discussion on the Nanjing massacre in Chapter 3). They used many people for slave labor in farms and factories and wiped out entire villages in their "three-alls" ("kill all, burn all, destroy all") campaigns.
- Warlords controlled much of the remaining territory. Impoverished peasants worked long hours on their lands, producing crops to be sold elsewhere, while local people starved (Buck, 2005). In areas administered by the Kuomintang, lineage leaders often dominated their entire community, or absentee landlords exploited poor tenants. Unions were banned in the cities, and people worked for low wages under harsh conditions.
- In contrast, the Communists worked with landlords to reduce their rents. They paid peasants for food and supplies used by their troops and warned their troops not to molest women. They created producer cooperatives, helped peasants pool their labor to build up fields and irrigation, and developed local industries (see Hinton, 1970, 1997). As a result, their numbers grew rapidly, and many students left the universities to help. Peasants in Japanese or KMT areas were eager to bring their regions into Communist hands or to escape into Communist-held territory. By 1941, Communist and Kuomintang forces were fighting one another. In 1942, Mao initiated the first of many rectification campaigns (based on the Confucian notion of rectifying your good name when you have shamed it, by apologizing and correcting your behavior), forcing

people to stand before their neighbors and admit their mistakes in an effort to enforce political solidarity. The Communists started letting peasants settle old scores by killing their landlords. If the land fell back into KMT control, landlords would in turn shoot peasants; the Japanese would kill them all and burn their villages. Fighting and recrimination among the three sides grew increasingly bloody.

Unity Nearly Restored

At war's end in 1945, much of China's countryside had been ravaged by war, deforestation, erosion, floods, and exploitative landlords. Many of its industries had been dismantled. The Communists had personnel trained and eager to tackle such problems and peasants willing to work long hours to restore fields and factories. In the communist areas, inflation was low and production quickly resumed. Many warlords and KMT leaders had their attention focused on other matters, and morale among their laborers was low. A portion of food that cost US$1 in KMT cities in mid-1947 cost over US$500 by the beginning of 1949, but strikes for higher wages were forbidden (see Spence, 1999:474–480). Against that background, KMT Nationalists battled Communist forces for control of China (Westad, 2003; Lynch, 2010). Morale also was low among many KMT troops, especially those who had not been paid. Even during the fight against Japan, US General Joseph Stilwell was "horrified at the campaigns of enforced conscription carried out by the Kuomintang armies, and at the sight of ragged, barefooted men being led to the front roped together, already weakened almost to death by beriberi or malnutrition" (Spence, 1999:453). Many officers fled to Taiwan before battles with Communist forces ended. After Japan's surrender, Stalin occupied Manchuria and then left it to the Red Army, and the Communists already occupied large pieces of terrain in northern China. Toward the end of 1948, the Red Army engaged the demoralized KMT troops to seize the railway connections linking the major cities, which (except for Harbin) were still under KMT control. In January 1949, after capturing nearby Tianjin in a focused assault, the Red Army persuaded the heavily outnumbered KMT troops guarding Beijing to surrender that city, and ten days later Chiang Kai-shek resigned as president. The Red Army swept southward to take strategic cities there; by year's end, the KMT regime had retreated to Taiwan. On October 1, 1949, Mao declared formation of the People's Republic of China.

China was ready for a restoration of order (Brown and Pickowicz, 2007). That required curbing inflation, restoring land to the peasants, rebuilding heavy industry, and creating a stable administrative structure. To accomplish this, the Communists needed the skills of landlords, managers, technicians, and able civil servants. Many Chinese returned from abroad to help with the reconstruction. In 1950, the regime seized and redistributed about 40 percent of cultivable land and may have killed over 2 million landlords (Dietrich, 1997:69); many friendly landlords were spared and allowed to keep their land. The government vigorously cracked down on the secret triad societies, whose corruption had been keeping urban fiscal and civil order at bay. Repeating a tactic pioneered during the Han dynasty, foreign and domestic business owners were forced to sell out for "back taxes" but then were hired to manage their former firms if they stayed. The country was divided into six military/administrative districts, each under separate command of officers of the Red Army, now renamed the People's Liberation Army (PLA). These commanders supervised both military and civil activities in their districts. The Communist Party was the "leading element" in the country but needed coordination with these military units and the civilian bureaucracy to rule. The party's top organs, the Central Committee and Politburo (see below) contained many military officers. Extending the Qing dynasty's *baojia* approach (households grouped together under a leader; see Chapter 5), all factories, offices, schools, and other places of employment were organized into work units that reported the activities of their members to those authorities (*danwei*) (see Walder, 1986). A common currency was created for the entire country, and government spending was brought under tight control. Inflation declined rapidly.

The next challenge was to root out opponents of the new regime and inspire the citizenry to set aside personal gain so as to restore the nation's vitality. The animosities surrounding the Korean War (see Chapter 7), which lasted from 1950 to 1953, provided a backdrop to these efforts. As the US Seventh Fleet patrolled the waters between Taiwan (whose regime was asserting its right to take back the mainland by force) and the mainland, and US aid helped Taiwan rearm and rebuild, the Communist government began a series of rectification campaigns. It wanted to be sure its citizens did not side with Taiwan and that they gave their all to promote national development and a new communist society that would be free from exploitation and that sought to better the lives of everyone rather than a select few (see Chapter 12). The 1951 "counterrevolutionary" campaign forced people to stand before their neighbors and confess that they had been disloyal to the new regime; tens of thousands of them were executed. Then the "three anti" campaign brought managers and bureaucrats before their work units to confess waste, corruption, and activities that obstructed development. The 1952 "five anti" campaign was aimed at foreign and domestic capitalists engaged in tax evasion, bribery, theft of state property, fraud on government contracts, and theft of state economic information (Thornton, 2007). The government needed their production for the Korean War and civil development and even helped pay many of their fines—making them more subservient and cautious about such practices. Few were killed. The campaigns attacked foreign enemies and called for patriotism and determination to rout those holding back China's development (for discussion of these campaigns, see Tiewes, 1993).

The Korean War also brought a trade blockade of China and removed it from access to foreign capital. The Soviet Union supplied capital and technical assistance for China's First Five-Year Plan (discussed further in Chapter 5). The separate military-political units of the country were abandoned, and planning was centralized to promote frugality and growth. Government agencies were placed on tight budgets, and resources were carefully targeted. Between 1953 and 1957, agencies invested extensively in state-operated heavy industries spread throughout the country, and in hydroelectric plants, railroads, and urban housing. Production focused on military hardware and then, increasingly, on machinery, construction materials, and basic consumer goods. Wages were kept low, and workers had to "contribute" heavy taxes and savings bond investments to the state, but employment was guaranteed. Little was spent on education or social welfare, but citizens were recruited for drives to wipe out pests, improve sanitation, combat common diseases, and promote literacy. Peasants were organized into mutual-aid teams composed of six or seven (later, fifty) families who kept title to their land while pooling their resources. They sold the government a fourth of their grain at low prices; the government, in turn, sold flour, rice, and cooking oil to urban workers for low prices (keeping inflation low). Wealthy peasants were excluded from these teams. Agricultural output rose, but not enough to keep pace with industrial production. People's diets steadily improved, but they could buy little beyond food.

Up to that point, the government's efforts had some historical precedents in China's long history of encouraging but regulating capitalist enterprises in a successful effort to restore social and economic stability. Many people had, in fact, been pleased to see individual excesses brought under control. But now the government was ready to move beyond that, testing dangerous new waters in its efforts to ratchet up agricultural production. Capitalism would be banned, not just reformed; the state and peasant organizations would own all production enterprises. By 1955, many mutual-aid teams were being incorporated into cooperatives comprising 200 to 300 families, and credit was being withheld from richer families. Much of the cooperatives' land was being farmed in common, though each family retained a private plot.

China had pulled itself together and left the war years behind, but it was facing a baffling dilemma it still cannot solve. The Chinese people are prepared to give support to strong leaders, especially when they remember periods of disarray. They have long experience at investing in and developing farms and businesses and will devote long hours to work. But they feel strongly about carrying out their *guanxi* obligations to their own families and others with whom they have special relationships. In the 1950s, they were being asked to sacrifice living standards for their own families when they knew others were passing favors to their friends. Given a choice to spend their efforts on common fields or on their own plots, many members of cooperatives chose the latter and then lied to the tax authorities about the income they derived from selling their own livestock and vegetables (and about how small the harvest was on the common land). The most fervent Communists saw this emphasis on one's own land and on jobs like hauling or hawking to earn extra money as putting capitalist family interests above those of the whole community. Communists also disliked religious practices that helped bond the community, because they held back material progress by wasting resources on extravagant funerals and weddings. The Communists had returned the land to the peasants but were imposing rules that ran counter to their traditional culture.

The year 1956 began on a hopeful note (see Macfarquar, 1974; Tiewes, 1993). According to the often-inflated reports, agricultural output seemed to be rising, so China's leaders followed Mao Zedong's guidance and rapidly pushed greater numbers of mutual-aid teams into the larger cooperatives. Soviet premier Nikita Khrushchev was secretly denouncing Stalin (who had died in 1953) in the Soviet Union's party congress and openly called for peaceful coexistence. Mao and others within China's ruling circle (hoping for reconciliation with Taiwan) secretly discussed allowing greater intellectual freedom and encouraging more openness to foreigners and minorities. Some of their colleagues strongly resisted such accommodation with bourgeois elements, and this debate was short-lived. The summer brought a severe drought and disastrous harvest. Peasants resisted the imposition of the badly managed large cooperatives. In the fall, the Hungarians rose against the Soviet Union, Tibetans rioted against Chinese rule (see Chapter 6), and the Chinese Communists held their first party congress since taking over China. The congress abruptly stopped converting mutual-aid teams into cooperatives, called for greater central control of the economy, supported those who opposed a Khrushchev-style united front with bourgeois elements, and challenged Mao's leadership. For a time, neither the Soviet Union nor China suffered from a "cult of personality."

Mao had been ostracized from inner party circles before (for interesting biographies, see Spence, 2000; Terrill, 1999; Li, 1994; Ji, 2008; Feigon, 2002; Meisner, 2007; Karl, 2010; Mao and Zizek, 2007; Mao, 2000; Ford, 2005; Chang and Halliday, 2006; Gao, 2008; Benton and Lin, 2009). Among the party's founders, he was the only one who came from a peasant background and had not studied in Europe. The others tended to associate with intellectuals and attempted to organize among workers in the cities where they lived, whereas Mao moved into the countryside to organize peasants. His work was largely ignored by his urban comrades. In 1927, after the Kuomintang attack on the Communists, Mao tried to lead a peasant uprising. The KMT quickly squelched it, and the Communist Party removed him from the Central Committee. While the KMT suppressed urban branches of the party, Mao simply continued organizing the peasants—thus providing the basis for the 1934 Long March. The survivors of that march formed the core group who would take over China. Mao was their natural leader—not the urban intellectuals.

Removed once again in 1956 from the inner circle, Mao returned to the source of his power, the peasants and workers. Early in 1957, he publicly delivered a speech drawing on one he had made privately the previous year, calling for greater intellectual freedom so that "a hundred flowers" could bloom and "a hundred schools of thought contend" (Spence, 1999:539–543). He said the country was now so united it could benefit from such a debate. The press, a natural ally in such an initiative, hesitated at first to print his words. When they did, criticism rushed forth. Mao had hoped the press and citizens would attack his adversaries leading the party and support his reforms. Instead, the students at Beijing University started a "Democracy Wall" and filled it with posters denouncing a wide range of Communist Party policies and even the right of the communists to rule. People around the country joined in; many were critical of Mao himself. Within weeks, Mao backed down and joined the inner circle in calling for a crackdown on the campaign and severe punishment of those making the criticisms. The antirightist rectification campaign that ensued led to 300,000 intellectuals (branded as "rightists") losing their jobs without hope of finding other employment and sending many of them into exile on farms. Their numbers included many of the youths who had been most zealous in supporting the initial rise to power of the Communists. They would not forget this humiliation.

Two Decades of Turmoil

In 1957, agricultural production moved to center stage as the primary concern of China's leaders. Industrial production had been growing far more rapidly than grain production, and the income of rural workers had outpaced that of peasants. Left once again to their own devices, peasants had focused on more profitable vegetables and livestock, leaving the country with inadequate flour, rice, and cooking oil to feed its burgeoning population. Mao was determined to end this lethargy and propel China into a communist utopia by increasing agricultural and industrial output to improve the lives of everyone and surpass the capitalist West. Late in 1957, the party mobilized millions of peasants into work gangs to irrigate and terrace millions of acres of new cropland. The effort was carried out through a mass rectification campaign; units outdid themselves to show their all-out commitment to pure "red" communism by reporting huge increases in production. Encouraged by these wildly inflated figures, the following year the party announced the Great Leap Forward (for alarming close-ups, see Macfarquar, 1983; Bachman, 2006; Domenach, 1995; Liu and Link, 2006; Thaxton, 2008; and Yang, 1996; for an overview, see Dietrich, 1997:110–142; Becker, 1997; Dikotter, 2010; Larus, 2012). Private plots were abolished. Mutual-aid teams and cooperatives were amalgamated into gigantic communes. Families were absorbed into large crews who worked in the fields and made their meals together. These crews were even mobilized to help develop an atomic bomb and increase steel production by melting scrap metal in backyard ovens, based on Mao's ideas that committed peasants could enhance industrial output more effectively than professionals working with central planners.

In the long run, the Great Leap Forward opened much new land for agricultural production and brought new industry and agricultural capabilities to formerly remote regions (for an account of how the Great Leap Forward improved life in one small village, after a period of great pain, see Chan, Madsen, and Unger, 1992; also see White, 1998; Seybolt, 1996; Huang, 2008). And it enlarged local militias, which competed with the PLA. In the short run—due to bad weather, diversion of labor to other projects, increased exports of grain to the Soviet Union based on the exaggerated output claims, layoff of skilled civil servants during the antirightist campaigns, and other mismanagement—agricultural production fell below even the disastrous levels of the prior two years. Millions of people were starving; over 20 million died (see Yang, 1996; Becker, 1997; Spence, 1999:553). Yet grain exports to the Soviet Union in payment for its aid in developing industry were increasing. Once again, the party leadership called off the campaign and removed Mao as head of state in 1959. Registration in the *danwei* was intensified to pull people back to the countryside. Private plots began to be distributed again, communes were divided among private production brigades, and rural markets reopened. Many inefficient rural industries and state enterprises were closed. Gradually, agricultural production and private entrepreneurship began to revive.

Meanwhile, the United States had begun supplying Taiwan with missiles. The Soviet Union, talking of "peaceful coexistence" with the capitalist nations, showed no signs of helping China develop an atomic bomb. Khrushchev had sent no assistance to the Great Leap Forward, which differed from his own new initiatives to provide workers with economic incentives. While China was having foreign policy disputes with India and Indonesia (discussed in Chapters 6 and 7), Khrushchev was warming relations with them. In 1960, the Soviet Union called home its technical advisers and cut off aid to China, bringing a halt to many projects.

The debate within China's inner circle of top Communist Party leaders defies simple summation. They decried the excesses that resulted from suppressing capitalist enterprises, yet did not want capitalism to return. They all largely agreed that Khrushchev's policy of accommodation with capitalists was the wrong tack for China and that China's peasants and workers needed more discipline, but they disagreed on how to achieve that discipline. Mao preferred those who were "red" (a true devotee of the communist cause) to those who were simply trained experts. As evidence mounted that the efforts to instill "redness" by organizing great communes and putting peasants and workers in charge was a disaster threatening their positions as leaders of government and party organs and popular support for Communist Party rule, the leaders struggled for a way out. They chose, at this point, to restore the use of expert bureaucrats, managers, and technicians in a central bureaucracy to plan allocation of resources, direct what should be grown and produced, and assist with distribution of finished products; meanwhile, they sought to give people more opportunity to profit from their output. Some in the party leadership felt China needed more technical expertise from the outside but feared that exposure to bourgeois capitalism would weaken people's resolve to serve their whole community.

To ensure that the renewed opportunities for profit were not at the expense of the community, national party leaders initiated a "socialist education campaign" in 1963, which attempted to reduce fraud both in accounting for grain and property and in distributing incentive pay to those who worked harder. The campaign, however, was carried out by local party leaders who themselves might have been guilty of those offenses. The communist leaders of communes, cooperatives, work teams, and state enterprises were made responsible for judging how to proceed and determining who among their own ranks was cheating; they were to discipline themselves (for an account of how local leaders found themselves involved in such national projects, see Siu, 1999). Thus local leaders could cheat without getting caught, but ordinary people were closely supervised, without assurance of extra rewards for hard work.

To challenge his opponents within the party leadership, Mao took advantage of citizens' resentment over leaders' abuses of power. He applauded his model village of Dazhai for increasing production through "red" ideological fervor rather than supervision by experts, even though a party inspection team found its production was down and many of its inhabitants were undernourished. He called once again for more open debate, to let the masses—not the local party leaders—ferret out the corruption among their leaders. His position gained support among troops within the People's Liberation Army who felt that their own power was being eclipsed by the party's civilian leaders, who were calling for stricter discipline and professionalism, and from the militias, who had grown in strength since the Great Leap Forward. And Mao had the ear of some groups who, ironically, were suffering from his own efforts: city people from "bourgeois" or former Kuomintang families who had lost university admissions, jobs, and party posts to individuals from the countryside who had more humble (and therefore presumably more "red") origins. He also gained support from many unemployed youth who had fled to the cities during the agricultural downturn Mao had helped create and now had been returned to the farms, where they were not always well received. Finally, the current batch of university students worried about their prospects in the wake of all the recent cataclysms.

Mao preached to these politically alienated listeners that they should assert themselves against their leaders, and they listened. In 1965, the PLA abandoned all ranks and insignia on their uniforms; officers and enlisted soldiers would be "equal" and share all work assignments. By spring 1966, Mao had stirred leading university campuses into protest, and protesting students began calling themselves "Red Guards." Soon they were joined by students and other supporters from throughout the country. By fall, they were dragging political leaders, teachers, bureaucrats, and others into the streets and making them confess crimes before kangaroo courts. Schools and universities were closed, workers were stealing property from their factories, historic buildings and monuments were being destroyed, production was grinding to a halt. The Great Proletarian Cultural Revolution had begun (Macfarquar, 1999; Perry and Li, 1996; Macfarquar and Schoenhals, 2008; White, 1989; Cunxin Li, 2004; Yuan, 1987; Dietrich, 1997:178–235; Wang, 1991; Wang, 1995; Chang, 1991; Chen, 1981; Chen, 2001, 2003; Yan and Gao, 1996; Gao, 1987; Gao, 2003; Cheng, 2010; Min, 2002; Yang, 1997; Yang, 1998; Liang, 1984; Jun, 1998; Ma, 1996; Ma, 2004; Esherick, Pickowicz, and Walder, 2006; Walder, 2009; Fens, 2007; Guo, Song, and Zhou, 2006; Clark, 2008; Han, 2008; Jacai, 1996; Zhengguo, 2008; Moise, 2008:165–196).

Mao had hoped to regain control of China's leadership and keep China's people focused on the good of the whole community. Instead, once again, he had roused (together with millions of people acting out of pure idealistic fervor) the anticommunist, anarchist, and disaffected citizens in the country to

Giant Mao statues like this one in Kashgar, Xinjiang, were common in China during the 1970s.

attack authority and seek their own personal gain—or at least disrupt community life. By February 1967, Mao was supporting efforts by the party leaders and the army to restore order. This time, it would take ten years. By the late 1960s, schools were beginning to reopen, and Mao was seeking ties with the United States. Many more students had been sent to work in the countryside alongside those sent there earlier in the 1960s; slowly they returned to the cities, bitter over their forced exile and long-disrupted education (Tiewes and Sun, 2007). Because the party's membership had expanded to include many Red Guards, a series of rectification campaigns first attacked those leading the Cultural Revolution and then those trying to bring it under control. Even top leaders of the party were subjected to beatings and imprisonment, and many were humiliated to the point of suicide.

In 1976, Zhou Enlai (who had led the restoration of party control) and Mao died. Mao's successor, Hua Guofeng, promptly arrested the "Gang of Four," four of the most prominent leaders of the Cultural Revolution; in their trial, they were blamed for all the excesses of that era (Terrill, 1997). A new era had begun. Within four years, Deng Xiaoping (for biographies, see Goodman, 1994; Shambaugh, 1995; Yang, 1997; and Vogel, 2011) had overcome strong challenges from his rivals to take control of the party, and the United States had extended diplomatic recognition to the People's Republic. Mao had paved the way for reforms more in keeping with tradition—such as encouraging limited capitalism—by weakening the central bureaucracies, returning land to the peasants, and helping even small communities develop consumer industries. The United States made reforms possible by helping Hong Kong, Taiwan, Japan, and Southeast Asian countries develop strong economies and currencies to invest in China; for more on this, see Chapter 6.

Into the World Economy

After Mao's era ended, China was free to pursue the added elements of economic strength that had eluded it before: foreign capital, technology, and markets. China's attempt to modernize its economy without changing its political system would confuse those in the West and would burden China with new social problems, but it would also bring China the broadest prosperity it had ever experienced.

To implement reform, Deng called for four modernizations—of agriculture, industry, defense, and science and technology—and initiated new economic policies, which are discussed in detail in Chapter 5 (see also Macfarquar, 1997; Misra, 1998; Huang, 2008; Li Lanqing, 2010). The household responsibility system allowed peasants to lease plots of land and sell their crops for profit. Groups of individuals or entire villages and townships could form cooperative enterprises to manufacture, transport, and sell goods (sometimes hiring workers from villages farther inland for low pay). In addition, foreign firms could create joint ventures with firms in China. Special economic zones were created where foreign businesses could buy land and get special breaks on taxes and regulations. And state industries were authorized to fire workers (Hurst, 2009; Gold et al., 2009), give incentive pay, and sell shares of stock to Chinese investors. These reforms brought China continuous and dynamic economic growth at a rate surpassing 10 percent a year (see Figure 5.1).

Meeting the Initial Challenges of Reform

The three groups initially most helped by Deng's reforms were the peasants, party bureaucrats in coastal provinces, and urban workers who could form cooperatives. The groups most harmed were students, intellectuals, urban youth still trapped in the countryside, central planners, and workers in state industries. To achieve power after Mao's death, Deng had to win support from factions with adherents in all these camps.

Mao's reforms allowed the land to be returned to peasant producers; Deng's responsibility system and cooperatives gave them the incentive to produce. They rapidly began bringing home profits. Intellectuals, bureaucrats, and skilled blue-collar workers with assigned jobs and fixed salaries, in contrast, found themselves making less than uneducated peasants and laborers. Rural workers used their incomes to build large new houses, whereas urban dwellers were crowded into small, dingy apartments. Many urban youths who had been sent to the countryside during the Cultural Revolution still could not get permission to return to the cities yet were not entitled to land or jobs where they were. The government had little money to invest in universities; students studied on drab campuses with few laboratory or library facilities, ate food ladled from buckets of gruel onto metal plates, and lived with six people in dorm rooms meant for two, without heat or air conditioning. Even graduates of the leading universities anticipated assigned jobs paying less than the income of a bicycle repairperson on a street corner or someone gathering scrap cardboard in a cart and selling it to a wholesaler. Many students had marched in demonstrations and hung posters on the "Democracy Wall" in 1976 and 1978 to help bring Deng to power and felt both unrewarded and betrayed by the arrest of Wei Jingsheng and others who had led those demonstrations (see Black and Munro, 1993; Ding, 2006; Wasserstrom, 1997; Zhang, 1996).

By 1986, students were marching again, against rigged elections, their poor living conditions, low pay for university graduates, the growth in inflation and the corruption of officials who were hiring their own children and diverting resources into the pockets of their factional cohorts. In the spring of 1989, students marched once more to raise these concerns. This time the foreign media was in Beijing to cover the historic reopening of relations with the Soviet Union as Mikhail Gorbachev flew in for a state visit, and reporters saw the students occupy and refuse to leave Tiananmen Square at the center of Beijing.

Robert E. Gamer

The 1989 demonstrations took place for several weeks in cities all over China. Hangzhou saw daily scenes like this.

Some of the leaders felt it was time to take a more tolerant view than had ever been taken in the past toward demonstrations and suggested inviting the leaders into public dialogue about the issues they had raised (Zhao, 2009). Most, however, worried that the situation might get out of hand as had happened during the prior two decades; the students' complaints about corruption and economic disparities and their ties to political factions within the party were reminiscent of the Red Guards, who had started the Cultural Revolution with similar demonstrations (for interviews with participants in such demonstrations going back to 1942, see Benton and Hunter, 1995). That approach prevailed, and the government responded with a bloody recapture of Tiananmen Square, arrests of and long prison sentences for demonstration leaders, a rectification campaign condemning the action, and requirements that students should serve stints in the army to remind them of the need for discipline (for inside reports, see Zhang, Nathan, and Link, 2001; Gamer, 1989; Pomfret, 2006:137–176; Calhoun, 1997; Brook, 1998; Wright, 2001:21–94; Feigon, 1999; Dingzin Zhao, 2004; Fewsmith, 2008; Li, Mark, and Li, 2007; and Cunningham, 2009).

The government then took steps to defuse the anger that lay behind the demonstrations (Béja, 2011). Part of this strategy focused on the PLA. The units who ran the tanks into the square were from inland rural areas that had not benefited from the reforms; they feared and distrusted the students, who lived better than they did and were taking actions country youths would not dream of. Some soldiers lost their lives on the square, raising the level of distrust and envy. When Deng came to power he had sought to reduce the influence of the PLA, which had greatly expanded during the Cultural Revolution, by separating police units from it, reducing the size of military forces and budgets, and removing officers from top party posts. Now he restored officers to some of these posts and gradually increased military spending. The PLA first was given rights to set up numerous joint ventures and sell arms abroad and later in the 1990s received large increases in its budget to procure weaponry, raising their morale.

Universities were mandated to start businesses (a policy since abandoned), charge wealthier students tuition, and raise money in other creative ways. University campuses acquired new gardens, paint, furniture, buildings, and equipment. Mess halls began serving a variety of foods. Occupancy of dorm rooms was reduced, and more buildings were heated and air conditioned. Later in the 1990s, some key universities received large grants from the government to give substantial raises to instructors, construct massive new campuses, and increase the size of their student bodies. New universities, and private primary and secondary schools, were created (Li Lanqing, 2004).

Rather than being assigned to low-paying government jobs as in the past, students were now free to seek jobs with joint ventures, and later private firms, after graduation (Postiglione, 2006). In 1992, Deng called for dramatic further expansion of economic liberalization. This set off a wave of construction; new housing, roads, public buildings, factories, airports, dams, and electrical power stations brought jobs and better living conditions all over the country (Gittings, 2006). Chapter 5 chronicles the dramatic changes in the 1990s.

Twenty-First-Century Political Challenges

As the new millennium dawned, China had come a long way. It had restored unity and set in motion dynamic economic growth. But it faced numerous challenges: inflation and deflation, environmental degradation, rising unemployment, overextended bank loans, the shrinking social safety net, widespread corruption, maintenance of adequate incomes, the increasing gap in economic growth and income between the coastal cities and inland provinces and between the rich and poor, and the restoration of national pride and cultural identities. These challenges are about improving the quality of people's lives.

China's government faces the task of maintaining unity and improving quality of life while loosening its grip on the economy. That involves new kinds of symbiotic relationships. The decentralization accompanying economic reform has given new freedoms to China's provincial leaders (Naughton and Yang, 2004; Zheng, 2006, 2010; Zhong, 2003). These freedoms have been made possible largely for the following reasons: China is once again unified;

it has been accorded diplomatic recognition by other governments; it has been able to ensure political stability; and it is now able to move people and resources from one region to another for manufacturing and marketing. In 2001, China was admitted into the World Trade Organization (WTO), making it a regular part of the world trading community, and Beijing was chosen as the site of the 2008 Olympics. New cars demand new roads, which often used to end at the city limit, so the central government initiated a vast program to build new freeways linking all the major cities; it also created more electric-generating capacity, numerous modern airfields, and other infrastructure. All this gave political leaders incentive to work together to achieve continuing economic growth; provinces cannot achieve these objectives on their own (Yang, 2004). At the same time, the central government gave provinces control over a lot of money and resources. Municipalities, townships, and provinces allied with former state industries and foreign multinational corporations have become the main recipients of investment capital. They collect most tax revenues as well, including internal tariffs on goods crossing their boundaries. Cities pass "health" and "quality control" laws banning goods from other provinces. They bypass laws banning foreign ownership of industries like mining, steel, telecommunications (including the Internet), and education by setting up variable interest entities (VIEs), which elaborately disguise foreign ownership stakes. Over a thousand disputes over internal boundary lines have sometimes led to bloodshed, as two provinces make claims on the same mines or timber. In addition, the country is divided into seven military regions whose boundaries do not correspond with provincial lines; though the central government frequently moves around senior officers, their troops have strong regional loyalties.

The government has also needed to deal with the ethnic minorities. Chapter 6 discusses Tibet, whose territory used to be much greater. On Tibet's eastern border, many Tibetans and other inhabitants of Sichuan and Yunnan provinces share in the religion and customs of Tibet and of areas in Southeast Asia. The regions to the north and east of Tibet—now the provinces of Xinjiang, Qinghai, and Gansu (see Map 2.2)—were occasionally penetrated by Chinese armies (see Map 3.1). Tang dynasty conquests brought in Chinese culture that local people continued to absorb even after military withdrawals. The Silk Roads (Map 2.1) made these provinces a meeting place for many cultures and of all the world's great religions (Hopkirk, 1984; Barber, 2000; Mallory and Mair, 2000; Starr, 2004; Rudelson, 1997; Dwyer, 2005; Beckwith, 2009; Millward, 2007; Kaltman, 2007; Dautcher, 2009; Bovingdon, 2010; Mackerras and Clarke, 2011). Many of their people are Muslim and share religious and family customs far different from those of the Han or the Tibetans.

During the seventeenth century, the Manchus, to the northeast of China above Korea (now the eastern part of Inner Mongolia, Heilongjiang, Jilin, and

Liaoning; see Map 2.2), crossed the Great Wall to conquer China; their rulers adopted the Confucian system but kept separate administrative units (and even separate official records, written in their own language) for Manchus (Elliott, 2001). Although they told the Han people they were imposing Confucian customs on people in the periphery, they in fact allowed those peoples much leeway in carrying out their own cultural traditions (Rawski, 1996; Rhoads, 2000). In 1911, much support for ending the empire came from southern Chinese who were tired of being ruled by these alien Manchus (see earlier in this chapter, and Chapter 6). Once they took power, they tried to impose their laws and customs more rigidly on those in the periphery, including the Manchus. These peoples strongly resisted that imposition, seeking to preserve old customs. Rank-and-file Manchus, who now constitute less than 10 percent of the populace in Jilin and Heilongjiang provinces, often failed to adopt Chinese ways. Thousands of Mongols were tortured and killed during the Cultural Revolution on suspicion that they were foreign agents.

During the Cultural Revolution, acting on communist ideological convictions that nationality traits must be removed if bourgeois society is to wither away and the dictatorship of the proletariat flourish, Red Guard activists aggressively sought to destroy places of worship, languages, clothing, music, and all other manifestations of these cultures. During the earlier years of the People's Republic and now again since the Cultural Revolution, China's Communist regime has sought to retain such expressions of cultural differences, while at the same time bringing modernization to these regions. It recognizes fifty-five minority nationalities. Whole provinces like Tibet, as well as individual prefectures, counties, and townships, are designated autonomous areas; they cover nearly two-thirds of China's territory (generally the least populous). Their legislatures have the right to create laws protecting local customs. In addition, citizens registered as cultural minorities have many special privileges unavailable to those officially classified as Han. They are exempt from family planning limits (see Chapter 8) and can gain admission to higher education and cadre posts with lower qualifications.

Today, Beijing sends large numbers of Han to Tibet and cities in the outer northern arc and the southwest in the belief that it is spreading modernization and civilization, but also to develop the vast natural resources in those regions (which some there would prefer to exploit themselves). Han sent to these regions often feel exiled from the best schools, housing, and food, and resent the special privileges enjoyed by inhabitants there. And local inhabitants deeply resent their destruction of old neighborhoods, hundreds of monasteries, and hillsides of timber; murders of religious leaders; insistence on communicating in Chinese rather than local languages; cultural arrogance; and growing numbers (Dillon, 2004; Tyler, 2004; Kaltman, 2007). Non-Han residents of autonomous areas often have lower incomes and rates of literacy than their Han compatriots; some of the nation's worst pockets of poverty are to be found among them. Numerous civil rebellions break out in Tibet, Xinjiang, and Inner Mongolia (Clarke, 2011). These regions border on countries and movements like al-Qaeda that may even stir up unrest to help them seize disputed territories (see Chapter 7); the Chinese authorities are determined to squelch the resistance. Since the September 11, 2001, attack on New York's World Trade Center, they have increased the intensity of their efforts to round up and execute individuals engaged in such resistance. All the while, the non-Han peoples in these regions are falling behind in sharing China's growing prosperity, and the growing cross-border trading increases contacts among radical groups fomenting cultural and religious separation.

So we look next at China's twenty-first-century leaders, how they are organized to face these challenges, and what they are doing to meet them.

The Fourth and Fifth Generations of Leadership

The Communist Party has about 80 million members, with about 2 million primary organizations meeting in villages, urban neighborhoods, *danwei,* and military divisions. These local branches elect a local secretary, a local party committee, and other officers, who select individuals to serve on the county and provincial party congresses. Those bodies send about 1,500 delegates (rising to 2,270 in 2012) to a National Party Congress, which meets every five years; about 200 of those delegates (it varies) form the Party Congress's Central Committee. Twenty-five of the Central Committee's members constitute its Politburo, nine of whom belong to the Standing Committee of the Politburo, which meets regularly. That body, headed by its general secretary, wields the highest authority in the land (Bo, 2010:17–90).

The Standing Committee of the Politburo works closely with the party's Military Affairs Commission—the top body directing the armed forces—and with leading government ministers in the State Council, headed by its premier (sometimes referred to as prime minister). A number of individuals hold posts on more than one of these bodies: both Deng Xiaoping and his successor Jiang Zemin (see Kuhn, 2004; Tien and Chu, 2000) simultaneously held the posts of general secretary of the Standing Committee, and as head of the Military Affairs Commission. During Jiang's tenure, Premier Zhu Rongji (see Brahm, 2003; Zhu, 2011) headed the State Council and Li Peng led the National People's Congress (Jiang, 2003). At the Sixteenth National Party Congress (Chu, Lo, and Meyers, 2004; Chen and Zhong, 2004), held in 2002, members of the Standing Committee resigned, except for fifty-nine-year-old Hu Jintao, who had become a member of the Standing Committee in 1992 and vice president in 1998. Hu, a former hydraulic engineer who had long been groomed for a leadership position, then replaced Jiang as general secretary of the Communist Party, and the other eight posts in the Standing Committee were filled with new individuals (then ranging in age from fifty-eight to sixty-seven, all engineers; Joel Andreas

[2009] explains why that profession dominates). Zhu Rongji's former deputy and close associate, Wen Jiabao, became premier. Half the members of the Central Committee were replaced, leaving a fifth under the age of fifty. This move had been planned for several years to allow for a peaceful succession of power to a younger generation. This was called the Fourth Generation of leadership, popularly known as "princelings" because they are direct descendants of the leaders who founded the People's Republic along with Mao Zedong.

There are about 4 million central government bureaucrats, along with 4 million party cadres. And about 3.2 million people serve as delegates to the 48,000 people's congresses, ranging from the township level to the National People's Congress. Thus the Communist Party, the government, and the armed forces intersect to govern China (McGregor, 2010).

The party's cadres, including the party secretaries, are paid functionaries of the party charged with supervising the work of the government bureaucracy (including provincial governors and mayors), the armed forces, and other elements of government and society. Many party members and cadres were chosen during the Cultural Revolution and often had little education. In 1992, Deng Xiaoping made a number of the older cadres retire (Lieberthal, 2003: 230–239), and that process has continued, accelerated again in 2002 with the ascension of the People's Republic's Fourth Generation of leadership under Hu Jintao and Wen Jiabao. There is still tension between the older-style cadres with less education (from Mao's, Deng's, and Jiang's generations) and the new elite with advanced degrees from universities. Party secretaries at the provincial, county, municipal, and township levels hold the power there and are served by dual government and party bureaucracies at those levels (Lieberthal, 2003:159–218; Blecher and Shue, 1996; Finkelstein and Kiviehan, 2003; Dreyer, 2011; Joseph, 2010:165–191; Guo, 2012). There is no government bureaucracy at the village level, but cadres and village committees serve there (Mohanty et al., 2007). Even today, it is easier for the most highly educated individuals to rise high in the ranks of government than it is for them to become a high party leader (Bo, 2010).

Local cadres help choose candidates for elections to party congresses, and citizens over eighteen have suffrage to nominate and vote directly for delegates to people's congresses at the township, county, or urban district level. Candidates need not belong to the CCP, but the party usually shortens the list of candidates and tends to keep independents off ballots. Internet blogging on Sina Weibo (see below) is increasingly being used to support candidacies, including independent write-in candidates. Delegates for people's congresses at levels above that are chosen by these local congresses, and they generally must belong to the CCP or to one of eight small parties that operate mostly among older city intellectuals who cooperated with the Communist Party before World War II. China's million villages are encouraged by the central government to hold elections with rival candidates competing to head the village council (O'Brien and

Zhao, 2010). An uncertain number are doing so, though nominations tend to be carefully controlled (He, 2007). Some villages are electing their local party leader in competitive elections (Hessler, 2010:249–254, 267–276). These moves are in response to rising unrest in rural China—discussed below—over corruption by local officials, tepid economic growth, high taxes, and other issues. Many of China's billionaires are National People's Congress delegates.

Each year, meetings of the National People's Congress (the national legislature, whose Standing Committee enforces martial law during domestic disturbances) and the national meeting of the People's Political Consultative Conference (chosen from among the 32,025 members of these conferences from the county level on up) showcase diversity. Though the main purpose of the week-long meetings is to rubber-stamp government programs, in recent years they have engaged in some lively debates about some of the divisive issues just discussed. The controversial Three Gorges Dam project discussed in Chapter 9 barely passed the People's Congress with a majority vote. Most of the time, the debate takes place behind the scenes. Many factions develop among these individuals, tying them and others together through *guanxi* (Huang, 2000; Yan, 1996; Friedman, Pickowicz, and Selden, 2007; Tsai, 2002; White, 2009:101–158). These connections, in turn, link the regions of the country with the center and one another. Kenneth Lieberthal makes a counterargument that people develop loyalty to their own *danwei* (now grouped into slightly larger neighborhood communities called a *shiqu*; see Heberer, 2009), whose leaders report to multiple bosses, causing the leaders to resist cooperation that might harm their own local interests; this results in "fragmented authoritarianism," with individual units living in "economic, social, and political cocoons" (Lieberthal, 2003:120, 169, 217–218). In recent years, instances of local and provincial people's congresses taking issue with government policies or appointments have increased.

Relations between the People's Liberation Army, with its 2.5 million personnel, and the government are more complex than most (Dreyer, 2011). Civilian ministries report directly to the State Council and also are supervised by the Communist Party. In contrast, the PLA reports directly to the Military Affairs Commission of the Communist Party. The Military Affairs Commission does not report to the State Council. The Ministry of Defense under the State Council has little real control over the military. So the armed forces are supervised by the party, but not by the government. PLA members serve on the party's Politburo (in 2012 only two and none on the Standing Committee) and Central Committee, and they are well connected with party leaders at provincial and local levels as well. Many of those connections were with the old guard, who developed close ties with the military in the early years of the revolutionary struggle; in 2002, at the Party Congress, all the top posts in the PLA were also passed to younger individuals who had entered the military since the PRC came into being—and were closely allied to Jiang Zemin.

Imperial China sought a new ruler only after the prior one died. Communist China has kept that tradition. Mao was no longer in control of China's government when he died in 1976, but the struggle to succeed him did not begin until after his death. Though Deng Xiaoping finally gave up all his formal titles during the 1980s, the mantle of rule could not fall on anyone until his death more than a decade later. Jiang Zemin, the former leader of Shanghai, became the general secretary of the Standing Committee of the Politburo of the Communist Party after his predecessor was removed over the 1989 demonstrations; though he was head of the Military Affairs Commission, he was not able to visit the headquarters of the PLA without direct permission from Deng (Lieberthal, 2003:189). He worked to strengthen his position by gaining support of various elements of the army, party, and bureaucracy in all areas of the country and placing his own followers in key positions (Tien and Chu, 2000). To do that he had to widen the spread of economic reforms while controlling the problems that arose along with them. He also had to show the networks that he was not selling out China to foreigners in any moves reminiscent of the period of foreign domination (see Chapter 7).

Jiang's successor, Hu Jintao, was prepared for this eventuality and mastered it skillfully. Jiang Zemin remained the head of the Military Affairs Commission for only one more year. He turned that post over to Hu and then quietly retired. Behind the scenes, he remains powerful. Six members of the 2002 Politburo were Jiang's strong allies: his closest ally, Zeng Qinghong, retained considerable control over patronage and appointments by taking Hu's former position as vice president. Jia Qinglin, reportedly best man at Jiang's wedding, also became head of the People's Political Consultative Conference. Wu Bangguo, former Shanghai party secretary, succeeded Li Peng as chair of the National People's Congress. Li Changchun became head of propaganda and a member of the Standing Committee. Wu Guanzheng also became head of the Central Commission for Discipline Inspection (the top agency for investigating corruption). These were all Jiang associates. None of the new top military commanders were in the new Politburo. Most of these former Jiang associates adapted quickly to the transition. One Jiang ally who did not work closely with Hu, Chen Liangyu, was dismissed as party chief in Shanghai on corruption charges in 2006; he was replaced by another Jiang ally, Xi Jinping, who supported Hu's policies.

At the Seventeenth Party Congress in 2007, Xi Jinping became a member of the Standing Committee (and subsequently state vice president and later vice chair of the Central Military Affairs Commission), positioned as the successor to Hu as general secretary of the Standing Committee at the Eighteenth Party Congress in 2012. Born in 1953, he served as party chief in Zhejiang province and Shanghai, presiding over rapid economic development in both. Li Keqiang, party chief of Liaoning province, an ally of Hu outside Jiang Zemin's circle, joined the Standing Committee poised to succeed Wen Jiabao as premier in

UN Photo/Marco Castro

General Secretary Hu Jintao addresses the general debate of the sixty-fourth session of the UN General Assembly.

2013. Jiang Zemin's allies Jia Qinglin, Wu Bangguo, and Li Changchun kept their posts. Two more engineers—He Guoqiang, head of the party's Organization Department, and Zhou Yongkang, public security minister, also joined the Standing Committee. The Central Committee changes membership frequently, and contains a handful of women and ethnic minorities. The twenty-five-member Politburo of the Seventeenth Party Congress contained one woman; seven of its members were "princelings," heirs of Mao's generation of party leaders. General Secretary Xi Jinping's wife, Peng Liyuan, is a popular folk singer and a member of the People's Consultative Conference.

The Fourth Generation leadership had a more direct approach than the prior generation to confronting China's domestic problems (Lam, 2006). In 2003, when Severe Acute Respiratory Syndrome (SARS, or bird flu) was spreading through Asia, Jiang Zemin was slow to acknowledge its existence. Hu Jintao, facing the first big political crisis of his regime, immediately called together medical experts and began public visits to inspect problem areas and personally organize governmental response to the disease (Kleinman and Watson, 2005; Wong and Yongnian, 2004). The government also responded rapidly to the massive earthquake that hit Sichuan in 2008 (Bo, 2010:271–322; Jeffries, 2010:758–820). Hu, Wen Jiabao, and the other seven engineers on the Politburo's Standing Committee proceeded to deal with problems like poverty, the gap between the coastal and inland provinces, and environmental degradation, with similar technocratic precision and attention to results. They vigorously continued the campaign to accelerate development in the western regions that Zhu Rongji began while Wen Jiabao was his deputy (Lu and Nielson, 2004; Su, 2009; Donaldson, 2011). Construction of roads, airports, railroads, shopping centers, urban housing, schools, parks, hotels, power stations, and other structures accelerated throughout China. As discussed in Chapter 1, the new system of toll roads and trains began to link the country together for rapid transit. Land leases to many peasants were extended. Government programs are improving irrigation channels, and roads give town access to farmers to transport crops. The government is raising subsidies to farmers growing grain. Peasant families can receive five-year loans to build themselves new houses. In 2007, the central government ended taxes on all peasants. Poor students receive the "three frees": food, board, and transportation. Some poorer families receive cash subsidies, as do unemployed and retired workers under some city plans. The government put in place a health insurance scheme available in most rural counties (but still unaffordable to most peasants) to pay a portion of participants' medical expenses (Wong, Lo, and Tang, 2005; Postiglione, 2006; Li and Wu, 2010). See Chapter 8.

Universities are building extensive new libraries, laboratories, classrooms, student housing, dining halls, and other facilities, with budgets for new books and equipment. In 2010, 31 million students were enrolled in junior colleges and universities—quadruple the number in 2003. Two-thirds of these graduates had jobs at graduation, with demand for engineers, accountants, doctors, lawyers, managers, and other professionals in the rapidly expanding economy—though increasing numbers of graduates cannot find work (Guo, 2005; Li Lanqing, 2004; Postiglione, 2006). As retail, office, construction, energy-sector, and other jobs expand, new positions are opening for clerks, couriers, cleaners and custodians, waiters, drivers, heavy equipment operators, unskilled laborers, mechanics, carpenters, masons, and many others. Rural people make extra money by buying a tractor or small utility vehicle to haul bricks, wood, farm produce, recycled materials, and other products. Connected by the new road network, these people have money to spend on everything from clothing and electronics to cars and condominiums (Yu, Chan, and Ireland, 2006). This is in addition to people employed in production for export. By 2007, China was running an annual trade surplus of US$300 billion a year.

This growth strengthened the wealth and power of local leaders and placed new strains on the environment (see Chapter 9). Unlike their predecessors, the Fourth Generation national leaders began to attempt serious measures for environmental protection (Chen, 2009). They intensified the national program of tree planting begun in the 1990s; billions of new trees have been planted. In 2008, the State Environmental Protection Administration was elevated to a Cabinet-level ministry under the State Council, the Ministry of Environmental Protection. The Central Bank of China now includes environmental impact in credit evaluation. As Chapter 5 discusses, through installing emission-controlling equipment on power plants and factories burning coal and closing thousands of older coal-fired power plants and outdated iron smelters, they achieved some reduction in acid rain. A fourth of railway right-of-way is electrified, and many cities mandate that all taxis operate on natural gas. Millions of homes and businesses, alerted by government officials to the environmental advantages and cost savings, are purchasing solar panels to heat water and run small appliances.

The central government's environmental initiatives are resisted by local officials, who profit from operating polluting factories and plants and do not want to pay to clean them up (Garrison, 2009). The environmental impact study—released in 2006 and showing that pollution is costing China US$64 billion a year, 3 percent of gross domestic product (GDP)—was quickly buried on bureaucrats' shelves without further action. The rapidly expanding economy is producing many new cars, power plants, factories, and other polluting devices. As Chapter 9 discusses at length, with such obstacles, China is not meeting its goals but is trying an array of initiatives.

All of this underscores the need for new unifying themes (Brady, 2007). The new economic freedoms have lessened the value of communism as a unifying ideology (Tang, 2005). Jiang turned instead to nationalism (Suisheng Zhao, 2004; He and Guo, 2000; Hughes, 2006) and Confucian values (see the "Religion and Chinese Society" section in Chapter 12) as unifying themes—first in the form of his 1996 "spiritual civilization" campaign and then in his incorporation of the "three representatives" into the constitution in 2002: "the people's interests, modern productive forces, and advanced civilization." China's greatness, it was argued, derives from its unique culture, which gives it both unity and dynamic drive. Jiang wanted China to become powerful in the world without outside challenges to its core values. He wanted it to combine concerns like environmental protection, appreciation for the arts, and family morality with an economic system that both addresses basic needs and promotes affluence. China's Communist Party quietly developed close ties with social democratic parties in Europe. At the Sixteenth National Party Congress in 2002, businesspeople were for the first time admitted to party membership.

Hu Jintao, while continuing to espouse Jiang's "one country three systems" nationalism, expanded on another unifying theme: "building a harmonious society" through "scientific development." (See also Chapters 1, 9, 12, and 14 for more on this Confucian concept.) Moving from a planned to a market economy, China must not allow crime, a "widening gap of ideas" among different strata of society, and security concerns from abroad to disrupt society. Everyone, including the more than 150 million living below the official minimal poverty line and the urban unemployed, should share in social wealth as the middle class grows (Dowling and Yap, 2009:263–284; Xu, 2011). That requires a partnership between government and the peasants throughout China and the rule of law so that officials can be held to high moral standards and the economy can run smoothly. Management skills, an adequate social security system, and competency in medicine and sports and science are basic to harmonious survival in a globalized world. A harmonious environment also means clean water, fresh air, and healthy food. Unlike Jiang's unifying themes, which emphasized China's greatness and rising affluence, Hu's themes centered on solving problems facing the country, being honest, helping one another, and living more simply.

In 2011, the National People's Congress adopted the Twelfth Five-Year Plan centered on the theme of "inclusive growth," with large expenditures on health, education, and pensions (now paid to a third of those over sixty-five; see Frazier, 2010) to bridge the growing gap between the rich and the poor. In the twenty-first century, China's leaders are more open about the problems the nation faces and are implementing policies directed at solving them—seeking not just development, but balanced development that includes even the country's poorest inhabitants (Shambaugh, 2008).

The Eighteenth Party Congress, in 2012, brought the Fifth Generation of "princelings" to power, though, as you will see at the end of this chapter and in Chapter 6, in a less tidy manner than in 2002. Vice President Xi Jinping succeeded Hu Jintao, who was also poised to step down as president by 2013 and as supreme military commander within a year or two after that. Xi's father was a member of the Politburo right after the Communist revolution but was jailed for sixteen years by Mao during the Great Leap Forward and Cultural Revolution. Premier Wen Jiabao passed his post along to another Fifth Generation princeling, Deputy Premier Li Keqiang. Many younger Chinese wish that the potential successors might at least include some individuals who are not related to the first generation of the party's leaders.

With this leadership in place, what are the chances for this balanced development?

What Will Endure and What Will Change?

China has a long tradition of limited, small-scale capitalism (Gates, 1996). Households produced crops and goods for their own use and to exchange with relatives and neighbors. They could also hire labor to produce surpluses sold in small markets or through brokers. The state taxed and regulated that trade. By combining resources of small producers, brokers could prevent large producers from monopolizing trade. Public officials could regulate the brokers and prevent the large producers from adopting technology they deemed inappropriate for maintaining the rural communities, who are the ideological backbone for Confucian social relations. The introduction of guilds also gave small craftspeople the power to hold back technical innovations that might threaten their jobs. State firms produced some goods needed by other components of the economy. The *baojia* system later allowed for the organization of larger groups of people. Leaders and members of each of these units developed special relationships and exchanged favors to get others to cooperate. The basic social unit, the family, relied on the cooperation of all its members to carry out their obligations in providing labor and distributing output. Even the wealthy accepted the governmental controls that helped keep alive a peaceful and orderly business climate, let them dominate the labor force, maintained the waterways, and operated the marketplaces. They could use their wealth to help their sons become officials and respected members of the community.

Many of China's leading enterprises today are derived from state industries led by party cadres. They include in their ranks many of China's new multimillionaires. China's largest petroleum companies (China National Petroleum Corporation and China Petrochemical Corporation), its three largest automobile manufacturers (First Automotive Works, Shanghai Automotive Industry Corporation, and Dongfeng Motors), its largest retail chains (the Bailian Group and Dalian Dashan), its largest telecommunications equipment company (Zhongxing Telecommunication Equipment Company), its largest cell phone provider (China Mobile), and its best-known appliance manufacturer (Haier) are all consortiums of state-owned enterprises. About 150 such companies control key sectors of the economy, including military and aerospace, minerals, banking, insurance, and transportation. They have issued stock, formed alliances with foreign corporations, and adapted to the Chinese market many management and fiscal practices and innovations developed overseas. Within their sectors, they maintain larger revenues from sales within China than any foreign firms investing there. They also maintain close ties with government, more in keeping with traditional Chinese capitalist practices than with those outside China (even in Germany, France, and Japan, where the state takes an active role in creating and maintaining corporations, but corporate leaders take a less active role in operating the state). They receive large loans from state banks. And foreign firms are subject to pressures, like theft of their intellectual property, without judicial recourse in courts that are stacked against them (Diamant, Lubman, and O'Brien, 2005; Eger, Faure, and Naigen, 2007; Peerenboom, 2002; Zhao, 2006).

More than 90 percent of China's 43 million companies are now private. Those in which the state does not own a majority of shares are much smaller but produce perhaps 70 percent of their combined contribution to GDP ("Let a Million Flowers Bloom," 2011). To function, all must create close alliances with local cadres, bureaucrats, and police (Chen, 2008). Millions of small entrepreneurs—often from modest rural backgrounds—operate plants using sophisticated machinery to sustain assembly lines of migrant laborers making simple products like buttons, socks, screws, pens, toys, playground equipment, bicycles, or small trucks in newly urbanizing industrial zones (Hessler,

2010:281–415; Chen, 2008; Chang, 2008). Government units build them new roads, airports, railroad lines, power generators and lines, and other infrastructure. *Guanxi* partners lend them money, sometimes involving high interest rates and bribes that may skirt the law and have them—like the enormously rich head of the giant chain of Gome stores, Huang Guangyu—hauled into court ("When Fund-raising Is a Crime," 2011; Tsai, 2004). They develop relationships with local officials to lease buildings, avoid heavy taxation, keep wages and benefits low, avoid paying for intellectual property, acquire raw materials, and much more (White, 2009). They often copy from abroad or their neighbors to create their own machinery. Some 260 million rural dwellers migrate from their homes to work in such enterprises, sometimes creating their own enterprises to sell food, clothing, and other goods or services in these newly urbanizing zones. Many millions more bring crops or locally produced goods to nearby towns to sell to brokers or in street markets. As Chapter 8 explains, they are eligible for few public services.

A large number of party and government ministries oversee these activities, each with its own special relationships (Lieberthal, 2003; Hsueh, 2011). Dan Breznitz and Michael Murphree (2011) call this "structured uncertainty," and contend that it gives China's firms, and foreign corporations operating in China, special advantages at "second generation" innovation. China's citizens may be poor at developing new technological breakthroughs, but they are adept at using personal networks to quickly pull together disparate resources and organizational capabilities, creating "on time" production and delivery of that technology. That includes training of workers to use ever more advanced levels of technology, with the expansion of universities and their research programs.

But as modern capitalism makes greater inroads within China, the features of China's society that initially created growth can become impediments to further development (Gilley, 2001; Chun, 2006; Dittmer and Liu, 2006; Gries and Rosen, 2010). Major impediments to continuing market dominance by these firms include the regulations that surround the older forms of capitalist enterprise and a judicial system that still protects the old special arrangements; the government is passing many new laws designed to attack those problems, but the big test will come with implementing them (Eger, Faure, and Naigen, 2007; Zheng, 2004; Diamant, Lubman, and O'Brien, 2005; Moody, 2007; Pei, 2006; Tubilewicz, 2006; Lynch, 2006; Zhao, 2006). An even greater impediment to more modern capitalism is the lack of an independent middle class.

The Industrial Revolution in Europe created a new middle class there separate from the old dominating nobility; the middle class used political revolution to overthrow the political ascendancy of the nobility. In contrast, China's entrepreneurs have not had to free themselves from wealthy landowning families with titles of nobility, whose dominance ended there over 2,000 years ago when the Qin dynasty overthrew the feudal system of the Zhou dynasty (see Chapter 3). Today's top business and political leaders have in fact descended from the same social orders that ruled imperial China, running government and business hand-in-hand (Pieke, 2009). Unlike its counterpart in the French Revolution, this China-style middle class brings with it the attitudes of the "old regime," rather than providing a radical alternative to it. Its members, and the members of the government bureaucracy, are more comfortable with the old capitalism than with the new (Dickson, 2008; Gallagher, 2005; Hessler, 2010:178–195, 225–276).

Many leading independent businesspeople are from Taiwan and Hong Kong. They know that full political independence for Taiwan would endanger all their business dealings in China, so they offer support to Beijing's government in resisting that (see Chapters 6 and 7). Those businesspeople and foreign firms want to introduce enforceable civil law and open exchange of currency. But they recognize the limits on China's ability to extend such reforms even as they push for them. They seldom advocate political reforms beyond that, especially when they threaten political stability. The leaders of China's adapting state firms have even less incentive to do so, given their strong connections with government. Their employees, who are the most affluent members of the new middle class, benefit from this new prosperity and also have little incentive to interfere with it.

The emperors' Mandate of Heaven was endangered by a breakdown of order and prosperity. Today, both rapid economic growth and potential economic slump threaten those conditions. Only 1.4 percent of urban households earn over US$15,000 (and 12 percent over US$5,000) a year, and three-fifths to four-fifths of the 675 million rural residents still make a living from selling crops off their tiny plots of land, with only a sixth the average income of urban dwellers (Orlik and Rozelle, 2009; "All Eyes on Chinese Aisles," 2011). Some 260 million rural migrants make an average of US$125–200 a month in their city jobs. A third of China's citizens live on less than US$2 a day—150 million on less than US$1 (Foroohar, 2010). Entrepreneurs want to keep wages low; government employees accept low wages in exchange for subsidized housing, health care, and other perquisites. That puts a strong damper on the size of the middle class and how much it has to spend on the consumer goods that stoke a modern economy. It keeps them and all those less fortunate highly vulnerable to inflation and deflation, layoffs, pay cuts, working for months without pay, and other side effects of rapid economic growth and downturns in world demand for China's products.

Only a third of China's GDP comes from consumer spending; two-thirds of the US economy does so. Another third of China's economy comes from real estate construction and land sales. As long as the economic growth depends on government loans and spending for construction, mining, and other aspects of the economy, and wage increases are kept low, there will be little change in that ratio. Between 2008 and 2011, the total amount of bank loans rose from 97 percent to 120 percent of GDP (Ferguson, 2011), much of which was spent on huge blocks of condos and apartments, built purely on speculation that they will sell in the future (see Figure 5.6).

The government has introduced policies to raise wages, dampen price swings, and give social support (Zhao and Lim, 2010; Ferguson, 2011). Even the new policies leave tens of millions of rural dwellers—and migrants to cities—without adequate income, housing, health care, schools, and protection from corrupt officials stealing their money, land, and labor (Hessler, 2010:343–348; Su, 2009; Li and Wu, 2010; Harney, 2008; Zhao and Lim, 2010:23–72, 119–140).

Peasants are upset and engaging in many forms of protest because the government and local officials are levying higher fees and taxes while reducing services and purchasing fewer goods from them (Chen and Wu, 2006; Johnson, 2005; Lee, 2007; O'Brien and Li, 2006; Sun, 2004). Rural schools are poor, books and transport and supplies are no longer free, and few peasants now make it to university (Hessler, 2010:153–154, 195–201, 215–224). Bus fares and school fees rise while officials pay peasants less than market prices for their crops and pocket the difference. At the same time, both peasants and workers are paying more for purchases. Village leaders control the distribution of leased land, which they increasingly confiscate and sell to urban institutions as urban growth creates demands for more land (Ho, 2005; Hsing, 2010; Zhao and Lim 2010:119–140). Or a dam has swamped their land and left them in a replacement house without a livelihood. Pollution brings them health problems and kills or poisons their fish. Every year 100,000 of them file lawsuits to protest such problems, but fewer than a third of these win in court (Lam, 2009).

About a third of new university graduates cannot find work in the new market economy, and housing (which rose in price five to ten times during the first decade of the twenty-first century) is too expensive for them. A central government push on local governments, begun in 2010 to build social housing, will do little to ease that problem. The jobs many do find are far from home, with poor pay and benefits (Kuruvilla, Lee, and Gallagher, 2011). In 2011, 6.6 million students graduated from colleges and universities; 1.4 million of them took the civil service exams to enter the privileged ranks of the government bureaucracy, competing for only 16,000 jobs (offering good benefits packages).

People complain about the lack of legal reforms to stop corruption, yet many benefit directly or indirectly from the money that changes hands outside official channels (on corruption, see Park, 1997; Kwong, 1997; Guo, 2006:61–88; Lu, 2000; Sun, 2004; Liao, 2009; Midler, 2009; Mexico, 2009:23–43, 273–292). They know the absence of such reforms slows growth, but although they may want to let that fresh air in, they also want to keep out anything that interferes with cultural reciprocities. Reforms like tightening legal procedures and allowing groups to register complaints threaten the very relationships that have allowed some to advance, or that may be used by unions and cadres to block further reform. Premier Zhu Rongji led a campaign against corruption, with some high-level officials and businesspeople condemned to death, yet charges of corruption crept close to the top leaders themselves, a widespread problem. The wife of Jia Qinglin, one of the Politburo members discussed above, was protected by Jiang against charges that she was involved in a major smuggling scandal. An internal party document said that 78 percent of fraud cases in amounts over US$600,000 involved senior officials and that 98 percent of them had relatives in key business or government posts. Some economists estimated that 14 percent of China's GDP bleeds into corruption. Products like lead-coated toys and contaminated pharmaceuticals and foods have harmed the reputation of Chinese goods (Midler, 2009; Zhao and Lim, 2010:195–210). Chinese media reported that 200,000 officials had been prosecuted since 1998 (Wang, Hu, and Ding, 2002; Liu, 2002).

Every year millions of people participate in tens of thousands of strikes, demonstrations, and riots to protest these problems (google "China protests" or "human rights in China"; Goldman, 2005; Lee, 2007; O'Brien, 2008b; Gilley, 2001; Perry and Goldman, 2007; Huang, 2008; Cai, 2010; Perry and Selden, 2010; Hessler, 2010:389–395; Zhong, 2011). Since 2006, official data records more than 90,000 protests each year ("The Next Emperor," 2010).

The government meets such activities with large numbers of police and arrest of leaders afterward (Wang, 1991; Dutton, 2004; Guo, 2006:89–116). Between 1997 and 1998, the number of armed police nearly doubled and a new Office on Maintaining Social Stability was created, which continues to grow and is supervised by the head of the Political and Legal Affairs Commission, Zhou Yongkang, a member of the Standing Committee of the Politburo. His commission also controls the judicial system—both the judges and the prosecutor's offices (the procuratorate). So the police, prosecutors, and courts, like the army, answer directly to the Communist Party (Xiaobing Li, 2010). Half the chief justices of the provinces have no legal background; most come from within the security apparatus of the CCP. Only about 10 percent of judges have graduate degrees. The president of the Supreme People's Court, Wang Shengjun, and the minister of justice, Wu Aiying, never attended law school (Lam, 2009). Many local judges have been appointed unlawfully.

This web of connections makes it hard for laws to be enforced fairly. Periodically, with prodding from the party's Central Commission for Discipline Inspection, judges and public officials are arrested for taking bribes or helping organized crime; those with the right connections can escape this fate (Lubman, 2001; Peerenboom, 2002; Trevaskes, 2007).

Falun Gong, a group that promotes *qigong* exercises but also recruits people for demonstrations against the government (Chang, 2004; Hessler,

Robert E. Gamer

Standing guard in Tiananmen Square, 2000.

2007:122–129, 199–202; Ownby, 2008) has effectively used the Internet to reach large numbers of peasants and workers. The government has responded with continuing arrests (Yang, 2009; Tong, 2009).

Several US companies helped it make an Internet firewall to block and tap undesired political content and arrest individuals sending it (Zhou, 2006; Xu, 2007; Zhao, 2008; Liu, 2004). Twitter and Facebook are blocked. Chinese sites like Sina Weibo, with over 250 million users, and Tencent's QQ, a chat service that claims to have 625 million user accounts, serve such purposes, along with Youku, a Chinese YouTube, and 163.com. After ethnic clashes in 2009, international Internet and mobile phone services were suspended in Xinjiang province for months. Google moved to Hong Kong in protest of these policies, leaving its Chinese competitor Baidu, which is cooperative with regulators, as the chief search engine. Cyber-security firm McAfee found widespread worldwide hacking of corporate and government websites emanating from China, accessing intellectual property, legal documents, e-mails, and much more (Gross, 2011).

After the crash of two new high-speed trains in 2011, bloggers, suspecting a cover-up of the cause and number of reported casualties, sent more than 20 million messages about the event on Sina Weibo. The government reversed its attempt to bury the train and prevent victims from suing (Winchester, 2011), and subsequently undertook a major review of the program. Then bloggers organized a large street protest when a chemical factory blew up; the government promptly announced it would close the factory.

Two months later two trains collided in Shanghai's new subway system, and then seventeen miners died in a coal mine explosion in Guizhou. Millions of bloggers spread first-hand accounts. By then, even the official party publication *China Daily* was lamenting "blood soaked GDP"—shoddily constructed show projects with poorly trained and disciplined staff. The Central Committee vowed to fix "serious flaws and problems" in Weibo causing "huge social harm." But the Internet is becoming harder to control. New requirements that users must register under their real names will be the biggest test of whether controls work.

Andrew Nathan and Bruce Gilley (2003), citing secret party files, assert that between 1998 and 2001 over 60,000 Chinese were executed, died in custody, or were shot by police while fleeing (Angle and Svensson, 2001; Bakken, 2007). Wu Lihong, once dubbed an "Environmental Warrior" by the National People's Congress, was jailed by local police, courts, and officials of the polluting chemical plants he was exposing (Kahn, 2007). Literary critic Liu Xiaobo got an eleven-year jail term, and the Nobel Peace Prize, for helping write Charter 08, a manifesto signed by over 350 intellectuals calling for more human rights. Many members of unregistered churches (see Chapter 12) have been arrested. The 2011 North African "jasmine revolutions" brought new crackdowns. Bloggers, activists, and defense lawyers were arrested, including Ai Weiwei, designer of the "birds nest" National Stadium for the 2008 Olympics and critic of shoddy construction of schools that collapsed in the 2008 Sichuan earthquake; he needed brain surgery in 2009 after being beaten by thugs. His poet father was a favorite of Chairman Mao. Many other political prisoners remain in prisons and labor camps, enduring beatings and other brutality. The number of executions, however, is declining—perhaps 4,000 in 2011 by outside estimates (Liu and Fish, 2011; Cohen, 2011; McConville, 2011; Keith and Lin, 2005).

China shows little sign of moving toward democracy. The only Politburo member with business experience is Zhou Yongkang, former minister of pubic security and head of China National Petroleum Corporation. Only one (alternate) member of the Central Committee has business experience. The Politburo has been run by engineers. General Secretary Xi Jinping has a law degree in addition to his engineering degree. Premier Li Keqiang has a degree in law and a doctorate in economics from Peking University—and a daughter who is a Harvard graduate. But the Fifth Generation leadership still does not contain individuals with a broad introduction to the social sciences and world politics. Strong forces resist the introduction of greater political freedom; local officials and entrepreneurs benefit from current economic policies and restrictions on political dissent (Zhong, 2003; Zheng, 2006, 2010; Wank, 2001; Gallagher, 2005; Pan, 2009). Yet China needs innovations in civil law, banking, election processes, administrative procedures, press freedoms, and academic freedom to sustain a vibrant role in the world economy (Wang, 2006). It is hard to fight corruption, assure businesses a fair trading environment, fund viable investment, and distribute economic gains to all sectors of society in the absence of such reforms.

China's security requires steady high economic growth and facing the social, economic, and ecological problems that growth has produced. In his annual address to the National People's Congress in 2011, Premier Wen Jiabao asserted (with objections from party hard-liners) that China's accelerated resource-guzzling growth is not balanced, coordinated, or sustainable. It relies too much on government investment in basic infrastructure. China must enhance creativity, enrich philosophy and innovation and human services, make sure its children get an hour of physical exercise in school each week, and become a moderately prosperous nonextravagant consumer society. Wen's address reprised earlier debate. In 1989, during the Tiananmen Square protests, intellectuals talked about the possibilities of a "new authoritarianism" that would be firm but more open to modern society (Gamer, 1994). In 1998 ("Hayek's Children," 1998), they discussed German thinker Friedrich Hayek's (1994) "civil society," a "spontaneous order" emerging from the bottom up rather than through planning by government. Today there is talk of "consultative Leninism," "soft authoritarian pluralism," and the "new left," which feels that capitalism has done away with the equality and national pride China experienced under Mao and wants to reprise some of the reforms of that era—but without the bad parts (Wang, 2010; Huang, 2008; see also Chapter 13)!

A "princeling" (son of a 1930s guerrilla leader who was purged and jailed in the Cultural Revolution but then directed the 1980s purges), Bo Xilai, party secretary of Chongqing municipality, gained populist "new left" fans with rallies singing Mao-era "Red songs," big public housing and welfare programs even for migrants, job-creating economic dynamism, and show-trials of corrupt "mafia" bosses. In 2012, those fans wanted him on the next Standing Committee. Since Mao's cult of personality, which Bo emulates, its members rule by consensus and keep a low profile. Suddenly, Bo's police chief sought asylum in a US consular office. Bo was removed from the Politburo and as Chongqing's party secretary, and his wife was accused of murdering an Englishman, who may have helped her smuggle millions of dollars into foreign bank accounts. Other shocking revelations and allegations (Coronel, 2012) jammed the Internet and world press. Bo's close ties with politically ambitious new left PLA generals alarmed leaders (Page and Wei, 2012). Those "mafia" were often rivals or critics, arrested on spurious charges, tortured, jailed, or executed, and their land and assets seized. Chongqing was deeply in debt. The big Ford, Coca Cola, BASF, Acer, and BP plants spurring Bo's "socialist" growth pay low wages. But Bo's wife, her sisters, and Bo's brother and first son—like hundreds of thousands of other "princelings" (Barboza and Frontiere, 2012; Garnaut, 2012a)—were secretly on boards of numerous Chinese and foreign enterprises, making millions of dollars. Bo's second son lived in lavish style in Harrow, Oxford, and Harvard University. But many bloggers supported Bo.

This rare public glimpse at the infighting, nepotism, and corruption behind the façade of rule by a team of wise elders shows how hard it is to secure reforms that narrow the gap between rich and poor and increase consumer spending. Strong local and capitalist interests oppose Bo's public housing, relaxing the *hukou* system, and expensive social benefit programs. Like Bo, they resist strikes and higher wages that deter private investment. Premier Wen, rallying the party around Bo's purge, warned that "excessive concentration of power and lack of effective oversight" brings "the biggest threat to the ruling party," corruption. Many bloggers agreed, but asked, Why, then, do Wen and other advocates of political and economic liberalization (Gernaut, 2012b) still help to crush lawful dissent? With their pervasive abuse of privilege, have princelings already lost the right to rule? But behind the scenes, Jiang Zemin intervened to assure Bo's purge did not spread to other corrupt princelings, or into a liberal assault on the new left (Lim and Buckley, 2012).

Liberals admire the "bottom up" approach of former factory worker Wang Yang, party secretary of another thriving province, Guangdong (Lam, 2012). Wang blogs. He mediates to get strikers higher wages. Security officers jailed villagers in Wukan fishing village for protesting local officials seizing their land; Wang negotiated their release and arranged a by-election that threw the officials out and put the protest leader in charge. "Giving power back to society," Wang simplified registration for nongovernmental organizations (NGOs). China has 250,000 "mass organizations" registered with the government, representing everything from economic interests to environmental groups (Chen, 2010; Chen, 2009:41–65; Zheng and Fewsmith, 2008; van Rooij, 2010). In addition, Matt Forney (1998) believes there may be an equal number of NGOs that have failed to register with the government; they shelter abused wives, give physical therapy rehabilitation, provide networking for divorcées and homosexuals, help the poor, stand up for women and migrant workers, try to preserve historic homes (Shi, 1997), help evicted tenants, and provide other educational and philanthropic services. Press reports, and bloggers on the Internet, increasingly focus on bureaucratic corruption and misbehavior, environmental degradation, and other ills (Mexico, 2009:1–22, 273–291; Shirk, 2011; Xie, 2011). Zhu Rongji encouraged submission of petitions to the government, and his protégé and successor Wen Jiabao continued that emphasis. Punk rockers bemoan government oppression (Mexico, 2009:251–172). More than 900 million Chinese have cell phones, and more than 500 million are online. Computer-based accounting makes fraud more difficult. There are over 2,000 newspapers, 8,000 magazines (including Chinese editions of many from the West), and 700 television stations—all registered with the government and aware that as of December

2010, Reporters Without Borders knew of 108 journalists and bloggers in prison for writing about forbidden topics.

Conceivably, a combination of those innovations and social changes could transform China into a pluralist democracy, but this process would probably take a long time (see Chapter 14). So far, aside from Wen Jiabao and his predecessor, Zhu Rongji (Zhu, 2011), none of China's top leaders have endorsed political liberalization. Meanwhile, the government's handling of rural-development unemployment and social services, housing, corruption, village and township elections, press and Internet censorship, dissidents, NGOs, ethnic conflict, and labor and peasant protest will provide clues as to how far liberalization, and China's efforts to remain a leading player in the world economy, can proceed (Zhou, 2010). So will a continuance of Beijing's present, somewhat frayed, policy (see Chapter 6) of refraining from overt interference in Hong Kong's and Taiwan's policies and encouraging (though still with strong resistance from among the ranks) enforcement of higher productivity, a modern bureaucracy, responsible banking and stock markets, intellectual property rights, and just civil and contract law.

Bibliography

"All Eyes on Chinese Aisles." 2011. *The Economist* 399 (May 21–27): 8734.

Andreas, Joel. 2009. *Rise of the Red Engineers: The Cultural Revolution and the Origins of China's New Class.* Stanford, CA: Stanford University Press.

Angle, Stephen C., and Marina Svensson (eds.). 2001. *The Chinese Human Rights Reader: Documents and Commentary, 1900–2000.* Armonk, NY: M. E. Sharpe.

Averill, Stephen C., Joseph W. Esterich, and Elizabeth J. Perry. 2005. *Revolution in the Highlands: China's Jingganshan Base Area.* Lanham, MD: Rowman and Littlefield.

Bachman, David M. 2006. *Bureaucracy, Economy, and Leadership in China: The Institutional Origins of the Great Leap Forward.* New York: Cambridge University Press.

Bakken, Berge (ed.). 2007. *Crime, Punishment, and Policing in China.* Lanham, MD: Rowman and Littlefield.

Barber, Elizabeth Wayland. 2000. *The Mummies of Urumchi.* New York: W. W. Norton.

Barboza, David, and Sharon LaFraniere. 2012. "'Princelings' in China Use Family Ties to Gain Riches." *New York Times,* May 17.

Barnouin, Barbara, and Yu Changgen. 2006. *Zhou Enlai: A Political Life.* Hong Kong: Chinese University Press.

Becker, Jasper. 1997. *Hungry Ghosts: Mao's Secret Famine.* New York: Henry Holt.

———. 2006. *Dragon Rising: An Inside Look at China Today.* Washington, DC: National Geographic.

Beckwith, Christopher I. 2009. *Empires of the Silk Road: A History of Central Eurasia from the Bronze Age to the Present.* Princeton, NJ: Princeton University Press.

Béja, Jean-Philippe (ed.). 2011. *The Impact of China's 1989 Tiananmen Massacre.* New York: Routledge.

Benton, Gregor, and Alan Hunter (eds.). 1995. *Wild Lily, Prairie Fire: China's Road to Democracy, Yan'an to Tian'anmen, 1942–1989.* Princeton, NJ: Princeton University Press.

Benton, Gregor, and Lin Chun (eds.). 2009. *Was Mao Really a Monster? The Academic Response to Chang and Hallidays "Mao: The Unknown Story."* London: Routledge.
Bergère, Marie-Claire. 2000. *Sun Yat-sen.* Trans. Janet Lloyd. Stanford, CA: Stanford University Press.
Black, George, and Robin Munro. 1993. *Black Hands of Beijing: Lives of Defiance in China's Democracy Movement.* New York: Wiley.
Blecher, Marc. 2009. *China Against the Tides: Restructuring Through Revolution, Radicalism, and Reform.* 3rd ed. New York: Continuum International.
Blecher, Marc, and Vivienne Shue. 1996. *Tethered Deer: Government and Economy in a Chinese County.* Stanford, CA: Stanford University Press.
Bo, Zhiyue. 2010. *China's Elite Politics: Governance and Democracy.* Singapore: World Scientific Publishers.
Bovingdon, Gardner. 2010. *The Uyghurs: Strangers in Their Own Land.* New York: Columbia University Press.
Brady, Anne-Marie. 2007. *Marketing Dictatorship: Propaganda and Thought Work in China.* Lanham, MD: Rowman and Littlefield.
Brahm, Laurence J. 2003. *Zhu Rongji and the Transformation of Modern China.* New York: Wiley.
Breznitz, Dan, and Michael Murphree. 2011. *Run of the Red Queen: Government, Innovation, Globalization, and Economic Growth in China.* New Haven, CT: Yale University Press.
Brook, Timothy. 1998. *Quelling the People: The Military Suppression of the Beijing Democracy Movement.* Stanford, CA: Stanford University Press.
———. 2007. *Collaboration: Japanese Agents and Local Elites in Wartime China.* Cambridge, MA: Harvard University Press.
Brown, Jeremy, and Paul G. Pickowicz (eds.). 2007. *Dilemmas of Victory: The Early Years of the People's Republic of China.* Cambridge, MA: Harvard University Press.
Buck, Pearl S. 2005. *The Good Earth.* New York: Pocket Books.
Cai, Yongshun. 2010. *Collective Resistance in China: Why Popular Protests Succeed or Fail.* Stanford, CA: Stanford University Press.
Calhoun, Craig. 1997. *Neither Gods nor Emperors: Students and the Struggle for Democracy in China.* Berkeley: University of California Press.
Chan, Anita, Richard Madsen, and Jonathan Unger. 1992. *Chen Village Under Mao and Deng.* Expanded and updated. Berkeley: University of California Press.
Chang, Iris. 1997. *The Rape of Nanking: The Forgotten Holocaust of World War II.* New York: HarperCollins.
Chang, Jung. 1991. *Wild Swans: Three Daughters of China.* New York: Simon and Schuster.
Chang, Jung, and Jon Halliday. 2006. *Mao: The Unknown Story.* New York: Anchor.
Chang, Leslie T. 2008. *Factory Girls: From Village to City in a Changing China.* New York: Spiegel and Grau.
Chang, Maria Hsia. 2004. *Falun Gong: The End of Days.* New Haven, CT: Yale University Press.
Chen, Calvin. 2008. *Some Assembly Required: Work, Community, and Politics in China's Rural Enterprises.* Cambridge, MA: Harvard University Asia Center.
Chen, Da. 2001. *Colors of the Mountain.* New York: Anchor.
———. 2003. *Sounds of the River: A Young Man's University Days in Beijing.* New York: Harper Perennial.
Chen, Gang. 2009. *Politics of China's Environmental Protection.* Singapore: World Scientific Publishing.

Chen, Guidi, and Wu Chuntao. 2006. *Will the Boat Sink the Water? The Life of China's Peasants*. New York: PublicAffairs.
Chen, Jie. 2006. "The NGO Community in China: Expanding Linkages With Transnational Civil Society and Their Democratic Implications" *China Perspectives* 68: 29–40.
———. 2010. "Transnational Environmental Movement: Impact on the Green Civil Society in China." *Journal of Contemporary China* 19(65): 503–523.
Chen, Weixing, and Yang Zhong. 2004. *Leadership in a Changing China*. New York: Palgrave.
Chen, Yuan-tsung. 1981. *The Dragon's Village: An Autobiographical Novel of Revolutionary China*. New York: Penguin.
Cheng, Nien. 2010. *Life and Death in Shanghai*. New York: Penguin.
Chu, Yun-han, Chi-Cheng Lo, and Ramon H. Meyers. 2004. *The New Chinese Leadership: Challenges and Opportunities After the 16th Party Congress*. Cambridge: Cambridge University Press.
Chun, Lin (ed.). 2000. *China*. 3 vols. Burlington, VT: Ashgate.
———. 2006. *The Transformation of Chinese Socialism*. Durham, NC: Duke University Press.
Clark, Paul. 2008. *The Chinese Cultural Revolution: A History*. New York: Cambridge University Press.
Clarke, Michael E. 2011. *Xinjiang and China's Rise in Central Asia*. London: Routledge.
Coble, Parks M. 2003. *Chinese Capitalists in Japan's New Order: The Occupied Lower Yangzi, 1937–1945*. Berkeley: University of California Press.
Cohen, Jerome. 2011. "Not a Pretty Picture." *South China Morning Post*, May 10.
Coronel, Sheila S. 2012. "The Bo Scandal: How We Got That Story." *Columbia Journalism Review* (May 2).
Cunningham, Philip J. 2009. *Tiananmen Moon: Inside the Chinese Student Uprising of 1989*. Lanham, MD: Rowman and Littlefield.
Dautcher, Jay. 2009. *Down A Narrow Road*. Cambridge, MA: Harvard University Asia Center.
Diamant, Neil J., Stanley B. Lubman, and Kevin O'Brien. 2005. *Engaging the Law in China: State, Society, and Possibilities for Justice*. Stanford, CA: Stanford University Press.
Dickson, Bruce J. 2008. *Wealth into Power: The Communist Party's Embrace of China's Private Sector*. Cambridge: Cambridge University Press.
Dietrich, Craig. 1997. *People's China: A Brief History*. 3rd ed. New York: Oxford University Press.
Dikotter, Frank. 2010. *Mao's Great Famine: The History of China's Most Devastating Catastrophe, 1958–1962*. New York: Walker.
Dillon, Michael. 2004. *Xinjiang: China's Muslim Far Northwest*. London: Routledge.
Ding, X. L. 2006. *The Decline of Communism in China: Legitimacy Crisis, 1977–1989*. Cambridge: Cambridge University Press.
Dittmer, Lowell, and Guoli Liu (eds.). 2006. *China's Deep Reform: Domestic Politics in Transition*. Lanham, MD: Rowman and Littlefield.
Domenach, Jean-Luc. 1995. *The Origins of the Great Leap Forward: The Case of One Chinese Province*. Boulder: Westview.
Donaldson, John A. 2011. *Small Works: Poverty and Economic Development in Southwestern China*. Ithaca, NY: Cornell University Press.
Dong, Stella. 2001. *Shanghai: The Rise and Fall of a Decadent City, 1842–1949*. New York: Harper Perennial.
Dowling, John Malcolm, and Yap Chin-Fang. 2009. *Chronic Poverty in Asia: Causes, Consequences, and Policies*. Singapore: World Scientific Publishers.

Dreyer, June Teufel. 2011. *China's Political System: Modernization and Tradition.* 8th ed. Englewood Cliffs, NJ: Prentice Hall.
Duara, Prasenjit. 1988. *Culture, Power, and the State: Rural North China, 1900–1942.* Stanford, CA: Stanford University Press.
———. 2004. *Sovereignty and Authenticity: Manchukuo and the East Asian Modern.* Lanham, MD: Rowman and Littlefield.
Dutton, Michael. 2004. *Policing Chinese Politics: A History.* Durham, NC: Duke University Press.
Dwyer, Arienne M. 2005. *The Xinjiang Conflict: Uyghur Identity, Language Policy, and Political Discourse.* Washington, DC: East-West Center.
Eger, Thomas, Michael Faure, and Zhang Naigen (eds.). 2007. *Economic Analysis of Law in China.* Northampton, MA: Edward Elgar.
Elliott, Mark. 2001. *The Manchu Way: The Eight Banners and Ethnic Identity in Late Imperial China.* Stanford, CA: Stanford University Press.
Elvin, Mark. 1973. *The Pattern of the Chinese Past.* Stanford, CA: Stanford University Press.
Esherick, Joseph W., Paul G. Pickowicz, and Andrew Walder. 2006. *The Chinese Cultural Revolution as History.* Stanford, CA: Stanford University Press.
Feigon, Lee. 1999. *China Rising: The Meaning of Tiananmen.* Lanham, MD: Rowman and Littlefield.
———. 2002. *Mao: A Reinterpretation.* Chicago: Ivan R. Dee.
Fenby, Jonathan. 2004. *Chiang Kai-shek: The Generalissimo and the Nation He Lost.* New York: Carroll and Graf.
Fens, Jacai. 2007. *Ten Years of Madness: Oral Histories of China's Cultural Revolution.* San Francisco: China Books and Periodicals.
Ferguson, Niall. 2011. "Gloating China, Hidden Problems." *Newsweek,* August 22, 29.
Fewsmith, Joseph. 2008. *China Since Tiananmen: From Deng Xiaoping to Hu Jintao.* 2nd ed. Cambridge: Cambridge University Press.
Finkelstein, David M., and Maryanne Kiviehan (eds.). 2003. *Chinese Leadership in the Twenty-First Century: The Rise of the Fourth Generation.* Armonk, NY: M. E. Sharpe.
Fitzgerald, John. 1996. *Awakening China: Politics, Culture, and Class in the Nationalist Revolution.* Stanford, CA: Stanford University Press.
Ford, James H. (ed.). 2005. *The Art of Warfare by Mao Zedong.* El Paso, TX: El Paso Norte Press.
Forney, Matt. 1998. "Voice of the People." *Far Eastern Economic Review* 161(19) (May 7).
Foroohar, Rana. 2010. "China's Wealth Worries." *Newsweek,* November 1.
Frazier, Mark W. 2010. *Socialist Insecurity: Pensions and Politics of Uneven Development in China.* Ithaca, NY: Cornell University Press.
Friedman, Edward, Paul G. Pickowicz, and Mark Selden. 1991. *Chinese Village, Socialist State.* New Haven, CT: Yale University Press.
———. 2007. *Revolution, Resistance, and Reform in Village China.* New Haven, CT: Yale University Press.
Fu, Zhengyuan. 1994. *Autocratic Tradition and Chinese Politics.* Cambridge: Cambridge University Press.
———. 1996. *China's Legalists: The Earliest Totalitarians and Their Art of Ruling.* Armonk, NY: M. E. Sharpe.
Gallagher, Mary E. 2005. *Contagious Capitalism: Globalism and the Politics of Labor in China.* Princeton, NJ: Princeton University Press.
Gamer, Robert E. 1989. "From Zig-Zag to Confrontation at Tiananmen: Tradition and Politics in China." *University Field Staff Reports* 10 (November): 1–11.

———. 1994. “Modernization and Democracy in China: Samuel P. Huntington and the ‘Neo-Authoritarian’ Debate.” *Asian Journal of Political Science* 2(1) (June): 32–63.

Gao, Anhua. 2003. *To the Edge of the Sky: A Story of Love, Betrayal, Suffering, and the Strength of Human Courage.* New York: Penguin.

Gao, Mobo. 2008. *The Battle for China’s Past: Mao and the Cultural Revolution.* Ann Arbor, MI: Pluto Press.

Gao, Wenqian. 2007. *Zhou Enlai: The Last Perfect Revolutionary.* New York: PublicAffairs.

Gao, Yuan. 1987. *Born Red: A Chronicle of the Cultural Revolution.* Stanford, CA: Stanford University Press.

Garnaut, John. 2012a. “In Thrall of the Empire of the Sons.” *Sydney Morning Herald*, May 26.

———. 2012b. “Meet Reformist Wang Yang, China’s New Guard.” *Sydney Morning Herald*, June 3.

Garrison, Jean A. 2009. *China and the Energy Equation in Asia: The Determinants of Policy Choice.* Boulder: Lynne Rienner.

Gates, Hill. 1996. *China’s Motor: A Thousand Years of Petty Capitalism.* Ithaca, NY: Cornell University Press.

Gilley, Bruce. 2001. *Model Rebels: The Rise and Fall of China’s Richest Village.* Berkeley: University of California Press.

Gittings, John. 2006. *The Changing Face of China: From Mao to Market.* Oxford: Oxford University Press.

Gold, Thomas. 2002. *Social Connections in China: Institutions, Culture, and the Changing Nature of Guanxi.* Cambridge: Cambridge University Press.

Gold, Thomas, William J. Hurst, Jaeyoun Won, and Qiang Li (eds.). 2009. *Laid Off Workers in a Worker’s State: Unemployment with Chinese Characteristics.* New York: Palgrave Macmillan.

Goldman, Merle. 2005. *From Comrade to Citizen: The Struggle for Political Rights in China.* Cambridge, MA: Harvard University Press.

Goodman, David S. G. 1994. *Deng Xiaoping and the Chinese Revolution: A Political Biography.* London: Routledge.

Gordon, David B. 2009. *Sun Yat-sen: Seeking a Newer China.* Englewood Cliffs, NJ: Prentice Hall.

Gries, Peter, and Stanley Rosen (eds.). 2010. *Chinese Politics: State, Society, and the Market.* London: Routledge.

Gross, Michael Joseph. 2011. “Enter the Cyber-Dragon.” *Vanity Fair,* September.

Guo, Jian, Yongyi Song, and Yuan Zhou. 2006. *Historical Dictionary of the Chinese Cultural Revolution.* Lanham, MD: Scarecrow.

Guo, Sujian. 2006. *China’s ‘Peaceful Rise’ in the 21st Century: Domestic and International Developments.* Burlington, VT: Ashgate.

———. 2012. *Chinese Politics and Government: Power, Ideology, and Organization.* London: Routledge.

Guo, Yu Gui. 2005. *Asia’s Educational Edge: Current Achievements in Japan, Korea, Taiwan, China, and India.* Lanham, MD: Lexington Books.

Hamilton, John Maxwell. 2003. *Edgar Snow: A Biography.* Baton Rouge: University of Louisiana Press.

Han, Dongping. 2008. *The Unknown Cultural Revolution: Life and Change in a Chinese Village.* New York: Monthly Review Press.

Harney, Alexandra. 2008. *The China Price: The True Cost of Chinese Competitive Advantage.* New York: Penguin.

Hayek, Friedrich A. 1994. *The Road to Serfdom.* Chicago: University of Chicago Press.

"Hayek's Children." 1998. *Far Eastern Economic Review* 161(20) (May 14): 82.
He, Baogang. 2007. *Rural Democracy in China: The Role of Village Elections*. New York: Macmillan Palgrave.
He, Baogang, and Yingjie Guo. 2000. *Nationalism, National Identity, and Democratization in China*. Burlington, VT: Ashgate.
Heberer, Thomas. 2009. "Evolvement of Citizenship in Urban China or Authoritarian Communitarianism? Neighborhood Development, Community Participation, and Autonomy." *Journal of Contemporary China* 18(61): 491–515.
Henriot, Christian, and Wen-hsin Yeh. 2003. *Shanghai Under Japanese Occupation*. Cambridge: Cambridge University Press.
Hessler, Peter. 2007. *Oracle Bones: A Journey Through Time in China*. New York: Harper Perennial.
———. 2010. *Country Driving: A Journey Through China from Farm to Factory*. New York: Harper.
Hinton, William. 1970. *Iron Oxen: A Documentary of Revolution in Chinese Farming*. New York: Vintage.
———. 1997. *Fanshen: A Documentary of Revolution in a Chinese Village*. Berkeley: University of California Press.
Ho, Peter. 2005. *Institutions in Transition: Land Ownership, Property Rights, and Social Conflict in China*. Oxford: Oxford University Press.
Honda, Katsuichi. 1999. *The Nanjing Massacre: A Japanese Journalist Confronts Japan's National Shame*. Armonk, NY: M. E. Sharpe.
Honig, Emily. 1986. *Women in the Shanghai Cotton Mills, 1919–1949*. Stanford, CA: Stanford University Press.
———. 1992. *Creating Chinese Ethnicity: Subei People in Shanghai, 1850–1980*. New Haven, CT: Yale University Press.
Hopkirk, Peter. 1984. *Foreign Devils on the Silk Road: The Search for the Lost Cities and Treasures of Chinese East Asia*. Amherst: University of Massachusetts Press.
Hsing, You-tien. 2010. *The Great Urban Transformation: Politics of Land and Property in China*. Oxford: Oxford University Press.
Hsueh, Roselyn. 2011. *China's Regulatory State: A New Strategy for Globalization*. Ithaca, NY: Cornell University Press.
Huang, Jing. 2000. *Factionalism in Chinese Communist Politics*. Cambridge: Cambridge University Press.
Huang, Yasheng. 2008. *Capitalism with Chinese Characteristics: Entrepreneurship and the State*. Cambridge: Cambridge University Press.
Hughes, Christopher R. 2006. *Chinese Nationalism in the Global Era*. London: Routledge.
Hurst, William. 2009. *The Chinese Worker After Socialism*. New York: Cambridge University Press.
Jacai, Fens. 1996. *Ten Years of Madness*. San Francisco: China Books.
Jeffries, Ian. 2010. *Political Developments in Contemporary China: A Guide*. London: Routledge.
Ji, Chaozhu. 2008. *The Man on Mao's Right: From Harvard Yard to Tiananmen Square, My Life Inside China's Foreign Ministry*. New York: Random House.
Jiang, Jinsong. 2003. *The National People's Congress of China*. San Francisco: China Books.
Johnson, Ian. 2005. *Wild Grass: Three Stories of Change in Modern China*. New York: Vintage.
Joseph, William A. 2010 (ed.). *Politics in China: An Introduction*. New York: Oxford University Press.

Jowett, Philip. 2010. *Chinese Warlord Armies 1911–30*. New York: Osprey.
Jun, Jing. 1998. *The Temple of Memories: History, Power, and Morality in a Chinese Village*. Stanford, CA: Stanford University Press.
Kahn, Joseph. 2007. "In China, a Lake's Champion Imperils Himself." *New York Times*, October 14.
Kaltman, Blaine. 2007. *Under the Heel of the Dragon: Islam, Racism, Crime, and the Uighur in China*. Athens: Ohio University.
Karl, Rebecca E. 2010. *Mao Zedong and China in the Twentieth-Century World: A Concise History*. Durham, NC: Duke University Press.
Keith, Ronald, and Zhiqiu Lin. 2005. *New Crime in China: Public Order and Human Rights*. London: Routledge.
King, Ambrose Y. C. 1991. "Kuan-hsi and Network Building: A Sociological Interpretation." *Daedalus* (Spring): 63–83.
Kipnis, Andrew B. 1997. *Producing Guanxi: Sentiment, Self, and Subculture in a North China Village*. Durham, NC: Duke University Press.
Kleinman, Arthur, and James L. Watson (eds.). 2005. *SARS in China: Economic, Political, and Social Consequences*. Stanford, CA: Stanford University Press.
Kuhn, Lawrence. 2004. *The Man Who Changed China: The Life and Legacy of Jiang Zemin*. New York: Crown.
Kuruvilla, Sarosh, Ching Kwan Lee, and Mary E. Gallagher (eds.). 2011. *From Rice Bowl to Informalization*. Ithaca, NY: Cornell University Press.
Kwong, Julia. 1997. *The Political Economy of Corruption in China*. Armonk, NY: M. E. Sharpe.
Lam, Willy Wo-Lap. 2006. *Chinese Politics in the Hu Jintao Era: New Leaders, New Challenges*. Armonk, NY: M. E. Sharpe.
———. 2009. "China's Political Feet of Clay." *Far Eastern Economic Review* 172 (October).
———. 2012. "Wang Yang: Future Torchbearer of Reform?" *China Brief* 12(11) (May 25).
Larus, Elizabeth Freund. 2012. *Politics and Society in Contemporary China*. Boulder: Lynne Rienner.
Lary, Diana. 2010. *The Chinese People at War: Human Suffering and Social Transformation, 1937–1945*. New York: Cambridge University Press.
Lee, Ching Kwan. 2007. *Against the Law: Labor Protests in China's Rustbelt and Sunbelt*. Berkeley: University of California Press.
"Let a Million Flowers Bloom." 2011. *The Economist* 398 (March 12–18): 8724.
Li, Cunxin. 2004. *Mao's Last Dancer*. New York: Putnam.
Li, Huayin. 2009. *Village China Under Socialism and Reform*. Stanford, CA: Stanford University Press.
Li Lanqing. 2004. *Education for 1.3 Billion: Former Chinese Vice Premier Li Lanqing on 10 Years of Education Reform and Development*. New York: Pearson.
———. 2010. *Breaking Through: The Birth of China's Opening Up Policy*. New York: Oxford University Press.
Li, Laura Tyson. 2006. *Madame Chiang Kai-shek: China's Eternal First Lady*. New York: Grove Press.
Li, Peter, Steven Mark, and Marjorie H. Li (eds.). 2007. *Culture and Politics in China: An Anatomy of Tiananmen Square*. New Brunswick, NJ: Transaction Publications.
Li, Xiaobing. 2010. *Civil Liberties in China*. Santa Barbara CA: ABC-CLIO.
Li, Yan, and Shufang Wu. 2010. "Migration and Health Restraints in China: A Social Strata Analysis." *Journal of Contemporary China* 19(64): 335–358.
Li, Zhisui. 1994. *The Private Life of Chairman Mao: The Inside Story of the Man Who Made Modern China*. London: Chatto and Windus.

Liang, Heng. 1984. *Son of the Revolution*. Trans. Judith Shapiro. New York: Vintage.

Liao, Yiwu. 2009. *The Corpse Walker: Real Life Stories. China from the Bottom Up*. Trans. Wen Huang. New York: Anchor.

Lieberthal, Kenneth. 2003. *Governing China: From Revolution Through Reform*. 2nd ed. New York: Norton.

Lim, Benjamin Kang, and Chris Buckley. 2012. "China Leadership Rules Bo Case Isolated, Limits Purge: Sources." Reuters, May 25.

Liu, Binyan, and Perry Link. 2006. *Two Kinds of Truth: Stories and Reportage from China*. Bloomington: Indiana University Press.

Liu, Kang. 2004. *Globalization and Cultural Trends in China*. Honolulu: University of Hawaii Press.

Liu, Melinda. 2002. "Party Time in Beijing." *Newsweek*, November 25.

Liu, Melinda, and Isaac Stone Fish. 2011. "Portrait of the Gulag." *Newsweek*, July 4.

Lu, Ding, and William A. W. Neilson (eds.). 2004. *China's West Region Development*. Singapore: World Scientific.

Lu, Xiaobo. 2000. *Cadres and Corruption: The Organizational Involution of the Chinese Communist Party*. Cambridge: Cambridge University Press.

Lubman, Stanley B. 2001. *Legal Reform in China After Mao*. Stanford, CA: Stanford University Press.

Lynch, Daniel C. 2006. *Rising China and Asian Democratization: Socialization to "Global Culture" in the Political Transformation of Thailand, China, and Taiwan*. Stanford, CA: Stanford University Press.

Lynch, Michael. 2010. *The Chinese Civil War 1945–49*. New York: Osprey.

Ma, Bo. 1996. *Blood Red Sunset: A Memoir of the Chinese Cultural Revolution*. New York: Penguin.

Ma, Jisen. 2004. *The Cultural Revolution in the Chinese Foreign Ministry: A True Story*. Hong Kong: Chinese University Press.

Macfarquar, Roderick. 1974. *The Origins of the Cultural Revolution: Contradictions Among the People, 1956–1957*. Vol. 1. New York: Columbia University Press.

———. 1983. *The Origins of the Cultural Revolution: The Great Leap Forward, 1958–1960*. Vol. 2. New York: Columbia University Press.

——— (ed.). 1997. *The Politics of China: The Eras of Mao and Deng*. 2nd ed. Cambridge: Cambridge University Press.

———. 1999. *The Origins of the Cultural Revolution: The Coming of the Cataclysm, 1961–1966*. New York: Columbia University Press.

Macfarquar, Roderick, and Michael Schoenhals. 2008. *Mao's Last Revolution*. Cambridg, MA: Harvard University Press.

Mackerras, Colin, and Michael Clarke (eds.). 2011. *China, Xinjiang, and Central Asia: History, Transition, and Crossborder Interaction in the 21st Century*. London: Routledge.

MacKinnon, Stephen R. 2008. *Wuhan, 1938: War, Refugees, and the Making of Modern China*. Berkeley: University of California Press.

Mallory, J. P., and Victor H. Mair. 2000. *The Tarim Mummies*. London: Thames and Hudson.

Mao Tse-tung. 2000. *On Guerrilla Warfare*. Trans. Samuel B. Griffith. Champaign: University of Illinois Press.

Mao Zedong. 2010. *The Red Book of Guerrilla Warfare*. Trans. Shawn Conners. El Paso, TX: El Paso Norte Press.

Mao Zedong, and Slavoi Zizek. 2007. *On Practice and Contradiction*. New York: Verso.

McConville, Mike. 2011. *Criminal Justice in China: An Empirical Enquiry*. Northampton, MA: Edward Elgar.

McGregor, Richard. 2010. *The Party: The Secret World of China's Communist Rulers*. New York: Harper.

Meisner, Maurice. 2007. *Mao Zedong: A Political and Intellectual Portrait*. New York: Polity.

Mexico, Zachary. 2009. *China Underground*. New York: Soft Skull Press.

Midler, Paul. 2009. *Poorly Made in China: An Insider's Account of the Tactics Behind China's Production Game*. New York: Wiley.

Millward, James A. 2007. *Eurasian Crossroads: A History of Xinjiang*. New York: Columbia University Press.

Min, Anchee. 2002. *Wild Ginger*. New York: Mariner Books.

———. 2006. *Red Azalea*. New York: Anchor.

Misra, Kalpana. 1998. *From Post-Maoism to Post-Marxism: The Erosion of Official Ideology in Deng's China*. London: Routledge.

Mitamura, Taisuke. 1970. *Chinese Eunuchs: The Structure of Intimate Politics*. Rutland, VT: Charles E. Tuttle.

Mitter, Rana. 2005. *A Bitter Revolution: China's Struggle with the Modern World*. Oxford: Longman.

Miyazaki, Ichisada. 1981. *China's Examination Hell: The Civil Service Examinations in Imperial China*. New Haven, CT: Yale University Press.

Mohanty, Monoranjan, Richard Baum, Rong Ma, and George Mathew (eds.). 2007. *Grass-Roots Democracy in India and China*. Thousand Oaks, CA: Sage.

Moise, Edwin. 2008. *Modern China*. 3rd ed. Harlow, UK: Pearson Education Limited.

Moody, Peter. 2007. *Conservative Thought in Contemporary China*. Lanham, MD: Rowman and Littlefield.

Nathan, Andrew J., and Bruce Gilley. 2003. *China's New Rulers: The Secret Files*. 2nd ed. New York: New York Review of Books.

Naughton, Barry J., and Dali L. Yang (eds.). 2004. *Holding China Together: Diversity and National Integration in the Post-Deng Era*. Cambridge: Cambridge University Press.

O'Brien, Kevin J. 2008a. *Reform Without Liberalization: China's National People's Congress and the Politics of Institutional Change*. Cambridge: Cambridge University Press.

——— (ed.). 2008b. *Popular Protest in China*. Cambridge, MA: Harvard University Press.

O'Brien, Kevin J., and Lianjiang Li. 2006. *Rightful Resistance in Rural China*. Cambridge: Cambridge University Press.

O'Brien, Kevin, and Suisheng Zhao (eds.). 2010. *Grassroots Elections in China*. London: Routledge.

Orlik, Tom, and Scott Rozelle. 2009. "Averting Crisis in the Countryside." *Far Eastern Economic Review* 172 (October).

Ownby, David. 2008. *Falun Gong and the Future of China*. New York: Oxford University Press.

Page, Jeremy, and Lingling Wei. 2012. "Bo's Ties to Army Alarmed Beijing." *Wall Street Journal*, May 17.

Pakula, Hannah. 2009. *The Last Empress: Madame Chiang Kai-shek and the Birth of Modern China*. New York: Simon and Schuster.

Pan, Philip C. 2009. *Out of Mao's Shadow: The Struggle for the Soul of a New China*. New York: Simon and Schuster.

Park, Nancy E. 1997. "Corruption in Eighteenth-Century China." *Journal of Asian Studies* 56(4) (November): 967–1005.

Peerenboom, Randall. 2002. *China's Long March Toward Rule of Law*. Cambridge: Cambridge University Press.

Pei, Minxin. 2006. *China's Trapped Transition: The Limits of Developmental Autocracy.* Cambridge, MA: Harvard University Press.

Perry, Elizabeth J. 1993. *Shanghai on Strike: The Politics of Chinese Labor.* Stanford, CA: Stanford University Press.

———. 2007. *Patrolling the Revolution: Worker Militias, Citizenship, and the Modern Chinese State.* Lanham, MD: Rowman and Littlefield.

Perry, Elizabeth J., and Merle Goldman (eds.). 2007. *Grassroots Political Reform in Contemporary China.* Cambridge, MA: Harvard University Press.

Perry, Elizabeth J., and Xun Li. 1996. *Proletarian Power: Shanghai in the Cultural Revolution.* Boulder: Westview.

Perry, Elizabeth J., and Mark Selden (eds.). 2010. *Chinese Society: Change, Conflict, and Resistance.* 3rd ed. New York: Routledge.

Pieke, Frank N. 2009. *The Good Communist: Elite Training and State Building in Today's China.* Cambridge: Cambridge University Press.

Pomfret, John. 2006. *Chinese Lessons: Five Classmates and the Story of the New China.* New York: Henry Holt.

Postiglione, Gerald A. (ed.). 2006. *Education and Social Change in China: Inequality in a Market Economy.* Armonk, NY: M. E. Sharpe.

Rawski, Evelyn S. 1996. "Reenvisioning the Qing: The Significance of the Qing Period in Chinese History." *Journal of Asian Studies* 55(4) (November): 829–850.

Rhoads, Edward J. M. 2000. *Manchus and Han: Ethnic Relations and Political Power in Late Qing and Early Republican China, 1861–1928.* Seattle: University of Washington Press.

Rudelson, Justin Jon. 1997. *Oasis Identities: Uyghur Nationalism Along China's Silk Road.* New York: Columbia University Press.

Saich, Tony. 2011. *Governance and Politics of China.* 3rd ed. New York: Palgrave Macmillan.

Schiffrin, Harold Z. 2010. *Sun Yat-Sen and the Origins of the Chinese Revolution.* Berkeley: University of California Press.

Seagrave, Sterling. 1987. *The Soong Dynasty.* New York: Harper Perennial.

Seybolt, Peter J. 1996. *Throwing the Emperor from His Horse: Portrait of a Village Leader in China, 1923–1995.* Boulder: Westview.

Shambaugh, David. 1995. *Deng Xiaoping: Portrait of a Chinese Statesman.* Oxford: Oxford University Press.

———. 2008. *China's Communist Party: Atrophy and Adaptation.* Berkeley: University of California Press.

Shi, Tianjian. 1997. *Political Participation in Beijing.* Cambridge, MA: Harvard University Press.

Shirk, Susan. (ed.). 2011. *Changing Media, Changing China.* New York: Oxford University Press.

Siu, Helen F. 1999. *Agents and Victims in South China: Accomplices in Rural Revolution.* New Haven, CT: Yale University Press.

Snow, Edgar. 1994. *Red Star over China.* Rev. ed. New York: Grove Press.

Spence, Jonathan. 1999. *The Search for Modern China.* 2nd ed. New York: W. W. Norton.

———. 2000. *Mao Zedong.* New York: Penguin.

Starr, Frederick. 2004. *Xinjiang: China's Muslim Borderland.* Armonk, NY: M. E. Sharpe.

Stranahan, Patricia. 1998. *Underground: The Shanghai Communist Party and the Politics of Survival, 1927–1937.* Lanham, MD: Rowman and Littlefield.

Su, Minzi. 2009. *China's Rural Development Policy: Exploring the "New Socialist Countryside."* Boulder: Lynne Rienner.

Sun, Yan. 2004. *Corruption and Market in Contemporary China*. Ithaca, NY: Cornell University Press.

Tang, Wenfang. 2005. *Public Opinion and Political Change in China*. Stanford, CA: Stanford University Press.

Taylor, Jay. 2009. *The Generalissimo: Chiang Kai-shek and the Struggle for Modern China*. Cambridge, MA: Belknap Press of Harvard University Press.

Terrill, Ross. 1997. *Madame Mao: The White-Boned Demon*. Rev. ed. Stanford, CA: Stanford University Press.

———. 1999. *Mao: A Biography*. Rev. ed. Stanford, CA: Stanford University Press.

Thaxton, Ralph A., Jr. 2008. *Catastrophe and Contention in Rural China: Mao's Great Leap Forward, Famine, and the Origins of Righteous Resistance in Da Fo Village*. New York: Cambridge University Press.

"The Next Emperor." 2010. *The Economist* 397 (October 23–29): 8705.

Thomas, Bernard S. 1996. *Season of High Adventure: Edgar Snow in China*. Berkeley: University of California Press.

Thornton, Patricia M. 2007. *Disciplining the State: Virtue, Violence, and State-Making in Modern China*. Cambridge, MA: Harvard University Asia Center.

Tien, Hung-mao, and Yun-han Chu. 2000. *China Under Jiang Zemin*. Boulder: Lynne Rienner.

Tiewes, Frederick C. 1993. *Politics and Purges in China: Rectification and the Decline of Party Norms, 1950–1965*. Armonk, NY: M. E. Sharpe.

Tiewes, Frederick, and Warren Sun. 2007. *The End of the Maoist Era: Chinese Politics During the Twilight of the Cultural Revolution 1972–1976*. Armonk, NY: M. E. Sharpe.

Tong, James W. 2009. *Revenge of the Forbidden City: The Suppression of the Falungong in China: 1999–2005*. Oxford: Oxford University Press.

Trevaskes, Sue. 2007. *Courts and Criminal Justice in Contemporary China*. Lanham, MD: Rowman and Littlefield.

Tsai, Kellee S. 2004. *Back-Alley Banking: Private Entrepreneurs in China*. Ithaca, NY: Cornell University Press.

Tsai, Lily Lee. 2002. "Cadres, Temple and Lineage Institutions, and Governance in Rural China." *China Journal* 48 (July): 1–27.

Tsai, Shih-Shan Henry. 1995. *The Eunuchs in the Ming Dynasty*. Binghamton: State University of New York Press.

Tubilewicz, Czeslaw. 2006. *Critical Issues in Contemporary China*. London: Routledge.

Tyler, Christian. 2004. *Wild West China: The Taming of Xinjiang*. Piscataway, NJ: Rutgers University Press.

van Rooij, Benjamin. 2010. "The People vs. Pollution: Understanding Citizen Action Against Pollution in China." *Journal of Contemporary China* 19(63): 55–77.

Vogel, Ezra F. 2011. *Deng Xiaoping and the Transformation of China*. Cambridge, MA: Belknap Press of Harvard University Press.

Wakeman, Frederick. 1996. *Policing Shanghai, 1927–1937*. Berkeley: University of California Press.

———. 2002. *The Shanghai Badlands: Wartime Terrorism and Urban Crime, 1937–1942*. Cambridge: Cambridge University Press.

Walder, Andrew George. 1986. *Communist Neo-Traditionalism: Work and Authority in Chinese Industry*. Berkeley: University of California Press.

———. 2009. *Fractured Rebellion: The Beijing Red Guard Movement*. Cambridge, MA: Harvard University Press.

Wang, Hui. 2006. *China's New Order: Society, Economy, and Politics in Transition*.

Trans. Rebecca E. Karl and Theodore Huters. Cambridge, MA: Harvard University Press.

———. 2010. *The End of Revolution: China and the Limits of Modernity.* New York: Verso.

Wang, Ruowong. 1991. *Hunger Trilogy.* Trans. Kyna Rubin and Ira Kasoff. Armonk, NY: M. E. Sharpe.

Wang, Shaoguang. 1995. *Failure of Charisma: The Cultural Revolution in Wuhan.* Oxford: Oxford University Press.

Wang, Shaoguang, Hu Angang, and Ding Yuanzhu. 2002. "Behind China's Wealth Gap." *South China Morning Post,* October 31.

Wank, David L. 2001. *Commodifying Communism: Business, Trust, and Politics in a Chinese City.* Cambridge: Cambridge University Press.

Wasserstein, Bernard. 1999. *Secret War in Shanghai: An Untold Story of Espionage, Intrigue, and Treason in World War II.* New York: Houghton Mifflin.

Wasserstrom, Jeffrey. 1997. *Student Protests in Twentieth-Century China: The View from Shanghai.* Stanford, CA: Stanford University Press.

Wei, Julie Lee, Ramon H. Myers, and Donald G. Gillin. 1994. *Prescriptions for Saving China: Selected Writings of Sun Yat-sen.* Stanford, CA: Hoover Institution Press.

Westad, Odd Orne. 2003. *Decisive Encounters: The Chinese Civil War, 1946–1950.* Stanford, CA: Stanford University Press.

"When Fund-raising Is a Crime." 2011. *The Economist* 399 (April 16): 8729.

White, Lynn T., III. 1989. *Policies of Chaos: The Organizational Causes of Violence in China's Cultural Revolution.* Princeton, NJ: Princeton University Press.

———. 1998 and 1999. *Unstately Power: Local Causes of China's Intellectual, Legal, and Governmental Reforms.* Vols. 1–2. Armonk, NY: M. E. Sharpe.

———. 2009. *Political Booms: Local Money and Power in Taiwan, East China, Thailand, and the Philippines.* Singapore: World Scientific Publishers.

Winchester, Simon. 2011. "How Fast Can China Go?" *Vanity Fair,* October.

Wong, Chack-kie, Vai Io Lo, and Kwang-leung Tang. 2005. *China's Urban Health Care Reform: From State Protection to Individual Responsibility.* Lanham, MD: Lexington Books.

Wong, John, and Zheng Yongnian (eds.). 2004. *The SARS Epidemic: Challenges to China's Crisis Management.* Singapore: World Scientific.

Wood, Alan T. 1995. *Limits to Autocracy: From Sung Neo-Confucianism to a Doctrine of Political Rights.* Honolulu: University of Hawaii Press.

Wright, Teresa. 2001. *The Perils of Protests: State Repression and Student Activism in China and Taiwan.* Honolulu: University of Hawaii Press.

Xie, Lei. 2011. *Environmental Activism in China.* London: Routledge.

Xu, Feng. 2011. *Looking for Work in Post-Socialist China: Governance, Active Job Seekers, and the New Chinese Labour Market.* London: Routledge.

Xu, Wu. 2007. *Chinese Cyber Nationalism: Evolution, Characteristics, and Implications.* Lanham, MD: Lexington Books.

Yan, Jiaqi, and Gao Gao. 1996. *Turbulent Decade: A History of the Cultural Revolution.* Trans. D. W. Y. Kwok. Honolulu: University of Hawaii Press.

Yan, Yunxiang. 1996. *The Flow of Gifts: Reciprocity and Social Networks in a Chinese Village.* Stanford, CA: Stanford University Press.

Yang, Benjamin. 1997. *Deng: A Political Biography.* Armonk, NY: M. E. Sharpe.

Yang, Dali L. 1996. *Calamity and Reform in China: State, Rural Society, and Institutional Change Since the Great Leap Famine.* Stanford, CA: Stanford University Press.

———. 2004. *Remaking the Chinese Leviathon: Market Transition and the Politics of Governance in China.* Stanford, CA: Stanford University Press.

Yang, Guobin. 2009. *The Power of the Internet in China: Citizen Activism Online*. New York: Columbia University Press.
Yang, Mayfair Mei-hui. 1994. *Gifts, Favors, and Banquets: The Art of Social Relationships in China*. Ithaca, NY: Cornell University Press.
Yang, Rae. 1998. *Spider Eaters: A Memoir.* Berkeley: University of California Press.
Yang, Xiguang. 1997. *Captive Spirits: Prisoners of the Cultural Revolution*. Oxford: Oxford University Press.
Young, Louise. 1999. *Japan's Total Empire: Manchuria and the Culture of Wartime Imperialism*. Berkeley: University of California Press.
Yu, Lianne, Cynthia Chan, and Christopher Ireland. 2006. *China's New Culture of Cool: Understanding the World's Fastest Growing Market*. Berkeley: New Riders.
Yuan, Gao. 1987. *Born Red: A Chronicle of the Cultural Revolution*. Stanford, CA: Stanford University Press.
Zhang, Liang, Andrew J. Nathan, and Perry Link (eds.). 2001. *The Tiananmen Papers: The Chinese Leadership's Decision to Use Force Against Their Own People*. New York: PublicAffairs.
Zhang, Wei-wei. 1996. *Ideology and Economic Reform Under Deng Xiaoping, 1978–1993*. New York: Columbia University.
Zhao, Dingzin. 2004. *The Power of Tiananmen: State-Society Relations and the 1989 Student Movement*. Chicago: University Press of Chicago.
Zhao, Litao, and Lim Tin Seng (eds.). 2010. *China's New Social Policy: Initiatives for a Harmonious Society.* Singapore: World Scientific Publishers.
Zhao, Suisheng. 2004. *A Nation-State by Construction: Dynamics of Modern Chinese Nationalism*. Stanford, CA: Stanford University Press.
———. 2006. *Debating Political Reform in China: Rule of Law vs. Democratization*. Armonk, NY: M. E. Sharpe.
Zhao, Yuezhi. 2008. *Communication in China: Political Economy, Power, and Conflict*. Lanham, MD: Rowman and Littlefield.
Zhao, Ziyang. 2009. *Prisoner of the State: The Secret Journal of Chinese Premier Zhao Ziyang*. Trans. Bao Pu and Renee Chiang. London: Simon and Schuster.
Zheng, Yongnian. 2004. *Globalization and State Transformation in China*. Cambridge: Cambridge University Press.
———. 2006. *De Facto Federalism in China: Reforms and Dynamics of Central-Local Relations*. Singapore: World Scientific.
———. 2010. *The Chinese Communist Party as Organizational Emperor: Culture, Reproduction, and Transformation*. London: Routledge.
Zheng, Yongnian, and Joseph Fewsmith (eds.). 2008. *China's Opening Society: The Non-state Sector and Governance*. New York: Routledge.
Zhengguo, Kang. 2008. *Confessions: An Innocent Life in Communist China*. Trans. Susan Wilf. New York: Norton.
Zhong, Yang. 2003. *Local Government and Politics in China: Challenges from Below.* Armonk, NY: M. E. Sharpe.
———. 2011. *Political Culture and Participation in Rural China*. London: Routledge.
Zhou, Jinghao. 2010. *China's Peaceful Rise in a Global Context: A Domestic Aspect of China's Road to Globalization*. Lanham, MD: Lexington Books.
Zhou, Yongming. 2006. *Historicizing Online Politics: Telegraphy, the Internet, and Political Participation in China*. Stanford, CA: Stanford University Press.
Zhu, Rongji. 2011. *Zhu Rongji Meets the Press*. New York: Oxford University Press.

5

China's Economy

Sarah Y. Tong and John Wong

During the past three decades, from 1978 to 2010, China's economy has grown at an amazing speed of nearly 10 percent a year. This translates into a more than twentyfold increase of the economy from 1978. However, as the economy rapidly increases, there have also been extensive structural changes and growing imbalances, including particularly the rising income inequality in recent years.

When Deng Xiaoping started the reform, Chinese people were quite poor, or perhaps "equally poor," with most workers making, at that era's rate of exchange, less than US$1 a day (though with a lot of welfare subsidies) regardless of their work and performance. Deng made a sharp departure from Mao's basic social tenet of egalitarianism and launched an economic reform program with the motto of "letting some people get rich first."

After more than thirty years of reform and development, Chinese society has become moderately affluent (*xiaokang*) but economically very unequal. While per capita gross domestic product (GDP) rose from 381 renminbi (the "people's money" or RMB; also call yuan, meaning "coin") (roughly US$230) in 1978 to nearly 29,762 RMB (about US$4,000) in 2010. Meanwhile, the Gini coefficient[1] measuring inequality rose considerately from less than 0.3 in the early 1980s to perhaps as high as 0.47. By 2007, China was perhaps already home to more billionaires than any country other than the United States, while at the same time there are more than 57 million people still living in poverty on incomes below US$125 a year, and 36 percent of the populace on incomes less than US$2 a day.[2] Credit Suisse estimates that a third of Chinese adults have a net worth between US$10,000 and US$100,000, compared with 7 percent in India. Only 2.7 percent have a net worth over US$100,000, while 5.8 percent have less than US$1,000 in assets. Over a million are millionaires.[3] The *Hurun Report* on the 2010 Rich

List named 189 Chinese billionaires, up from three in 2004 and 106 in 2007.[4] And perhaps 10 percent of Chinese wealth goes unreported.

In this chapter, we explore in greater detail the extent of China's economic growth, what has led up to it, and whether it can be expected to continue. The easiest way to comprehend the full extent of this phenomenon is to first look at several sets of rather dramatic numbers. Then we shall briefly examine China's economic history and look at some of the problems facing its economy.

China's Dynamic Growth in Perspective

The Chinese economy has experienced spectacular growth since it started economic reform and its open-door policy more than three decades ago. Real growth during 1978–2010 was at an annual rate of 9.9 percent, compared to an average annual rate of less than 3 percent for the world economy as a whole.

Even when compared to the rest of East Asia, China's performance was remarkable. In the late 1990s, while the Asian financial crisis brought down many Asian economies, China was hardly affected and continued to grow at 9.3 percent in 1997 and 7.8 percent in 1998. Between then and the early 2000s, economic growth in most of Asia was falling to very low or negative growth, and the world economy at large crept toward recession; China's economy alone still steamed ahead with strong growth.

Since 2001, when China became a member of the World Trade Organization (WTO) later that year, the economy has gained strong new momentum. Between 2002 and 2007, the economy grew by more than 10 percent a year for five consecutive years. Even when the world economy was hard hit in 2008 by a serious financial and economic crisis, China's economy continued to grow at more than 10 percent a year, while the rest of the world economy dipped into recession (see Figure 5.1).

China's economy has been much less affected by the global economic downturn, mainly because of its large size and population: on average, over 80 percent of its growth is generated by domestic demand, including personal consumption and real estate investment. However, this does not mean that external demand (i.e., exports of goods and services) is not important for China's economic growth. In fact, China's economy is becoming ever more export-oriented, and export dependency has risen considerably since the early 2000s.

Indeed, China's exports have been increasing at an annual rate of over 17 percent (or more than twice the world average), from US$9.8 billion in 1978 to US$1.6 trillion in 2010 in nominal terms (see Figure 5.2). By 2002, China had become the world's sixth-largest exporting nation. Over the subsequent eight years, China's exports further accelerated and China had become the

Figure 5.1 Economic Growth of China, Developing East Asia and Pacific, and the World, 1978–2010

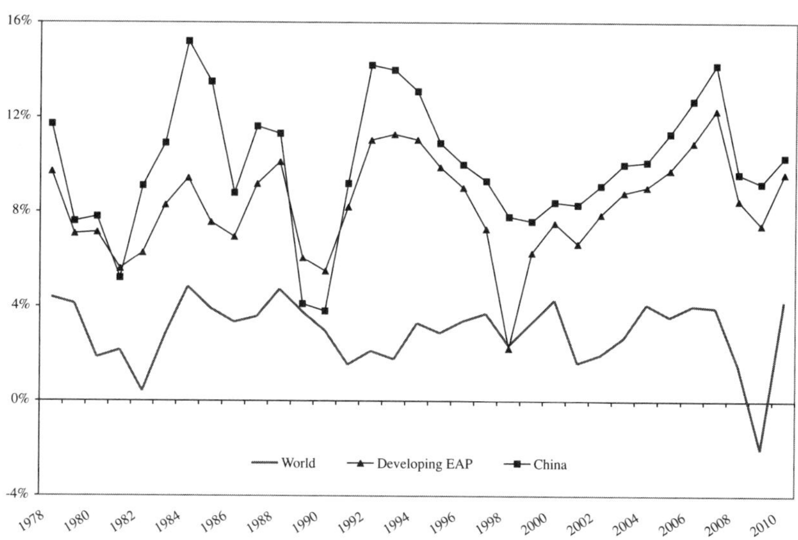

Source: World Bank, *World Development Indicators*, http://data.worldbank.org/data-catalog/world-development-indicators.

Note: Developing East Asia and the Pacific includes twenty-four economies of American Samoa, Cambodia, China, Fiji, Indonesia, Kiribati, Democratic Republic of Korea, Lao PDR, Malaysia, Marshall Islands, Federated States of Micronesia, Mongolia, Myanmar, Palau, Papua New Guinea, Philippines, Samoa, Solomon Islands, Thailand, Timor-Leste, Tuvalu, Tonga, Vanuatu, and Vietnam.

world's largest exporter in 2009. In 2010, China's exports made up roughly 10 percent of the world total, up from less than 1 percent in the late 1970s.

While exports are expanding rapidly, China's export structure has also experienced far-reaching changes. When China embarked on its open-door policy in 1978, primary commodities (i.e., agricultural products and natural resources such as coal and petroleum) constituted 55 percent of its total exports. In recent years, manufactured products made up roughly 95 percent of China's total exports, reflecting China's extensive industrialization progress.[5] Even more dramatically, the export structure within manufactured goods has also undergone a radical transformation. In the early 1990s, China's exports were dominated by labor-intensive manufactured products, particularly textiles, clothing, footwear, and toys. Since the second half of the 1990s, these traditionally labor-intensive manufactures have been gradually overtaken by nontraditional items such as electronics and machinery, whose share in total exports rose to 50 percent in recent years, from roughly a third in the early 2000s. Furthermore, in 2010, the export of high-technology products

Figure 5.2 China's Exports and Export Growth, 1978–2010

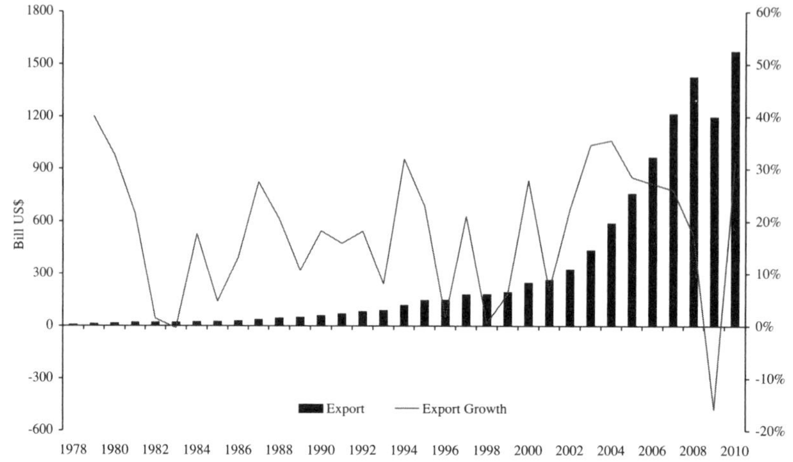

Source: CEIC Data, China Premium Database, at http://www.ceicdata.com/China.html.

accounted for 31 percent of China's total exports, up from around 15 percent in the early 2000s (Chen and Shih, 2005; Ling, 2006; Sigurdson, Jiang, and Kong, 2006; Hsu, Zhang, and Lok, 2007; Haiyang Li, 2006). In other words, along with China's successful industrial upgrading, Chinese exports today are no longer confined to low-technology intensive and low value-added products.

In addition to trade expansion, foreign investment[6] has also contributed significantly to China's past economic growth. Since 1993, China has become the most-favored destination among developing countries for foreign direct investment (FDI).[7] China's realized inward FDI has grown steadily, except for the years immediately after the Asian financial crises, and has further accelerated since 2001 to attract more than US$60 billion a year in the mid-2000s and more than US$90 billion a year since 2008 (Wang, 2001; Thun, 2006; Huang, 2005; Fung, Iizaka, and Tong, 2004) (see Figure 5.3). By the end of 2010, the accumulated FDI in China reached a total of more than US$1 trillion. Between 1990 and 2010, China captured roughly one-third of all FDI to Asia, in addition to around 17 percent for Hong Kong, part of which will eventually end up in China (see Figure 5.4). China's share of the total accumulated stock of FDI in Asia nearly tripled in twenty years—from 6 percent in 1990 to about 15 percent in 2010.[8]

One result of such a large influx of FDI, coupled with China's persistent and growing trade surplus in the past decade, is that China's foreign exchange reserves have increased gradually and steadily since the mid-1990s. After China's accession to the WTO in late 2001, there was a significant surge in

Figure 5.3 China's Foreign Direct Investment Inflow, 1979–2010

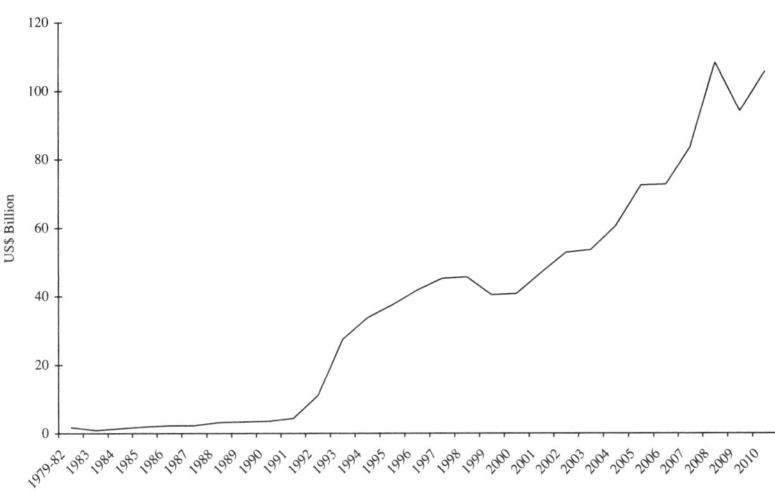

Source: CEIC Data, China Premium Database, at http://www.ceicdata.com/China.html.

Figure 5.4 Shares of Mainland China and Hong Kong in Total FDI to Asia, 1990–2010

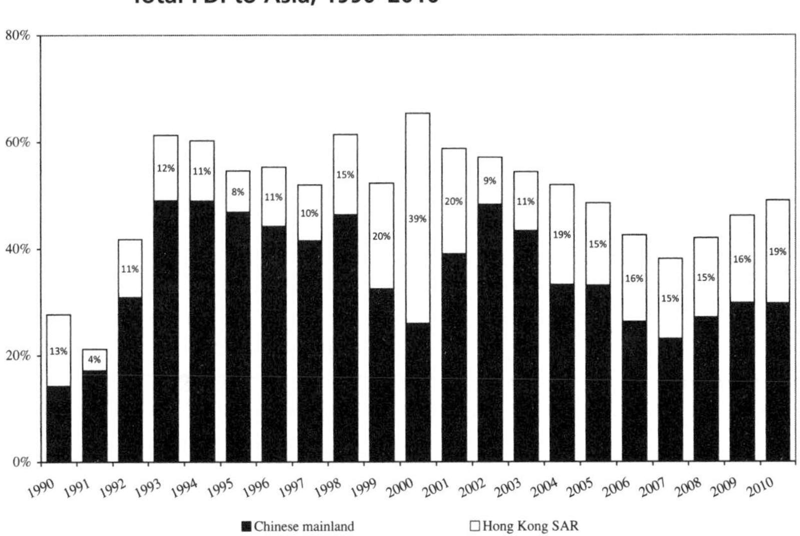

Source: UN Conference on Trade and Development (UNCTAD), FDI Statistics Division on Investment and Enterprise database, at www.unctad.org/fdistatistics.

China's foreign reserves over the next five years, from US$212 billion in 2001 to US$1.07 trillion in 2006. In less than five years, they nearly tripled to reach more than US$3.2 trillion in June 2011. In 2011, China owned, directly and through intermediaries, US$1.6 trillion in US Treasury securities—17 percent of the US national government's debt[9]—and exported a record US$365 billion of goods to the United States, while importing $92 billion of goods from the United States. At the same time, China's foreign debt by the end of 2010 amounted to only US$549 billion, with 32 percent of it being long-term debt.

Consequently, in recent years, China has been under growing pressure to appreciate its currency, the Chinese RMB, which had been under a de facto fixed exchange rate between the mid-1990s and the mid-2000s (Liew and Wu, 2008). In July 2005, Chinese authorities instituted a one-time appreciation of the RMB against the US dollar by about 2.1 percent, from 8.27 to 8.11, and have subsequently widened the daily trading band of the RMB. Since then, the RMB has continued to appreciate against the US dollar, reaching a level of around 6.41 in August 2011, representing an accumulated depreciation of around 28 percent since July 2005. The Chinese RMB, however, has appreciated only modestly or even depreciated against other major currencies, along with the depreciating US dollar.[10] Therefore, China continues to run a trade surplus and to accumulate foreign reserves; the pressure for China to appreciate its currency remains strong.

China is facing a dilemma in managing its huge amount of foreign reserves, where a large portion is in US assets, including US Treasury Bills. If it were to sell off some of its large US T-Bill holdings to diversify, it might push the US dollar further down in value and lose both on the sale and on its remaining holdings. If it maintains its current position, it might also face large potential losses as the US dollar continues its downslide. While China is exploring using its foreign reserve to buy non-US foreign assets, as suggested by the establishment of the China Investment Company (CIC) in 2007, it is unlikely that China will dump its US dollar holdings wholesale.

Economic growth means increases in GDP. As in compounding interest rates, when an economy grows at 9.9 percent annually, it doubles its GDP in less than eight years. As a result of sustained high economic growth, China's nominal GDP increased from 365 billion RMB in 1978 (when it started economic reform) to 40 trillion RMB in 2010, which translates into roughly US$5.9 trillion, ranking China the world's second-largest economy, after the United States. In terms of purchasing power parity (PPP),[11] the Chinese economy since 1999 has been the world's second largest, after the United States.

However, China's current per capita GDP, at just about US $4,400 in 2010, remains relatively low due to its large population base. More importantly, there is considerable variation of per capita GDP among provinces and cities. As can be expected, the more developed and the more open provinces and cities along China's east coast have per capita incomes way above the national average, while those in the interior and the western region have per capita incomes considerably below the national average. The per capita incomes of Guangzhou, Shanghai, and Beijing, at over US$10,000, have reached the level the World Bank has classified as upper-middle-income economies.

Beyond the rise in GDP, China's high rates of economic growth are clearly reflected in its industrial statistics. Since the mid-1990s, China's industrial sector has accounted for roughly 46 percent of its total GDP on average, a proportion that is much higher than the average for the developing world, which is about 35 percent over the same period. In the meantime, the service sector has continued to rise in its contribution to the overall economy. Its share in GDP has risen from 33 percent in 1995 to 46 percent in 2010.[12] Nonetheless, producing roughly half of the country's output, industry remains highly significant. In 2010, China was able to produce 3.2 billion tons of coal, 590 million tons of steel, 118 million color television sets, 73 million refrigerators, 109 million air conditioners, 998 million cell phones, 245.8 million personal computers, and 18.3 million automobiles.[13] Indeed, as a result of its rapid industrialization progress, China is fast becoming the world's foremost manufacturing base. Back in 2001, China passed the United States as the world's largest mobile phone market and, with more than 500 million Chinese online, has become the world's largest "Web population."

Not surprisingly, the meteoric rise of China's economy has since the early 2000s become a hot topic in international and regional media. It has also, at times, become a real concern to certain Asian countries.[14] Many commentators see the emergence of China as a disruptive force for the Asian economies. In particular, Japan has grown increasingly apprehensive about the rise of China as a manufacturing powerhouse.[15] For example, in 2008, China's production of air conditioners accounted for roughly 80 percent of the world total and that of refrigerators about 40 percent.[16]

Some Western journalists and scholars, however, have taken issue with Chinese official statistics. They contend that the official numbers are grossly inaccurate and therefore exaggerate China's economic performance.[17] Interestingly, this argument stands in sharp contrast to the "China as economic threat" thesis that is also found in print and in the blogosphere. US-Chinese lawyer Gordon Chang's book *The Coming Collapse of China* (2001) points to every possible negative aspect of reports on China's development.

How reliable are official Chinese statistics? Especially during the Great Leap Forward in the late 1950s,[18] central planning involved setting targets for enterprises to fulfill, putting pressure on underperforming production units to make false reports. With the emergence of the "socialist market economy," China's National Bureau of Statistics (NBS) is under less and less political and ideological pressure to produce inflated numbers. In fact, as the Chinese government is becoming more technocratic, it demands more accurate statistical figures for effective macroeconomic management.[19] Since under the market system Chinese enterprises are no longer required to fulfill production targets, there is also no incentive for enterprise managers to exaggerate output figures, which would lead to higher taxes. Furthermore, the NBS today has become a modern organization, run by professionals and employing modern methodologies (e.g., conducting frequent sample surveys as counterchecks) and up-to-date computation and communication facilities (e.g., using fax and Internet technologies for reporting).

All this does not mean that Chinese official statistics are entirely accurate. Underqualified statistical officers, especially at local levels, make mistakes gathering data. Some enterprises underreport output and profits to evade taxes, while others hide their losses, underreport imports, or overreport exports, all for various reasons. The mathematical laws of large numbers can normally take care of such discrepancies, with overreporting being balanced by underreporting so that the final macroeconomic data at the national level are not compromised by local irregularities. International organizations and most China scholars have continued to use official figures, particularly those related to trade, investment, and GDP. In recent years, some even argue that, in view of the existence of a large underground economy and widespread activities of smuggling and capital flight, China's official GDP figures, if anything, actually tend to underestimate rather than overestimate the true size of its economy.

Employing a more comprehensive test of the relationship between China's GDP and fifteen other major indicators (including variables on not only energy, but also electricity, grain, steel, freight, civil aviation, long-distance telephone, and so on) for the period 1980–2000, Lawrence R. Klein (a Nobel Laureate) and Suleyman Ozmucur (2002) confirm that the movements of these major economic components "are consistent with the movements of real GDP as officially estimated." Klein has qualified that their study has not "proved" the Chinese official GDP measure correct, as no one knows the "correct estimate,"[20] but that it should provide additional confidence in China's official statistics.

China today is a fairly open country, which in 2010 received around 27 million foreign tourists (in addition to 107 million visits—some daily—from ethnic Chinese in Hong Kong, Macau, and Taiwan) and allowed 57 million of its own citizens to tour overseas. Foreign tourists can see for themselves the hectic economic activities, including the incessant construction of roads, skyscrapers, and houses, not just in big cities like Shanghai and Guangzhou, but also in numerous regional cities formerly classified as rural county towns. Tourists can also see the massive industrial sprawl, along with the smog and suffocating traffic congestion, not just in the Pearl River Delta and the Yangtze Delta, but also in many other locations.

In fact, China's high economic growth of the past two decades as reflected in its official GDP statistics, though very impressive, is actually not exceptional in the historical context of many high-performance East Asian economies. As shown in Table 5.1, Japan had double-digit rates of growth in

Table 5.1 China's Economic Performance Indicators in East Asian Context

	Population in millions, 2010	GNP per Capita		Annual GDP Growth (%)					Annual Export Growth (%)			Manufacturing Exports as % of Total Merchandise Export			Exports as % of GDP		
		Current US$, 2010	PPP-based Constant 2005 International $, 2010	1960–1970	1970–1980	1980–1990	1990–2000	2000–2010	1980–1990	1990–2000	2000–2010	1990	2000	2009	1990	2000	2010 (2009)
China	1,338	4,260	6,810	3.6	6.2	9.3	10.4	10.5	13.1	14.9	20.3	72	88	94	16	23	29
Japan	128	42,130	30,903	9.8	4.5	4.6	1.2	0.8	7.9	2.8	2.0	96	93	88	10	11	(13)
NIEs																	
South Korea	49	19,890	27,027	8.2	7.2	8.7	6.1	4.1	14.0	10.2	10.5	94	91	90	28	39	(50)
Hong Kong	7	32,780	41,714	10.2	9.6	6.7	3.9	4.0	15.3	9.4	6.8	95	95	79	130	143	223
Singapore	5	41,430	51,969	10.0	9.0	7.7	7.2	5.6	10.5	10.1	9.8	72	86	74	177	192	211
ASEAN-4																	
Indonesia	240	2,500	3,880	4.1	7.9	6.4	4.2	5.2	0.7	9.2	9.2	35	57	41	25	41	25
Malaysia	28	7,760	13,186	6.5	7.8	6.0	7.1	4.6	8.6	12.8	7.3	54	80	70	75	120	(96)
Philippines	93	2,060	3,560	4.9	5.9	1.7	2.9	4.8	3.5	17.2	2.6	38	92	86	28	51	35
Thailand	69	4,150	7,672	8.2	6.9	7.8	4.5	4.3	13.5	11.6	11.0	63	75	75	34	67	71
India	1,171	1,340	3,240	6.4	3.0	5.6	5.5	7.8	7.7	9.0	17.7	71	78	67	7	13	18

Sources: World Bank, *World Development Indicators*, http://data.worldbank.org/data-catalog/world-development-indicators.

the 1960s. The four newly industrialized economies (NIEs) of South Korea, Taiwan, Hong Kong, and Singapore had similar high growth for more than three decades—the 1960s through the 1980s—while several economies of the Association of Southeast Asian Nations (ASEAN) also experienced high growth performance in the 1970s and 1980s.

To a large extent, China followed the other successful East Asian economies in pursuing export-led growth. It has differed from the others in its active promotion of process trade—importing components and assembling them into finished products for export. Japan, Korea, Taiwan, and Hong Kong have provided a good deal of FDI for this activity. Foreign invested enterprises (FIEs) shift part of their production to China to take advantage of various beneficial policy measures as well as low labor cost. Export processing was particularly welcome, as the government wanted to minimize the negative shock to relatively inefficient domestic industry. As a result, China's expansion has been associated with a rising share by FIEs, especially for information technology (IT) products.

Since the early 2000s, China's foreign trade has become a critical link in the East Asian supply chains. It can further be argued that China, as shown in Figure 5.5, is becoming an important "integrator" of global production networks. Thus, China's exports embody raw materials, parts and components, technology, and financial services from different Asian economies, converting "Made in Asia" into "Made in China" products for the world markets.

China is a much larger country than its East Asian neighbors. China should have greater internal dynamics to sustain an even longer period of high growth, as it has virtually a whole continent to develop. Skeptical views of China's economy are thus inconsistent with the historical experiences of other East Asian economies.

Figure 5.5 China's Foreign Trade in Global Economic Integration

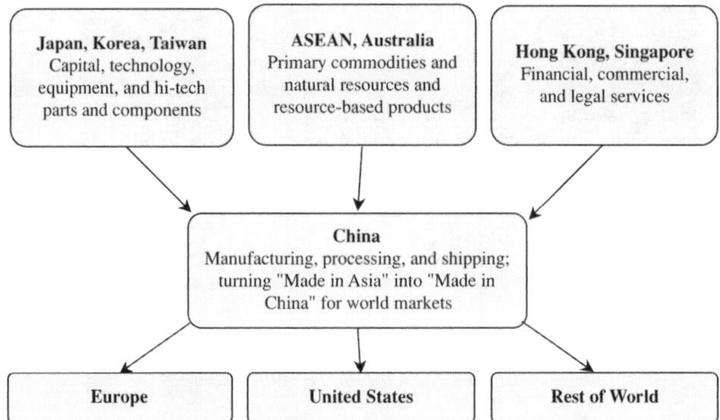

Note: Arrows indicate direction of surplus for each country.

China's Traditional Mixed Economy

China's economy has long involved, and eluded, state planning. From the earliest dynasties, it has centered on agriculture (Chao, 1987; Kamachi, 1990; Perdue, 1987; Brook, 1989). Already during the Qin and Han dynasties, feudalism, with serfs working the land of nobles, had largely ended. Until the Song dynasty, however, large landowners controlled much of the land, expecting their tenants to furnish them with labor and loyalty; this dominance receded slowly in later centuries (see Elvin, 1973). The land produced little surplus and what there was went mostly to enrich landowners and public officials and pay taxes. Agricultural workers were also required to devote long hours in forced corvée labor to fulfill their tax obligations to the state. The state created large factories, mines, franchises, and monopolies to produce and distribute salt, porcelain, armaments, bricks, timber, coal, gold, and copper (Wagner, 2002). Periodically, reforming emperors would attempt to redistribute land or regulate interest rates; those reforms were short-lived. Merchants bought and sold goods largely for sale to public officials and wealthy landowners (Lufrano, 1997; Shiba, 1969; Mann, 1987).

The introduction of double and triple crops of rice each year during the Song dynasty, made possible by new rice strains from Southeast Asia, enabled China to support a much larger population and paved the way for major economic and social changes. Gradually the large estates gave way to smaller owner-occupied plots suitable for intensive agricultural cultivation. Greater agricultural surpluses allowed for an expanded market economy (Shiba, 1969). Already during the Song, a fifth of China's population had moved to towns and cities, which began to produce a great variety of household products on which ordinary people came to depend (see Ma Rong's discussion in Chapter 8; Chao, 1987; Shiba, 1969). Many such goods were produced by family groups who regulated sales and set up apprenticeships open to new residents. In the countryside, large numbers of agricultural families sent some of their members to work in cottage industries producing silk, cotton, and other textiles.

The state issued franchises to brokers, who were authorized to witness all wholesale transactions in agricultural commodities, cotton, and silk. This allowed them to ensure that prices were not fixed by large extended families that came to control such trade in their regions and that proper taxes were paid. These brokers, the holders of franchises for state monopolies, and the public officials to whom taxes were paid, were in a position to accumulate wealth along with the many new merchants and heads of extended agricultural families. They formed a market for a growing array of luxury consumer goods. They could use their surplus capital to extend credit at high interest rates or to run pawnshops, but they failed to invest in new technologies that would spur an industrial revolution. Much of the capital was distributed among merchants and officials as *renqing*—special favors to fulfill the reciprocal obligations owed to family, officials, and special friends (see Chapters 4 and 12). As a result, life did not improve for most members of the populace.

Northern China had been under control of the Mongols since the tenth century; they had reduced a portion of the rural populace there to virtual serfs living on the estates of Mongol nobles. Under Kublai Khan, they tried to extend this system southward. By the seventeenth century, large landowning lineages were running their own schools and charities and keeping much (though gradually declining portions) of the rural populace tied to the land as virtual serfs (Elvin, 1973:235–267; Kamachi, 1990; Huang, 1985:85–87; Huang, 1990; Naquin, 1987:146). But private urban businesses kept growing, still within a controlled atmosphere (Gates, 1996; Deng, 1999; Redding, 1990). Artisans in state-directed, guild-controlled small workshops produced an array of consumer goods. Chapters 3 and 4 discuss the enormous role those goods played in world trade (Pomeranz, 2000). The entrepreneurs defended themselves against excessive demands from officials and fixed wages and prices (see Rowe, 1989; Marme, 2004; Fewsmith, 1983; Faure, 2006; Yang, 2007). Nicholas Kristof and Sheryl WuDunn (1994) cite evidence that these artisans also discouraged the introduction of inventions that might displace their jobs. Pawnshops and brokers extended loans and credit. As Manchu conquerors founded the Qing dynasty, they kept the Confucian system in place but added an important new social and political resource, the *baojia* system. All households were grouped together under the supervision of a headperson, who reported their activities to the authorities and organized them for activities such as building dikes. All members of a *bao* were responsible if one of their members engaged in a criminal activity.

During the nineteenth century, the Europeans built modern infrastructure in China's treaty ports, which in turn led to the establishment of some modern factories. But this did not spark off an industrial revolution. Modern factories were too few, and some actually had the effect of disrupting the rural economy. Peasants started to leave farms to work in coastal factories for low pay. Cheap new factory-made textiles competed with textiles made in villages and thus depressed local economies (Rowe, 1984; Honig, 1986; Bell, 1999; Fewsmith, 1983; Richardson, 2000; Smith, 2001; Feuerwerker, 1996). Regions came under control of warlords who siphoned off taxes from the new enterprises for their own use. Some local enterprises thrived (Zelin, 2006). Clan leaders and absentee landlords often sold goods outside their regions, where they could get higher prices. Whole regions were increasingly ravaged by warfare, often paid for by high taxes on agriculture (Prazniak, 1999). The state granaries, established during the Song dynasty (Will, 1991) to provide peasants with grain during times of hardship, as well as irrigation facilities, waterways, and other public services, were often not maintained. Soil exhaustion, erosion, deforestation, floods, and droughts added to the problems (Perkins, 1969; Perdue, 1987). The new republic established in 1911 tried to address these problems but, as Robert Gamer discusses in Chapter 4, found it hard to take back control from regional warlords and foreign powers and in addition found itself confronting Japanese invaders.

After the 1934 Long March, Mao Zedong led his dwindling communist forces to establish a small base in Yan-an in the arid region of China's northwest. The Japanese invasion of China touched off a strong nationalism, which provided Mao a good opportunity to recoup and expand. Mao promised land to the peasants and he carried out land reform in areas occupied by the communist forces. In effect, this enabled Mao to enlist the support of the peasant masses, to fight first the Japanese invaders and subsequently the Kuomintang. After the Japanese surrender, the urban areas occupied by the Kuomintang were suffering from strikes, social unrest, hyperinflation, and desperate shortages of agricultural and manufactured goods. Such economic and social instability hastened the demise of the Kuomintang regime.

From Revolution to Reform

When Mao Zedong formally declared the formation of the People's Republic of China on October 1, 1949, he found himself taking over an economy poorly adapted to modernization and much ravaged by a long period of war and internal strife. In the cities, his first order of business was to bring down high inflation and reestablish production and distribution of manufactured goods (Spence, 1999; Eckstein, 1977; Hua-yu Li, 2006). He set in place a disciplined bureaucracy and fiscal measures that curbed inflation, and he worked with factory owners, whose plants he had seized, to start up production. In 1953, as the economy had completed this stage of rehabilitation, the government launched the First Five-Year Plan (FYP), which was a typical replica of the Soviet industrialization strategy under Joseph Stalin, putting strong emphasis on the development of some key capital-intensive industries like iron and steel, railroad trains, and agricultural equipment. Large state-owned industries were created throughout China to manufacture these, employing large numbers of workers who would be housed and offered social services and lifetime employment by their employers (guarantees now dubbed the "iron rice bowl") (Frazier, 2002; Bray, 2005; Lu and Perry, 1997; Walder, 1986).

The First FYP was a great success, with the economy growing at an average annual rate of 8.5 percent during the plan period. But Mao was unhappy. He saw inherent "contradictions" in the Soviet development strategy, which was biased against small industry and labor-intensive technology as well as rural development. In Mao's view, the Soviet development strategy was fundamentally at odds with China's basic development conditions and resource endowment, because China had started off as a much more backward economy with a huge population and a lower level of technological development.

Mao started to experiment with his own developmental model. In the rural areas, after land reform, he organized the peasants first into small production teams and agricultural cooperatives and then collectives. Subsequently, he transformed the collectives into the "people's communes" (Eckstein, 1977; Rawski, 1972; Wong, 1973). The height of this collectivization came during the Great Leap Forward in 1958–1960, which called for a simultaneous development of both agriculture and industry, both small and large industry—what Mao propagandists called "walking on two legs." The people's communes mobilized peasants en masse for large-scale capital construction projects like building dams and irrigation systems, as well as making iron and steel by native methods (the so-called backyard furnaces). Not just wasteful of resources, these mass activities also resulted in a serious neglect of farming and cultivation (Tiewes and Sun, 1998; Yang, 1996).

The Great Leap Forward collapsed in 1959 with disastrous economic consequences, particularly a dive in agricultural production and widespread food shortages in the countryside (Chan, Madsen, and Unger, 1984; Tiewes and Sun, 1998; Bramall, 1993; Yang, 1996). The other party leaders tried to return to more traditional production methods, making industrial goods in factories and producing food on collectivized farms, but Mao was undaunted and unconvinced. As Chapter 4 explains, in 1966 he tried again by starting the Great Proletarian Cultural Revolution (Cultural Revolution), which he also used as a means of ridding himself of his dissenting senior party colleagues, who were considered to be revisionist. Thus, millions of students were organized as Red Guards to attack the country's power structures, including government and party establishments. Virtually all senior party leaders except Zhou Enlai were attacked or purged at one time or another by the Red Guards. The excesses of the Cultural Revolution are only now becoming known to the public.

Unlike the Great Leap Forward, the Cultural Revolution was primarily political in nature. In the economic arena, it merely emphasized certain ideological attributes in the overall economic development strategy, such as "self-reliance," "ideology and politics to take precedence over economics," or "ideological incentive to be a substitute for material incentive." Consequently, the Cultural Revolution brought much less direct disruption to economic production, particularly in the rural areas, though it resulted in long-term economic damage to government administration and factory management as well as the country's education system (Riskin, 1987).

However, the Cultural Revolution did leave behind at least one positive legacy. Many of the old guards, like Deng Xiaoping, emerged from this nightmare to finally realize that political and social stability are most crucial to economic development, whereas incessant class struggle and ideological contention were inimical to economic growth. Thus, when Deng finally regained power, he was determined to open a new chapter in China's modern economic history, which he did by launching economic reform and the open-door policy in December 1978 (Wong, 1993). Chapter 4 points to some entrepreneurship quietly spreading amid all the fury, which would help him do so.

The Successful Transition to a Market Economy

China's transition to the market system since the late 1970s has been immensely successful, especially compared to the dismal performance of the economic reform programs of the former Soviet Union and Eastern European countries. Numerous books and articles have been written about the different reform experiences of China and Eastern Europe.[21] Most discussion is focused on the gradual and incremental strategy adopted by China, versus the "Big Bang" approach in Eastern Europe, where major political and economic reforms were initiated side by side. It has also been argued that the initial conditions on the eve of their respective reforms were much more favorable for China than for the other economies in transition; China was less industrialized, its economy was much less tightly planned, and its people had a long history of individual entrepreneurship (Woo, Parker, and Sachs, 1996; Wu, 1994; Lai, 2007; McCormick and Unger, 1995; Wank, 1999; Lin, Cai, and Li, 2001, 2003; Yang, 2007).

In a more concrete sense, the Chinese success was the product of its unique reform strategies, which were carried out with great flexibility ("taking two steps forward and—if in trouble—one step back") and great pragmatism (Liu, 2001; Clegg, Wang, and Berrell, 2007).[22] It can also be argued that China's past reform success owes a great deal to its entrepreneurial style, as opposed to the largely bureaucratic reform process characteristic of the Eastern European approach (Wong, 1995; Sheff, 2002; Chow, 2007:47–90; Cheung, 2002; Liu, 2001; Skoggard, 1996; Tsai, 2004)

From the start, Chinese reformers recognized that there would be no textbooks to teach them how to "un-plan" a socialist economy (Clissold, 2006; Chen, 2003; Zhang, 1996). China's reform process was therefore open-ended, not accompanied by any detailed plans or complicated blueprints. Since reforming a socialist economy inevitably involves a great deal of risk and uncertainty, the best strategy for Chinese reformers was to grope their way around with a gradual trial-and-error approach and then to exploit opportunity for reform breakthroughs, much like true entrepreneurs making their business decisions.

Furthermore, China owed its smooth progress to the right sequencing of reform policies to suit its economic and institutional conditions. Thus China chose to start with agricultural reform first, by instituting the "household responsibility system" (Garnaut, Guo, and Ma, 1996; Croll, 1994; Kelliher, 1992; Zweig, 1997; Lyons, 1994; Lyons and Need, 1994; Powell, 1992; Oi, 1999). The communes returned the control of land to the townships, which in turn leased it to community members (see Oi, 1989b:155–226; Zhou, 1996).

They would initially sell a portion of their crops to state marketing agencies, which in turn sold basic grains and oils to urban dwellers at much lower prices (with the government subsidizing the difference). The rest they could sell privately in farmers' markets. The impact was almost immediate: a rapid growth of agricultural productivity and rural incomes. This in turn led to the mushrooming of township and village enterprises (TVEs), which soon became the driving force for China's economic growth (see Yabuki and Harner, 1999; Zhou, 1996; Wei, 1998; Yang, 1996; Thun, 2006; Wong, Ma, and Yang, 1995; Gore, 1999; Bramall, 2000; Vermeer, Pieke, and Chong, 1997; Walder, 1998; Whiting, 2000; White, 1998; Zhou and White, 1995). These unique nonstate businesses created new jobs, provided many cheap consumer products to meet rising demand, and contributed to regional development. By the late 1990s, the TVEs had accomplished their development objectives, and thus most were subsequently privatized.

In retrospect, the Chinese reform strategy based on trial and error had worked well in the initial phases. But many critical macroeconomic reform measures like taxation, banking, finance, and foreign exchange did not effectively lend themselves to the gradualist approach by experimentation (Deyo, Doner, and Hershberg, 2001; Kim, 2000; Chai and Roy, 2006; Young, 1995; Wang and Hu, 2001; Oi and Walder, 1999; Riedel, Jin, and Gao, 2007). Reforms of these areas are interrelated and have to be dealt with in one blow rather than piecemeal, the strategy of the earlier phase. The recognition of this fact actually paved the way for the Third Party Plenum in November 1993 to adopt the fifty-article "Decision" for a comprehensive reform of China's economic structure, which is, in a way, the Chinese equivalent of the "Big Bang" approach to economic reform (Yabuki and Harner 1999).

Overall, in putting economic liberalization ahead of political liberalization and phasing in reform changes gradually, China was better able to interface political changes with economic reform. In fact, China has followed closely the East Asian tradition of "economic growth first and political changes later" (see Park, 2006). Successful economic reform is used to boost the legitimacy of the political leadership, which is, in turn, under strong pressure to achieve good economic performance. In contrast, Russia put *glasnost* (political reform) before *perestroika* (economic reform). As a result, its vital reform measures were delayed and often bogged down by politics and polemics.

Since the Eighth National People's Congress in March 1993, China has officially become a "socialist market economy," which is conceptually devoid of meaning or just as contradictory as the journalistic term "Red capitalism." But such semantics are insignificant. China's "socialist market economy" increasingly looks like a conventional mixed economy; government controls big industries while leaving many light and consumer-oriented economic activities to a competitive marketplace. In 1994, the prices of over 90 percent of China's consumer goods, 80 percent of raw materials, and 79 percent of agricultural produce were no longer fixed by the state but set by market forces.[23] This, along with the rapid decline of the state sector, has actually rendered the Chinese economy more and more capitalistic in operation.

When economic reforms started in the late 1970s, state-owned industry accounted for over 70 percent of China's gross industrial output (Ash and Kueh, 1996); by 2000, the proportion came down to only 24 percent, with the state ownership mainly confined to the large strategic industries. In terms of operational units, by the end of 1999, state enterprises accounted for 9.7 percent, collective enterprises (including urban collectives and TVEs) 23.5 percent, private (*siying*) and individual (*getihu*) enterprises 21.9 percent, shareholder enterprises 32.5 percent, and others 12.4 percent (Guiheux, 2002).

Up to the mid-1990s, it was not so much the relative decline of the state sector but rather the rapid expansion of the nonstate sector in the Chinese economy that was the most important, or "growing out of the plan" (Naughton 1995; Lin and Song, 2007). Beginning in 1995, Chinese leadership started serious restructuring of its large state-owned sector (Chiu and Lewis, 2006; Fernández and Fernández, 2006; Yusuf, Nabeshima, and Perkins, 2005; Hassard et al., 2006; Holz, 2003; Lin, Cai, and Li, 2001; Naughton, 2007). For ideological reasons, "privately managed" enterprises (*siying qiye*) first appeared in the party document only in 1987. The Thirteenth Party Congress in October 1987 recognized the importance of encouraging the development of the private economy in order to supplement the growth of the state sector. It was only after the Fourteenth Party Congress in 1992 (which adopted the socialist market economy) that the private economy in China was able to develop and expand freely without political hindrances. In September 1997, at the Fifteenth Party Congress, private enterprises were formally legitimized as an "important element" of China's socialist economy, and this was subsequently written into the modified constitution in 1999. At the eightieth anniversary celebration of the Chinese Communist Party (CCP) on July 1, 2001, General Secretary Jiang Zemin went a step further by calling on the party to admit into its ranks capitalists ("outstanding elements" of society such as private entrepreneurs, professionals, technical and managerial personnel from nonstate firms and multinational corporations [MNCs]). Jiang's move to embrace capitalists partly represented his efforts to strengthen the party by ensuring that it can adapt itself to changing economic and social needs (see Chapter 4). It was also partly designed to leave his own ideological legacies (based on his "Three Represents") to the younger Fourth-Generation leaders under Hu Jintao (Wong and Zheng, 2001). Thus, in his keynote address at the Sixteenth Party Congress on November 8, 2002, Jiang urged all ranking party members to "keep pace with the times" by embracing his new theory of "Three Represents" for broadening the social base of the party and admitting capitalists.[24] In short, China has politically and economically gone a long way in developing its own brand of socialism (Guthrie, 2002; Gates, 1996; Hamilton, 2006; Ikels, 1996; Lin, 2004; Sheff, 2002; Brodsgaard and Young, 2001).

In October 1995, the Fifth Plenary Session of the Fourteenth Central Committee of the Chinese Communist Party adopted the Ninth FYP (1996–2000) and the Long-Term Vision of China's Economic and Social Development for 2010. It was envisaged that China's real per capita GDP (total economic output divided by the number of people) by the year 2000 would have quadrupled from the 1980 level, despite the addition of over 300 million people. The goal was, in fact, reached three years earlier than scheduled, in 1997. From 2000 to 2010, China expected to double its per capita income so that within fifteen years it will have developed into a moderately affluent middle-income economy.[25] At the Sixteenth Party Congress in November 2002, Jiang Zemin reiterated that "China would concentrate on building a well-off society (i.e., *xiao-kang*) of a higher standard in an all-round way in the first twenty years of this century."[26] From 2000 to 2010, per capita GDP rose from 7,858 yuan to 29,992 yuan in normal terms, representing an increase of more than 150 percent in real terms, again surpassing the goal.

Traditionally, a five-year plan has been regarded as an integral part of a command communist economy. With the growth of the market since economic reform, the Chinese economy is no longer taking to mandatory central planning. This is very much evidenced by the grossly reduced economic role of the government over the years (Lin, 2004; Leong, 1998). The share of government expenditure declined from 32 percent of GDP in 1979 to 18 percent in 2006. The proportion of industrial output from the state sector declined from 77 percent in 1978 to 33 percent in 1996.[27] The relative importance of state-owned enterprises (SOEs), measured as share of total above-scale industrial output,[28] continues to decline, from 50 percent in 1998 to about 38 percent in 2006. This, along with the inevitable uncertainty that accompanies an increasingly market-oriented Chinese economy, has rendered central planning much less relevant. At best, a five-year plan is to serve only as a kind of "perspective plan," or as a rough indicator of government policy direction. The last few FYPs have already functioned much like indicative plans found in other mixed economies. Indeed, in 2006, the word "Program" has replaced "Plan" in the economic planning for the years 2006–2010 (the Eleventh Five-Year Program) to stress the changing nature of FYPs.

Is High Growth Sustainable?

It is sufficiently clear that China has become the world's most successful "transitional economy" in terms of both dynamic growth and the reform of its economic systems. The next question is: Is China's dynamic economic growth sustainable?

In the 1990s, toward the end of four consecutive years of double-digit rates of growth (1992–1995), the Chinese economy became overheated, with inflation (measured by the consumer price index) rising to a 27 percent record high in 1994 and 14.8 percent in mid-1995. In 1995, a number of tough macroeconomic stabilization measures, including a credit squeeze and the reimposition of control on prices of certain essential commodities, were introduced by then Premier Zhu Rongji to bring down the rampant inflation. By November 1997, inflation had been reduced to 1.1 percent, with only a small reduction in economic growth, which was still 9 percent for 1997. In common economic parlance, the Chinese economy achieved a "soft landing."

Nonetheless, doubts about the sustainability of China's rapid economic growth have long existed. In the late 1990s, affected by the Asian Financial Crisis, China's growth slid down from its peak of 14.2 percent in 1992 to just 7.6 percent in 1999. While economic downturns had hit other Southeast Asian economies much more severely, the Chinese government had countered sluggish domestic consumption demand by artificially priming the economy with a vigorous program of domestic fixed-asset investment (Park, 2006). Economic growth recovered gradually to reach 9.1 percent in 2002. Since then, fueled by continued growth in fixed asset investment and the post-WTO surge in external demand, economic growth remained at more than 10 percent a year for five consecutive years, between 2002 and 2007. Since late 2008, the world economy has been hit by an even more serious financial and economic crisis. As China's economy decelerated, from 14.2 percent in 2007 to 9.6 percent in 2008, 9.2 percent in 2009, 10.4 percent in 2010 and 9.2 percent in 2011, the question rose again. Can China's high growth be taken for granted? Can China again achieve a soft landing?

It should be noted that even before the reform, the Chinese economy was growing at a rather modest rate of 5.7 percent (during 1952–1978), despite all its inherent socialist economic inefficiencies and the disruptions caused by numerous political campaigns.[29] Moreover, reform has set free the latent dynamic economic and social forces to fuel China's further economic growth. This expansion can be readily analyzed from both demand and supply side perspectives.

On the demand side, China's high economic growth stems from its high levels of domestic investment, which are matched by equally high levels of domestic savings. According to the World Bank, China's gross capital formation grew at 10.2 percent in the 1990s and 13.3 percent in the 2000s, and this gave rise to GDP growth of 10.4 percent and 10.5 percent, respectively. In 2010, China's gross domestic savings as a proportion of its GDP was 50 percent, while its gross capital formation was 45 percent. Thus, China's domestic investment and domestic savings levels are among the highest in the world.[30] High investment and high savings creates what may be called the "virtuous circle of growth": high savings, high investment, high output and export growth, high GDP growth, and then high savings. It provides the simplest explanation of the arithmetic of China's high economic growth. This is in fact similar to the high growth experience of Hong Kong, Taiwan, South Korea, and Singapore (Brodsgaard and Young, 2001; Deyo, Doner, and Hershberg, 2001).

Still very much a developing economy, China certainly has need for infrastructural investment in transportation, communications, ports, airports, and power plants. Figure 5.6 captures the major sources of China's growth for the period 1990–2010. External demand, measured by net exports, plays a relatively minor role in China's economic growth (Bardhan, 2010). For domestic demand, fixed investment is most crucial. During the heady years of double-digit rates of growth in the early 1990s, fixed asset investment increased by over 20 percent a year and was the major source of China's GDP growth. Between the late 1990s and early 2000s, China's economic growth was less investment-driven, while exports and household consumption were becoming increasingly more important. Since the early 2000s, however, investment has again become the most important source of growth. This is especially true after 2008 when the government instituted a strong stimulus package to avert a sharp slowdown in face of a global economic crisis.

Apart from fixed investment, China still has a potential for increasing domestic consumption as a source of its future growth, particularly in the rural areas and small towns, where millions of peasants are in need of basic household consumer durables like televisions, refrigerators, and cell phones. In the

Figure 5.6 Contribution of Domestic Demand and External Demand to China's GDP Growth, 1990–2010

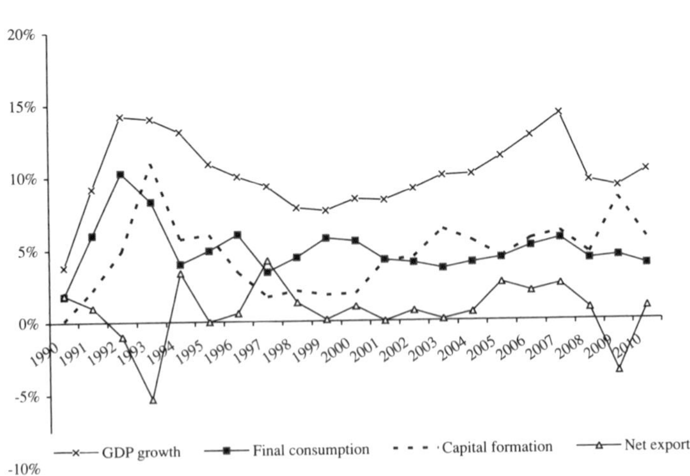

Source: China Statistical Abstract 2011 (Beijing: China Statistical Press).

more developed coastal region, economic affluence has created a burgeoning middle class, whose consumption of those basic consumer durables has by and large been satisfied. However, the affluent urban middle class are now shifting their consumption patterns toward residential housing, household goods, and automobiles, which can be a new source of consumption demand growth (Fleisher et al., 2008; McGregor, 2007; Prestowitz, 2005; Latham, Thompson, and Klein, 2006; Dikotter and Dwyer, 2007). Apart from the consumption of goods, demand for services such as education and vacations has also been rising rapidly in recent years. The government has actively promoted domestic tourism by encouraging people to take extended leave for the Chinese New Year (usually falling in February), Labor Day (May), and National Day (October) in order to boost the so-called holiday economy. Total domestic travelers rose from 280 million in 1990 to 2.1 billion in 2010.

In the long run, the Chinese economy has to grow mainly by relying on domestic demand, especially on household consumption. This is different from China's smaller Asian neighbors, whose economic growth can be mainly propelled by export growth or external demand. Since economic reform began in 1978, as mentioned earlier, China's exports have been growing at an average annual rate of 18 percent, and this provides additional impetus for China's economic growth. However, the world market simply cannot continue to absorb such a massive onslaught of manufactured goods from China. It is therefore fortunate for China that its sheer size and diversity can provide sufficient internal dynamics to generate its own growth in the long run.

Viewed from the supply side, China's economic growth can also be sustained on its own, while at probably a slower rate, by a growing labor force and increasing productivity. As has happened to Japan and South Korea before, growth in productivity is associated with the shift of labor from low-productivity agriculture to high-productivity manufacturing. In China, the rural sector has been a huge reservoir of millions of underemployed laborers (commonly known among economists as "rural disguised unemployment"). Although a large portion of the underemployed rural laborers have been gradually reallocated into the modern industrial sector, agriculture still accounted for 38 percent of China's total labor force in 2010, while contributing only 10 percent of GDP. This suggests that rural underemployment persists and can be an important source of future economic growth.

However, the key element on the supply side for long-term sustainable growth lies in productivity improvement. Clearly, continuing high economic growth cannot be sustained by just dumping more and more capital (i.e., more fixed investment) into an increasingly large labor force. What is more crucial to the process of sustained economic growth is the condition of technological progress resulting from the acquisition of knowledge. Such is the "endogenous growth theory," which emphasizes improvement in productivity through investment in human capital.[31]

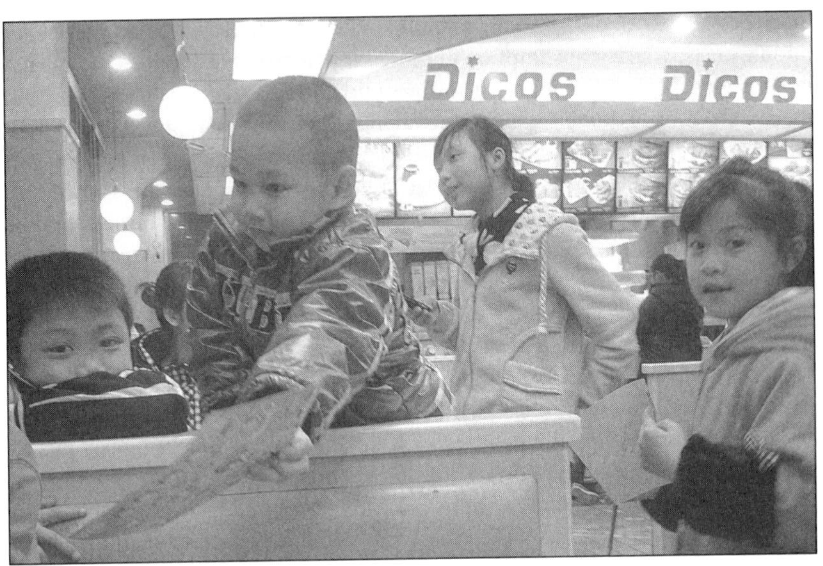

Robert E. Gamer

Children in a fast food restaurant in Kaili, Guizhou.

Paul Krugman has argued that East Asian growth has been based exclusively on the accumulation of capital per worker rather than on increases in output per worker, that is, productivity growth. Accordingly, he argued that East Asian growth could be a flawed strategy of growth without improvement in total factor productivity (TFP)—the amount of measured overall growth that cannot be explained by such factors as capital or labor—and would eventually bring about a collapse in growth as in the former Soviet Union (Krugman, 1994). His observation stirred up a lively debate among economists and commentators. Several researchers argued that Krugman exaggerated the TFP problem of East Asia and that many East Asian economies have in fact experienced real TFP growth.[32]

Productivity or technological progress is admittedly a nebulous concept, which is also empirically difficult to measure or quantify. In the case of China, for instance, its high growth since 1978 has indeed been accompanied by substantial productivity gains.[33] For example, in accounting for China's 9.4 percent growth between 1978 and 1995, the World Bank has identified that 3.5 percentage points, 0.8 percentage points, and 0.7 percentage points were contributed by capital formation, human capital improvement, and labor force increases, respectively. This leaves the unexplained share of growth at 46 percent, or 4.3 percentage points, which is unusually large, compared to South Korea and Japan for the appropriate periods. A substantial part of this residual portion could be the TFP improvement or efficiency increase, which was generated from economic reform and the open-door policy.[34] In other words, China's high growth for the past three decades has been sustained by a productivity boom (see Brandt and Rawski, 2008:829–886).

The argument runs as follows. High savings and high investment alone would not have generated such sustained high growth for China. Operating under socialist planning before 1978, China also had relatively high savings and high investment by controlling consumption. But China's average annual growth during 1952–1978 was considerably lower, at around 5.7 percent, which was achieved with gross inefficiency coupled with a great deal of fluctuation. After 1978, by introducing market forces to economic decisionmaking, economic reforms had brought about greater allocative efficiency. Moreover, by reintegrating China into the global economy, the open-door policy had exposed China to greater external competitive pressures (Gallagher, 2005; Shou, 2010). These have led to higher TFP growth, and the economy started to take off by consistently chalking up near double-digit rates of growth (Nazrul, Dai, and Sakamoto, 2006).[35]

All in all, we can be justifiably optimistic about the overall growth prospects of China's economy over the medium and long run. In many ways, it is developing in a manner similar to the past growth pattern of other high-performance East Asian economies. But, unlike them, China is a vast country with a huge resource base and a huge domestic market. Up to then, most growth had been concentrated in the coastal region, which stood to gain the most from Deng's open-door policy. China's new frontiers of growth could come from its interior.

The turning point in the strategy came in 1999. Faced with overinvestment and overproduction in the coastal region, Chinese policymakers realized the need to spread development into the country's less-developed interior so as to cultivate new sources of economic growth. The western region, comprising the ten provinces of Xinjiang, Gansu, Qinghai, Ningxia, Shaanxi, Tibet, Sichuan, Yunnan, Guizhou, and Chongqing, occupied 57 percent of China's total area but accounted for only 23 percent of China's total population and only about 14 percent of China's total GDP. Furthermore, the whole western region in 1999 absorbed only 12 percent of the country's total domestic investment and 3 percent of the country's total FDI.[36] Clearly economic development had bypassed the western region. Viewed from a different angle, the western region provided new growth opportunities.

In January 2000, the State Council set up a high-level interministerial Western Development Committee, headed by Premier Zhu Rongji. The committee was charged with the mission of planning long-term development strategies to guide China's western development over the next fifteen years (Lu and Neilson, 2004). The involvement of Premier Zhu underscored China's determination to develop its western region as its new frontier for future development.[37] Clearly, it will take years for China to exhaust its total development potential. So far, the go-west campaign has not yet produced significant economic outcome. While the shares of the western ten provinces in total fixed asset investment and in total inward FDI increased modestly to 19 percent and 7 percent in 2010, respectively, they still accounted for only 15 percent of China's GDP. However, the roads, railroad lines, airports, power plants, commercial buildings, and rural development schemes being generated by this initiative (discussed in Chapters 1, 4, and 8) are laying the groundwork for future growth in that ratio.

Overcoming Challenges and Constraints

Thus, China's economy rests on a strong footing, favorable to continuing growth. However, it also faces some serious problems—problems that China's government is addressing. We now turn to discuss these problems.

Human Resource Development

First, China's population growth has been slowing down considerably from the average natural growth rate of 1.5 percent in the 1980s to 1.0 percent in the 1990s and further to 5.6 percent in the 2000s,[38] due in part to the successful implementation of its "one-child policy" (discussed in Chapter 8). Accordingly, China's total fertility rate came down from 2.5 in 1980 to 1.6 in recent years, which is well below the replacement level of fertility. This also means that China's population is not just slowing down in growth but could eventually reach zero growth after a certain time lag. But before this, the population will become rapidly aging during the second decade of the twenty-first century. This will change its labor force structure and pose an ultimate constraint on industrial development in the longer run.

Second, as shown in Table 5.2, China's human resource development is still weak compared to other leading countries in East Asia (Harney, 2008). China's adult illiteracy in 2009 stood at 6 percent, down from 9 percent in 2000. This translates into some 64 million people who cannot read and write (Li, 2004). In the same year, only 25 percent of the relevant age group in China was receiving tertiary education (Alon and McIntyre, 2005), compared to 90 percent in South Korea, 59 percent in Japan, 13 percent in India, 84 percent in Taiwan, and 44 percent in Singapore.[39] This may, in time, constrain attempts to restructure and upgrade the Chinese economy into more skill-intensive and higher value-added activities. In short, China's manpower gaps, in quantitative as well as in qualitative terms, could well operate to moderate its long-term growth potential.

The WTO and Globalization

On December 11, 2001, China was formally admitted into the World Trade Organization as its 143rd member, ending China's fifteen years of efforts to

Table 5.2 China's Social Indicators in East Asian Context

	Total Fertility Rate (%), 2009	Life Expectancy at Birth (years), 2009	Infant Mortality Rate (per 1,000 births), 2005	Physicians (per 1,000 people)	Adult Illiteracy Rate (%), 2009	Percentage of Age Group Enrolled in School			Human Development Index	
						Primary, 2009	Secondary, 2009	Tertiary, 2009	HDI	World Ranking, 2010
China	1.61	73	15.8	707 (2009)	6	113	78	25	0.663	89
Japan	1.37	83	2.4	485 (2006)	1 (2005)	103	101	59	0.884	11
NIEs										
South Korea	1.15	80	4.2	508 (2008)	2 (2005)	104	97	100	0.877	12
Hong Kong	1.04	83	2	758 (1995)	7 (2005)	104	82	57	0.862	21
Singapore	1.22	81	2.1	546 (2009)	5				0.846	27
ASEAN-4										
Indonesia	2.15	68	27.2	3,472 (2007)	8 (2008)	121	79	24	0.600	108
Malaysia	2.67	74	5.4	1,063 (2008)	8	95 (2008)	69 (2008)	26 (2008)	0.744	57
Philippines	3.19	68	23.2	867 (2004)	5 (2008)	110 (2008)	82 (2008)	29 (2008)	0.638	97
Thailand	1.60	74	11.2	3,460 (2004)	6 (2005)	91	76	45	0.654	92
India	2.66	65	48.2	1,669 (2005)	37 (2006)	117 (2008)	60 (2008)	13 (2007)	0.519	119
Average of low-income countries	4.14	58	69.7	5,319 (2009)	39	104	39	7		
Average of middle-income countries	2.37	69	38.0	1,242 (2009)	17	109	69	24		

Sources: World Bank, *World Development Indicators*, http://data.worldbank.org/data-catalog/world-development-indicators; World Bank, *World Development Report*, various years; UN Development Programme, *Human Development Report*, various years, http://hdr.undp.org/en/statistics.

Note: Human Development Index combines life expectancy, educational attainment, and income indicators to give a composite measure of human development.

join this multilateral trading body. There have since been numerous discussions and debates on the impact of WTO membership on China's overall economy and its sectors (Cass, Williams, and Barker, 2003; Panitchpakti and Clifford, 2002; Moore, 2002; Zweig, 2002; Bao, Lin, and Zhao, 2006; Bhattasasalis, Li, and Martin, 2004; Ching and Ching, 2003; Chu and Wong, 2007; Fung, Pei, and Zhang, 2006; Kong, 2002). Inevitably, there are both opportunities and risks, and the outcome depends very much on how well China responds to global economic challenges brought about by its WTO membership and how well the rest of the world responds to China's integration into the world trading system.

Even before China's formal accession into the WTO, the country already stepped up its efforts to intensify its trade reforms, including lowering tariff rates and merging the dual exchange rate. Reforms also started in the financial sector to meet the upcoming WTO obligations. In anticipation of China's imminent WTO membership, foreign firms from Taiwan, South Korea, and Japan, as well as from Western countries, flocked to China to set up "beachheads" (Bramson, 2000; Buderi and Huang, 2006; Chang and Goldstein, 2007; Gu, 2006; Guo, 2006; Huang, 2005; Kynge, 2006; Mann, 1997; Studwell, 2002; Luo, 2001; Ambler and Witzel, 2003; Blackman, 2001; Watson, 2006; Chan, 2011). In 2001, FDI to China surged to an all-time high of US$47 billion. The surge has since continued, and China's annual inward FDI reached $60 billion in 2005 and $109 billion in 2010 (see Figure 5.3).

Many foreign businesses saw China's WTO accession as a good opportunity to establish a stronghold in the China market. Starting from January 1, 2002, China reduced its average tariff rate to 12 percent from the then existing 15.3 percent. By 2009, the average (bound) tariff level had come down to 10 percent: 15.7 for agricultural products and 9.2 for nonagricultural products. In 2008, trade-weighted average tariff rate was less than 4.3 percent (10.3 percent for agricultural products and 4.0 percent for nonagricultural products).[40]

In the early 2000s, many foreign and Chinese commentators were also concerned about the disruptive WTO effects: How could China's ailing state-owned enterprises and inefficient financial sector survive foreign competition? What will be the fate of millions of small-business owners and small-scale farmers (Chen and Song, 2006; Heberer, 2007; Shih, 2009)?

To cope with the adverse WTO impact, the Chinese government continued its efforts to reform the economy. In fact, WTO accession had served as an external force to push for China's economic reform and restructuring, as well as increasing integration with the world economy. With a grace period of three to five years before full implementation of WTO obligations, China implemented various trade and investment liberalization measures to prepare its sectors to compete domestically and internationally for the post-WTO era.

More importantly, as indicated earlier in this chapter, the external balance of the Chinese economy has been exceptionally strong: (1) for many years in a row, China has continued to chalk up a huge trade surplus; (2) the influx of FDI has continued unabated, and will continue for at least a number of years; and (3) China's total foreign exchange reserves have kept on rising. Not surprisingly, China was able to manage its post-WTO economy with full confidence.

Indeed, WTO membership represents a new phase in China's open-door policy, often referred to as the third wave of China's opening up to the world. Previously, China's open-door policy was based on selective and unilateral liberalization, but since the early 2000s, its policy has become more comprehensive and rule-based liberalization. Such extensive liberalization serves to promote China's overall economic efficiency through greater competition and technological progress (Gallagher, 2005; Garnaut et al., 2005; Jeffries, 2010:385–596). On the one hand, as a WTO member, China now has easier access to world markets for its exports, and Chinese products are subjected to less unfair treatment or discrimination in certain markets. On the other hand, as China is committed to open its domestic market, many Chinese industries, particularly those SOEs in less competitive sectors such as chemicals, automobiles, pharmaceuticals, and agriculture, face fierce competition (Holz, 2003; Wedeman, 2003). Service industries such as banking, insurance, and telecommunications, which used to be highly protected, are particularly vulnerable. This means that China needs to urgently deal with the remaining reform problems in connection with its SOEs and state banks (Chiu and Lewis, 2006; Yang, 2006; Tong, 2005; Tong and Zheng, 2006).

Until the late 1990s and early 2000s, progress on reforming China's SOEs and the financial sector had been slow (Chan, Fung, and Liu, 2007; Walter and Howie, 2010). Efforts to reform state enterprises were initially directed at improving their efficiency by restructuring management, which included introducing measures to define enterprise rights under law and to free management from government supervision. This culminated in the promulgation, on July 1, 1994, of a new Company Law, which provides the needed legal framework for the formation of "shareholding companies," the Chinese method of privatization (Oi and Walder, 1999).

However, mere focus on ownership reform cannot ensure the efficiency and profitability of state enterprises, which eventually have to go through a fundamental management reform in order to transform SOEs into profit-maximizing companies (Yi and Ye, 2003; Moore, 2002; Gallagher, 2005; Brown, Waldron, and Longworth, 2005; Dutta, 2005; Engardio, 2007; Tong and Liang, 2004; Jeffries, 2010:287–385). In other words, state enterprises would ultimately have to operate under "hard budget constraints," where hopelessly unprofitable state enterprises have to be shut down. China passed a bankruptcy law as early as 1986; but before 1997, the government was extremely reluctant to allow the ailing state enterprises to fold up for fear of social instability that would result from massive layoffs (*xiagang*).

Since 1997, Beijing's basic strategy for reform of state enterprises has been *zhua-da fang-xiao* (grasp the large and let go of the small), which enabled the government to get rid of many nonstrategic and loss-making small and medium-sized SOEs (Lin, Cai, and Li, 2001). Moreover, in fulfilling its commitment to open its banking sector, the government has speeded up the restructuring of state banks since 2001.

The state-owned commercial banks had incurred a high proportion of nonperforming loans (NPLs) because of political pressures to lend to SOEs ("policy lending"). In fact, NPLs of China's four state banks increased from 21.4 percent in 1995 to 29.2 percent in 2000. To cope with rising NPLs, the government set up four state-run assets management corporations (AMCs) in 2000, one for each of the four big state banks, and introduced the "debt-equity" swap scheme. By 2001, the level of NPLs was brought down to 25.4 percent. Nonetheless, in August 2002, the People's Bank of China admitted that China's total NPLs still amounted to 18 percent of its GDP.[41] Some Western credit-rating agencies gave much higher estimates.[42] The government implemented numerous other measures as well, including the writing off of US$500 billion of the NPLs, the corporatization and ownership diversification of the state-owned commercial banks, and the participation of foreign banks in restructuring the banking sector (Jeffries, 2010:135–286). As a result, the level of NPLs in the state commercial banks was reduced to less than 6 percent in 2008, on official account.[43] There are also signs that the corporate governance of the state banks has been significantly improved and strengthened. All four state-owned banks—the Industrial and Commercial Bank of China (ICBC), the Bank of China (BOC), the People's Construction Bank of China (CCB), and the Agriculture Bank of China (ABC)—have already been listed on the Shanghai Stock Exchange and/or the Hong Kong Stock Exchange.

Moreover, the government can take comfort from the fact that Chinese people are big savers, leaving huge deposits in the banking system: total household savings deposits in banks amounted to over 30 trillion yuan in 2010—that is, 77 percent of total GDP. As the economy has been growing at double-digit rates each year, the accumulated bad loans could be gradually absorbed, as long as the new lending (discussed in the next section) is based on sound economic principles.

Strengthening and restructuring the state sector, the weakest link of China's economy, have helped China to better weather the adverse effects of increased global competition, though it is difficult in practice to pinpoint the exact impact of WTO membership on various sectors. Apart from the lack of reliable data, the winners and losers cannot be determined with any certainty, as much depends not only on how an industry restructures or positions itself for post-WTO challenges, but also on the dynamism of external demand and potential trade conflicts. Many new opportunities do present themselves to foreign firms, as the Chinese economy has sustained high growth for a sustained long period, but risks, such as lax enforcement of intellectual property rights, abound (Mann, 1997; Mertha, 2005; Navarro, 2006:21–45; Shenkar, 2006:81–100; Tse, 2010; Cheung, 2011). Similarly, some Chinese SOEs would fold up under mounting foreign competition; but most manage to survive, as they continue to enjoy many of the existing "native" competitive advantages.

Rising Unemployment

One serious concern to Beijing in post-WTO China is the growing structural unemployment (Lee and Warner, 2006; Sato and Li, 2006). As the economy is undergoing more vigorous macroeconomic reform and as businesses are forced to restructure for greater efficiency in order to meet WTO challenges, there have been more layoffs (Chan, 2001; Lee and Warner, 2006). This pool of unemployed competing for jobs in turn holds down wages, which makes it difficult to expand domestic consumption; people do not have enough discretionary income to spend on new goods and services, especially automobiles and housing.

Since 1997, when Premier Zhu Rongji stepped up SOE reform, about 7–8 million urban workers have been laid off every year under the *xiagang* scheme (actually a disguised means of laying off redundant workers). By mid-2002, about 24 million workers had been laid off as their SOEs were restructured. In 2004, for example, those unemployed due to bankruptcy and layoff accounted for half of all urban registered unemployment.[44] At the same time, about 6 to 8 million new jobs have been created every year since 1997, which, however, is inadequate to meet the rising number of new entrants to the labor force (roughly about 10 million a year), not to mention the numerous underemployed rural laborers ("disguised unemployment").

For years, the official "registered" urban unemployment rate stayed at a very low level, edging up from 1.8 percent in 1985 to 3.6 percent in 2001; it increased to 4.3 percent in 2003, the highest since 1981, and has since fluctuated at between 4.0 and 4.3. However, China's actual urban unemployment rate realistically should be significantly higher, if the past laid-off workers from SOEs are included, to reach 8 to 10 percent for the years 1996–2002 when the number of laid-off workers was the largest.[45] A survey of more than 7,000 people in mid-2008 by the Chinese Academy of Social Sciences found that 9.4 percent of its urban sample would be considered "economically active" but without work—that is, formally unemployed.[46]

That situation persists. And besides such open urban unemployment, there is also growing rural underemployment or disguised rural unemployment, aggravated by China's WTO membership. Many small farmers in China suffer as a result of greater competition from the world's more efficient agricultural producers. In recent years, rural discontent has been rising in many areas due to widening rural-urban income inequalities as well as local misgovernment. Indeed, there have been rising incidents of labor protests in recent years (discussed in Chapter 4), both in the rust belt in the northeast and in the vibrant southeast of China (Lee, 2007).

The Chinese government has started to pay attention to human resource development programs, including job retraining. The government has also stepped up its social security reform in recent years. For example, efforts to establish a national minimum living guarantee scheme (*dibao*) for urban residents started in 1993. The scheme was officially launched in 2000, following the promulgation of the Minimum Living Guarantee Ordinance in 1999. The number of people included in the scheme rose from 4.0 million in 2000 to around 22 million since 2003.[47] A similar scheme for rural residents was later enacted, and the number of people covered rose from less than 5 million in 2004 to over 52 million in 2010. Steps are also being taken to establish pension systems for urban and rural residents and insurance schemes for unemployment, health care, and work-related injuries (Hu, 2006:97–207). The vast majority of workers are still not covered by these programs. Chapter 8 discusses this more fully.

In the end, the government still depends on sustaining high economic growth to ameliorate the unemployment problem. Not surprisingly, the government will always stand ready to prime the economy through massive spending on infrastructural investment and speculative loans to stimulate real estate construction whenever signs of economic slowdown appear, as they did during the 2008 world economic recession; this sharply diminished China's exports and new FDI (see Figures 5.1, 5.2, 5.3, and 5.6). Chinese bank loans rose from 97 percent of GDP in 2008 to 120 percent of the still higher GDP in 2011.[48] Much of this US$7.5 trillion in loans can become nonperforming if the massive new blocks of condominiums built purely on speculation do not sell and the new toll roads and high-speed trains do not attract enough traffic. With the price of housing inflating five to ten times during the 2000s, with food and household goods costing more, with unemployment rising, and with wages stagnating, the market for these units is limited. Chapter 4 discusses this dynamic in greater detail. It raises concerns among many Chinese citizens, and foreign journalists and bankers, about the danger of a "hard landing" for China's economy if combined with a continuing worldwide downturn that once again lowers demand for China's exports. For the first time since 1998, China's foreign exchange reserves declined during the fourth quarter of 2011 as investors worried about China's economic future. China's government and banks have enough assets to soften such a landing, and are keenly focused on finding solutions. But they worry about what hardships and instability such a combination of factors might create (Sharma, 2012).

Social Constraints

China's rapid economic growth in recent years has given rise to many negative social externalities, from rising social expectations to rising crime and ris-

Robert E. Gamer

Long rows of high-rise condos, and superhighways, are proliferating in cities throughout China.

ing superstition. As a result of the unprecedented growth of materialism, a sense of general "moral crisis" is sweeping China. To what extent does all this represent a transitional phenomenon? Will it go away by itself once the economy and society develop further?

Most China scholars take the view that many of those negative social externalities may create frictions in the economic growth process, but they will not, on their own, be serious enough to disrupt the development process. Chinese authorities understandably place a high priority on maintaining social order, which is crucial for economic growth and economic reform. It is often the case that the best way to deal with the by-products of rapid economic growth is to continue with rapid economic growth, which will generate more resources to deal with social problems.

However, there are other critical problems that will create strains in Chinese society even with continuing high economic growth. First, the leadership must mobilize all its institutional resources to combat corruption, which is rampant in China today[49] (Wang, 2001; Kwong, 1997; Oi, 1989a). Economic reform in all transitional economies generates opportunities for extortion, profiteering, and open graft and corruption. But the problem in China is becoming so serious that it threatens to undermine the social fabric of the country as well as the moral authority of the CCP. In late 2010, the Chinese government issued its first Anticorruption White Paper.[50] It stated that within the first eleven months of that year, a total of 119,000 investigations led to administrative and party disciplinary punishments on 113,000 individuals. Among them, 4,332 people were transferred to the judicial system. That is just the tip of the iceberg.

More than a mere social evil, corruption hampers economic growth by increasing transaction costs and reducing efficiency (Kwong, 1997; Zweig, 2002; Hughes, 2002; Chu, 2006; McGregor, 2007). Rampant corruption also slows trade and investment (Oi, 1989a; Yan, 2004; Luo, 2007; McGregor, 2007). Although there have been numerous publicized anticorruption cases, there is little sign that the problem is sufficiently and effectively addressed.

A second major social issue with serious economic and political consequences is the growing income disparity between urban and rural areas, or between industrial and agricultural sectors. Rural income has grown significantly slower then urban income. Between 1998 and 2010, average rural household net per capita income increased by an annual rate of 6.3 percent (in real terms), from 2,161 yuan to 5,919 yuan. In the same period, average urban household disposable income per capita increased by 9.4 percent a year, from 5,425 yuan to 19,109 yuan. At the start of economic reform in 1978, the rural-urban per capita income gap was 1 to 2.57. By 2010, the gap had increased to 1 to 3.23, implying that China's pattern of economic growth has been blatantly urban-biased. Income gaps have also widened within cities and within the countryside. Among urban dwellers, the ratio of per capita disposable income of the top 20 percent to the bottom 20 percent went up from 3.4 in 1999 to 5.4 in 2010. Among rural dwellers, the figure rose from 6.5 in 2000 to 7.1 in 2010.

The economic plight of the rural people is actually much worse than indicated by the aggregate official statistics (Riskin, Zhou, and Li, 2001). First, the rural household income is not "disposable income" as for the urban dwellers, but "gross income," which includes "imputed elements" of food and livestock as well as working capital like payment for seed and fertilizer for the next production period. Second, unlike urban households, rural households receive little state welfare for education, housing, and medical care. Worse still, the rural population is subjected to burdensome levies and taxes, both lawful and unlawful. While agricultural levies have been gradually abandoned since 2004, the resulting reduction of local government revenue may inevitably lead to either higher unlawful burdens or lower public services.

In short, while China's high post-1978 economic growth has brought about a perceptible measure of material affluence to the urban sector, particularly to the middle class in the many large coastal cities, the same is not true for the masses in the rural areas, particularly those in the interior provinces; and rural income growth for the past few years has actually stagnated (Golley, 2007). To escape poverty and search for a better future, some 260 million young peasants have flocked to the urban areas to seek nonfarm employment as migrant labor; in the 1990s, these peasants were called the *liudong renkou* ("floating population") (Zhang, 2001; Murphy, 2002). However, instead of economically and socially absorbing the surplus rural labor as in other industrial countries during their industrialization process, the Chinese urban sector has continued to use the old practice of *hukou* (household registration) to discriminate against rural migrant labor, hence aggravating the rural problem (see Chapters 4 and 8).

Not surprisingly, since the early 2000s, the rural problem has become a hotly debated subject in China. Most Chinese discussion of the rural problem involves three complicated aspects (the *san-nong* issue): the agricultural problem (*nongye*); the village problem (*nongcun*); and the peasant problem (*nongmin*). The agricultural problem is mainly an economic issue involving food production and agricultural trade, while the village problem is largely caused by the rapid deterioration of the overall economic and social conditions in the countryside as a result of China's rapid economic modernization (Dong, Song, and Zhang, 2006). The peasants also have a problem, basically because their income is not rising fast enough to keep pace with their increasing output.

China today has by and large resolved its food production problem. As a result of rising agricultural productivity brought about by greater mechanization and technological progress, China has developed the capacity to feed itself, despite its growing population and shrinking cultivated acreage. Ironically, increased agricultural productivity has rendered many rural laborers redundant, so they must leave their village for nonfarm employment. The share of agricultural activity in employment, GDP, and exports is declining.

In a nutshell, the whole rural problem is basically a development problem. Many of the economic and social problems in the rural areas can only be resolved by further development of the nonfarm sectors. In the short run, however, the government can devise more effective policy measures to manage the rural decline without squeezing the peasants too hard and too fast. The government can also channel some resources back to the rural areas for the building of social infrastructure such as schools and health care facilities, not just to relieve rural poverty but also to prepare the young peasants for future nonfarm employment.

In reality, the Chinese leadership in the past has done precious little to help the peasants. Mao and most of his Long March comrades were either peasants in origin or highly experienced in working with the peasants. China's younger generation of leaders, in contrast, are basically urban intellectuals, with little or no rural background in their previous careers. Since 2003, when the Hu-Wen leadership came to power, there has been a serious discussion about shifting the development focus from purely growth-centered to a more balanced approach, or to what is referred to as the "scientific views of development." The government's attention has been increasingly focused on the many negative consequences of China's past unbridled economic growth, including rural poverty and widening income disparities. Chapters 4 and 8 discuss some of the programs they initiated.

Physical Constraints to Long-Term Growth

In the longer run, physical constraints may be the biggest challenge to China's growth and development. The country's worsening air and water pollution, and lowering of water tables, combined with increasing droughts and melting glaciers, threaten its food production and the health of its people (Ho and Vermeer, 2006; Song and Woo, 2008). And it is becoming increasingly dependent on imported oil, food, and natural gas to fuel economic growth. Chapter 9 deals with all these issues in greater detail.

When it comes to energy, China still enjoys a relatively low degree of external dependency. Overall, net energy imports, measured by million tons of standard coal, amounted to 13 percent of total energy consumption in 2009, up from less than 5 percent in the early 2000s,[51] but still much lower than that of other East Asian economies. For crude oil, however, China's degree of external dependency has risen sharply in recent years, from less than 30 percent in the early 2000s to over 50 percent in 2009.[52]

China has become a major contributor to global greenhouse emissions. Having surpassed the United States as the world's largest emitter of CO_2, the country is facing increasing pressure to take more action to reduce greenhouse emissions.[53]

This is due largely to concerns over the rapid deterioration of China's own environment and its social as well as economic implications. In 2004, China experimented with computing a crude "Green GDP" index, which shows that the cost of pollution in 2004 was about 3 percent of GDP; water and air pollution were the most significant contributors.[54] According to a report by China's Environmental Protection Ministry, one-third of 113 cities surveyed failed to meet the national air standards in 2009. A 2011 report from the World Health Organization, that looked at data from about 1,100 cities worldwide, found that the average levels of particulate matter in the air in China was nearly five times higher than WHO air quality standards—much worse than the world average of about three and half times higher.

The Chinese government has reinforced its efforts to tackle environmental issues. During the March 2008 National People's Congress in Beijing, the State Environmental Protection Administration (SEPA) was upgraded to the Ministry of Environmental Protection (MOEP), a cabinet-level ministry under the State Council. Also in 2008, a number of targets on reducing pollution were specified for the period 2006–2010 (Jeffries, 2010:613–648). One is to reduce chemical oxygen demand (COD) in water and sulphur dioxide (SO_2) emissions, each by 2 percent a year, or 10 percent by 2010, to reduce acid rain. The Eleventh Five-Year Program (2006–2010) also aimed to reduce energy consumption by 20 percent per unit of GDP. By closing hundreds of small inefficient coal-fired plants and introducing scrubbers and desulfurization facilities to all state-owned coal-fired plants and factories, these targets were largely met.[55] By 2010, energy consumption per unit of GDP went down by 19.1 percent, slightly short of the government's objective. SO_2 emissions and COD in water dropped by 14.29 percent and 12.45 percent, respectively. But levels still far exceed international standards, and further progress will meet resistance from local officials. As construction of new coal-fired power plants and automobiles proliferated the emission of CO_2 and nitrogen oxide (NO_x) into the air kept rising. In 2011, the State Council announced its intention to introduce energy consumption quotas relying on cap-and-trade mechanisms and initiated a 5–10 percent nationwide sales tax on petroleum, natural gas, and coking coal.

Since the mid-1990s, grain production has stagnated, increasing at roughly 1 percent per annum, due to both distorted market incentives and changing consumption patterns. In contrast, production of economic crops and aquaculture has expanded twice as fast or more. Rises in food prices contributed significantly to China's inflation in 2004, 2008, and 2011. Since agricultural production is highly cyclical, it can respond to high prices. But it faces another more intractable problem: water shortage and pollution. China's average freshwater resource per head is 2,200 cubic meters, 31 percent below the world average, roughly the level in Israel. Worse, the distribution of China's water resources is highly uneven. About 60 percent of China's cultivated land is in north China, which enjoys only 16 percent of total water resources, while south China has only 40 percent of the arable land but 84 percent of the water supply.

North China depends on underground water, which is overextracted; its water table is dropping at the rate of a meter a year. Major rivers in north China are overused. The world average utilization ratio is around 40 percent, while in China there is an 80 percent utilization ratio for the Hai and Liao Rivers and 70 percent for the Yellow River. As a result, Chinese rivers often dry up. In the south, rivers are heavily polluted. In 2006, 30 million tons of waste water and industrial waste were dumped into the Yangtze River.

Currently, about 400 cities out of about 1,500 large and small cities face serious water shortages. Even for Beijing, only two out of its sixteen major lakes meet the good-quality standard of grade 2, while half of them are heavily polluted. Cities in north China pin their hopes on the gigantic and expensive South-to-North Water Diversion Project. As Chapter 9 explains, glacial melting threatens all the water supplies.

In the past, the strategy has been "growth first and clean up later." With a quickly aging population and rapidly deteriorating physical environment, China has no other option but to maximize its growth for the next decade in order to generate enough wealth and resources to cope with all those problems. It seems to have reached a point where "growth at all costs" is no longer a viable option. China has to manage the two demanding tasks—growing and cleaning up—at the same time (Dahlman, 2007; UNDP, 2002; Yusuf and Nabeshima, 2006; Song and Woo, 2008).

In 2007, the government launched the Clean Development Mechanism (CDM) Fund and aimed to invest more in antipollution projects. There have also been efforts to include achievement in environmental protection as part of the performance index for local officials. This is aimed at modifying the incentives and behavior of local governments from growth focus alone to a more balanced approach. There have also been efforts to raise public awareness about environmental issues. With the water tables dropping, the glaciers melting, and much of the remaining water polluted, those efforts have become an urgent priority. It is to China's credit, and benefit, that they are being made.

Notes

1. The Gini coefficient is a measure of inequality of income distribution (or, using different equations, of wealth distribution) with values between 0 and 1. A low Gini coefficient indicates more equal income or wealth distribution. 0 corresponds to perfect equality (everyone has the same income) and 1 corresponds to perfect inequality (one person has all the income). While developed nations tend to have relatively low Gini coefficients below 0.4, some poor countries may have Gini coefficients over 0.6. According to the United Nations Development Programme, China's Gini coefficient was 0.415 in 2007, up from 0.400 in 2000 (UNDP, *Human Development Report 2009*). China has not published a Gini coefficient since 2000, when they announced that it was 0.412, so the estimates vary, but 0.47, an estimate in a 2005 Chinese Academy of Social Science report, is used by the *China Daily, the CIA World Factbook*, and other periodicals (Fang Xuyan and Lea Yu, "China Refuses to Release Gini Coefficient: Government Cites Incomplete Data on High-Income Earners," Caixin Online, January 19, 2012; *Wall Street Journal,* Market Watch, http://articles.marketwatch.com/2012-01-19/economy/30788275_1_income-gap-china-reform-foundation-gini-coefficient). A Gini coefficient higher than 0.4 is considered a potential trigger for unrest in a developing country. The US Census Bureau, "Income, Poverty, and Health Insurance Coverage in the US, 2009," *Newsroom*, September 16, 2010, estimates the US Gini coefficient at 0.468—unusually high for a developed nation. The UK is around 0.34 and Germany 0.27.

2. Some 21.5 million of China's rural population live below the official "absolute poverty" line (approximately US$90 per year); an additional 35.5 million of the rural population live above that level but below the official "low income" line (approximately US$125 per year). See UNDP, *Human Development Indices: A Statistical Update 2008*. According to Nan Zhenzhong, vice chair of the Foreign Affairs Committee of the National People's Congress, China is "second only to India in terms of the numbers of poor people. In this sense, the only role we can play in international affairs is the role of a large developing nation." See Rana Foroohar, "China's Wealth Worries," *Newsweek*, November 1, 2010.

3. "Average Wealth in China at US$21,000: Credit Suisse," available at http://english.caijing.com.cn/2011-10-20/110904317.html. See also Niall Ferguson, "Gloating China, Hidden Problems," *Newsweek,* August 22 and 29, 2011.

4. Forbes' China's 400 Richest 2011 counted 146 Chinese billionaires.

5. National Bureau of Statistics of China, *China Statistical Abstract 2011* (Beijing: China Statistical Press, 2011).

6. Foreign investment hereafter refers to all investment from outside mainland China, including those from Hong Kong, Macau, and Taiwan.

7. Foreign direct investment refers to "foreign investment that establishes a lasting interest in or effective management control over an enterprise." "International Monetary Fund (IMF) guidelines consider an investment to be a foreign direct investment if it accounts for at least 10 percent of the foreign firm's voting stock of shares. However, many countries set a higher threshold because 10 percent is often not enough to establish effective management control of a company or demonstrate an investor's lasting interest." (World Bank, http://www.worldbank.org/depweb/english/beyond/global/glossary.html#24).

8. UN Conference of Trade and Development, *World Investment Report 2010* (Geneva: United Nations), available at www.unctad.org.

9. Niall Ferguson, "Washington Proves the Communists Right," *Newsweek,* August 15, 2011.

10. Between July 2005 and August 2011, the RMB appreciated by 8 percent against the euro, 12 percent against the Japanese yen, and 8 percent against the Australian dollar. In real terms, the RMB's effective exchange rate appreciated by 21 percent between July 2005 and August 2011, according to the Bank of International Settlement.

11. Purchasing power parity (PPP) is a measure of long-term equilibrium exchange rates based on relative price levels of two countries. The idea is that in the absence of transaction costs and official barriers to trade, identical goods will have the same price in different markets when the prices are expressed in terms of one currency. The PPP conversion factor is the number of units of a country's currency required to buy the same amount of goods and services in the domestic market as a US dollar would buy in the United States. PPP-based GDP is internationally more comparable since it takes into account different relative prices in different countries. It is important to be aware of the problem of overstating China's real GDP by the PPP measure; see World Bank, *World Development Report 2000/2001* (New York: Oxford University Press, 2001.)

12. World Bank, *World Development Indicators 2011* (Washington, DC: World Bank, 2011).

13. *China Statistical Abstract 2011* (Beijing: China Statistical Press, 2011).

14. "Analysing China's Economy: Is China a Threat?" *Journal of Japanese Trade and Industry* (September–October 2002).

15. "China's Rise Threatens Japanese Industry," *Nikkei Weekly* (Japan), August 19, 2002.

16. "Opinions on Accelerating the Upgrading of China's Household Appliance Industry by the Ministry of Industry and Information, available at http://www.xxgxj.gov.cn/zcfg/2011-03-11/381.html (accessed October 14, 2011).

17. See, for example, Brian Palmer, "China by the Numbers," *Fortune*, December 6, 1999; "Beijing Has HK$54 b Chasm in Key Data," *South China Morning Post*, July 24, 2000; Thomas Rawski, "What Is Happening to China's GDP Statistics?" *China Economic Review* 12(4) (December 2001): 347–354; and "Why China Cooks the Books?" *Newsweek,* April 1, 2002.

18. Dwight H. Perkins, *Market Control and Planning in Communist China* (Cambridge, MA: Harvard University Press, 1966.)

19. See, for example, Nai-Ruenn Chen, "An Assessment of Chinese Economic Data: Availability, Reliability, and Usability," in *China: A Reassessment of the Economy*, Joint Economic Committee, US Congress (Washington, DC: US Government Printing Office, 1985); Carsten A. Holz, "OECD-China Project: The Institutional Arrangements for the Production of Statistics," OECD Statistics Working Papers 2005/1 (Paris: OECD, 2005); Gregory C. Chow, "Are Chinese Official Statistics Reliable?" *CESifo Economic Studies*

52(2) (2006): 396–414; and Gregory C. Chow, *Interpreting China's Economy* (Singapore: World Scientific, 2010), pp. 119–140.

20. Lawrence R. Klein and Suleyman Ozmucur, "The Estimation of China's Economic Growth Rate," *Journal of Economic and Social Measurement* 28 (2002–2003): 187–202.

21. See, for example, Lawrence R. Klein, "Experiences in the Transition to a Market Economy," *Journal of Comparative Economics* (June 1994); and Thomas G. Rawski, "Implications of China's Reform Experience," Working Paper No. 295, Department of Economics, University of Pittsburgh, 1995.

22. Deng's well-known adage is, "It does not matter if the color of the cat is black or white so long as she can catch mice."

23. *China Price Yearbook* (Beijing, 1995).

24. "Keep Pace with Times, Jiang Urges Party Forum," *International Herald Tribune*, November 9–10, 2002.

25. For the full text of the plan in English, see Xinhua News Agency (Beijing), October 4, 1995, 0702 GMT.

26. "Congress Draws Nation's Blueprint," *China Daily*, November 9, 2002.

27. Barry Naughton, *The Chinese Economy: Transitions and Growth* (Cambridge, MA: MIT Press, 2007).

28. Since 1998, the official statistics report the combined output of state-owned enterprises and corporations controlled by the state.

29. This official growth rate tends to overstate China's actual growth as it was estimated by revaluing Chinese GDP at 1980 prices rather than at earlier-year prices and hence inflates the contribution of industry to GDP growth. A more realistic average growth should be around 4.5–5.0 percent, which is still quite a respectable performance.

30. World Bank, *World Development Report 2010/2011* (New York: Oxford University Press, 2011).

31. See, for example, Paul Romer, "Increasing Returns and Long-run Growth," *Journal of Political Economy* (October 1986); and Philippe Aghion and Peter Howitt, "A Model of Growth Through Creative Destruction," *Econometrica* 60(2) (1992): 323–512.

32. See, for example, Alwyn Young, "The Tyranny of Numbers: Confronting the Statistical Realities of the East Asian Growth Experience," *Quarterly Journal of Economics* 110(3) (1995): 641–680; and Barry Bosworth, Susan Collins, and Yu-Chin Chen, "Accounting for Differences in Economic Growth," Brookings Discussion Papers in International Economics, No. 115 (Washington, DC: Brookings Institution, 1995).

33. A study by the World Bank attempted to evaluate the source of China's rapid growth of 9.4 percent between 1978 and 1995. It identified that during the seventeen years, physical capital grew by 8.8 percent a year, while labor force and human capital grew by 2.4 and 2.7 percent. With elasticity of 0.4 (which means a 1 percentage increase of capital is translated into 0.4 percentage increase of GDP), 0.3, and 0.3, the three components jointly contributed to 5.1 percent of GDP growth. It then concluded that the remaining 4.3 percent is unexplained by growth of input and thus attributable to productivity increase. This seems to be unusually large, compared to South Korea and Japan for the appropriate periods but possible due to large efficiency gains from China's economic reform and the open-door policy.

34. World Bank, *China 2020: Development Challenges in the New Century* (Washington, DC: World Bank, 1997).

35. See Hu Zuliu and Mohsin Khan,"Why Is China Growing So Fast?" Economic Issues No. 8 (Washington, DC: International Monetary Fund, 1997).

36. *Statistical Yearbook of China 2000* (Beijing: China Statistics Press).

37. See Tian Xiaowen, "China's Drive to Develop Its Western Region (I) and (II)," in *China's Economy into the New Century: Structural Issues and Problems*, edited by John Wong and Lu Ding, 237–272 (Singapore: Singapore University Press and World Scientific, 2002).

38. *China Statistical Abstract 2011* (Beijing: China Statistics Press).

39. The figures for South Korea, Taiwan, and Singapore are those for 2005; those for India are for 2007.

40. "Tariff Profiles: China," World Trade Organization, available at http://stat.wto.org (accessed October 6, 2011).

41. *Beijing Review*, August 29, 2002.

42. "On the Road to Ruin," *Far Eastern Economic Review*, November 14, 2002.

43. "Annual Report on Nonperforming Loans in China's Commercial Banks," various years, China Banking Regulatory Commission, available at http://www.cbrc.gov.cn (accessed October 7, 2011).

44. *China Labour Statistical Yearbook 2005* (Beijing: China Statistics Press).

45. Barry Naughton (2007). Indeed, even government officials admitted that China's urban unemployment is the early 2000s was as high as 7 percent; see "Beijing Tally of Jobless Far Too Low, Aide Admits," *International Herald Tribune*, November 12, 2002.

46. "Calculating China's Unemployment Rate," *Wall Street Journal*, April 2, 2009, available at http://blogs.wsj.com (accessed October 3, 2011).

47. *China Statistical Abstract, 2005, 2011* (Beijing: China Statistics Press). The number of urban residents covered by the scheme has remained relatively stable since 2003, ranging between 22.0 million and 23.5 million.

48. Niall Ferguson, "Gloating China, Hidden Problems," *Newsweek*, August 22 and 29, 2011.

49. An article in *China Daily* is actually titled "Fight Against 'Rampant Corruption' Stepped Up," March 6, 2011, available at http://www.chinadaily.com.cn.

50. See "China's Issuing of First Anticorruption White Paper: A Manifesto to Fight Corruption," *China News*, December 29, 2010, available at http://www.chinanews.com.

51. *China Statistical Abstract 2011* (Beijing: China Statistics Press, 2011).

52. CEIC, China Premium Database, at http://www.ceicdata.com/China.html.

53. It has been reported that China has already been the world's largest emitter of CO_2 from consumption of energy since 2007, overtaking the United States. See, for example, "World Carbon Dioxide Emissions Data by Country: China Speeds Ahead of the Rest," *The Guardian*, available at http://www.guardian.co.uk.

54. "Green GDP Accounting Study Report 2004 Issued," September 11, 2006; available at the Chinese government's official web portal, at www.gov.cn. The effort was later scrapped in 2007, for two main reasons: (1) calculating green GDP and their indices with high accuracy may be very difficult; and (2) there will be political concerns, since green GDP growth rate could be considerably lower than targeted.

55. Christina Larson, "China Takes First Steps in the Fight Against Acid Rain," *Environment 360*, October 20, 2010, Yale School of Forestry and Environmental Studies, available at http://e360.yale.edu.

Bibliography

Alon, Ilan, and John R. McIntyre (eds.). 2005. *Business and Management Education in China: Transition, Pedagogy, and Training*. Singapore: World Scientific.

Ambler, Tim, and Morgen Witzel. 2003. *Doing Business in China*. 2nd ed. London: Routledge.

Ash, Robert, and Y. Y. Kueh (eds.). 1996. *The Chinese Economy Under Deng Xiaoping*. Oxford: Oxford University Press.

Bao, Shuming, Shuanglin Lin, and Changwen Zhao (eds.). 2006. *The Chinese Economy and WTO Accession*. Burlington, VT: Ashgate.

Bardhan, Pranab. 2010. *Awakening Giants: Feed of Clay: Assessing the Economic Rise of China and India*. Princeton, NJ: Princeton University Press.

Bell, Lynda S. 1999. *One Industry, Two Chinas: Silk Filatures and Peasant-Family Production in Wuxi County, 1865–1937*. Stanford, CA: Stanford University Press.

Bhattasasalis, Deepak, Shangtong Li, and William J. Martin. 2004. *China and the WTO: Accession, Policy Reform, and Poverty Reduction Strategies*. Washington, DC: World Bank.

Blackman, Carolyn. 2001. *China Business: The Rules of the Game*. London: Allen and Unwin.

Bramall, Chris. 1993. *In Praise of the Maoist Economic Planning: Living Standards and Economic Development in Sichuan Since 1931*. New York: Oxford University Press.

———. 2000. *Sources of Chinese Economic Growth, 1978–1996*. New York: Oxford University Press.

Bramson, Christopher Bo. 2000. *Open Doors: Vilhelm Meyer and the Establishment of General Electric in China*. London: Curzon Press.

Brandt, Loren, and Thomas G. Rawski (eds.). 2008. *China's Great Economic Transformation*. Cambridge: Cambridge University Press.

Bray, David. 2005. *The Danwei System from Origins to Reform*. Stanford, CA: Stanford University Press.

Brodsgaard, Kjeld Erik, and Susan Young (eds.). 2001. *State Capacity in East Asia: China, Taiwan, Vietnam, and Japan*. Oxford: Oxford University Press.

Brook, Timothy. 1989. *The Asiatic Mode of Production in China*. Armonk, NY: M. E. Sharpe.

Brown, Colin G., Scott A. Waldron, and John W. Longworth (eds.). 2005. *Modernizing China's Industries: Lessons from Wool and Wool Textiles*. Northampton, MA: Edward Elgar.

Buderi, Robert, and Gregory T. Huang. 2006. *Guanxi (The Art of Relationships): Microsoft, China, and Bill Gates' Plan to Win the Road Ahead*. New York: Simon and Schuster.

Cass, Deborah Z., Brett Gerard Williams, and George Barker (eds.). 2003. *China and the World Trading System: Entering the New Millennium*. Cambridge: Cambridge University Press.

CEIC Data. 2012. China Premium Database. http://www.ceicdata.com/China.html.

Chai, Joseph C. H., and Kartik C. Roy. 2006. *Economic Reform in China and India: Development Experience in a Comparative Perspective*. Northampton, MA: Edward Elgar.

Chan, Anita. 2001. *China's Workers Under Assault: The Exploitation of Labor in a Globalizing Economy*. Armonk, NY: M. E. Sharpe.

——— (ed.). 2011. *Walmart in China*. Ithaca, NY: Cornell University Press.

Chan, Anita, Richard Madsen, and Jonathan Unger. 1984. *Chen Village: The Recent History of a Peasant Community in Mao's China*. Berkeley: University of California Press.

Chan, Kam C., Hung-Gay Fung, and Qingfeng Liu (eds.). 2007. *China's Capital Markets: Challenges from WTO Membership*. Northampton, MA: Edward Elgar.

Chang, Gordon. 2001. *The Coming Collapse of China*. New York: Random House.

Chang, Julian, and Steven M. Goldstein (eds.). 2007. *Economic Reform and Cross-Straits Relations: Taiwan and China in the WTO*. Singapore: World Scientific

Chao, Kang. 1987. *Man and Land in Chinese History: An Economic Analysis*. Stanford, CA: Stanford University Press.

Chen, Aimin, and Shunfeng Song (eds.). 2006. *China's Rural Economy After WTO: Problems and Strategies*. Burlington, VT: Ashgate.

Chen, Chien-Hsun, and Hui-Tzu Shih. 2005. *High-Tech Industries in China*. Northampton, MA: Edward Elgar.

Chen, Ming-jer. 2003. *Inside Chinese Business: A Guide for Managers Worldwide*. Cambridge, MA: Harvard Business School Press.

Cheung, Gordon C. K. 2011. *Intellectual Property Rights in China*. London: Routledge.

Cheung, Tai Ming. 2002. *China's Entrepreneurial Army*. Oxford: Oxford University Press.

China Statistical Abstract 2011. Beijing: China Statistical Press.

Ching, Cheong, and Hung-Yee Ching. 2003. *Handbook on China's WTO Accession and Its Impacts*. Singapore: World Scientific.

Chiu, Becky, and Mervyn K. Lewis (eds.). 2006. *Reforming China's State-owned Enterprises and Banks*. Northampton, MA: Edward Elgar.

Chow, Gregory C. 2007. *China's Economic Transformation*. 2nd ed. London: Blackwell.

Chu, Tianshu, and Kar-yiu Wong (eds.). 2007. *China's Accession to the WTO: Impacts on China and the Asia-Pacific Region*. Northampton, MA: Edward Elgar.

Chu, Yiu-kong. 2006. *The Triads as Business*. London: Routledge.

Clegg, Stewart R., Karen Wang, and Mike Berrell (eds.). 2007. *Business Networks and Strategic Alliances in China*. Northampton, MA: Edward Elgar.

Clissold, Tim. 2006. *Mr. China: A Memoir*. New York: HarperCollins.

Croll, Elisabeth. 1994. *From Heaven to Earth: Images and Experiences of Development in China*. London: Routledge.

Dahlman, Carl J. (ed.). 2007. *Enhancing China's Competitiveness Through Lifelong Learning*. Washington, DC: World Bank.

Deng, Gang. 1999. *The Premodern Chinese Economy: Structural Equilibrium and Capitalist Sterility*. London: Routledge.

Deyo, Frederick C., Richard F. Doner, and Eric Hershberg (eds.). 2001. *Economic Governance and the Challenge of Flexibility in East Asia*. Lanham, MD: Rowman and Littlefield.

Dikotter, Frank, and Michael J. Dwyer. 2007. *Exotic Commodities: Modern Objects and Everyday Life in China*. New York: Columbia University Press.

Dong, Xiao-yuan, Shunfeng Song, and Xiaobo Zhang (eds.). 2006. *China's Agricultural Development: Challenges and Prospects*. Burlington, VT: Ashgate.

Dutta, Manoranjan. 2005. *China's Industrial Revolution and Economic Presence*. Singapore: World Scientific.

Eckstein, Alexander. 1977. *China's Economic Revolution*. Cambridge: Cambridge University Press.

Elvin, Mark. 1973. *The Pattern of the Chinese Past*. Stanford, CA: Stanford University Press.

Engardio, Peter (ed.). 2007. *Chinia: How China and India Are Revolutionizing Global Business*. New York: McGraw Hill.

Faure, David. 2006. *China and Capitalism: A History of Business Enterprise in Modern China*. Hong Kong: University of Hong Kong Press.

Fernández, Juan Antonio, and Laurie Underwood. 2006. *China CEO: Voices of Experience from 20 International Business* Leaders. New York: Wiley.
Fernández-Stembridge, Leila, and Juan Antonio Fernández. 2006. *China's State-Owned Enterprise Reforms: An Industrial and CEO Approach*. London: Routledge.
Feuerwerker, Albert. 1996. *Studies in the Economic History of Late Imperial China: Handicraft, Modern Industry, and the State*. Ann Arbor: University of Michigan Monographs in Chinese Studies.
Fewsmith, Joseph. 1983. "From Guild to Interest Group: The Transformation of Public and Private in Late Qing China." *Comparative Studies in Society and History* 25:617–640.
Fleisher, Belton M., Nicholas C. Hope, Anita Alves Pena, and Dennis Tao Yang (eds.). 2008. *Policy Reform and Chinese Markets: Progress and Challenges*. Northampton, MA: Edward Elgar.
Frazier, Mark W. 2002. *The Making of the Chinese Industrial Workplace: State Revolution and Labor Management*. Cambridge: Cambridge University Press.
Fung, Hung-Gay, Changhong Pei, and Kevin H. Zhang (eds.). 2006. *China and the Challenge of Economic Globalization: The Impact of WTO Membership*. Armonk, NY: M. E. Sharpe.
Fung, K. C., Hitomi Iizaka, and Sarah Y. Tong. 2004. "Foreign Direct Investment in China: Policy, Recent Trend, and Impact." *Global Economic Review* 33(2): 99–130.
Gallagher, Mary Elizabeth. 2005. *Courageous Capitalism: Globalization and the Politics of Labor in China*. Princeton, NJ: Princeton University Press.
Garnaut, Ross, Ligang Song, Stayan Tenet, and Yang Yao. 2005. *China's Ownership Transformation: Process, Outcomes, Prospects*. Washington, DC: World Bank.
Garnaut, Ross, Shutian Guo, and Guonan Ma (eds.). 1996. *The Third Revolution in the Chinese Countryside*. Cambridge: Cambridge University Press.
Gates, Hill. 1996. *China's Motor: A Thousand Years of Petty Capitalism*. Ithaca, NY: Cornell University Press.
Gittings, John. 2006. *The Changing Face of China: From Mao to Market*. New York: Oxford University Press.
Golley, Jane. 2007. *The Dynamics of Chinese Regional Development: Market Nature, State Nurture*. Northampton, MA: Edward Elgar.
Gore, Lance L. P. 1999. *Market Communism: The Institutional Foundation of China's Post-Mao Hyper-Growth*. Oxford: Oxford University Press.
Gu, George Zhibin. 2006. *China and the New World Order: How Entrepreneurship, Globalization, and Borderless Business Are Reshaping China and the World*. Stanford, CA: Fultus Corporation.
Guiheux, Gilles. 2002. "The Incomplete Crystallization of the Private Sector." *China Perspectives* 42 (July–August): 24–36.
Guo, Yuantao. 2006. *Global Big Business and the Chinese Brewing Industry*. London: Routledge.
Guthrie, Doug. 2002. *Dragon in a Three-Piece Suit: The Emergence of Capitalism in China*. Princeton, NJ: Princeton University Press.
Hamilton, Gary G. 2006. *Commerce and Capitalism in Chinese Societies: The Organisation of Chinese Economics*. London: Routledge.
Harney, Alexandra. 2008. *The China Price: The True Cost of Chinese Competitive Advantage*. London: Penguin.
Hassard, John, Jonathan Morris, Jackie Sheehan, and Rose Zhou (eds.). 2006. *Chinese State Enterprise Reform*. London: Routledge.
Heberer, Thomas. 2007. *Doing Business in Rural China: Liangshan's New Ethnic Entrepreneurs*. Seattle: University of Washington Press.

Ho, Peter, and Eduard B. Vermeer (eds.). 2006. *China's Limits to Growth: Greening State and Society*. New York: Wiley-Blackwell.

Holz, Carsten A. 2003. *China's Industrial State-Owned Enterprises: Between Profitability and Bankruptcy*. Singapore: World Scientific.

Honig, Emily. 1986. *Sisters and Strangers: The Cotton Textile Workers of Shanghai*. Stanford, CA: Stanford University Press.

Hsu, Chen-Min, Wei-Guo Zhang, and Leslie Lok. 2007. *The Business and Investment Environment in Taiwan and Mainland China: A Focus on the IT and High-Tech Electronic Industries*. Singapore: World Scientific.

Hu, Angang. 2006. *Economic and Social Transformation in China: Challenges and Opportunities*. London: Routledge.

Huang, Philip C. C. 1985. *The Peasant Economy and Social Change in North China*. Stanford, CA: Stanford University Press.

———. 1990. *The Peasant Family and Rural Development in the Yangzi Delta, 1350–1988*. Stanford, CA: Stanford University Press.

Huang, Yasheng. 2005. *Selling China: Foreign Direct Investment During the Reform Era*. Cambridge: Cambridge University Press.

Hughes, Neil C. 2002. *China's Economic Challenge: Smashing the Iron Rice Bowl*. Armonk, NY: M. E. Sharpe.

Ikels, Charlotte. 1996. *The Return of the God of Wealth: The Transition to a Market Economy in Urban China*. Stanford, CA: Stanford University Press.

Jeffries, Ian. 2010. *Economic Developments in Contemporary China: A Guide*. London: Routledge.

Jiang, Fuming, and Bruce W. Stening. 2006. *The Chinese Business Environment: An Annotated Bibliography*. Northampton, MA: Edward Elgar.

Kamachi, Noriko. 1990. "Feudalism or Absolute Monarchism? Japanese Discourse on the Nature of State and Society in Later Imperial China." *Modern China* 87(3): 330–370.

Kelliher, Daniel. 1992. *Peasant Power in China: The Era of Rural Reform, 1979–1989*. New Haven, CT: Yale University Press.

Kim, Samuel S. (ed.). 2000. *East Asia and Globalization*. Lanham, MD: Rowman and Littlefield.

Klein, Lawrence R., and Suleyman Ozmucur. 2002. "The Estimation of China's Economic Growth Rate." *Journal of Economic and Social Measurement* 28(4): 187–202.

Kong, Qingjiang. 2002. *China and the World Trade Organization: A Legal Perspective*. Singapore: World Scientific.

Kristof, Nicholas, and Sheryl WuDunn. 1994. *China Wakes: The Struggle for the Soul of a Rising Power*. New York: Random House.

Krugman, Paul. 1994. "The Myth of Asia's Miracle." *Foreign Affairs* 73(6) (November–December): 62–75.

Kwong, Julia. 1997. *The Political Economy of Corruption in China*. Armonk, NY: M. E. Sharpe.

Kynge, James. 2006. *China Shakes the World: A Titan's Rise and Troubled Future and the Challenge for America*. New York: Houghton Mifflin.

Lai, Hongyi Harry. 2007. *Reform and the Non-State Economy in China: The Political Economy of Liberalization Strategies*. New York: Palgrave.

Latham, Kevin, Stuart Thompson, and Jakob Klein (eds.). 2006. *Consuming China: Approaches to Cultural Change in Contemporary China*. London: Routledge.

Lee, Ching Kwan. 2007. *Against the Law: Labor Protests in China's Rustbelt and Sunbelt*. Berkeley: University of California Press.

Lee, Grace, and Malcolm Warner (eds.). 2006. *Unemployment in China*. London: Routledge.
Leong, Liew. 1998. *The Chinese Economy in Transition: From Plan to Market*. Cheltenham, UK: Edward Elgar.
Li, Haiyang. 2006. *Growth of New Technology Ventures in China's Emerging Market*. Northampton, MA: Edward Elgar.
Li, Hua-yu. 2006. *Mao and the Economic Stabilization of China, 1948–1953*. Lanham, MD: Rowman and Littlefield.
Li, Lanqing. 2004. *Education for 1.3 Billion*. New York: Penguin.
Liew, Leong H, and Harry X. Wu (eds.). 2008. *The Making of China's Exchange Rate Policy: From Plan to WTO Entry*. Northampton, MA: Edward Elgar.
Lin, Justin Yifu, Fang Cai, and Zhou Li. 2001. *State-owned Enterprise Reform in China*. Hong Kong: Chinese University Press.
———. 2003. *The China Miracle: Development Strategy and Economic Reform*. Rev. ed. Hong Kong: Chinese University Press.
Lin, Shanglin, and Shunfeng Song (eds.). 2007. *The Revival of Private Enterprise in China*. Burlington, VT: Ashgate.
Lin, Yi-min. 2004. *Between Politics and Markets: Firms, Competition, and Institutional Change in Post-Mao China*. Cambridge: Cambridge University Press.
Ling, Zhijun. 2006. *The Lenovo Affair: The Growth of China's Computer Giant and Its Takeover of IBM-PC*. New York: Wiley.
Liu, Xiuwu R. 2001. *Jumping into the Sea: From Academics to Entrepreneurs in South China*. Lanham, MD: Rowman and Littlefield.
Lu, Ding, and William A. W. Neilson (eds.). 2004. *China's West Region Development: Domestic Strategies and Global Implications*. Singapore: World Scientific.
Lu, Xiaobo, and Elizabeth J. Perry. 1997. *Danwei: The Changing Chinese Workplace in Historical and Comparative Perspective*. Armonk, NY: M. E. Sharpe.
Lufrano, Richard John. 1997. *Honorable Merchants: Commerce and Self-Cultivation in Late Imperial China*. New York: Columbia University Press.
Luo, Yadong. 2001. *How to Enter China: Choices and Lessons*. Ann Arbor: University of Michigan Press.
———. 2007. *Guanxi and Business*. 2nd ed. Singapore: World Scientific.
Lyons, Thomas P. 1994. *Poverty and Growth in a South China County: Anxi, Fujian, 1949–1992*. Ithaca, NY: Cornell University Press.
Lyons, Thomas P., and Victor Need (eds.). 1994. *The Economic Transformation of South China: Reform and Development in the Post-Mao Era*. Ithaca, NY: Cornell University Press.
Mann, Jim. 1997. *Beijing Jeep: A Case Study of Western Business in China*. Boulder: Westview.
Mann, Susan. 1987. *Local Merchants and the Chinese Bureaucracy, 1750–1950*. Stanford, CA: Stanford University Press.
Marme, Michael. 2004. *Suzhou: Where the Goods of All the Provinces Converge*. Stanford, CA: Stanford University Press.
McCormick, Barrett L., and Jonathan Unger (eds.). 1995. *China After Socialism: In the Footsteps of Eastern Europe or East Asia?* Armonk, NY: M. E. Sharpe.
McGregor, James. 2007. *One Billion Customers: Lessons from the Front Lines of Doing Business in China*. New York: Free Press.
Mertha, Andrew C. 2005. *The Politics of Piracy: Intellectual Property in Contemporary China*. Ithaca, NY: Cornell University Press.
Moore, Thomas G. 2002. *China in the World Market: Chinese Industry and*

International Sources of Reform in the Post-Mao Era. Cambridge: Cambridge University Press.

Murphy, Rachel. 2002. *How Migrant Labor Is Changing Rural China*. Cambridge: Cambridge University Press.

Naquin, Susan. 1987. *Chinese Society in the Eighteenth Century*. New Haven, CT: Yale University Press.

Naughton, Barry. 1995. *Growing Out of the Plan: Chinese Economic Reform, 1978–1993*. Cambridge: Cambridge University Press.

———. 2007. *The Chinese Economy: Transitions and Growth*. Cambridge, MA: MIT Press.

Navarro, Peter. 2006. *The Coming China Wars: Where They Will Be Fought and How They Can Be Won*. Upper Saddle River, NJ: FT Press.

Nazrul Islam, Erbiao Dai, and Hiroshi Sakamoto. 2006. "Role of TFP in China's Growth," *Asian Economic Journal* 20(2): 127–157.

Oi, Jean C. 1989a. "Market Reforms and Corruption in Rural China." *Studies in Comparative Communism* 22 (Summer–Autumn): 221–233.

———. 1989b. *State and Peasant in Contemporary China: The Political Economy of Village Government*. Berkeley: University of California Press.

———. 1999. *Rural China Takes Off: The Institutional Foundations of Economic Reform*. Berkeley: University of California Press.

Oi, Jean, and Andrew G. Walder (eds.). 1999. *Property Rights and Economic Reform in China*. Stanford, CA: Stanford University Press.

Panitchpakti, Supachai, and Mark L. Clifford. 2002. *China and the WTO: Changing China, Changing World Trade*. New York: John Wiley.

Park, Yung Chul. 2006. *Economic Liberalization and Integration in East Asia: A Post-Crisis Paradigm*. Oxford: Oxford University Press.

Perdue, Peter C. 1987. *Exhausting the Earth: State and Peasant in Hunan, 1500–1850*. Cambridge, MA: Harvard University Press.

Perkins, Dwight. 1969. *Agricultural Development in China, 1368–1968*. Chicago: Aldine.

Pomeranz, Kenneth. 2000. *The Great Divergence: China, Europe, and the Making of the Modern World Economy*. Princeton, NJ: Princeton University Press.

Powell, Simon. 1992. *Agricultural Reform in China: From Communes to Commodity Economy, 1978–1990*. Manchester: Manchester University Press.

Prazniak, Roxann. 1999. *Of Camels and Kings and Other Things: Rural Rebels Against Modernity in Late Imperial China*. Lanham, MD: Rowman and Littlefield.

Prestowitz, Clyde. 2005. *Three Billion New Capitalists: The Great Shift of Wealth and Power to the East*. New York: Basic Books.

Rawski, Evelyn Sakakida. 1972. *Agricultural Change and the Peasant Economy of South China*. Cambridge, MA: Harvard University Press.

Rawski, Thomas G. 1995. *Implications of China's Reform Experience*. Working Paper No. 295, Department of Economics, University of Pittsburgh.

Redding, S. Gordon. 1990. *The Spirit of Chinese Capitalism*. Berlin: Walter de Gruyter.

Richardson, Philip. 2000. *Economic Change in China, c. 1800–1950*. Cambridge: Cambridge University Press.

Riedel, James, Jing Jin, and Jian Gao. 2007. *How China Grows: Investment, Finance, and Reform*. Princeton, NJ, and Oxford: Princeton University Press.

Riskin, Carl. 1987. *China's Political Economy: The Quest for Development Since 1949*. Oxford: Oxford University Press.

Riskin, Carl, Renwei Zhao, and Shi Li (eds.). 2001. *China's Retreat from Equality: Income Distribution and Economic Transition*. Armonk, NY: M. E. Sharpe.

Rowe, William T. 1984. *Hankow: Commerce and Society in a Chinese City, 1796–1889*. Stanford, CA: Stanford University Press.

———. 1989. *Hankow: Conflict and Community in a Chinese City, 1796–1895*. Stanford, CA: Stanford University Press.

Sato, Hiroshi, and Shi Li (eds.). 2006. *Unemployment, Inequality, and Poverty in Urban China*. London: Routledge.

Sharma, Ruchir. 2012. *Breakout Nations: In Pursuit of the Next Economic Miracles*. New York: W. W. Norton.

Sheff, David. 2002. *China Dawn: The Story of a Technology and Business Revolution*. New York: HarperBusiness.

Shenkar, Oded. 2004. *The Chinese Century: The Rising Chinese Economy and Its Impact on the Global Economy*. Philadelphia: Wharton School Publishing.

Shiba, Yoshinobu. 1969. *Commerce and Society in Sung China*. Trans. Mark Elvin. Ann Arbor: University of Michigan Abstracts of Chinese and Japanese Works on Chinese History.

Shih, Victor C. 2009. *Factions and Finance in China: Elite Conflict and Inflation*. Cambridge: Cambridge University Press.

Shou, Huisheng. 2010. *Race to the Bottom or Move to the Middle? Globalization and Welfare Regime Transformation in the Developing World*. PhD diss., University of Illinois.

Sigurdson, Jon, Jiang Jiang, and Xinxin Kong. 2006. *Technological Superpower China*. Northampton, MA: Edward Elgar.

Skoggard, Ian A. 1996. *The Indigenous Dynamic in Taiwan's Postwar Development: The Religious and Historical Roots of Entrepreneurship*. Armonk, NY: M. E. Sharpe.

Smith, S. A. 2001. *Like Cattle and Horses: Nationalism and Labor in Shanghai, 1895–1927*. Chapel Hill, NC: Duke University Press.

Song, Ligang, and Wing Thye Woo (eds.). 2008. *China's Dilemma: Economic Growth, the Environment, and Climate Change*. Washington, DC: Brookings Institution.

Spence, Jonathan. 1999. *The Search for Modern China*. New York: W. W. Norton.

Studwell, Joe. 2002. *The China Dream: The Quest for the Last Great Untapped Market on Earth*. New York: Atlantic Monthly Press.

Thun, Eric. 2006. *Lanes in China: Foreign Direct Investment, Local Governments, and Auto Sector Development*. Singapore: World Scientific.

Tiewes, Frederick C., and Warren Sun. 1998. *China's Road to Disaster: Mao, Central Politicians, and Provincial Leaders in the Unfolding of the Great Leap Forward, 1955–1959*. Armonk, NY: M. E. Sharpe.

Tong, Sarah Y., 2005. "Ethnic Networks in FDI and the Impact of Institutional Development." *Review of Development Economics* 9(4): 563–580.

Tong, Sarah Y., and Ruobin Liang. 2004. "Strengthening Corporate Governance: China's Strategy for Completing Its Unfinished Business of State-Owned Enterprise Reform." EAI Background Brief No. 218. Singapore: National University of Singapore.

Tong, Sarah Y., and Yi Zheng. 2006. "How Ready Are China's Banks to Meet Full WTO Obligations?" EAI Background Brief No. 310. Singapore: National University of Singapore.

Tsai, Kellee S. 2004. *Back-Alley Banking: Private Entrepreneurs in China*. Ithaca, NY: Cornell University Press.

Tse, Edward. 2010. *The China Strategy: Harnessing the Power of the World's Fastest-Growing Economy*. New York: Basic Books.

UNDP (United Nations Development Programme). 2002. *China Human Development Report: Making Green Development a Choice*. Oxford: Oxford University Press.

———. 2010. *Human Development Report: 20th Anniversary*. New York: Palgrave Macmillan.

———. 2011. *Human Development Report: Sustainability and Equity: Towards a Better Future for All*. New York: Palgrave Macmillan.

Vermeer, Eduard B., Frank N. Pieke, and Woei Lien Chong. 1997. *Cooperative and Collective in China's Rural Development*. Armonk, NY: M. E. Sharpe.

Wagner, Donald B. 2002. *The State and the Iron Industry in Han China*. Oslo: Nordic Institute of Asian Studies.

Walder, Andrew G. 1986. *Communist Neo-traditionalism: Work and Authority in Chinese Industry*. Berkeley: University of California Press.

——— (ed.). 1998. *Zouping in Transition: The Process of Reform in Rural North China*. Cambridge, MA: Harvard University Press.

Walter, Carl, and Fraser Howie. 2010. *Red Capitalism: The Fragile Financial Foundation of China's Extraordinary Rise*. New York: Wiley.

Wang, Hongying. 2001. *Weak State, Strong Networks: The Institutional Dynamics of Foreign Direct Investment in China*. Oxford: Oxford University Press.

Wang, Shaoguang, and Hu Angang. 2001. *The Chinese Economy in Crisis: State Capacity and Tax Reform*. Armonk, NY: M. E. Sharpe.

Wank, David L. 1999. *Commodifying Communism: Business, Trust, and Politics in a Chinese City*. Cambridge: Cambridge University Press.

Watson, James L. (ed.). 2006. *Golden Arches East: McDonalds in East Asia*. 2nd ed. Stanford, CA: Stanford University Press.

Wedeman, Andrew. 2003. *From Mao to Market: Rent Seeking, Local Protectionism, and Marketization in China*. Cambridge: Cambridge University Press.

Wei, Pan. 1998. *The Politics of Marketization in Rural China*. Lanham, MD: Rowman and Littlefield.

White, Lynn T., III. 1998. *Unstately Power: Local Causes of China's Economic Reform*. Vol. 1. Armonk, NY: M. E. Sharpe.

Whiting, Susan. 2000. *Power and Wealth in Rural China: The Political Economy of Institutional Change*. Cambridge: Cambridge University Press.

Will, Pierre-Etienne. 1991. *Nourish the People: The State Civilian Granary System in China, 1650–1850*. Ann Arbor: Center for Chinese Studies, University of Michigan.

Wong, John. 1973. *Land Reform in the People's Republic of China: Institutional Transformation of Agriculture*. New York: Praeger.

———. 1993. *Understanding China's Socialist Market Economy*. Singapore: Times Academic Press.

———. 1995. "China's Entrepreneurial Approach to Economic Reform." IEAPE Internal Study Paper No. 8 (Singapore), February 16.

Wong, John, and Zhiyu Bo. 2010. *China's Reform in Global Perspective*. Singapore: World Scientific.

Wong, John, and Zheng Yongnian. 2001. "Embracing the Capitalists: The Chinese Communist Party to Brace Itself for Far-Reaching Changes." EAI Background Brief No.100. Singapore: National University of Singapore.

Wong, John, Rong Ma, and Mu Yang. 1995. *China's Rural Entrepreneurs: Ten Case Studies*. Singapore: Times Academic Press.

Woo, Wing Thye, Stephen Parker, and Jeffrey Sachs (eds.). 1996. *Economies in Transition: Comparing Asia and Europe*. Cambridge, MA: MIT Press.

World Bank. Various years. *World Development Report*. New York: Oxford University Press.

———. 2007. *Cost of Pollution in China: Economic Estimates of Physical Damages*. Washington, DC: World Bank.

World Health Organization. 2011. Tackling the Global Clean Air Challenge. http://www.who.int/mediacentre/news/releases/2011/air_pollution_20110926/en/index.html.

Wu, Yu-Shan. 1994. *Comparative Economic Transformations: Mainland China, Hungary, the Soviet Union, and Taiwan*. Stanford, CA: Stanford University Press.

Yabuki, Susumu, and Stephen M. Harner. 1999. *China's New Political Economy: The Giant Awakes*. 2nd ed. Boulder: Westview.

Yan, Sun. 2004. *Corruption and the Market in Contemporary China*. Ithaca, NY: Cornell University Press.

Yang, Dali L. 1996. *Calamity and Reform in China: Rural Society and Institutional Change Since the Great Leap Famine*. Stanford, CA: Stanford University Press.

Yang, Gu. 2006. *Financial System and Institutions in China*. London: Routledge.

Yang, Keming. 2007. *Entrepreneurship in China*. Burlington, VT: Ashgate.

Yi, Jeannie Jingheng, and Shawn X. Ye. 2003. *The Haier Way: The Making of a Chinese Business Leader and a Global Brand*. Dumont, NJ: Homa and Sekey Books.

Young, Susan. 1995. *Private Business and Economic Reform in China*. Armonk, NY: M. E. Sharpe.

Yusuf, Shahid, and Kaoru Nabeshima. 2006. *China's Development Priorities*. Washington, DC: World Bank.

Yusuf, Shahid, Kaoru Nabeshima, and Dwight H. Perkins. 2005. *Under New Ownership: Privatizing China's State-Owned Enterprises*. Washington, DC: World Bank.

Zelin, Madeleine. 2006. *The Merchants of Zigong: Industrial Entrepreneurship in Early Modern China*. New York: Columbia University Press.

Zhang, Li. 2001. *Strangers in the City: Reconfigurations of Space, Power, and Social Networks Within China's Floating Population*. Stanford, CA: Stanford University Press.

Zhang, Wei. 1996. *Ideology and Economic Reform Under Deng, 1978–1993*. Geneva: Kegan Paul International.

Zheng, Yongnian, and Sarah Y. Tong (eds.). 2010. *China and the Global Economic Crisis*. Singapore: World Scientific.

Zhou, Kate Xiao. 1996. *How the Farmers Changed China: Power of the People*. Boulder: Westview.

Zhou, Kate Xiao, and Lynn T. White III. 1995. "Quiet Politics and Rural Enterprise in Reform China." *Journal of Developing Areas* 29 (July): 461–490.

Zweig, David. 1997. *Freeing China's Farmers: Rural Restructuring in the Reform Era*. Armonk, NY: M. E. Sharpe.

———. 2002. *Internationalizing China: Domestic Interests and Global Linkages*. Ithaca, NY: Cornell University Press.

6

China Beyond the Heartland

Robert E. Gamer

Having overviewed China's geography, history, politics, and economy, in this chapter we will take a closer look at four special topics: overseas Chinese, Hong Kong, Taiwan, and Tibet. These elements are all part of China, and yet not. They figure prominently in China's defense, foreign policy, economy, and culture. Even before reading this book, you were probably already aware that Hong Kong reverted to China in 1997, that Taiwan and China are engaged in vigorous diplomatic and military competition, and that Tibetans have resisted China's presence in their territory. The outcome of these issues will have enormous consequences in determining China's future. We will look at some historical background on each and then examine present and future trends. But the topic we begin with, perhaps a less familiar one, will help you comprehend China's extraordinary economic growth and some of the threads that tie together China, Hong Kong, and Taiwan: overseas Chinese. As Chapter 1 indicated, there are some 65 million Han Chinese who have left or whose ancestors left China, including those in Taiwan and Hong Kong. The richest among them control large amounts of investment capital. As you will see, most of China's foreign direct investment comes from them. How have they become so wealthy? How have they come to figure so prominently in China's affairs?

Overseas Chinese

For thousands of years, Chinese merchants have been trading in Indochina (Vietnam), Cambodia, Siam (Thailand), Malaya (mainland Malaysia), and Java (part of Indonesia)—all in Southeast Asia (see Map 2.1)—and in Korea and Japan. Their trade brought great prosperity to China's leading families during the Tang, Song, Yuan, Ming, and Qing empires (see Table 3.1). Most simply traveled there on business trips; a few settled, married native women, and became absorbed into local society. When the Europeans arrived in the sixteenth century, they created or captured Macau (across the bay from Hong Kong), Manila in the Philippines (the big island group north of Indonesia; see Map 2.1), Melaka (Malacca) in Malaya, and Batavia (Jakarta) and other ports in Java, and encouraged Chinese merchants and artisans (largely from the southern provinces of Fujian, Guangdong, and Zhejiang; see Map 2.2) to move there (Suryadinata, 1985; Wang, 2000, 2001; Cheung, 2005; Kuhn, 2008). These settlers brought Chinese wives and established or expanded Chinese communities; many became prosperous from their trading activities (Wang, 2000; Reid, 2001; Redding, 1995). As China's population burgeoned during the nineteenth century, relatives from their home provinces and unemployed urban youth moved to those communities and to the newly founded ports of Penang and Singapore in Malaya. They filled jobs as laborers, miners, plantation workers, teachers, journalists, traditional opera performers, house servants, and retailers. Others went to the Americas and Australia to construct railroads and work on farms. Some settled in Tokyo, smaller Pacific islands (Dye, 1997; Chang, 1988), Sydney (Ang, 2001; Cunningham and Sinclair, 2000), Calcutta, Europe (Pieke et al., 2004), London (Benton and Pieke, 1998), San Francisco (Cassel, 2002; Tong, 1994, 2000; Lee, 2003; Chen, 2002; Li, 2006; Yung, Chang, and Lai, 2006), Vancouver (Chong, 1996), the West Indies, and Lima. Those working on farms, plantations, mines, and railroads often experienced cruel treatment, harsh conditions, and tight restrictions on entering the country and obtaining citizenship (Lee, 2003; Phaelzer, 2007; Kwong and Miscevic, 2007; Thuno, 2007; Daniels, 1988; Sandmeyer, 1991; McClain, 1996; Wong and Chan, 1998). Those who did not perish or return home stayed to set up laundries or small shops or work for other Chinese in "Chinatowns," which began to emerge even in cities beyond the port of original entry into the country (Dirlik, 1998a; Chang, 2004; Chen and Omatsu, 2006; See, 1996; Yung, 1995, 1999; Zhao, 2002; Chan and Hsu, 2008; Lee, 2007).

The principal source of income for overseas Chinese communities was trade with China. The wealthiest families made their fortunes serving as intermediaries in trade transactions between China and non-Chinese in Asia, Europe, or the Americas (Tan, 2006; Seagrave, 1995; Fong and Luk, 2006; Gambe, 2000; Brown, 2000; Koehn and Yin, 2002). They became patrons to Chinese-language schools, newspapers (Sun, 2002, 2006), temples, festivals and other cultural activities; welfare and legal aid societies; and cemeteries (Chung and Wegars, 2005). Siam and the Philippines encouraged Chinese to intermarry and mingle with indigenous people in places of work; elsewhere they met with greater wariness and prejudice. The British in Malaya and Singapore hired Chinese and other ethnic groups for some bureaucratic posts; most of the remaining Chinese in these settlements worked for themselves or for other Chinese. Most Chinese sent money home to poorer relatives in China.

In the second half of the nineteenth century, prominent Chinese families began sending some of their children abroad to study. Those students discovered that except in the Philippines, where the Spanish had established schools and universities for native inhabitants, few Chinese born overseas were studying outside their own communities. Most who attended school were taught in Chinese dialects. In contrast, US missionary schools in China introduced their students to English and a modern Western curriculum; their best graduates were welcomed into leading US, British, and European colleges and universities. Japan, too, welcomed students from China (Bieler, 2004). Upon their return home, many of these graduates became prominent in China's government, commerce, and cultural life. Their exposure to Japanese, US, and European languages and cultures was far deeper than that of most Chinese living abroad.

The Chinese studying abroad returned home wanting to introduce China to techniques and ideas they had learned on their sojourns—to change Chinese culture. In contrast, leaders of Chinese communities abroad wished to preserve Chinese traditions among their families, workers, and neighbors. In exchange for cash remitted to their families in China, they asked China's leaders for assistance in dealing with the governments and societies of their adopted lands. Both these responses were very new. Until the second half of the nineteenth century, educated Chinese did not venture abroad to study, and China did not concern itself with the needs of Chinese who had moved abroad. To control piracy and rebels, the Ming and Qing governments had forbidden emigration under penalty of death. The treaties imposed after the Opium Wars (discussed below and in Chapter 7) changed that. They forced the emperors to allow emigration, while giving China the right (as a new participant in European-created international law) to protect its subjects living abroad. For the first time, China sent ambassadors and consuls to foreign capitals and trading cities. There they discovered the great prosperity of the overseas Chinese. The Qing government began to support schools for Chinese in Southeast Asian countries and conferred citizenship on overseas Chinese and their children. Chinese consular officials were available to assist Chinese when they encountered problems in their adopted countries and to intercede against abuses of laborers. After centuries of being cut off from their homeland, under threat of the death penalty imposed since the Ming dynasty for being illegal emigrants, overseas Chinese were being treated as compatriots. In exchange, the Qing government encouraged them to send money home to relatives.

This created precedents that continue to affect China's foreign relations and the lives of overseas Chinese. It encouraged the predisposition of overseas Chinese to isolate themselves from the social and political life of their adopted lands and to interest themselves in the politics and economy of China (Freedman, 2000; Garth, 1973; Barabantseva, 2010). It reinforced the inclination of China's governments to treat the overseas Chinese as continuing subjects of China and the lands where some of them reside as part of China's domain. Most important, it also helped end the Qing dynasty. The Revive China Society, which started the Kuomintang (KMT) and the Republican movements, was born among Chinese studying abroad and benefited from substantial financial contributions from overseas Chinese. Its founder, Sun Yat-sen, grew up in Hawaii studying in an Anglican school, and lived in exile in Japan, Europe, the United States, Canada, Singapore, and Penang.

After the Qing dynasty was overthrown in 1911 (see Chapter 4), all political factions in China sought financial and moral support among overseas Chinese, who helped set up schools for their children. The Kuomintang government promoted equal treatment for overseas Chinese in their countries of residence, helped them send their children to China for study, and gave special incentives to overseas Chinese for establishing businesses in China. It focused heavily on establishing schools, training teachers, and setting standards for the children of overseas Chinese and criticized the governments of those countries for "interfering" in this education, which was conducted entirely in the Chinese language, when they sought assurance that it would help integrate pupils into their adopted lands (Fitzgerald, 1972:8; Charney, Yeoh, and Tong, 2003:101–162).

From 1921 to 1927, the Communists and Nationalists cooperated in a "united front" in China; after that, they vied with each other and with the warlords for control of territories. All these factions sought financial and moral support from the overseas Chinese. In 1936, to counter the Japanese, they once again declared a united front, with both the Kuomintang and the Communists proclaiming that overseas Chinese were included in their efforts to cooperate. By giving their attention and resources variously to the Kuomintang and the Communists, overseas Chinese remained within China's orbit and roused suspicions among their new compatriots that they were not entirely loyal to their adopted lands. They also found themselves caught up in the ideological battle between communism and the Western democracies, even though many of them had thought little about such issues.

That problem of divided loyalties would continue after World War II. Both China and Taiwan, now ruled respectively by the Communists and the Kuomintang Nationalists, would need the deep pockets and the economic connections of these overseas Chinese as they sought to spread their economic and political influence in the region. And an island that was almost barren when China sought to control the opium trade in 1839 would play a pivotal role. So we fit it into the story here.

Hong Kong

Beginnings

In 1839, the Qing emperor appointed Lin Zexu as special commissioner in Guangzhou, the only port open to foreign trade (as Chapter 7 explains), and ordered him to stamp out the opium trade. Thus began China's humiliation by foreign powers. Guangzhou (Canton) is located near the Pearl River Delta of the West River (see Maps 2.2 and 2.4), just upstream from the Portuguese-founded city of Macau. Lin sent troops to the foreign wharves where trading took place and refused to let anyone leave until they surrendered the opium inside and promised not to import more. Among those in attendance was Captain Charles Elliot, Britain's trade representative. After six weeks of stand-off, Elliot surrendered 3 million pounds of opium to Lin, who had it flushed into the sea. Elliot retreated downstream to Macau, where the Portuguese did not wish to become involved. Hence he headed across the Pearl River Delta to a sparsely inhabited 423 square mile (1,095 kilometers) island called Hong Kong. It contained an excellent protected harbor, where he and his companions stayed aboard ship. When some Chinese war junks tried to expel his crews from the harbor, Elliot's ships sank them. The following summer, the British sent a fleet commanded by Elliot's cousin, Admiral George Elliot, to avenge the action (Hoe and Roebuck, 1999). His ship, the *Nemesis,* an all-iron steam-powered gunboat, far outclassed wooden junks with sails (Marks, 2006:116–117). Because they would not sign pledges declaring they would no longer trade in opium, Lin had all of Elliot's ships expelled from Macau. They headed across the bay, where by now Captain Elliot had established a village on a Hong Kong harbor. Though the British had declared an embargo on trade with China, the United States acted as intermediary for the British, which signed bonds promising to obey Chinese laws.

Admiral Elliot blockaded Guangzhou's harbor, headed north to blockade the mouth of the Yangtze River, and then entered the city of Tianjin unopposed (see Map 2.2). This was the first Opium War. In the negotiations that followed, China ceded the island of Hong Kong to Britain and offered to pay some war indemnity and reopen Guangzhou's trade with Britain. When the word reached Britain, foreign secretary Lord Palmerston was furious about these terms; the only real concession of the Chinese was modified rights to "a barren island with hardly a house on it"—though, as Michael Ingham (2007) chronicles, it in fact contained a millennia-old fishing community. Palmerston dismissed Elliot, refused to sign the treaty, and sent another expedition that reopened hostilities, decisively defeating Qing forces and signing the 1842 Treaty of Nanjing (Hibbert, 1970:73–182; Tsang, 2007:3–28).

This treaty became the basis for all China's relations with foreign powers. It opened Guangzhou, Fuzhou and Xiamen in Fujian province, Ningbo in

Zhejiang province, and Shanghai for residence by British subjects. It also created British consulates there and let British merchants carry on trade with whomever they chose and not merely with official trading organizations (*cohongs;* see Chapter 7). It let Chinese subjects reside with and work for the British and promised to protect British living in China, along with their property. It limited taxation on imported goods to "a fair and regular tariff" at customs halls in the five "treaty ports" and stipulated that foreigners need no longer use terms like "I beg you" in correspondence with Chinese officials (Spence, 1999:160–163). Deviating from his instructions, the British negotiator also forced the Chinese to cede Hong Kong Island to Britain "in perpetuity." Further treaties would increase the number of treaty ports, extend these privileges to other nations, and allow missionaries to come to China and foreigners to learn Chinese. Foreign countries would also be able to establish embassies in Beijing. And the treaties would expand the principle of extraterritoriality—that any foreigner accused of a crime should be turned over to officials of his or her own government for punishment. Chapter 7 elaborates on these developments.

Among the treaty ports, only one would maintain prominence: Shanghai, then a small fishing village and now China's largest city. Its chief rival was that "barren island," Hong Kong. Immediately after Elliot's arrival, trading ships operators like Alexander Matheson, Lancelot Dent, and William Jardine began to build warehouses there, where they could store opium and other goods they traded with China, away from the reach of Chinese officials (see Brook and Wakabayashi, 2000). Soon a frontier community, composed of Chinese and a few British subjects, was growing along the harbor. The many islands on the seacoast north of the Pearl River Delta had provided refuge for pirates and smugglers, who had plied these waters for centuries. During the decades following establishment of Hong Kong, the island community became a neutral place where British and Chinese traders, pirates, bankers, and officials could meet to do business. More wars and skirmishes were to ensue before diplomatic and trade relations with China stabilized; even when they were at their most intense, ships moved in and out of Hong Kong harbor carrying goods between China and the rest of the world. British traders imported 6.5 million pounds of opium into China each year (Marks, 2006:127). Crowded streets emerged on the hillsides that rise steeply from the harbor.

Rising Stature

In 1860, the British received a lease on Kowloon, the small, flatter peninsula on the mainland just across from Hong Kong harbor (Tsang, 2007:29–44). There they had room to lay out military barracks. In 1896, the Chinese (smarting from the Treaty of Shimonoseki after their defeat by Japan in the Sino-Japanese War) signed a secret agreement with Russia, agreeing to take common action against the Japanese in case of attack and allowing Russian ships to use any Chinese port. The Germans then used the murder of two missionaries as an excuse to send in warships and force China to lease them the port of Qingdao on the Shandong peninsula (Map 2.2) for ninety-nine years. Across the bay, the Russians seized Lushun in Manchuria and negotiated a treaty ceding it to them (they renamed it Port Arthur) for twenty-five years. South of the Pearl River on Hainan Island (Map 2.2), the French signed a lease ceding France a harbor for ninety-nine years. Feeling the need for more land to defend Kowloon harbor from the Russian and French warships now plying Chinese waters, in 1898 the British obtained a ninety-nine-year lease for the New Territories—365 square miles of land north of Kowloon and 235 surrounding islands (Hayes, 2006). The Kowloon-Canton railway, completed in 1912, linked Kowloon with the New Territories and China. It helped encourage more of Hong Kong's expanding populace (now surpassing a quarter million) to move across into Kowloon.

Hong Kong's unique position as a meeting place between China and the outside world was maturing (see Brown and Foot, 1997; Hibbert, 1970; Carroll, 2007; Lee, 2008). The 90,000 inhabitants of the New Territories had a history of independence from China—there is little record of them being under Chinese rule before the eleventh century. Since many had been engaged in smuggling activities and rebelled fiercely against the new Qing dynasty, the emperor forced them to move inland from the sea in 1662. Later, coastal fishermen and farmers from farther north joined them. By the end of the nineteenth century, other rebels had gravitated to the area. Hong Kong had already become a place where China and the outside world could meet. The Hong Kong and Chinese Bank, founded in 1865, had grown into the biggest bank in China by the end of the century. Hong Kong and Macau facilitated contact, remittances, investment, and trade with overseas Chinese in countries that did not have diplomatic relations with China. Hong Kong's non-Chinese populace still did not exceed 20,000; fewer than 1,500 were British. Chinese in Hong Kong could study and discuss new ideas without worrying about political consequences; they could learn about parliamentary government and speak English as their principal language. The Red House, located in the New Territories, became the center where several coups against the Qing dynasty were planned (see Chung, 1997; Tsai, 1995; Tsang, 2007:73–101). Hundreds of individuals involved in those aborted attempts sought refuge there. Sun Yat-sen studied medicine at Hong Kong's College of Medicine for the Chinese, which would expand into Hong Kong University in 1911, the year he founded the republic (see Chapter 4).

The Suez Canal opened in 1869, making the voyage from Western Europe to India and the Far East much shorter. Between 1880 and 1890, Britain's foreign investment rose to three-quarters of its domestic investment. Its foreign trade was greater than that of France, Germany, and the United States combined. Still, by the end of the century, Britain's exports to China constituted only 1.5 percent of its total exports; Britain and all its colonies combined exported less to China than to Holland (Welsh, 1993:282, 318). This would not change markedly before the end of World War II. Hong Kong's trade in opium and other goods made it basically profitable, but not among Britain's greatest sources of colonial income. Britain decided to concentrate its military forces in Singapore rather than Hong Kong. Shanghai's volume of trade came to match that of Hong Kong.

Many Chinese became wary of Britain's imperialism and the strict social segregation it maintained between Chinese and white inhabitants of its colonies. The Whampoa Military Academy, just outside Guangzhou, became the launching ground in 1925 for Chiang Kai-shek's attempt to take China back from the warlords, who had removed power from Beijing. Using weapons and advisers supplied by the Soviet Union, he swept out from Guangzhou to take territory. This was accompanied by strikes and student demonstrations. On May 30, 1925, British troops fired on some demonstrators in Shanghai, killing and wounding several, and this precipitated strikes against the British in many cities. During one of those strikes in Hong Kong, British troops killed over fifty Chinese and wounded a hundred more. For sixteen months China boycotted Hong Kong ships and goods, crippling its economy. Soon China's united front had split apart, Japanese aggression grew, and the republic sought aid from the United States and Britain. Hong Kong's trade resumed.

When Japan occupied Hong Kong in 1941 after a short battle, it had 1.6 million inhabitants (Snow, 2003). Britain returned to liberate the island in 1945 and quickly restored law and order, a stable currency, public utilities, adequate supplies of food, and a stable business climate. This contrasted sharply with the situation in Chinese cities. And Britain's policy of continuing good relations with the Kuomintang while establishing early diplomatic relations with the new communist regime contrasted with the behavior of other Western powers in the region. That set the stage for a new and important phase in Hong Kong's history. As civil war erupted in China, hundreds of thousands of refugees poured across Hong Kong's border, until both sides shut off the flow by 1950. Many of these refugees, fleeing Shanghai and other former commercial centers, were experienced in business. The immigration created a huge housing problem, spurring Hong Kong's government into a massive housing construction program. Thousands of small industries employed many of the new workers. By 2011, its population stood at 7.1 million.

Living with the People's Republic

China contended that Hong Kong had been the result of treaties imposed on China and was therefore a part of China temporarily under foreign occupation. There was always a conflict for the People's Republic of China (PRC) between its anti-imperialism and its relations with Britain (Jain, 1976:158–183; Chan and Young, 1994). Although the PRC was slow to create full diplomatic links with Britain due to Britain's refusal to break off relations with Taiwan, it never broke the relations it established with Britain early on. Britain reluctantly went along with the US call for an embargo of China, yet trade continued through Hong Kong (Boardman, 1976; Schenk, 2001; Tsang, 2007:161–206). The Bank of China building in Hong Kong housed the New China News Agency; in the absence of formal diplomatic relations, it acted as the representative of the PRC for relations with Britain. The US consulate in Hong Kong became the largest in the world, gathering intelligence on China and seeking to keep communist goods from reaching the United States through Hong Kong. The consulate's presence helped encourage cooperation between smugglers and Hong Kong revenue officers. Meanwhile, many prominent Shanghai business-people opened small workshops producing clothing and small consumer goods. In contrast to Britain and China, they were free to make purchases in stable US dollars (to which the Hong Kong dollar has been pegged since 1983, at a rate of 7.8 Hong Kong dollars to one US dollar). Taxes were low, wages were rising, and profits could be sent out of the colony freely. The civil disturbances of the Cultural Revolution (see Chapters 4 and 7) spread into Hong Kong in 1967 and disrupted the economy briefly. The island gradually increased its exports to the outside world and remained the easiest point of entry for visitors to China. Hong Kong manufacturers, seeking more cheap labor, began to establish factories in the nearby province of Guangdong.

When China's opening to the world began in 1978, Hong Kong was perfectly positioned to become the hub of the reforms taking place in the special economic zones, where the initial experiments in a freer market took place before they were extended to all of China (Meyer, 2006). Two of the first four zones to be established—Shenzhen and Zhuhai (adjoining Macau)—are close to Hong Kong. A Hong Kong resident who had made billions in the Hong Kong real estate market, Gordon Wu, immediately began construction on a six-lane turnpike linking Shenzhen to Hong Kong, using his own money. At that point, Shenzhen was just a farming village. The colossal gamble spurred colossal growth. Today Shenzhen is filled with factories, skyscrapers, amusement parks, hotels, and office buildings, with a population exceeding 10 million (versus 7.1 million in Hong Kong and the New Territories). Hong Kong's new US$7 billion airport was constructed along with highways, bridges, tunnels, and towns. Guangdong's government is building roads, bridges, airports, and vast swamp reclamation projects. Hong Kong and Kowloon are packed with new luxury office complexes, hotels, convention centers, wharves, and shopping malls. The Pearl River Delta and the Yangtze River Delta around Shanghai, farther north, became the fastest-growing economic regions in the world, often surpassing 20 percent increases in gross domestic product (GDP) a year. By the time it was handed over to China in 1997, Hong Kong had become the world's eighth-largest trading economy, accounting for about a sixth of China's total GDP (Patten, 1997). Hong Kong was the largest foreign investor in the Philippines, the second largest in Vietnam, and the third largest in Indonesia, Thailand, and Taiwan.

Between 1970 and 2010, Hong Kong's economy more than quadrupled in size. Its 2010 per capita GNP of US$45,900 in purchasing power parity surpassed that of Switzerland ($42,600), Australia ($41,000), Canada ($39,400), Germany ($35,700), Taiwan ($35,700), United Kingdom ($34,800), Japan ($34,000), France ($33,100), and China ($7,600), and is close to that of Singapore ($62,100), Norway ($54,600), the United Arab Emirates ($49,600), and the United States ($47,200) (CIA, 2011; see also Table 5.1). But the percentage of its GDP deriving from manufacturing dropped from 31 percent to less than 2 percent, with its fastest growth in the financial and insurance sector (which rose to 15 percent of GDP) and export, import, and retail trade. Hong Kong benefits from re-exporting (i.e., passing through its harbor, storage facilities, and its financial system) goods manufactured elsewhere. Ninety-one percent of the re-exports were to or from mainland China, which accounted for 49 percent of Hong Kong's trade value in 2009.

In 2010, 4.3 million foreign tourists and businesspeople came through Hong Kong on the way to the mainland, and in 2010, citizens of China made 22.7 million trips into Hong Kong. As mainland China's fourth-largest trading partner (after the European Union, the United States, and Japan), Hong Kong accounts for 8 percent of China's total trade value. Forty-two percent of China's foreign investment came from or through Hong Kong by the end of 2010 (US$456 billion). The total amount of foreign investment coming into Hong Kong amounted to 488 percent of its GDP at the end of 2010; 36 percent (US$341 billion) came from the mainland. Hong Kong's new airport is the world's busiest in terms of international cargo tons carried and the third busiest in terms of international passengers, and Hong Kong harbor is one of the world's busiest container ports. Hong Kong is the tenth-largest trading entity in the world; China is the second-largest. Between 1990 and 2010, Hong Kong's real GDP grew an average of 4 percent a year, surpassing the world average of 3.4 percent (*Hong Kong Yearbook 2010*).

To adapt to its roles as China's financier, marketer, raw materials supplier, quality controller, packager, and shipper, Hong Kong's government invested heavily in developing harbor and airport facilities, office and convention space, education, housing, and health care. Between 1963 and 2011, the portion of government expenditures devoted to health, education, housing, and social welfare grew from 21 percent to over 50 percent (see Chan and Postiglione, 1996; Shek, 2002; Wong, White, and Gui, 2004; *Hong Kong Yearbook 2010*). Health care at family planning, child, and maternal health centers, social hygiene clinics, tuberculosis clinics, mental health clinics, and emergency wards is provided free of charge or for low fees, and other health services are heavily subsidized by the government. Hong Kong's infant mor-

Robert E. Gamer

Hong Kong harbor, 2011.

tality rate of 1.6 per 1,000 births and its life expectancy of eighty for males and eighty-six for females are among the best in the world (*Hong Kong Yearbook 2010*). The government spends 23 percent of its recurrent budget on education to ensure that the workforce adapts to the new demands of technology and the service economy. Students with inadequate means receive grants to pay for school fees, travel, and textbooks from primary school through university. Hong Kong had one university at the end of World War II; twelve additional degree-granting institutions of higher education have been founded since, along with nine other junior and technical colleges. Secondary schools offer many technical, industrial, and business courses, with apprenticeships and training for the disabled. Buildings and equipment are modern and advanced. In 1987, only one young person in thirty-three pursued a postsecondary higher education; today over 60 percent do (Patten, 1997; Ho, Morris, and Chung, 2005; *Hong Kong Yearbook 2010*).

Hong Kong's government balances its budget. Its ability to do so depends on high and constantly increasing land prices. All of Hong Kong's land belongs to the government. Nearly half of the government's income comes from auctioning off long-term leases to this land and renewing these leases; changing zoning designations on leases; collecting taxes on rents and mortgages, on property, and on profits from land development companies; and collecting rents from public housing and other government-owned buildings. Very low taxes on land that is not generating income encourages large investors to buy land or flats for hoarding until prices rise. Both the government and land-related investors benefit from rising prices. So do the bureaucrats, contractors, laborers, and other service enterprises that build the infrastructure from portions of these land taxes dedicated to public works projects—which themselves raise the value of the land around them. But all this has radically raised the cost of housing for the general public, especially young professionals just trying to set up families. Thirty percent of the populace live in public housing, but few new units are being built for low-income workers. There are 1.2 milllion people below the poverty line. Corporate profits taxes and income taxes are capped at about 15 percent, and 60 percent of the workforce pay nothing. There is no capital gains tax, sales tax, hotel room tax, or (since 2006) estate tax (*Hong Kong Yearbook 2010*).

The Transition to Chinese Rule

Hong Kong was ruled by a governor appointed by Britain from 1841 to 1997. Initially, he was assisted by a Legislative Council, also composed of appointed individuals. In 1884, one Chinese was appointed to the council; the number grew to three (out of eighteen) in 1929. In 1984, the British and Chinese governments issued a joint declaration on the future of Hong Kong. At that point, all members of Hong Kong's Legislative Council were still appointed (though elections for some members of a sanitation board, later broadened into an urban council and then into 18 district boards, had been held since 1883, with very few eligible to vote).

The 1984 Sino-British Joint Declaration agreed to return Hong Kong to China on July 1, 1997 (Jeffries, 2010:134–160). Hong Kong would be part of China but would maintain a separate system—"one country, two systems." Beijing would retain control over defense and foreign affairs. A joint liaison group would conduct consultations to prepare for the turnover. (On December 20, 1999, Portugal returned Macau to China in a similar manner.) Never in modern history has a handover of territory been agreed on so far in advance. Hong Kong would be a special administrative region guaranteed an "open and free plural society" with its own laws, institutions, and freedoms for fifty years (Bueno de Mesquita, Newman, and Rabushka, 1996; Chan and Postiglione, 1996; Chang and Chuang, 1998; Chung, 2001; Herschensohn, 1999; Li, 2000; Lam, 2007; Tsang, 2007:211–277; Lee, 2006; Ma, 2007). It could maintain its liberal policies on exchange controls; join international trade and cultural organizations; collect its own taxes and use them for its own purposes; and determine its own policies on international air travel, land rights, passports, and shipping rights.

Then, without consulting the joint liaison group, Hong Kong's governor, for the first time in Hong Kong's history, agreed to hold elections for some seats on the Legislative Council and established a new elected regional council for the New Territories. The 1984 offer of "one country, two systems" in the Sino-British Joint Declaration, as with the similar offer to Taiwan in 1981 (discussed in the next section), had assumed that both systems would restrain democracy (Lam, 2004).

In 1994, China's government indicated that, after the transfer in 1997, it would ignore Hong Kong's reforms. In 1996, China appointed a preparatory committee composed of owners of major Hong Kong companies, professional people, and people from China to choose the governor's replacement. They picked the owner of a major shipping company, Tung Chee-hwa, to replace the governor and endorsed Beijing's plan to cancel all the new changes in the legislature and abolish the urban and regionals, but to elect a new legislature the following year on its own terms. That election in 1998 brought a record 53 percent of the electorate (as of 2011, Hong Kong had 3.3 million registered voters) to the polls to directly elect twenty of the new body's sixty members; thirty more were indirectly elected by approximately 100,000 corporate and professional voters in twenty-eight "functional constituencies" representing insurance, health care, transport, education, real estate and contractors, social welfare, labor, and other sectors (Loh, 2006.) Parties critical of the government won more than two-thirds of the votes (and a third of the legislature's seats under complex voting rules) and called for a speedup of electoral reform; when legislative elections were held again in 2000 (this time for twenty-four seats), only 43 percent of the electorate participated, and support for the prodemocratic parties declined. In the 2004 legislative elections, thirty seats were directly elected; eighteen of these (and seven more from the functional constituency seats) went to prodemocratic parties (which garnered 60 percent of the votes). In 2008, nineteen of the thirty directly elected seats (and four of the functional constituency seats) went to prodemocratic parties (with 57 percent of the votes). Forty-five percent of registered voters participated in both those elections. To avoid any appearance of direct interference, China's Communist Party has not contested these elections. However, it has given support to parties sympathetic to its preferences and is stepping up that support.

In 2002, an 800-member election committee composed of business and professional people, and Hong Kong members of the Legislative Council and the National People's Congress and People's Consultative Committee, chose Tung Chee-hwa to serve a second five-year term. At that time, only 16 percent of respondents in one poll wanted him to seek another term. Under Hong Kong's Basic Law, it could hold direct elections for a majority of legislative seats and for its chief executive after 2007 if the chief executive and two-thirds of the members of the legislature agreed. However, in 2004, the National People's Congress of China declared this would not happen. Hong Kong demonstrators took to the streets to protest this and oppose a law proposed by Beijing that would have greatly loosened the definition of treasonable acts, threatening civil liberties of journalists who write freely in Hong Kong, of companies selling weapons components to Taiwan, and of groups like Falun

Gong who demonstrate in front of the Legislative Council building every weekend (Currie, Petersen, and Mok, 2006). In response to massive street demonstrations in Hong Kong and opposition by Hong Kong's legislature, Tung Chee-hwa resigned, after withdrawing the proposed treason law, and was replaced by civil servant Donald Tsang Yam-kuen, who was reelected by the 800-member election committee in 2007. Sir Tsang was the first Chinese to hold the position of financial secretary under colonial British rule and was knighted by the queen. He was opposed in this election by a candidate backed by the prodemocratic reform parties but won most of the votes.

On the last day of 2007, Beijing announced that direct elections for the chief executive could not begin until 2017, and all candidates would have to be approved by Beijing. Direct elections for all legislative seats might begin in 2020. However, limited democratic reforms might be allowed before the 2012 elections. In 2010, Hong Kong's legislature passed legislation raising the number of its members from sixty to seventy, with the ten new seats all directly elected by the voters. Five of them are divided among the five regional districts, and five of them—dubbed "super-legislators"—are directly elected by all the voters, except those few who vote for functional constituency delegates. And the size of the election committee for choosing the chief executive was increased from 800 to 1,200 members, 200 of them directly elected. Plans are also progressing to hold the 2017 election for chief executive; for the first time, Hong Kong's chief executive will be chosen by universal suffrage. The election committee, or a committee based on it, is likely to nominate the candidates. Because under the Basic Law two-thirds of the legislature must vote for amendments to suffrage rules, it may be hard to obtain enough votes from among the functional constituency members to change their seats into directly elected ones in 2020. That could radically shift power away from powerful economic groups. According to the Hurun Report, in 2011 alone, the richest 70 members of the Legislative Council increased their wealth by US$90 billion, more than the total combined net worth of the entire US Congress, Cabinet, and Supreme Court (De Golyer, 2011; Martin, 2011; *Hong Kong Yearbook 2010*; Pesek, 2012).

A new Court of Final Appeals was created in Hong Kong to replace the British High Court in London, which had formerly been the highest court of appeals, though China's National People's Congress retains the ultimate right to amend Hong Kong's Basic Law should it wish to do so (Tsang, 2001). A Committee of Twelve (with six members chosen by Beijing and six by Hong Kong) reviews the constitutionality of laws passed by Hong Kong's legislature. In 1999, the National People's Congress overruled a decision by Hong Kong's Court of Final Appeals on a case regarding who is entitled to reside in Hong Kong, thus setting a precedent for potential cases in the future on more sensitive issues (see Tsang, 2001). At the 1997 handover, Hong Kong's professional civil servants, who had been running the government, retained their jobs so long as they declared loyalty to the new regime (Burns, 2005). In 2001, Anson Chan, head of the civil service, resigned because she felt Beijing was exerting too much pressure on their operations; in 2002, top civil servants were placed on five-year contracts rather than serving for life. This raises concerns about the independence of the civil service.

The 1997 Asian economic turndown brought a sharp drop in Hong Kong's real estate prices, exports, and tourism, which recovered briefly in 2000, only to confront the economic downturn and September 11, 2001, attacks in the United States, the SARS (severe acute respiratory syndrome) outbreak in 2003, and the world banking crisis of 2008, which again depressed all these economic activities in Hong Kong, while Shanghai's economy continued to grow at a 10 percent annual rate. Those setbacks proved to be temporary. Hong Kong's economy is growing in tandem with China's booming economy. Tourism is rising rapidly, with 36 million visitors in 2010. Hong Kong's heavy investment in education, its established rule of law, and its comprehensive financial network, combined with a convertible currency, transportation and communications infrastructure, simple tax system and low tax rate—and its reputation as a free economy friendly to business—leave its position highly competitive. Hong Kong and the Pearl River Delta have ten times the number of Asian headquarters for multinational corporations as either Shanghai or Beijing. But soaring rent and real estate prices, and an increasingly competitive job market, have taken a toll on the government's popularity. In 2011, large numbers again took to the streets to stop a proposed change in by-election laws, demanding more democracy and access to affordable housing. A third of those aged over 65 live in poverty. While the government held back spending on social problems, it pursued expensive airport and highway projects, and supported a provision in the constitution filling hospital maternity wards with mainland mothers because children born in the territory have a right to permanent residence. Only a third of citizens told pollsters they were satisfied with Sir Tsang's government (De Golyer, 2011:77), and his support took further beatings with reports of his lavish 6,500-square-foot retirement penthouse and rides on yachts and private planes that were furnished by wealthy business leaders. During his last month in office, satisfaction with government had dropped to 19 percent of respondents, and a committee of the Legislative Council was considering whether to impeach him.

In March 2012, the election committee selected a successor to Sir Tsang as chief executive, choosing between two top civil servants with close ties to Beijing: Henry Tang Ying-yen, the son of a wealthy textile manufacturer, and Leung Chun-ying, the son of a police officer. Both are wealthy, top-level civil servants. Leung is a member of the Standing Committee of the Chinese People's Political Consultative Conference. He had high approval ratings in polls, promising to build more public housing, alleviate poverty, and assert independence. This angered the richest real estate tycoons, who endorsed Tang, with close ties to them and Jiang Zemin. Media charges flew. Leung was accused of using his public office to benefit his surveying company, of being a secret member of the Communist Party, and advocating using riot police to tear gas the 2003 treason-law protesters. His poll approval ratings fell from two-thirds to one-third. The press also carried sensational reports of Tang's extramarital affair, an illegitimate child, and his failure to get permits for his palatial home improvement project. In one poll, he had 16 percent approval. A third candidate, Albert Ho Chun-yan, head of the Democratic Party (who thus can't even get a visa to visit the mainland) was representing all the pro-democratic parties; with discontent over policies supported by those parties he got little support in the polls. Faced with a public relations debacle, Premier Wen Jiabao publicly asserted that the election committee should choose the most popular candidate and sent a Politburo member to lobby for Leung, who then won a majority of votes on the election committee and was selected to succeed Sir Tsang. Amid massive street demonstrations protesting his selection and the heavy-handed interference by Beijing, Leung was summoned to Beijing to receive an "instrument of appointment" from Premier Wen. The legislative elections were held in September of 2012. Finding a balance among pleasing Beijing, the real estate developers, and Hong Kong's public will be a difficult task for them. Their handling of surging housing prices, shortages of public housing, stagnant wages, rising unemployment, environmental issues, immigration from the mainland, and declining social services for the poor and elderly will be essential. None of the political parties have easy solutions, and tension over those issues is high. It is difficult for a chief executive to govern Hong Kong without popular support. This has strengthened the argument of those calling for democratic election of the chief executive in 2017 and of all legislators in 2020.

Meanwhile, nearby Macau is also experiencing economic good fortune (Chan and Lo, 2006; Lo, 2007; Berlie, 2000; Gunn, 1996; McGivering, 1999; Porter, 1999). Since 2007, it has welcomed over 25 million tourists a year, half from China and another third from Hong Kong. New high-speed rail and superhighways opening in 2012 make it increasingly accessible. Most visitors come to enjoy its more than thirty casinos. Their VIP rooms offer the opportunity to exchange large amounts of currency outside the strict confines of China's laws, which forbid its free exchange (although about half of China's illegal foreign exchange seems to take place in nearby Shenzhen). Under a 2002 law, Las Vegas owners have been opening large new casinos, helping to turn Macau gambling revenues into the world's highest. So far, Macau is the only place in China with legalized casino gambling. With a liberal monetary control policy, and banks welcome from around the globe, Macau is a popular tax haven for investors.

Taiwan

We turn now to the other focal point for overseas Chinese—Taiwan, formerly Formosa (Map 2.2). At the end of World War II, mainland Chinese took power there. Like Hong Kong, it is heavily involved in China's economy. But is it a part of China or a separate nation? Why does this small island figure so prominently in Chinese and world affairs? Are its former mainland Chinese still part of the mainland, or have they become overseas Chinese?

China has never succeeded in establishing cultural or political dominance over the island of Formosa. In the seventeenth century, Chinese traders from Guangdong and Fujian began crossing the strait to Formosa, purchasing deer hides and horns from hunters and traders there (Andrade, 2005). These Chinese established some small settlements along Formosa's southwest coast. Chinese and Japanese pirates and Spanish traders also sought refuge in nearby harbors, and in 1624 Dutch traders established the fort of Zeelandia on one of them. Chinese settlers moved to these towns. They brought with them from Fujian province the Hokkien and Hakka languages, which—along with the ten languages spoken by the island's half million aborigines—have become the language of the 80 percent of Taiwan's populace. During the following two decades, the Ming dynasty was falling to Manchu invasion. A Fujian pirate with a trading empire extending to Japan had a son, Koxinga, by a Japanese wife. Koxinga turned his father's home of Xiamen (in Fujian; see Map 2.2) into a major trading port, but as the Qing armies moved toward his city, he set his eyes and guns on Zeelandia. Although the Dutch resisted his assault for several months, in 1662 they surrendered. When the Qing conquerors pursued their policy of removing coastal Chinese of Fujian and Guangdong inland to cut off their independent trading activities, tens of thousands of them fled to Zeelandia. In 1683, a large Qing fleet finally brought it under submission.

The Qing established a new city, Tainan, near Zeelandia and declared it the capital of the island, which would now be a part of Fujian province. They largely left it alone, restricting further Chinese immigration and declaring that the lands belonging to the native aboriginal Formosans should be retained by them. After a revolt during the eighteenth century, the emperors, hoping to make it less of a frontier society, allowed wives and children to join the Chinese men on the island and the Chinese to rent land from the native islanders. In 1858, an "unequal treaty" (see Chapter 7), the Treaty of Tianjin, opened additional treaty ports, including two on Formosa. By that time, numerous Chinese were crossing the strait to settle cities and farms there; today significant portions of the populace have blood and linguistic ties to those immigrants (Brown, 2004; Constable, 2005; Harrison, 2007; Hsieh, 2006). In 1871, Formosan aborigines killed fifty-four shipwrecked Ryukyu sailors (the Ryukyu Islands are located between Taiwan and Japan; see Map 2.1). Japan asserted its right to seek justice for the Ryukyuans. The Ryukyu

Islands had been paying tribute (see Chapter 7 on that custom) to China since 1372 but had also been paying tribute to Japan since 1609 (without China's knowledge). The Japanese sent a fleet to Formosa in 1874. The Chinese fleet defending Formosa contained only guns for firing salutes that would burst if real shells were fired from them; it could not mount a defense. The treaty that followed gave Japan the right to build barracks on Formosa, paid for by China. The Japanese then occupied Formosa but, after protests from the British, retreated. In 1879, they annexed Okinawa and the other Ryukyus. In 1885, China declared Formosa a full province. Within a decade, the Japanese soundly defeated the Chinese navy in the Sino-Japanese War. The Treaty of Shimonoseki (Gordon, 2007; Paine, 2005), signed in 1895, forced China to give Japan Formosa (which they renamed Taiwan), the Pescadores Islands (in the strait between Formosa and the mainland), and the Liaodong peninsula of Manchuria (the southern tip of Liaoning; see Map 2.2).

The Japanese forced the Chinese inhabitants of Taiwan to learn the Japanese language and customs (Ching, 2001; Liao and Yang, 2006). They used the island to supply Japan with food, wood, minerals, and chemicals; its economy prospered as Japan's Co-Prosperity Sphere took over Asia during World War II (Edmonds and Goldstein, 2002; Ho, 1978). At the Cairo Conference in 1943, anticipating Japan's defeat, Franklin D. Roosevelt and Winston Churchill agreed to the demand of Chiang Kai-shek that Taiwan be awarded to his Kuomintang Nationalists. Nationalist troops entered the island in 1945, but their corruption and inefficiency soon eroded its stability and economy. When riots erupted in 1947, they suppressed them brutally, executing thousands of intellectuals and prominent citizens and contributing to enduring resentment of the KMT by the Formosans who already lived there. By 1949, the Communists were overwhelming the KMT Nationalist troops on the mainland (see Chapter 4); 2 million of them fled to Taiwan's capital, Taipei, where Chiang Kai-shek set up his government in exile. Having cleared him and his armies from the mainland, the Communists vowed to take Taiwan as well and complete their victory. The Nationalist base closest to mainland was on the island of Quemoy, part of a group of fourteen islands just outside Amoy Bay, outside the old Chinese treaty port of Xiamen. Just beyond Quemoy lies the Taiwan Strait, which separates Taiwan from the mainland. The Communists began shelling that island group in October 1949 but did not have the military capability to mount an immediate invasion of those islands or of Taiwan. In the months that followed, both the Communist and Nationalist forces ceased hostilities while they assessed their options. The US secretary of state, Dean Acheson, gave a speech outlining US strategic interests in the area without mentioning South Korea and Taiwan.

Then, on June 25, 1950, North Korea attacked South Korea. Two days later, the United States extended protection to Taiwan. It gave Taiwan military assistance and patrolled the strait between Taiwan and the mainland

(Accinelli, 1997; Tucker, 1994; Bush, 2004; Cole, 2006; Huang and Li, 2010:11-87). In 1954, China shelled islands in the Taiwan Strait; in response, the United States signed a treaty with Taiwan guaranteeing to defend it and the Pescadores Islands, just to the west of it within the strait, from invasion, in exchange for a pledge that Taiwan would not attack the mainland without approval by the United States. Six months later, China pledged it would use only peaceful means to liberate Taiwan and declared that Kuomintang members were even welcome to visit China. Until the Cultural Revolution began, China gave official receptions for all visiting groups of overseas Chinese, but this did not stop further hostilities. When China began bombarding the offshore islands of Quemoy and Matsu in 1958, the United States sent in troops. In 1962, Chiang Kai-shek threatened to invade the mainland; the United States restrained him, and the Soviet Union threatened to support China against an invasion.

The United States initiated a massive program of military and civilian aid to Taiwan (Tucker, 1994). Chiang Kai-shek initiated land reforms to give land to native Formosan farmers, restricted imports, and helped foreign industries in a special economic zone obtain credit and avoid taxes and regulations on exports. (This zone, created in the 1960s, would become a model for mainland China's special zones after 1978, where the reform experiments began.) With exports of manufactured goods surging, Taiwan's gross national product (GNP) quadrupled between 1950 and 1980 (Marsh, 1996; Gold, 1986; Clark and Tan, 2011; Rigger, 2011:41–58). When US president Richard Nixon visited Beijing in 1972, he agreed to let Taiwan and the mainland work out the integration between them. When the United States resumed full diplomatic relations with China in 1979, it broke off formal relations and its defense treaty with Taiwan; its troops had to leave Taiwan, and it could supply it with only "defensive" weapons. Taiwan also lost its seats on the International Monetary Fund and the World Bank. Since Taiwan claims to represent all of China (calling itself the Republic of China, not the Republic of Taiwan), and mainland China also claims Taiwan as one of its provinces, the bodies had to choose which regime represented China. Recognizing the People's Republic of China as the government of China required breaking off formal relations with the Republic of China. This was a dramatic switch.

By 1979, Taiwan's per capita GNP was six times that of mainland China; even in purchasing power parity terms it was still over four times that of China (US$35,700 vs. US$7,600) in 2009. But discontent was growing on the island. Riots in 1971 and 1972 had protested Taiwan's loss of its United Nations seat and special relationship with the United States, as the United States and the People's Republic of China warmed relations. People were angry over corruption and lack of freedoms under KMT rule, and native Formosans were expressing resentment over the takeover of their island by Chinese born on the mainland; many of them wanted Taiwan to declare itself independent of the mainland, with no aspirations to become a part of or to take over China. Then it could gain diplomatic recognition and join international bodies like any other nation. The KMT claimed the right to put down these demonstrations with strict military measures because it was still engaged in a civil war to regain the mainland. In 1975, Chiang Kai-shek died and was succeeded by his son, Chiang Ching-kuo, who in turn died in 1988 (Huang and Li, 2010:88-122).

Meanwhile, investment continued to pour into Taiwan, and its trade rose markedly. Two of China's first four special economic zones, created in 1980, Shantou (in Guangdong) and Xiamen (in Fujian), are on the coast opposite Taiwan (Lee, 2000; Tsai and Cheng, 2006). The initial investment response was slow, but by the end of the decade Taiwan was picking up speed rapidly, and by 2000 its GNP ranked sixteenth in the world, 30 percent greater than Russia's, nearly the same as that of the Netherlands and Australia, a third of that of China (with a population fifty-six times smaller), and a thirtieth of that of the United States. Due to the political tensions, Taiwanese trade and investment on the mainland had to be done quietly through Hong Kong. In 1987, just before his death, Chiang Ching-kuo lifted the ban on travel to the mainland, opening a flood of Taiwan investment and tourism there. He also lifted the strict martial law that had tightly restricted civil liberties for years (Rigger, 2011:59–94). For the first time, Taiwan's longer-term inhabitants could speak Hokkien and Hakka in public, form opposition parties, print opposing views, run for office, and hold legislative seats. Many of them backed the Democratic Progressive Party (the DPP).

Chiang's successor to the presidency and control of the Kuomintang, Lee Teng-hui, was a native Hakka-speaking Chinese. He held the first open elections for a fully elected national legislature, which left the Kuomintang with a slim majority of seats, and in 2000 held elections for president. Chen Shui-bian, the DPP candidate, also a native Taiwanese, won that election, and for the first time in history a new government came to power via an election (Goldstein and Chang, 2008; Lee, 2010:41–68; Clark and Tan, 2011; Fell, 2011). A year later, elections for the legislature left the KMT with only 30 percent of the seats, versus 39 percent to the DPP. The core support for the KMT comes from descendants of those who fled the mainland in 1949. Lee Teng-hui left the KMT to join the new proindependence Taiwan Solidarity Union, which gained 6 percent of the seats in the new legislature and became allied with the DPP (Dickson and Chao, 2002). The third largest number of seats in the new legislature, 20 percent, went to the newly formed People First Party, which obtained most of its votes in the heavily indigenous southeast corner of the island and has worked with the KMT in opposition to the DPP. The New Party, advocating closer ties with China, won only one seat.

Chen Shui-bian barely won the 2004 presidential election, which involved an incident in which he was shot; the opposition charged that he arranged the injury himself to gain sympathy votes. His control of the legislature was further weakened in the 2004 legislative election, which gave nearly 51 percent of the seats to a coalition between the KMT, the Pan-Blue Coalition, and the People First Party, but only 45 percent to a coalition of the DPP, the Pan-Green Coalition, and the Taiwan Solidarity Union (Bedford and Hwang, 2006; Fell, 2005).

Many leaders of the DPP call for total independence for Taiwan (Huang and Li, 2010:217–295). They would simply declare Taiwan a sovereign nation, with no formal links to overseas Chinese and no claim over the mainland. Lacking a majority in the parliament, President Chen softened those demands and initiated the Three Direct Links policy to develop government-to-government links with the mainland for trade, the postal service, and transportation, so that these activities would no longer have to be carried out through intermediaries like Hong Kong. Beginning in 2001, goods could be shipped to and from the mainland through Taiwan harbors and airports, and restrictions on Taiwan investments in the mainland were eased, including direct banking. In 2002, both China and Taiwan joined the World Trade Organization (WTO) (see Chang and Goldstein, 2007). By 2008, the mainland had become Taiwan's largest trading partner, with two-way trade surpassing US$132 billion, and US$100 billion of Taiwan business.

But both sides continued to build up their weaponry, and suspicions remained high (Edmonds and Tsai, 2006; Bush, 2004, 2005; Cole, 2006; Copper, 2008; Tian, 2006; Tsang, 2005; Tucker, 2005). President Chen continued to suggest that the question of independence should be decided in a referendum. That issue again emerged in his 2008 referendum to ask voters if Taiwan should seek membership in the United Nations; only a third of voters turned out, so the initiative failed. Chapter 7 discusses this enduring source of tension in the region.

The issue of Taiwan's relationship with China inextricably enmeshes the 65 million overseas Chinese, most of whom live in Hong Kong (with 7.1 million inhabitants), Taiwan (whose population is 23 million), and Southeast Asia. Some of them are billionaires, leading guilds and trading associations that dominate the economies of Indonesia, Singapore, Malaysia, Thailand, the Philippines, Burma, and China itself. They can move themselves and their money at will. They have intimate connections with the leaders and bureaucracies of all these governments (Brown, 2004; Redding, 1995; Gambe, 2000; Weller, 2001). Leaders of both mainland China and Taiwan know they cannot go it alone without the full input from the overseas Chinese; their prosperity depends on the investment capital and trading links of that widely dispersed community.

Two-thirds of voters turned out for the 2008 legislative and presidential elections, bringing dramatic change. The KMT and five parties aligned with it, boosted by a stagnant economy (4–5 percent GDP growth, with 4 percent unemployment) in Taiwan, and running on a platform opposing independence and favoring improved relations with the mainland, received 72 percent of the vote in the legislative elections, to the DPP's 24 percent. That gave them eighty-seven seats to the DPP's twenty-seven in the legislature, ending deadlock there. In the presidential election that followed, the KMT's candidate Ma Ying-jeou (with 58 percent of the vote) swept past the DPP's candidate, Frank Hsieh (with 42 percent), to become Taiwan's president. Ma, with graduate degrees from New York University and Harvard, ran on a platform of seeking a peace accord to bring to a formal end the state of hostility, confidence-building military exchanges, direct flights, postal service, and cultural and economic exchanges with China, including a common market, while agreeing to disagree about unification (his slogan for the campaign was "no independence, no unification, no military conflict"). His election was welcomed by China. It paved the way for a quick resolution of more issues (Cai, 2010; Lee, 2010:185–226; Jeffries, 2010:47–133). Within months, agreements were concluded to expand mainland tourism to Taiwan (1.6 million Chinese visited Taiwan in 2010, and 4 million Taiwanese visited the mainland), expand free trade, cooperate on banking and crime fighting, regulate securities trading, and other matters; the number of weekly flights between Taiwan and mainland destinations surpassed 270. Mayors of major Chinese cities led delegations to Taiwan, announcing large new economic projects. More than a million Taiwanese businesspeople live in Shanghai and other mainland cities, 800,000 Taiwanese have residences in China, and 40 percent of Taiwan's exports go to China and Hong Kong, surpassing Japan as Taiwan's largest trading partner. In 2010, Taiwan's GDP grew by 10.9 percent, and that trend continues. In 2009, Chen Shui-bian was jailed for corruption and ordered to serve nineteen years.

Still, Taiwan persists in seeking recognition by international bodies as the legitimate government of China. It has sought readmission to the United Nations, formal visits by its president to other nations, and unofficial and informal relations with as many countries as possible. Only twenty-three countries (largely poor nations from Central America, the South Pacific, and Africa) still maintain diplomatic relations with it. Beijing strongly resists all moves by other countries to maintain informal relations with Taiwan, although, as Chapter 7 explains, it has softened its rhetoric.

The biggest hurdle is how to place the question of unification in the background. In public opinion polls, fewer than 20 percent of Taiwan's citizens want to someday reunite with the mainland, while on the mainland, unification has widespread support. Beijing has 1,600 missiles aimed at Taiwan, and both Taipei and Beijing continue to make and buy more arms.

These facts were on voters' minds as the 2012 presidential and parliamentary election approached. Economic growth spurred by the new economic ties with China had not reached the average Hakka-speaking voter. Unemployment had not declined, housing prices were skyrocketing, and wages were the lowest in thirteen years. The DPP candidate—Tsai Ing-wen, a Hakka-speaking university professor—distanced herself from those in her party who want to push for immediate independence. From a mainland family and born in Hong Kong, Ma's first Cabinet had contained only Mandarin-speakers. However, Ma had not been touched by scandal, while Tsai's role in a questionable business startup reminded voters of past DPP misconduct. And she failed to present an alternative agenda for dealing with China. With public opinion polls showing the race to be close—especially after Ma floated the idea of signing a peace pact with China within the next ten years—200,000 Taiwan business people who were benefiting from the warming relations with China flew home to cast ballots. Ma was elected to a second term with 52 percent of the vote, compared to 46 percent for Tsai, a margin of 800,000 votes. The KMT retained control of the parliament, but reduced to 64 seats out of 113. This provides President Ma with a mandate to cautiously continue his new initiatives with China. For the first time, Beijing did not censor Internet coverage of the Taiwan election, and many millions of mainlanders followed it closely on Sina Weibo.

Tibet

China, Hong Kong, and Taiwan carry out a shadow play with thrusts and parries of defiance, although in reality they share many cultural ties and commercial transactions. Tibet represents a sharp contrast: it is an area without such clear historic cultural or economic ties to China (Blondeau and Buffetrille, 2008), and here the thrusts and parries have resulted in real warfare since the founding of the People's Republic, highly visible to the outside world, with strong partisans on either side. And Westerners have long viewed Tibet through misty eyes, which often makes it hard to separate myth from reality (Baker, 2006; Brauen, 2004; Dodin, 2001; Feigon, 1998; Lopez, 1999). As Chapter 8 explains, China's government recognizes fifty-five minority nationalities, many of which have a long history of resisting Han rule. The ninth largest of these recognized nationalities, with 5.4 million members, is classified as "Tibetan." These "Tibetans" are spread out into four provinces, speak a variety of different languages, and have fought fiercely among themselves for centuries. Tibet's ties to China are complex, as are the animosities that separate them.

The Tibetans are a people living on a high, sparsely settled plateau (see Chapter 2, especially Map 2.4). Along the drier northern portions of the plateau—in Kham, Amdo, and Chantang—they make their living by herding sheep and yak. Along the river valleys and mountain passes to the south, a feudal nobility and the king parceled out lands in exchange for rent and labor services. The king presided over the region, while shamans associated with the native Bon religion, storytellers, and singers of riddles propagated religious beliefs associated with totemism, animism, and occultism (see Chapter 12).

The seventh to tenth centuries CE brought power and culture to Tibet (Stein, 1995:56–75; van Schaik, 2011). In the seventh century, Buddhism (also examined in Chapter 12) was introduced to Tibet from India (Snellgrove, 2003; Novick, 1999:14–29). The country developed a written alphabet, based on the script of Kashmir. Tibetan kings, beginning with the legendary Songsten Gampo, conquered territory in Nepal, Turkistan, and far north and east into what is now Yunnan, Sichuan, Xinjiang, Qinghai, Gansu, and Shaanxi (Map 2.2); married daughters of Chinese emperors and of rulers from other surrounding principalities; and welcomed scholars from Persia, China, and elsewhere (Beckwith, 1993). They signed peace treaties delineating borders with China—then much wider than Tibet's present boundaries—in 734 and 822 CE.

In about 775 CE, the king presided over the construction of a great Buddhist monastery at Samye, brought in a monk from Nepal to be its abbot, ordained several noblemen as monks, and arranged for monks from China to come in and preach. In 791, he decreed Buddhism to be the official state religion. Monks would have special privileges and were to receive gifts. Several hundred people took religious vows. In the succeeding centuries, disputes severely weakened the power of the kings. Some nobility resisted the adoption of Buddhism, whereas others (sometimes claiming divine descent) took charge of the monasteries that sprouted up all over Tibet and surrounding regions, passing the post of abbot from uncle to nephew. Many people joined these monasteries, which began to acquire much land and wealth. Doctrinal disputes arose among the monks; some became morally decadent. Traditional Bon religious practices continued and were absorbed into Buddhism (Kapstein, 2002; Davidson, 2005; Thurman, 1996; Tuttle, 2005; Goldstein, 1997:1–29; van Schaik, 2011).

At the start of the thirteenth century, Genghis Khan, who was to conquer China (see Chapter 3), sent his troops deep into Tibet, whose leaders agreed to send him tribute and thus symbolically recognized his power. Genghis Khan, in turn, invited the Tibetan scholar Sakya Panchen to Mongolia, where he helped him devise an alphabet. In 1270, Kublai Khan granted Sakya's followers rulership of all Tibet; meanwhile, Genghis's descendants were fighting among themselves for control of Mongolia, and various Tibetan monasteries allied with some of them to contest for power, often joining in with their own fighting forces. Two orders, the Black Hats and Red Hats, started looking in villages shortly after the death of a holy individual (a bodhisattva) to seek a baby into which his soul had been reborn, or reincarnated; those individuals were brought into monasteries to be raised as lamas (superior ones). In 1283, the Red Hats declared one of these lamas ruler of Tibet. In keeping with Tantric traditions popular at the time in India, these orders used mantras (repetition of mystical words and revolutions of prayer wheels) and mandalas (sacred diagrams) in rituals and meditations.

In 1403, a monastic scholar, concerned with these two orders' emphasis on worldly power and wealth, founded the Geluk-pa (Yellow Hat) order, which also emphasized the need for monastic discipline, personal morality, and good works as part of the search for total liberation from the world. Armed with this reforming zeal, armies from its monasteries fought with the Red Hats, with the followers of Sakya and the remaining Bon orders, and with the weak kings and princes for political control.

In 1578, the Mongol ruler Altan Khan, seeking an ally among the contending forces, declared the head of the Yellow Hats to be the Dalai (ocean-wide, all-embracing) Lama; Altan's influence was extended further upon the death of this Dalai Lama, when the monks found his reincarnated successor to be none other than a great-grandson of Altan Khan! But this did not stop the bitter fighting for control among the various sects and the kings, who in turn allied with rival Mongol princes. In the seventeenth century, a Mongol ruler sent his armies into Tibet, killed the king, helped the fifth Dalai Lama build the great Potala Palace (Namgyal, 2002; Maher, 2010; van Schaik, 2011), which still dominates the valley above the capital of Lhasa, and, in 1641, declared him the sovereign of Tibet (with a governor nominated by the Mongols to assist him). The Manchu ruler who founded the Qing dynasty in 1644 also was his ally. After his death, bitter fighting broke out among various Tibetan factions, Mongol princes, and Chinese emperors over his successors and who should choose them. When Dzungar Mongol forces invaded Tibet in 1717 to drive out another Mongol prince who had killed the sixth Dalai Lama and was trying to replace him with his own candidate, China attacked Tibet and established small military garrisons there.

The Dalai Lama ruled with assistance from ministers, a council composed of monks and nobles, another monastic council, and a National Assembly composed of high officials; important decisions required the approval of all these bodies (Rahul, 1969:22–72; Richardson, 1984:14–27). Between the death of a Dalai Lama and the growth into manhood of the next, regents were chosen to assume his office. Nobles held power and supervised administration in various regions of Tibet; Kham and Amdo to the northeast remained under Mongol control. China sent to Lhasa two formal representatives (*ambans*), who exerted influence over governance of the kingdom; when they killed a Tibetan official in 1750, Tibetans massacred Chinese living there. Chinese troops intervened to restore order. Chinese troops also helped Tibet repel an invasion by Gurkhas (from Nepal) in 1788 to capture Ladakh (east Kashmir, on Tibet's western border), dictated the peace terms, and closed the borders to the British—who may have instigated the invasion. The Chinese also successfully helped the Tibetans resist invasions from Dogras (out of Kashmir) in 1841. In 1847, despite that loss, the British marked the boundaries between

Tibet and Dogra; the Chinese did not recognize those boundaries, which later became the focus of China's dispute with India. But another Gurkha attack in 1855 was more successful, forcing Tibet to give them trading rights.

The Dalai Lama is believed (along with Songsten Gampo, Tibet's first centralizing Buddhist king) to be the indirect reincarnation of Avalokitesvara, Tibet's patron bodhisattva (one who has achieved a degree of enlightenment but has returned to earth to help living mortals achieve spiritual progress). Tibet's second great lama is the Panchen Lama, abbot of one of the great monasteries, who is the reincarnation of Amitabha, before whom Avalokitesvara took his original bodhisattva vow to return to Tibet and help all beings (Richardson, 1984:38–60). In exchange for helping repulse the 1788 Gurkha invasion, China demanded the right to dictate the candidates from whom the Dalai Lama and Panchen Lama would be chosen. They also allowed those two worthies to open new monasteries in Mongolia and China and welcomed lamas in the imperial court at Beijing. Panchen Lamas began to make that trek, developing ties to China's emperors. The Tibetans continued to ignore the Chinese when choosing Dalai Lamas.

The thirteenth Dalai Lama, who lived from 1875 to 1933, befriended a Russian lama who put him into contact with the Russian czar (Richardson, 1984:73–90, 268–273). This frightened the British, who tried to enter into negotiation with China and Tibet to define Tibet's western and southern borders. When this failed, they sent a military expedition that captured Lhasa in 1904 (Batt, 2001). The Dalai Lama fled to Mongolia, but the British government (before withdrawing its troops) forced his officers to sign a convention delineating the borders it preferred and opening Tibet to trade with Britain. Two years later, the British signed a treaty with China, to which Tibet was not a party, recognizing the 1904 treaty and China's suzerainty (dominance; see Chapter 7) over Tibet, and in 1907 Britain concluded a similar treaty with Russia. Then, in 1910, a Chinese general began to conquer territory in eastern Tibet and then Lhasa itself, forcing the Dalai Lama to flee to India. When the new republic was formed in China in 1911, it declared that Tibet was now an integral part of China, but it could not control or defend China's troops there, now under attack from Tibetan forces. China withdrew its troops, and the Dalai Lama expelled the Chinese *ambans* and renounced all Chinese connections with Tibet. In 1914, Sir Henry McMahon obtained a Tibetan, but not a Chinese, signature on a convention signed in Simla, India, which defined boundaries and still—over Tibet's continuing objections—declared China suzerain over Tibet and even declared large portions of former Tibetan territory to be a part of China (Shakabpa, 1967:246–259; Goldstein, 1991; McKay, 1997; Smith, 2008).

Except for the continuing British representative in Lhasa, who had a radio transmitter, Tibet largely cut itself off from the outside world. This isolation was enforced by a ban on selling food to outsiders and reinforced by the absence in Tibet of any roads or wheeled vehicles; only about twenty Europeans and Americans are known to have entered Tibet during this entire period (Hopkirk, 1995; Harrer, 1954). In 1915, the Khams rose in revolt and captured back some of the terrain taken from them by Chinese troops in 1910. Tibet created no ministry of foreign affairs and exchanged no ambassadors. Few Tibetans spoke any foreign language. Four students were sent to study in England, and in 1948 a few more were selected to study in India. An English school begun in Lhasa in 1945 had to close when the monasteries objected that it might interfere with religious beliefs. Tibet did not issue a passport until 1948, when it sent out a trade delegation in an attempt to alert the world to its pending troubles (Shakabpa, 1967:289–290).

After the death of the thirteenth Dalai Lama in 1933, China sent an informal delegation to Lhasa with a radio transmitter. They stayed until the Tibetan council seized the radio transmitter and expelled them in 1949, after the leader of the Sera monastery, who had ties to the Chinese, attempted a coup to overthrow the young Dalai Lama's regent (Shakabpa, 1967:290–294; Harrer, 1954:222–231; Lin, 2007), and after the new Communist regime in China declared again that Tibet was a province of China. In 1950, with some assistance from Kham rebels who resented Lhasa's rule, Chinese troops entered Tibet, defeated the Dalai Lama's troops, and forced his government to sign a 1951 agreement on "the peaceful liberation of Tibet," declaring it an integral part of China. The Dalai Lama and the "existing political system in Tibet" would stay in place and freedom of religion would be guaranteed, but foreign affairs would be handled by Beijing (Richardson, 1984:290–293). As we discuss below, many Tibetans would like to return to the terms of that treaty. El Salvador wanted the topic of Tibet's status placed on the agenda of the United Nations, but other countries—following India's lead in contending that China's right to suzerainty over Tibet was already established—refused to allow such a debate (Richardson, 1984:186).

China's new government wished to repudiate the treaties imposed on China's emperors by Britain and other imperial powers (see Chapter 7). The 1914 Simla convention had declared that the Dalai Lama had spiritual authority over all believers in his faith but removed his political authority from Nepal, Ladakh, Bhutan, and Sikkim; the Dalai Lama had been reluctant to accept that latter provision and China had refused to sign the convention. When India achieved independence in 1947, its government, led by Pandit Jawaharlal Nehru, moved quickly to establish good relations with China (Moraes, 1960:117–143; Patterson, 1960; Rahul, 1969:88–100). After initial objection, it acquiesced in the agreement signed between China and Tibet in 1951 and signed an agreement in 1954 giving up rights British India had claimed in Tibet, contending that China had long had suzerainty over Tibet. This treaty, however, did not precisely define the border between Tibet and India. Nehru was somewhat disturbed when he discovered that Chinese maps still showed large portions of India and those border states within Chinese territory; China's foreign minister, Zhou Enlai, assured him the maps were simply old (Richardson, 1984:199, 215; see Chapter 7 for more).

Under Tibet's traditional social system, about a third of the land had belonged to the state, a third to the nobility, and a third to the monasteries who parceled their land out to families (Tung, 1996; Carrasco, 1959; Cassinelli and Ekvall, 1969). Commoners (i.e., those not monks, nuns, or nobility) turned over portions of their agricultural output for rent and taxes and were asked to contribute labor to civic projects; otherwise they were free to move about Tibet and engage in commerce with the traders who regularly traversed the kingdom. They could also serve as administrators or rise within the hierarchy of the monasteries, though top positions usually went to nobility. Local administrators settled civil disputes and tried criminal cases, often with an ear to local public opinion; severe punishments were rare (Cassinelli and Ekvall, 1969:153–185; Richardson, 1984:16–17; Harrer, 1954:88–90). Though people lived on meager diets, starvation was uncommon because granaries and seed supplies were maintained by public authorities for distribution in time of need or emergency (Cassinelli and Ekvall, 1969:98, 115; Harrer, 1954:234). Although the Dalai Lama was both the chief sovereign and the leader of his own religious order (the Yellow Hats), many monasteries belonged to other Buddhist orders or followed traditional Bon practices, and some adhered to Islam, Hinduism, and other religions, which they were free to do. Many regions were headed by nobility or monasteries that did not belong to the Yellow Hat order (Cassinelli and Ekvall, 1969:65–72; Harrer, 1954:179). The monasteries, which subjected nuns and monks to stern discipline, maintained their own militias and stored large quantities of weapons (Harrer, 1954:246–247; Goldstein, Seibenschuh, Tsering, 2006). Young men were conscripted to serve in the army and monasteries (Cassinelli and Ekvall, 1969:294–301). The vast majority of people inside and outside the monasteries were illiterate. The monasteries resisted the introduction of modern medicine, fearing it would endanger their hold on power; infant mortality in Tibet was among the highest in the world. They also resisted introducing motor vehicles, electricity, and industry. People moved from village to village on foot or horseback and carried goods on the backs of yaks.

Around Lhasa and along the southern river valleys of Tibet, China initially left this social system largely intact, though it immediately began demanding the appointment of its supporters within the administration (Richardson, 1984:191–192). It opened new clinics and schools and rapidly proceeded to build Tibet's first road, through the Amdo and Kham regions of eastern Tibet. The road soon brought in new settlers from other parts of China as well as reforming communists. In the regions along the road, China began to take traditional grazing lands and pastures from monasteries and nobility for redistribution to commoners and new settlers. Chinese leaders talked about rescuing serfs from exploitation by feudal lords and corrupt and cruel religious leaders and returning land to the people (Strong, 1976).

In 1955, Beijing established a Preparatory Committee for the Autonomous Region of Tibet, headed by the Dalai Lama, to plan for new administrative procedures in Tibet; many traditional leaders feared this meant a further weakening of their powers. The fiercely independent Kham and Amdo people, who had helped the Chinese take over Tibet in 1950, resented these attacks on their religion and traditional way of life (Harrer, 1954:109–131; Laird, 2003). They began physically and verbally attacking Chinese troops sent to their outposts (Patterson, 1960:125–128; Richardson, 1984:200–205; Goldstein, 2007; Shakya, 1999:1–45). By 1954, the road reached Lhasa, and, by 1956, open rebellion had broken out among the Kham and Amdo; Chinese troops struck back with brutal force, shelling monasteries and jailing and killing rebels. Little mercy was shown by either side (Patt, 1992:50–53; Patterson, 1960:125–135; Goldstein, Sherap, and Siebenschuh, 2004). Guerrilla forces and stockpiles of arms grew in number and strength. In March 1959 came a final showdown; the Dalai Lama fled to Dharamsala, India, where he still resides (Patterson, 1960:148–191; Richardson, 1984:199–214, 242; Patt, 1992:143–166; Shakabpa, 1967:322–363; Shakya, 1999:185–211). From his new exile home in India, the Dalai Lama announced that 65,000 Tibetans had died in the fighting and 1,000 monasteries had been destroyed. His government in exile, which includes a cabinet and parliament, has sought not independence but "true autonomy" for Tibet along the lines of Hong Kong's special "one country, two systems" relationship (Dalai Lama, 1991; Dalai Lama and Ford, 1997; Schell, 2000; Powers, 2004; Craig, 1997; Avedon, 1994).

In 1962, war broke out between China and India on the Ladakh border. China was angry that India was giving exile to the Dalai Lama and the Tibetan rebels, that Indian intelligence officers cooperated with the CIA to arm and supply them (see US Department of State, 1996; Knaus, 1999; Morrison and Conboy, 2002; Sperling, 2004; Dunham, 2004; McGranahan, 2010), and that Ladaki Indians were in Tibet illegally. China made some small territorial gains (Richardson, 1984:224–243).

Meanwhile in Tibet, large numbers of monks, lamas, members of the nobility, and other educated people were imprisoned, executed, and subjected to brutal treatment (Patt, 1992:205–209). Most monks were removed from monasteries, the monasteries' wealth was taken, and the people were discouraged from religious practices. Public rectification campaigns forced people to attack their family members and village notables. Tibetans were restricted to their villages and organized into communes and into teams to carry out public works projects. Food was strictly rationed, and many suffered from hunger and starvation. Large numbers of Chinese troops were stationed throughout Tibet. Despite all this, resistance activities continued (Richardson, 1984:194,

237–258; Patt, 1992:210; Barnett, 1994; Heath, 2005; Khetsun, 2008; Rinpoche, 2010). In 1965, the Preparatory Committee for the Autonomous Region of Tibet changed Tibet's administration: the new Tibetan Autonomous Region (TAR) would be divided into eight military zones. The Panchen Lama, who had previously been used to counter the Dalai Lama, refused to cooperate further and was placed in custody. The onset of the Cultural Revolution in 1966 brought in the Red Guards, who looted and razed thousands of the remaining monasteries (there had been 2,700 in Tibet and 3,800 more in Sichuan, Qinghai, Gansu, and Yunnan) and dismissed the military government. They finally turned on themselves in factional fighting, and the People's Liberation Army tried to restore order. Some nobility and former Tibetan officials were called back to positions of prominence and some monasteries and holy places were restored.

In 1987, Tibetans staged another uprising (Schwartz, 1994; Barnett, 2006). China declared martial law, which it has continued with varying degrees of intensity (and of formal recognition) since that time. News and travel from the outside world are strictly censored and controlled; foreign journalists are very rarely allowed in. The Dalai Lama travels throughout the world urging support (though not independence) for Tibet, and many socially prominent individuals support his cause. Heads of state (including the prime minister of Mongolia) continue to support China's claims over Tibet while urging China's leaders to show restraint in their treatment of Tibetans. China contends that Tibet is its internal affair, not the business of foreign nations that have sought to dominate Tibet and many other countries themselves in the past. Since 1988, China and the Dalai Lama have carried on nine rounds of talks, without result. In 1995, the Dalai Lama announced that a six-year-old boy was the reincarnation of the Panchen Lama; Beijing promptly arrested the boy and announced that another six-year-old was the actual reincarnated Panchen Lama (Jeffries, 2010:171–325). One is being held in a secret location, while the other is kept from his home monastery. He lives in Beijing.

Today's Tibet is a far cry from the Tibet of the 1940s, when there were no roads, automobiles, electricity, airports, or hospitals (Sautman and Dreyer, 2006). Its 3 million inhabitants (probably twice the population in 1950 [Yan, 2000]) are still 90 percent Tibetans, most of whom live in rural areas. A third are still illiterate. But life expectancy has risen from thirty-five years to sixty-seven years, and the GDP is thirty times higher, growing at a rate of 10 percent in recent years. The streets of its two largest cities, Lhasa and Shigatse, are filled with traffic and lined with modern stores, public buildings, and parks, though factories have failed to appear. Construction crews are hard at work rebuilding old houses, fitting them with modern plumbing, electrical outlets, and other amenities. In the countryside, the government is encouraging Tibetan families to own their own farms and lending them money to rebuild their homes as large modern family complexes. Yak and sheepherders compete

Robert E. Gamer

A Tibetan family's farm compound. The government offers Tibetan farmers and herders low-interest loans for home construction, electricity, irrigation, and new roads.

with them for land and water (Bauer, 2003). Demand for Tibet's rare caterpillar fungus (used in traditional Chinese medicine) was enriching people even in some obscure rural areas. New roads (now totaling 13,600 miles or 22,500 kilometers) are being built at a rapid rate. In 2006, the new railroad connection between Lhasa and Beijing was completed (Lustgarten, 2008). The oxygen-enhanced trains reach a height of 16,640 feet (5,072 meters) on their forty-seven-hour trip between the two cities, on track carefully constructed to avoid environmental degradation, and to adapt to permafrost. Most of the passengers (like the workers who built the right-of-way) are Chinese, coming as tourists or to pursue business ventures in Lhasa, often for short stays.

Monasteries, now much smaller and fewer in number, accommodate monks, who continue to learn and recite sutras, while faithful Tibetans turn the prayer wheels, hang flags, and leave tablets in front of the Buddhas, while contributing food, cash, and other gifts to the monks (Baker, 2006; Kolas and Thowsen, 2006). In the cities, these participants may work in offices, drive cars, carry cell phones, watch soap operas on television, and shop in superstores. Such individuals, like other Tibetans, revere the Dalai Lama; they also live in the modern world that has been created by the connection with the PRC. The PRC maintains a large presence of police and military personnel (not counted in the official statistics on residency), alert to any sign of civil disobedience. It also is not uncommon to find them chatting with Tibetan and Hui Muslim men playing cards. In the morning, older Han Chinese like to perform tai chi exercises or carry out social dancing beneath the north wall of Lhasa's Potala (the exiled Dalai Lama's palace, now a popular tourist site), while to the east of that palace, Tibetan men and women take an early morn-

Robert E. Gamer

Potala Palace, former residence of the Dalai Lamas, in Lhasa.

ing *kora* (pilgrimage), visiting the sacred sites on a hillside before joining friends in a nearby coffeehouse or teahouse.

Nearly all the shops, hotels, and offices in Lhasa and other Tibetan towns and cities are run by immigrant Han, who now constitute a majority of the capital's inhabitants (Ma, 2010). They have come far from their home provinces to this harsh land for the traditional reasons Chinese have always migrated overseas: they can make far more money, with fewer taxes and political restrictions on their commerce. The city culture is transformed by the presence of hundreds of Chinese restaurants, teahouses, and medicine shops, and billboards advertising China Mobile cell phones. The Chinese make little effort to learn the Tibetan language. They often stay only long enough to save some money before returning to their home provinces (Hansen, 2005). Before 1959, high percentages (at times, perhaps a third) of the male populace were celibate monks; now very few boys become monks, but those who do not often do not progress far in school. That is gradually improving, as more Tibetans graduate from high school and universities and take jobs as office workers or tour guides, or work in small factories and the like (Ma, 2010). A number of them own cars and modern condominiums. Religious practices are once again allowed, but with restrictions: it is unlawful to display a picture of the Dalai Lama (a rule many Tibetans disobey); monks must take "patriotic education" exams, requiring them to renounce the Dalai Lama; and civil servants are not allowed to participate in religious practices. The Chinese complain that their

Robert E. Gamer

Shops along this street in Lhasa were burned during the 2008 riots.

religion leaves Tibetans with attitudes not conducive to discipline and economic endeavor; without liberation, the monks would have denied modernization to Tibet. Young monks sometimes carry cell phones; they compare themselves with peers who are engaged in modern careers and are starkly aware that the role of monasteries in society has been vastly reduced under Chinese dominance.

Early in 2008, with the Olympics approaching, some monks in Lhasa staged a demonstration to mark the anniversary of the 1959 uprising; their arrests touched off demonstrations by hundreds of other monks and rioting by Tibetan civilians in Lhasa, who wrecked Han and Hui retail stores and burned their inventory in great pyres on the streets, along with vehicles and buildings ("Trashing the Beijing Road," 2008; Wang and Shakya, 2009:191–270; Smith, 2009; Bo, 2010:199–270). During the following week, demonstrations led by monks and accompanied or cheered by thousands of students, townspeople, and rural nomads and farmers spread to many other cities and monasteries in Tibet, Qinghai, Sichuan, Yunnan, and Gansu. There were some incidents of youths burning vehicles and hurling stones at or burning government buildings. The Chinese authorities sent out numerous convoys filled with troops to quell the disturbances and closed those areas to the outside world. Since 2008, China has maintained tight security, with a heavy presence of troops and carefully controlled access to journalists and foreign tourists. In 2011, the sixtieth anniversary of the signing of the 1951 agreement on "the peaceful liberation of Tibet," activism flared up again. In two autonomous prefectures in the western portion of Sichuan, populated by Khams, protesters turned to setting themselves on fire, and police started new roundups of monks for participating in the 2008 uprising. Monks are being forced to renounce the Dalai Lama.

Chinese hoped that economic advance would reduce political protest. It is strikingly evident that although the economy is growing even more rapidly than the rest of China's economy, Tibetans remain politically restless. The growth has been accompanied by high inflation and has helped some Tibetans more than others. The conspicuous proliferation of Han businesses selling expensive goods, owning vehicles, and controlling the top political posts are obvious sources of resentment. But above all, repression of religious liberty is deeply resented. Other regions of China experience similar disparities, but since 1989, demonstrations in those regions (discussed in Chapter 4) have never spontaneously flared out to include thousands of people on the main streets of numerous towns and cities. Here, demands for religious freedom continue to grow along with the economy (Makley, 2007).

Many Tibetans do not want to be entirely detached from China—to become a landlocked country with stalled economic development. The Dalai Lama wants a "one country, two systems" solution along the lines of Hong Kong, giving his chosen successors control of Tibet's monasteries and cultural development, with restrictioned migration into its cities, high-end rather than mass tourism, bilingual education in schools, and celebration of its unique essence. More radical young activists want full independence and democracy, and continuing police raids on monasteries strengthen their resolve.

In 2011, the Dalai Lama, retaining his role as spiritual leader, stepped down as political leader of the government in exile, and its parliament organized an election, with 82,000 exiled Tibetans around the world voting to choose a new prime minister. A forty-three-year-old fellow at Harvard Law School, Lobsang Sangay, narrowly defeated a Stanford scholar to assume this post for a five-year term. The government in exile renamed itself the Tibetan Administration. Then the Dalai Lama ordered an end to the tradition of lamas finding the infant reincarnated successor to a Dalai Lama after his death. Instead, he will choose one of the most scholarly monks to succeed him when he dies.

Lobsang Sangay and the Dalai Lama speak out against the self-immolations that have resulted in at least twenty-nine monks and nuns burning themselves to death. But both voice support for the cause of those protesters. They encourage foreign governments to help them bring back dialogue with Chinese authorities to reach a "one country, two systems" solution. The Chinese government denounces the acts of the protesters as terrorism and continues to denounce the "separatist" activities of the Dalai Lama. Many of the protesters believe his activities are not separatist enough.

Conclusion

The Han migrants into Lhasa and Shigatse are a new breed of overseas Chinese, this time living in their own land. They bring with them economic skills and networks and tremendous personal drive. They foment vast economic change, but they also leave in their wake resentment from local peoples and environmental degradation as they exploit natural resources. Since they often make little attempt to mingle with or understand those whose cultural zones they have entered, the source of that resentment is hard for them to comprehend. Chapter 7 explores this further while examining China's foreign policy in Southeast Asia.

In this chapter, we have noted similar tensions in Taiwan between the KMT who arrived after World War II and those already living there. Much of Taiwan's economy depends on investments in and by other regions of Asia and on selling goods on the world market; however, this helped the KMT immigrants more than the earlier Han settlers and aboriginals, until they revolted and received US aid. Lhasa's new economy, too, depends heavily on the world market of tourism and precious metals; this money flows more to Han immigrants than to native Tibetans. Once established, this inherent economic dependence on the outside world can help restrain the harshest behavior and parochial instincts of Han rulers; it is hard, for example, to maintain the strictest martial law while increasing, or even allowing, tourism. But such economic growth also widens the gap between rich and poor, Han and native, even with the many new initiatives to improve their living standards.

Hong Kong provides a unique environment for interaction between Han and outsider. Largely uninhabited until recent times, lying off the shores of China, and provided with a large and secure harbor area, it was able to develop its own culture. From the beginning, its entire economy revolved around entrepôt trade, selling goods to the outside world. It was outside China and smoothly connected with the world beyond. It contains no hostile natives whose economy once depended on something else; most of its immigrants came because they wanted more freedom to carry out such commerce. Still, its prosperity has depended on remaining apart from the rules and relationships that restrict commerce in China. For thousands of years, China has depended on merchants who would venture outside its shores, using their cultural skills to make deals and connections for the homeland. Its own culture zone has encouraged investment and trade but has also confined it within a regulatory grid and circle of obligations that limits their size and scope (see Chapters 4 and 7). The real money can be made in places where those regulations and obligations are not in force. China knows that pulling Hong Kong inside the orbit could endanger that arrangement. That is the logic behind the "one country, two systems" formula.

In Chapter 7, we shall take a broader look at China's connections with the outside world as we survey its overall foreign policy. A similar question persists: Is China seeking to take economic, political, and strategic control of this outside environment? Or is it seeking to join a community of nations that encourages both individual and national competition, with respect for the sovereignty of other nations? The fight between the PRC and the Republic of China over who represents all of China and (as we will examine more in Chapter 7) over who represents all the overseas Chinese, highlights this dilemma.

Bibliography

The Pacific Rim and Overseas Chinese

Ang, Ien. 2001. *On Not Speaking Chinese: Living Between Asia and the West.* London: Routledge.

Barabantseva, Elena. 2011. *Overseas Chinese, Ethnic Minorities, and Nationalism: De-Centering China.* London: Routledge.

Benton, Gregor, and Frank N. Pieke (eds.). 1998. *The Chinese in Europe.* London: Palgrave Macmillan.

Bieler, Stacey. 2004. *"Patriots" or "Traitors"? A History of American-Educated Chinese Students.* Armonk, NY: M. E. Sharpe.

Brown, Rajeswary Ampalavanar. 2000. *Chinese Big Business and the Wealth of Asian Nations.* New York: Palgrave.

Cassel, Susie Lan. 2002. *The Chinese in America: A History from Gold Mountain to the New Millennium.* Lanham, MD: Rowman and Littlefield.

Chan, Sucheng, and Madeline Y. Hsu (eds.). 2008. *Chinese Americans and the Politics of Race and Culture.* Philadeplphia: Temple University Press.

Chang, Iris. 2004. *The Chinese in America: A Narrative History.* New York: Penguin.

Chang, Tong Len. 1988. *Sailing for the Sun: The Chinese in Hawaii, 1789–1989.* Honolulu: University of Hawaii Press.

Charney, Michael W., Brenda S. A. Yeoh, and Chee Kiong Tong. 2003. *Chinese Migrants Abroad: Cultural, Educational, and Social Dimensions of the Chinese Diaspora.* Singapore: World Scientific.

Chen, Edith Wen-Chu, and Glenn Omatsu (eds.). 2006. *Teaching About Asian-Pacific Americans: Effective Activities, Strategies, and Assignments for Classrooms and Communities.* 2nd ed. Lanham, MD: Rowman and Littlefield.

Chen, Yong. 2002. *Chinese San Francisco: 1859–1943: A TransPacific Commmunity.* Stanford, CA: Stanford University Press.

Cheung, Gordon C. K. 2005. "Involuntary Migrants, Political Revolutionaries, and Economic Energisers: A History of the Image of Overseas Chinese in Southeast Asia." *Journal of Contemporary China* 14(42): 55–66.

Chin, Ung-Ho. 1997. *Chinese Politics in Sarawak: A Study of the Sarawak United People's Party.* Oxford: Oxford University Press.

Chong, Denise. 1996. *The Concubine's Children.* New York: Penguin.

Chow, Claire S. 1998. *Leaving Deep Water: The Lives of Asian American Women at the Crossroads of Two Cultures.* New York: Dutton.

Chung, Sue Fawn, and Priscilla Wegars. 2005. *Chinese American Death Rituals: Respecting the Ancestors.* Lanham, MD: Alta Mira Press.

Constable, Nicole (ed.). 2005. *Guest People: Hakka Identity in China and Abroad.* Seattle: University of Washington Press.

Cunningham, Stuart, and John Sinclair (eds.). 2000. *Floating Lives: The Media and Asian Diasporas*. Melbourne: University of Queensland Press.

Daniels, Roger. 1988. *Asian American: Chinese and Japanese in the United States Since 1850*. Seattle: University of Washington Press.

Dirlik, Arif (ed.). 1998a. *Chinese on the American Frontier*. Lanham, MD: Rowman and Littlefield.

———. 1998b. *What Is in a Rim? Critical Perspectives on the Pacific Region Idea*. 2nd ed. Lanham, MD: Rowman and Littlefield.

Dye, Bob. 1997. *Merchant Prince of the Sandalwood Mountains: Afong and the Chinese in Hawaii*. Honolulu: University of Hawaii Press.

Fitzgerald, Stephen. 1972. *China and the Overseas Chinese: A Study of Peking's Changing Policy, 1949–1970*. Cambridge: Cambridge University Press.

Fong, Eric, and Chiu Luk. 2006. *Chinese Ethnic Business: Global and Local Perspectives*. London: Routledge.

Freedman, Amy L. 2000. *Political Participation and Ethnic Minorities: Chinese Overseas in Malaysia, Indonesia, and the United States*. London: Routledge.

Gambe, Annabelle. 2000. *Overseas Chinese Entrepreneurship and Capitalist Development in Southeast Asia*. New York: Palgrave.

Garth, Alexander. 1973. *The Invisible China: The Overseas Chinese and the Politics of Southeast Asia*. New York: Macmillan.

Koehn, Peter, and Xiao-huang Yin (eds.). 2002. *The Expanding Roles of Chinese Americans in U.S.-China Relations: Transnational Networks and Trans-Pacific Interactions*. Armonk, NY: M. E. Sharpe.

Kuhn, Philip A. 2008. *Chinese Among Others: A History of Chinese Emigration in Modern Times*. Lanham, MD: Rowman and Littlefield.

Kwong, Peter, and Dusanka Miscevic. 2007. *Chinese America: The Untold Story of America's Oldest New Community*. New York: New Press.

Lee, Erika. 2003. *At America's Gates: Chinese Immigration During the Exclusion Era, 1882–1943*. Chapel Hill: University of North Carolina Press.

Lee, Josephine Tsui Yueh. 2007. *New York City's Chinese Community*. Charleston, SC: Arcadia Publishing.

Li, Veronica. 2006. *Journey Across the Four Seas: A Chinese Woman's Search for Home*. Paramus, NJ: Homa and Sekey.

Ma, Laurence J. C., and Carolyn Cartier (eds.). 2002. *The Chinese Diaspora: Space, Place, Mobility, and Identity*. Lanham, MD: Rowman and Littlefield.

McClain, Charles J. 1996. *In Search of Equality: The Chinese Struggle Against Discrimination in Nineteenth Century America*. Berkeley: University of California Press.

Pan, Lynn (ed.). 1999. *The Encyclopedia of the Overseas Chinese*. Cambridge, MA: Harvard University Press.

Phaelzer, Jean. 2007. *Driven Out: The Forgotten War Against Chinese Americans*. New York: Random House.

Pieke, Frank, Pal Nyiri, Mette Thuno, and Antonella Ceccagno. 2004. *Transnational Chinese: Fujianese Migrants in Europe*. Stanford, CA: Stanford University Press.

Redding, S. Gordon. 1995. *The Spirit of Chinese Capitalism*. Berlin: Walter de Gruyter.

Reid, Anthony (ed.). 2001. *Sojourners and Settlers: Histories of Southeast Asia and the Chinese*. London: Allen and Unwin.

Sandmeyer, Elmer. 1991. *The Anti-Chinese Movement in California*. Urbana: University of Illinois Press.

Seagrave, Sterling. 1995. *Lords of the Rim: The Invisible Empire of the Overseas Chinese*. New York: G. P. Putnam.

See, Lisa. 1996. *On Gold Mountain: The One-Hundred-Year Odyssey of My Chinese-American Family.* New York: Vintage.
Sun, Wanning. 2002. *Leaving China: Media, Migration, and Transnational Imagination.* Lanham, MD: Rowman and Littlefield.
——— (ed.). 2006. *Media and the Chinese Diaspora: Community, Communications, and Commerce.* London: Routledge.
Suryadinata, Leo. 1985. *China and the ASEAN States: The Ethnic Chinese Dimension.* Singapore: Singapore University Press.
Tan, Chee-Beng (ed.). 2006. *Chinese Transnational Networks.* London: Routledge.
Thuno, Mette (ed.). 2007. *Beyond Chinatown: New Chinese Migration and the Global Expansion of China.* Copenhagen: Nordic Institute of Asian Studies.
Tong, Benson. 1994. *Unsubmissive Women: Chinese Prostitutes in Nineteenth Century San Francisco.* Norman: University of Oklahoma Press.
———. 2000. *Chinese Americans: The New Americans.* New York: Greenwood Press.
Wang, Gungwu. 2000. *The Chinese Overseas: From Earthbound to the Quest for Autonomy.* Cambridge, MA: Harvard University Press.
———. 2001. *Don't Leave Home: Migration and the Chinese.* Singapore: Times Academic Press.
Wong, K. Scott, and Sucheng Chan. 1998. *Claiming America: Constructing Chinese American Identities During the Exclusion Era.* Philadelphia: Temple University Press.
Yung, Judy. 1995. *Unbound Feet: A Social History of Chinese Women in San Francisco.* Berkeley: University of California Press.
———. 1999. *Unbound Voices: A Documentary History of Chinese Women in San Francisco.* Berkeley: University of California Press.
Yung, Judy, Gordon H. Chang, and Him Mark Lai. 2006. *Chinese American Voices: From the Gold Rush to the Present.* Berkeley: University of California Press.
Zhao, Xiaojian. 2002. *Remaking Chinese America: Immigration, Family, and Community, 1940–1965.* Piscataway, NJ: Rutgers University Press.

Hong Kong

Abbas, Ackbar. 1997. *Hong Kong: Culture and the Politics of Disappearance.* Minneapolis: University of Minnesota Press.
Berlie, Jean (ed.). 2000. *Macao 2000.* Oxford: Oxford University Press.
Boardman, Robert. 1976. *Britain and the People's Republic of China, 1949–74.* London: Macmillan.
Brook, Timothy, and Bob Tadashi Wakabayashi (eds.). 2000. *Opium Regimes: China, Britain, and Japan, 1839–1952.* Berkeley: University of California Press.
Brown, Judith M., and Rosemary Foot. 1997. *Hong Kong's Transitions, 1842–1997.* New York: St. Martin's.
Bueno de Mesquita, Bruce, David Newman, and Alvin Rabushka. 1996. *Red Flag over Hong Kong.* Chatham, NJ: Chatham House.
Burns, John P. 2005. *Government Capacity and the Hong Kong Civil Service.* Oxford: Oxford University Press.
Carroll, John M. 2007. *A Concise History of Hong Kong.* Lanham, MD: Rowman and Littlefield.
Chan, Ming K., and Gerard A. Postiglione (eds.). 1996. *The Hong Kong Reader: Passage to Chinese Sovereignty.* Armonk, NY: M. E. Sharpe.
Chan, Ming K., and John D. Young. 1994. *Precarious Balance: Hong Kong Between China and Britain, 1842–1992.* Armonk, NY: M. E. Sharpe.
Chan, Ming K., and Shui-hing Lo. 2006. *Historical Dictionary of the Hong Kong SAR and the Macao SAR.* Lanham, MD: Scarecrow.

Chang, David Wen-Wei, and Richard Y. Chuang. 1998. *The Politics of Hong Kong's Reversion to China*. New York: St. Martin's.
Cheung, Gordon C. K. 2007. *China Factors: Political Perspectives and Economic Interactions*. New Brunswick, NJ: Transaction Publications.
Chung, Stephanie P. Y. 1997. *Chinese Business Groups in Hong Kong and Political Changes in South China, 1900–1920s*. New York: St. Martin's.
Chung, Sze-yuen (ed.). 2001. *Hong Kong's Journey to Reunification: Memories of Sze-Yuen Chung*. Hong Kong: Chinese University Press.
CIA (Central Intelligence Agency). 2011. *CIA World Factbook*. Washington, DC: Central Intelligence Agency.
Currie, Jan, Carole J. Petersen, and Ka Ho Mok. 2006. *Academic Freedom in Hong Kong*. Lanham, MD: Lexington Books.
De Golyer, Michael. 2011. *Elections 2011/2012: Political Challenges, Political Opportunities*. Hong Kong: Hong Kong Transition Project. http://www.hktp.org/list/elections_20112012_june.pdf.
Gunn, Geoffrey C. 1996. *Encountering Macau: A Portuguese City-State on the Periphery of China, 1557–1999*. Boulder: Westview.
Hayes, James. 2006. *The Great Difference: The New Territories and Its People, 1898–2004*. Hong Kong: Hong Kong University Press.
Herschensohn, Bruce. 1999. *Hong Kong at the Handover*. Lanham, MD: Lexington Books.
Hibbert, Christopher. 1970. *The Dragon Awakes: China and the West, 1793–1911*. New York: Harper.
Ho, Lok-Sang, Paul Morris, and Yue-Ping Chung (eds.). 2005. *Education Reform and the Quest for Excellence: The Hong Kong Story*. Hong Kong: University of Hong Kong Press.
Hoe, Susanna, and Derek Roebuck. 1999. *The Taking of Hong Kong: Charles and Clara Elliot in China Waters*. London: Curzon Press.
Hong Kong Census and Statistics Department. 2011. *Statistical Tables*. http://www.censtatd.gov.hk/hong_kong_statistics/statistical_tables/index.jsp.
Hong Kong 1995: A Review of *1994*. 1995. Hong Kong: Government Printing Department.
Hong Kong Yearbook 2010. Hong Kong: Government Printing Department.
Ingham, Michael. 2007. *Hong Kong: A Cultural History*. New York: Oxford University Press.
Jain, J. P. 1976. *China in World Politics: A Study of Sino-British Relations, 1949–1975*. New Delhi: Radiant Press.
Jeffries, Ian. 2010. *Political Developments in Contemporary China: A Guide*. London: Routledge.
Lam, Wai-man. 2004. *Understanding the Political Culture of Hong Kong: The Paradox of Activism and Depoliticization*. Armonk, NY: M. E. Sharpe.
——— (ed.). 2007. *Contemporary Hong Kong Politics: Governance in the Post-1997 Era*. Hong Kong: University of Hong Kong Press.
Lee, Leo Ou-fan. 2008. *City Between Worlds: My Hong Kong*. Cambridge, MA: Belknap Press of Harvard University.
Lee, Pui-tak. 2006. *Colonial Hong Kong and Modern China: Interaction and Reintegration*. Hong Kong: University of Hong Kong Press.
Li, Pang-kwong. 2000. *Hong Kong from Britain to China: Political Cleavages, Electoral Dynamics, and Institutional Changes*. Burlington, VT: Ashgate.
Lo, Shui-Hing. 2007. *Political Change in Macau*. London: Routledge.
Loh, Christine (ed.). 2006. *Functional Constituencies: A Unique Feature of the Hong Kong Legislative Council*. Hong Kong: University of Hong Kong Press.

Ma, Ngok. 2007. *Political Development in Hong Kong: State, Political Society, and Civil Society.* Hong Kong: University of Hong Kong Press.

Marks, Robert B. 2006. *The Origins of the Modern World: A Global and Ecological Narrative from the Fifteenth to the Twenty-First Century.* 2nd ed. Lanham, MD: Rowman and Littlefield.

Martin, Michael F. 2011. *Prospects for Democracy in Hong Kong: The 2012 Election Reforms.* Washington, DC: Congressional Research Service. http://www.fas.org/sgp/crs/row/R40992.pdf.

Mathews, Gordon, Eric Ma, and Tai-lok Lui. 2008. *Hong Kong, China: Learning to Belong to a Nation.* New York: Routledge.

McGivering, Jill. 1999. *Macao Remembers.* Oxford: Oxford University Press.

Meyer, David R. 2006. *Hong Kong as Global Metropolis.* Cambridge: Cambridge University Press.

Patten, Christopher. 1997. "Farewell to My Hong Kong." *Newsweek,* March 3.

Pepper, Suzanne. 2007. *Keeping Democracy at Bay: Hong Kong and the Challenge of Chinese Political Reform.* Lanham, MD: Rowman and Littlefield.

Pesek, William. 2012. "Basement-Gate Points to Shaky Future." *Bloomberg View,* February 28. www.bloomberg.com.

Porter, Jonathan. 1999. *Macau: The Imaginary City.* Boulder: Westview.

Schenk, Catherine R. 2001. *Hong Kong as an International Financial Centre: Emergence and Development, 1945–1965.* London: Routledge.

Shek, Daniel T. L. (ed.). 2002. *Entering a New Millennium: Advances in Social Welfare in Hong Kong.* Hong Kong: Chinese University Press.

Snow, Philip. 2003. *The Fall of Hong Kong: Britain, China, and the Japanese Occupation.* New Haven, CT: Yale University Press.

Spence, Jonathan. 1999. *The Search for Modern China.* 2nd ed. New York: Norton.

Tsai, Jung-fang. 1995. *Hong Kong in Chinese History: Community and Social Unrest in the British Colony, 1842–1913.* New York: Columbia University.

Tsang, Steve (ed.). 2001. *Judicial Independence and the Rule of Law in Hong Kong.* London: St. Anthony's.

———. 2007. *A Modern History of Hong Kong, 1841–1998.* London: Tauris.

Welsh, Frank. 1993. *A History of Hong Kong.* London: HarperCollins.

Wong, Linda, Lynn T. White, and Gui Shixun (eds.). 2004. *Social Policy Reform in Hong Kong and Shanghai: A Tale of Two Cities.* Armonk, NY: M. E. Sharpe.

Taiwan

Accinelli, Robert. 1997. *Crisis and Commitment: United States Policy Toward Taiwan, 1950–1955.* Chapel Hill: University of North Carolina Press.

Andrade, Tonio. 2005. *How Taiwan Became Chinese: Dutch, Spanish, and Han Colonization in the Seventeenth Century.* New York: Columbia University Press.

Aspalter, Christian. 2002. *Democratization and Welfare State Development in Taiwan.* Burlington, VT: Ashgate.

Bedford, Olwen, and Kwang-Kuo Hwang. 2006. *Taiwanese Identity and Democracy: The Social Psychology of Taiwan's 2004 Elections.* New York: Palgrave.

Brown, Melissa J. 2004. *Is Taiwan Chinese? The Impact of Culture, Power, and Migration on Changing Identities.* Berkeley: University of California Press.

Bush, Richard C. 2004. *At Cross Purposes: U.S.-Taiwan Relations Since 1942.* Armonk, NY: M. E. Sharpe.

———. 2005. *Untying the Knot: Making Peace in the Taiwan Strait.* Washington, DC: Brookings Institution Press.

Cai, Kevin G. (ed.). 2010. *Cross–Taiwan Straits Relations Since 1979: Policy*

Adjustment and Institutional Change Across the Straits. Singapore: World Scientific.

Chang, Julian, and Steven M. Goldstein (eds.). 2007. *Economic Reform and Cross-Straits Relations: Taiwan and China in the WTO.* Singapore: World Scientific.

Ching, Leo T. S. 2001. *Becoming Japanese: Colonial Taiwan and the Politics of Identity Formation.* Berkeley: University of California Press.

Clark, Cal, and Alexander C. Tan. 2011. *Taiwan's Political Economy: Meeting Challenges, Pursuing Progress.* Boulder: Lynne Rienner.

Cole, Bernard. 2006. *Taiwan's Security: History and Prospects.* London: Routledge.

Constable, Nicole (ed.). 2005. *Great People: Hakka Identity in China and Abroad.* Seattle: University of Washington Press.

Copper, John F. 2008. *Taiwan: Nation-State or Province?* 5th ed. Boulder: Westview.

Dickson, Bruce, and Chien-min Chao. 2002. *Assessing the Lee Tung-hui Legacy in Taiwan's Politics.* Armonk, NY: M. E. Sharpe.

Edmonds, Martin, and Michael M. Tsai (eds.). 2006. *Taiwan's Defense Reform.* London: Routledge.

Edmonds, Richard Louis, and Steven M. Goldstein (eds.). 2002. *Taiwan in the Twentieth Century: A Retrospective View.* Cambridge: Cambridge University Press.

Fell, Dafydd. 2005. *Party Politics in Taiwan: Party Change and the Democratic Evolution of Taiwan, 1991–2004.* London: Routledge.

———. 2011. *Government and Politics in Taiwan.* London: Routledge.

Gambe, Annabelle. 2000. *Overseas Chinese Entrepreneurship and Capitalist Development in Southeast Asia.* New York: Palgrave.

Gilley, Bruce, and Larry Diamond (eds.). 2008. *Political Change in China: Comparisons with Taiwan.* Boulder: Lynne Rienner.

Gold, Thomas B. 1986. *State and Society in the Taiwan Miracle.* Armonk, NY: M. E. Sharpe.

Goldstein, Stephen M., and Julian Chang. 2008. *Presidential Politics in Taiwan: The Administration of Chen Shui-bian.* Norwalk, CT: Eastbridge.

Gordon, Leonard H. D. 2007. *Confrontation over Taiwan: Nineteenth-Century China and the Powers.* Lanham, MD: Rowman and Littlefield.

Harrison, Mark. 2007. *Legitimacy, Meaning, and Knowledge in the Making of Taiwanese Identity.* New York: Palgrave.

Ho, Samuel. 1978. *Economic Development in Taiwan, 1860–1970.* New Haven, CT: Yale University Press.

Hsieh, Jolan. 2006. *Collective Rights of Indigenous Peoples: Identity-Based Movement of Plain Indigenous in Taiwan.* London: Routledge.

Huang, Jing, and Xiaoting Li. 2010. *Inseparable Separation: The Making of China's Taiwan Policy.* Singapore: World Scientific.

Jeffries, Ian. 2010. *Political Developments in Contemporary China: A Guide.* London: Routledge.

Lee, David Tawei. 2000. *The Making of the Taiwan Relations Act: Twenty Years in Retrospect.* Oxford: Oxford University Press.

Lee, Wei-chin (ed.). 2010. *Taiwan's Politics in the 21st Century: Changes and Challenges.* Singapore: World Scientific.

Liao, Ping-hui, and David Der-Wei Yang. 2006. *Taiwan Under Japanese Colonial Rule, 1895–1945: History, Culture, Memory.* New York: Columbia University Press.

Manthorpe, Jonathan. 2005. *Forbidden Nation: A History of Taiwan.* New York: Palgrave Macmillan.

Marsh, Robert. 1996. *The Great Transformation: Social Change in Taipei, Taiwan, Since the 1960s*. Armonk, NY: M. E. Sharpe.
Paine, S. C. M. 2005. *The Sino-Japanese War of 1894–95: Perceptions, Power, and Primacy*. New York: Cambridge University Press.
Redding, S. Gordon. 1995. *The Spirit of Chinese Capitalism*. Berlin: Walter de Gruyter.
Rigger, Shelley. 2011. *Why Taiwan Matters: Small Island, Global Powerhouse*. Lanham, MD: Rowman and Littlefield.
Roy, Denny. 2003. *Taiwan: A Political History*. Ithaca, NY: Cornell University Press.
Rubinstein, Murray A. (ed.). 2006. *Taiwan: A New History*. Expanded ed. Armonk, NY: M. E. Sharpe.
Taiwan Yearbook. 2009. Taipei: Republic of China Information Office.
Tian, John Q. 2006. *Government, Business, and the Politics of Interdependence and Conflict Across the Taiwan Strait*. New York: Palgrave.
Tsai, Terence, and Borshivan Cheng. 2006. *The Silicon Dragon: High-Tech Industry in Taiwan*. Northampton, MA: Edward Elgar.
Tsang, Steve (ed.). 2005. *If China Attacks Taiwan: Military Strategy, Politics, and Economics*. London: Routledge.
Tucker, Nancy Bernkopf. 1994. *Taiwan, Hong Kong, and the United States, 1945–1992*. New York: Maxwell Macmillan.
———. 2005. *Dangerous Strait: The U.S-Taiwan-China Crisis*. New York: Columbia University Press.
Weller, Robert P. 2001. *Alternate Civilities: Democracy and Culture in China and Taiwan*. Boulder: Westview.

Tibet

Avedon, John F. 1994. *In Exile from the Land of the Snows: The Definitive Account of the Dalai Lama and Tibet Since the Chinese Conquest*. New York: Harper Perennial.
Baker, Ian. 2006. *The Heart of the World: A Journey to the Last Secret Place*. New York: Penguin.
Barnett, Robert (ed.). 1994. *Resistance and Reform in Tibet*. Bloomington: University of Indiana Press.
———. 2006. *Lhasa: Streets with Memories*. New York: Columbia University Press.
Batt, Herbert J. (ed.). 2001. *Tales of Tibet: Sky Burials, Prayer Wheels, and Wind Horses*. Lanham, MD: Rowman and Littlefield.
Bauer, Kenneth Michael. 2003. *High Frontiers: Himalayan Pastoralists in a Changing World*. New York: Columbia University Press.
Beckwith, Christopher I. 1993. *The Tibetan Empire in Central Asia: A History of the Struggle for Great Power Among Tibetans, Turks, Arabs, and Chinese During the Early Middle Ages*. Princeton, NJ: Princeton University Press.
Blondeau, Anne Marie, and Katia Buffetrille. 2008. *Authenticating Tibet: Answers to China's 100 Questions*. Berkeley: University of California Press.
Bo, Zhiyue. 2010. *China's Elite Politics: Governance and Democracy*. Singapore: World Scientific Publishers.
Brauen, Martin. 2004. *Dreamworld Tibet: Western Illusions*. Boston: Weatherhill.
Carrasco, Pedro. 1959. *Land and Polity in Tibet*. Seattle: University of Washington Press.
Cassinelli, C. W., and Robert B. Ekvall. 1969. *A Tibetan Principality: The Political System of Sa sKya*. Ithaca, NY: Cornell University Press.
Coleman, Graham, and Thupten Jinpa (eds.). 2007. *The Tibetan Book of the Dead: First Complete Translation*. Trans. Gyurme Dorjie. New York: Penguin.

Craig, Mary. 1997. *Kundun: A Biography of the Family of the Dalai Lama.* Washington, DC: Counterpoint.

Cuevas, Bryan J. 2006. *The Hidden History of the Tibetan Book of the Dead.* New York: Oxford University Press.

Dalai Lama. 1991. *Freedom in Exile: The Autobiography of the Dalai Lama.* San Francisco: Harper Perennial.

———. 1995. *The World of Tibetan Buddhism: An Overview of Its Philosophy and Practice.* Somerville, MA: Wisdom Publications.

Dalai Lama, and Melissa Mathison Ford. 1997. *My Land and My People: The Original Autobiography of His Holiness the Dalai Lama of Tibet.* New York: Warner Books.

Davidson, Ronald W. 2005. *Tibetan Renaissance: Tantric Buddhism in the Rebirth of Tibetan Culture.* New York: Columbia University Press.

Dawa, Norbu. 1987. *Red Star over Tibet.* 2nd ed. New York: Envoy Press.

Diemberger, Hildegard. 2007. *When a Woman Becomes a Dynasty: The Samding Dorje Phagmo of Tibet.* New York: Columbia University Press.

Dodin, Thierry. 2001. *Imagining Tibet: Realities, Projections, and Fantasies.* Somerville, MA: Wisdom Publications.

Dunham, Mikel. 2004. *Buddha's Warriors: The Story of the CIA-Backed Tibetan Freedom Fighters, the Chinese Communist Invasion, and the Ultimate Fall of Tibet.* New York: Penguin.

Feigon, Lee. 1998. *Demystifying Tibet: Unlocking the Secrets of the Land of the Snows.* Chicago: Ivan R. Dee.

Goldstein, Melvyn C. 1991. *A History of Modern Tibet, 1913–1951: The Demise of the Lamaist State.* Berkeley: University of California Press.

———. 1997. *The Snow Lion and the Dragon: China, Tibet, and the Dalai Lama.* Berkeley: University of California Press.

———. 2007. *A History of Modern Tibet, Volume 2: The Calm Before the Storm: 1951–1955.* Berkeley: University of California Press.

Goldstein, Melvyn C., Dawei Sherap, and William R. Siebenschuh. 2004. *A Tibetan Revolutionary: The Political Life and Times of Bapa Phuntso Wangye.* Berkeley: University of California Press.

Goldstein, Melvyn C., William R. Siebenschuh, and Tashi Tsering. 2006. *The Struggle for Modern Tibet: The Autobiography of Tashi Tsering.* Armonk, NY: M. E. Sharpe.

Hansen, Mette Halskov. 2005. *Frontier People: Han Settlers in Minority Areas of China.* Vancouver: University of British Columbia.

Harrer, Heinrich. 1954. *Seven Years in Tibet.* Trans. Richard Graves. New York: E. P. Dutton.

———. 1997. *Lost Lhasa: Heinrich Harrer's Tibet.* New York: Harry N. Abrams.

———. 1998. *Return to Tibet: Tibet After the Chinese Occupation.* Trans. Ewald Osers. New York: J. P. Tarcher.

Heath, John. 2005. *Tibet and China in the Twenty-First Century: Non-Violence vs. State Power.* London: Saqi Books.

Hopkirk, Peter. 1995. *Trespassers on the Roof of the World: The Secret Exploration of Tibet.* New York: Kodansha International.

Jeffries, Ian. 2010. *Political Developments in Contemporary China: A Guide.* London: Routledge.

Kapstein, Matthew T. 2002. *The Tibetan Assimilation of Buddhism: Conversion, Contestation, and Memory.* Oxford: Oxford University Press.

———. 2006. *The Tibetans.* London: Blackwell.

Khetsun, Tubten. 2008. *Memories of Life in Lhasa Under Chinese Rule*. Trans. Mathew Akester. New York: Columbia University Press.
Knaus, John Kenneth. 1999. *Orphans of the Cold War: America and the Tibetan Struggle for Survival*. Washington, DC: PublicAffairs.
Kolas, Ashild, and Monika P. Thowsen. 2006. *On the Margins of Tibet: Cultural Survival on the Sino-Tibetan Frontier*. Seattle: University of Washington Press.
Laird, Thomas. 2003. *Into Tibet: The CIA's First Atomic Spy and His Secret Expedition to Lhasa*. New York: Grove.
Lhalungpa, Lobsang P. 1983. *Tibet: The Sacred Realm: Photographs 1880–1950*. Millerton, NY: Aperture.
Lin, Hsiao-ting. 2007. *Tibet and Nationalist China's Frontier: Intrigues and Ethnopolitics, 1928–49*. Vancouver: University of British Columbia Press.
Lopez, Donald S., Jr. 1999. *Prisoners of Shangri-La: Tibetan Buddhism and the West*. Chicago: University of Chicago Press.
Lustgarten, Abraham. 2008. *China's Great Train: Beijing's Drive West and the Campaign to Remake Tibet*. New York: Times Books.
Ma Rong. 2010. *Population and Society in Tibet*. Seattle: University of Washington Press.
Maher, Derek F. 2010. "Sacralized Warfare: The Fifth Dalai Lama and the Discourse of Political Violence." In *Buddhist Warfare*, edited by Michael Jerryson and Mark Juergenmeyer, 77–90. New York: Oxford University Press.
Makley, Charlena. 2007. *The Violence of Liberation: Gender and Tibet Buddhist Revival in Post-Mao China*. Berkeley: University of California Press.
McGranahan, Carole. 2010. *Arrested Histories: Tibet, the CIA, and Memories of a Forgotten War*. Durham, NC: Duke University Press.
McKay, Alex. 1997. *Tibet and the British Raj: The Frontier Cadre, 1904–1947*. London: Curzon Press.
Moraes, Frances Robert. 1960. *The Revolt in Tibet*. New York: Macmillan.
Morrison, James, and Kenneth J. Conboy. 2002. *The CIA's Secret War in Tibet*. Lawrence: University of Kansas Press.
Namgyal, Phuntsok. 2002. *Splendor of Tibet: The Potala Palace*. Paramus, NJ: Homa and Sekey.
Novick, Rebecca McClen. 1999. *The Fundamentals of Tibetan Buddhism*. New York: Crossing Press.
Patt, David. 1992. *A Strange Liberation: Tibetan Lives in Chinese Hands*. Ithaca, NY: Snow Lion.
Patterson, George N. 1960. *Tibet in Revolt*. London: Faber and Faber.
Perry, Art, and Robert A. F. Thurman. 1999. *The Tibetans: Photographs*. New York: Viking Press.
Powers, John. 1995. *Introduction to Tibetan Buddhism*. Ithaca, NY: Snow Lion.
———. 2004. *History as Propaganda: Tibetan Exiles vs. the People's Republic of China*. New York: Oxford University Press.
Rahul, Ram. 1969. *The Government and Politics of Tibet*. Delhi: Vikas.
Richardson, Hugh E. 1984. *Tibet and Its History*. 2nd ed. Boston: Shambhala.
Rinpoche, Arjia. 2010. *Surviving the Dragon: A Tibetan Lama's Account of 40 Years Under Chinese Rule*. New York: Rodale Press.
Sautman, Barry, and June Teufel Dreyer (eds.). 2006. *Contemporary Tibet: Politics, Development, and Society in a Disputed Region*. Armonk, NY: M. E. Sharpe.
Schell, Orville. 2000. *Virtual Tibet: Searching for Shangri-La from the Himalayas to Hollywood*. New York: Henry Holt.

Schwartz, Ronald David. 1994. *Circle of Protest: Political Ritual in the Tibetan Uprising, 1987–92*. New York: Columbia University Press.
Shakabpa, Tsepon W. D. 1967. *Tibet: A Political History*. New Haven, CT: Yale University Press.
Shakya, Tsering. 1999. *The Dragon in the Land of Snows: A History of Modern Tibet Since 1947*. New York: Columbia University Press.
Smith, Warren W., Jr. 2008. *China's Tibet? Autonomy or Assimilation*. Lanham, MD: Rowman and Littlefield.
———. 2009. *Tibet's Last Stand? The Tibetan Uprising of 2008 and China's Response*. Lanham, MD: Rowman and Littlefield.
Snellgrove, David. 2003. *Indo-Tibetan Buddhism: Indian Buddhists and Their Tibetan Successors*. Boston: Shambhala.
Sperling, Elliot. 2004. *The Tibet-China Conflict: History and Polemics*. Washington, DC: East-West Center.
Stein, R. A. 1995. *Tibetan Civilization*. Stanford, CA: Stanford University Press.
Strong, Anna Louise. 1976. *When Serfs Stood Up in Tibet*. 2nd ed. San Francisco: Red Sun.
Thurman, Robert A. F. 1996. *Essential Tibetan Buddhism*. New York: HarperOne.
"Trashing the Beijing Road." 2008. *The Economist* 386 (March 22–28): 8572.
Tung, Rosemary Jones. 1996. *A Portrait of Lost Tibet*. Berkeley: University of California Press.
Tuttle, Gray. 2005. *Tibetan Buddhists in the Making of Modern China*. New York: Columbia University Press.
US Department of State. 1996. *Foreign Relations of the United States, 1958–1960*. Vol. 19. Washington, DC: US Government Printing Office.
van Schaik, Sam. 2011. *Tibet: A History*. New Haven, CT: Yale University Press.
Wang, Lixiong, and Tsering Shakya (eds.). 2009. *The Struggle for Tibet*. London: Verso.
Yan, Hao. 2000. "Tibetan Population in China: Myths and Facts Reexamined." *Asian Ethnicity* 1(1): 11–36.

7

International Relations

Robert E. Gamer

At the end of Chapter 6, I suggested that China is torn between its new desire to become a part of the world community and its traditional wishes to establish cultural and political dominance over its surrounding territories. The notion of being part of a world community composed of sovereign nations is something that has come into focus in China only during your lifetime. For most of its long history, China had little contact with the outside world. Its southern coastal communities developed trading contacts through the South China Sea. Its northern capitals sought to conquer, or protect themselves from conquest by, groups in the regions on China's borders. Abruptly and unexpectedly, all that changed in the nineteenth century (as we discussed in Chapter 6) when Beijing was brought to its knees by a small fleet of British ships. China spent the next century trying to free itself from domination by countries about which it had little prior knowledge and with which it had little prior contact. Then it spent three decades trying to reestablish rule without outside domination. Then, suddenly, during the last decades of the twentieth century, China emerged as a premier participant in world trade and a player in regional crises of importance to the major powers; it is surrounded by small, newly independent nation-states dependent on its economic output and competes with Taiwan for seats on international bodies and the investments of enormously wealthy overseas Chinese families. It is scrambling to take full advantage of those opportunities while maintaining unity and stability at home. Those goals sometimes conflict, especially in a nation so recently thrust upon the world stage.

China's Foreign Relations Before the Opium Wars

Throughout most of China's history, the country's leaders had little contact with regions beyond those on the western borders, but had extensive contact with those regions (Cohen, 2001). Largely isolated from the rest of the world, it had much reason to think of itself as the "Middle Kingdom" in the universe. It fought wars with some neighbors, while accepting tribute missions from others. As Chapter 6 indicated, long before the Roman Empire, China's merchants began trade with Java (in the Indonesian archipelago; see Map 2.1), Europe, India, and points between. In the twelfth century BCE, towns stretching from Guangzhou (Canton) to Fuzhou began extensive sea trade with Southeast Asia (see Maps 2.1, 2.2). In the fourth century BCE, a kingdom along China's southern coast—and during the third century BCE the Qin dynasty (Chapter 3)—sent out fleets of rafts full of settlers who might even have reached North America (Needham, 1971). Early in the Han dynasty, Chinese garrisons began to protect traders along the Silk Roads into inner Asia (Map 2.1). In the sixth century CE, Arab, Jewish, Christian, and Turkish merchants started settling in China's coastal cities. Chinese ship captains (most notably, Admiral Zheng He, whose expeditions into the Indian Ocean early in the fifteenth century are discussed in Chapter 3) accepted gifts from local rulers, which they passed on as tribute to Chinese emperors. Merchants coming overland brought the emperors tribute, as did emissaries from some kings of bordering states. As we saw in Chapter 6, China sought to control the administration and territorial expansion of Tibet. Beyond this, China had no formal relations with foreign governments, even though it produced a third of the world's manufactured goods sold by these merchants (Marks, 2006:123–127).

Like those of Siam (Thailand), Tibet, Japan, and Turkey, traditional Chinese leaders received tribute from lesser kingdoms around them. This solemnized their trade and foreign relations (Cohen, 2010). Emissaries or merchants from the lesser kingdoms brought gifts to the leader of the dominant one. China's emperors assumed these gifts were an indication that the kingdoms sending them recognized China's cultural superiority. To emphasize this, emissaries carrying the gifts were required to kneel before the emperor, hit their heads against the ground three times, and then lie flat (prostrate themselves) on the ground nine times. This was called the "kowtow." After that, the emperor would hold a banquet for the emissaries, give them gifts of greater value than those they had brought, and accord them the right to trade with China. The emperors interpreted this to mean that the barbarians who brought this tribute had "come to be transformed" and were recognizing China as the center of world civilization. The emperors believed any kingdom sending such gifts was a "vassal" recognizing China's "suzerainty" (dominance) over it. Korea, the kingdom of Melaka (Malacca) on the Strait of Malacca (near the southern tip of peninsular Malaysia; see Map 2.1), Siam (Thailand), Burma, and Vietnam (all in Southeast Asia; see Map 2.1), Japan, the Ryukyu Islands (stretching between Taiwan and Japan, containing Okinawa), and bordering kingdoms of Central Asia all sent emissaries to China's emperors bearing tribute; in exchange, China traded with them. Several ports were open for this trade; foreigners had to reside and stay within neighborhoods reserved for them. Ships came from as far as India and Arabia.

The sixteenth century brought major challenges to this system; new outside forces, coming by sea, challenged China's suzerainty. In 1511, Portuguese ships took over one of China's vassal states, the kingdom of Melaka, and then established a fort on an island off southern China. The emissary they sent to Beijing was rebuffed and jailed. By 1557, in the Pearl River Delta below Guangzhou (see Map 2.2), the Portuguese had established the colony of Macau, which was sending emissaries to Beijing with tribute in exchange for trading privileges. In 1555, Japanese pirates sacked the city of Nanjing, near the mouth of the Yangtze River (Map 2.2). In 1592 and 1597, the Japanese emperor Hideyoshi invaded China's vassal Korea and some Chinese ports; the threat subsided with Hideyoshi's sudden death (Swope, 2009). These provocations caused China's emperor to close most ports to trade. Macau became the principal port for China's trade with Japan, until Japan closed its ports to Portugal in 1639. In 1637, a British flotilla shot its way up the Pearl River toward Guangzhou, hoping to open the port. Then in 1685, China decided to open all its ports to foreign trade, and they remained open until 1757.

During the seventeenth century, the expanding Russian Empire arrived at China's border; the Ming emperors granted trading rights. When the Mongols, whose territories had bordered those of Russia, took Beijing and established the Qing dynasty in 1644, they created the Lifan Yuan, an agency (staffed entirely by Manchus and Mongols) to deal with Russia and inner Asian rulers. The Russian emperors were not comfortable having their emissaries prostrate themselves before the Chinese emperors; they preferred a relationship between empires of equal stature. After some protracted wrangling over kowtowing and some border skirmishes, Jesuit court advisers helped the Lifan Yuan negotiate a treaty—China's first—to demarcate China's western boundaries and stabilize China's relations with Russia. It was signed in Nirchinsk in 1689 and was followed by another at Kiakhta in 1729. The treaties prescribed that, in exchange for kowtows in Beijing by Russia's emissaries, China's emissaries would kowtow at the czar's court in St. Petersburg. The trade missions, which crossed the borders in increasing numbers, would simply exchange gifts without court appearances. In a great break from precedent, Russia was allowed to send a permanent emissary to reside in Beijing, but it was not allowed to trade by sea.

As the volume of outside trade began to expand rapidly during the eighteenth century, China's government found it necessary to create new ways of dealing with the outside world. In 1720, Guangzhou merchants formed the first of the trading organizations (*cohongs*), which became the official points of contact between China and European merchants. After 1757, Guangzhou

(Canton) became the only port legally open for foreign trade. But no foreigners were allowed to live there; the employees of their firms had to reside in nearby Macau. Women were not to be allowed in the foreigners' Guangzhou warehouse wharves, and men could leave the area, for an escorted walk in a park, only three times a month. By 1784, the United States began trade with Guangzhou (Cohen, 2010).

The *cohongs* had to pay government officials large sums of money from their profits; they recovered this by demanding bribes and arbitrary fees from the foreigners. And the Chinese government kept creating new regulations to control the personal behavior of foreigners, restricting their movement outside Macau. In 1741, a disabled British ship had pulled into Hong Kong harbor and was refused assistance. Complaints about unfair trade practices had to be mediated by the very *cohongs* with which the foreigners were trading. In 1759, Britain's East India Company sent an emissary to the emperor to complain about these trade restrictions; he was imprisoned. With Britain now the largest seafaring trader in China, King George III sent an expedition to Beijing in 1793 to ask for the right to exchange ambassadors, let British live in Guangzhou and create warehouses to trade in other ports, allow missionaries to preach Christianity, and establish an outpost on an island near the mouth of the Yangtze River. Its leader, Lord Macartney, came laden with tribute consisting of Britain's latest manufactures. Qianlong, China's longest-serving emperor and one of its greatest, greeted him warmly (dispensing with a kowtow) and sent him home with many boxes of gifts and a long letter addressed to King George (Cameron, 1975:22–45; Hevia, 2005), turning down all his requests. It explained the following:

- All foreigners living in China must live in special neighborhoods that they cannot leave, must wear Chinese garb, cannot open businesses or interact with Chinese subjects, and are never permitted to return home. Ambassadors could not function that way, and China does not need other religious doctrines. The letter adds, "The distinction between Chinese and barbarian is most strict" (Cameron, 1975:33).
- Europeans are permitted to reside in Macau and trade through Guangzhou *cohongs*. They can buy what they want there and are making large profits. Provisions have been made for settling disputes to the satisfaction of Europeans. Rules forbidding Europeans to set foot in Guangzhou and other parts of China cut down on the chance for disputes between Chinese and barbarians and give foreign trading organizations control over their own people.

From the Opium Wars to the People's Republic

These rules prevailed until the British fleet forced the Chinese to sign the Treaty of Nanjing in 1842, ending the first Opium War, which is discussed in

Chapter 6 (Grasso, Corin, and Kort, 2004; Elleman, 2001:13–34). During the subsequent half-century, European powers invaded China on numerous occasions; after the peace negotiations that followed, China signed twenty more treaties reinforcing the new rules created by the Treaty of Nanjing and extending them to interaction with Japan, the United States, Peru, Brazil, Russia, and all the major European nations (Bau, 2010:93–180; Cameron, 1975:45–52; Cohen, 2010:8–28). Though it was greatly weakened, none of these countries acquired China as a colony. But its sovereignty and interaction with foreign lands had been completely transformed (Lydia Liu, 2006). Suddenly foreigners were able to reside in special neighborhoods in a variety of "treaty ports" (Johnson, 1995). They were able to learn Chinese, dress and behave as they pleased, open businesses, trade with anyone, travel in other parts of the cities where they lived, interact with Chinese subjects and propagate their religion, and travel to their homelands whenever they wished. They built industries and railroad lines and hired Chinese workers for jobs at home and overseas. Their boats plied inland waterways. Consuls appointed by foreign governments communicated directly with Chinese officials. Under new rules of "extraterritoriality," foreigners accused of crimes were tried under their own laws.

The new rules required China, for the first time, to establish a national customs office and foreign affairs ministry (in 1861) and to open a school (soon transformed into a college) to train interpreters for Chinese officials dealing with foreigners. By the 1870s, China was sending ambassadors abroad and no longer requiring ambassadors received by the emperor to kowtow (Hsu, 1980:81–82). Smarting from its military defeats and loss of sovereignty, the Qing government took steps at "self-strengthening" by acquiring a modern navy, establishing naval and military academies, and sending students abroad to learn about modern technical subjects (Lydia Liu, 2006; Cameron, 1975:95–111).

Meanwhile (as Chapters 3, 4, 6, and 8 explain), China faced civil wars, disintegration of Beijing's control from the center, extensive migration by many able people, and social and economic problems caused by rapid population growth and economic change. Seeing its weakness, foreign powers took control of countries that had once been China's vassals and of territory within China. Some examples follow.

- As discussed in Chapter 6, the Japanese took Formosa (Taiwan), the Ryukyu Islands (Okinawa), the Pescadores Islands, and the Liaodong peninsula in Manchuria (Elleman, 2001:94–115).
- The French took control of Vietnam (Elleman, 2001:82–93). They also demanded and received a lease for a port on Hainan Island (Map 2.2).
- The British took Burma. They also leased a port city on the north side of Shandong (Map 2.2) and Kowloon and the New Territories on the mainland opposite Hong Kong.

• Germany forced the Qing to lease it the port of Qingdao (now famous for its beer, commonly known as Tsingtao) and surrounding territory on the Shandong peninsula (Map 2.2).

• Nearby in Manchuria, the Russians received a lease for Port Arthur (Lushun, on the southern tip of Liaoning; Map 2.2).

In retaliation for some missionaries being killed during the Boxer Uprising (see Chapter 12), foreign troops actually occupied Beijing's Forbidden City from 1900 to 1901, forcing the emperor and empress dowager to flee. Supported by France and Germany, Russia used the chaos to occupy Manchuria (Heilongjiang, Jilin, and Liaoning provinces; see Map 2.2), which prompted an alliance between Britain and Japan to protect their interests (Hsu, 1980:115–138; Cameron, 1975:163–186).

In 1905, Japan defeated Russia in a war; the two signed a peace treaty in Portsmouth, New Hampshire, mediated by President Theodore Roosevelt. Roosevelt and the European powers were concerned about protecting the territorial integrity of China. The treaty acknowledged that Korea was under Japan's sphere of influence and agreed to the withdrawal of all foreign troops from Manchuria, except for some territory containing railway lines whose lease Russia was to transfer to Japan. Both Russia and Japan were to be allowed to station some troops in Manchuria to protect the railway. The Japanese received Port Arthur. This set the stage for forty-five years of conflict (Hsu, 1980:138–141; Xiao Liu, 2006; Howe, 1996) in which Japan would play a major role (see Table 7.1).

In 1910, Japan annexed Korea. For supporting Britain in World War I (and despite China's strong objection), the 1919 Treaty of Versailles gave Germany's land leases in China's Shandong peninsula to Japan, kicking off the May Fourth Movement of protest discussed in Chapter 13 (Wang, 1966:306–361; Bau, 2010:181–283). To counter the Soviet takeover of Russia, Japan occupied land bordering Manchuria. The Soviets kept claim to Russian railroad lines running through Manchuria, which angered Japan. In 1931, Japan occupied Manchuria and set it up as the puppet state of Manchukuo (Duara, 2003). In 1937, Japan attacked China and occupied large portions of it (as discussed in Chapter 4) until Japan's surrender to the Allied Forces in 1945 (Hsiung and Levine, 1997; Elleman, 2001:194–216; Mitter, 2000; Tuchman, 2001).

Foreign Policy Under Mao

During the "united front" between the Communists and Chiang Kai-shek's Nationalists, which lasted from 1936 until the end of World War II, the United States and the Soviet Union could deal with the Communists and the Nationalists at the same time. Even when the united front broke down, both gave technical and military assistance to the Nationalists while maintaining

Table 7.1 Important Dates in China's Foreign Policy

1842	Treaty of Nanjing ends first Opium War
1861	Founding of Customs Office and Foreign Affairs Ministry
1895	Treaty of Shimonoseki cedes Formosa to Japan
1900	British occupy Forbidden City after Boxer Uprising
1905	Treaty of Portsmouth allows Japanese troops in Manchuria
1919	Treaty of Versailles gives Japan Shandong land leases
1931	Japan occupies Manchuria
1945	End of World War II brings KMT-Communist combat
1950	Start of Korean War and US Seventh Fleet in Taiwan Strait
1953	Korean War armistice
1955	Bandung Conference of "nonaligned" states
1956	Tibetan rebellion
1960	Break in relations with USSR
1962	Sino-Indian border war
1964	China explodes atomic bomb
1965	United States enters Vietnam War
1970	China takes Taiwan's United Nations seat
1972	US president Richard Nixon visits China
1975	End of Vietnam War
1979	United States and China establish diplomatic relations
1987	Tibetan rebellion
1989	USSR general secretary Mikhail Gorbachev visits China
1997	Hong Kong joins China
1997	Chinese oil companies begin heavy investment abroad
1999	Macau joins China
2001	Beijing chosen as site of 2008 Olympics
2001	China and Taiwan join World Trade Organization
2008	Beijing Olympics
2009	China and Taiwan accelerate the signing of trade and travel agreements
2009	China declares the South China Sea within its "core interests"
2011	South Sudan becomes independent from Sudan with assistance from China

friendly contact with the Communists (Sheng, 1998). As the Japanese surrendered, the Nationalist and Communist armies turned to fight one another for control of China (Elleman, 2001:217–232). The United States assisted only the Nationalists (Westad, 1992; Tucker, 2001; Cohen, 2010:89–114), while Joseph Stalin attempted to play both sides. He turned over control of enormous arms stockpiles and the city of Harbin to the Communists and trained and supplied Mao Zedong's troops; he gave the Nationalists command of all the other Manchurian cities (after dismantling many industries and seizing many assets for shipment to the Soviet Union) and maintained good relations with Chiang Kai-shek. Thus, once Stalin captured Beijing and Chiang's Kuomintang (KMT) government fled to Taiwan in 1949, Mao felt uneasy taking on Stalin as an ally, but he had nowhere else to turn because he found himself isolated diplomatically. Britain quickly recognized the People's Republic of China

(PRC) but also continued to recognize the legitimacy of Chiang's regime in Taiwan. Though Mao made overtures to President Harry Truman, the United States did not respond (Garver, 1993:40; Chen, 2012). The spread of communism in Eastern Europe was making the United States hesitant to carry on further relations with communist regimes. Therefore, needing foreign assistance, Mao accepted aid from the Soviet Union; this uneasy relationship lasted until 1960 (Heinzig, 2004). Two days after North Korea attacked South Korea in June 1950, the US Seventh Fleet moved into the Taiwan Strait to protect the Nationalists from invasion by Mao's forces; the United States would not recognize the PRC until 1979 (Cohen, 2010:148–214). Before exploring these developments further, we should assess Mao's strategic considerations as he assumed power.

After a hundred years of division and foreign intrusion, Mao sought to reestablish China's traditional borders and to reassert influence over all the regions that once paid tribute to China. That tribute had recognized China's moral and cultural superiority as well as its physical dominance. As a communist, Mao wanted to rid China and its neighbors of imperialist masters and to persuade its neighbors of the superiority of China's communist system. At the same time, he wanted to continue to attract capitalist investment so as to rebuild China's economy and to develop friendly trade relations with foreign nations. That combination of goals called for a delicate balancing act that involved several elements.

- The 11 million overseas Chinese, mostly residing in Southeast Asia, might provide technical skills and investment capital. But as their countries received independence from the colonial powers, they wished to incorporate their Chinese populace into their own citizenry. If the PRC were to continue treating these overseas Chinese as its own citizens, it risked alienating the governments of these new nations.
- Guerrilla movements were challenging the legitimate governments in many of these countries. As China's leader, Mao realized they could help him assert China's dominance over the region. As a communist, he was sympathetic to their revolutionary aspirations of returning power to the exploited lower classes, but he also wanted peace on his borders while he consolidated power and fought outside challengers. He did not want to force neighboring governments into treaties that would give the United States bases on China's borders or into retaliation against their Chinese communities. He wanted the support of the wealthy Chinese living in those countries, who hated the guerrillas and were also being wooed by Chiang Kai-shek to support the KMT in Taiwan. And the guerrillas also had loyalties to their own countries and might not ultimately side with China.
- The PRC wanted admission into the United Nations and other bodies that could provide it with access to world markets and participation in interna-

tional decisionmaking. But it was determined to defeat Chiang Kai-shek's Nationalist forces, which had fled to the island of Taiwan while insisting (as explained in Chapter 6) that they were still the rightful government of all China. Only one could hold China's United Nations seat, and both had supporters there.

• Mao wanted to abrogate "unequal treaties" drawn up between imperial powers and former Chinese governments, but he also wanted trade, investment, and assistance from those imperial powers.

Overseas Chinese, discussed in Chapter 6, stood squarely at the center of all those concerns, so Mao's government could not walk away from them (Storey, 2011). More overseas Chinese had contact with the KMT and other parties in China than with the Communists; both sides needed their money and support to continue fighting one another. Many overseas Chinese were facing political repression and finding it hard to get education or employment; some were joining guerrilla movements in their own countries. The new Communist regime initially responded with a simple offer: come back home and help rebuild China. It offered them inexpensive education if they stayed to become residents of China, and higher salaries than locals. It created special banking arrangements, housing, shops, grain allotments, and travel privileges for overseas Chinese and for local relatives of overseas Chinese receiving monetary remittances from them. It urged them to create enterprises in China (Peterson, 2011). Nearly half a million Chinese came back (Fitzgerald, 1972:33). In addition, the government encouraged Chinese families with relatives abroad to write them to solicit money. It still looked upon all these overseas Chinese as China's citizens; they could become citizens of other nations and still retain (dual) citizenship in China.

By 1957, the People's Republic had discovered that the amount of technical talent, money, and political support it could attract through these policies was limited, and many Chinese who had stayed home resented the special privileges accorded those who had left, so it reversed course, unleashing a rectification campaign (see Chapter 4) to limit the rights of these returnees and urge Chinese to cut off their contacts with overseas relatives. By then, it also was negotiating agreements with Burma and Indonesia, the only Southeast Asian countries with which it had diplomatic relations, allowing (for the first time in history) overseas Chinese who became citizens of those nations to break their affiliation with China if they chose to do so. Those choosing this course would no longer receive favors or protection from China and would no longer be considered Chinese citizens. Furthermore, China now encouraged schools to be built for Chinese students by wealthy Chinese in Southeast Asian countries to teach local languages, history, and skills that would prepare them for local employment.

Events in Korea and Vietnam made this normalization possible. North

Korea invaded South Korea in June 1950. Until then, Mao's government had shown little interest in Korean affairs; the Soviet Union was North Korea's principal ally. China had been informed by those two countries shortly before the invasion took place and let North Korean troops stationed on its territory return home to participate. But the entry of United Nations forces on the side of South Korea and the US Seventh Fleet into the Taiwan Strait, as well as imposition of a trade blockade, roused China's concern (Chen, 1994; Cumings, 1981, 1990; Chang, 1990; Zhang, 2001). In August, the United Nations proposed to China that it mediate a truce in exchange for a United Nations Security Council seat. However, in October, General Douglas MacArthur's troops crossed into North Korea and headed toward the Yalu River (the same river the Japanese had crossed when they invaded Manchuria; see Spanier, 1965). Beijing lies within 400 miles of that border. China immediately mobilized troops and sent them secretly into North Korea; they succeeded in pushing the United Nations forces back into South Korea (Scobell, 2003:79–93; Elleman, 2001:235–253; Garver, 1993:285–286; Zhang, 1995; Goncharov, 1995; Li, 2007:79–112). A truce was signed three years later, leaving Korea divided. The United States suffered 160,000 casualties and China over 700,000 (including one of Mao's sons), leaving deep antagonism and suspicion on both sides (Perlmutter, 2007). The United States was now firmly committed to "containing" China, holding it within its boundaries and isolating it diplomatically (Xu, 2007). But China was also angry at the Soviet Union for starting a war on its borders in which China—not the USSR—suffered deep casualties (Nelsen, 1989; Sheng, 1998). Hence China now made an all-out effort to improve relations with smaller neighboring Asian countries.

In Vietnam, Ho Chi Minh began guerrilla warfare against the French at the end of World War II. In 1949, Chinese Red Army troops moved to the Vietnamese border to chase remaining Kuomintang Nationalist troops from China (Whiting, 2001; Elleman, 2001:284–298). In the next few years, China's government gave Ho's forces small amounts of technical assistance. After the Korean War armistice was signed in 1953, this aid grew dramatically (Karnow, 1984; Roberts, 2007; Womack, 2006; Zhai, 2000). Ho was attacking governments supported first by the French and then by the United States, which now was moving to encircle China. Though many leaders of newly independent nations had themselves begun by resisting colonial rulers and therefore might have sympathy for Ho's attempts, they also were wary of attempts by the Soviet Union, the United States, or China to involve them in the Cold War. And communist guerrillas threatened their regimes as well. So China was careful to restrict its support to the Viet Minh in Vietnam, declaring that communist forces in Laos (an area of interest to India) and in Cambodia, where China lent support to Prince Sihanouk, should seek separate settlements (Zhai, 2000). Meanwhile, remnants of KMT troops remained in those areas, supported by the United States.

In 1955, China agreed to end support for communist guerrillas operating in Burma (which, in 1949, had been the first Asian government to recognize Mao's regime); China gave little support thereafter. During talks in 1960, Burma and China agreed to some concessions on territory they claimed. When a more radical socialist government gained power in Burma in 1963, defeating the Maoist guerrillas, it took a harder line against China.

In 1955, leaders of African and Asian nations held a conference in Bandung, Indonesia, to declare a neutral path toward "peaceful coexistence," avoiding alliance with either the Soviet Union or the United States. Zhou Enlai (Han, 1994; Shao, 1996; Gao, 2007), representing China, was a major presence at this conference, declaring China's intent to sign agreements with these nonaligned nations to settle differences over dual citizenship by overseas Chinese, guerrilla warfare waged against independent nations, border disputes, and other contentious issues. As part of these efforts, China distributed hundreds of millions of dollars in aid to developing nations (Garver, 1993:221; Jain, 1976:112–156). Zhou Enlai was competing for allegiance of these nations with India, which also declared its neutrality while seeking aid from the Soviet Union.

Taiwan's continuing insistence that foreign governments allow Chinese residents to fly Nationalist flags and obey their policies strengthened the PRC's position on normalizing relations. Taiwan's legislature contained seats representing overseas Chinese. As late as 1970, the KMT kidnapped two Manila newspapermen of Han ancestry in the Philippines who did not consider themselves citizens of Taiwan and placed them on military trial for violating Taiwan's emergency regulations (Fitzgerald, 1972:76). Many Southeast Asians saw these assertions and actions as interference with the sovereignty of their own nations. By taking steps to break off ties with overseas Chinese, the PRC was attempting to distance itself from this approach (which had been habitual with Chinese governments during the past century) and thus gain more confidence among governments that feared subversion by overseas Chinese. In addition, few Chinese were now emigrating from the mainland into Southeast Asia.

Acts by surrounding countries made the PRC's attempts at normalization more difficult. Thailand had outlawed separate educational institutions for overseas Chinese. Many Southeast Asian countries suppressed Chinese newspapers. The 1955 nationality treaty with Indonesia allowed Chinese who had accepted Indonesian citizenship to regain Chinese citizenship by moving out of Indonesia, leaving many Indonesians wondering whether naturalized Chinese would remain loyal to their adopted country (Sukma, 1999:16–43). In 1956, South Vietnam forced all Chinese to declare Vietnamese citizenship and excluded them from Chinese education and most retail trade. In 1960, Indonesia also banned Chinese from retail trade, their principal source of livelihood, and closed many Chinese schools and newspapers. The heat over this controversy sparked riots; the Chinese government sent ships to carry 100,000 refugees to asylum in China. After 1963, China also extricated refugees when repression in India followed the Sino-Indian border skirmishes (discussed in the last section of Chapter 6).

To quell these fears about the loyalty of overseas Chinese, Zhou Enlai announced that Chinese everywhere were free to choose their own citizenship; he encouraged them to become citizens of and obey the laws of the lands where they resided and to marry local people. Overseas Chinese who chose to retain Chinese citizenship would be expected to obey the laws of the lands where they resided, but ultimately they were subject to the jurisdiction of the PRC and not of Taiwan. And no Chinese should be forced to accept citizenship against their will (Fitzgerald, 1972:112–114, 140–161).

In 1960, China and the Soviet Union broke off relations. The Soviet Union, concerned about China's Great Leap Forward (see Chapter 4) and development of an atomic bomb, refused it further aid (Lewis and Xue, 1991). Seeking to gain influence in South and Southeast Asia under its own policy of "peaceful coexistence," Khrushchev supported Indonesia and India—which was also developing atomic weaponry—in their disputes with China (see Chapter 6 on the dispute with India). Cut off now from all the great powers and arguing with its neighbors, China gave even higher priority to becoming a nuclear power (Lewis and Xue, 1991; Li, 2007:147–176). By 1963, the Soviet Union had moved troops to protect the Outer Mongolian border (see Mongolia on Map 2.1) from uncertainties in China; meanwhile, it was airlifting supplies to North Vietnam and Laos. An increasingly militant China was sending aid to forces fighting white colonialists in Rhodesia and Mozambique, to Albania, and to the neutral Sihanouk regime in Cambodia. In 1964, China exploded an atomic bomb. This helped it restore dignity and greatness in the eyes of smaller countries of the region but heightened the determination of the United States to halt its projection of power, and caused some in the United States to regret not invading China when it had the chance.

In the fall of 1964, Khrushchev was removed from office in the Soviet Union; his successors returned to a militant communism closer in spirit to that of Mao (Chen, 2000). The new leaders invited Zhou Enlai to see whether relations could now be improved and to enlist China's support in the Soviet Union's new resolve to substantially aid North Vietnam, but Mao remained suspicious (Nathan and Ross, 1997:35–55). Soviet troops remained on the Mongolian border. In the summer of 1965, regular US forces entered the Vietnam War for the first time. Once again, the United States was actively countering an invasion backed by the Soviet Union in a country on China's border. Hard lines were being drawn.

The Cultural Revolution

In 1966, Mao launched the Cultural Revolution (see Chapter 4). For a time in 1967, elements of the extreme left within the Red Guards took over the

Foreign Ministry. By the end of that year, Zhou Enlai reemerged as a conciliator to begin restoring order, but for much of the next decade, China's domestic and foreign policy had to accommodate the wishes of the extreme left (Barnouin and Yu, 1997). This brought mistrust even among nations that had begun to feel more comfortable with China's policies. The radical elements were holding rallies and pillorying officials throughout China, talking about extending permanent revolution to all the rest of the world. Pol Pot in Cambodia, Sendero Luminoso guerrillas in Peru, and the Naxalite rebels in India sent emissaries to Beijing.

Such militant behavior and rhetoric helped the United States amass more support in the region for fighting the Viet Minh in Vietnam. Ironically, China was trying hard to stay out of the Vietnam War. Having sustained enormous losses in Korea, fearing an attack by the Soviet Union on its western border, and facing disruption at home from the Cultural Revolution, Mao avoided sending Chinese troops but increased military aid to the Viet Minh and resisted US attempts to achieve a peace settlement (Karnow, 1984:452–453; Zhai, 2000:130–157; Li, 2007:205–240). The main proponents of greater intervention were professional elements of the military displeased that their troops were bogged down at home carrying out public works and propaganda. They advocated spending more on weapons and equipment that could be used for armed conflict.

The radicals' desire for worldwide revolution caused problems for the Chinese in Indonesia. In the confusion surrounding a 1965 military coup in Indonesia, local inhabitants in many places slaughtered large numbers of Chinese neighbors. Initially, refugees were welcome in China; China's policy was to repatriate Chinese rather than encourage them to revolt. After the 1967 seizure of the Foreign Ministry, however, this policy changed; the radicals now encouraged overseas Chinese to rebel. This only increased resistance abroad. By the end of 1967, Outer Mongolia was expelling overseas Chinese. Chinese in Burma, Cambodia, Penang, Macau, and Hong Kong clashed with authorities. Red Guards harassed overseas Chinese visiting China from abroad on trade missions and wrote to some of them, informing them that their houses and property in China were being seized. Letters and parcels from abroad were confiscated, and Chinese were discouraged from writing to relatives abroad. By 1969, suspicion of China in Indonesia grew so great that its government declared the 1955 nationality treaty null and void.

The radicalization of China's Foreign Ministry was short-lived, however. By late 1967, Mao was calling upon Zhou Enlai and the army to reestablish some order and restrain the Red Guards (Zhu, 1998). Overseas Chinese engaged in rebellion would not receive material support from China. A 1969 border incursion by radical Chinese troops was decisively trounced by Soviet troops (Jones and Kevill, 1985:92–96). Slowly, China sought to restore normal relations with the outside world. In 1970, Mao asked US journalist Edgar

Snow to stand with him on the reviewing stand for National Day. The following year, Zhou Enlai met secretly with Henry Kissinger; in October, China took Taiwan's seat in the United Nations. Richard Nixon's visit to Beijing in 1972 dramatized the changing relationship (Holdridge, 1997; Tucker, 2001; Garrison, 2005; MacMillan, 2007; Kissinger, 2011; Baum, 2010:61–81). Soon Japan and a host of other nations established diplomatic relations. Japan was especially well poised to take advantage of the new era. Since the end of World War II, it had quietly resumed trade and diplomatic contacts with China. Now those relations were legitimized, and Japanese businesspeople had a head start on setting up new enterprises in China.

In 1975, North Vietnamese troops entered Saigon, and the last US troops were airlifted out. The following year, both Zhou Enlai and Mao died. On January 1, 1979, the United States and China established full diplomatic relations. Weeks later, relations between Vietnam and China were in disarray. China crossed the border with troops; within a month, their ill-equipped and poorly trained troops were beaten back by superior Vietnamese forces (Scobell, 2003:119–143). This was the ultimate proof of how weak Mao's policies had made China. After three decades of hostility, China and the United States were renewing relations, both smarting from defeat by a nation that had long pitted them as adversaries (Ross, 1995). Ironically, the United States had fought North Vietnam as part of an effort to stop China from extending its political power into Southeast Asia; now Vietnam was holding back China's troops from entering Vietnam.

Joining the World Community

Chapters 4–6 discussed the enormous economic growth China has experienced since Deng Xiaoping took the reins of power by 1980. Deng brought an end to the Cultural Revolution, freeing China to try his economic reforms. China's new position in the international community also facilitated reform. It was now a member of the United Nations Security Council and had diplomatic relations with the United States. And the Cold War was coming to an end. China was free to assume a normal position in world affairs (Sutter, 2010:65–95). It could press aggressively to establish trade ties for its reforming economy. With the Soviet Union disintegrating, large numbers of traders were crossing the borders of its former republics to buy goods for their depleted economies. China set out to ease trade across the borders with Nepal, Mongolia, Burma, Laos, and Thailand (bringing a flood of unwelcome opium along with other goods). In 1989, Soviet leader Mikhail Gorbachev visited Beijing and, in 1992, China settled part of a border dispute with Russia (which resulted in the signing of a formal border agreement in 1997) and started importing Russian technology. China helped Thailand fight Moscow-backed Vietnamese and Cambodian forces until a Cambodian peace settlement in

1991 allowed it to withdraw support from Khmer Rouge guerrilla forces there and cut all ties with Thai communists. No longer a military ally or adversary, Vietnam gradually emerged as a trading partner with China and the West; China opened trade across its border in 1990 (Womack, 2006). In 1989, China ended support for Malaysian communist guerrillas, and in 1990 Singapore and Indonesia established diplomatic relations with China. Businesspeople from around the world began to explore the "China market."

The military intervention at Tiananmen Square in 1989 brought a chill to China's foreign relations for a time (see Chapter 4; Scobell, 2003:144–170; Baum, 2010:118–137). But after Deng toured the Pearl River Delta region early in 1992 and announced that in the new "socialist market economy" the reform efforts would be speeded, and that China's people should explore capitalist techniques, investment began to pour in (see Chapter 5). Now China carries on trade (and diplomatic relations) with virtually every foreign nation. It belongs to the World Bank and World Trade Organization and signed the nuclear nonproliferation treaty in 1984 (though it has continued to sell nuclear materials abroad).

Only North Korea remains a hard-core communist nation. China treats it with respectful reserve, urging restraint when South Korea (which established diplomatic relations with China in 1992) or the United States has sought serious retaliation or sanctions against its nuclear program or military threats. Since 1997, it has worked with the United States, Japan, and South Korea in negotiations to control North Korea's nuclear buildup, but that buildup seems to continue. China has also aided North Korea with grain, oil, and fertilizer and is North Korea's biggest trading partner (Sutter, 2007:247–253; Snyder, 2009).

As we saw in Chapter 6, Hong Kong and Taiwan have become China's biggest partners in investment and trade. Japan, the United States, Western Europe, and Singapore joined in more slowly but have grown into sizable partners as well. However, a number of controversies still clouded this interaction.

Regional Relations

China maintains a traditional concern about the regions to its south (in Southeast Asia) and west (in Central Asia) (see Map 2.1). Since the second century BCE, some of China's greatest emperors have extended its borders in those directions (Womack, 2006, 2010:369–510). Its main traditional enemies—the Annamese and Champas (from Vietnam), Turks, Mongols, Manchus, Zunghars, Tanguts, Tartars, Russians, and Tibetans (from Central Asia)—lived in or invaded territory there. Those areas remain of great strategic concern to China (Yahuda, 2011:137–159). China has recently accommodated some of its disputes in Southeast Asia, but its relations with Tibet Autonomous Region and nations that border it remain very tense (see Chapter 6). It also faces unrest among Muslims and other minorities in Xinjiang

Autonomous Region, who are influenced by Islamic fundamentalists in regions to the west of China. China sold arms to Iran, Pakistan, and Iraq in hopes of cooperation on keeping border security (Garver, 2006). It outbid US oil companies for rich oil fields in Indonesia and in Kazakhstan, which take on increasing strategic importance.

Chapter 6 discussed some of China's historical disputes with India; relations between the two countries remain tentative and complex (Dittmer, 2005; Frankel and Harding, 2004; Garver, 2002; Lal, 2006; Ramesh, 2006; Sidhu and Yuan, 2003; Whiting, 2001; Sutter, 2007:295–308; Cooney and Sato, 2009:177–213; Pant, 2011; Malik, 2011). While India courted support from the Soviet Union, China supplied arms to India's adversaries in Pakistan, Saudi Arabia, Iran, and Iraq, helping Afghan forces fight the Soviet invasion in the 1980s. When it became apparent in 1989 that China was selling Pakistan nuclear materials, India stepped up its arms race with China. China remains angry that the Dalai Lama, along with many Tibetan refugees, has political asylum in India. In 1997, China agreed to cut back arms sales to Pakistan, but has continued to supply them, even with fighter jets and guided-missile frigates.

In 2001, during the US war to overthrow the Taliban in Afghanistan, heavy fighting broke out in Kashmir, and Pakistan and India threatened to use nuclear weapons against each other (Dittmer, 2005). The only valley connecting Xinjiang and Tibet passes through a segment of Kashmir controlled by China and claimed by India. But China feared the rise of Islamic militancy, and threat of nuclear conflagration, on its borders. It did not take sides in the Kashmir dispute but sought to ease tensions. For the first time, direct flights between China and India commenced. And direct trade began to grow. In 1992, India's trade with China accounted for four-tenths of 1 percent of its total exports and imports; in 2010, it amounted to over 10 percent—US$40 billion in imports from China and US$20 billion in exports to China ("A Strategy to Straddle the Planet," 2011). China's economy is three times the size of India's, and its export of manufactured goods is ten times greater than India's (Sally, 2009). Seventy percent of India's exports to China are raw materials, principally iron ore. But the world's two most populated nations find themselves engaged in a competition to expand their economies and alliances (Meredith, 2008; Ramesh, 2006; Denoon, 2007; Holslag, 2009; Emmott, 2009; Sieff, 2010; Pant, 2009, 2011; Chellaney, 2009, 2010; Bahl, 2010). That means they need expanding amounts of increasingly scarce resources, especially oil and water, new markets for their goods, and allies in their quest to obtain these and to maintain security against the many ethnic and religious factions that threaten both of their border regions with growing militancy and terrorism (Wayne, 2009). Both nations have vied for support from the Maoist rebels in Nepal. China's new network of railroads, superhighways, and airports has reached near the borders of India, Nepal, Afghanistan, and

Pakistan. China's new dams on the Brahmaputra River hold back more and more water from Bangladesh and India downstream. As the Dalai Lama ages, the disputed area in Kashmir, and India's eastern state of Arunachal Pradesh, which has welcomed many Tibetan refugees and contains the Tawang valley linking Lhasa with India, grow in strategic importance in the eyes of China. It has also sent a lot of troops into Tibet and western Xinjiang. It has become more aggressive about its territorial demands by interfering with an international loan to Arunachal Pradesh, denying visas to its citizens, and sending troops to aggressively patrol the borders. India has responded by sending more divisions of troops to border areas. The United States has added to these tensions by signing agreements to sell India sophisticated weapons systems and nuclear fuel and reactors, recognizing their right to a nuclear arms program, endorsing India's bid for permanent membership in the UN Security Council, and sharing military intelligence—while maintaining neutrality with regard to this territorial claims standoff. Still, trade between India and China expands.

In 1996, China helped create the Shanghai Cooperation Organization (SCO) to settle border disputes with Russia, Kazakhstan, Kyrgyzstan, Tajikistan, and Uzbekistan (Sutter, 2007:308–319; Lanteigne, 2005:115–142; Marketos, 2009; Hao and Chou, 2011:47–68; Zhao, 2011). These nations hold joint military exercises and work together on crime, terrorism, drug trafficking, and energy policy. In 2011, Russia was supporting India's admission into the group, while China was endorsing Pakistan. China has also worked with

Robert E. Gamer

Military vehicles in Gansu; part of China's patrol of its western regions.

Japan and ASEAN (Association of Southeast Asian Nations) to resolve regional border and trade disputes. China has worked to make ASEAN nations partners in contracts for manufactured goods, supplying components that let them share in the economic growth (Beeson, 2008; Zhao, 2011).

Oil plays a major role in China's policy toward the Middle East, which supplies over half of China's imported oil and natural gas, much of that from Saudi Arabia and Iran (Sutter, 2007:355–367; Kong, 2010; Garrison, 2009; Andrews-Speed and Dannreuther, 2011). Oil and arms policies are heavily intertwined. China supplies Iran with missiles, fighter planes, and other arms, along with subways, dams, and electricity grids. Oman buys Chinese rocket guns and launchers. Saudi Arabia buys its missiles, Yemen buys its fighter planes, the United Arab Emirates rocket launchers, and Kuwait self-propelled guns. China takes care not to offend any of these countries. It used its position on the UN Security Council to weaken sanctions against Iran over its nuclear program but, in 2010, joined in support for those sanctions. China helped Pakistan build a deep-sea port, now operated by the Singapore Port Authority, at the mouth of the Persian Gulf; it has plans to build an oil pipeline from there to Xinjiang. In 2009, China's navy joined in the hunt for Somali pirates; on the way to the Gulf of Aden its submarine was tailed by Indian ships, testing their sonar defenses (Pant, 2009). China has coordinated with India in bidding for African oil supplies. All this affects United States foreign policy in that region and worries India (Simpfendorfer, 2009; Alterman and Garver, 2008; Kemp, 2010).

China's relations with Burma are controversial. The generals there renamed the country Myanmar, placed the winner of the 1990 election Aung San Suu Kyi under house arrest, brutally suppressed all political opposition, and cut the country off from the outside world. Most of the world's nations ceased trading with it. Meanwhile China, Thailand, and India continued border trade, often of banned trade items like teakwood, bear paws, tiger and leopard skins, and elephant tusks—and heroin and opium. Thailand and China helped it build environmentally harmful dams and gold mines. China has built a deep water port for oil tankers at the mouth of the Irrawaddy River and is beginning to tap the rich oil and gas fields off its coast and is building pipelines to route it into China. China refused to go along with UN sanctions against Burma in 2007, when it acted as mediator in international attempts to soften a brutal crackdown on students and monks who engaged in demonstrations. In 2009, China allowed some Kokang, a Han Chinese minority, to cross into China during their fighting against Myanmar government troops. As many as 2 million Chinese live in northern Burma, dominating the gem and jade trade, running illegal casinos, and causing resentments as they flaunt their wealth (Hao and Chou, 2011:253–274). Since Burma's elections in 2010, its more moderate leaders have closed a large Chinese dam project and sought to close the illegal casinos, while continuing the oil and gas projects.

Another serious point of tension lies in the waters east and south of China, which carry about half of the world's merchant cargo ship tonnage, including much crude oil bound for the United States (Bateman and Emmers, 2009; Storey, 2011). The South China Sea (see Map 2.4), extending from Taiwan to Singapore, is dotted with hundreds of tiny islands, islets, and reefs, which are potential launching points for military assaults and control of the vast petroleum reserves on the ocean floor. The Portuguese began the eventual European domination of China by occupying islands there. China, Taiwan, Malaysia, Brunei, the Philippines, and Vietnam lay claim to the Spratly and Paracel Island chains north of Borneo and to various parts of the South China Sea surrounding them. By some estimates, the seabed around these islands contains more oil and natural gas reserves than Kuwait, and during the 1990s, these countries were contracting with US oil companies to drill there. This led to disputes. In addition, these countries send commercial fleets to fish in the abundant waters of the area. During the 1990s, China, for the first time since the Ming dynasty, sent a navy into the open sea as part of its improved training and deployment of troops. Visits by those ships to the Spratly, Paracel, and Natuna Islands caused concern to the governments of Malaysia, the Philippines, Indonesia, and Taiwan.

Meanwhile, China, Taiwan, and Japan all claim ownership of the Diaoyu Islands in the East China Sea northeast of Taiwan (Map 2.4) (Bush, 2010); Hao and Chou, 2011:117–163). After a radical nationalist Japanese group erected a lighthouse there in 1996, Japan (declaring the islands their "exclusive economic zone") set up a coast guard patrol nearby, which in 1998 sank a vessel carrying twenty-five Hong Kong protesters, who were rescued by accompanying Taiwanese protest ships. To ease some of these concerns, in 1998 the United States signed an accord with China designed to avoid naval and air conflicts at sea, and United States navy vessels maintain a continuing presence there. A decade later, in 2009, hostilities reemerged when China declared the South China Sea to be a "core interest" and presented the UN with a declaration of intent to enforce its right to 80 percent of it. It began harassing fishing boats, including the US navy ship *Impeccable*, which triggered an intense diplomatic standoff (Dutton and Garofano, 2009). In 2010, a Chinese fishing boat collided with two Japanese coast guard vessels, and China cut off shipments of rare earth to Japanese high-tech companies when Japan detained the fishing boat captain. In 2011, the tsunami and nuclear meltdown in Japan helped lead to agreements between the countries on cooperation in disaster relief, nuclear safety, and future drilling, but both countries stuck to their claims on the islands.

Meanwhile, the nations of the region are surveying the sea for oil and gas and building fortifications of the small islands they seized during the 1990s. In 2011, China cut the multimillion-dollar seismic survey cables of a Vietnamese research ship. Serious protests erupted. Later that year Vietnam instituted a military draft and ordered six Russian submarines for its navy. Also in 2011,

China unloaded oil rig building materials on a barren reef near the Philippines, which sparked controversy. Vietnam, the Philippines, and South Korea held joint naval drills with the United States, which—now declaring its "national interest" in maintaining freedom of navigation there—has been increasing its naval presence by setting up a marine base in northern Australia, deploying new amphibious assault vessels in Singapore, acquiescing to Vietnam enriching its own uranium, joined the Philippines by referring to the South China Sea as the "West Philippines Sea," and resuming links to Indonesia's army special forces in light of these tensions.

Japanese nationalists—who look back with pride to the World War II era when Japan projected its power throughout Asia and who fear China's growing military capacity, nuclear testing, and skirmishes with Taiwan—play an important role in Japan's overall relationship with China (Howe, 1996; Bush, 2010). Chinese nationalists remember Japan's mass killings of civilians, the Chinese women forced to be "comfort women" for the Japanese soldiers, and general brutality during World War II (see Chapter 4). They also object to Japan deploying military forces to support UN and US initiatives, seeking its own approach to alliances with ASEAN nations and India, expressing support for Taiwan, and increasing aid to countries in regions where China was also competing for support (Sutter, 2007:217–247; Heazle and Knight, 2007; Liao, 2006). Both pressure their governments to avoid looking weak by making concessions to the other side. Yet their governments, like Vietnam's and South Korea's, have strong reasons for restraint. China is Japan's largest trade partner, and Japan is China's second-largest after the United States; in 2010, they conducted US$300 billion in trade. That represents 20 percent of Japan's foreign trade, versus 5 percent in 1992. Vietnam, which has the fastest economic growth in Southeast Asia, had US$20 billion in trade with China in 2009; 22 percent of South Korea's 2010 trade was with China, versus 4 percent in 1992 ("A Strategy to Straddle the Planet," 2011).

A Serious "Internal" Conflict

The most difficult controversy obstructing China's efforts to join the world community is its puzzling relationship with Taiwan—the unresolved civil war (see Chapter 6). Their only point of agreement is that both are part of the same country. China insists that Taiwan is part of mainland China, and its public supports that policy. Taiwan's leaders are divided, as is Taiwan's public. Some insist that Taiwan is the rightful ruler of China, others want Taiwan to be an independent nation, while many prefer to leave the issue unresolved until a later time. Countries establishing diplomatic relations with China are forced to end relations with Taiwan (which now has relations with twenty-three small countries—in Latin America, Africa, and the South Pacific). Taiwan is the largest investor in China. Chapter 6 discusses the diplomatic moves under way to try to bridge these radical differences.

The United States, ever since it brought the Seventh Fleet into the Taiwan Strait in 1950, has pledged to defend Taiwan against attack by China (Cole, 2006). It extended diplomatic recognition to China in 1979 with the stipulation that it would allow Taiwan and China to settle their differing interpretations of what "one China" meant—so long as neither party launched a military attack on the other—and that the United States would still continue to supply Taiwan with "defensive" weapons (Huang and Li, 2010:88–122).

In 1999, intervening in Yugoslavia, US planes bombed the Chinese embassy in Belgrade, killing a number of staff members there. This provoked outrage on campuses and among citizens in China and began a period of especially strained relations between China and the United States (Gries, 2005; Huang and Li, 2010:217–266). Only months later, Chen Shui-bian came to power in Taiwan, and China threatened to invade if his new government sought to declare independence. Meanwhile, China is making a major push to add to its arsenal of cruise and land-based missiles, supersonic jets, helicopters, hovercraft, destroyers (13), frigates (more than 65), submarines (more than 60), missile-armed fast attack boats (more than 85), amphibious landing ships, aircraft carriers, tanks, satellites, and other advanced weaponry, together with radar and the most advanced software and electronics. Much of it comes from Russia, but Israeli, British, French, and even US firms are vying to sell it advanced weapons and the technology needed to design and operate them (Cole, 2001). China itself is building new aircraft and ships, many of which are the most advanced possessed by countries in the region (Erickson et al., 2007; Erickson, Goldstein, and Lord, 2009; Erickson, Goldstein, and Nan, 2010; Howarth, 2006; Cordesman and Klieber, 2007; Collins et al., 2008; Holmes and Yoshihara, 2009; Yoshihara and Holmes, 2010; Kaplan, 2010; US Military, 2011). In 2007, it successfully shot down one of its own satellites with a missile (Handberg, 2006).

In response, the United States agreed to sell Taiwan new classes of weaponry. Members of Congress called for supplying Taiwan, in addition, with submarines, antisubmarine aircraft, a new class of Aegis destroyers, and a highly advanced "theater" missile system. When President George W. Bush took office in 2001, China feared he would let Taiwan purchase these additional weapons. It also rejected US assertions that it was helping Iraq improve its air defenses. Then in April, a US spy plane was rammed by a Chinese plane and forced to land in China; China demanded a full apology from the United States before returning the crew (Goldstein, 2005). The United States issued a cautious apology but also allowed Chen Shui-bian to visit the United States, over China's protests, and agreed to sell him new weaponry.

After this high drama, a new phase began in relations between the United States and China. By the end of 2001, Beijing had been chosen as the site of the 2008 Olympics, China and Taiwan were admitted into the World Trade Organization, and—after September 11—China was cooperating with the

United States in the war against terrorism. By the end of 2002, President Bush had visited China twice, Hu Jintao had visited the White House, and Jiang Zemin had visited Bush's Texas ranch shortly before stepping down as general secretary of the Communist Party. A Beijing exhibition celebrated the thirtieth anniversary of Nixon's visit to China. A US Navy ship visited a port in China, and top military commanders exchanged visits. And US secretary of state Colin Powell reiterated US support for "one China" and against independence for Taiwan. And President Chen began the series of steps, discussed in Chapter 6, that led to China being Taiwan's largest trading partner. With the return to power of the KMT in 2008, these steps toward cooperation intensified. However, the United States pressured China to increase the exchange rate of the yuan. President Barack Obama continued similar cordial exchanges with China and Taiwan. The 2011 US military budget was US$740 billion.

Meanwhile, the top leadership of the People's Liberation Army (PLA) continues to push for high military spending (the Pentagon estimates that China spent US$150 billion on its military in 2009—less than it spent on its internal security apparatus) and vigilance against Taiwan (Blasko, 2011; Finkelstein and Gunness, 2007; Prabhakar, Ho, and Bateman, 2006; Hao and Chou, 2011:163–198; Li, 2007:271–300; Fallows, 2011:51), while the United States helps Taiwan add to its arms capacities. Both these entities continue to have a military capacity far below that of the United States (though China is fast catching up to Japan's military capacity; see Bush, 2010), and their training and technical support lag behind the capacity of the new weaponry. But their relative capacities in relation to each other grow more even, and more lethal (Shambaugh, 2006; Fisher, 2010). Both actively spy on each other (Wise, 2011). The great danger is that they could trigger warfare, and that casualties for all participants could be high if it breaks out. The rising trade, investment, travel, and communication between Taiwan and China, the entry of both into the World Trade Organization, and the increased cooperation between the United States and China reduce, but do not eradicate, that threat (Hao and Su, 2006; Huang and Li, 2010:267–341; Ong, 2011).

China's Role in the World

In 1997, the value of Thailand's currency collapsed, sparking the Asian economic crisis (see Chapter 5). Soon Malaysia, Indonesia, and other Southeast Asian countries had similar difficulties, and stock markets fell in Hong Kong, Japan, and other countries of the region. China immediately offered Thailand US$1 billion in loans to help stabilize the value of its currency and promised aid to Indonesia as well; later the International Monetary Fund (IMF) stepped in with many billions of dollars in loans. These devalued currencies meant that products from Southeast Asia could sell for less in the United States and Europe. China was tempted to devalue its own currency to remain competitive but chose not to. Knowing that this might further deflate all the region's currencies and standards of living, it chose instead to raise interest rates and take other uncomfortable measures to hold the value of their currencies firm. Unlike Japan, it cooperated closely with the IMF to bolster Asia's currencies. It has also invested heavily in Southeast Asia and Australia (Thomas, 2004), buying oil and gas fields, timber, coal and copper mines, palm oil plantations, and other resources, and setting up manufacturing plants for its products. That helps surrounding countries, along with overseas Chinese who invest heavily in China, but also fuels old resentments against the Chinese (Cooney and Sato, 2009:159–176).

In 2002, China and ASEAN nations signed an accord creating a free trade area. Some of its members envision this as the beginning of a common market that will eliminate all tariffs within the region. That will be difficult to achieve. But this agreement contributes to stability in the area. China also gives foreign aid to Cambodia. It is criticized by countries along the Mekong River for its series of hydroelectric dams upstream (one of which is second in size only to the largest of the Three Gorges dams—see Chapter 9). It worked with those countries on a program to dynamite the rapids and shoals in the Mekong to improve navigation, over the objections of environmentalists and the Thai army (Thakur and Newman, 2004:209–242). While at home it pursues the environmental measures discussed in Chapters 4 and 9, it harvests and buys tropical trees and opens environmentally invasive mines in Burma. It is spending billions to connect the countries of the region with China and each other via high-speed trains.

China has many problems to overcome as it seeks to become a major player in the international economy and community of nations. Its abuses of human rights (Mann, 2007; Chan, 2006; Womack, 2010:37–60), infringements of copyright laws, official corruption, uncertain legal protections on contracts, crackdowns on political expression, treatment of children in orphanages, mislabeling of products to circumvent trade quotas, restrictions on foreign companies, defective and harmful products, and breaking of promises not to sell certain arms abroad or goods made in prisons all cause concern abroad. During the first year after entry into the World Trade Organization, it passed 2,300 new laws and abolished 830 others to address some of these problems. That process continues. However, Beijing does not always have control over the activities in the provinces where many of these abuses emanate. And its fear of disruption makes it hesitant to allow much extension of political freedoms. In fact, China's top leaders, in keeping with centuries of tradition, are so keen to maintain control over foreign policy that China's foreign minister, Yang Jiechi, is not even a member of the Politburo!

Beijing's government wants to restore unity and power to China, and it wants to make its people prosperous (Ong, 2007; Kuhn, 2009). The two objectives are hard to accomplish simultaneously. It wants its own populace to feel—after the era of "unequal treaties" and Japanese occupation—that their nation is strong and able to resist outside pressure. And it wants to assert control over the offshore oil in the South China Sea and to expand its military capacity. Yet it does not want to frighten overseas Chinese and European investors and traders. With over 10 percent of the world's exports, it is the world's biggest exporter. After the Korean and Vietnam Wars, and decades of US military aid to Taiwan, it remains wary of US military and political intentions in the region. Whenever the US government criticizes, or acts to counter, China's military buildup, arms sales, infractions of contract or international law, or violations of human rights, it reinforces those fears. Yet China wants US economic and political support, and it benefits from selling to the US market, which absorbs about a fifth of its exports. Its new, more open relationship with Taiwan, discussed in Chapter 6, has toned down the rhetoric used by both sides against one another, but harsh language about invading Taiwan and installing new missiles aimed in that direction still raises doubts about whether China can be trusted as a partner in international affairs (Blum, 2006; Bush, 2006; Bush and O'Hanlon, 2007; Carpenter, 2006; Dillon, 2007; Kynge, 2006; Navarro, 2006; Goldstein, 2005; Howarth, 2006; Page and Xie, 2010; Halper, 2010).

The powers that played the most dominant roles in opening China to international relations—Portugal, Spain, Britain, Japan, Russia, France, and Germany—have stopped exerting major military and political power in the region. Today the United States is the principal player, and its role is vital (Doyle, 2007). Unless Japan takes on a greater military and political role, the United States stands as the main power that can prevent China from dominating its own region, because the United States has the world's most sophisticated weaponry and controls China's entry into international trade organizations, access to advanced technology, and acceptance as a part of the world community.

It is important for the United States to understand China's approach to foreign policy, which, as discussed earlier in this chapter, historically centered on vassal states bringing tributes and kowtowing, before quietly working out agreements. Direct public challenges cause leaders to lose face. China has the skills for negotiating behind the scenes, but it has little familiarity with negotiating amid a sea of criticism from Western media and public officials not directly involved in the negotiations (Overhold, 2007; Solomon, 1999; Lampton, 2001, 2008; Wachman, 2007; Clegg, 2009; Wasserstrom, 2010:103–136; Li, 2008; Bell, 2008:3–56; Rozman, 2010; Callahan, 2010; Wang, 2011; Yan, Bell, and Zhe, 2011; Yahuda, 2011:269–313; Kissinger, 2011; Brzezinski, 2012). China's classic *The Art of War* by Sun Tze, written in the sixth century BCE, tells how to use resourcefulness, cunning, the profit motive, flexibility, people's sense of responsibility, secrecy, speed, positioning, surprise, deception, and artful manipulation to win without fighting.

Actual warfare was confined to the areas outlined on Map 3.1; China did not attempt to rule beyond those territories (Sun Tze, 2005; Sawyer, 1993, 2011; Graff, 2001; Perdue, 2005; Tao, 2007; Bloodworth and Bloodworth, 2004; Hui, 2005; Waley-Cohen, 2006; Mott and Kim, 2006; Ng, 2004; Yan, Bell, and Sun Zhe, 2011). The rest of the world needs to learn about that, and China must learn more about the written (e.g., Thucydides, 1954; Machiavelli, 1992; Clausewitz, 1984) and unwritten fundamentals of European diplomacy, which depend on nations, on a regular basis, issuing direct challenges to one another's policies before working things out behind the scenes. European countries conducted warfare, conquered, and ruled territories far from their homelands. Both cultures use carefully coded language to convey what they really mean. They need to learn each other's codes. When to kowtow, and when to challenge, and how to move to the next step takes cross-cultural learning. The same words and actions can carry different messages in different cultures. Both sides must learn to adapt to the other's techniques of negotiating (Carlson, 2005; Chan, 2006; Gill, 2007; Kornberg and Faust, 2005; Hutton, 2006; Swaine and Zhang, 2007; Tkacik, 2007; Zhu, 2006; Nathan and Ross, 1997; Flower, 2008; Rosecrance and Gu, 2009; De Mente, 2009; Keith, 2009).

If other powers want China or its government to disintegrate or change faster than it is prepared to, or if both sides distrust each other's fundamental motives, they will be on a collision course (Carpenter, 2006; Copper, 2006; Lewis and Xue, 2006; Tsang, 2006; Tucker, 2009; Wu and Zheng, 2006). Even if all major players agree on goals, as seems more evident in recent years, danger lurks. Traditional posturing among China's leaders has crossed over into bloodshed in the past. So has modern diplomacy. When those two traditions meet, a misstep or misreading of body language can have disastrous results. This is why it is important for each side to learn the rules of the other's game.

That can happen. In 2012, after the Chongqing police chief sought asylum in a US consular office, sparking the purge of Bo Xilai (see Chapter 4), the US maintained official silence about the well-publicized incident. Both sides kept China's arrest of a high-level officer in China's security ministry accused of spying for the CIA a secret. A few weeks later, Chen Guangcheng, a blind self-trained peasant lawyer, took refuge in the US Embassy after a dramatic escape from hired minders who were illegally holding him under house arrest in his village for exposing brutality and corruption by local officials. Diplomats braced for a major confrontation between the two countries. In China, asylum-seeking carries a maximum penalty of exile or death, but both governments quietly worked out a deal letting Chen move to another province to pursue law studies. Chinese officials were furious when Chen changed his mind after the agreement was reached, but did not say so publicly, and negotiated a new one that allowed Chen and his family to go to the United States for studies. Silent diplomacy combined with a common interest in maintaining good economic and diplomatic relations, and China's desire for a good image abroad amid a torrent of Weibo blogs and world press headlines about Chen's maltreatment, brought a positive negotiated outcome. Hardliners still used their arsenal. The Foreign Ministry asked the United States to apologize for interfering in China's internal affairs and guarantee that "things like this will never happen again." Security chief Zhou Yongkang placed a number of Chen's relatives and associates—joining a million others his agency deems a security threat (Hutzler, 2012)—under illegal house arrest, declaring that the law "should always adhere to the party's cause first" and China should resist "erroneous political views in the West" (Beech, 2012). Zhou's ministry had already spent US$11 million on Chen's house arrest. Chen calls that "a lawless police state . . . stability before all else." His nephew was charged with "intentional homicide" for wielding a knife when agents burst into his home and beat up his family. Beijing, stoking nationalist sentiments, initiated a crackdown on foreigners working without proper visas. And the United States bolstered its South China Sea fleet. But Chen and his family were free, under the terms of the agreement.

Until recently, much of China's foreign policy has focused on the European powers, the United States, and the countries immediately adjoining it. Today, it also has a strong focus on other parts of the world, including Africa, Latin America, and the Middle East (Pant, 2011; Hearn and León-Manríquez, 2011; Dittmer and Yu, 2010). It has operated in those regions with a doctrine of "noninterference" and "peaceful development," supporting whatever government and social system is in power. China wants markets for its goods, sites for Chinese businesses and investment, oil and other raw materials, support in the United Nations and other international bodies, and goodwill, from nations worldwide. While it continues to buy US Treasury bonds backed by the US dollar and investments backed by the euro, China wants to lessen its dependence on those two currencies and is taking steps to make international loans and bilateral trading transactions using the Chinese yuan instead of dollars.

In keeping with that spirit is its new "soft power" initiatives, highlighted by the 2008 Olympics (Kurlantzick, 2007; Lampton, 2008; Gurtov, 2002; Congressional Research Service, 2008; Bergsten et al., 2009; Rosecrance and Gu, 2009:23–34; Ding, 2008; Womack, 2010:61–74; Li, 2009; Chan, Lee, and Chan, 2011). The Chinese Young Volunteers Serving Africa sends Chinese to Africa to help in medicine, education, agriculture, sports, and other fields. Several thousand Chinese serve in Africa as doctors, medical consultants, UN peacekeepers, agricultural extension officers, and the like. China advocates the UN Millennium Goals to reduce poverty, the UN Human Rights Council, and the admission of more African nations into the World Trade Organization. China has waived US$1.2 billion in African debt, sent hundreds of doctors and teachers, and agreed to bring 10,000 African students to China for study. In 2000, it joined with forty-four African nations to form the China-Africa

Cooperation Forum, which is sponsoring numerous economic and cultural exchange initiatives. China has opened Confucius Institutes all over the world to teach Mandarin and foster exchange. Chinese students are studying in many countries (285,000 in 2011, more than 128,000 of them in the United States), and China is bringing increasing numbers of students from around the world to study at its universities (Cheng, 2005). The African Human Resources Development Fund has trained over 15,000 African professionals. China welcomed 56 million foreign tourists in 2010, while Chinese tourist groups are increasingly visible abroad—including in many African countries (Arlt, 2006).

China's government has provided the funds for many public works projects. It is building railroads, bridges, highways, power stations, electricity grids, dams, pharmaceutical plants, environmental restoration, and mobile phone networks in most of Africa's fifty-four countries and in many other countries as well. In 2009 and 2010, two Chinese banks lent US$110 billion for projects in developing nations—more than the World Bank, and on more generous terms (Dyer, Anderlini, and Sender, 2011). This included loans-for-oil deals in Russia, Kazakhstan, Burma, Venezuela, and Brazil; railroads in Argentina; infrastructure in Ghana; and much more. Chinese firms and workers are also flocking into Africa and Latin America, buying up mines, building factories, selling Chinese goods, and working on these development projects (Michel and Beuret, 2009; Sutter, 2007:367–389; Eisenman, Higinbotham, and Mitchell, 2007; Brautigam, 2010; Rotberg, 2008; Ellis, 2009; Lederman, Olarreaga, and Perry, 2009; Gallagher and Porzecanski, 2010; Dittmer and Yu, 2010; Fung and Herrero, 2011). China has become Brazil's, Chile's, and Argentina's largest trading partner; in 2010, it had 11 percent of Latin American foreign trade. In 2010, its trade with Africa surpassed US$120 billion.

However, this approach can lead to new distrust and puzzlement. China faces increasing criticism that it does not hire enough locals, pays low wages to and provides dangerous working conditions for those it does hire, sabotages union organization, constructs shoddy roads and buildings (or fails to construct promised projects), pollutes the environment, puts local businesses out of work, and strips away and pays too little for precious raw materials. The Chinese government is also critized for ignoring civil war, corruption, human rights violations, and the ineptitude of African leaders in order to curry their favor (Ampiah and Naidu, 2008; Raine, 2009; Taylor, 2006, 2010; Cheru and Obi, 2010; Alden, 2008; Manji and Marks, 2007; "The Queensway Syndicate," 2011; Taylor, Kopinski, and Polus, 2011). While other nations imposed sanctions on the oppressive regime in Zimbabwe, China opened direct flights between China and Zimbabwe, where it rebuilt the electricity grid and built a palatial residence for Robert Mugabe and provided him with equipment to jam the broadcasts of his political opponents and with off-road vehicles to pursue them. A third of China's imported oil comes from Angola, Sudan, and Nigeria. China has become Sudan's largest arms supplier, including ammunition, tanks, helicopters, and fighter aircraft, making it possible for them to pursue brutal warfare against rebels in Darfur and the south. It used its position on the UN Security Council to support Sudan's military suppression of opposition in Darfur. In a like manner, it has helped the Democratic Republic of Congo's government fight its rebels.

China's growing economic influence and military capacity gives it clout to work with other nations on settling disputes and solving problems (Kang, 2007; Chung, 2010). And it wants to be considered a major part of the international community. In that context, it has started to make some exceptions to its policies of noninterference. In 2007, after long ignoring the issue and under intense pressure from the international community, China began to assist in efforts to curb the violence in Darfur and quietly supported the process that allowed south Sudan to become independent in 2011. Also in 2011, the "jasmine revolution," which started in Tripoli and Egypt brought a new challenge. Many Chinese citizens were also using the Internet to discuss similar reforms. But China did not want to lose its clout by failing to support rebels who succeeded in overthrowing regimes. It responded with new crackdowns on political dissent at home, while joining in the UN vote for sanctions against Muammar Qaddafi in Libya and meeting with the rebels. However, it also condemned NATO air strikes and allowed Chinese companies to sell missiles to Qaddafi. China, calling it a "distinctly Chinese approach," joined with the other BRICS nations (Brazil, Russia, India, China, and South Africa) to oppose UN sanctions against President Bashar al-Assad's regime in Syria but instead backed a cease-fire arranged by former UN Secretary-General Kofi Annan with China's help in conjunction with the Arab League. Throughout the process China refused to endorse any joint resolution that called for the ouster of Assad.

In 2011, China's government had US$3 trillion in reserve capital, growing at a rate of US$800 billion a year. A study by China Merchant Bank estimates that wealthy individuals in China have US$9.6 trillion in investible assets, which they are increasingly investing abroad ("Streaks of Red," 2011). Most of this investment has been in Asia, Latin America, and Africa, but their investment in European real estate and companies is growing at a rapid pace as well. China is saving increasing amounts of assets in euros instead of dollars; European countries, like the United States, are relying on some of those purchases to finance their deficit spending. This makes China an ever-growing presence in world finance.

China's Cold War isolation is over. It is beginning to experience the rewards and problems, and assume the responsibilities, of a nation with economic clout and growing military capacity (Jacques, 2009; Deng, 2008; Rosecrance and Gu, 2009). There are those who regard that rise as beneficial (Cole, 2001; Kang, 2007; Chung, 2010; Fravel, 2008; Ross and Zhu, 2008; Page and Xie, 2010; Li, 2010; Kissinger, 2011; Brzezinski, 2012), and others who fear it (Carpenter, 2006; Copper, 2006; Lewis and Xue, 2006; Tsang, 2006; Tucker, 2009; Wu and Zheng, 2006; Navarro, 2006). The two largest economies in the world are now the United States and China, and those economies are tightly entwined (Karabell, 2009; Steinfeld, 2010). US companies, which controlled half of the world's foreign direct investment in 1967, still own over 20 percent of it; China's firms own 6 percent of it ("Being Eaten by the Dragon," 2010). China holds about 7 percent of US national debt and provides a fifth of its imports. The two nations are also the largest consumers of energy and sources of environmental pollution. The United States has military spending larger than the next seventeen nations combined and is likely to remain the most influential player in world politics for decades to come (Foot and Walter, 2011; Womack, 2010). The United States must stand up to China when it steals intellectual property, undervalues its currency, ignores treaty obligations, obstructs international sanctions against dictators, abuses human rights, and otherwise defies international norms. But China's geopolitical position gives it ever-increasing power to affirm its own position in the face of US military and diplomatic maneuvers. As common stakeholders in the world economy, both sides have strong reasons to avoid all-out war. Yet confrontation can result in dangerous mistakes. That makes responsible stakeholding ever more imperative for these two powers.

Bibliography

Abramowitz, Morton, and Stephen Bosworth. 2006. *Chasing the Sun: Rethinking East Asian Policy.* New York: Century Foundation Press.

Alden, Chris. 2008. *China in Africa: Partner, Competitor, or Hegemon?* New York: Palgrave Macmillan.

Alterman, John, and John Garver. 2008. *The Vital Triangle: China, the United States, and the Middle East.* Washington, DC: Center for Strategic and International Studies.

Ampiah, Kweku, and Sanusha Naidu (eds.). 2008. *Crouching Tiger, Hidden Dragon: Africa and China.* Scottsville, South Africa: University of Kwazulu Natal Press.

Andrews-Speed, Philip, and Roland Dannreuther. 2011. *China, Oil, and Global Politics.* London: Routledge.

Arlt, Wolfgang. 2006. China's Outbound Tourism. London: Routledge.

"A Strategy to Straddle the Planet." 2011. *Financial Times,* January 18.

Bahl, Raghav. 2010. *Superpower? The Amazing Race Between China's Hare and India's Tortoise.* New York: Portfolio/Penguin.

Barnouin, Barbara, and Yu Changgen. 1997. *Chinese Foreign Policy During the Cultural Revolution.* New York: Columbia University Press.

Bateman, Sam, and Ralf Emmers (eds.). 2009. *Security and International Politics in the South China Sea.* New York: Routledge.

Bau, Mingchien Joshua. 2010. *The Foreign Relations of China: A History and a Survey (1922).* 2nd ed. Cornell University Library Digital Collections. New York: Fleming H. Revell.

Baum, Richard. 2010. *China Watcher: Confessions of a Peking Tom.* Seattle: University of Washington Press.

Beech, Hannah. 2012. "Murder, Lies, Abuse of Power and Other Crimes of the Chinese." *Time*, May 14.

Beeson, Mark. 2008. *Regionalism and Globalization in East Asia: Politics, Security, and Economic Development.* New York: Palgrave Macmillan.

Bell, Daniel. 2008. *China's New Confucianism: Politics and Everyday Life in a Changing Society.* Princeton, NJ: Princeton University Press.

"Being Eaten by the Dragon." 2010. *The Economist* 397 (November): 8708.

Bergsten, Fred, Charles Freeman, Nicholas Lardy, and Derek Mitchell. 2009. *China's*

Rise: Challenges and Opportunities. Washington, DC: Peterson Institute for International Economics.

Blackman, Carolyn. 1997. *Negotiating China: Case Studies and Strategies.* London: Allen and Unwin.

Blasko, Dennis J. 2011. *The Chinese Army Today: Tradition and Transformation in the Twenty-First Century.* 2d ed. London: Routledge.

Bloodworth, Ching, and Dennis Bloodworth. 2004. *The Chinese Machiavelli: 3000 Years of Chinese Statecraft.* New Brunswick, NJ: Transaction Publications.

Blum, Susan D. 2006. *Lies that Bind: Chinese Truth, Other Truths.* Lanham, MD: Rowman and Littlefield.

Bradie, Anne-Marie (ed.). 2010. *Looking North, Looking South: China, Taiwan, and the South Pacific.* Singapore: World Scientific.

Brautigam, Deborah. 2010. *The Dragon's Gift: The Real Story of China in Africa.* New York: Oxford University Press.

Broadman, Harry G. (ed.). 2007. *Africa's Silk Road: China and India's New Economic Frontier.* Washington, DC: World Bank.

Brzezinski, Zbigniew. 2012. *Strategic Vision: America and the Crisis of Global Power.* New York: Basic Books.

Bush, Richard C. 2006. *Untying the Knot: Making Peace in the Taiwan Strait.* Washington, DC: Brookings Institution Press.

———. 2010. *The Perils of Proximity: China-Japan Security Relations.* Washington, DC: Brookings Institution Press.

Bush, Richard C., and Michael E. O'Hanlon. 2007. *A War Like No Other: The Truth About China's Challenge to America.* New York: Wiley.

Callahan, William A. 2010. *China: The Pessoptimist Nation.* New York: Oxford University Press.

Cameron, Nigel. 1975. *From Bondage to Liberation: East Asia 1860–1952.* Hong Kong: Oxford University Press.

Carlson, Allen. 2005. *Unifying China, Integrating with the World: Securing Chinese Sovereignty in the Reform Era.* Stanford, CA: Stanford University Press.

Carpenter, Ted Gale. 2006. *America's Coming War with China: A Collision Course Over Taiwan.* New York: Palgrave.

Chan, Gerald. 2006. *China's Compliance in Global Affairs: Trade, Arms Control, Environmental Protection, Human Rights.* Singapore: World Scientific.

Chan, Gerald, Pak K. Lee, and Lai-ha Chan. 2011. *China Engages Global Governance: A New World Order in the Making?* London: Routledge.

Chang, Gordon H. 1990. *Friends and Enemies: The United States, China, and the Soviet Union, 1948–1972.* Stanford, CA: Stanford University Press.

Chellaney, Brahma. 2009. "Three's a Crowd in the India-China Theater." *Far Eastern Economic Review* 172 (November): 7.

———. 2010. *Asian Juggernaut: The Rise of China, India, and Japan.* New York: HarperCollins.

Chen, Dean. 2012. *US Taiwan Strait Policy: The Origins of Strategic Ambiguity.* Boulder: Lynne Rienner.

Chen, Jian. 1994. *China's Road to the Korean War: The Making of the Sino-American Confrontation.* New York: Columbia University Press.

———. 2000. *Mao's China and the Cold War.* Chapel Hill: University of North Carolina Press.

Cheng, Li. 2005. *Bridging Minds Across the Pacific: U.S.-China Educational Exchanges, 1978–2003.* Lanham, MD: Lexington Books.

Cheru, Fantu, and Cyril Obi (eds.). 2010. *The Rise of China in Africa: Challenges, Opportunities, and Critical Interventions.* New York: Zed Books.

Chung, Chien-peng. 2010. *China's Multilateral Cooperation in Asia and the Pacific: Institutionalizing Beijing's "Good Neighbor Policy."* New York: Routledge.

Clausewitz, Carl von. 1984. *On War.* Trans. and ed. Michael Howard and Peter Paret. Princeton, NJ: Princeton University Press.

Clegg, Jenny. 2009. *China's Global Strategy: Toward a Multipolar World.* New York: Pluto Press.

Cohen, Warren I. 2001. *East Asia at the Center: Four Thousand Years of Engagement with the World.* New York: Columbia University Press.

———. 2010. *America's Response to China: A History of Sino-American Relations.* 5th ed. New York: Columbia University Press.

Cole, Bernard D. 2001. *The Great Wall at Sea: China's Navy Enters the Twenty-First Century.* Annapolis, MD: Naval Institute Press.

———. 2006. *Taiwan's Security: History and Prospects.* London: Routledge.

Collins, Gabriel B., Andrew S. Erickson, Lyle J. Goldstein, and William S. Murray (eds.). 2008. *China's Energy Strategy: The Impact on Beijing's Maritime Policies.* Annapolis, MD: Naval Institute Press.

Cooney, Kevin, and Yoichiro Sato (eds.). 2009. *The Rise of China and International Security.* London: Routledge.

Congressional Research Service, Library of Congress. 2008. *China's Foreign Policy and "Soft Power" in South America, Asia, and Africa.* Washington, DC: Government Printing Office. http://biden.senate.gov/imo/media/doc/CRSChinaReport.pdf.

Copper, John F. 2006. *Playing with Fire: The Looming War with China over Taiwan.* New York: Praeger.

Cordesman, Anthony H., and Martin Klieber. 2007. *China's Military Modernization: Force Development and Strategic Capabilities.* Washington, DC: Center for Strategic and International Studies.

Cumings, Bruce. 1981, 1990. *The Origins of the Korean War.* 2 vols. Princeton. NJ: Princeton University Press.

De Mente, Boye Lafayette. 2009. *The Chinese Mind: Understanding Traditional Chinese Beliefs and Their Influence on Contemporary Culture.* North Clarendon, VT: Tuttle.

Deng, Yong. 2008. *China's Struggle for Status: The Realignment of International Relations.* Cambridge: Cambridge University Press.

Denoon, David B. H. 2007. *The Economic and Strategic Rise of China and India.* New York: Palgrave Macmillan.

Dillon, Dana. 2007. *The China Challenge: Standing Strong Against the Military, Economic, and Political Threats That Imperil America.* Lanham, MD: Rowman and Littlefield.

Ding, Sheng. 2008. *The Dragon's Hidden Wings: How China Rises with Its Soft Power.* Lanham, MD: Lexington Books.

Dittmer, Lowell (ed.). 2005. *South Asia's Nuclear Security Dilemma: India, Pakistan, and China.* Armonk, NY: M. E. Sharpe.

Dittmer, Lowell, and George T. Yu (eds.). 2010. *China, the Developing World, and the New Global Dynamic.* Boulder: Lynne Rienner.

Doyle, Randall. 2007. *America and China: Asia Pacific–Rim Hegemony in the Twenty-first Century.* Lanham, MD: Rowman and Littlefield.

Duara, Prajenjit. 2003. *Sovereignty and Authenticity: Manchukuo and the East Asian Modern.* Lanham, MD: Rowman and Littlefield.

Dutton, Peter, and John Garofano. 2009. "China Undermines Maritime Laws." *Far Eastern Economic Review* 172 (April): 3.

Dyer, Geoff, Jamil Anderini, and Henny Sender. 2011. "China's Lending Hits New Heights." *Financial Times,* January 18.

Eisenman, Joshua, Eric Higinbotham, and Derek Mitchell (eds.). 2007. *China and the Developing World: Beijing's Strategy for the Twenty-First Century*. Armonk, NY: M. E. Sharpe.
Elleman, Bruce. 2001. *Modern Chinese Warfare*. London: Routledge.
Ellis, R. Evan. 2009. *China in Latin America: The Whats and Wherefores*. Boulder: Lynne Rienner.
Emmott, Bill. 2009. *Rivals: How the Power Struggle Between China, India, and Japan Will Shape our Next Decade*. New York: Mariner Books.
Erickson, Andrew S., Lyl J. Goldstein, and Nan Li (eds.). 2010. *China, the United States, and 21st Century Sea Power: Defining a Maritime Partnership*. Annapolis, MD: Naval Institute Press.
Erickson, Andrew S., Lyl J. Goldstein, and Carnes Lord (eds.). 2009. *China Goes to Sea: Maritime Transformation in Comparative Historical Perspective*. Annapolis, MD: Naval Institute Press.
Erickson, Andrew S., Lyl J. Goldstein, William S. Murray, and Andrew P. Wilson (eds.). 2007. *China's Future Nuclear Submarine Force*. Annapolis, MD: Naval Institute Press.
Fallows, James. 2011. "Arab Spring, Chinese Winter." *The Atlantic*, September.
Finkelstein, David M., and Kristen Gunness (eds.). 2007. *Civil-Military Relations in Today's China: Swimming in the New Sea*. Armonk, NY: M. E. Sharpe.
Fisher, Richard. 2010. *China's Military Modernization: Building for Regional and Global Reach*. Stanford, CA: Stanford Security Studies.
Fitzgerald, Stephen. 1972. *China and the Overseas Chinese: A Study of Peking's Changing Policy, 1949–1970*. Cambridge: Cambridge University Press.
Flower, Kathy. 2008. *China–Culture Smart: The Essential Guide to Customs and Culture*. Rev. ed. London: Kuperard.
Foot, Rosemary, and Andrew Walter. 2011. *China, the United States, and the Global Order*. New York: Cambridge University Press.
Frankel, Francine R., and Harry Harding (eds.). 2004. *The India-China Relationship: What the United States Needs to Know*. New York: Columbia University Press.
Fravel, M. Taylor. 2008. "China's Search for Military Power." *Washington Quarterly* 31(3): 125–141.
Fung, K. C., and Alice Garcia Herrero (eds.). 2011. *Sino–Latin American Economic Relations*. London: Routledge.
Gallagher, Kevin, and Roberto Porzecanski. 2010. *The Dragon in the Room: China and the Future of Latin American Industrialization*. Stanford, CA: Stanford University Press.
Gao, Wenqian. 2007. *The Last Perfect Revolutionary*. New York: PublicAffairs.
Garrison, Jean A. 2005. *Making China Policy: From Nixon to G. W. Bush*. Boulder: Lynne Rienner.
———. 2009. *China and the Energy Equation in Asia: The Determinants of Policy Choice*. Boulder: Lynne Rienner.
Garver, John W. 1993. *Foreign Relations of the People's Republic of China*. Englewood Cliffs, NJ: Prentice-Hall.
———. 2002. *Protracted Conflict: Sino-Indian Rivalry in the Twentieth Century*. Seattle: University of Washington Press.
———. 2006. *China and Iran: Ancient Partners in a Post-Imperial World*. Seattle: University of Washington Press.
Gill, Bates. 2007. *Rising Star: China's New Security Diplomacy*. Washington, DC: Brookings Institution Press.

Goldstein, Avery. 2005. *Rising to the Challenge: China's Grand Strategy and International Security.* Stanford, CA: Stanford University Press.
Goncharov, Sergei. 1995. *Uncertain Partners: Stalin, Mao, and the Korean War.* Stanford, CA: Stanford University Press.
Graff, David A. 2001. *Medieval Chinese Warfare, 300–900.* London: Routledge.
Grasso, June, Jay Corrin, and Michael Kort. 2004. *Modernization and Revolution in China: From the Opium Wars to the World Power.* 3rd ed. Armonk, NY: M E. Sharpe.
Gries, Peter Hays. 2005. *China's New Nationalism: Pride, Politics, and Diplomacy.* Berkeley: University of California Press.
Gurtov, Melvin. 2002. *Pacific Asia: Prospects for Security and Cooperation in East Asia.* Lanham, MD: Rowman and Littlefield.
Halper, Stefan. 2010. *The Beijing Consensus: How China's Authoritarian Model Will Dominate the 21st Century.* New York: Basic Books.
Han, Suyin. 1994. *Eldest Son: Zhou Enlai and the Making of Modern China, 1898–1976.* New York: Farrar, Straus, and Giroux.
Handberg, Roger. 2006. *Chinese Space Policy: A Study in Domestic and International Politics.* London: Routledge.
Hao, Yufan, and Bill K. P. Chou (eds.). 2011. *China's Policies on Its Borderlands and the International Implications.* Singapore: World Scientific.
Hao, Yufan, and Lin Su (eds.). 2006. *China's Foreign Policy Making: Societal Force and Chinese American Policy.* Burlington, VT: Ashgate.
Hearn, Adrian H., and José Luis León-Manríquez (eds.). 2011. *China Engages Latin America: Tracing the Trajectory.* Boulder: Lynne Rienner.
Heazle, Michael, and Nick Knight (eds.). 2007. *China-Japan Relations in the Twenty-First Century: Creating a Future Past?* Northampton, MA: Edward Elgar.
Heinzig, Dieter. 2004. *The Soviet Union and Communist China 1945–1950: The Arduous Road to the Alliance.* Armonk, NY: M. E. Sharpe.
Hevia, James L. 2005. *Cherishing Men from Afar: Qing Guest Ritual and the Macartney Embassy of 1793.* Durham, NC: Duke University Press.
Holdridge, John H. 1997. *Crossing the Divide: An Insider's Account of the Normalization of US-China Relations.* Lanham, MD: Rowman and Littlefield.
Holmes, James R., and Toshi Yoshihara. 2009. *Chinese Naval Strategy in the 21st Century: The Turn to Mahan.* London: Routledge.
Holslag, Jonathan. 2009. *China and India: Prospects for Peace.* New York: Columbia University Press.
Howarth, Peter. 2006. *China's Rising Sea Power: The PLA Navy's Submarine Challenge.* London: Routledge.
Howe, Christopher (ed.). 1996. *China and Japan: History, Trends, and Prospects.* Oxford: Oxford University Press.
Hsiung, James C., and Steven I. Levine (eds.). 1997. *China's Bitter Victory: The War with Japan, 1937–1945.* Armonk, NY: M. E. Sharpe.
Hsu, Immanuel C. Y. 1980. "Late Ch'ing Foreign Relations, 1866–1905." In *The Cambridge History of China,* vol. 2, *Late Ch'ing, 1800–1911,* pt. 2, edited by John K. Fairbank and Kwang-Ching Liu, 70–141. Cambridge: Cambridge University Press.
Huang, Jing, and Xiaoting Li. 2010. *Inseparable Separation: The Making of China's Taiwan Policy.* Singapore: World Scientific.
Hui, Victoria Tin-bor. 2005. *War and State Formation in Ancient China and Early Modern Europe.* Cambridge: Cambridge University Press.
Hutton, Will. 2006. *The Writing on the Wall: Why We Must Embrace China as a Partner or Face It as an Enemy.* New York: Free Press.

Hutzler, Charles. 2012. "Dissident Monitoring Business Is Booming in China." *Huffington Post*, May 28.
Jacques, Martin. 2009. *When China Rules the World: The End of the Western World and the Birth of a New Global Order.* New York: Penguin.
Jain, J. P. 1976. *China in World Politics: A Study of Sino-British Relations, 1949–1975.* New Delhi: Radiant Press.
Johnson, Linda Cooke. 1995. *Shanghai: From Market Town to Treaty Port, 1074–1858.* Stanford, CA: Stanford University Press.
Jones, Peter, and Sian Kevill. 1985. *China and the Soviet Union, 1949–84.* Harlow, UK: Longman.
Kang, David C. 2007. *China Rising: Peace, Power, and Order in East Asia.* New York: Columbia University Press.
Kaplan, Robert D. 2010. *Monsoon: The Indian Ocean and the Future of American Power.* New York: Random House.
Karabell, Zachary. 2009. *Superfusion: How China and America Became One Economy and Why the World's Prosperity Depends on It.* New York: Simon and Schuster.
Karnow, Stanley. 1984. *Vietnam: A History.* New York: Penguin.
Keith, Ronald C. 2009. *China from the Inside Out: Fitting the People's Republic into the World.* New York: Pluto Press.
Kemp, Geoffrey. 2010. *The East Moves West: India, China, and Asia's Growing Presence in the Middle East.* Washington, DC: Brookings Institution Press.
Kissinger, Henry. 2011. *On China.* New York: Penguin.
Kong, Bo. 2010. *China's International Petroleum Policy.* New York: Praeger.
Kornberg, Judith F, and John R. Faust. 2005. *China in World Politics: Policies, Processes, Prospects.* 2nd ed. Boulder: Lynne Rienner.
Kuhn, Robert. 2009. *How China's Leaders Think: The Inside Story of China's Reform and What This Means for the Future.* New York: Wiley.
Kurlantzick, Joshua. 2007. *Charm Offensive: How China's Soft Power Is Transforming the World.* New Haven, CT: Yale University Press.
Kynge, James. 2006. *China Shakes the World: A Titan's Rise and Troubled Future.* New York: Houghton Mifflin.
Lal, Rollie. 2006. *Understanding China and India: Security Implications for the United States and the World.* New York: Praeger.
Lampton, David M. 2001. *Same Bed, Different Dreams: Managing US-China Relations, 1989–2000.* Berkeley: University of California Press.
———. 2008. *The Three Faces of Chinese Power: Might, Money, and Minds.* Berkeley: University of California Press.
Lanteigne, Marc. 2005. *China and International Institutions: Alternate Paths to Global Power.* London: Routledge.
Lederman, David, Marcello Olarreaga, and Guillermo Perry (eds.). 2009. *China's and India's Challenge to Latin America.* Washington, DC: World Bank.
Lewis, John Wilson, and Xue Litai. 1991. *China Builds the Bomb.* Stanford, CA: Stanford University Press.
———. 2006. *Imagined Enemies: China Prepares for Uncertain War.* Stanford, CA: Stanford University Press.
Li, Mingjiang (ed.). 2009. *Soft Power: China's Emerging Strategy in International Politics.* Lanham, MD: Lexington Books.
———. 2010. "China and Maritime Cooperation in East Asia." *Journal of Contemporary China* 19(64): 291–310.
Li, Minqi. 2008. *The Rise of China and the Demise of the Capitalist World Economy.* New York: Monthly Review Press.

Li, Nan (ed.). 2005. *Chinese Civil-Military Relations: The Transformation of the People's Liberation Army.* London: Routledge.
Li, Xiaobing. 2007. *A History of the Modern Chinese Army.* Lexington: University of Kentucky Press.
Liao, Janet Xuanli. 2006. *Chinese Foreign Policy Think Tanks and China's Policy Toward Japan.* Hong Kong: Chinese University Press.
Liu, Lydia. 2006. *The Clash of Empires: The Invention of China in Modern World Making.* Cambridge, MA: Harvard University Press.
Liu, Xiao Yuan. 2006. *Reins of Liberation: An Entangled History of Mongolian Independence, Chinese Territoriality, and Great Power Hegemony, 1911–1950.* Stanford, CA: Stanford University Press.
Machiavelli, Niccolo. 1992. *The Prince.* 2d ed. Trans. Robert M. Adams. New York: Norton.
MacMillan, Margaret. 2007. *Nixon and Mao: The Week That Changed the World.* New York: Random House.
Malik, Mohan. 2011. *China and India: Great Power Rivals.* Boulder: Lynne Rienner.
Manji, Firoze, and Stephen Marks (eds.). 2007. *African Perspectives on China in Africa.* Oxford: Pambazuka Press.
Mann, James. 2007. *The China Fantasy: How Our Leaders Explain Away Chinese Oppression.* New York: Viking.
Marketos, Thrassey N. 2009. *China's Energy Geopolitics.* New York: Routledge.
Marks, Robert B. 2006. *The Origins of the Modern World: A Global and Ecological Narrative from the Fifteenth to the Twenty-First Century.* 2nd ed. Lanham, MD: Rowman and Littlefield.
Meredith, Robyn. 2008. *The Elephant and the Dragon: The Rise of India and China and What It Means for All of Us.* New York: Norton.
Michel, Serge, and Michel Beuret. 2009. *China Safari: On the Trail of Beijing's Expansion in Africa.* Trans. Raymond Valley. New York: Nation Books.
Mitter, Rana. 2000. *The Manchurian Myth: Nationalism, Resistance, and Collaboration in Modern China.* Berkeley: University of California Press.
Mott, William H., IV, and Jae Chang Kim. 2006. *The Philosophy of Chinese Military Culture: Shih vs. Li.* New York: Palgrave.
Nathan, Andrew J., and Robert S. Ross. 1997. *The Great Wall and the Empty Fortress.* New York: Norton.
Navarro, Peter. 2006. *The Coming China Wars: Where They Will Be Fought and How They Can Be Won.* Upper Saddle River, NJ: FT Press.
Needham, Joseph W. 1971. *Science and Civilization in China,* vol. 4, pt. 3. Cambridge: Cambridge University Press.
Nelsen, Harvey. 1989. *Power and Insecurity: Beijing, Moscow, and Washington, 1949–1988.* Boulder: Lynne Rienner.
Ng, Ka Po. 2004. *Interpreting China's Military Power: Doctrine Makes Readiness.* London: Frank Cass.
Ong, Russell. 2007. *China's Security Interests in the 21st Century.* London: Routledge.
———. 2011. *China's Strategic Competition with the United States.* London: Routledge.
Overhold, William H. 2007. *Asia, America, and the Transformation of Geopolitics.* New York: Cambridge University Press.
Page, Benjamin I., and Tao Xie. 2010. *Living with the Dragon: How the American Public Views the Rise of China.* New York: Columbia University Press.
Pant, Harsh V. 2009. "China Tightens the Screws on India." *Far Eastern Economic Review* 172 (September): 7.

———. 2011. *China's Rising Global Profile: The Great Power Tradition.* Eastbourne, UK: Sussex Academic Press.

Perdue, Peter C. 2005. *China Marches West: The Qing Conquest of Central Eurasia.* Cambridge, MA: Belknap Press of Harvard University Press.

Perlmutter, David D. 2007. *Picturing China in the American Press: The Visual Portrayal of Sino-American Relations in Time Magazine 1949–1973.* Lanham, MD: Lexington Books.

Peterson, Glen. 2011. *Overseas Chinese in the People's Republic of China.* London: Routledge.

Prabhakar, Lawrence W., Joshua H. Ho, and Sam Batemen. 2006. *The Evolving Maritime Balance of Power in the Asia-Pacific.* Singapore: World Scientific.

Raine, Sarah. 2009. *China's African Challenge.* London: Routledge.

Ramesh, Jairam. 2006. *Making Sense of Chindia: Reflections on China and India.* New Delhi: India Research Press.

Roberts, Priscilla (ed.). 2007. *Behind the Bamboo Curtain: China, Vietnam, and Cold War.* Stanford, CA: Stanford University Press.

Rosecrance, Richard, and Gu Guoliang (eds.). 2009. *Power and Restraint: A Shared Vision for the U.S.-China Relationship.* New York: Perseus.

Ross, Robert S. 1995. *Negotiating Cooperation: The United States and China, 1969–1989.* Stanford, CA: Stanford University Press.

Ross, Robert, and Zhu Feng (eds.). 2008. *China's Ascent: Power, Security, and the Future of International Politics.* Ithaca, NY: Cornell University Press.

Rotberg, Robert (ed.). 2008. *China into Africa: Trade, Aid, and Influence.* Washington, DC: Brookings Institution Press.

Rozman, Gilbert. 2010. *Chinese Strategic Thought Toward Asia.* New York: Palgrave Macmillan.

Sally, Razeen. 2009. "Don't Believe the India Hype." *Far Eastern Economic Review* 172 (May): 4.

Sawyer, Ralph D. 1993. *The Seven Military Classics of Ancient China.* Boulder: Westview.

———. 2011. *Ancient Chinese Warfare.* New York: Basic Books.

Scobell, Andrew. 2003. *China's Use of Military Force: Beyond the Great Wall and the Long March.* Cambridge: Cambridge University Press.

Shambaugh, David. 2006. *Power Shift: China and Asia's New Dynamics.* Berkeley: University of California Press.

Shao, Kuo-Kang. 1996. *Zhou Enlai and the Foundations of Chinese Foreign Policy.* New York: St. Martin's.

Sharma, Shalendra D. 2009. *China and India in the Age of Globalization.* Cambridge: Cambridge University Press.

Sheng, Michael M. 1998. *Battling Western Imperialism: Mao, Stalin, and the United States.* Princeton, NJ: Princeton University Press.

Sidhu, Pal Singh, and Jing Dong Yuan. 2003. *China and India: Cooperation or Conflict?* Boulder: Lynne Rienner.

Sieff, Martin. 2010. *Shifting Superpowers: The New and Emerging Relationship Between the United States, China, and India.* New York: Cato Institute.

Simpfendorfer, Ben. 2009. *The New Silk Road: How a Rising Arab World Is Turning Away from the West and Rediscovering China.* New York: Palgrave Macmillan.

Snyder, Scott. 2009. *China's Rise and the Two Koreas: Politics, Economics, Security.* Boulder: Lynne Rienner.

Solomon, Richard H. 1999. *Chinese Negotiating Behavior: Pursuing Interests Through "Old Friends."* Herndon, VA: US Institute of Peace Press.

Spanier, John W. 1965. *The Truman-McArthur Controversy and the Korean War.* New York: W. W. Norton.
Steinfeld, Edward S. 2010. *Playing Our Game: Why China's Rise Doesn't Threaten the West.* New York: Oxford University Press.
Storey, Ian. 2011. *Southeast Asia and the Rise of China: The Search for Security.* London: Routledge.
"Streaks of Red." 2011. *The Economist* 400 (July 2): 8740.
Sukma, Rizal. 1999. *Indonesia and China: The Politics of a Troubled Relationship.* London: Routledge.
Sun Tze. 2005. *The Illustrated Art of War.* Trans. Samuel B. Griffith. New York: Oxford University Press.
Sutter, Robert G. 2007. *Chinese Foreign Relations: Power and Policy Since the Cold War.* Lanham, MD: Rowman and Littlefield.
———. 2010. *U.S.-Chinese Relations: Perilous Past, Pragmatic Present.* Lanham, MD: Rowman and Littlefield.
Swaine, Michael D., and Zhang Tuosheng (eds.). 2007. *Managing Sino-American Crises: Case Studies and Analysis.* Washington, DC: Carnegie Endowment for International Peace.
Swope, Kenneth M. 2009. *A Dragon's Head and a Serpent's Tail: Ming China and the First Great East Asian War, 1592–1598.* Norman: University of Oklahoma Press.
Tao, Hanzhang. 2007. *Sun Tzu's Art of War: The Modern Chinese Interpretation.* Trans. Yuan Shibing. New York: Sterling Innovation.
Taylor, Ian. 2006. *China and Africa: Engagement and Compromise.* London: Routledge.
———. 2010. *China's New Role in Africa.* Boulder: Lynne Rienner.
Taylor, Ian, Dominik Kopinski, and Andrzek Polus (eds.). 2011. *China's Rise in Africa: Perspectives on a Developing Connection.* London: Routledge.
Terrill, Ross. 2004. *The New Chinese Empire: And What It Means for the United States.* New York: Basic Books.
Thakur, Ramesh, and Edward Newman (eds.). 2004. *Broadening Asia's Security Discourse and Agenda: Political, Social, and Environmental Perspectives.* Washington, DC: Brookings Institution Press.
"The Queensway Syndicate and the Africa Trade." 2011. *The Economist* 400 (August): 8746.
Thomas, Nicholas (ed.). 2004. *Re-Orienting Australia-China Relations: 1972 to the Present.* Burlington, VT: Ashgate.
Thucydides. 1954. *The History of the Peloponnesian War.* Trans. Rex Warner. New York: Penguin.
Tkacik, John J. (ed.). 2007. *Reshaping the Taiwan Strait.* Westminster, MD: Heritage Books.
Tsang, Steve. 2006. *If China Attacks Taiwan: Military Strategy, Politics, and Economics.* London: Routledge.
Tuchman, Barbara. 2001. *Stilwell and the American Experience in China, 1911–1945.* New York: Grove Press.
Tucker, Nancy Bernkopf. 2001. *China Confidential: American Diplomats and Sino-American Relations, 1945–1996.* New York: Columbia University Press.
———. 2009. *Strait Talk: United States–Taiwan Relations and the Crisis with China.* Cambridge, MA: Harvard University Press.
US Military, Department of Defense. 2011. *Department of Defense Reports on Military and Strategy Involving the People's Republic of China 2006 Through 2010: People's Liberation Army (PLA), Communist Party, Weapons, Tactics.* San Rafael, CA: Progressive Management Publications.

Wachman, Alan. 2007. *Why Taiwan? Geostrategic Rationales for China's Territorial Integrity.* Stanford, CA: Stanford University Press.
Waley-Cohen, Joanna. 2006. *The Culture of War in China: Empire and the Military Under the Qing Dynasty.* New York: Palgrave.
Wang, Y. C. 1966. *Chinese Intellectuals and the West, 1872–1949.* Durham: University of North Carolina Press.
Wang, Yuan-Kang. 2011. *Harmony and War: Confucian Culture and Chinese Power Politics.* New York: Columbia University Press.
Wasserstrom, Jeffrey N. 2010. *China in the 21st Century: What Everyone Needs to Know.* New York: Oxford University Press.
Wayne, Martin I. 2009. "Inside China's War on Terrorism." *Journal of Contemporary China* 18(59): 249–261.
Westad, Odd Arne. 1992. *Cold War and Revolution: Soviet-American Rivalry and the Origins of the Chinese Civil War, 1944–1946.* New York: Columbia University Press.
Whiting, Allen S. 2001. *The Chinese Calculus of Deterrence: India and Indochina.* Ann Arbor: Center for Chinese Studies, University of Michigan.
Wilson, Dick. 1984. *Zhou Enlai: A Biography.* New York: Viking.
Wise, David. 2011. *Tiger Trap: America's Secret Spy War with China.* New York: Houghton Mifflin.
Womack, Brantly. 2006. *China and Vietnam: The Politics of Asymmetry.* Cambridge: Cambridge University Press.
———. 2010. *China Among Unequals: Asymetric Foreign Relationships in Asia.* Singapore: World Scientific.
Wu, Raymond Ray-kuo, and Yongnian Zheng. 2006. *Sources of Conflict and Cooperation in the Taiwan Strait.* Singapore: World Scientific.
Xu, Guangqui. 2007. *Congress and the U.S.-China Relationship, 1949–1979.* Akron, OH: University of Akron Press.
Yahuda, Michael. 2011. *The International Politics of the Asia-Pacific.* 3rd ed. New York: Routledge.
Yan, Xuetong, Daniel Bell, and Sun Zhe. 2011. *Ancient Chinese Thought, Modern Chinese Power.* Trans. Edmund Ryden. Princeton, NJ: Princeton University Press.
Yoshihara, Toshi, and James R. Holmes. 2010. *Red Star Over the Pacific: China's Rise and the Challenge to U.S. Maritime Strategy.* Annapolis, MD: Naval Institute Press.
Yu, Peter Kien-hong. 2002. *The Crab and Frog Motion Paradigm Shift: Decoding and Deciphering Taipei and Beijing's Dialectical Politics.* Lanham, MD: University Press of America.
Zhai, Qiang. 2000. *China and the Vietnam Wars, 1950–1975.* Chapel Hill: University of North Carolina Press.
Zhang, Shu Guang. 1995. *Mao's Military Romanticism: China and the Korean War, 1950–1953.* Lawrence: University of Kansas Press.
———. 2001. *Economic Cold War: America's Embargo Against China and the Sino-Soviet Alliance, 1949–1963.* Stanford, CA: Stanford University Press.
Zhao, Suisheng (ed.). 2011. *China and East Asian Regionalism: Economic and Security Cooperation and Institution-Building.* London: Routledge.
Zhu, Fang. 1998. *Gun Barrel Politics: Party-Army Relations in Mao's China.* Boulder: Westview.
Zhu, Zhiqun. 2006. *US-China Relations in the 21st Century: Power, Transition, and Peace.* London: Routledge.

8

Population Growth and Urbanization

Ma Rong

Each of the prior chapters has dealt with some common themes that, taken together, provide a basis for understanding the growth and dispersion of China's populace. China has long been divided between more prosperous and populous coastal regions and interior regions with fewer people, harsher conditions, and vast untapped natural resources. It has long had entrepreneurs in cities and the countryside producing an abundance of crops and goods, mostly in those coastal regions. And the market economy they supply has been at its liveliest when effective rulers unify great portions of the country; since those rulers usually have emerged from interior parts of the continent, this creates both a tie and a tension between the interior and the coast.

China's prosperity has hinged on three balancing acts: between city and country, between population and food, and between regions of hardship and regions of prosperity. Americans have heard of China's spectacular building boom in its cities, its controversial "one-child" birth control policy, and the contrast between life in modern areas like Shanghai and Hong Kong and the more traditional life in minority areas of the interior. China had extensive urbanization long before the rest of the world; but cities have always depended on the countryside for their prosperity, and the line between city and countryside has always been blurred. One cannot thrive without the other. China must grow or import enough food to feed its rising population and find ways to spread prosperity inland if its current boom is to continue. These are not new problems or new solutions, but the magnitude of both is far greater than ever in the past. Food production and population have long risen simultaneously, but ultimately they reach a point where they cannot sustain one another, bringing social crisis. And China has never been able to survive with two nations, one rich and one poor; it needs social service networks linking the capital and regional cities to keep that kind of polarization from occurring. China's future success depends on maintaining these fine balances, but it will not be easy.

City and Countryside in History

China has always been a country on the move. Its history brought a succession of droughts, floods, plagues, famines, rebellions, conquerors, and great public works projects. All of these involved movement of great numbers of people. Emperors and soldiers built cities, moving people by force for their construction and occupation (Barbieri-low, 2007); in times of rebellion, angry peasants burned those cities. People in leaner regions of the north moved south and west to seek greater prosperity, often creating new cities in the regions they entered or settling close to existing ones (Gaubatz, 1996). Cities were generally built by soldiers and rulers, but they were sustained by commerce, which moved both people and goods.

In *The City in Late Imperial China*, William G. Skinner (1977) makes the case that a principal role of cities in late imperial China was as commercial centers. In these cities, public officials and merchants interacted to tap and regulate markets and means of production, creating wealth both for citizens and for government. However, the cities were not the only place that generated wealth. Many villages, in fact, produced goods in cottage industries, raised crops, and helped maintain canals, roads, and streams that served as transportation networks to move their goods to and from the cities. Nearly everyone in and around the urbanized areas helped supply, and purchased from, this trade.

Cities were often located along major canals or rivers (Xu, 2000). The short Miracle Canal (Ling Qu) linked the Xiang River, which flows into the Yangtze, with the Gui River, which flows toward Guangzhou; it was begun in the third century BCE. The Grand Canal (begun much later, in the sixth century CE, using 2 to 3 million laborers) linked the Yangtze River valley with the Yellow River and later Beijing. Over the centuries, these and other canals were frequently rerouted to fit the needs of commerce and conquest, and their maintenance required extensive labor (Van Slyke, 1988:69–72). Huge quantities of grain moved along these waterways, along with troops, all manner of manufactured goods, small merchants, and thousands of boatmen and their families. Officials extracted taxes and tolls, and merchants extracted profits, from this trade. The roads and waterways helped rulers hold China together and conquer people along the periphery.

To keep their rule alive, officials also established towns in areas with less commerce to control the populace and maintain defense networks. In contrast to the commercial centers, many of these centers cost the government a good deal of money to maintain while generating little revenue. As one moved inland, the number of such cities tended to increase (see Skinner, 1977:221; Skinner, 2001). It was not the case that these centers were associated with poverty and the commercial cities were associated with wealth. Many of the laborers who contributed to the prosperity of the commercial cities worked very hard for little income. Many of the clans living around the administrative towns engaged in little commerce beyond their villages but may have supported themselves adequately on their small farms. City inhabitants had to garner money either from the capital or from outside commerce to prosper. Threats of outside attack or social unrest could help attract such funds to cities that had little outside commerce; the capital might also send money if the town formed a useful link to control neighboring regions.

The role of cities as centers of trade and administration began very early in China's history (Lewis, 2006; Friedmann, 2005:1–18). In Chapter 3, Rhoads Murphey discussed the rise of cities as early as the Shang dynasty (see Table 3.1); his mention of the battle for dominance between the commercial towns and cities of the state of Qu in the Yangtze River valley and the frontier feudal fiefdom of Qin, which finally unified China, highlights their dual role as political and commercial centers. Cities surrounded by tall walls and "defense-rivers" were the settlements for governmental offices and the army. Cities were built to protect both urban and rural residents during wartime. Towns with no significance in administration, whose main occupation was trade, did not have walls and large populations (Elvin and Skinner, 1974). Since the Qin unification of China in 221 BCE, the country has needed to establish a strong administration system to manage the large territory. Therefore, big cities developed in China much earlier than in Europe (Steinhardt, 1999). During the Tang dynasty (752 CE), the population of the capital city, Chang'an (present-day Xi'an; see Map 3.1), was around 2 million (Chao and Xie, 1988:191); it was a center of both governance and commerce. In comparison, big cities developed in Europe much later, and their main expansion occurred after the Industrial Revolution in the eighteenth century (Chandler, 1987).

As indicated in Chapters 3 and 4, the Song dynasty was a period of great commerce, with a fifth of the populace moving to towns and cities to engage in these pursuits (Chao, 1987:56; Kiang, 1999). In the centuries following, urbanization increased as overall population began to rise rapidly (see Table 8.1). At the beginning of the nineteenth century, China had 1,400 cities of over 3,000 people; more than half of the cities with a population above 10,000 were the seats of prefectures and provincial administrations (Rozman, 1982:209). China's population exceeded 300 million people by 1800 (Chao and Xie, 1988:378). In western and northern China, where the economy is less developed and population density is low, the main function of cities and towns is still administrative (Reardon-Anderson, 2005; Wang, 2003). Manufacturing and services were limited there, and a large proportion of the urban labor force worked in governmental institutions.

In contrast, many "market towns" in the coastal regions (especially in Jiangsu, Zhejiang, Fujian, and Guangdong provinces) have a more prosperous

Table 8.1 Historical Changes in China's Population (thousands)

Year	Population	Year	Population
2140 BCE	13,554	1500	92,746
1063	13,715	1552	96,225
684	11,847	1602	98,780
334	32,000	1646	88,486
221	20,000	1671	94,515
162	31,200	1695	100,525
90	30,600	1710	111,428
2 CE	58,006	1730	129,081
13	59,850	1749	182,625
31	15,056	1768	226,807
188	59,780	1774	263,690
221	14,083	1796	297,611
263	18,853	1805	329,128
290	22,223	1812	367,219
370	27,000	1830	400,716
520	42,300	1840	418,880
577	39,650	1850	436,299
585	43,860	1860	417,967
604	50,780	1870	357,736
624	17,697	1880	367,023
652	25,729	1890	380,636
764	31,274	1898	396,432
825	32,584	1911	405,484
845	38,069	1922	447,150
959	24,793	1931	468,842
1004	38,069	1942	467,610
1044	53,971	1949	549,066
1067	66,063	1950	559,514
1106	94,931	1959	682,501
1124	98,324	1962	684,462
1178	93,419	1970	844,596
1188	99,356	1975	924,200
1210	108,178	1980	987,050
1234	71,875	1985	1,058,510
1275	54,748	1990	1,143,330
1293	79,816	1995	1,211,210
1368	63,827	2000	1,267,430
1398	71,867	2005	1,307,560
1420	79,238	2008	1,328,020
1470	89,895	2009	1,340,055

Sources: Before 1984, Zhao Wenlin and Xie Shujun, *Population History of China* (Beijing: People's Press, 1984), pp. 535–544. After 1985, Population and Development Study Center, *Data Handbook of Population and Family Planning* (Beijing: Population Press of China, 2009), p. 89.

economy and high population densities. Trade, manufacture, handicraft, transportation, and services are important functions of these towns. Some of them grew up rapidly and even became large cities (Finnane, 2004). After the Opium Wars (1839–1842), the population of the treaty ports along the coast began to rise rapidly. Shanghai was only a country town with a few thousand people at the beginning of the eighteenth century, but it became the largest city in East Asia a century later because it served as the main trade center and transportation port between China and other countries (Henriot, 1993; Yeh, 2007; Dong and Goldstein, 2006; Logan, 2002; Wasserstrom, 2009; Bergère, 2009). Today China has a number of big cities in its coastal regions. By 2010, the population of Guangzhou reached 25 million, Beijing exceeded 18 million, and Shanghai's population 20 million. There were forty-two cities in China with a population over 2 million, and more than 170 with over 1 million (National Bureau of Statistics of China, 2011).

Population and Food

It is well known that China is the most populous country of the world, with 1.337 billion people in 2011—about one-fifth of the world's total population, which stood at 7 billion. China's population exceeded the combined populations of the United States (313 million), Russia (140 million), Japan (127 million), Indonesia (246 million), and all of Europe and Central Asia (474 million). The country with the world's second-largest population is India, with 1.189 billion. Because of India's higher annual birthrates (21 per 1,000 versus 12 per 1,000 in China), its population is expected to surpass China's soon.

By world standards, China's population has been high throughout recorded history; but its absolute numbers have been much lower than at present. China's population exceeded 100 million in 1685, based on census and other records of population accounting during different dynasties for the purpose of tax collection and army recruitment, which are not entirely accurate but give some general sense of population sizes. From the first "census" (household accounting) in 2 CE to the one in 1400, China's population experienced a long process of instability. Sometimes the population increased at an annual rate of 4 to 5 percent under peaceful and prosperous social conditions, perhaps even exceeding 100 million during the twelfth century at the height of the Song dynasty; sometimes wars and famines decreased it by 30 to 40 percent. By the height of the Ming dynasty in the fifteenth century, it had risen again to around 100 million, dipped again with the wars that brought the Qing dynasty to office, and then moved into steady growth after those wars ended in 1681. It took seventy-nine years to exceed 200 million (in 1759), another forty-one years to exceed 300 million (in 1800, a third of the world's population), and another thirty years to exceed 400 million by 1830—doubling in seventy-one years (Chao and Xie, 1988:378). Because of foreign invasion (such as the Opium Wars and the

1931–1945 Japanese occupation) and civil wars (the "Taiping Heavenly Kingdom," and the war between the Communist Party and Kuomintang; see Chapter 4), "the century between 1851 and 1949 was one of societal breakdown . . . an annual average population growth rate of only 0.3 percent" (Banister, 1987). Then China entered into a period of spectacular rise in population.

Food was a major factor in determining population. As Rhoads Murphey pointed out in Chapter 3, China's civilization was able to sustain itself because of the cultivation of rice and wheat. Wars, epidemics, and floods killed people directly. Along with droughts, they also destroyed fields and crops, leading to starvation, lower fertility rates, and infanticide (killing babies at birth) to avoid having to share food with newborn infants. For many centuries, China's population rose and fell on the basis of how much grain it could grow and store. Then, in the eighteenth century, new plants arrived from the New World and Europe: sweet potatoes, maize (corn), Irish potatoes, and peanuts—all of which could grow abundantly on previously unused terrain—along with new, more productive strains of rice from Southeast Asia. Especially in southern China, more people could marry at earlier ages and have more children, who had an increased chance to live because of better nutrition for both mother and infant.

One tactic used by armies in the civil wars and foreign invasions from which China suffered from the mid-nineteenth to mid-twentieth centuries was to break dikes and cause flooding. Bad weather also brought periodic droughts. Granary storage systems were emptied and extended families and communities scattered. Combined with the disease, direct killings, and other hardships brought by war and social disorder, these losses of crops brought great loss of life. Chapters 3 and 4 gave some estimates of those losses. Yet despite all this hardship, China's population crept upward during this period, adding more people than all of China had supported before the seventeenth century. The new crops helped this to happen.

The arrival of the People's Republic of China (PRC) in 1949 brought peace, the economic stabilization measures discussed in Chapter 4 that ended the high inflation of food prices, the return of peasants to the land, and measures to provide basic medicine and hygiene. The first modern census, conducted in 1953, showed a population of 582 million. Twenty-nine years later, in 1982, it surpassed 1 billion.

From 1958 to 1961, there was a serious famine in China (see Chapter 4). Both natural disasters (drought) and policies of rural development (the "commune system" and the Great Leap Forward) impacted the famine and resulted in negative population growth rates in the early 1960s. The mortality rate was very high (Banister and Hill, 2004). The high birthrates in the late 1960s and 1970s are called "compensative births" by demographers, since many people who did not bear children during the famine wanted to have them right after (Tien, 1983:16). The total fertility rate (expected average number of children per woman at the end of her childbearing years) decreased to 3.3 in 1960 and jumped back to 5.8 in 1970. The general trend is for the birthrate to exceed the death rate and for population to rise faster in rural areas than in urban.

There has always been a basic argument or debate within the government and among demographers in the PRC over whether family planning is necessary and what should be the "proper standard" or limitation in family planning programs. In other words, how many children should a couple have? The most famous debate was between the president of Peking University, Ma Yinchu, and Chairman Mao Zedong in 1957.

Citing his study and population projections, Ma (an economist) called on China to control births and encourage family planning. At a meeting of the National People's Congress, he warned that China's population would reach 1.5–2.6 billion (at an annual growth rate of 2 to 3 percent) in fifty years, and that such a huge population would become an intolerable burden preventing China from becoming a prosperous industrialized nation. To solve the problem, he suggested setting a goal of two children per family (Ma Yinchu, 1957). His suggestion was supported by some senior officials, including Zhou Enlai; a movement was organized, mainly to call people's attention to population issues without policy enforcement. This was the first family planning campaign, from 1955 to 1957 (see Figure 8.1), just before the terrible famine.

At the time, Mao was worried about the possibility of war between China and the United States. The Korean War had not formally ended, and the situation on the Taiwan Strait was hostile and fragile, as explained in Chapters 6

Figure 8.1 Demographic Dynamics During China's Family Planning Campaigns

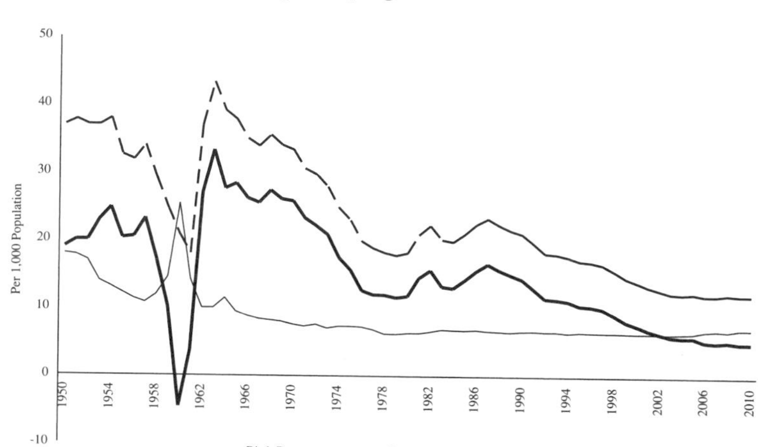

Source: Population and Development Study Center, *Data Handbook of Population and Family Planning* (Beijing: Population Press of China, 2009), pp. 89–90.

and 7. He believed China needed to maintain a large population to survive a nuclear war, since it had no nuclear weapons to deter such an attack. Mao said that even if nuclear bombs killed half the population, China would still have millions left to continue fighting. Mao rejected Ma's suggestion on the basis of this strategic thinking. Then Ma was criticized very seriously as "the new Malthus" and lost his position and influence. (Malthus was an eighteenth-century thinker who gave a gloomy forecast that the world's population is destined to grow faster than food supplies.)

But China was not involved in nuclear war with either the United States or the Soviet Union. As can be seen in Figure 8.1, the birth rate shot up after the period of famine during the Great Leap Forward (1958–1960) and the government called for a second family planning campaign. Fertility rates declined again during the Cultural Revolution (1966–1976). After those periods of chaos, they rose once more, as Ma Yinchu had predicted. The government announced the third family planning campaign with a new slogan: *wan, xi, shao* (late marriage, long birth intervals, and fewer births).

As the population pressure on land, urban jobs, housing, and social spending became more serious, it was clear that a rapidly growing population would make the "four modernizations" (of agriculture, industry, the military, and science and technology) announced in 1978 an impossible dream. So in the 1980s, the Chinese government finally set up a more restrictive birth control policy, the one-child campaign (Greenhalgh and Winckler, 2005:47–165; Scharping, 2002; Greenhalgh, 2008; White, 2009; Poston et al., 2009). China's fertility rates, birthrates, and mortality rates all stabilized (as Table 8.2 and Figure 8.1 show), resulting in a low natural rate of population increase—rising just 0.57 percent a year between 2000 and 2010 ("Only and Lonely," 2011). Unlike the experiences of industrialized countries, where social and economic development gradually lead to low fertility, government policy and enforcement have played a key role in this transition in China.

Some argue that low fertility will be spontaneously adopted by people after economic and societal development and that no policy enforcement is really needed (see Beaver, 1975; "Only and Lonely," 2011). But in China's case, the huge population and a high birthrate obviously hinder social and economic development. In 1982, 80 percent of China's population was traditional farmers and more than 32 percent of the populace over the age of twelve were illiterate. Such individuals are apt to have large families, straining food supplies and government support services at a time when resources need to be devoted to building an infrastructure for modernization that could bring societal and economic development (Hansen, 1999).

Since Han people, especially farmers, have a strong preference for boys, the sex ratio at birth increased from 108.5 boys in 1982 to 110.2 boys in 1990, and then to 116.9 in 2000 for every 100 girls. One of the reasons is the higher possibility that couples will decide to have an abortion when they learn the new baby will be a girl. But it is also very likely that many rural households did not report the births of girls, which may in turn make the ratio more even. In regions where local administrators are more zealous about enforcing birth control, people often fail to report births of both sexes, and it is difficult to estimate the total number that were not reported to administration and registered by censuses.

When the Chinese government recognized the difficulties in enforcing the one-child policy in rural areas, it made many local adjustments in birth regulations to allow farmers to have more than one child. For example, if the first child is a girl or has some disease or if the father is the only son of his family, a second child is allowed. By estimation, there are generally two children per family in most rural areas in China, whereas the one-child policy is generally followed in cities (Peng, 1991; Greenhalgh and Winckler, 2005: 45–165; Hessler, 2010:150–153). In Chapter 11, Laurel Bossen discusses this topic further.

As can be seen in Tables 8.2 and 5.2, the Chinese population has two major characteristics: large size and low education. Among the total population above age fifteen in China in 2010, 4 percent of males and 11 percent of females were illiterate. Because many rural primary schools have very poor teaching conditions and many teachers received only primary school education themselves, the quality of education for a large proportion of graduates of rural primary schools is considered very low. With such low quality in education, skill training, and social experiences, a huge population will have a more negative than positive impact on China's development.

The importance of family planning becomes even clearer if we carefully examine the connection between natural resources in China and population growth. Arable land in China covers less than 250 million acres (101.2 hectares) and has continually decreased because of urban expansion and construction of dams, roads, bridges, and new factories. The arable land per capita in 1998 was 0.26 acres (0.1 hectares) in China, one-seventh that of the United States, one-fifteenth that of Canada, and one-twenty-eighth that of Australia (Qu and Li, 1992:53). India, with 432 million acres (174.4 million hectares) of arable land, has fewer people than China. Therefore, the pressure of population on grain production is worse in China than in India. The Chinese government argues that, with 7 percent of the world's arable land and the need to feed 21 percent of the world's population, family planning was the only choice for China to maintain its social stability and proceed into modernization.

The outlook for other natural resources in China is equally grim. Only 22 percent of China's territory has forest cover (up from 12 percent twenty years ago, thanks to an aggressive reforestation program), compared to 33 percent for the United States, 68 percent for Japan, 50 percent for Russia, and 31 percent for the world as a whole (*World Bank, Development Indicators,* 2011).

Table 8.2 Selected Development and Demographic Trends in China

	1950	1960	1970	1980	1990	2000	2008
Total population (in millions)	552.00	662.00	830.00	987.00	1,120.00	1,266.00	1,328.02
GNP per capita (US$)	—	—	—	290.00	370.00	884.75	3263.00
% urban[a]	11.20	19.70	17.40	19.40	26.00	36.33	45.70
Infant mortality per 100 births[b]	13.80	8.56	5.15	3.76	3.70	3.00	2.01
Crude birthrate (% increase)	3.70	2.09	3.34	1.82	2.10	1.52	1.21
Crude death rate (% decrease)	1.80	2.54	0.7	0.63	0.63	0.64	0.71
Rate of population growth (%)	1.90	–0.45	2.58	1.19	1.44	0.76	0.71
Total fertility rate per childbearer[c]	5.80	3.30	5.80	2.20	2.30	1.9	1.8
Life expectancy (female)[b]	49.20	58.00	63.20	69.20	71.10	72	74
Life expectancy (male)[b]	46.70	56.00	61.10	66.20	67.80	68	70

Sources: World Bank (ed.), *World Development Report* (New York: Oxford University Press, 1982–2011).

a. Xiangming Wang, "Urbanization of China's Population," in *Almanac of China's Population 1985* (Beijing: Chinese Social Sciences Publishing House [in Chinese], 1986), p. 284; National Bureau of Statistics, *International Statistical Yearbook (2001)* (Beijing: China Statistics Press, National Bureau of Statistics of China, 2001), p. 91.

b. Fude Lin, "An Analysis of China's Birth Rates," in *Almanac of China's Population* 185 (Beijing: Chinese Social Sciences Publishing House [in Chinese], 1986), p. 238; World Bank (ed.), *World Development Indicators* (Washington, DC: World Bank, 2011).

c. Rui Yan and Cheng Shengqi, "Age-Specific Death Rates and Life Expectancy in the Past Forty Years," in *Collected Papers Presented at International Conference on Fertility Sampling Surveys of China*, edited by Chinese Association of Population Studies (Beijing: Population Press of China [in Chinese], 1993); Rongqing Huang, "The Mortality of China in the 1980s," in *Selected Papers Presented at the Sixth National Conference on Population Science of China*, edited by Chinese Association of Population Studies (Beijing: Chinese Association of Population Studies [in Chinese], 1993); World Bank (ed.), *World Development Indicators* (Washington, DC: World Bank, 2001); National Bureau of Statistics of China, *International Statistical Yearbook (2009)* (Beijing: China Statistics Press, National Bureau of Statistics of China, 2009), pp. 101–108.

Water is one of the most important natural resources. The per capita surface water runoff—the amount of water that flows on the surface to use for drinking, agriculture, sanitation, and industry—is only one-fourth the world average and one-fifth that of the United States (Qu and Li, 1992:117). Furthermore, China's water resources are unequally distributed. Most of the cities in northern China experience serious water shortages, whereas southeastern China is often threatened by floods. Beijing, where the population is growing by a million people every two years, has 26,000 gallons of water available per person; a standard used by the United Nations classifies any urban area with less than 260,000 gallons per person as experiencing chronic scarcity (in Chapter 9, Richard Edmonds discusses all these problems in greater detail.) With such shortages and imbalanced geographic distribution between population and natural resources, birth control and family planning are necessary measures. The difficulties of increasing food production for a growing population are substantial.

Despite the one-child policy, China's population continues to grow and has been predicted to become stable around 2033, after reaching 1.5 billion people (Chang, 2011). China's population was 723 million in 1964; if the fertility rate, mortality rate, and natural growth rate had stayed the same as they were that year, China would have had a population of 2.075 billion by 1995. Now, with the fertility rate a third of what it was then, the expected population by 2015 is 1.4 billion. The decrease in births means fewer workers and offspring to help retired parents and grandparents.

City and Countryside Today

To feed its population, China must have enough people in the countryside to maintain the food supply while managing the gravitation to towns and cities that naturally accompanies modernization. Because of the geographic characteristics and distribution of natural resources, China's population is not equally distributed. The plateau and deserts in the western part of China can support only a very small population. As can be quickly grasped by looking at Maps 2.2 and 2.3 and drawing a diagonal line from western Heilongjiang to western Yunnan, 94 percent of the total population live in the southeastern part of China (about 36 percent of the total territory), whereas 6 percent live in the northwestern part (about 64 percent of total territory). This pattern has not changed for centuries. Furthermore, the most populous cities lie to the southeast. Although China's average density is 125 persons per square kilometer (325 per square mile), its coastal regions are considered among the most crowded places in the world, with a population density of over 600–1,000 persons per square kilometer (1,500–2,600 per square mile). Anyone who visits Beijing, Shanghai, or even rural areas in the coastal regions will certainly have a very strong impression about the high population density there. It is even difficult for urban people to move on streets and in shops on weekends and holidays, and there are very short distances between villages in rural areas (Dutton, Lo, and Wu, 2010; Edelmann, 2008; Gil, 2008).

In 1949, the PRC established a centrally planned economic system on the model of the Soviet Union. In order to manage food and housing supplies, employment, education, and other public facilities under the governmental plans, a residential registration system was created in 1953 to control the size of urban populations and the volume of rural-urban migration (Goldstein and Goldstein, 1985:9–12; Lu, 2006; Fong and Murphy, 2005:27–40). Under this policy, the proportion of urban residents in the total population was kept around 20 percent for a long period, much lower than in other nations.

The Great Leap Forward, which began in 1958 (see Chapter 4), resulted in about 20 million rural people migrating into cities to participate in an urban industrial expansion. Since the factories were established in a hurry and there were many problems in management and the quality of the labor force, many new factories did not make profits and had to be closed. Then the government had to tell the 20 million new urban residents to move back to rural areas (Tien, 1983:28). After this crisis, the government set up a very restricted system of urban population control. Anyone who wanted to move from one place to another had to apply for an official transfer, and it was difficult to obtain approval for a move from the countryside into a town or city, especially into big cities. Kam Wing Chan (1996) argues that this system helped stabilize cities as they industrialized.

During the Cultural Revolution (1966–1976), the government arranged a special type of urban-rural migration for city middle-school graduates. They were sent to rural areas in the periphery, to army reclamation farms, and to urban suburbs for "reeducation." They were compelled to learn from farmers and herders and work as one of them. The total number of these students was around 1.2 million. After the Cultural Revolution, a large portion of these students returned to the cities of their origin, resulting in a rural-urban return migration.

Following the new economic reforms in the 1980s, migration control loosened. The grain coupons (which were province specific) and hotel clerks' requests for "travel approval" for checking into hotels were abandoned. Now people may travel anywhere in the country, though official local residential status is still needed when applying for a formal job in governmental institutions. Migration abroad has also become more convenient if the visa is approved by foreign countries. According to the 2000 national census, 756,726 persons were living abroad and had temporarily canceled their local residential registration (Population Census Bureau of China, 2002:13). That number is growing. Yet all this new freedom of movement comes with a price: the social guarantees and stability of neighborhoods and communities that the regulations helped establish are not as firm.

Health Care

One guarantee under pressure is health care. Life expectancy at birth has increased significantly in China since 1950. At that time, it was only 49.2 years for women and 46.7 years for men; by 2011, it had risen to 77 years and 73 years. The improvements in income and housing have had a positive impact on people's nutrition and health. The general improvement of mass education has also had some indirect impact on reducing mortality. More children attend school.

The health care facilities managed by the government also play an important role in reducing mortality and increasing life expectancy. After 1949, university-educated doctors and nurses became available to urban workers. "Barefoot doctors," who received basic paramedical training and were supported by their local villages, proved very helpful in controlling infectious diseases and offering simple treatment of urgent cases in rural areas. But the gap between the quality of health care facilities in rural areas and cities remained wide. Before the reforms of the 1980s, there were two different health care systems in rural and urban China. In rural areas, a system called the "collective health care system" was in practice. At that time, all rural dwellers belonged to communes, which controlled management of the land; they were divided into brigades and finally into smaller production teams. Brigade members all contributed equal levies to a fund that supported their health care. When they became ill, the fund paid half their bill; they paid the rest. Urban workers had better coverage than that. The ministries, schools, and state-owned factories and shops, for which over 90 percent of urban employees worked, paid all medical expenses and provided employees with doctors and hospitals near their workplace. The work units also covered 70 to 80 percent of the health care expenses of employee dependents. So urban workers had better access than rural dwellers to hospitals and fully trained doctors and paid few of their own medical bills.

Since the system reform in the early 1980s, the collective health care system has lost its financial base because all lands and properties were redistributed among peasants. Now peasants pay most of their own health care expenses (Liu and Rao, 2006; "Dipping Into the Kitty," 2012). The former "barefoot doctors" now either open their own private clinics and make money from their services or switch to other activities. These clinics are under the regulation of county bureaus of public health care. The New Rural Cooperative Medical Care system instituted in 2005 offers rural dwellers subsidized low-cost insurance, but it pays only 40 percent of very basic coverage. In some poor areas, local doctors with medical degrees left their villages and moved to rich regions, and even cities, to earn higher incomes. Poorer regions are suffering from a serious shortage of doctors and health care services. At the same time, widespread smoking, tainted food, and pollution have helped make cancer the leading cause of death.

In urban areas, state-owned enterprises are now facing serious financial problems as they compete with private companies and joint ventures. Often they must cut back drastically on the health coverage they offer their employees. Fifty-eight cities have established health insurance programs, which they encourage all factories to join; their employees must pay monthly premiums in exchange for coverage. In rich regions along the eastern coast, where township enterprises prosper, local health insurance systems are successfully established at town and even village levels. In other regions of China, the urban and rural health care facilities have been largely maintained by subsidies from central or provincial governments, whose budgets are increasingly strained. High percenages of urbanites now have government-subsidized health insurance but copay about a third of the cost for basic services. Benefits are capped, so they do not cover serious illnesses (Gu and Zhang, 2006; "Dipping Into the Kitty," 2012). Many new hospitals with advanced equipment are being built in cities; their patients have private insurance or pay for all or most of their care. One reason for the appeal of Falun Gong and of Dr. Hong Zhaoguang, whose self-help health books (emphasizing exercise, diet, and "right thinking") have sold millions of copies and whose inspirational lectures are jammed with listeners, is their promise of simple and inexpensive ways to cure diseases and stay healthy. Unlicensed and unregulated illegal clinics, dispensing low-cost advice and drugs of uncertain value, have also sprung up (Li and Wu, 2010).

Housing

The housing system in rural China, like health care, differs from that in towns and cities. Under the PRC, with the exception of a few private houses that residents built or bought before 1949, all houses and apartment buildings in urban areas were managed by government institutions. These apartments were assigned to employees who needed to pay only a very small amount for "rent." In rural areas, the peasants built their houses themselves after obtaining official permission from village, town, and county authorities for land use.

When the economic reforms were first instituted after 1978, this worked to the advantage of rural dwellers. Under the household responsibility system, which let them lease land and sell crops in markets, many of them acquired savings that they used to build themselves houses; these are often quite large (especially in more sparsely populated areas like Yunnan). Sometimes this is done by families themselves, and sometimes by the village or township leaders. Meanwhile, urban dwellers remained confined to the apartments assigned them—often only one or two rooms for a family, with a tiny kitchen and toilet sometimes shared with another family. Since low rents cannot cover the expenses of maintenance, the buildings were often in poor repair. Sometimes young workers live in dormitories for several years, even after marriage, before being assigned an apartment. Hence reform of the urban housing system became one of the key issues in the 1980s. During the 1990s, urban governments rapidly accelerated the building of tall housing blocks with larger, more modern apartments. Since 1998, all workers moving to new apartments must purchase them, while rents are gradually rising for those in older apartments. The final goal of housing reform is to sell most apartments to the residents with subsidies from the institutions that employ them. Now the skylines of cities and towns all over China are filled with modern apartment buildings and even some landscaped gated communities (Zhang, 2010). They are served by corner convenience stores, indoor and outdoor markets, shops, malls, and superstores that sell everything one would find in US retail outlets. Some categories, like pharmaceuticals, include few of the same items to be found in a comparable US store. In others, like electronics and water heaters, the choice is greater than in a comparable US store.

Meanwhile, many villages located close to larger cities have created new factories and other cooperative enterprises under the reforms (Pei, 2005). They, too, are using the income to build blocks of apartment buildings, along with schools, retirement homes, hospitals, and other amenities. Hence these rural areas are coming to look more like cities, and their inhabitants are being assigned housing in a manner resembling cities.

Redefining the Distinction Between City and Countryside

The relaxation of restrictions on travel from the countryside into cities and towns has resulted in some 260 million temporary laborers moving from villages into cities; these people are called "rural laborers" and are not counted as "permanent urban residents." Between the 2000 and 2010 censuses, their number rose by 83 percent. It is estimated that more than 6 million temporary residents or migrants live in Beijing; Shanghai has about that number as well. Under the *hukou* household-registration system, outsiders cannot make use of urban schools, subsidized housing, and other amenities until they are formally registered as urban citizens, which can take years and means losing their land plots back in their village (Solinger, 1999; Zhang, 2002; Research Institute of State Council, 2006:3; Hoy, 2006; Iredale, Bilik, and Guo, 2003; Murphy, 2002; Oates and Schein, 2005; Pieke and Mallee, 2000; Meyer, 2009; National Bureau of Statistics of China, 2001–2011). Some of them have lived and worked in cities for several years, purchased or rented apartments, and have no intention of returning to villages. They are hired for construction teams, by city factories, and as domestic servants in residents' houses, or they set up small shops and businesses.

Many of them still live in makeshift housing they construct themselves or in crude dormitories provided by their temporary employer. Having grown up in the countryside, many of them may find it difficult to adapt to urban life. They must send their children to often illegal private schools with low standards. City dwellers are inclined to shun them. They often leave their families at home initially. Some of them may engage in crime or even become involved in criminal syndicates. Resentments against them by long-term city residents sometimes lead to confrontation. When they travel back to villages for spring festival and then return to the cities where they usually work, the trains and railway stations throughout China become highly congested.

These "rural laborers" are part of even bigger changes in urban life. Wrecking balls and tall cranes (often jokingly referred to as the "national bird") rising from construction sites herald a complete transformation in the way urban people live and the way cities blend with surrounding towns and villages. Unlike in Europe or the United States, city planners in China need not contend with long legal battles to acquire property for development projects. Much of the land is not private and is available for conversion to public uses, so entire city streets and blocks are frequently torn down to make way for public development projects.

Many of China's ancient cities had walls, which were still in place in 1949. Most urban dwellers then lived in small, low-rise houses within those walls. To make way for new roads, public squares, government buildings, factories, and high-rise housing, many sections of those walls were torn down, and building extended outward from the center (Hung Wu, 2005; Chan, 1996; Clausen and Thogersen, 1995; Davis et al., 1995). Still, some of the older urban neighborhoods remained. Today, such old-style buildings and houses, and the original round of postwar construction, are being rapidly torn down and replaced with modern freeways, bridges, high-rise offices, shopping centers, hotels, and apartment buildings. Beijing, Shanghai, and other large cities have been nearly entirely rebuilt, with only small patches of old neighborhoods remaining. This has provided residents with better housing and hygiene, but it has also scattered the population, made it harder to maintain neighborhood activities, and destroyed many historic buildings (du Cros and Lee, 2006; Campanella, 2011; Meyer, 2009; Bergère, 2009; Chen, 2009) and, as the development moves outward, much farmland. Often people are moved to an apartment miles from where they work, requiring them to use buses, bicycles, subways, or cars to commute long distances. Private cars became very popular in Chinese cities in the new century. The total number of private cars in Beijing increased from 0.62 million in 2001 to 4.76 million in 2010; 15,000 are added each week.

With new cars rapidly being added to the mix, traffic jams grow in intensity; extensive new construction of elevated highways, subways, high-speed trains, and large bridges is seldom adequate to keep up with the rising demand. But they allow the size of cities to expand. China has become the world's largest car market. In 2002, 1 million cars were sold in China; in 2010, 18 million. Between 1988 and 2009, China built 40,400 miles (65,000 kilometers) of multilane expressways (toll roads); by 2030, it plans to triple that number. It has also been extensively improving and expanding its total paved road system of 1.8 million miles (3 million kilometers).

In Shanghai, the entire rural area to the east of the city has been converted into the Pudong Development Zone, transforming the farms that formerly occupied the land into industrial parks, apartment and office blocks, motorways, and port facilities; begun in 1990, this zone already covers an area as large as that occupied by Shanghai itself (Yeung and Sung, 1996; Gamer, 1998; Lu, 2004; Campanella, 2011; Wasserstrom, 2009; Bergère, 2009; Pridmore, 2008; Warr, 2008; den Hartog, 2010). In addition, developers have been building suburban housing estates spreading out in all directions, featuring luxurious two- and three-story single-family "villas" with private yards and parking decks. The same phenomenon is occurring around many large cities, both coastal and inland (Davis et al., 1995; Chen, Liu, and Zhang, 2004a; Wu, Xu, and Yeh, 2006; Yeung, 2000; Hessler, 2010: 338–348). Workmen are constructing ring roads, which soon become clogged with traffic and surrounded by new high-rise buildings, airports, shopping malls, amusement parks, and other urban amenities. High-speed trains allow people to commute 150 miles (240 kilometers) in less than an hour. Shanghai boasts the world's first magnetic levitation train, which covers the 30 miles (48 kilometers) from downtown to the main airport in seven minutes. Guangzhou has plans to consolidate 42 million people in nine cities that account for a tenth of China's economy into a megacity the size of Wales or the Netherlands, crisscrossed by 3,100 miles (4,988 kilometers) of railway (Moore and Foster, 2011). Village and urban leaders bargain intently over the land rights to accommodate this urban sprawl; billions of yuan are at stake (Hsing, 2010) All this brings with it an increasingly cosmopolitan lifestyle (Elfird, 2001; Broudehoux, 2004; Bergère, 2009;

Robert E. Gamer

Pudong's financial district, viewed from Shanghai. In the 1980s, this was all farmland.

Haarman, 2010; Gifford, 2008; Hessler, 2006, 2007, 2010; Dutton, Lo, and Wu, 2010; Scocca, 2011).

Within this maze of construction may lie the outlines of older towns and villages, caught up in a megalopolis; surrounding the construction are villages a few miles away that are carrying out similar construction to support new township enterprises (Friedmann, 2005:35–76; Guldin, 1997). Much of the development is, in fact, directed by local authorities rather than the national government. This can result in considerable confusion about what is local and what is metropolitan, and in urban sprawl. There has been a debate on the strategy of future urbanization in China for several years. The official strategy put forth by the government in 1980 is to "control the population size of large cities, properly develop middle-sized cities, and encourage the development of small cities and towns" (Ma Rong, 1992:141). Some experts emphasized the importance of small towns since they could absorb surplus rural laborers by developing township enterprises and could depend on their own revenues without much provincial or national governmental investment. Instead, much of the emphasis has been on developing the large cities.

Changes in the government's definition of what constitutes an urban area emphasize the difficulty of coming to grips with these problems. The definition may change to accommodate policy needs. For example, in 1963, when 20 million people were asked to return to rural areas after the failure of the Great Leap Forward, the criteria for setting up a "township" and a "city" became more restricted (to become a township, a village needed at least 2,100 nonagricultural residents rather than the prior 750), so that villages could not declare themselves one of these to keep out migrants. Cities were required to have 100,000 inhabitants rather than the 20,000 needed previously, so that suddenly the portion of the populace officially living in towns and

Robert E. Gamer

Suburban villas such as these single-family homes surround many of China's cities.

cities was radically reduced, showing "compliance" with the shift back to the countryside.

After 1980, however, the government wished to encourage the formation of townships so that they could set up township enterprises and take over responsibilities like education and health care, which were formerly handled by communes. Under the law implemented in 1984, any seat of county government could become a town, as could any former rural commune with a nonagricultural population over 2,000, and many border posts, mine settlements, tourist places, and villages in minority ethnic group regions. Under the new standards, the total number of towns increased from 2,781 in 1983 to 6,211 in 1984. And by 1986, towns with a permanent nonagricultural population over 60,000 and whose total value of annual domestic production exceeded 200 million yuan could apply for city status—down from 100,000 (Ma Rong, 1992:120, 128–129). Suddenly, many more people officially lived in towns and cities that could include them in plans for township and urban enterprises, health care, education, new housing blocks, and other initiatives (Friedmann, 2005:19–34).

The 2000 and 2010 censuses classified as urban all people living in towns and cities, including both "urban residents" and "rural laborers." By that standard, in 2011, 51.3 percent of China's population (about 690 million people) were found to be urban, an increase of 14 percent over 2000 figures. (By comparison, 82 percent of the United States and 50 percent of the world populace live in urban areas). It is clear that cities, towns, and villages in China are increasingly intertwined in their governance, economies, and social connections. In 2010, 171 cities had populations over 1 million. As cities grow out of their former boundaries, as towns build modern buildings and amenities, and as factories in the countryside produce expanding quantities of goods for the world market, the populations and social support programs of villages, towns, and cities will increasingly need to coordinate their efforts. Furthermore, the rapid decline of employment in the state sector leaves many unemployed and without support programs. Some of the older industrial towns and cities are crumbling rather than developing. Finding a balance here, like finding a balance between a rising population, urban sprawl destroying farmland, and food supply, will not be easy.

As just indicated, over 260 million migrants flock to urban areas from the countryside seeking temporary work; some 200 million urban workers, including both migrants and permanent residents, are probably unemployed or underemployed (Murphy, 2002; Whyte, 2010). As of 2009, Minimum Standard Living Allowances, a program to assist those in poverty, reached only 35 million urban (and 75 million rural) families.

Permanent residents in the cities often live in government housing, access municipal health services, and have access to schools for their children. But "rural laborers" and their dependents are usually denied these services (Carillo, 2011; Carrillo and Duckett, 2011). It was reported that the total num-

Robert E. Gamer

Miles of development accompany new highways like this one outside Shanghai.

ber of "temporary migrants" in cities reached 260 million in 2011, and many of them have already lived in cities for longer than ten years and still cannot be treated as "urban residents." Several issues related to these "temporary migrants" have caught attention in Chinese society: their access to urban welfare programs, their health care, their employment and living conditions, and the education of their children. A study in Nanjing found a third of all migrants living below the poverty line. A third of unemployed permanent urban residents also had earnings below that level but at least could access some of these benefits (Liu, He, and Wu, 2008). And migrations to towns and cities can leave villages with fewer resources for such services for those who remain, especially when they are far from urban markets where they can sell their produce, and when they have marginal dry or hilly land. Since much of this migration involves movement from poorer inland areas toward the coast, and since those most in need of such public services are in those villages or have left them, failure to adequately address these problems can increasingly leave China polarized between rich and poor (Whyte, 2010). The middle class is growing, but the poor are a larger group and growing even faster. Strikes and protests are on the rise. Chapters 4 and 5 address those issues.

Ethnic Minorities

Deeply entwined in these attempts to find balance between urban and rural is the need to keep the less urbanized inland provinces, largely inhabited by ethnic minorities, from falling behind the more urbanized and prosperous coastal provinces as modernization continues. China is a multiethnic country. As Chapter 3 discussed, even the Han majority is culturally divided, especially between south and north. Nonetheless, the Chinese government classifies about 92 percent of the populace as "Han," and divides the remaining "minorities" into fifty-five ethnic groups. This creates a somewhat artificial distinction between Han and everyone else, ignoring similarities shared by Han and minorities, and differences within the group classified as Han; ironically, it also helps rebel leaders give minority groups that have historically been divided reasons to unite (see Gladney, 2004; Litzinger, 2000; Schein, 2000; Harrell, 1996, 2002; Blum and Jensen, 2002). For an excellent introduction into how government officials drew up these distinctions, see Dreyer (1976). The central government also established many autonomous areas for the different ethnic minority groups: five autonomous provinces, thirty autonomous prefectures, and 120 autonomous counties. These areas—mostly in inland areas away from the coastal plains—cover about 64 percent of China's total territory. Even in those autonomous areas, much of the population is often from the Han majority group, who also tend to be among those in the most modernized sectors of the economy (Hansen, 2005).

In 2000, there were nine ethnic minority groups with populations over 4 million (see Table 8.3), while twenty-two groups contained fewer than 10,000 people. Table 8.3 makes it apparent that several groups had a very high growth rate between 1982 and 1990, though between 1990 and 2000, that growth slowed substantially (Harrell, 2001, 2002; Kaup, 2000). This stems largely from the fact that ethnic minorities receive special treatment under the new

Robert E. Gamer

A Dong minority mother watches her children in the village of Ma'an, Guangxi.

Table 8.3 Ethnic Minorities with a Population of More than 4 Million (millions)

	1982	1990	2000	Growth (%) 1982–1990	Growth (%) 1990–2000	Annual Growth Rate (%) 1982–1990	Annual Growth Rate (%) 1990–2000
Zhuang	13.38	15.49	16.18	15.7	4.5	1.8	0.4
Manchu	4.30	9.82	10.68	128.2	8.8	10.9	0.8
Hui	7.23	8.60	9.82	19.0	14.2	2.2	1.3
Miao	5.02	7.40	.94	46.9	20.8	5.0	1.4
Uyghur	5.96	7.21	8.40	21.0	16.5	2.4	1.5
Yi	5.45	6.57	7.76	20.4	18.1	2.4	1.7
Tujia	2.83	5.70	8.03	101.2	40.9	9.1	3.5
Mongolian	3.41	4.81	5.81	40.7	20.8	4.4	1.9
Tibetan	3.85	4.59	5.41	18.6	17.9	2.2	1.7

Sources: Population Census Bureau of China (Beijing: Chinese Statistical Publishing House, 1985, 1993); Provincial Statistical Yearbooks, various provinces (Beijing: China Statistics Press, 2001).

family planning program (see Chapter 10). Not only are they having more children than the rest of the populace, but investigations have found that during the 1980s, many individuals who had been classified as Han, but had a blood relationship with a minority, registered themselves as a minority (Manchu, Tujia, Miao, Mongolian, etc.) so as to have more children and to take advantage of other special privileges enjoyed by ethnic minorities. The central government allows ethnic minorities to enter colleges and universities with lower test scores, gives them priority for promotions in government institutions, and affords them other advantages to help them rise economically. However, many of them are not familiar with Mandarin, the language in which higher education is conducted, and come from families too poor to send them to school—or they attend crowded rural schools with low standards and high dropout rates (Bhalla and Qiu, 2006). This gives a special edge to Mandarin-speakers classified as minority.

The central government and the National People's Congress established a basic law for the autonomy of ethnic minorities, which pledges respect for the language, religion, and traditional customs of ethnic minorities and guarantees them equal rights (Davis, 2005). Among the fifty-five ethnic minority groups, two (Manchu and Hui) use the Mandarin language of the Han majority; fifty-three groups speak their own languages. Before 1949, only eighteen had written languages. In 1956, the government helped twelve groups create a new written language and helped three others revise their written language. There is also diversity of religion among ethnic minority groups in China. Of the fifty-five minorities, four are largely Tibetan Buddhists, four are Hinayana Buddhists, and ten are Muslim (Israeli, 2007; Benson and Svanberg, 1998); others adhere to religions such as shamanism. The government has also instituted programs to provide financial subsidies and investment to autonomous regions and to give more favorable consideration in education, housing, employment, cadre selection, social welfare, and childbearing to individuals belonging to ethnic minority groups.

Urbanization in minority regions developed rapidly after 1949. The population of Hohhot (the capital city of Inner Mongolia Autonomous Region) and Urumqi (the capital city of Xinjiang Uyghur Autonomous Region) more than doubled as those cities became newly industrialized and radically modernized. In Inner Mongolia Autonomous Region as a whole, urban population was 15.1 percent in 1953 and increased to 28.9 percent in 1982 and to 48.5 percent in 2007. The urban area of Lhasa (the capital city of Tibetan Autonomous Region) has expanded at least twelve times since 1952—when the Agreement on Measures for the Peaceful Liberation of Tibet was signed—to about half a million, but Tibet's population still remains largely rural (see Chapter 6).

The rapid growth of urban populations in ethnic minority regions is due partly to in-migration from Han majority regions, partly to natural increase of urban residents, and partly to rural-urban migration of local minorities. By moving into cities and living with Han urban residents—who have lived in cities and towns in many minority regions for centuries—these ethnic minorities gradually adapt to urban life and integrate with the Han (Mackerras, 1995; Hansen, 2005). Their language, religion, culture, and customs are respected by others under the law, but when they adopt a modern urban lifestyle, some of their customs gradually disappear. Many of them now wear suits, use telephones and computers, listen to popular music, and believe that modernization is the only way for the future of their groups. Some elderly people have difficulties adapting to urban life, and the generation gap that exists among all Chinese people extends to China's ethnic minorities as well.

Although the basic situation in coastal areas and cities has greatly improved with regard to income, housing, and public health care facilities, the Chinese government's 2006 Report on the Development of an Overall Well-off Society estimates that 48 million people in China still have income under 25 cents a day, while 135 million live on less than $1 a day. That problem persists. These people usually have high birthrates, high mortality rates, and a low life expectancy. Most of them are rural, and many live in these autonomous regions, largely outside the monetary economy. Promoting the development of these "poverty regions" is a key issue in China today. The government has initiated new programs for poorer rural dwellers, such as free tuition, rides to school, and relief from all taxation.

In 2000, the government launched a strategic plan to "develop the West" that resulted in huge investment and construction projects in Tibet, Xinjiang, and other inland provinces. Many projects are related to energy production, infrastructure, and urbanization. This resulted in a large number of Han majority migrating from coastal and central regions to western parts of China. The rapid economic development changed the cultural environment and traditional economic orders of local minority communities. In order to protect minority languages and traditional culture, the government established a parallel school system just for local minorities. Initially, minority students (Tibetan, Uyghur, Mongolian, Kazak, etc.) could complete their education from primary school to university in their mother tongue. This policy resulted in another problem: these minority graduates cannot speak fluent Mandarin (Putonghua, the common language in China, used by 95 percent of the total population) and they face difficulties in today's job market. Hence, the Chinese government has mandated bilingual education in Xinjiang and Tibet (Ma Rong, 2012). In the period of a planned economy, these graduates were guaranteed jobs by government assignment. When market mechanisms replaced a planned economy during the reform in the 1980s, employment of minority students became a serious social issue. The government enforced many programs to help these minority students to find jobs, and professional training is always a part of the "programs of province-minority region pair-partnership." The central government also established "inland Tibetan school/class" and "inland Xinjiang school/class" in coastal cities where minority students enjoy better educational resources (Chen, 2008; Zhu Zhiyong, 2007).

The "opening up" policy allows Chinese residents to travel abroad, including Muslim residents to travel to Pakistan, Afghanistan, and Saudi Arabia for pilgrimage. The impact of religious extremism and terrorism has been found in minority regions in China. Recent rioting in Xinjiang, Tibet, and elsewhere has caused some scholars to call for a review of the "nationality theory" and the Soviet model in designing ethnic relationships that China adopted from Stalin and the USSR from the 1950s (Ma Rong, 2007).

Challenges

At the beginning of the chapter, I referred to three "balancing acts" China must perform—between city and country, between population and food, and between regions of hardship and regions of prosperity. By now it must be evident that these three issues are themselves interrelated. The main challenges China faces in the twenty-first century regarding population and urbanization are as follows:

- China's population will continually increase even under the one-child policy designed to keep it down, reaching 1.5–1.6 billion in the 2030s. These people must have food, jobs, housing, health care, and social services.
- Because of family planning and the one-child policy, China is facing the problem of dealing with an aging population. The percentage of the population aged sixty or older was 10.3 percent of the total population of China (about 125 million) in 2000, rising to 13.3 percent in 2010 (175 million). Meanwhile,

those under fifteen shrunk from 32 percent (390 million) to 16.6 percent (220 million). As this progresses, along with the rise in life expectancy, more single children will be responsible for their aging parents and grandparents, and the number of working-age individuals will start to decline.

- About 250–300 million laborers will switch from agriculture to the nonagricultural sector in the next ten to fifteen years, which will result in a huge volume of rural-urban migration.
- Because of the rapid growth in the urban population due to both natural increase and migration, the pressure on housing and public services (including health care, schools, transportation, water and energy supply, and pollution control) will become very serious.
- Since most human resources and capital move from poor regions to prosperous regions under the market economy system, poverty in western China and ethnic minority regions will remain a problem of great concern.

Whether the national goal of modernization of China can be reached in the twenty-first century will largely depend on how successfully the Chinese government handles these challenges.

Bibliography

Banister, Judith. 1984. "An Analysis of Recent Data on the Population of China." *Population and Development Review* 10(2): 241–271.

Banister, Judith, and Kenneth Hill. 2004. "Mortality in China, 1964–2000." *Population Studies* 58(1): 55–75.

Barbieri-low, Anthony J. 2007. *Artisans in Early Imperial China*. Seattle: University of Washington Press.

Beaver, Steven E. 1975. *Demographic Transition Theory Reinterpreted*. Lexington, MA: Lexington Press.

Benson, Linda, and Ingvar Svanberg. 1998. *China's Last Nomads: The History and Culture of China's Kazaks*. Lanham, MD: M. E. Sharpe.

Bergère, Marie Claude. 2009. *Shanghai: China's Gateway to Modernity*. Stanford, CA: Stanford University Press.

Bhalla, Ajit S., and Shufang Qiu. 2006. *Poverty and Inequality Among Chinese Minorities*. London: Routledge.

Blum, Susan Deborah, and Lionel M. Jensen (eds.). 2002. *Mapping the Margins of the Middle Kingdom*. Honolulu: University of Hawaii Press.

Broudehoux, Anne, 2004. *The Making and Selling of Post-Mao Beijing*. London: Routledge.

Campanella, Thomas J. 2011. *The Concrete Dragon: China's Urban Revolution and What It Means for the World*. Princeton, NJ: Princeton Architectural Press.

Carrillo, Beatriz Garcia. 2011. *Small Town China: Rural Labour and Social Inclusion*. New York: Routledge.

Carrillo, Beatriz Garcia, and Jane Duckett (eds.). 2011. *China's Changing Welfare Mix: Local Perspectives*. New York: Routledge.

Carroll, Peter J. 2006. *Between Heaven and Modernity: Reconstructing Suzhou, 1895–1937*. Stanford, CA: Stanford University Press.

Chan, Kam Wing. 1996. *Cities with Invisible Walls: Reinterpreting Urbanization in Post-1949 China*. Oxford: Oxford University Press.
Chandler, Tertius. 1987. *Four Thousand Years of Urban Growth: An Historical Census*. Lewiston, ME: Edward Mellen.
Chang, Gordon G. 2011. "China's New Census: The Ancient Country Is Growing Old." *Forbes*, May 1.
Chao, Kang. 1987. *Man and Land in Chinese History: An Economic Analysis*. Stanford, CA: Stanford University Press.
Chao, Wenlin, and Xie Shujun. 1988. *History of China's Population*. Beijing: People's Press (in Chinese).
Chen, Aimin, Gordon G. Liu, and Kevin H. Zhang (eds.). 2004a. *Urban Transformation in China*. Burlington, VT: Ashgate.
——— (eds.). 2004b. *Urbanization and Social Welfare in China*. Burlington, VT: Ashgate.
Chen, Xiangming (ed.). 2009. *Shanghai Rising: State Power and Local Transformations in a Global Megacity*. Minneapolis: University of Minnesota Press.
Chen, Yangbin. 2008. *Muslim Uyghur Students in a Chinese Boarding School*. New York: Lexington Books.
China Population and Information Research Center. 1985, 2001, 2008. *Handbook of Population and Family Planning Data*. Beijing: Population Press of China.
Clausen, Soren, and Stig Thogersen. 1995. *The Making of a Chinese City: History and Historiography in Harbin*. Armonk, NY: M. E. Sharpe.
Davis, Deborah S., Richard Kraus, Barry Naughton, and Elizabeth J. Perry. 1995. *Urban Spaces in Contemporary China: The Potential for Autonomy and Community in Post-Mao China*. Cambridge: Cambridge University Press.
Davis, Sara L. M. 2005. *Song and Silence: Ethnic Revival on China's Southwest Borders*. New York: Columbia University Press.
den Hartog, Harry. 2010. *Shanghai New Towns: Searching for Identity in a Sprawling Metropolis*. Hong Kong: 010 Publishers.
"Dipping Into the Kitty." 2012. *The Economist* 403 (May 26): 8786.
Dong, Madeleine Yue. 2003. *Republican Beijing: The City and Its Histories*. Berkeley: University of California Press.
Dong, Madeleine Yue, and Joshua Goldstein (eds.). 2006. *Everyday Modernity in China*. Seattle: University of Washington Press.
Dong, Stella. 2001. *Shanghai: The Rise and Fall of a Decadent City, 1842–1949*. New York: Harper Perennial.
Dreyer, June Teufel. 1976. *China's Forty Millions: Minority Nationalities and National Integration in the People's Republic of China*. Cambridge, MA: Harvard University Press.
du Cros, Hilary, and Yok-shiu F. Lee (eds.). 2006. *Cultural Heritage Management in China: Preserving the Cities of the Pearl River Delta*. London: Routledge.
Dutton, Michael, Hsiu-Ju Stacy Lo, and Dong Dong Wu. 2010. *Beijing Time*. Cambridge, MA: Harvard University Press.
Edelmann, Frederik. 2008. *In the Chinese City: Perspectives on the Transmutation of an Empire*. New York: Actar.
Efird, Robert. 2001. *China Urban: Ethnographies of Contemporary Culture*. Durham, NC: Duke University Press.
Elvin, Mark, and G. William Skinner (eds.). 1974. *The Chinese City Between Two Worlds*. Stanford, CA: Stanford University Press.
Fan, Jie, Thomas Heberer, and Wolfgang Taubmann. 2006. *Rural China: Economic and Social Change in the Late Twentieth Century*. Armonk, NY: M. E. Sharpe.

Finnane, Antonia. 2004. *Speaking of Yangzhou: A Chinese City, 1550–1850*. Cambridge, MA: Harvard University Asia Center.
Fong, Vanessa. 2004. *Only Hope: Coming of Age Under China's One-Child Policy*. Stanford, CA: Stanford University Press.
Fong, Vanessa, and Rachel Murphy. 2005. *Chinese Citizenship: Views from the Margins*. London: Routledge.
Friedmann, John. 2005. *China's Urban Transition*. St. Paul: University of Minnesota Press.
Gamer, Robert E. 1998. "The Continuing Transformation of the Welfare State: Planning and Funding Housing and Transportation in Shanghai, London, Paris, and Kansas City." *Political Crossroads* (Australia) 6(1): 57–77.
Gaubatz, Piper Rae. 1996. *Beyond the Great Wall: Urban Form and Transformation on the Chinese Frontiers*. Stanford, CA: Stanford University Press.
Gifford, Rob. 2008. *China Road: A Journey into the Future of a Rising Power*. New York: Random House.
Gil, Iker. 2008. *Shanghai Transforming*. New York: Actar.
Gladney, Dru C. 2004. *Dislocating China: Muslims, Minorities, and Other Subaltern Subjects*. Chicago: University of Chicago Press.
Goldstein, Sidney, and Alice Goldstein. 1985. *Population Mobility in the People's Republic of China*. Papers of the East-West Population Institute No. 95. Honolulu: East-West Center.
Greenhalgh, Susan. 2008. *Just One Child: Science and Policy in Deng's China*. Berkeley: University of California Press.
Greenhalgh, Susan, and Edwin A. Winckler. 2005. *Governing China's Population: From Leninist to Neoliberal Biopolitics*. Stanford, CA: Stanford University Press.
Gu, Edward, and Jianjun Zhang. 2006. "Health Care Regime Change in Urban China: Unmanaged Marketization and Reluctant Privatization." *Pacific Affairs* 79(1): 49–71.
Guldin, Gregory Eliyu (ed.). 1997. *Farewell to Peasant China: Rural Urbanization and Social Change in the Late Twentieth Century*. Armonk, NY: M. E. Sharpe.
Haarman, Anke. 2010. *Shanghai Urban Public Space*. New York: Jovis.
Hansen, Mette Halskov. 1999. *Lessons in Being Chinese: Minority Education and Ethnic Identity in Southwest China*. Seattle: University of Washington Press.
———. 2005. *Frontier People: Han Settlers in Minority Areas of China*. Vancouver: University of British Columbia.
Harrell, Stevan (ed.). 1996. *Cultural Encounters on China's Ethnic Frontiers*. Seattle: University of Washington Press.
———. 2001. *Perspectives on the Yi of Southwest China*. Berkeley: University of California Press.
———. 2002. *Ways of Being Ethnic in Southwest China*. Seattle: University of Washington Press.
Haw, Stephen. 2006. *Beijing: A Concise History*. London: Routledge.
Henriot, Christian. 1993. *Shanghai, 1927–1937*. Berkeley: University of California Press.
Hessler, Peter. 2006. *River Town: Two Years on the Yangtze*. New York: Harper Perennial.
———. 2007. *Oracle Bones: A Journey Through Time in China*. New York: Harper Perennial.
———. 2010. *Country Driving: A Journey Through China from Farm to Factory*. New York: HarperCollins.
Hoy, Caroline. 2006. *Migration and Populations in China: Moving Peoples and Creating Change*. London: Routledge.

Hsing, You-tien. 2010. *The Great Urban Transformation: Politics of Land and Property in China*. Oxford: Oxford University Press.
Huang, Rongqing. 1993. "The Mortality of China in the 1980s." In *Selected Papers Presented at the Sixth National Conference on Population Science of China*, edited by Chinese Association of Population Studies, 137–143. Beijing: Chinese Association of Population Studies (in Chinese).
Iredale, Robyn, Naran Bilik, and Fei Guo (eds.). 2003. *China's Minorities on the Move: Selected Case Studies*. Armonk, NY: M. E. Sharpe.
Israeli, Raphael. 2007. *Islam in China: Religion, Ethnicity, Culture, and Politics*. Lanham, MD: Rowman and Littlefield.
Kaup, Katherine Palmer. 2000. *Creating the Zhuang: Ethnic Politics in China*. Boulder: Lynne Rienner.
Kiang, Heng Chye. 1999. *Cities of Aristocrats and Bureaucrats: The Development of Cityscapes in Medieval China*. Honolulu: University of Hawaii Press.
Lague, David. 2003. "The Human Tide Sweeps into Cities." *Far Eastern Economic Review* 166(1) (January 9): 24–28.
Lewis, Mark Edward. 2006. *The Construction of Space in Early China*. Albany: State University of New York Press.
Li, Yan, and Shufang Wu. 2010. "Migration and Health Restraints in China: A Social Strata Analysis." *Journal of Contemporary China* 19(64): 335–358.
Lin, Fude. 1986. "An Analysis of China's Birth Rates." In *Almanac of China's Population 185*, 237–246. Beijing: Chinese Social Sciences Publishing House (in Chinese).
Litzinger, Ralph. 2000. *Other Chinas: The Yao and the Politics of National Belonging*. Durham, NC: Duke University Press.
Liu, Yuanli, and Keqin Rao. 2006. "Providing Health Insurance in Rural China: From Research to Policy." *Journal of Health Politics, Policy, and Law* 31(1): 71–92.
Liu, Yuling, Shenjing He, and Fulong Wu. 2008. "Urban Pauperization Under China's Social Exclusion: A Case Study of Nanjing." *Journal of Urban Affairs* 30(1): 21–36.
Logan, John. 2002. *The New Chinese City: Globalization and Market Reform*. New York: Wiley-Blackwell.
Lu, Ding (ed.). 2011. *The Great Urbanization of China*. Singapore: World Scientific.
Lu, Duanfang. 2006. *Remaking Chinese Urban Form: Modernity, Scarcity, and Space, 1949–2005*. London: Routledge.
Lu, Hanchao. 2004. *Beyond the Neon Lights: Everyday Shanghai in the Early Twentieth Century*. Berkeley: University of California Press.
Ma Rong. 1992. "The Development of Small Towns and Their Role in the Modernization of China." In *Urbanizing China*, edited by Gregory E. Guldin, 119–154. New York: Greenwood Press.
———. 2007. "A New Perspective in Guiding Ethnic Relations in the 21st Century: 'De-politicization' of Ethnicity in China." *Asian Ethnicity* 8(3): 199–218.
———. 2012. "The Development of Minority Education and the Practice of Bilingual Education in Xinjiang Uyghur Autonomous Region." In *China's Assimilationist Language Policy*, edited by Gulbahar H. Beckett and Gerard Postiglione, 33–44. New York: Routledge.
Ma Yinchu. 1957 and 1981. "New Essay on Population." In *Collected Works of Ma Yinchu on Economics*, vol. 2, 174–195. Beijing: Peking University Press (in Chinese).
Mackerras, Colin. 1995. *China's Minority Cultures: Identities and Integration Since 1912*. New York: St. Martin's.

Meyer, Michael. 2009. *The Last Days of Old Beijing: Life in the Vanishing Streets of a City Transformed.* New York: Walker.

Ministry of Education of China. 2005. *Statistical Yearbook of Education.* Beijing: People's Education Press.

Moore, Malcolm, and Peter Foster. 2011. "China to Create Largest Megacity in the World with 42 Million People." *Telegraph,* January 24.

Murphy, Rachel. 2002. *How Migrant Labor Is Changing Rural China.* Cambridge: Cambridge University Press.

National Bureau of Statistics of China. 1950–2011. *Statistical Yearbook of China (1950–2011).* Beijing: China Statistics Press.

———. 2001 and 2009. *International Statistical Yearbook (2001, 2009).* Beijing: China Statistics Press.

Oates, Tim, and Louisa Schein (eds.). 2005. *Translocal China: Linkages, Identities, and the Reimagining of Space.* London: Routledge.

"Only and Lonely." 2011. *The Economist* 400 (July 23): 8743.

Pei, Xiaolin. 2005. "Collective Landownership and Its Role in Industrialization." In *Developmental Dilemmas: Land Reform and Institutional Change in China,* edited by Peter Ho, 203–227. London: Routledge

Peng, Xizhe. 1991. *Demographic Transition in China.* Oxford: Clarendon Press.

Pieke, Frank N., and Hein Mallee (eds.). 2000. *Internal and International Migration.* London: Curzon Press.

Population and Development Study Center. 1985. *The Data Sets of Population and Family Planning Statistics.* Beijing: Population Press of China.

———. 1993. *The Tabulation of the 1990 Population Census of the People's Republic of China.* Beijing: China Statistics Press.

———. 2009. *Data Handbook of Population and Family Planning.* Beijing: Population Press of China.

Population Census Bureau of China. 2002. *Tabulation on the 2000 Population Census of the PRC.* Beijing: Chinese Statistical Publishing House.

Poston, Dudley L., Che-fu Lee, Cheung-fang Chang, Sherry L. McKibben, and Carol S. Walther (eds.). 2009. *Fertility, Family Planning, and Population Policy in China.* London: Routledge.

Pridmore, Jay. 2008. *Shanghai: The Architecture of China's Great Urban Center.* New York: Abrams.

Qian, Wenbao. 1996. *Rural-Urban Migration and Its Impact on Economic Development in China.* Brookfield, VT: Ashgate.

Qu, Geping, and Li Jichang. 1992. *Population and Environment in China.* Beijing: Chinese Press of Environmental Sciences (in Chinese).

Reardon-Anderson, James. 2005. *Reluctant Pioneers: China's Expansion Northward, 1644–1937.* Stanford, CA: Stanford University Press.

Research Institute of State Council. 2006. *Report on Farm Workers in Cities in China.* Beijing: China Yanshi Press (in Chinese).

Rossabi, Morris (ed.). 2005. *Governing China's Multiethnic Frontiers.* Seattle: University of Washington Press.

Rozman, Gilbert (ed.). 1982. *The Modernization of China.* New York: Free Press.

Rudelson, Justin Jon. 1997. *Oasis Identities: Uyghur Identities: Uyghur Nationalism Along China's Silk Road.* New York: Columbia University Press.

Scharping, Thomas. 2002. *Birth Control in China: 1949–2000.* New York: Routledge.

Schein, Louisa. 2000. *Minority Rules: The Miao and the Feminine in China's Cultural Politics.* Durham, NC: Duke University Press.

Scocca, Tom. 2011. *Beijing Welcomes You: Unveiling the Capital City of the Future.* New York: Riverhead.

Skinner, William G. (ed.). 1977. *The City in Late Imperial China.* Cambridge, MA: Harvard University Press.

———. 2001. *Marketing and Social Structure in Rural China.* New York: Association for Asian Studies.

Solinger, Dorothy J. 1999. *Contesting Citizenship in Urban China: Peasant Migrants and the Logic of the Market.* Berkeley: University of California Press.

State Statistical Bureau. 1950–2010. *Statistical Yearbook of China.* Beijing: China Statistics Press.

Steinhardt, Nancy Shatzman. 1999. *Chinese Imperial City Planning.* Honolulu: University of Hawaii Press.

Strand, David. 1993. *Rickshaw Beijing: People and Politics in the 1920s.* Berkeley: University of California Press.

Tang, Wengfang, and William L. Parish. 2000. *Chinese Urban Life Under Reform: The Changing Social Contract.* Cambridge: Cambridge University Press.

Tang, Wing-Shing. 2007. *The Government of Urban Planning in Pre-Reform China.* London: Routledge.

Tien, H. Yuan. 1983. "China: Demographic Billionaire." *Population Bulletin* 38:2.

Unger, Jonathan. 2002. *The Transformation of Rural China.* Armonk, NY: M. E. Sharpe.

Van Slyke, Lyman P. 1988. *Yangtze: Nature, History, and the River.* Reading, MA: Addison-Wesley.

Wang, Di. 2003. *Street Culture in Chengdu: Public Space, Urban Commoners, and Local Politics, 1870–1930.* Stanford, CA: Stanford University Press.

Wang, Xiangming. 1986. "Urbanization of China's Population." In *Almanac of China's Population 1985,* 283–292. Beijing: Chinese Social Sciences Publishing House (in Chinese).

Warr, Anne, 2008. *Shanghai Architecture.* New York: Watermark Press.

Wasserstrom, Jeffrey. 2009. *Global Shanghai: 1850–2010.* London: Routledge.

White, Tyrene. 2009. *China's Longest Campaign: Birth Planning in the People's Republic, 1949–2005.* Ithaca, NY: Cornell University Press.

Whyte, Martin King (ed.). 2010. *One Country, Two Societies: Rural-Urban Inequality in Contemporary China.* Cambridge, MA: Harvard University Press.

World Bank (ed.). 1982–2011. *World Development Report.* New York: Oxford University Press.

——— (ed.). 1997–2011. *World Development Indicators.* Washington, DC: World Bank.

Wu, Fulong (ed.). 2005. *Globalization and the Chinese City.* London: Routledge.

Wu, Fulong, Jiang Xu, and Anthony Gar-On Yeh (eds.). 2006. *Urban Development in Post-Reform China: State, Market, Space.* London: Routledge.

Wu, Hung. 2005. *Remaking Beijing: Tiananmen Square and the Creation of Political Space.* Chicago: University of Chicago Press.

Xu, Yinong. 2000. *The Chinese City in Space and Time: The Development of Urban Form in Suzhou.* Honolulu: University of Hawaii Press.

Yan, Rui, and Cheng Shengqi. 1993. "Age-Specific Death Rates and Life Expectancy in the Past Forty Years." In *Collected Papers Presented at International Conference on Fertility Sampling Surveys of China,* edited by Chinese Association of Population Studies. Beijing: Population Press of China (in Chinese).

Yeh, Wen-hsin. 2007. *Shanghai Splendor: Economic Sentiments and the Making of Modern China: 1843–1949.* Berkeley: University of California Press.

Yeung, Yue-man. 2000. *Globalization and Networked Societies: Urban-Regional Change in Pacific Asia*. Honolulu: University of Hawaii Press.

Yeung, Yue-man, and Sung Wun-wing. 1996. *Shanghai: Transformation and Modernization under China's Open Policy*. Hong Kong: Chinese University Press.

Zhang, Li. 2002. *Strangers in the City: Reconfigurations of Space, Power, and Social Networks Within China's Floating Population*. Stanford, CA: Stanford University Press.

———. 2010. *In Search of Paradise: Middle Class Living in a Chinese Metropolis*. Ithaca, NY: Cornell University Press.

Zhu Zhiyong, 2007. *State Schooling and Ethnic Identity: The Politics of a Tibetan Neidi Secondary School in China*. New York: Lexington Books.

9

China's Environmental Problems

Richard Louis Edmonds

Chapter 8 discussed human problems; this one discusses the environment in which humans live and their interactions with it. The overall quality of China's environment has deteriorated considerably since the founding of the People's Republic of China (PRC) in 1949. More than doubling the population and rapid economic growth since 1949 has hastened deforestation, desertification, soil erosion, water shortages, glacial retreat, and pollution. The current population of over 1.34 billion already may have exceeded the number that the country can hope to support at a good standard of living relying on its own resources (Kitzes et al., 2008). Moreover rapid unequal economic growth has led to environmental social unrest increasing significantly since 2000 (Watts, 2007; Mertha, 2008). Environmental protests could destabilize the regime, and greenhouse gas emission growth could bring China into conflict with other nations. Meanwhile, the political system remains relatively unchanged, with thousands of local decisions affecting the environment largely beyond central government control. Even the most positive observers see the combination of huge population, economic growth, and lack of political transparency placing serious strains on China's environment.

Modification of China's environment, moreover, goes back a long way, as Rhoads Murphey explained in Chapter 3. When humans first settled on the Loess Plateau in north-central China (see Map 2.4), the area was probably covered with a mixture of forests and grasslands. Intensive use of some of these lands led to a reduction in vegetation and serious erosion on the plateau centuries ago. Similar problems occurred elsewhere as the proto-Chinese people proliferated, spread out from the Loess Plateau and the North China Plain, and incorporated other groups over the past 2,000 years (Edmonds, 1994:28–35). Even though the Han Chinese did evolve some ecologically sound agricultural practices that improved the quality of the soil, they stripped the land of forests as they spread southward (Vermeer, 1998:247–259). As they spread more slowly to the north and west, they began to farm virgin land and substantially degraded many of these fragile areas. Moreover, the pace of farming intensified as the population grew (Marks, 1998; Elvin and Liu, 1998; Elvin, 2004).

During the 1950s, the Chinese focused on reconstructing a war-torn country and devising means to promote rapid economic growth. Although these efforts led to better attempts at hygiene and health care, the government generally viewed natural resources as a commodity to be exploited to create wealth. After the creation of communes during the mid-1950s, many hillsides were cleared and wetlands filled to create new farmland. During the years of the so-called Great Leap Forward (1958–1961), huge numbers of trees were felled for fuel to produce low-quality steel in small, highly polluting home furnaces. From 1960 to 1962, China was hit with a drought that, combined with these policies, produced the Three Bad Years (1960–1962) of widespread famine and staggering estimations of death rates in the tens of millions (Dikötter, 2010). In 1966, just as the country was devising policies designed to avoid recurrence of such a catastrophe, Chairman Mao Zedong proclaimed the Cultural Revolution. Close to a decade of political unrest and lawlessness followed, and ecological degradation became commonplace (Shapiro, 2001; Li, 2007).

More vigorous efforts to deal with ecological problems began in a modest way in the early 1970s. In 1973, the government created the National Environmental Protection Agency, and environmental planning became included in national plans. Some Chinese academics and policymakers argued that economic development could not continue without considering its impact on the environment; others argued that China must follow the "pollute first and clean up later" phase that the developed world had experienced before pollution control received high priority. In 1979, the government promulgated an Environmental Protection Law (for trial implementation). Under this law, the agency began to write environmental impact statements on proposed heavy industry, manufacturing, and infrastructure projects. However, the recommendations of these impact statements generally were ignored and were not available to the public.

From 1982, the concept of harmonious development (*xietiao fazhan*), similar to the idea of sustainable development formulated by the Bruntland Commission, was adopted as official policy. It was supposed to increase efficiency by initiating recycling and pollution-abatement measures. However, the new small entrepreneurs who flourished after economic reform did not comply with the plan. A full-fledged Environmental Protection Law was adopted in 1989, but environmental policy decisions continued to be held back by vagueness of the laws, local priorities that accentuated economic growth and corruption, as well as the relative weakness of many local environmental protection bureaus in the local bureaucracy (Ma and Ortolano, 2000; Ross, 1988; Chen, 2009:16–32).

In the 1990s, the Chinese system began to open in a restricted way with the formation of nongovernmental organizations (NGOs), although many were either "government-organized NGOs" or had to register under the supervision of government sponsors leading to what could be called an embedded structure (Ho and Edmonds, 2007). New laws such as the 2003 Environment Impact Assessment Law and the 2006 Provisional Measures for Public Participation in Environmental Impact Assessment allowed for a modest increase in public participation in environmental matters (Moore and Warrant, 2006:5–6; Chen, 2009:33–52) but, as already mentioned in Chapter 4, protest has grown considerably. The rapid growth of China's role in the international economy in the last two decades has been accompanied by growing demands from the international community for China to adhere to international environmental standards at the level of a developed country. At the same time, however, there is evidence that China's pollution problems sped up in the early years after joining the World Trade Organization in 2001 (Chen, 2009:26–32).

Contemporary Environmental Problems

Pollution has grown rapidly in China while water supply, vegetation, soil quality, and other natural resources are dwindling. Urbanization also is rapid, with plans to relocate hundreds of millions of rural people to cities by 2030. These people most likely will increase their energy consumption as they move into cities. There may well be a metacity stretching all the way from Beijing in the north through Shanghai to Hong Kong in the south by 2020 (Stamoran, 2010). China already has much less land area, forest cover, and water resources per person than the average country. Cropland accounts for only 10 percent of China's total area, and both the per capita level and the total quantity of arable land are decreasing despite attempts to reclaim wastelands. In the twenty-first century, China has begun to get around some of these problems by importing resources, which has facilitated environmental degradation in other countries.

Water Shortages

China's water shortage has grown steadily throughout the reform period (Ma, 2004; Gleick 2009; Zhao and Seng, 2010:165–194). The country currently supports 20 percent of the world's population with only 8 percent of the world's water. Many rivers, lakes, reservoirs, and aquifers have shrunk or dried up during the last three decades, and China has stopped expanding its irrigated area since the beginning of the 1980s. Water shortage is at its worst north of the Huai River (roughly, in a line due west along the mouth of the Yangtze River; see Map 2.4), where 64 percent of China's cultivated land has access to only 19 percent of the country's water, and there is considerable annual variation in precipitation. The water table in northern China has fallen more than 200 feet (60 meters) since 1970 and is currently estimated to be falling a meter a year (Qiu, 2010). Some eastern and northern cities have sunk as the earth settles to adjust to this loss of water and the construction of large buildings. For example, land in Shanghai (Map 2.2) subsided at a rate of 5–7 millimeters per year from 2001 to 2006 (Lee, 2006). Subsiding can lead to floods during storms and can destroy building foundations. Although rising sea levels, increased erosion, and geological movements of the earth's crust can be responsible for this condition, the lowering of the water table also is a key factor.

The water supply problem is most acute around big cities in northern China, where precipitation levels are lower than in the south. It is said that two-thirds of China's official 660 cities are water short and 108 of those suffer severe shortages (Cheng, Yuanan, and Jianfu, 2009:241). Major efforts to save water by recycling or to increase water through diversion projects began in the 1980s. The Huang (Yellow) River has stopped flowing virtually every year since 1985, and dried up for seven months in 1998, resulting in the August 2002 announcement of a ten-year project to tackle environmental problems. Flow rate has improved recently, and there are estimates that climate change will lead to increased flow in the river due to faster glacier melt—while the glaciers last (Loeve and Immerzeel, 2009). Whether flow shortages are avoided or not, a project to move water north via the Grand Canal is likely to be completed by 2013, as well as along a second, central route from the Three Gorges (Sanxia) Dam after the 2014 flood season (Demick, 2010). As northern China's water shortages continue to grow, conservation of existing water resources is of primary importance. Because irrigation water is often used in an inefficient manner, the government has modestly increased charges and advocated dry-land farming, and water quotas assigned to industries have resulted in some savings; water associations have also helped improve water management in rural areas. So far, household water use has not been very wasteful compared to agriculture. As incomes continue to increase, however, and more people move from older housing into homes with modern plumbing, domestic water consumption increases. Recent studies suggest that industrial water pollution contributes more to China's water shortages than was previously assumed (World Bank, 2007:xvi). The water shortage problem has even become an international issue as China increasingly builds dams in the upper reaches of rivers that flow into other countries, causing concern in Southeast and South Asia (see Chapter 7; Chellaney, 2007).

Forest Loss and Recovery

All major basins now experience annual floods and drought, due in part to forest loss. The State Forestry Administration indicated in 2009 that a national survey revealed that China had forest cover equal to 20.36 percent of the country's total area, which is roughly two-thirds of the world average (Hou, 2009), and less than the cover in 1949 but higher than the 18.21 percent coverage in 2003. The forestry responsibility system established in the early 1980s, with quotas and fines, stopped the decline. But in some remote areas, lack of state control rules out enforcement of laws. Illegal logging activities have been widespread, especially as the market economy makes it easy to sell timber. The state wood-supply system was excessively wasteful due to a lack of realistic pricing mechanisms. Recent moves toward higher, more appropriate timber prices appear to have reduced waste but have added to the incentive to log. Fire and disease also continue to reduce vegetation cover. Forest management has been corrupt and inefficient; the natural forests that remain today have been saved largely by inaccessibility.

China aims to reach 26 percent forest coverage by 2050. There are several large projects to plant trees along 77,000 square miles (200,000 square kilometers) along the middle and upper reaches of the Yangtze River, around Beijing, in the north, and elsewhere (Yin and Yin, 2009:1–12). These programs have planted billions of trees.

In addition, the Obligatory Tree-Planting Program, adopted in 1981, requires all Chinese citizens above eleven years old to plant three to five trees each year or do other relevant forestry work, although reports suggest only a little over half the targeted population participated in the obligatory tree planting programs. Most Chinese cities, and many areas in the countryside, show the benefits of urban tree-planting programs along streets and highways.

Soil Erosion and Nutrient Loss

China has one of the most serious soil erosion problems in the world. Conservative estimates suggest that one-sixth of the nation's arable land is affected. Between 5,000 and 10,000 million metric tons of soil are washed down rivers each year. Rapid soil erosion has contributed to China's overall environmental degradation in several ways. Riverbeds, lakes, and reservoirs are silting up and have had their hydroelectric and flood control storage capacity reduced. The loss of good-quality topsoil has reduced arable land and threatens to cause serious food shortages in the near future.

Some of the most severe erosion occurs in northern portions of the semiarid Loess Plateau of north-central China (see Map 2.4). According to some reports, the plateau loses about a third of an inch (0.838 centimeters) of topsoil each year. The Chang (Yangtze) River valley in central China and Heilongjiang and eastern Inner Mongolia in the northeast are other badly affected areas. A 2007 report stated that the chernozem black soil belt of the northeast had been reduced in thickness from 31 inches (80 centimeters) to less than 12 inches (30 centimeters) between the 1940s and the 2000s, while in the same period the organic content had dropped by 12 percent. Even areas in the far south that once had little erosion—such as Yunnan, Hainan, and Fujian—have had severe soil erosion in the last three decades.

China has made considerable effort to stem the flow of topsoil. A massive area of eroded land that has been improved since the mid-1950s has been planted with trees or terraced. In addition, tens of thousands of check dams have been built across small gullies to control erosion. Today the focus has shifted from individual plots to entire river basins and from central to local government. The problem is the massive scale of the effort required. As the erosion is being checked in one area, it may be increasing in another.

The increased erosion largely resulted from policies implemented since the 1950s that opened steep slopes, formerly forested areas, and wetlands to farming; population growth also makes it difficult to reduce the population numbers on the land (Shapiro, 2001). Still, some of those areas that were opened up are being returned to forests and herding. However, many of the areas where such policy needs to be carried out are generally poor and hard to reach with grain shipments during the transition from agriculture to forestry or herding. Therefore, it is hard to persuade peasants to change or to enforce policies.

China's soils lack nutrients even where they are not yet degraded to a point that crops will not grow. For example, the rich yields of southern China have been obtained only through heavy labor inputs and the widespread use of manure and composted matter. The natural organic content of China's soil averages less than 1.5 percent. However, there is great regional variety in China's soils. Today, some peasants are beginning to practice "ecological agriculture," combining farming, animal husbandry, and forestry with local food processing and reuse of residual materials.

On Hainan Island (Map 2.2) and in nearby regions of the south, peasants have grown three rounds of crops a year in a field. When the only crop they grow is rice in flooded wet-paddy fields and drainage is poor, gleization (depletion of oxygen from iron compounds in the soil) can reduce the land's ability to grow rice or other crops. Approximately one-sixth of China's paddy lands suffer from gleization.

Desertification and Salinization-Alkalinization

Approximately one-quarter of China's land is degraded by dry climate and sand or rocky desert. Despite some progress in recent years, an almost continuous belt of degraded land stretches for 3,400 miles (5,500 kilometers) from northwest to northeast China (see Map 2.4). Desertification already affects millions of people and vast areas of pasturage, cropland, and rangeland, as well as railway lines, roads, and even the Great Wall (Williams, 2002). Sandstorms related to desertification cause considerable economic damage. Most notably, the government worries about dust storms that affect the Beijing and Tianjin areas and has been investing considerable amounts of funds in the areas to the northwest of Beijing to stop this. The Lhasa to Beijing rail line, which opened in 2006, is built atop complex erosion control terraces and nitrogen-filled tubing to counteract melting of the permafrost.

Desertification over the past two decades has largely occurred on agricultural land that can be restored. However, the northwest arid region is also showing a modest increase in desertification that will be hard to rectify.

Desertification and water shortages go hand-in-hand. A twenty-four-year study completed in 2004 by the Chinese Academy of Sciences found 46,298 glaciers throughout China totaling 22,936 square miles (59,406 square kilometers). That represents a reduction of 5.5 percent in total square miles, and 7 percent in total amount of ice, over the prior forty years. Annual mean temperatures have been rising in the northwest at a rate of .7 degrees Fahrenheit every ten years, causing glaciers there to recede nearly twice as fast as when the study began, triggering dust storms and diminishing the flow of the Yellow, Yangtze, West, Brahmaputra, Mekong, Ganges, Salween, Irrawaddy, and Indus Rivers, all of which have their source in the mountains of this region. If this rate of melt continues, nearly all the glaciers could be gone by the end of the twenty-first century, leaving these rivers without a steady water source and rapidly speeding desertification. The UN Intergovernmental Panel on Climate Change, as well as others, predict a much faster rate of melt than that ("Glacier Study," 2004; "Tibetan Glacier Melt," 2006; Collier, 2007; Intergovernmental Panel, 2007; Morton, 2011).

Robert E. Gamer

A view of one of China's 46,298 glaciers, which are rapidly shrinking due to climate change.

Although China has improved an estimated 15,000 square miles (39,000 square kilometers) of salinized-alkalinized land since 1949, problems of salinization and alkalinization are becoming more serious due to inefficient drainage and excessive irrigation, which have increased the levels of salts in the soil. Various estimates indicate that a fifth of China's irrigated cropland is salinized and some counties in the drier counties of Northeast China have more than 20 percent of their land salinized (Li et al., 2007:422). Crops sensitive to salt cannot grow on this land. It appears that the total area affected by salinization is continuing to grow. Overpumping in coastal areas has also allowed saltwater to seep into the groundwater supply. The major land reclamation projects carried out during the Great Leap Forward in the late 1950s destroyed many wetlands that had helped dissipate excess water during flood periods (Shapiro, 2001). This led to increased flooding and salinization of flooded areas. Today, more wetland areas are being filled for industrial development and housing.

Pollution

China's industries are major polluters. By 2009, over 42 percent of the tested sections of China's major river systems was categorized in the lowest two grades of water quality, with the Hai, Liao, Songhua, and Huai Rivers having the worst quality; and close to 54 percent of China's lakes failed to meet China's Grade III standard, with over a third failing to even make the lowest Grade V (Government of China, 2010). A sensitive figure was removed from a World Bank report, *Cost of Pollution in China* (2007), suggesting over 60,000 premature deaths were attributable to poor-quality water annually, largely in rural areas (McGregor, 2007a). The same report noted that water scarcity and pollution resulted in more than US$21 billion a year in losses (Barboza, 2007:A3). Pollution of surface water in the cities remains serious.

Water pollution is more serious in populous eastern China than in the west and in the northeastern quarter of the country in particular. An estimated 115 million rural people rely on surface water, which makes them particularly vulnerable to possible pollution (World Bank, 2007). In general, only lakes and reservoirs that provide drinking water have been protected, and even some of these have levels of ammonia nitrogen higher than the national standards. Pollution is especially severe in small lakes near urban areas. Problems in many large lakes, such as Tai Lake, Chao Lake, and Dianchi Lake, appear to be spreading from smaller bodies of water. The summer of 2007 saw these lakes hit with severe blue-green algae pollution, rendering water supplies to some cities and towns undrinkable. (For Tai Lake, see Chen, 2009:76–87.)

There have been some alarming recent cases of pollution of the coastal seas and some estuaries and bays. The most poignant case was pollution of the Bo Sea off the northern China coast, which had become so serious that a fifteen-year cleaning program was launched in 2001. However, pollution off the

China coast around Shanghai and Hangzhou, and farther south around Guangzhou, Hong Kong, and Macau, is probably the worst in China today.

Pollution from organic chemicals and heavy metals has been serious in places, although heavy metal pollution has been reduced in recent years. Inorganic nitrogen and phosphorus generally exceed the Chinese maximum limit in coastal waters. Oil concentrations above fishery standards have been found in coastal waters such as the Pearl River Delta around Guangzhou, Dalian Bay, and Jiaozhou Bay. Red tides, which refer to seawater discolored by certain types of marine plankton that feed on pollution and are fatal to many forms of marine life, continue to increase along China's coastline.

The groundwater around some cities has been found to contain phenols, cyanides, chromium, chlorides, nitrates, sulfates, and an increasing degree of hardness. Wells have had to be shut down. In recent years, this pollution has improved in some cities and grown worse in others. Lowered water tables around some coastal cities have added to salinization of groundwater. In many cases, people have taken to drinking bottled water, but fake bottled water has undermined confidence in this source (Zhao, 2007).

Water pollution problems are by no means confined to urban areas. In suburban and rural areas with relatively high densities of farm animals, an increase in nitrates can be detected in the soil and water. Many small rivers have become anoxic—no longer able to sustain aquatic life. As mentioned above, many lakes such as Tai and Dianchi are suffering from eutrophication—overloads of organic pollution.

Although China has undertaken increased efforts to improve soils in a wide range of environments, soil pollution has negated much of this initiative. It has been said that one-tenth to one-fifth of all cropland is suffering from heavy-metal pollution (Xie and Li, 2010:8).

Increased and improper applications of chemical fertilizers, coupled with growing livestock production, have also led to degradation of soil quality in rural areas. China's fertilizer usage is higher than the world average, and peasants often use nitrogen-rich human and animal wastes as fertilizer. Combining human and animal wastes with fertilizer made of plant and rock materials results in balanced enhancement of crop output, but when human and animal wastes are combined with nitrogen-rich chemical fertilizer, the soil receives too much nitrogen and crop yields drop (Smil, 2005). As of the late 2000s, China produces almost one-quarter and consumes over a third of the chemical fertilizer used in world agriculture (Niu, 2010).

Pesticide use remains heavy and excessive in some areas, surpassing levels used in most Asian countries but on a par with Japan and South Korea. Between 2000 and 2008, production of pesticides in China increased 2.8-fold (Jin et al., 2010:139). In recent years, despite the growth of a pesticide monitoring system, lack of oversight and rapid growth have led to unscrupulous entrepreneurs selling foods processed with cheap substitutes and additives, many of which are poisonous; cases of people dying both inside China and in other countries from Chinese foods and other products have been reported.

During the period of communization, the Chinese had considerable success using various combinations of plants and animals, instead of pesticides, as a method of integrated pest management. Such integrated pest management can only be effectively practiced over a wide area; by 1979, they were using this method over a larger area than any country in the world (Sanders, 2000). With the demise of communes and the return to family farming, though, individual farmers have reverted to using pesticides. However, since around 2003, China has seen some success at introducing foxes, weasels, and starlings to eat pests such as rats and locusts, principally in northwestern China.

When chemical fertilizers became more available around 1980, many peasants stopped using human waste as fertilizer, and "night soil" collection became a problem in cities used to disposing of waste by carrying it out to the fields. The use of manure and human wastes as fertilizer increased moderately from the mid-1980s, but worries that now more industrial wastes from the increasing number of rural enterprises are mixed in appear to be justified.

Biogas appears to be a good but minor solution to both the solid waste and the energy shortage problems in rural China, which goes through cycles of promotion and relative abandonment. Biogas, also known as marsh gas or gobar gas, is methane produced by the decomposition of organic matter. The gas can be generated in reactors into which crop waste, animal and human excrement, and a fermenting agent are placed. The residual sludge from this process is organic and makes an excellent fertilizer.

At its height in 1978, the Chinese said there were 7 million biogas small-scale reactors in use, mostly in southern China. The transformation to family farming generally hurt the production of biogas, since the communes provided a larger-scale operation for reactors, and the labor force needed to maintain them. Although biogas made a small comeback in the early 1990s, the number of reactors in use was still below the totals for the late 1970s. In 1999, the UN Development Programme (UNDP) began to help Chinese livestock and poultry farms commercialize biogas. The Chinese government is giving subsidies to farmers to build larger-scale biogas reactors to control stock farm pollution in part because of greenhouse gas concerns, although the number of such operations remains small and residue water from the process can still be polluting (Barclay, 2010). Another solution to emerge on the scene in recent years is shale gas, which China is beginning to pursue in Sichuan, Liaoning, and other areas (Liu and Turner, 2011). However, there are questions about water usage and pollution in connection with this new gas extraction method that suggest it might not be the best solution for a water-short country like China. Yet another area of expansion is in biofuels and, most notably for China, "second generation biofuels," which are oils made from agricultural wastes instead of agricultural food products. Second-generation biofuels could be produced on a commercial scale in China by 2013, with bioethanol and biodiesel expected to grow in use over the subsequent decade and all automotive gasoline planned to be made from biofuel by 2020 (Wang Xiaotan, 2011).

Total household rubbish is increasing rapidly and has reach 190 million metric tons a year, or roughly 30 percent of the world's total (Zhuang et al., 2008). Although there is still a tendency toward more wet rubbish in Chinese cities, trash in Shanghai and many other urban areas contains as much heavy metals and other inorganic matter as that found in any city in Europe or North America. Around mining sites in rural areas, tailings of milled ore residues create reservoirs of polluted water. A considerable proportion of the waste released by industry is dumped directly into rivers and streams.

China's refuse generally contains a larger amount of coal ash than is found in developed countries. Although some of this is being put to use for paving roads, more is generated than can be used. Although China is attempting to shift from solid fuels to gas, especially in urban areas, this is offset by the growth of city populations and rural development, such that the refuse problem still grows. In order to increase natural gas supply to keep up with rapid demand, China is importing considerable amounts, both by pipeline and as liquefied natural gas (China was self-sufficient up to 2006 and may be importing 25–45 percent of its total supply by 2030) (Collins and Erickson, 2010: Kopits 2011). It is also expanding coalbed methane production and is experimenting with coalbed methane liquification.

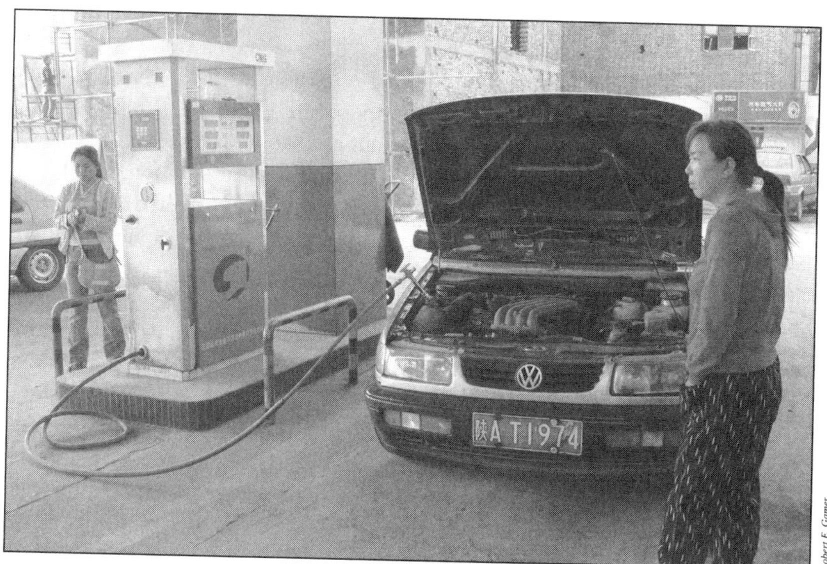

Robert E. Gamer

Filling up on natural gas.

Most urban refuse is removed by truck or boat to farms or rural dumping sites at ever-increasing distances from cities. Plastic containers and other non-degradable forms of refuse are increasing. China has a shortage of incinerators and of systems for lining dump sites to prevent polluted water from the trash from seeping into the surrounding groundwater. Research into how to bury rubbish in lined landfills began only in 1986, and the first modern incineration plant was built in Shenzhen in 1987. China only began to set up toxic waste storage sites during the 1990s and the number of brownfield sites is increasing, with some dating from the 1950s and penetrating the soil up to 10 meters in depth (Xie and Li, 2010:3).

A nuclear power station became operational at Qinshan in Zhejiang province during 1991; by 2011, thirteen were in operation and twenty-seven under construction, although China's future nuclear plans may be curtailed in light of the Fukushima nuclear disaster in Japan. So far, the Chinese say that monitoring at power plants has indicated no perceivable impacts on the surrounding environment. Nuclear power as of 2009 accounted for only 1.9 percent of China's power supply, compared to 20.2 percent in the United States, 28.9 percent in Japan, and 75.2 percent in France. While China's plans to build new plants may be scaled back, it is highly likely that the amount of energy produced from nuclear fuel will still increase significantly during the next two decades.

Meanwhile, new coal-fired power stations are coming into operation at a rapid rate. New cement plants, steel mills, aluminum smelters, and petrochemical, glass, paper, and other energy-intensive industries are constantly opening. And 26,000 new automobiles go into service each day. Together they are responsible for creating greenhouse gases, which include CO_2, methane, and nitrous oxide. China's total carbon dioxide emissions of 6.2 billion tons surpassed that of the United States at 5.8 billion tons around 2006. The US Energy Information Service has predicted an almost doubling of China's CO_2 emissions between 2006 and 2030 (World Nuclear Association, 2011). In 2009, annual sales of automobiles surpassed sales in the United States, and some expect Chinese growth to continue at 15 percent per annum to 2016 (Yang and Yu, 2011:17–36). In 1992, China produced 1 million cars, growing to 18 million cars in 2010, by which time the country had over 95,000 gasoline stations. China's oil demand in 2009 was close to 8.6 million barrels of oil a day (vs. 18.6 million in the United States), and the amount keeps growing as new vehicles pour onto the road.

Coal combustion is responsible for two-thirds of the nitrogen oxides (NO_x) emitted in China. Nitrogen oxide pollution is not yet serious when compared with CO_2, particles and sulfur dioxide, but traffic congestion in cities has created levels of NO_x at intersections that often exceed the safety level. Use of gasoline for cars and industry is increasing rapidly, so emissions of carbon monoxide, hydrocarbons, and nitrogen oxides will increase; catalytic converters on new vehicles became mandatory in 2000. Car numbers in mid-2010 were growing at a rate of more than 26,000 a day.

Particle levels in Chinese cities, about half of which is caused by coal combustion, are worse than in most urban areas in industrialized countries. In 2009, China accounted for 46 percent of the world's coal consumption compared to 13 percent for the United States. About 70 percent of China's energy was produced by burning coal; that is not likely to change much until at least 2025, when pipelines from newly acquired oil fields in Kazakhstan are completed and make petroleum more steadily available. Much coal is unwashed and burned in small-to-medium–sized furnaces often with poorer efficiency than is the case of Japan, the United States, or India. Progress made in particle control has been negatively offset largely by increased coal consumption. Particulate levels are higher in the cities and provinces of the north (Beijing, Tianjin, Qinghai, Liaoning, and Ningxia) but, by 2009, 82 percent of China's major monitored sites officially had reached acceptable levels. But there are serious questions about the accuracy of China's air pollution monitoring growth in the number of the more dangerous small-sized particulates and a view that the situation has not improved in recent years (Andrews, 2008–2009; Lin et al., 2010). Problems are also relatively severe in Chongqing and Hunan in the south.

Older homes in Chinese cities use coal. Lung cancer rates among housewives in such homes are higher than in any other segment of the population, with the heavy use of hot oils for cooking also contributing to the problem. The World Bank (2007) report, *Cost of Pollution in China,* written with the cooperation of Chinese ministries, had about 30 percent of the text cut, including a sensitive finding that 750,000 people die prematurely each year from urban air pollution, with perhaps 300,000 of those dying from poor air indoors (McGregor, 2007b; World Bank, 2007; Ho and Nielsen, 2007). While newer housing is relatively more efficient, new appliances mean that urban Chinese are using far more energy than their rural cousins—and efficiency still remains well below Germany's or Japan's. Cancer rates from air and water pollution are said to be rising rapidly. In 2011, the Ministry of Health revealed that cancer had become the leading cause of death in China—responsible for close to a fourth of all deaths (Larsen, 2011).

China is now thought to be the largest emitter of sulfur dioxide (SO_2) in the world. Sulfur dioxide, like particulate, is closely connected with coal smoke, which produces the vast majority of SO_2 emissions. Sulfur dioxide causes acid rain, which is estimated to cost China more than $4 billion a year in crop damage (Barboza, 2007:A3), as well as close to $1 billion in material damage (World Bank, 2007:xvi). More than 30 percent of the country's total area is subject to acid rain. The problem is most serious in the area east of the Qinghai-Tibetan Plateau, including the Sichuan Basin and south of the Yangtze River (see Map 2.4). Because of the high temperatures in the atmos-

Robert E. Gamer

Despite national regulations, many smokestacks remain unscrubbed.

phere there, sulfur dioxide converts to acid faster than in most northern industrial countries. More than half of the rainfall in southern China is now overly acidic. There has been some minor reduction in acidity in recent years with a regional air quality monitoring program launched in 2005 (Chan and Yao, 2008:30–31; see Chapters 4 and 5).

New wind-powered electrical generating plants are also under construction, and solar buildings as well as bases have been constructed; manufacturing is growing with China now the largest producer of solar panels (Campana, 2010; Yang and Yu, 2011:81–100, 137–198). China is also the largest geothermal energy producer and is talking about producing much more. Still, the proportions of solar and geothermal in domestic use remain small compared to conventional energy generation.

Noise has received low priority compared with other forms of pollution but regulations have toughened in recent years. Before 1982, there were no standards set for construction materials. Many buildings were built with steel-reinforced concrete panels little more than an inch (3 or 4 centimeters) thick. When one walked on the stairs in these buildings, the noise produced sounded like drumbeats. Economic development over the last two decades has added significant amounts of high-tech living to the mix—most notably mechanized transport. As of 2009, a little under one-quarter of the 113 key Chinese cities were considered noise polluted by Chinese standards (Government of China, 2010). The average equivalent sound levels of road traffic in these key cities ranged between 63.0 and 71.6 A-weighted decibels (dBA). For reference, at constant exposure, the level considered damaging to the ear is 75 dBA; serious hearing impairment can occur after eight hours of exposure at 100 dBA (Jones, Forbes, and Hollier, 1990:107–108, 300).

Citizen complaints about noise have mushroomed in the twenty-first century, making noise control a major issue in urban China. The government is concentrating on reducing noise from traffic, construction, and industry, as well as residential noise, and most rigorously in urban areas. Despite a slight improvement in noise statistics in the last decade, most Beijing residents feel noise has worsened in recent years ("China Tackles Worsening Pollution," 2011). Nationally, more attention is being paid to constructing noise barriers along high-speed expressways and other transport corridors as well as enforcing bans on nighttime construction. The government also has required that each of the 113 key cities have at least one billboard that will inform cities of noise levels (Li, 2011).

Pollution problems in general are compounded by the favoritism that many industries receive from local government, which allows them to operate inefficient equipment without scrubbers or sewage treatment (Ho and Vermeer, 2006). Official statistics suggest that progress has been made in the treatment of industrial wastes and that levels of air, water, and noise pollution in many major Chinese cities has dropped since 1989. The picture in rural China is less clear and varies from region to region.

Many waste-producing industries have relocated from the urban areas to the countryside over the past three decades. There has been some moderate local success in the control of rural pollution, but streams of consumer wastes and agricultural runoff, along with illegal dumping of industrial and municipal wastes, are growing problems (Fan, 2008). Many rural areas, particularly along the prosperous east coast, have employed complex and intensive waste-recycling systems to produce high-value products such as silk and freshwater fish. In some cases, pollution in rural areas has been reduced by consolidating small plants so their wastes can be treated and minerals recycled. However, the number of serious cases of untreated rural wastes being discharged is still growing. Many rural villages continue to freely dump and burn their waste without sorting. Sewage monitoring has increased since the 1990s. Automatic water-monitoring systems had been set up, but the level of equipment manufactured on the ground remains over a decade behind that in much of the developed world, though that is rapidly improving (Innovation Center Denmark, 2009:20). There have been cases where control facilities are installed but then, to cut costs, are not run. Moreover, local governments, which have close ties to industries, often resist enforcement. Pollution problems continue to grow or at best stabilize in China despite significant efforts in recent years to address them. The costs of pollution have been tremendous in economic terms. Progress has been made in relative reductions of certain pollutants at certain times, but overall the situation is still getting worse. The task for the future is to experiment with methods to regulate emissions effectively, including raising local government accountability and cutting energy consumption per unit of GDP.

Nature Conservation

China is known as a treasure house for many rare species of wildlife. The first nature reserve and laws directly dealing with nature conservation appeared in 1956. In the early 1980s, the government set up a wildlife protection bureau, an office to control import and export of endangered species, and the China Wildlife Conservation Association (Enderton, 1985). In 1988, the government devised China's first wildlife protection law, which stipulated details of administration and punishments. In 1992, the State Council promulgated Regulations on the Protection of Terrestrial Wild Fauna of the People's Republic of China, and the government published the first volume of China's *Redbook on Flora: Rare and Endangered Flora*. Local governments have followed suit with similar laws and regulations, but many species continue to dwindle. At the end of 2009, there were 2,541 nature reserves in China covering about 14.7 percent of China's national land territory. Nature reserves are organized into three types: wildlife, natural ecosystem, and natural monuments, with wildlife occupying the largest area (McBeath and Leng, 2006). In addition, as of 2010, there was an expanding system of a hundred wetland parks and close to 750 national forest parks geared toward tourism. In 2002, the State Bureau of Forestry established a Forest Parks Administration Office for their management.

The administration of nature reserves in China is not uniform, however. Many of China's nature reserves are considered national nature preserves (319 in 2010), and others are classified as provincial or local. Different reserves are often administered by different organizations and at different government levels. On the whole, the forestry bureaus tend to dominate because nature conservation work began in the Ministry of Forestry (now called the State Forestry Administration), although oversight of the system is now under the Ministry of Environmental Protection. Other government organs involved in nature reserve management and supervision include the Ministry of Land and Resources, the Ministry of Water Resources, the Ministry of Agriculture, the Chinese Academy of Natural Sciences, and the State Oceanic Administration.

Vertebrate species are protected in the PRC at first-class or second-class levels of protection. China also has three categories of protected plant species. Animals and plants receiving first-class protection are those that are endemic, rare, precious, or threatened. Those accorded second-class protection are species whose numbers are declining or whose geographical distribution is becoming more restricted. The third-class species are plants of economic importance, and thus harvesting is to be limited. In general, the preservation method has been to establish nature reserves in the areas where the wildlife lives and breeds or to establish artificial breeding centers. Certain endangered species are recovering. However, some animal populations continue to remain low or to decrease. For example, increased nutrient loading and industrial pollution in lakes, along with the construction of dams and weirs, have led to drastic reductions in fish and crustacean yields and species. Often, in order to increase food production, crab and carp eggs have been stocked in lakes, leading to a reduction of indigenous species and, in some cases, extinction. A photo taken with a digital camera by a man working for a decoration company confirmed that there was only one Yangtze dolphin (*baiji*) in the Chang River after a group of experts could not find any during a 2007 survey ("Extinct Dolphin," 2007).

China is a member of the Man and the Biosphere Program of the UN Educational, Scientific, and Cultural Organization (UNESCO), has signed the Convention on International Trade in Endangered Species (CITES) of Wild Fauna and Flora, has sites on the UNESCO World Heritage Commission's list, and has nature reserves included on the International Important Wetlands List. Many of the larger reserves have research organizations attached, often with international cooperation.

In 1981, an agreement was signed with the World Wildlife Fund to protect and study the giant panda (Schaller, 1993). Although archaeological evidence indicates that pandas once were distributed widely over southern China, their range now has shrunk to small areas in southern Shaanxi, Gansu, and Sichuan. During 1975 and 1976, 138 giant pandas were found dead along the Sichuan-Gansu border (Map 2.2) due to deterioration of the arrow bamboo and square bamboo groves that provide their food (Enderton, 1985). This panda famine stimulated a series of attempts to preserve the animal's habitat. The total giant panda population of China is now estimated to be under 2,000, with about 300 bred in captivity. As of 2010, there were approximately forty reserves protecting the giant panda in southwest China. The World Wildlife Fund has committed more funds to increase the number of panda reserves in China by 2013. Despite this, the range of the animal has continued to decrease.

China's cooperation with other countries and multinational corporations in conserving animals has been increasing since the 1980s. However, as ecotourism grows, the desire to bring in tourist revenue can compromise the conservation aspects of nature parks. Cases of national parks being turned into tourist spots have been all too common. The effects of tourism on China's nature preserves have rarely been positive. Wealthy Hong Kong, Macau, and Taiwan residents and overseas Chinese have been known to pay large amounts for tiger bones, elephant tusks, and parts of other endangered species, risking the species' survival all over the world (Coggins, 2003).

The various units that administer the nature reserves have had a tendency to look for short-term economic advantage or to protect only those aspects of the environment beneficial to their bureau's interests. Often, state forests or forest parks are located next to nature reserves; joint management of these could bring increased conservation benefits. Sometimes reserves are zoned for various revenue-generating or productive purposes, compromising their conservation role.

Laws standardizing procedures for establishing nature reserves, management procedures, and penalties for violations have been on the books since the late 1980s, but there still is a need for clear enforcement of local versions pertinent to specific circumstances.

For laws and their enforcement to be successful, the nature reserve managers must consider solving the economic and social problems of the local inhabitants. Attempts have been made in many of the larger nature reserves to compensate and relocate local dwellers. The government has been trying to solve employment problems for some local people by training them as forest rangers or nature reserve staff. Still, some nature reserves are reserves in name only. In many cases, logging and hunting are still happening in areas where such activities are prohibited by law.

Most Chinese environmentalists point to the long-term economic value that improved management of nature conservation brings. This is the only argument that will attract the attention of a government intent on rapid economic development. China's policymakers have come to understand that nature conservation is a necessity for the country's long-term survival. So far, overseas help and the dedication of Chinese researchers have moved the agenda forward. In recent years, China also has become concerned about invasive foreign species.

The Three Gorges Dam

In spite of recent international controversies over dam building on rivers in southwestern China that flow into Southeast and South Asian neighboring states (discussed in Chapter 7), the most controversial hydrological project in China today remains the construction of the Three Gorges (Sanxia) Dam on the Yangtze River in western Hubei province. The Sanxia area, which extends for 125 miles (200 kilometers) along the river, is rich in historical sites and evokes many ancient Chinese legends (see Hengduan Shan on Map 2.4). It contained six historic walled cities, ancient plank roads cut into cliffs, Stone Age archaeological village sites, many old temples and burial sites, and miles of spectacular caves. It was home to a multitude of plants and animals. The sublime beauty and strategic significance of the Three Gorges was celebrated for centuries in the works of China's poets and travelers (for photos prior to reservoir impounding, see Benson 2006; Zorn 2006). To build a dam in an area of such cultural and natural treasures was bound to cause irredeemable damage.

Robert E. Gamer

Wu Gorge, the center of the Three Gorges, before construction of the dam.

Proposals for building a dam in the Sanxia area date to the 1920s, and arguments for and against the project persisted among various ministries and provinces from that time (Edmonds, 1992; Dai, 1997). The climate of repression in the aftermath of the Tiananmen demonstrations in 1989 helped stifle public opposition. The 1991 Yangtze and Huai River floods brought the issue to the fore; since a principal objective of the dam was flood control, the stance of proponents was strengthened. Defiant gestures in the National People's Congress during formal approval in the spring of 1992 over the dam issue included a record-breaking number of delegates voting against the project, or abstaining, and an unprecedented walkout by two delegates.

Construction began in December 1994. The main course of the Yangtze River was successfully dammed in 1997, with the first generator installed in 2001. The final stage of reservoir clearance began in 2001 and the reservoir started filling in April 2002; in 2003, the dam's first turbines began generating electricity, the coffer dam was dismantled, and, in 2006, the reservoir water reached 156 meters. The original planned components of the project were finished in October 2008 in line with the 2008 Beijing Olympics. All debts on the dam were due to be repaid by 2012. The city of Chongqing, standing at the western end of the proposed reservoir, was separated from Sichuan province and given the same national municipal status as Beijing, Tianjin, and Shanghai. China has planned to use this project to facilitate inland economic growth. Arguments as to whether the dam should have been constructed concentrated on several key questions: flood control, water supply, navigation, energy supply, safety, human dislocation, and ecological damage.

The Sanxia Dam controls about half of the Yangtze River valley's annual flow volume. The 12 million people and 2,000 square miles (5,200 square kilometers) of good fields in the Jianghan Plain just below the dam site receive the greatest flood protection from the project. The dam supposedly gives the Jianghan Plain 100-year flood protection instead of the forty-year flood protection calculated as the optimum obtainable from further investment in existing dikes without the dam. In addition, water will be diverted to water-deficient northern China via the central route of the South-north Water Diversion Project now under construction. At the same time, the Sanxia Dam can allow 10,000 dead-weight metric ton (dwt) vessels to get as far as Chongqing for more than half the year if there are no major drought conditions.

The Sanxia Dam has an 18,200-megawatt generating capacity, making it the world's largest hydroelectric generating plant (and the world's largest dam in terms of tons of poured concrete). It is built to supply about one-eighth as much electricity as was generated in China during 1991. In the debate about the project, proponents stressed that building a large dam at Sanxia was more cost-effective than building a series of small dams on tributaries upstream or constructing coal-fired plants. Moreover, the centrally located site was deemed the best on the river for distributing electricity around China.

Proponents stated that the dam would be safe from military attack, denied that it lies in an earthquake zone, and asserted that it would not induce earthquakes nor burst in the event of an earthquake. They also argued that resettlement costs would be low because more than half of those displaced came from small towns, and their incomes would skyrocket through the sale of goods and services to construction workers.

During the proposal phase, proponents also argued that ecological damage would be minimal and the loss of good agricultural land would not be serious. Air and water pollution that would have been generated by coal-fired power plants would be avoided, and they stated there was little evidence to suggest that the reservoir would create breeding grounds for disease-carrying parasites. The reservoir was considered to have great fish-raising potential and a positive effect on local microclimates. Some historical artifacts currently sited below the new water level have been moved to higher locations.

Opposition to the Sanxia Dam from within China persisted during construction, though little opposition aired in the official press until 2007. In contrast, overseas opposition was considerable. Opponents argued that flood control is relevant only to the area directly below the dam. Major rainstorms upstream could flood areas there, and clear-water releases from the dam could lead to undercutting of dikes downstream. Some suggested that dikes already being raised in height on lower portions of the river combined with several dams on tributaries would have been a far more effective and less expensive means of flood control, with less aesthetic and environmental harm. For the first time in the history of any hydraulic project, manila grass is being grown on Sanxia-project dike banks to stop erosion—a cheap and simple solution that opponents say should have been used more widely before more drastic solutions were attempted. They also pointed out the mutually exclusive functions of a flood prevention dam and a power-generating dam: a dam used for hydropower generation should have its reservoir largely full of water, whereas one used primarily for flood control should be kept almost empty.

Others argued that building a series of small dams along the Yangtze, using smaller ships, and extending hours of navigation would have increased efficiency without as big a risk. Opponents also suggested that the buildup of silt upstream could lead to increased flooding above the dam or actually burst it. Considerable amounts of electricity could be lost in transmission over long distances, and there were questions about the efficiency of such large generators. Critics cited past Chinese big-dam construction experiences that did not inspire confidence. Gezhouba Dam, just downstream, took eighteen years to finish at a cost close to four times the original estimate. Its locks have experienced serious failures, which appear to be due to basic design flaws and lack of maintenance. If this ever happens at the Sanxia Dam, with water depths of over five times more on either side of its locks, such an incident could result in a great disaster.

Approximately 1.4 million people living in the area were relocated by 2008. There was significant opposition to resettlement in the Sanxia area, and there were cases of peasants refusing to move and being forcibly evicted as well as reports of misuse and embezzlement of resettlement funds. More than 150 towns and a portion of Chongqing were flooded, and the land submerged generally is more productive than the land given to compensate peasants. Many peasants were moved to apartments in town, away from jobs or land. In spite of this, soil erosion had become so serious by 1998 that reforestation of some newly cultivated land, banning of cultivation on slopes over 25 degrees, and resettlement of people out of the region became necessary (Steil and Duan, 2002).

Some postulated that the reservoir might cause the water table to rise and trigger landslides, and evidence since construction suggests that they were correct. Opponents also pointed out that there are geological fault belts near the reservoir area. Earthquakes greater than 4.75 on the Richter scale have been recorded, and increased pressure on the bottom of the new reservoir could cause stronger earthquakes (Chen and Talwani, 1998). Officials have acknowledged that seismic activity has increased slightly since the reservoir began filling in 2002, and there are Chinese scientists who have cited dams as responsible for over a dozen earthquakes since 1949 (Naik and Oster, 2009; Pellman, 2008). Research also exists that suggests that the dam has induced a large number of earthquakes in the region during times of rising and falling water levels in the reservoir (Dai et al., 2010; Probe International, 2011).

There were worries about the effect of the dam on climate, the creation of disease-fostering habitats, pollution from submerged mines, impacts on downstream ecosystems, and the future of some forms of wildlife. A slowed flow rate may reduce the ability of the river to flush out rubbish and a growing number of pollutants, which appears to now be a problem. It could also result in land being lost along the coast because the balance between silt being deposited from the river and wave erosion will be altered. In September 2007, for the first time, the Chinese government's official Xinhua News Agency and People's Daily Online issued press releases noting that "officials and experts have admitted the Three Gorges Dam project has caused an array of ecological ills, including more frequent landslides and pollution, and, if preventive measures are not taken, there could be an environmental 'catastrophe'" (People's Daily Online, 2007). The report notes that this was the conclusion of all the participants at a conference held in Wuhan. The report admits that erosion has triggered ninety-one landslides along the banks of the reservoir, that clear water discharges are threatening downstream embankments, and that the water on tributaries has deteriorated. In spring 2011, drought forced authorities to close a 140-mile (225-kilometer) segment of the middle reaches of the Yangtze to traffic as water levels reached the lowest level since the dam began operating in 2003, demonstrating that the project has been unable to successfully manage water flow. All this has been more serious and costly than experts predicted and required further resettlement of 70,000 people out of landslide-prone areas. In spring 2011, the Chinese State Council released a statement admitting that there were significant flaws in the project, and there has been considerable criticism of the project on the Internet (Wang Xiangwei, 2011). The unreliability of flood control also has led to the cancellation of a nuclear power plant at Xianning in Hubei province about 350 miles (550 kilometers) east of the dam and 20 miles (30 kilometers) from the banks of the Yangtze (Xinhua, 2011). Thus, at this late date, the Chinese government finally admitted what many experts predicted all along. Although things seems to be slowly changing, the political situation in the PRC remains such that domestic public opinion cannot block a project for long if the leadership is in favor of it.

As the Sanxia project comes to a close, and antidam efforts in China continue, China is constructing the Xiluodu Dam on the Jinsha River, an upstream tributary of the Yangtze on the Sichuan-Yunnan border. When completed, Xiluodu will be China's second-largest hydropower project. China is also focusing on plans for a recently revived series of thirteen staircase dams on the Nu (Salween) River, eight dams on the Lancang (Mekong) River in Yunnan province (Magee, 2006), and five along Yarlung Zangbo (Brahmaputra) River in Tibet. All these dams have international implications, and concerns have been expressed by Southeast and South Asian states through which these rivers pass. China is also involved in 250 dam projects in sixty-eight countries—something unimaginable twenty years ago.

Prospects for China's Environment

The Chinese government took a stand on international environmental cooperation at the UN Conference on Environment and Development, held in Rio de Janeiro in June 1992. China ratified the UN Framework Convention on Climate Change and the Kyoto Protocol, which aimed to cut greenhouse gas emissions, but because China was classified as a developing country in both cases, it had no binding emissions levels. It argued that poverty was the main cause of environmental degradation in developing countries, and thus it was not reasonable to expect these countries to maintain lower emissions levels or install expensive equipment to control emissions on their own. Instead, the developed nations should transfer funds and technology to help poorer countries reduce emissions levels, since in the case of China it is thought that by 2050 global warming may submerge all of its coastal areas, which are currently less than 13 feet (4 meters) above sea level, forcing relocation of about 67 million people. This viewpoint was part of a foreign policy initiative to assume leadership of developing countries' environmental bloc as well as to gain relief for China's pollution and resource degradation reduction, with outside help. To accomplish the latter, China has joined global environmental change programs and set up its own organizations. Of the big energy-use countries with potential to produce greenhouse gases, China is the most likely to have its energy use grow significantly over the next forty or so years.

Observed data show that nationwide mean surface temperatures increased markedly during the twentieth century with changes of 0.9–1.5 degrees Fahrenheit (0.5–0.8 degrees Celsius) and predictions of a further 6 degrees Fahrenheit (3.2 degrees Celsius) rise possible by 2080 (Lin et al., n.d.:1–2). The rates of sea-level rise since the 1950s are put at 1.4–3.2 millimeters per annum (about an inch per decade), while drought has generally increased in north China and flooding has increased in the south. Water flows in the major rivers also appear to have decreased (Lin et al., n.d.:3). The Chinese further predict that agricultural production could be seriously affected over the next fifty years with production down 5–10 percent by 2030, and there could be an increase in arid land area with a reduction in permafrost areas, inland lakes, coastal land, wetlands, and biodiversity as well as more increases in drought and floods. However, some flora and fauna, such as grassland and forestry, might actually increase although species would vary, and growth pattern change could be disruptive.

China has modified its tough developing-country stand as it moves up in the world order and begins to lose developing-country status (Jiang, 2007). By the 2009 Copenhagen climate summit, China's international presence had become multifaceted, with no less than fifteen NGOs sending delegates and with considerable Chinese media coverage on site. Stiffer regulations aimed at conservation and efficiency are being promulgated. China released its own National Climate Change Program in June 2007; the predictions include a 30 percent drop in precipitation in the Huai, Liao, and Hai river valleys in the coming century. The country already had goals for reducing energy intensity in its Eleventh Five-Year Plan released in 2006, and most of the National Climate Change Program suggestions were already in place before the plan was released (Chen, 2009:115–117).

China itself is likely to be seriously affected by climate change because of the country's continuing dependence on agriculture. Chinese research suggests that a doubling of CO_2 output will have a negative impact on wheat, rice, and cotton production. If oceans rise by 3 feet (1 meter), China's coast below 12 feet (4 meters) above the current sea level would be flooded (an area the size of Portugal) resulting in much good agricultural land being lost and major cities being submerged. Predictions made public in 2007 suggest that by 2050 the coastline of Guangdong in the south will rise by a foot (30 centimeters) and temperatures in the area will rise by 5 degrees Fahrenheit (2.8 degrees Celsius) leading to economic losses both in agriculture and industry.

Still, the overall effect of global warming on Chinese agriculture would be mixed. Warmer temperatures mean that growing seasons would be lengthened. It is also likely that in many places precipitation would increase and even the glacial melt would lead to short-term moisture increases followed by serious aridity in later times. Even in the moister areas, evaporation should make soil drier and thus reduce water supply. Pests, weeds, and more severe storms could also reduce farm and fish yields in many places.

At the same time, despite recent crackdowns against political dissidents, the social atmosphere in China is changing in ways that favor environmental activism (Weller, 2006; Moore and Warrant, 2006). Citizen-based environmental groups are becoming more tolerated, although the pace of change is sporadic, and they remain closely watched if their activities are deemed to be political (see Chapter 4).

As previously mentioned, one of the most threatening of China's environmental problems is the continuing destruction of resources, particularly in poor western and central areas. The fragile ecosystems of the western and border areas are under great strain. Since the 1950s, the expansion of settled agriculture and industry in traditional herding pastures and oases of the west and the proliferation of new roads and highways have led to serious degradation. Population densities in parts of the west must be reduced and emphasis put on animal husbandry and forestry where possible. Thus, the "Go West" policy of the Chinese government could have very serious ecological implications for this region (Harris, 2007; Watts, 2010).

Although resource degradation also is serious in the east, the immediate problem facing the better-off population of eastern China is pollution. Pollution is widespread in rural areas. Most rural enterprises use outdated equipment, cannot afford or lack the political will to spend money on pollution abatement, and are inefficient energy users. In particular, rural industries have caused serious water-quality degradation. The appearance of "cancer villages" has been most alarming (Liu, 2010). Dealing with the rural industry pollution problem will require a tremendous investment by the Chinese government as well as strict enforcement of regulations. On an optimistic note, progress is being made in some of the more wealthy eastern rural areas.

The best that can be hoped for China as a whole is that the pace of water depletion, deforestation, soil erosion, and desertification will slow in coming years. If efforts at reforesting and population control begun in the 1980s prove successful, that will help. Efficient management and stricter enforcement of environmental laws also would help—for example, carrying out environmental assessments on construction projects, imposing fines, and implementing the new environmental programs and goals. In addition to more funds being properly spent and more personnel, there is a need for more public openness to assessment information. Raising prices of polluting fuels and industrial inputs will increase economic efficiency and improve China's environmental problems. Such pricing policies have helped to control some forms of degradation, such as pollution by state-run industries, and have aided in the promotion of environmentally friendly products. Although an array of price reforms has been introduced, pressure from government nonetheless remains the main force regulating investment in environmental control, since many inputs are still underpriced.

Ultimately, if the country is to feed and clothe all its people and provide a good standard of living in the next century, China needs strict population control, extensive environmental education, financial and infrastructural resources, political stability, and a more open society where information can be obtained and opinions freely expressed. It also needs to develop political and corporate cultures that feel it is in their best interest to control environmental degradation.

Bibliography

Andrews, Steven Q. 2008–2009. "Seeing Through the Smog: Understanding the Limits of Chinese Air Pollution Reporting," *China Environment Series* 10: 5–29.

Barboza, David. 2007. "China Reportedly Urged Omitting Pollution-Death Estimates." *New York Times,* July 5, A3.

Barclay, Eliza. 2010. "China Turns to Biogas to Ease Impact of Factory Farms." *Yale Environment 360*, November 11. http://e360.yale.edu.

Bauer, Joanne (ed.). 2006. *Forging Environmentalism: Justice, Livelihood, and Contested Environments.* Armonk, NY: M. E. Sharpe.

Benson, Steven. 2006. *The Cost of Power in China: The Three Gorges Dam and the Yangtze River Valley.* Lake Orion: Black Opal Press.

Berrah, Noureddine (ed.). 2007. *Sustainable Energy in China: The Closing Window of Opportunity.* Washington, DC: World Bank.

Campana, Alan. 2010. *Solar Technology and Markets: Illuminating the Prospects for China and the U.S.* Washington, DC: Woodrow Wilson International Center for Scholars, China Environment Forum.

Cary, Eve. 2011. "China's Policy Impasse: The Case of the 'Green GDP' Initiative." *China Brief* 11–8 (May 6): 4–6.

Chan, Chak K., and Xiaohong Yao. 2008. "Air Pollution in Mega Cities in China." *Atmospheric Environment* 42(1) (January): 1–42.

Chellaney, Brahma. 2007. "China Aims for Bigger Share of South Asia's Water Lifeline." *Japan Times,* June 26.

Chen, Gang. 2009. *Politics of China's Environmental Protection: Problems and Progress.* Singapore: World Scientific.

Chen, Linyue, and Pradeep Talwani. 1998. "Reservoir-induced Seismicity in China." *Pure and Applied Geophysics* 153(1): 133–149.

Cheng, Hefa, Hu Yuanan, and Zhao Jianfu. 2009. "Meeting China's Water Shortage Crisis: Current Practices and Challenges." *Environmental Science and Technology* 43(2): 240–244.

"China Tackles Worsening Pollution." 2011. *China Economic Review*, January 27. www.chinaeconomicreview.com.

Coggins, Chris. 2003. *The Tiger and the Pangolin: Nature, Culture, and Conservation in China.* Honolulu: University of Hawaii Press.

Collier, Robert. 2007. "Warming of Glaciers Threatens Millions in China." *San Francisco Chronicle,* August 1.

Collins, Gabe, and Andrew Erickson. 2010. "China's Natural Gas Approach: Pipelines Are Best Way to Resolve Shortages." *China SignPost*, December 10. www.chinasignpost.com.

Dai Miao et al. 2010. "A Study on the Relationship Between Water Levels and Seismic Activity in the Three Gorges Reservoir." *Journal of the Changjiang Water Resources Commission* 41(17): 12–14 (in Chinese). www.rmcjzz.com.

Dai, Qing. 1997. *The River Dragon Has Come! The Three Gorges Dam and the Fate of China's Yangtze River and Its People.* Trans. Ming Yi. Armonk, NY: M. E. Sharpe.

Day, Kristen A. (ed.). 2005. *China's Environment and the Challenge of Sustainable Development.* Armonk, NY: M. E. Sharpe.

Demick, Barbara. 2010. "China Moving Heaven and Earth to Bring Water to Beijing." *Los Angeles Times*, September 29. http://articles.latimes.com.

Dikötter, Frank. 2010. *Mao's Great Famine: The History of China's Most Devastating Catastrophe, 1958–1962.* London: Bloomsbury.

Economy, Elizabeth C. 2005. *The River Runs Black: The Environmental Challenge to China's Future.* Ithaca, NY: Cornell University Press.

Edmonds, Richard Louis. 1992. "The Sanxia (Three Gorges) Project: The Environmental Argument Surrounding China's Super Dam." *Global Ecology and Biogeography Letters* 4(2): 105–125.

———. 1994. *Patterns of China's Lost Harmony: A Survey of the Country's Environmental Degradation and Protection.* London: Routledge.

——— (ed.). 2000. *Managing the Chinese Environment.* Oxford: Oxford University Press.

Elvin, Mark. 2004. *The Retreat of the Elephants: An Environmental History of China.* New Haven, CT: Yale University Press.

Elvin, Mark, and Ts'ui-jung Liu. 1998. *Sediments of Time: Environment and Society in Chinese History.* Cambridge: Cambridge University Press.

Enderton, Catherine Shurr. 1985. "Nature Preserves and Protected Wildlife in the People's Republic of China." *China Geographer* 12:117–140.

"Extinct Dolphin Spotted in the Yangtze River." 2007. *Xinhua News Agency,* August 29.

Fan Feng. 2008. "'Garbage Villages': Growing Waste Problem in Rural China." Wilson Center China Environmental Health Project Research Brief, April. www.wilson center.org.

"Glacier Study Reveals Chilling Prediction." 2004. *China Daily,* September 23.

Gleick, Peter H. 2009. "China and Water." In *The World's Water 2008–2009* by Peter H. Gleick et. al, 79–100. Washington, DC: Island Press.

Government of China. 2010. "2009 Report on the Environment in China." http://english.mep.gov.cn/standards_reports/soe/soe2009/201104/t20110411_208 976.htm.

Harris, Richard B. 2007. *Wildlife Conservation in China: Preserving the Habitat of China's Wild West.* Armonk, NY: M. E. Sharpe.

Ho, Mun S., and Chris P. Nielsen (eds.). 2007. *Clearing the Air: The Health and Economic Damages of Air Pollution in China.* Cambridge, MA: MIT Press.

Ho, Peter, and Richard Louis Edmonds. 2007. "Perspectives of Time and Change: Rethinking Embedded Environmental Activism in China." In *Embedded Activism: Opportunities and Constraints of a Social Movement in China,* edited by Peter Ho and Richard Louis Edmonds. London: Routledge.

Ho, Peter, and Eduard B. Vermeer (eds.). 2006. *China's Limits to Growth: Greening State and Society.* New York: Wiley Blackwell.

Hou, Li (ed.). 2009. "Diaocha jieguo xianshi: Zhongguo senlin fugailü dadao 20.36%" (Investigative results show: China's forest coverage reaches 20.36 percent). *Zhongguo Guangbowang, Zhongguo zhi Sheng*, November 17. http://china.cnr.cn.

Innovation Center Denmark, Shanghai. 2009. "Wastewater Treatment in China." Shanghai: Innovation Center Denmark, Shanghai. http://www.shanghai.um.dk.

Intergovernmental Panel on Climate Change. 2007. *Climate Change, 2007: The Physical Science Basis, Summary for Policy Makers.* Geneva: World Meteorological Organization.

Jiang, Wenran. 2007. "China Debates Green GDP and Its Future Development Mode." *China Brief* 7(16): 4–6.

Jin, Fen, et al. 2010. "Pesticide Use and Residue Control in China." *Journal of Pesticide Science* 35(2): 138–142.

Jones, Alan Robertson, Jean Forbes, and Graham Hollier. 1990. *Collins Reference Dictionary: Environmental Science.* London: Collins.

Kitzes, Justin, et al. 2008. *Report on Ecological Footprint in China.* Beijing: China Council for International Cooperation in Environment and Development, Global Footprint Network, and WWF in China.

Kopits, Steven. 2011. "Statement of Steven Kopits, Managing Director Douglas-Westwood LLC Before the US House of Representatives Subcommittee on Energy and Power, 'The American Energy Initiative' regarding China's Oil and Gas Outlook," April 4. http://republicans.energycommerce.house.gov.

Larsen, Janet. 2011. "Cancer Now Main Cause of Death in China," May 26. www.peopleandplanet.net.

Lee, Seungho. 2006. *Water and Development in China: The Political Economy of Shanghai Water Policy.* Singapore: World Scientific.

Lee, Yok-shiu F., and Alvin Y. So. 1999. *Asia's Environmental Movements: Comparative Perspectives.* Armonk, NY: M. E. Sharpe.

Li Jing. 2011. "Big Cities Urged to Curb Noise Pollution." *China Daily,* January 26. www.chinadaily.com.cn.

Li, Lillian M. 2007. *Fighting Famine in North China: State, Market, and Environmental Decline, 1690s–1990s.* Stanford, CA: Stanford University Press.

Li, Xianyan, et al. 2007. "Assessment for Salinized Wasteland Expansion and Land Use Change Using GIS and Remote Sensing in the West Part of Northeast China." *Environmental Monitoring and Assessment* 131(1–3): 421–437.

Lin Erda, Xu Yinlong, Wu Shaohong, Ju Hui, and Ma Shiming. n.d. "Synopsis of China National Climate Change Assessment Report (II): Climate Change Impacts and Adaptation." Panel for China National Climate Change Assessment Report. Berkeley: School of Law, University of California.

Lin, Jintai, et al. 2010. "Recent Changes in Particulate Air Pollution over China Observed from Space and the Ground: Effectiveness of Emission Control." *Environmental Science and Technology* 44(20): 7771–7776.

Liu, Kexin, and Jennifer L. Turner. 2011. *Shale We Dance? Exploring a New Era of U.S.-China Energy Collaboration.* Washington, DC: Woodrow Wilson International Center for Scholars, China Environment Forum.

Liu, Lee. 2010. "Made in China: Cancer Villages." *Environment* (March–April). http://www.environmentmagazine.org.

Loeve, Ronald, and Walter Immerzeel. 2009. "Climate Change: Future Water Resources of the Yellow River." Paper prepared for the 4th International Yellow River Forum, October 20–23, Zhengzhou, China. www.watercycle.nl.

Ma, Jun. *China's Water Crisis.* 2004. Norwalk, CT: Eastbridge.

Ma, Xiaoying, and Leonard Ortolano. 2000. *Environmental Regulation in China: Institutions, Enforcement, and Compliance.* Lanham, MD: Rowman and Littlefield.

Magee, Darrin. 2006. "Powershed Politics: Yunnan Hydropower Under Great Western Development." *China Quarterly* 185 (March): 23–41.

Marks, Robert. 1998. *Tigers, Rice, Silk, and Silt: Environment and Economy in Late Imperial South China.* Cambridge: Cambridge University Press.

McBeath, Gerald A., and Tse-Kang Leng. 2006. *Governance of Biodiversity Conservation in China and Taiwan.* Northampton, MA: Edward Elgar.

McGregor, Richard. 2007a. "750,000 a Year Killed by Chinese Pollution." *Financial Times,* July 2.

———. 2007b. "Beijing Clouds the Pollution Picture." *Financial Times,* July 2.

Mertha, Andrew C. 2008. *China's Water Warriers: Citizen Action and Policy Change.* Ithaca, NY: Cornell University Press.

Moore, Allison, and Adria Warrant. 2006. "Legal Advocacy in Environmental Public Participation in China: Raising the Stakes and Strengthening Stakeholders." Woodrow Wilson International Center for Scholars, China Environment Series No. 8, July 7.

Morton, Katherine. 2011. "Climate Change and Security at the Third Pole." *Survival* 53(1): 121–132.

Naik, Gautam, and Shai Oster. 2009. "Scientists Link China's Dam to Earthquake, Renewing Debate." *Wall Street Journal*, February 6. http://online.wsj.com.

National Environmental Protection Agency. 2006. *Report on the State of the Environment in China 2005.* Beijing: National Environmental Protection Agency.

Niu, Shuping. 2010. "China Needs to Cut Use of Chemical Fertilizers: Research." Reuters, January 14. http://www.reuters.com.

Pellman, Tom. 2008. "Are Dams to Blame for Sichuan's Quake?" *China Economic Review*, May 15. http://www.chinaeconomicreview.com.

People's Daily Online. 2007. "China Warns of Environmental 'Catastrophe' from Three Gorges Dam," September 26.

Probe International. 2011. "Chinese Study Reveals Three Gorges Dam Triggered 3,000 Earthquakes, Numerous Landslides." June 1. http://journal.probeinternational.org.
Qiu, Jane. 2010. "China Faces Up to Groundwater Crisis." *Nature* 466 (July 13): 308.
Ross, Lester. 1988. *Environmental Policy in China*. Bloomington: Indiana University Press.
Sanders, Richard. 2000. *Prospects for Sustainable Development in the Chinese Countryside: The Political Economy of Chinese Ecological Agriculture*. Burlington, VT: Ashgate.
Schaller, George. 1993. *The Last Panda*. Chicago: University of Chicago Press.
Shapiro, Judith. 2001. *Mao's War Against Nature: Politics and the Environment in Revolutionary China*. Cambridge: Cambridge University Press.
Smil, Vaclav. 2005. *Enriching the Earth: Fritz Haber, Carl Bosch, and the Transformation of World Food*. Cambridge, MA: MIT Press.
Stamoran, Bogdan. 2010. "The State of Cities in China." *International Institute of Asian Studies: The Newsletter* 55 (Autumn–Winter): 22–23.
Steil, Shawn, and Duan Yuefang. 2002. "Policies and Practice in Three Gorges Resettlement: A Field Account." *Forced Migration Review* 12 (January 2002): 10–13.
"Tibetan Glacier Melt Leading to Sandstorms." 2006. *China Daily,* May 5.
Tsai, Terence. 2001. *Corporate Environmentalism in China and Taiwan*. New York: Palgrave.
Vermeer, Eduard B. 1990. "Management of Environmental Pollution in China: Problems and Abatement Policies." *China Information* 5(1): 34–65.
———. 1998. "Population and Ecology Along the Frontier in Qing China." In *Sediments of Time: Environment and Society in Chinese History,* edited by Mark Elvin and Ts'ui-jung Liu, 235–279. Cambridge: Cambridge University Press.
Wang Xiangwei. 2011. "State Council's Statement on Flaws in Massive Project Is a Significant Admission from the Top." *South China Morning Post,* updated May 23. http://www.scmp.com.
Wang Xiaotian. 2011. "China Set to Increase Use of Biofuels." *China Daily,* updated April 28. http://www.chinadaily.com.cn.
Watts, Jonathan. 2007. "China Blames Growing Social Unrest on Anger Over Pollution." *The Guardian,* July 6.
———. 2010. *When a Billion Chinese Jump*. London: Guardian Books.
Weller, Robert P. 2006. *Discovering Nature: Globalization and Environmental Culture in China and Taiwan*. Cambridge: Cambridge University Press.
Williams, Dee. 2002. *Beyond Great Walls: Environment, Identity, and Development on the Chinese Grasslands of Inner Mongolia*. Stanford, CA: Stanford University Press.
World Bank. 2007. *Cost of Pollution in China: Economic Estimates of Physical Damage*. Beijing: World Bank, Rural Development, Natural Resources, and Environment Management Unit, February. http://siteresources.worldbank.org.
World Nuclear Association. 2011. "Nuclear Power in China." May. http://www.world-nuclear.org/info/default.aspx?id=320&terms=China.
Xie, Jian, and Fasheng Li. 2010. *Overview of the Current Situation on Brownfield Remediation and Redevelopment in China*. Washington, DC: World Bank.
Xinhua. 2011. "Flood Risks Might Postpone Construction of China's First Inland Nuclear Power Station," edited by Zhi Chen. China-Wire, May 12. http://china-wire.org/?p=13157.
Yao Weijie. 2002. "Shui wuran yaosuan jingji zhang" (Water pollution must have an economic cost). *Kexue Ribao* (Science Times), December 5.

Yang, Mu, and Hong Yu (eds.). 2011. *China's Industrial Development in the 21st Century.* Singapore: World Scientific.

Yin, Runsheng, and Guiping Yin. 2009. "China's Ecological Restoration Programs: Initiation, Implementation, and Challenges." In *An Integrated Assessment of China's Ecological Restoration Programs*, edited by Runsheng Yin, 1–19. New York: Springer.

Zhao, Litao, and Lim Tin Seng (eds.). 2010. *China's New Social Policy: Initiatives for a Harmonious Society.* Singapore: World Scientific.

Zhao, Michael. 2007. "Yenei renshi baoguang Beijing bansu tongzhuangshui zaojia" (People in the industry expose the fact that half of Beijing's bottled water is fake). *Jinghua Shibao,* July 9.

Zhuang, Ying, et al. 2008. "Source Separation of Household Waste: A Case Study in China." *Waste Management* 28(10): 2022–2030.

Zorn, Bill. 2006. *The Three Gorges.* Saint Simons Island, GA: Flat Edge Press.

10

Family, Kinship, Marriage, and Sexuality

Zang Xiaowei

The family is a fundamental social unit in every society. In no aspect of culture are the diversities of human societies more striking than in the institutions of family and marriage. Families meet basic human needs of mating, reproduction, the care and upbringing of children, care for the aged, and the like, but families in different societies meet these needs in differing ways. For example, in 1950, only 4 percent of all births in the United States took place outside of marriage. By 1970, the figure was 11 percent; by 1990, it was 28 percent and by 2003, 35 percent (Cherlin, 2005:33, 35; see also Rosenfeld, 2006). In China, too, premarital sex, divorce, and staying single are also on the increase—but at a much slower rate compared with the United States. Hollywood, rock music, and individual paychecks sing their siren songs in China, too, but have been slower to disrupt family life. Loyalty to one's family takes precedence over other obligations. Even China's constitution contains detailed provisions about the family, discussing the care of the elderly and the upbringing of young children. In doing so, it echoes the emphasis of Confucius on the primary role of the family. That emphasis is weakening in China's culture, but its roots are so deep that the changes are likely to remain gradual.

Family Structure

Sociologists usually divide families into four basic structural categories. The first category is single men and women living alone, including those who have not married and those who are widowed or divorced. The second category, the nuclear family, consists of a couple and their unmarried children; it also includes childless couples or one of the parents (widowed or divorced) living with one of their married or unmarried children. The third category is a stem structure of an extended family, containing an aged parent or parents, one married child and his or her spouse, and perhaps grandchildren as well. Finally, the extended family differs by having two or more married siblings living together with their children and a grandparent or two.

In traditional China, the ideal family was an extended family consisting of five generations living together under one roof, sharing one common purse and one common stove, under one family head (Knapp and Kai-Yin, 2005). Confucianism expressed a preoccupation with familial relations and ethics. Families that were organized on the basis of "proper" relationships were considered by Confucian scholars to be fundamental to the maintenance of social harmony and political stability in China. The younger generation was ethically bound to support, love, and be obedient to their seniors (Hsiung, 2005; Spence, 2005; Watson, 1982; Watson and Ebrey, 1991).

The Chinese imperial state, which relied on Confucianism as its ideological foundation, strongly supported the traditional family institution (Faure, 2007). A local magistrate, for example, might erect a large memorial arch testifying to a widow's virtue for her refusal to remarry, or give an extended family a placard of honor to promote the ideal of five generations living harmoniously under one roof. Dividing the extended family, especially when aging parents were still alive, was strongly discouraged because it went against Confucian ethics (Mann, 1987).

Parents arranged marriages for their offspring, sometimes before they were old enough to live together and consummate the marriage. When a boy married, he brought his bride to live with his parents. When the father died, his estate was divided equally among his sons. Thus marriage did not lead to the creation of a new household. Usually, new families were created through partition of the family estate after the death of the father. Each son might use his share as the economic foundation for a new, smaller family he now headed, moving out of the parent's house to establish a nuclear family. One son might stay with or take in the widowed mother to create a stem family. Because of this cyclical process, at any given time most families were small. Some included parents (or one surviving parent) living with one or more married sons and perhaps their children. Others were limited to parents and their unmarried children and were thus similar to many present-day Western families in size and composition. Extended families with five generations living together were rare (Baker, 1979; Zang, 1993).

Family size was restricted not only because of divisions but also because of high infant mortality rates in imperial China and low life expectancy. However, rich families were more successful than the less well-to-do in raising their children to maturity. Rich families also tended to have higher birthrates than the less well-to-do because of better nutrition and the practice of polygamy (i.e., a man having two or more wives at the same time); the presence of additional women greatly increased the likelihood of more children. Although polygamy was generally acceptable in precommunist China, rich families were far better able to afford it. Consequently, rich families were larger than average in size; many of them were extended families that included several generations and could be extremely large. For example, in 1948, two US scholars claimed after their fieldwork in a Chinese village that "the Kwock and Cheung families are very nearly of equal size, having an estimated 500 to 750 members each, while the smallest unit is Choy, with about 200 to 300 members" (Baker, 1979:1; see also Tsui, 1989; Watson and Ebrey, 1991; Huang, 1992).

In the late nineteenth century, because of Western penetration into China, new bourgeois and working classes emerged in Chinese coastal cities along with a new intellectual elite. Since they obtained their incomes through employment outside the family, these individuals were freed from control by family elders. They were exposed and receptive to the new cultural and intellectual forces entering China from Japan and the West. Hence they agitated for legal and cultural reforms to promote the ideals of marriage based on free and romantic attachments and equality of men and women with respect to marriage, property, and inheritance (Lee, 2007; see also Huang, 2000). The reforms led to an increasing trend in urban China toward smaller nuclear family units and growing freedom of choice for men and women in choosing marriage partners. Since the 1930s, most urban Chinese have resided as nuclear families (Zang, 1993; Tsui, 1989; Whyte and Parish, 1984:chap. 6). My research on changes in family structure between 1900 and the 1980s documented that trend (Zang, 1993). By 1900, over half of urban families included in those surveys had already taken the nuclear form; by the 1980s, this had grown to two-thirds.

Chapters 4 and 8 discussed the increasing urbanization and rapid industrialization that followed the establishment of the People's Republic of China (PRC) in 1949. Those trends contributed further to the separation of nuclear families from control by their elders, especially in cities. There nuclear families tend to make decisions about and engage in reproduction, residence, food preparation, consumption and expenditure, and child rearing with little involvement by their elders (Hershatter, 2004; Parish and Whyte, 1978; Whyte, 1992:317–322; Whyte and Parish, 1984:chap. 6).

The stem family structure has not disappeared in urban China, however. Young couples may choose to live with their retired parents for free child care; housing prices may force young couples to live, at least for a few years, with their parents who have housing units. These considerations may stabilize or even increase the number of stem households temporarily (Riley, 1994:798–801; Knapp and Kai-Yin, 2005; Zhang, 2004). Today, many young people are even delaying marriage until they can afford to buy a flat. But increasing numbers of young couples are able to do so. The number of residences occupied by single families is on the rise.

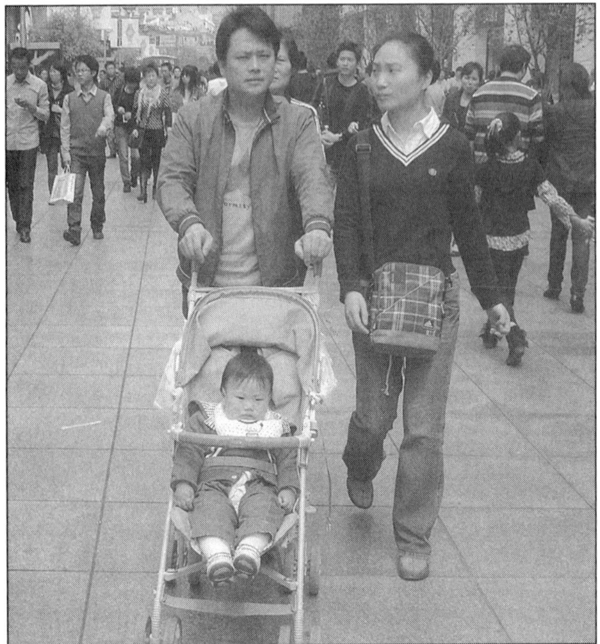
Robert E. Gamer

Taking baby for a stroll in Shanghai.

In rural areas, families continued to be organized along traditional lines until 1949. This is not surprising, given that the rural Chinese economy before 1949 was overwhelmingly based on traditional technologies and organizations. Traditional family forms were changed after 1949 (Hershatter, 2004; Potter and Potter, 1990; Wolf, 1985). An important factor causing the change in rural areas was the long period of collectivization (1955–1980). Prior to it, the father's indisputable authority in the family had been based on his control over and management of family property, farmwork, and dealings with the outside world. Collectivization abolished the private ownership of the means of production and transformed peasants into wage earners in collectives organized by the Communist Party. The farming family was no longer a production enterprise. With the family's well-being based mainly on the earnings of individual family members working for their collective unit or in other ways outside the family context, the father's authority was reduced significantly. There were no large family landholdings that would encourage brothers to stay together under their father's authority. Brothers tended to move out of their parents' house shortly after marriage, being constrained only by the cost and availability of new housing. However, the stem family structure survived the collectivization campaign as some parents continued to live with one of their married sons for old-age support and security.

Parental authority did not disappear totally during the collectivization period. Sons generally stayed in their father's village. Many peasant parents remained deeply involved in the marriage of a child, even if they had not chosen the spouse. Parental power over a child's marriage derived from the fact that a groom usually required his parents to give his bride's family a large cash gift before marriage, which could be worth several years of his family's earnings (Croll, 1984). Parental power was also based on the parents' responsibility for preparing the wedding ceremony and housing for their son and would-be daughter-in-law.

In the late 1970s, in a truly dramatic policy shift, the government instituted a process of decollectivization to stimulate China's rural economy. As Chapters 4 and 5 explained, by the early 1980s, agriculture in China once again became the undertaking of individual families, who now lease their plot of land on a long-term basis, or own it outright (fifteen-year or twenty-five-year contracts are common, and are often extended) from the townships where they worked previously. This policy shift has had unintended implications for family organization (Liu, 2000; Zeng, 2002). Although most families are still nuclear and stem in form, rich families are reappearing in the countryside, with some larger than average and similar to the typical extended family since they contain married brothers (Cohen 1992a:370–373). Rural houses, both old and new, are often designed to hold stem or extended families; in villages near cities, extra space may be rented to migrant laborers who have left their village to work in construction.

My 1993 survey found that most urban married couples surveyed either lived by themselves (neolocal) or close to the groom's family (patrilocal). William Lavely and Xinhua Ren (1992:378–391) pointed to similar trends in rural China. Only a small minority of Chinese couples choose to stay with the bride's family (matrilocal residence). However, in Yunnan province in southwestern China, matrilocal residence has been the norm among some minorities. In these matrilineal societies, a groom moves into his bride's house and has no control over household possessions and other assets. In sum, although nuclear families are the norm, many stay in close contact with parents and grandparents. And few Chinese live alone. Massive urban construction, however, increasingly moves couples to parts of the city distant from their parents' residence.

Marriage

Traditionally, 96 percent of people in China who reached adulthood married (Kohrman, 2005:chap. 6), though, as we are about to discuss, the growing unbalanced ratio of males to females is lowering that percentage. In imperial

China, marriage was not based on love and romance. Young people had very little say regarding marriage, either about timing or about partners. Many marriages were arranged by parents and thus were "blind," with the bride and the groom not even meeting each other until the wedding day. Frequently, two sets of parents contracted marriages between young children, who did not begin to cohabit until they were older. All this gave parents effective control over the marriages of their offspring. Arranged marriage was a crucial part of a family's strategy for success. Through marriage, old alliances between families could be strengthened and new ones formed. Parents secured support in their old age. Resources were transferred from one family to another (Xu and Whyte, 1990:714; Riley, 1994:792; Croll, 1984, 2005).

Parental influence in the marriage institution was gradually eroded after the turn of the twentieth century as reformers and revolutionaries denounced the personal misery and suicides that had resulted from arranged marriages. Especially in cities, young people struggled to change traditional practices like the Confucian ideals of filial piety, arranged marriage, and the subordinate role of women in the family. These struggles led to significant changes in the marriage institution, one of which was the age at which youths married. In my survey data, published in 1993, I found that about 10 percent of my respondents who had been brides during the 1930s were less than fifteen years of age; by 1950, that practice was reduced significantly (Zang, 1993; Whyte, 1990; Whyte and Parish, 1984:chap. 5). Early marriage has not been entirely eliminated under the communist regime, however. In 1990, China still had over 8 million marriages of girls under the age of fifteen in rural areas; this figure was halved by 1994. More than 90 percent of early marriages were found in rural areas ("China's Current Marriage Patterns," 1995).

Freedom of choice in choosing one's mate has radically increased in urban China since 1900 (Lee, 2007). Proceedings dominated by parents arranged more than half of all marriages between 1900 and 1938; by 1982, such practices almost disappeared. By then, four in every five couples married of their own volition. Data from my survey conducted in Lanzhou in 2001 show that 8.5 percent of Han women in that city reported arranged marriage (Zang, 2004). Chinese women today enjoy much more freedom in selecting mates than their counterparts who married before 1949 (Diamant, 2000; Xia and Zhou, 2003).

Parents and older associates still played a major role in this process, however. First, introductions by friends and coworkers were important for young people to find prospects. Studies indicate that workplace officials did their best to serve the needs of young people, including their marital concerns, in exchange for their political loyalty and obedience (Whyte, 1990; Whyte and Parish, 1984:chap. 5). US anthropologist William Jankowiak did fieldwork in a city in Inner Mongolia in the 1980s and reports that Chinese mothers were often a deciding force in their children's choices of marital

Robert E. Gamer

A date in the park.

partners (Jankowiak, 1993:chap. 8; Riley, 1994:794–798; Pimentel, 2000; Zang, 2004).

Casual dating was rare prior to the 1990s; dating was viewed by the public as an ad hoc agreement to marry rather than as a mechanism for selecting an eventual partner, as in the United States (Hsu, 1981). A survey found that nine out of ten Chinese women never had another person they considered marrying besides their eventual husbands. Less than 30 percent had other boyfriends. Many women said they rarely or never dated their future husbands; even for those who did, the dates almost always came after the decision to marry, rather than prior to it (Xu and Whyte, 1990). Data from a large sample (1,778 couples) collected in Beijing in the early 1990s show that most respondents did not date often—77 percent of women and 66 percent of men dated no one or only their spouse prior to marriage—and 56 percent of couples knew each other less than one year before marrying (Pimentel, 2000). Thus, many Chinese young people had to make a vital decision about their lives without being able to gain experience first through casual dating.

That pattern is changing rapidly. As explained in Chapter 13, movies, novels, and magazines are introducing Western ideas of love and marriage. As clubs, restaurants, dance halls, movie theaters, fast food joints, karaoke bars, and other entertainment spots multiply, and young people have more spending money, dating becomes easier. The new road system, urban sprawl, and the proliferation of motorcycles and cell phones give many rural youths the opportunity to take advantage of these urban attractions as well (Stanat, 2006; Farrer, 2007; Chang, 2008:207–245). Young people also are connected via cell phones and the Internet. Some 500 million Chinese post photos, blog, and chat on Renren, Baidu, Sina Weibo, and other sites. There are 180 million bachelors in China; over half are registered to use one of the three most popular dating services, Jiayuan.com, Zhenai.com, and Baihe.com. Because they must pay high fees for blogging, chatting (including with online matchmakers), and dating, only a fraction of them use these services at any one time. But with 120 males for every 100 females, as a result of the one-child policy, for many bachelors those fees seem worthwhile. The Chinese Academy of Social Science conservatively estimates that by 2020 there will be 24 million more unmarried men than women of marriage age, with declining prospects of marriage (Jiang, 2011; Zhang, 2012).

Children usually live with their parents until they marry. This pattern is both expected by cultural norms and the fact that few young people can afford to rent or purchase an apartment before they are married. Young people live in close physical proximity to their parents during the time when they choose a spouse, thus giving their parents ample opportunity to meet, judge, and comment on their boyfriends or girlfriends. Young Chinese would not want their parents to arrange their marriages, and almost all parents agree. However, they show little obvious resistance to, and seem to genuinely accept, a certain amount of parental influence and involvement.

Similar changes in mate choice also occurred in rural China (Lavely and Ren, 1992; Yan, 2003). Working in a collective gave young peasants opportunities for daily contact unavailable to them in the past, which increased their freedom to marry someone of their own choosing. Decollectivization has not changed this situation; young peasants still have greater freedom of choice. A marriage may be arranged by the parents, but the son and daughter will be given the opportunity to meet and agree to the match, or a young couple may become acquainted on their own through dating and ask their parents to prepare the wedding (Fan and Li, 2002; Murphy, 2004; Yuen, Law, and Ho, 2004; Yan, 2003, 2010).

High percentages of China's over 260 million migrants are young rural women who have left their villages to work in urban factory assembly lines in new coastal "boomtowns." Unlike their male counterparts, they have little opportunity to advance on the job or to retain this work past the age of twenty-five. Most of them return home to marry. But working on their own far from home creates an incentive to find and choose their own mate, and to set up housekeeping near their work. As children they attended school, perhaps in a nearby town, and knew little about farming. Working many hours a week, living in a dormitory, and having mostly women coworkers in the plant, these women have little chance of finding a mate. If they do meet someone, he may well be from another province, or be a local man who is older or less able to attract a mate. Urbanites often view poor rural people as outsiders. Some factories provide housing for married couples, but most couples must rent a small apartment at an exorbitant price. Many women return home for childbirth and have their grandparents visit them to help with their infants. They have little contact with their in-laws, who may even speak a different dialect. It is easier for men than women to achieve promotions at work, and their pay is generally much higher. The most successful wives in this situation may start a hair salon, restaurant, or movie rental store near the factory or one of their home villages. Those wives with good income may send home cash to help support their parents. But once these couples become used to shopping malls and big-city life, it is often hard for them to return to their villages. All this social mobility is speeding up independent dating, and living, for these migrants. But they lack the right to permanent residence and to the social services that are reserved for permanent urban residents under the *hukou* registration system (Wang, 2005). Migrants must pay far more than permanent residents for school fees, in inferior schools set up just for migrants, so they may find it necessary to send the children back to one of their home villages for education. And they often miss their families (Chang, 2008:360–376, 404–407; Gaetano and Jacka, 2004; Bossen, 2007; Zhang, 2009). Chapter 8 discusses this further.

A problem facing all prospective young couples in urban areas is the cost of housing, which is rising rapidly as old buildings are torn down to make way for new expensive ones built by real estate developers. And newly married couples living away from their parents must find funds to pay for child care while they are at work and for commuting long distances to and from work. Middle-class young men often feel the need to own a flat and car and have some savings before getting married.

Marital Breakdown

Divorce is another trend that mirrors the experiences of other countries. Causes of marital breakdown in China include the failure to deliver emotional support or a gratifying sexual relationship, family violence, the fading of romantic love after marriage, and extramarital affairs. In addition, political changes have had great impact on divorce in China. In 1953, China experienced a surge in divorces. Scholars interpret it as a consequence of the promulgation of the Marriage Law in 1950, which for the first time allowed women to ask for divorce. Many married women regarded divorce as a way out of intolerable arranged marriages. In rural areas, enforcement of the law was short-lived, as explained in Chapter 11. After the mid-1950s, divorce tended to be an urban phenomenon and, even there, remained rare (Conroy, 1987:54–55; Stacey, 1983).

Many China experts claim that a large number of divorces occurred during the Cultural Revolution (1966–1976). The impact of the Cultural

Revolution on divorce is difficult to assess with accuracy because of the lack of data. The extraordinary social upheavals and fear of persecution often led one partner to sue for divorce when the other got into political trouble. The implications for the whole family of one member's political wrongdoing were potentially disastrous. Divorce proceedings were initiated not because of a lofty sense of ideological outrage against the offending spouses but for the purpose of social survival and protection of the children's future (Conroy, 1987:55–56; Liang and Shapiro, 1983; Thurston, 1987).

Divorce has been on the upswing in China since the 1978 economic reforms (Conroy, 1987:58; Li, 2002). Extramarital affairs have increased. At the same time, contemporary Western ideas on marriage have gradually entered China. All these are said to have contributed to a rising divorce rate. From 1987 to 1990, divorces increased fourfold. Married people in their thirties exhibited the highest divorce rate. In 1994, there were 6.19 million divorced people, living mostly in cities. Divorce rates were lowest on the east coast and in eastern areas, highest in the northwest and the northeast, and moderate in the middle and southern parts of the country (Zeng and Wu, 2000). There have been 2 million divorces a year since 2000, 1.5 per thousand people vs. 5.2 in the United States (Jiang, 2011). In Shanghai, about 40 percent of divorces were filed because of extramarital affairs, 38 percent because of personality conflicts, and only 3 percent because of an unhappy sex life. They are usually initiated by the wife (Li, 2002:6; Beech and Hua, 2006). Overall, the divorce rate is growing in China at a much slower pace than in the West (Dong, Wang, and Ollendick, 2002).

Family Relations

The traditional Chinese family was most emphatically male-centered with respect to the distribution of authority, patterns of employment, residence, inheritance, a pronounced preference for male offspring, and oppression of women. In imperial China, even illiterate farmers knew about the Confucian Three Obediences by which women were to be governed: as an unmarried woman she must obey her father, as a married woman she must obey her husband, and as a widow she must obey her adult sons (Stacey, 1983:chap. 1; Mann, 1987; Saso, 1999). As Laurel Bossen points out in Chapter 11, in some regions and households, women found ways to assert some independence, but these opportunities were limited.

Female infanticide—the killing of female babies at birth—was practiced among some poor families before 1949 (Mungello, 2008). Poor parents might sell their daughters into slavery at three or four years of age or as prostitutes or concubines at twelve or fourteen (Johnson, 1993; Wolf, 1980). Even marriage did not bring women a higher status in the family. If a wife displeased her husband or her mother-in-law, she could be returned to her parents, and in times of economic stress, she might be rented, leased, or sold outright to a more prosperous man. She would obtain a degree of authority in her own right only after the passage of many years. Her position was weakest when she was still childless (sonless); it improved when she bore a son, and it grew even stronger when a daughter-in-law came under her direction. And by the time she entered into advanced age, her authority began to approximate that of her husband; if his was the earlier death, full power within the family might sometimes then be in her hands (Wolf, 1985:chap 1).

Women's oppression resulted from Confucian patriarchal ideology and women's economic dependence on men. The roots of women's subordination were undermined by the communist revolution of 1949 and subsequent economic and social changes. Yet gender discrimination in the workplace still exists. In addition, the Chinese government started the one child per household family planning policy in the late 1970s, discussed in Chapters 8 and 11. Persons not in compliance with the family planning policy face heavy fines or demotions or, on rare occasions, forced abortions. However, in most of rural China, where there is virtually no social security, peasants rely on their sons for old-age support. In rural areas enforcement of the one-child policy is not uniform, and a number of female births simply go unreported. But a study of abortion decisions and reported sex ratios at birth in a rural Yunnan county, found a male bias in the abortion pattern. As a result, sex ratio at birth rose from 107 males to 100 females in 1984–1987 to 110 to 100 in 1988–2000 (Löfstedt, Luo, and Johansson, 2004). Selective abortions of female fetuses may contribute most to the extremely high sex ratio for males among newborns (Wu, Viisainen, and Hemminki, 2006; see also Chu, 2001; Li, Zhu, and Feldman, 2004). This ratio is lowering the marriage prospects for young men, and leaving a shortage of women to work the farmland. In comparison, sex-selective abortions occur in urban China on a much less frequent basis because of the existence of social security systems there (discussed in Chapter 8). Today the increase in sexual freedom discussed in the next section has shifted the prevalence of urban abortions to unmarried young girls, who often have sex without protection or knowledge about contraception and face serious social taboos about young women having children out of wedlock, while there is more widespread acceptance of abortion (Nie and Kleinman, 2005).

Despite these unfortunate instances, blatant discrimination against Chinese women has been reduced significantly under the communist regime. In particular, since 1949, Chinese women have achieved a degree of economic independence as they work with men in state- or collective-run organizations. In urban China, it is unusual for women not to work outside the home. Chinese wives make more decisions than husbands, or the couple make decisions together despite unequal spousal statuses and widespread patriarchal values and practices (Zuo and Bian, 2005; see also Pimentel, 2000; Yu, 2004; Andors, 1983; Zuo and Bian, 2001). Zuo and Bian (2005) explain the unique

Chinese pattern with "family collectivism." They argue that women's labor-force participation and income-leveling programs in the post-1949 era shifted wives' financial dependence on husbands to the mutual financial interdependence of working husbands and wives. It also determined their equal sharing of household decisionmaking power. Since wives did more housework and knew more about family needs, they thus made more decisions than husbands.

Furthermore, urban young people in China today mainly rely on social institutions outside the family for employment and education, but live with their parents. Mothers are the center of the family's communication network; they are the glue that binds families together. Chinese youth adore and confide in their mothers. Children usually do not challenge orders from their fathers, who seldom issue direct orders to their children. Both parties carefully seek to avoid direct confrontation. A mother usually functions as the intermediary between her husband and their children. As the status of mothers evolves, the traditional hierarchical family authority structure is gradually disappearing in China.

Sexuality

The sexual bond between husband and wife is part of the basis of marriage, which in turn is the basis of the family. In China before the 1980s, an extremely high premium was placed on premarital virginity and conjugal fidelity. If an individual was caught in premarital sex or adultery, he or she would face serious punishments: mass criticism, forced confessions, demotions, or dismissal. Occasionally, an adulterer would be brought to court and sentenced to imprisonment on a verdict of hooliganism or rape (Cui, 1995:15–18).

Generally speaking, sex was a taboo topic in China before the 1980s (Dikotter, 1995). Any materials relating to sex, even nude works of art, were strictly forbidden. Even marital sex was not discussed. Today many people still avoid talking about sex either privately or publicly. A 1990 survey reported that over half of respondents never discussed sex with others (Zhao and Geng, 1992:1–4). More recent surveys show that these habits are not changing rapidly (Zhang et al., 2007; Yan et al., 2007; Lonn et al., 2007; Higgins and Sun 2007). The most comprehensive survey on the subject, interviewing more than 3,000 individuals from both urban and rural areas, including migrant laborers, found urbanites and younger respondents (under forty) reporting greater sexual activity than the rural folk. Thirty-five percent of males aged thirty to thirty-four reported having premarital sex, versus 14 percent of males over forty and 9 percent of urban females (Pan, 2005:23). Another study in the city of Changchun, among adolescents and parents from various social classes, found that most adolescents surveyed had not talked about sex with their parents (Zhang et al., 2007). Another in Jiangsu found that high percentages of college students spend several hours a week on the

Internet, but only 10 percent of the men and almost none of the women admitted to watching pornography (Yan et al., 2007). Respondents expressed high tolerance for premarital sexual behavior. Another national study of university students from differing social backgrounds found urban professionals more liberal in their views on sex than rural respondents (Higgins and Sun, 2007). A study of Uyghur students found that, like respondents in these other surveys, they knew how AIDS was transmitted sexually and via needles, but their knowledge was superficial (Lonn et al., 2007). Generally, well below 20 percent of total samples in any of these surveys admitted to having had premarital sex. AIDS is a growing problem in China, but until 2005, the government was reticent to have it discussed.

Public discourse on sexuality has occurred in the Chinese media since the 1980s (Cui, 1995:15–18; Honig and Hershatter, 1988:51–59). The focus of the discussion was once on chastity and self-restraint, emphasizing that improperly managed sexual feelings can lead to physical harm and social ruin. Today, the media is still filled with government-supported sex counselors who, while less inclined to focus on chastity, still emphasize the importance of managing sexual feelings so as to properly manage the body and one's role in society (McMillan, 2005; Xinran, 2003). James Farrer (2002), in his study of patrons of Shanghai dance halls and sex shops, found that many of them were there (as in the 1930s) to find a rich man or trophy mate. There is still much discussion of promiscuous foreign culture. This is a conservative sexual revolution—straying little from Confucian ideals (Slote and De Vos, 1998; Farquhar, 2002). It is difficult to determine to what extent premarital sex is still looked on with disfavor by the public in China today; the patterns observed in the 1980s and 1990s are certainly changing, but slowly.

After marriage, wives were required to play a traditional role in sexual activities, passively waiting to have sex when the husband wanted it; their task in marital intercourse was to satisfy their husbands' sexual needs (Honig and Hershatter, 1988:182; Jankowiak, 1993:233; Zhao and Geng, 1992:15). Those attitudes persist. Women in the Higgins and Sun survey (2007) expressed the importance of male superiority in marriage. In the comprehensive Pan survey (2005), fewer than 3 percent of male respondents in any age group reported experiencing kissing or sexual foreplay (women were not asked)! Research done in the 1980s and 1990s shows that although many urban Chinese do not think that husbands should insist on sexual intercourse when their wives are very reluctant, in reality many wives are inclined to satisfy their husbands' needs whenever they want intercourse. Jankowiak (1993:230–234) reports that when a wife does not like her husband, she may show more inclination to resist his advances and spend more time with her children or friends. The enhanced knowledge about sex among the population is accompanied by a more tolerant attitude toward premarital sex and cohabitation since the 1990s. Some university students move out of student dormitories and rent flats outside the campus to live with their sweethearts without any commitment to marriage. Such unions dissolve, without any bitterness, as soon as they graduate. Looser sexual restrictions, along with drug usage (Mexico, 2009:75–94, 231–250, 293–303; Jing and Worth, 2010), sex trafficking, careless blood transfusions, and prostitution (Gifford, 2007:76–85; Hessler, 2010:167–174; Zheng, 2009b; Mexico, 2009:23–58, 231–250, 278–282; Jing and Worth, 2010; Chang, 2008:231–241; Zhou, 2010:71–100) are contributing to a growing AIDS problem in China and are discussed later in this chapter. Still, there is little formal education about sex. Few use condoms. The government has instituted an advertising campaign to advocate their use.

Attitudes toward homosexuality are also changing. Such behavior has a long social history (Hinsch, 1992; Sang, 2003; Kang, 2009; Ho, 2011) but remains unpopular (Chou, 2000). In 2001, the Chinese Psychiatric Association ceased to define homosexuality as a mental disorder. Gay bars and social clubs have sprung up in the major cities, with a lively subculture (Rofel, 2007:111–156; Yau, 2010). Though no laws outlaw homosexuality, these establishments are subject to periodic police raids (Jeffreys, 2006:chap. 4). Numerous websites are available to China's gay community, and numerous Chinese films reference homosexuality (Lim, 2007; Martin, 2003). Very few gays or lesbians are open about their sexuality (Chou, 2000; Sang, 2003; Mexico, 2009:115–131).

Ethnic Minorities

In 2001, I conducted urban fieldwork (Zang, 2011a) comparing patterns in marriage and household structure between the majority Han and the Hui, the third largest minority group in China, who are Muslims (see Chapter 8). In my sample (comparing couples in one city), I found that few Han or Hui couples (27.2 percent versus 29.4 percent) used friends or relatives for introductions before their marriage. However, the Hui were much more likely than the Han to use parental arrangements or matchmakers to find a prospective mate (23.5 percent versus 8.5 percent, and 7.6 percent versus 3.7 percent, respectively). In comparison, the Han were more likely than the Hui to find a mate through coworkers (6.8 percent versus 2.6 percent). Also, 48.5 percent of the Han met their spouses on their own, compared with 32.8 percent of the Hui. It seems that the Hui rely more on traditional approaches in finding a mate than the Han. That helped shorten the average courtship time of the Hui couples—sixty-one weeks versus eighty-three weeks.

The Hui insist on marrying fellow Muslims or persons who promise to convert to Islam after marriage. This requirement reduces the odds for a Hui to meet a sweetheart from among his or her workmates (8.6 percent of the Hui couples in the sample were workmates, versus 17.6 percent of the Han), since there may not be many workers of the Hui ethnicity in his or her workplace.

Robert E. Gamer

This Yao minority grandfather is out for a walk with one of his grandsons in the village of Huangluo, Guangxi.

And there are no incentives for Han women to convert to Islam and marry Hui men, since the level of educational and economic attainment among the Han tends to be higher than that among the Hui.

Finally, I found rather similar patterns of living arrangements between the Han and Hui families. Nearly 70 percent of the Han live with their spouses and unmarried children, as compared with 65.5 percent of the Hui. Only 5.2 percent of the Han and 4.2 percent of the Hui were childless couples. Also, more than 11 percent of the Han and 12 percent of the Hui shared the same roof with spouses, married children, and parents; more than 25 percent of the Hui families and 13.3 percent of the Han families contain five to six persons.

I have also conducted surveys among Uyghur Muslims in Urumchi, the capital of the Xinjiang Uyghur Autonomous Region, and examined intergroup differences between the Uyghur and Han Chinese on arranged marriages. I found a rapid decline in parental arrangement for both Uyghur Muslims and Han Chinese in Urumchi. I also found that, in general, Han Chinese were less likely than Uyghur Muslims to report arranged marriages. However, the differences between Uyghur men and Han men fade away when people with the

Robert E. Gamer

A Uyghur family enjoys a fresh yogurt treat on a Sunday outing in Kashgar, Xinjiang.

same background characteristics were compared. That does not hold true for women. In addition, Uyghur women were more likely than Uyghur men to report arranged marriages (29 percent versus 22.9 percent). These findings indicate that Uyghur women have a lower degree of autonomy in the marriage market than their brothers. Uyghur parents influenced or controlled daughters more than sons with regard to marriage decisions, probably because the traditional Muslim family was often described as based on an authoritarian, patriarchal hierarchy, where women were viewed as the repository of the family honor. Muslim motherhood was regarded as a key safeguard of Islamic culture. The preservation of family honor traditionally entailed gender separation, the supervision of women, and restrictions on women's behavior, particularly as regards dress, mobility, and contact with men outside the immediate family. Uyghur men, however, are given more power and autonomy, since they have to compete with Han Chinese in the labor market. Uyghur women were also more likely than their Muslim brothers to report arranged marriages because Muslim women had a lower level of autonomy. Parents were less capable of controlling or influencing the marriage decisions of higher-status children (who were likely to be men) than those of lower-status children (who were likely to be women) (Zang, 2007, 2012; Dautcher, 2009).

I also studied whether modernization and urbanization have similar effects on family size for Uyghur and Han Chinese. I found that the Uyghurs were more likely than Han to live in large households. This may be partly due to the fact that the Chinese government has restricted every urban Han couple to one child and has privileged urban Uyghurs with an entitlement to have two children per couple. In addition, I found that Uyghur Communist Party members, professionals, and cadres were less likely than other Uyghurs to reside in a large family compound. This is consistent with the general tendency of families to have lower fertility rates and family size when they become more exposed to modernization (Fong, 2004:26; Zang, 2005).

Culture, and perceptions of culture, also link AIDS and minorities in the minds of many Chinese (Hyde, 2007). The first AIDS case in China was identified in Yunnan in 1985. The government immediately suspected that it emanated from minority groups—Tai, Lahu, and Wa—who live along the border and have members who indulge in promiscuous sex and use unsterilized needles to inject heroine. It set up a working group to track AIDS among these individuals, and for twenty years the official line suggested that this was the source of AIDS and that the rest of the country had no problem (Hyde, 2007). In fact, by that time, over a million people, in every province of the nation, were HIV positive and the problem was spreading because promiscuous sex—both with prostitutes and among other consenting adults—quietly takes place throughout China (Hershatter, 1997; Zheng, 2009a; Mexico, 2009:115–132, 273–292; Jing and Worth, 2010; Sutherland and Hsu, 2011). In 2005, the government began to address AIDS as a national and urgent problem. By 2009, official statistics placed the number of individuals HIV positive at 740,000, a third of them homosexuals. That is probably a conservative estimate (Jing and Worth, 2010).

Conclusion

As is true everywhere, radical changes in politics, the economy, and society brought on by modern life are affecting China's families and marriages. In rural China, the collectivization campaign changed peasants into wage earners who derived incomes from production teams, leading to the simplification of family structure and reduction in family size. The Marriage Law of 1950 and the Cultural Revolution during the 1960s made it acceptable for rural women to divorce. Since the 1980s, the government has decollectivized production teams, so that many economic functions have once again devolved to the family level and facilitated the reemergence of extended families in rural China. Yet rural youth have greater freedom than before to choose their own mates and make decisions about whether to stay or move to the city.

The family revolution occurred first in urban China as it experienced the penetration of Western influence and rapid industrialization. The lack of technological development in rural China kept out many of the forces of change that challenge traditional concepts of family life. This is still true today. In cities, families are changing more quickly. Urban youth can meet prospective marriage partners without help from their parents and even engage in premarital sex, and they can set up households and nuclear families that give them some distance from parental influence. Yet they are still strongly inclined to heed advice from their parents and to keep in close contact with them. And women, who are freed by this from economic dependence on their fathers and husbands, remain deferential to the advice of parents and husbands. The heavy emphasis of the Chinese on obedience to fathers and loyalty to family is a strong leash holding back the pull toward individualism.

Bibliography

Andors, Phyllis. 1983. *The Unfinished Liberation of Chinese Women, 1969–1980.* Bloomington: Indiana University Press.

Baker, Hugh. 1979. *Chinese Family and Kinship.* New York: Columbia University Press.

Beech, Hannah, and Bu Hua. 2006. "Breaking Up Is Easy to Do." *Time,* November 6.

Bossen, Laurel. 2007. "Village to Distant Village: The Opportunities and Risks of Long Distance Marriage Migration in Rural China." *Journal of Contemporary China* 16(50): 97–115.

Chang, Leslie T. 2008. *Factory Girls: From Village to City in a Changing China.* New York: Spiegel and Grau.

Chen, Nancy N., Constance D. Clark, Suzanne Z. Gottschang, and Lyn Jeffery (eds.). 2001. *China Urban: Ethnographies of Contemporary Culture.* Durham, NC: Duke University Press.

Cherlin, Andrew J. 2005. "American Marriage in the Early Twenty-First Century." *The Future of Children* 15(2): 33–55.

"China's Current Marriage Patterns." 1995. *Beijing Review,* August 14–20.

Chou, Wah-Shan. 2000. *Tongzhi: Politics of Same-Sex Eroticism in Chinese Societies.* Binghamton, NY: Haworth Press.

Chu, Junhong. 2001. "Prenatal Sex Determination and Sex-Selective Abortion in Rural Central China." *Population and Development Review* 27(2): 259–282.

Cohen, Myron. 1992a. "Family Management and Family Division in Contemporary Rural China." *China Quarterly* 130:357–377.

———. 1992b. "Family Organization in China." In *Case Studies in the Social Sciences,* edited by Myron Cohen, 3–16. Armonk, NY: M. E. Sharpe.

Conroy, Richard. 1987. "Patterns of Divorce in China." *Australian Journal of Chinese Affairs* 17:53–75.

Croll, Elizabeth. 1984. "The Exchange of Women and Property: Marriage in Post-Revolutionary China." In *Women and Property: Women as Property,* edited by Renée Hirschon. London: Croom Helm.

———. 2005. *Kinship, Contract, Community, and State: Anthropological Perspectives on China.* Stanford, CA: Stanford University Press.

Cui, Lili. 1995. "Sex Education No Longer Taboo." *Beijing Review,* April 3–16.

Dautcher, Jay. 2009. *Down a Narrow Road: Masculinity and Identity in a Uyghur Community in Xinjiang China.* Cambridge, MA: Harvard University Asia Center.

Diamant, Neil J. 2000. *Revolutionizing the Family: Politics, Love, and Divorce in Urban and Rural China, 1949–1968.* Berkeley: University of California Press.

Dikotter, Frank. 1995. *Sex, Culture, and Modernity in China: Medical Science and the*

Construction of Sexual Identities in the Early Republican Period. Honolulu: University of Hawaii Press.

Dong Qi, Yanping Wang, and Thomas H. Ollendick. 2002. "Consequences of Divorce on the Adjustment of Children in China." *Journal of Clinical Child and Adolescent Psychology* 31(1): 101–110.

Fan, C. Cindy, and Ling Li. 2002. "Marriage and Migration in Transitional China." *Environment and Planning A* 34(4): 619–638.

Farquhar, Judith. 2002. *Appetites: Food and Sex in Post-Socialist China*. Durham, NC: Duke University Press.

Farrer, James. 2002. *Opening Up: Youth Sex Culture and Market Reform in Shanghai*. Chicago: University of Chicago Press.

———. 2007. "China's Women Sex Bloggers and Dialectic Sexual Politics on the Chinese Internet." *Journal of Current Chinese Affairs* 36(4): 9–44.

Faure, David. 2007. *Emperor and Ancestor: State and Lineage in South China*. Stanford, CA: Stanford University Press.

Fong, Vanessa L. 2004. *Only Hope: Coming of Age Under China's One-Child Policy*. Stanford, CA: Stanford University Press.

Gaetano, Arianne M., and Tamara Jacka (eds.). 2004. *On the Move: Women in Rural-to-Urban Migration in Contemporary China*. New York: Columbia University Press.

Gifford, Rob. 2007. *China Road: A Journey into the Future of a Rising Power*. New York: Random House.

Hershatter, Gail. 1997. *Dangerous Pleasures: Prostitution and Modernity in Twentieth-Century Shanghai*. Berkeley: University of California Press.

———. 2004. "State of Field: Women in China's Long Twentieth Century." *Journal of Asian Studies* 63(4): 991–1065.

Hessler, Peter. 2010. *Country Driving: A Journey Through China from Farm to Factory*. New York: HarperCollins.

Higgins, Louise T., and Chunghui Sun. 2007. "Gender, Social Background, and Sexual Attitudes Among Chinese Students." *Culture, Health, and Sexuality* 9(1): 31–42.

Hinsch, Bret. 1992. *Passions of the Cut Sleeve: The Male Homosexual Tradition in China*. Berkeley: University of California Press.

Ho, Loretta Wing Wah. 2011. *Gay and Lesbian Subculture in Urban China*. London: Routledge.

Honig, Emily, and Gail Hershatter. 1988. *Personal Voices: Chinese Women in the 80s*. Stanford, CA: Stanford University Press.

Hsiung, Ping-Chen. 2005. *A Tender Voyage: Children and Childhood in Late Imperial China*. Stanford, CA: Stanford University Press.

Hsu, Francis. 1981. *Americans and Chinese*. Honolulu: University of Hawaii Press.

Huang, Chang-Ling. 2000. "Freedom, Rights, and Authority in Chen Duxiu's Thinking." *Issues & Studies* 36(3): 130–158.

Huang Shu-min. 1992. "Re-examining the Extended Family in Chinese Peasant Society." *Australian Journal of Chinese Affairs* 27:25–38.

Hyde, Sandra Teresa. 2007. *Eating Spring Rice: The Cultural Politics of AIDS in Southwest China*. Berkeley: University of California Press.

Jankowiak, William. 1993. *Sex, Death, and Hierarchy in a Chinese City*. New York: Columbia University Press.

Jeffreys, Elaine (ed.). 2006. *Sex and Sexuality in China*. London: Routledge.

Jiang, Chengcheng. 2011. "Why More Chinese Singles Are Looking for Love Online." *Time*, April 25.

Jing, Jun, and Heather Worth (eds.). 2010. *HIV in China: Understanding the Social Aspects of the Epidemic*. Sydney: University of New South Wales Press.

Johnson, Kay Ann. 1993. "Chinese Orphanages: Saving China's Abandoned Girls." *Australia Journal of Chinese Affairs* 30 (July): 61–87.
Johnson, Kay, Huang Banghan, and Wang Liyao. 1998. "Infant Abandonment and Adoption in China." *Population and Development Review* 24(3): 469–510.
Kang, Wenqing. 2009. *Obsession: Male Same-Sex Relations in China, 1900–1950.* Hong Kong: Hong Kong University Press.
Knapp, Ronald G., and Kai-Yin Lo (eds.). 2005. *House, Home, Family: Living and Being Chinese.* Honolulu: University of Hawaii Press.
Kohrman, Matthew. 2005. *Bodies of Difference: Experiences of Disability and Institutional Advocacy in the Making of Modern China.* Berkeley: University of California Press.
Lavely, William, and Xinhua Ren. 1992. "Patrilocality and Early Marital Co-Residence in Rural China, 1955–1985." *China Quarterly* 130: 378–391.
Lee, Haiyan. 2007. *Revolution of the Heart: A Genealogy of Love in China 1900–1950.* Stanford, CA: Stanford University Press.
Li, Raymond. 2002. "'Till Death Us Do Part' Forgotten as Revolution Shakes Society." *South China Morning Post,* April 20.
Li, Shuzhuo, Chuzhu Zhu, and Marcus W. Feldman. 2004. "Gender Differences in Child Survival in Contemporary Rural China: A County Study." *Journal of Biosocial Science* 36(1): 83–109.
Liang, Heng, and Judith Shapiro. 1983. *Son of the Revolution.* New York: Knopf/Random House.
Lim, Song Hwee. 2007. *Celluloid Comrades: Representations of Male Homosexuality in Contemporary Chinese Cinema.* Honolulu: University of Hawaii Press.
Liu, Xin. 2000. *In One's Own Shadow: An Ethnographic Account of the Condition of Post-Reform Rural China.* Berkeley: University of California Press.
Löfstedt, Petra, Luo Shusheng, and Annika Johansson. 2004. "Abortion Patterns and Reported Sex Ratios at Birth in Rural Yunnan, China." *Reproductive Health Matters* 12(24): 86–95.
Lonn, Bin, Karin Sahlholm, Rena Maiminti, Kaisaier Abdukarim, and Rune Andersson. 2007. "A Traditional Society in Change Encounters HIV/AIDS: Knowledge, Attitudes, and Risk Behavior Among Students in a Northwestern City." *AIDS, Patient Care, and STDs* 21(1): 48–56.
Makley, Charlene E. 2002. "On the Edge of Respectability: Sexual Politics in China's Tibet." *Positions: East Asia Cultural Critique* 10(3): 575–630.
Mann, S. 1987. "Widows in the Kinship, Class, and Community Structures of Qing Dynasty China." *Journal of Asian Studies* 46(1): 37–56.
Martin, Fran. 2003. *Situating Sexualities: Queer Representation in Taiwanese Fiction, Film, and Public Culture.* Hong Kong: Hong Kong University Press.
McMillan, Joanna. 2005. *Sex, Science, and Morality in China.* London: Routledge.
Mexico, Zachary. 2009. *China Underground.* New York: Soft Skull Press.
Mungello, David. 2008. *Drowning Girls in China: Female Infanticide Since 1650.* Lanham, MD: Rowman and Littlefield.
Murphy, Rachel. 2004. "The Impact of Labor Migration on the Well-Being and Agency of Rural Chinese Women: Cultural and Economic Contexts and the Life Course." In *On the Move: Women and Rural-to-Urban Migration in Contemporary China,* edited by Arianne M. Gaetano and Tamara Jacka, 243–276. New York: Columbia University Press.
Nie, Jing-Bao, and Arthur Kleinman. 2005. *Behind the Silence: Chinese Voices on Abortion.* Lanham, MD: Rowman and Littlefield.
Pan, Suiming. 2005. "Transformations in the Primary Life Cycle: The Origins and

Nature of China's Sexual Revolution." In *Sex and Sexuality in China,* edited by Elaine Jeffreys, 21–42. London: Routledge.

Parish, William, and Martin Whyte. 1978. *Village and Family in Contemporary China.* Chicago: University of Chicago Press.

Pimentel, Ellen Efron. 2000. "Just How Do I Love Thee? Marital Relations in Urban China." *Journal of Marriage and the Family* 62(1): 32–48

Potter, Salamith H., and Jack M. Potter. 1990. *China's Peasants: The Anthropology of a Revolution.* Cambridge: Cambridge University Press.

Riley, Nancy. 1994. "Interwoven Lives: Parents, Marriage, and Guanxi in China." *Journal of Marriage and the Family* 56: 791–803.

Rofel, Lisa. 2007. *Desiring China: Experiments in Neoliberalism, Sexuality, and Public Culture.* Durham, NC: Duke University Press.

Rosenfeld, Michael J. 2006. "Young Adulthood as a Factor in Social Change in the United States." *Population and Development Review* 32(1): 27–51.

Sang, Tze-Lan D. 2003. *Female Same-Sex Desire in Modern China.* Chicago: University of Chicago Press.

Saso, Michael. 1999. *Velvet Bonds: The Chinese Family.* Honolulu: University of Hawaii Press.

Shin, Eun-young. 2001. "The Effect of the Chinese Reform Policy on the Status of Rural Women." *Asian Journal of Women's Studies* 7(3): 63–92.

Slote, Walter H., and George A. De Vos (eds.). 1998. *Confucianism and the Family.* Albany: State University of New York Press.

Sommer, Matthew H. 2000. *Sex, Law, and Society in Late Imperial China.* Stanford, CA: Stanford University Press.

Spence, Jonathan. 2005. "Cliffhanger Days: A Chinese Family in the Seventeenth Century." *American Historical Review* 110(1): 1–10.

Stacey, Judith. 1983. *Patriarchy and Socialist Revolution in China.* Berkeley: University of California Press.

Stanat, Michael. 2006. *China's Generation Y: Understanding the Future Leaders of the World's Next Superpower.* Paramus, NJ: Homa and Sekey.

Sutherland, Dylan, and Jennifer Hsu. 2011. *HIV/AIDS in China: The Economic and Social Determinants.* London: Routledge.

Thurston, Ann. 1987. *Enemies of the People.* New York: Knopf.

Tsui, Ming. 1989. "Changes in Chinese Urban Family Structure." *Journal of Marriage and the Family* 51: 737–747.

Wang, Fei-Ling. 2005. *Organizing Through Division and Exclusion: China's Hukou System.* Stanford, CA: Stanford University Press.

Watson, James. 1982. "Anthropological Perspectives on Historical Research." *China Quarterly* 92: 589–622.

Watson, Ruby, and Patricia Ebrey (eds.). 1991. *Marriage and Inequality in Chinese Society.* Berkeley: University of California Press.

Whyte, Martin. 1990. "Changes in Mate Choice in Chengdu." In *Chinese Society on the Eve of Tiananmen,* edited by Deborah Davis and Ezra Vogel, 181–213. Cambridge, MA: Council on East Asian Studies, Harvard University.

———. 1992. "Introduction: Rural Economic Reforms and Chinese Family Patterns." *China Quarterly* 130: 317–322.

Whyte, Martin, and William Parish. 1984. *Urban Life in Contemporary China.* Chicago: University of Chicago Press.

Wolf, Arthur P. 1980. *Marriage and Adoption in China, 1845–1945.* Stanford, CA: Stanford University Press.

Wolf, Margery. 1985. *Revolution Postponed.* Stanford, CA: Stanford University Press.

Wu, Zhuochun, Kirsi Viisainen, and Elina Hemminki. 2006. "Determinants of High Sex Ratio Among Newborns: A Cohort Study from Rural Anhui Province, China." *Reproductive Health Matters* 14(27): 172–180.

Xia, Yan R., and Zhi G. Zhou. 2003. "The Transition of Courtship, Mate Selection, and Marriage in China." In *Mate Selection Across Cultures,* edited by Raeann Hamon and Bron Ingoldsby, 231–246. Thousand Oaks, CA: Sage.

Xinran, Xinran. 2003. *The Good Women of China: Hidden Voices.* New York: Anchor.

Xu, Xiaohe, and Martin Whyte. 1990. "Love Matches and Arranged Marriages: A Chinese Replication." *Journal of Marriage and the Family* 52: 709–722.

Yan, Hong, Xiaoming Li, Rong Mao, and Bonita Stanton. 2007. "Internet Use Among Chinese College Students: Implications for Sex Education and HIV Prevention." *Cyberpsychology and Behavior* 10(2): 161–169.

Yan, Yungxian. 2003. *Private Life Under Socialism: Love, Intimacy, and Family Change in a Chinese Village, 1949–1999.* Stanford, CA: Stanford University Press.

———. 2010. *The Individualization of Chinese Society.* London: Berg.

Yau, Ching (ed.). 2010. *As Normal As Possible: Negotiating Sexuality and Gender in China and Hong Kong.* Seattle: University of Washington Press.

Yu, Xiong. 2004. "The Status of Chinese Women in Marriage and the Family." In *Holding Up Half the Sky: Chinese Women Past, Present, and Future,* edited by Tao Jie, Zheng Bijun, and Shirley L. Mow, 172–192. New York: Feminist Press.

Yuen, Sun-pong, Pui-lam Law, and Yuk-ying Ho. 2004. *Marriage, Gender, and Sex in a Contemporary Chinese Village.* Trans. Fong-ying Yu. Armonk, NY: M. E. Sharpe.

Zang, Xiaowei. 1993. "Household Structure and Marriage in Urban China: 1900–1982." *Journal of Comparative Family Studies* 24(1): 35–43.

———. 2004. "Ethnic Differences in Marriage and Household Structure in a Chinese City." *New Zealand Journal of Asian Studies* 6(1): 64–82.

———. 2005. "Ethnic Variation in Family Size in Urban China." *Sociological Focus* 38(4): 223–239.

———. 2007. "Gender and Ethnic Variation in Arranged Marriages in a Chinese City." *Journal of Family Issues* 29(5): 615–638.

———. 2011a. *Ethnicity and Urban Life in China: A Comparative Study of Hui Muslims and Han Chinese.* London: Taylor and Francis.

——— (ed.). 2011b. *Understanding Chinese Society.* London: Taylor and Francis.

———. 2012. *Islam, Family Life, and Gender Inequality in Urban China.* London: Routledge.

Zeng, Yi. 2002. "A Demographic Analysis of Family Households in China, 1982–1995." *Journal of Comparative Family Studies* 33(1): 15–34.

Zeng, Yi, and Wu Deqing. 2000. "Regional Analysis of Divorce in China Since 1980." *Demography* 37(2).

Zhang, Dan. 2012. "Cyber-dating Industry Dating in China." *CNTV*, February 14. http://english.cntv.cn.

Zhang, Hong. 2009. "Labor Migration, Gender, and the Rise of Neo-Local Marriages in the Economic Boomtown of Dongguan, South China." *Journal of Contemporary China* 18(61): 639–656.

Zhang, Liying, Xiaoming Li, H. Iqbal, Wendy Baldwin, and Bonita Stanton. 2007. "Parent-Adolescent Sex Communication in China." *European Journal of Contraception and Reproductive Health Care* 12(2): 138–147.

Zhang, Qian Forrest. 2004. "Economic Transition and New Patterns of Parent-Adult

Child Coresidence in Urban China." *Journal of Marriage and the Family* 66(5): 1231–1245.

Zhao, Bo, and Geng Wenxiu. 1992. "Sexuality in Urban China." *Australian Journal of Chinese Affairs* 28: 1–20.

Zheng, Tiantian. 2009a. *Ethnographies of Prostitution in Contemporary China: Gender Relations, HIV/AIDS, and Nationalism.* New York: Palgrave Macmillan.

———. 2009b. *Red Lights: The Lives of Sex Workers in Post-socialist China.* Minneapolis: University of Minnesota Press.

Zhou, Jinghao. 2010. *China's Peaceful Rise in a Global Context: A Domestic Aspect of China's Road Map to Democratization.* Lanham, MD: Lexington Books.

Zuo, Jiping, and Yanjie Bian. 2001. "Gendered Resources, Division of Housework, and Perceived Fairness: A Case in Urban China." *Journal of Marriage and the Family* 63(4): 1122–1133.

———. 2005. "Beyond Resources and Patriarchy: Marital Construction of Family Decision-Making Power in Post-Mao Urban China." *Journal of Comparative Family Studies* 36(4): 601–622.

11

Women and Development

Laurel Bossen

In Chapter 10, Zang Xiaowei introduced you to family and kinship in China and discussed the central role they play. He explained that, except in some regions like western Yunnan, China's families have been patriarchal, with property generally passing through the male line and the bride coming to live with the groom's family, which in turn defers to the authority of his father. As Zang indicated, that system still gave the mother-in-law some control over family affairs but made younger women vulnerable to abuses. Gradually, urbanization and economic development are giving women increased clout; to a greater extent than is true in most nations, politics has played a role as well. In this chapter we shall focus more closely on how life is changing for women as economic reform progresses.

The study of women and development in China during the past century must be viewed in the context of China's political movements and the challenge of transforming China from a disintegrating imperial power into a modern nation. The most ambitious political transformations were introduced by the Communist Party when it took power in 1949. Unlike many other developing nations that have placed little or no priority on integrating women into development, China, under the leadership of the Communist Party, made explicit commitments to improving the status of women as part of its socialist agenda of promoting social and economic equality. China's self-proclaimed effort to "liberate" women has long generated a great deal of interest as a possible model for other nations. Those who favor government intervention to raise women's status while promoting economic development initially looked to China for inspiration and signs of success. Skeptics and critics of China's central planning and state control over information scrutinized China's claims and looked for independent evidence of achievement or failure. Since the 1980s, China's greater openness has led to better assessments of women's gains.

A long historical tradition of male dominance and patriarchal authority is deeply embedded in China's culture and institutions and is not easily overturned. For the first two and a half decades of revolutionary state planning and promotion of egalitarian goals, there was much talk about equality between the sexes. After Mao Zedong's death in 1976, the public emphasis on gender equality subsided, and liberalizing reforms have permitted a return of market forces and revival of earlier cultural practices. From the start of the reforms there has been concern that old patriarchal patterns and abuses of women would resurface, and, indeed, a more open society has allowed gender inequalities to become more visible. During nearly three decades of reform, many critics in China and abroad have publicized China's persisting structural inequalities and the unequal treatment of women both in the family system and in society at large (Andors, 1983; Croll, 1983; Honig and Hershatter, 1988; Johnson, 1983; Sargeson and Jacka, 2011; Stacey, 1983; Wolf, 1985; Xue 2003; Xinran, 2010). Moreover, China's strict family planning policies, discussed in Chapter 8, target women for control and place heightened pressure on women to give birth to sons (Attané, 2005; Greenhalgh and Winckler, 2005). As a result of strict family planning quotas, the sex ratio of reported births in the 1990s shows an increasing problem of "missing girls"—a clear sign that males and females are not treated equally (Bossen, 2002, 2006; Croll, 2001). At the same time, as explained in Chapter 10, increasing levels of female literacy, education, and urbanism, along with smaller families and greater economic autonomy, bring new benefits to women and may undermine patriarchal traditions even where earlier policies failed. When reviewing the changes from the early twentieth century to the early twenty-first century, there are many reasons to consider this a period of significant, if not always revolutionary, changes for women as well as men. These changes, aiming toward development and modernity, have brought greater equality and opportunity for women, but they continue to be contested by entrenched interests. From the perspective of a single generation, the movement toward greater gender equality may appear to be slow and to fall short of the revolutionary claims of the Maoist period, but the accelerating developments of the last century have indeed initiated momentous changes in gender relations.

The "Traditional" Portrait of Chinese Women

Any assessment of women's participation and of the benefits they have gained in China's development must choose a starting point for comparison. In China, historical sources emphasize the stability and tenacity of patriarchal authority, tracing it back to Confucian times. There is relatively little information, however, about local forms of gender inequality and family organization among

China's nonliterate populations. Not until the twentieth century have social scientists systematically begun to investigate the condition of women of different classes and subcultures within Chinese society. Thus the "traditional" portrait of Chinese women is usually a generalized and timeless abstraction that ignores processes of historical change and regional variation in the ways gender was experienced.

In this traditional portrait, most women held positions in society that were greatly devalued and relatively powerless compared to those of men. Women's low status derived from the classical Chinese family and kinship system, with its emphasis on the centrality of males within an enduring framework of patriarchal households based on patrilineal descent (inheritance through the male line) and patrilocal residence (in the household of the groom's father) after marriage (Bernhardt, 1999). The model Chinese family denied power and individual agency to women and youth; women as individuals lacked legal rights to own property such as land and were themselves liable to be transacted as property. Their parents arranged their marriages without their consent and transferred them as girls or young women to the homes of husbands who were strangers, there to live in a community dominated by their husband's patrilineal kin group. Parents also bound their daughters' feet, stunting their growth and hampering their mobility, to conform to an oppressive standard of female beauty and improve their daughters' chances in marriage. Women entered marriage with few resources and were required to submit to the authority of their husband's household, earning their keep by working obediently, preserving respect through marital fidelity, and gaining stature through the production of sons. Sons were generally considered far more valuable than daughters. When poverty threatened, infanticide, abandonment, the sale of children into servitude, or early marriage befell girls with much greater frequency than boys. The state did little to protect the rights of women and girls as such; rather it vested men with considerable powers as heads of households and patrilineal kin groups to manage the affairs of subordinate household members. Women had to look to fathers, brothers, husbands, or sons for whatever protection these men might offer.

This portrait depicts women's experience in Chinese history as one of universal, unremitting oppression and victimization. However, recent writings uncover considerable historical and regional variation in women's activities and rights and explore the degrees of flexibility within patriarchal structures (Jaschok and Miers, 1994; Ko, 1994; Watson, 1994; Hinsch, 2002; Tung, 2000). Rather than a single, unchanging system of patriarchy, contemporary studies reveal that earlier centuries witnessed significant shifts in women's economic activities, dowry and property rights, forms of marriage, legal rights, and even suicide patterns, as well as differences in women's condition according to class (Bernhardt, 1996, 1999; Ebrey, 1993; Gates, 1989, 1996; Huang, 1990; Mann, 1991, 1994, 1997; T'ien, 1988; Theiss, 2005). These studies illustrate the difficulty of determining precisely whether women in general gained or lost ground during previous historical periods. For instance, during the Song dynasty (960–1269), women gained the advantages of increased transmission of dowry property to daughters, of sustained ties to women's kin after marriage, of opportunities for elite daughters to learn to read and write, and of growing opportunities for women to earn money producing textiles and art (Lee, 2010). How does this progress weigh against the evidence of diminishing autonomy as indicated by the spread of foot binding and a growing market in women sold into various forms of servitude during that period (Ebrey, 1993:268)?

Although historians can trace some of the ways that women's rights became more limited in the subsequent Ming and Qing dynasties (Bernhardt, 1996; Watson and Ebrey, 1993), it is risky to apply descriptions written by and for privileged elites (usually from a male perspective) to the population as a whole. Indeed, the standard notion that rural Chinese women made minimal contributions to the agrarian economy is now challenged by recognition of their significant roles in commercial textile production over the centuries (Gates, 1997, 2005; Huang, 1990; Shih, 1992). The stereotype of women as domestic subordinates, politically powerless and economically burdensome, is increasingly modified by evidence that Chinese women were not easily restrained; they were productive and expressive, and they found ways to pursue their own interests (Cass, 1999). Although historical studies do reveal recurrent patterns of patrilineal, patrilocal, and patriarchal institutions, they are also shown to change over time. Because the evidence on the ways different classes of women behaved and responded to these institutions is so incomplete, the direction of change over long periods of Chinese history remains elusive (Ebrey, 1993; Chaffee, 1991; Hershatter, 2007; Mann, 1991).

Women in the Late Nineteenth and Early Twentieth Centuries

In the mid-nineteenth century, gender relations varied according to regional conditions. For example, northern China developed an economic system in which women had more limited roles in dry-land farming and other work outside the home than women in the rice-farming south (Buck, 1937; Davin, 1975; Johnson, 1983:15; Potter and Potter, 1990). Female foot binding was more pervasive in northern China than in southern China, making it hard for women in the north to help in the fields (Davin, 1975; Johnson, 1983). Recent research links the regional distribution and intensity of female foot binding to economic changes that influenced parental decisions to prepare their daughters for spinning and weaving indoors or for manual labor in the fields (Bossen, 2002; Gates, 1997, 2001). Where spinning cotton into thread was a major form of household production, girls with bound feet could not stray far from the spinning wheel. Variations on the stereotypical patriarchal family and marriage system have also been reported in different regions. In particular, peripheral areas with ethnic minorities have often favored atypical marriage patterns. Well-known regional variations include villages with high rates of uxorilocal marriage, in which a man joined his wife's household, or minor marriage, in which parents adopted a young girl and raised her to become the future bride of their son (Fei, 1949; Li et al., 2006; Pasternak, 1985; Wolf and Huang, 1980; Gates, 1996; Ono, 1989). The discovery that women in villages of southern Hunan embroidered poetic messages in their own unique "women's script" on fans and handkerchiefs for gift exchange between households contrasts with the prevailing image of universal illiteracy among rural women (Silbur, 1994; Yang, 1999; Mann, 2007).

Women from different classes had sharply contrasting lifestyles. Urban women from elite families had access to education and wealth, but respectability demanded that they not move beyond their doorways or interact with strange men. Meanwhile, women in rural rebel movements took an active part in public life. Women were active in rebel organizations in the Taiping Rebellion, the Red Spears movement, and the Boxer Rebellion of 1900 (Ono, 1989:10, 49; Perry, 1980:67, 204). The Taiping Rebellion (1851–1864), which is discussed further in Chapter 12, was a vast revitalization movement commingling Western Christianity with Chinese rebel traditions. It swept northward across China from the south, incorporating women as generals and soldiers under an ideology that stressed sexual equality. The Taiping rebels required followers to reject traditional patriarchal family structures, private property, polygamy, and foot binding and to live according to a radical system of sexual equality and segregation that prefigured communist experiments in social planning a century later. Women's participation in these movements suggests that even in the mid-nineteenth century patriarchal constraints on women were not completely accepted. As Maria Jaschok and Suzanne Miers observe, "The once ubiquitous stereotype of the long-suffering, meek, submissive Chinese woman as simply a victim of family interests, a vision of compliance and self sacrifice [*sic*], stands thus revealed for what it is—a stereotype in need of reappraisal and an empirical context" (1994:9).

Although the state occasionally attempted to protect women (with decrees forbidding foot binding and infanticide), state policies generally offered women little protection. As Rubie Watson notes:

> They could be divorced, although it was nearly impossible for them to divorce; they had no rights to family property, yet they could be pawned or sold. They could not take the imperial exams and were barred from holding office. Their legal status was rather like that of a jural minor; even as adults they remained under the authority of a husband, or if he was dead, a son. If a woman remarried or was divorced, she was likely to lose control of, and even access to, her children. (1994:27)

The legal limitations on women prior to 1949 indicated that the state supported the system of male authority.

Through the nineteenth and early twentieth centuries, China experienced growing external pressures for change. Increasing foreign trade, political intervention, urbanization, and cultural contact pried open some parts of China's inward-looking social system and shifted the balance of power in different directions (Judge, 2008). Europeans, and particularly European missionaries, encountering Chinese culture were convinced that one factor contributing to China's backwardness was the low status of women, as symbolized by their bound feet and lack of education (Ko, 2005). This perception was shared by Chinese reformers, who also began to argue that China's development required an end to foot binding and the elevation of women's status so that they could perform their role as mothers of a modern nation more effectively (Ono, 1989:23–47; Zhang and Wu, 1995).

Behind female foot binding and lack of education lay the patriarchal family system that deprived women and young people of individual rights and power. China still permitted family heads to buy and sell lesser members: as concubines, bondservants, and slaves (Jaschok, 1988; Jaschok and Miers, 1994; Watson, 1994; Gates, 1997, 2001). Women were duty bound to produce a male heir; if all they could produce were daughters, a concubine might be brought in to perform this duty. Although children of both sexes could be sold by their parents, the preference for sons in a patrilineal kinship system meant that girls were more likely than boys to be wrenched from their natal homes at a tender age. And at marriage age, the daughters were required to move out to join their husband's household and to take orders from their husband and mother-in-law. Widely repeated proverbs regarding the worthlessness and powerlessness of women reinforced women's subordination in the family. Thus daughters were described as "goods you lost money on," and advice for wives was that "if you marry a dog, follow the dog; if you marry a chicken, follow the chicken."

Accounts of captive women and sayings such as these illustrate the worst possibilities—warning of what could and did happen in extreme cases and of what was legally allowed to happen. But they do not enable us to envision the lives of ordinary women in ordinary times and do not help us to assess the rate and direction of change. Much as modern newspapers headline the most attention-grabbing crimes, many writings on China repeat the most disturbing images and sayings as evidence of Chinese women's general oppression and victimization. These negative images have provided grist for the mill of foreign and Chinese nationalist reformers. These more extreme images might have exotic appeal to a travel writer or provide moral justification to the missionary, but they did not accurately describe the situation of the majority of women. Along with those who were its obvious victims, many women lent their support to the patriarchal system. Scholars are beginning to assemble sys-

An elderly farm woman with bound feet, Yunnan, 1989.

tematic and reliable accounts of the range of economic and social roles that women in China played, including the ways that they defended themselves from abuse and sought to better their lives.

One example is a biography showing that when faced with an evil husband, a woman might not submit to his decisions and sometimes had outside recourse, as Ning Lao did when her opium-addict husband sold her three-year-old daughter in 1889:

> "I have sold her."
>
> I jumped out of bed. . . . I seized him by the queue [the long hair braid mandated by the Qing as the proper hairstyle for men]. I wrapped it three times around my arm. I fought him for my child. We rolled fighting on the ground.
>
> The neighbors came and talked to pacify us.
>
> "If the child has not left the city and we can keep hold of this one, we will find her," they said.
>
> So we searched. The night through we searched. . . . We walked a great circle inside the city, and always I walked with my hands on his queue. He could not get away. (Pruitt, 1967:68)

Ning Lao recovered her child with the help of neighbors, not the law, though the buyers of her child threatened to sell her along with her daughter to recover her husband's debt. This account suggests that a woman's lack of legal means to contest a husband's authority was only one dimension. Local social support could shore up a mother's determination to oppose a husband's action.

In evaluating the impact of development and commercialization, it is hard to estimate the changing proportions of girls and women who were sold by their families on a commercial basis rather than married with well-defined rights and dowries (Gates, 1996:132–133; Watson, 1994; Jaschok and Miers, 1994; Honig and Hershatter, 1988). Although many authors described the nastier sides of life for Chinese women at the turn of the century—female infanticide, sales of women and girls, servitude, abduction, prostitution, and concubinage—it is difficult to know if these problems were constant, getting worse, or just getting more publicity. In addition, the harsh conditions faced by women need to be assessed against the harsh conditions that men faced, particularly among China's vast peasantry.

From the mid-eighteenth century, China's population grew rapidly from around 275 million in 1779 to 549 million by 1949 (Smith, 1990). Overpopulation, land shortage, soil exhaustion, and economic dislocation compounded the problems of China's peasants, who continued to farm with preindustrial technology. Although a few prospered, large numbers did not. From the nineteenth to the mid-twentieth century, agricultural crises affected China's political and economic instability, contributing to famines, banditry, rebellions, and warfare. From 1932 to 1949, the Japanese occupation and China's war against Japan, followed by the civil war between the Communists and Nationalists, led to further dislocation.

Rural impoverishment and turmoil spelled misery for rural families. Infant girls were often abandoned, and young girls and women were frequently abducted, raped, and sold into various forms of servitude. Boys could also be sold as adopted sons or servants, and many men were dispossessed, impoverished, unable to form families, and condemned to wander in search of a livelihood. In addition, men could be conscripted and obliged to kill each other on behalf of China's competing armies (Mao, 1990; Stacey, 1983:198; Watson, 1976; Watson, 1994). Thus population growth and political instability in combination with overcrowded farms and declining incomes from traditional handicrafts meant that not only women were deprived of family support; large populations of surplus men, unmarried and unwanted, became beggars, bandits, soldiers, laborers, and lifelong bachelor-migrants and emigrants. In fact, exploring work and culture in the Pearl River Delta, Rubie Watson observes that "it is not altogether surprising to find that the boundaries that separated servile men from free men were more rigidly drawn than those that delineated servile women from free women." However, she adds: "Whether we can argue therefore that male servitude was harsher than female servitude requires further analysis" (1994:41).

Because the forms of dislocation were different for males and females, it is very difficult to determine whether women were singled out for bad treatment. There is simply insufficient information to show whether Chinese men or women experienced forced labor, poverty, malnutrition, and physical brutality in different proportions. Detailed demographic research comparing male and female life expectancies (such as Ts'ui-jung Liu's study of two Zhejiang clans from 1550 to 1850, in Hanley and Wolf [1985:58], which shows male life expectancies were lower) could provide some insights. The frequent references to female infanticide and abandonment, child marriage, and the abduction and sale of women found in nineteenth- and early-twentieth-century reports indicate that many women suffered dehumanizing experiences (Jaschok, 1988; Spence, 1999). Describing China in the 1930s, Jonathan Spence writes: "In the absence of accurate data, all one can do is acknowledge that the variations of suffering were endless, and that as impoverished families died out, others emerged to take over their land and struggle for survival in their turn" (1999:384).

Traditional Chinese gender inequality has often been illustrated by comparing the most distressed groups of young women with the most advantaged groups of senior men. This procedure exaggerates gender inequality by confounding it with age and class inequalities. Juxtaposition of such sharply contrasting images of women and men makes it relatively easy to proclaim improvements for women and to "measure" change by showing that most women are now better off than the appalling traditional image. This method of viewing Chinese women stacks the deck toward finding that modernism (whether begun during the Republican first or Communist second half of the twentieth century) improves women's status and also fosters the appearance that government policies promoting gender equality have been highly effective. One needs to keep this common source of distortion in mind when evaluating the communist revolution as a watershed.

Numerous women were experiencing very positive changes in the prerevolutionary period. By the early twentieth century, the demise of female foot binding had begun in parts of China in response to broad economic changes and industrialization, spurred on by government and missionary efforts to eradicate it (Bossen, 2002; Bossen et al., 2011; Gates, 1997, 2001; Gamble, 1968). Among the urban elite, following the demonstrations of May 4, 1919, protesting China's treatment at the Versailles Peace Conference, a growing revolutionary movement (discussed at length in Chapter 13) saw women's equality as important for national development. Opportunities for women to achieve formal education were expanding, along with exposure to Western concepts of modernization and sexual equality. Western missionaries encouraged Chinese women to abandon the practice of foot binding, to pursue higher education, and to reject arranged marriages. By 1922, the number of Chinese women receiving a university education had climbed to 887 out of a total 34,880 students, with women accounting for almost 9 percent of the students in Christian and foreign colleges. Western female missionaries also became role models and teachers for Chinese women, providing exposure to new concepts of public service and careers for women (Spence, 1999). Although government and missionary efforts to prohibit foot binding had some effect (Ko, 2005), early-twentieth-century processes of economic change, the decline of handcrafts, and industrial employment probably had a more significant impact (Bossen, 2002; Gates, 2001; Gamble, 1968). By the 1920s, some of the coastal areas where foot binding once was prevalent had abandoned the practice. Eradication of the custom in remote areas, however, would wait until the communists achieved power.

One of the major changes experienced by rural women in the early twentieth century was the decline in their ability to contribute to the household through cottage industries (Bossen, 2002; Bossen et al., 2011; Ono, 1989:7; Fei, 1949; Honig, 1986:62–64). As traditional handicrafts were displaced by industrial products, households had to shed surplus labor. Underemployed men typically migrated to cities seeking work. They might return with wealth or remain away for years. For underemployed women, risks of childbearing and child rearing and other considerations made migration a less viable option. Young, unmarried women risked abduction and illegitimate pregnancy if they worked outside the home, and young married mothers also risked the health of their children if they brought them along or risked losing their ties to the children if they entrusted them to others (Pruitt, 1967). But a daughter or wife kept virtuously at home had declining value. Thus the early twentieth century witnessed significant movements of women out of the rural family setting. Sometimes they were traded as commodities for their sexuality or labor, and sometimes they acted as independent agents seeking work in urban industries or services, begging, peddling, working as fortune-tellers, or migrating overseas. Young girls, in particular, could be sold by their parents as domestic slaves, entertainers, or prostitutes (Jaschok and Miers, 1994); the girls were obliged to pay back the money given to their parents and so transferred their dependency to their purchasers.

Young women who managed to migrate to find industrial work in cities or overseas to plantations often formed sisterhoods of various types that provided mutual support outside the protective umbrella of the patriarchal family (Jaschok and Miers, 1994:14; Honig, 1986:210). In the silk-producing areas of southern China, industrial employment provided young women with opportunities to delay or evade marriage by earning their own incomes (Topley, 1975; Sankar, 1984; Stockard, 1989). Jaschok and Miers (1994:23, 40) refer to these women as "marriage resisters." Growing numbers of women found employment in the textile factories that had displaced their cottage industries.

However, the depression of the 1930s brought falling world demand for silk, so rural and urban women again found themselves unemployed (Fei, 1949; Hershatter, 1986, 1991; Watson, 1994:33). Under such circumstances, girls and women could be compelled to join the ranks of young women providing domestic and sexual services in cities, where even greater numbers of displaced men also congregated seeking employment (Hershatter, 1991; Li, 2010). To thrive and compete in this economy, literacy, mobility, steady work performance, new skills, and connections were required. Most rural women, newly arrived in the cities, were poorly prepared to compete.

Women's Status After the Communist Revolution

The communist revolution set out to transform China by creating an egalitarian society and promoting rapid development. Shortly after taking power, China's leaders began to transform the system of property rights, marriage rights, and labor relations. In retrospect it is clear that many of these changes were economically ill advised and based on an oversimplified conception of rural life. For instance, the move from private to collective forms of agricultural production was expected to increase economic efficiency and productivity, yet for much of the revolutionary period, agricultural output only kept pace with population growth. The measures to produce social equality and to place women on a par with men were not thoroughly implemented; they left sufficient power concentrated in male hands to vitiate the reforms designed to benefit women.

The land reform program was intended to give peasants equal ownership of land. In 1950, the new Marriage Law gave "unmarried, divorced or widowed women the right to hold land in their own names" (Spence, 1999), which would enable them to become independent farmers. However, revolutionary theory soon gave way to pragmatism: rural men did not want to surrender control of family property. Enforcement of the law would have been very costly, requiring many educated officials as well as time and resources to register and protect titles for every rural adult as an individual. The party backed off and settled for a system in which women were counted as members of households to whom the land was distributed. Then the land and households were combined into collectives. The decision of how household income was to be distributed within the family remained, per tradition, in male hands.

The Marriage Law aimed to abolish the legal standing of arranged marriage, child marriage, and polygamy and to establish marriage as a voluntary contract between two equal adults, as well as to permit them to divorce. This measure, too, met with opposition, as peasant men labeled it "the divorce law" or the "women's law" (Ladany, 1992). Women who had been previously married by parental arrangements were thereby entitled to divorce their husbands. Combined with the newly acquired rights to land, women thought the law offered them a chance to break away from patriarchal control. Young rural women did attempt to use the new law and the courts to advance their interests (Diamant, 2000). However, women who sought to divorce faced strong opposition from their husband's family and the cadres. This led to considerable turmoil and violence against women—variously reported as violence by men who refused to accept divorce by their wives (Stacey, 1983:181), or by men who wanted to divorce and turned reluctant wives over to village militia for opposing the revolution (Ladany, 1992:60):

> Women had to fight their battles all alone, even under the threat of possible bloodshed. Many women were killed by their husbands or mothers-in-law, and many women chose to struggle to their deaths. During the year following the promulgation of the Marriage Law, more than 10,000 women were killed in South-Central China; in East China in 1950–1952 the figure reached 11,500. During the two or three years following the Law's enactment some 70,000–80,000 people per year were killed over marriage-related issues throughout the country. (Ono, 1989:181)

Judith Stacey similarly comments that "in a shocking number of cases women were murdered or driven to suicide when they attempted to gain their freedom" (1983:178).

The combined effect of the land and marriage reforms was perceived by married peasant men as a threat to their control over both land and labor. In 1953, the state gave orders to halt the violence, and campaigns to implement the Marriage Law were curtailed (Ladany, 1992:60; Stacey, 1983:181). The Marriage Law was intended to establish a more equitable basis for future marriages and to place the interests of the marriage partners above those of their parents. Older women, wanting control over the labor of their daughters-in-law, often objected to the increased freedom it offered younger women.

Following Marxist theory, the Chinese Communist Party held that women must work in the public sphere in order to achieve equality and contribute to socialist construction. Thus it became important symbolically to bring women out of the isolation of the household, where they worked for their husbands and families, and into production for society. Throughout the 1950s, women were increasingly pulled into nondomestic forms of labor intended to make them more productive. They joined agricultural work teams, and during the Great Leap Forward they participated in massive construction projects. In this respect, the Communist Party achieved a reversal of the direction of development seen in many Western countries where women were initially excluded from agricultural development plans (Momsen, 1991:66). In China, women were deliberately targeted and required to participate in farming in order to obtain income for their households.

In many parts of southern China, where rural women already participated in the public sphere in both agricultural and nonagricultural activities, the policy would have had no effect on women's economic equality—although some women claimed collective labor organization promoted equality by getting men to do their share of the farmwork (Bossen, 1994a). In areas where men were unaccustomed to seeing women do agricultural work, the fact that women were able to earn work points, a form of income, from the collective probably softened their opposition.

Communist theory took little account of the labor-intensive nature of housework in houses that lacked running water and modern stoves. In addition to hauling water, tending wood fires, and doing laundry by hand, rural women often engaged in a variety of home-based semicommercial activities like food processing, textile production, gardening, and raising courtyard livestock. All this was on top of the hours women spent working on the collective farm. The policies to bring women into agricultural work with status equal to men did not require men to take care of an equal share of the domestic work.

Countless reports from villages across China indicated that the local systems of allocating work points for collective work discriminated against women. Women were awarded only a fraction of the work points that men were awarded for similar types and quantities of work. The work point rate, like a wage rate, was in almost all cases an attribute of gender. When the maximum work point rate for men was ten points, the maximum for women would be seven or eight. Where men got twenty, women would get fifteen, and so forth, in village after village. Furthermore, the work points of members of a household were tallied together by village leaders, and their value was then paid to the household head. This system was blatantly discriminatory and did not establish women as independent actors in the labor force. Women were unable to exercise any direct control over the income they earned.

The unchallenged custom of patrilocal residence also kept patriarchal authority intact in the vast majority of rural marriages (Diamond, 1975). Daughters still had to marry out of their natal villages, leaving only their brothers to inherit housing and family savings. Men remained in the village where they were born and retained effective power over collective village land and politics, making decisions about work points, and allocating other village resources (Bossen, 1994a, 1994b, 1994c, 2002; Croll, 1995; Judd, 1994b; Potter and Potter, 1990). Patrilocal residence has helped to preserve male predominance in the definition of justice and retarded the extension of civil rights to women.

Of all the measures taken by China to improve the status of women, one that seems the least controversial will probably prove to have the largest impact over the long run: the policy of promoting equal education for girls and extending primary school education to the rural areas. China's early and consistent commitment to secular mass education has greatly benefited women of all regions. Before 1949, over 80 percent of women were illiterate. By 2004, the illiteracy rate for women dropped to 13.5 percent for women, and 5 percent for men (UNDP, 2006:6). In 1951, the proportion of girls among primary school students was 28 percent. By 1976, girls made up 45 percent of the primary school population. A quarter century later, in 2002, the proportion of girls in primary school, at 47 percent, was just slightly higher; it had still not reached 50 percent (NBS, 2004:57–63). However, this ratio reflects the shortage of girls due to demographic sex selection (discussed below) more than discrimination against girls in access to primary and middle school. In 2002, the enrollment rate of girls in primary school was 98.5 percent, essentially equal to that of boys. In middle school, female participation climbed to 47 percent by 2002. In college and university, the rise has also been impressive; the proportion of women in university rose from 21 percent in 1951 to 44 percent in 2002 (All-China Women's Federation, 1991:124, 136; NBS 2004:63). The gap between the sexes in university is relatively small today, but gender difference reappears at the higher levels. Female students outnumbered males at technical and teaching secondary schools, accounting for 54 and 71 percent of all students, respectively. At the highest educational levels, between 1991 and 2002, males accounted for 61 percent of the master's degrees and 74 percent of the PhDs (NBS, 2004:64) even though the proportion of women has been rising. China's pattern increasingly resembles that of Western developed nations where women predominate as teachers of the youngest children and men dominate the high-paying positions at the higher grade levels. In comparison to other large agrarian nations, China is doing well in promoting women's education and has narrowed the gender gap (UNDP, 2006; NBS 2004:63).

Continuing a process that began in the early twentieth century, during the revolutionary period women became an increasingly important part of the urban industrial workforce. The participation of women in urban industrial work did not bring sexual equality, however. Under state planning, women largely remained in segregated industries with lower salaries (Hershatter, 2007). Women were also less likely to be assigned to large state-run factories where health, pension, and housing benefits were provided. Rather, their jobs were concentrated in the lower-paying, less prestigious community—and neighborhood-run industries that offered fewer benefits (Whyte and Parish, 1984; Wolf, 1985). They sometimes had access to day care facilities, but this benefit was never very widespread. Most urban women worked outside industry; their total package of wages and benefits remained significantly lower and less secure than men's. Men continued to control the greater incomes and monopolize managerial positions. Unlike rural women, however, urban working women did collect their own wages.

Under state planning, urban women faced another task that consumed a great deal of time: standing in line at government stores for rationed products or locating scarce supplies on the black market. They also had to produce at home the goods they could not purchase. The predominantly male bureaucratic planners did not place high priority on inventing or producing labor-saving products to reduce housework. Women in revolutionary China did not have access to washing machines or even to laundromats and commercial hand-laundry services. Rather, they faced traditional chores such as hand-washing clothes for their family in a basin without in-home plumbing. They did all the housework, cooking, and minding the children.

Women and Economic Reform

During three decades of post-Mao reform, China has implemented many reforms, gradually liberalizing the economy, reviving markets and private sector activities. In the rural sector, the most significant reform was the dismantling of collective farm management. Individual households were allowed to contract former collective lands and farm them under household management, taking responsibility for meeting state quotas or taxes in grain production. In recent years, government taxes on the farmers have been reduced and eliminated. The household thus keeps surpluses for its own benefit. This incentive system has increased output while reducing labor committed to agricultural production. Households increasingly engage in labor migration as well as profitable sidelines or cottage industries, commerce, transport, construction, and service activities located off-farm in towns, cities, and distant provinces (Davin, 1999; Gaetano and Jacka, 2004; Jacka, 2005; Zhang, 2001).

In the reform period, village governments no longer require women to work in the fields in order to earn work points and contribute to household income. This does not mean women have stopped farming. The 2000 census showed that 69 percent of all women were still employed in farming, compared to 61 percent of all men (NBS, 2004:44), but women and men have gained greater flexibility in the disposal of their time and more opportunities to earn individual income through migrant labor and commercial activities. The reforms initially unleashed a mass exodus of men from farming to more lucrative occupations. Young men in particular set out for cities and towns—not encumbered, as women were, by social concerns for their sexual conduct and reputations—to look for work where they could find it (Zhou, 1996:137). This revived the pattern of seasonal male labor migration that was well established before the revolution (see Chapter 8).

Eventually, young unmarried women also joined this stream, although in lesser numbers and with greater risk. Generally, young women migrated in search of urban employment through relatives or personal contacts, helping in family businesses or providing domestic service and child care (Gaetano and Jacka, 2004; Zhang, 2009). Some set off simply to take their chances on finding work in informal urban labor markets, clustering on city streets, waiting for employers to arrive seeking young women to work, usually as domestic servants. These young women, often unsophisticated and illiterate, are easy prey for those ready to recruit them as brides for rural bachelors or as prostitutes, often through deception (Wong, 1996; Zhou, 1996:221; Mexico, 2009:43–58). Married rural women have had much less freedom to migrate due to their responsibilities for child care and the lack of housing for rural families (who have no urban household registration) in the cities. Married women have disproportionately stayed on the farms, working and managing the land allocated to their households. However, even married women are now entering the migrant stream when their families need greater cash income (Gaetano and Jacka, 2004).

Farming has become feminized in the sense that women in most regions of China supply the bulk of agricultural labor (Bossen, 1991, 1994c; Wolf, 1985; Judd, 1994a, 1994b), yet they have had little control over the land they farm. Village land is controlled by the village government. During the reform period, village leaders commonly allocated land on a per capita basis (so women are counted along with men) to individual households formed by married sons of the village, but individuals and households could not buy or sell their shares (Bossen, 2006). Thus, successful women farmers cannot purchase land to increase production, and women who are poor, inexperienced farmers or who hate farming cannot sell their shares and use the capital to finance other activities. The land remains firmly under village ownership and under the control of the patrilocal households they joined at marriage; it is not an asset women can own as individuals. Moreover, when they transfer their residence from their parents' to their husband's village at marriage, it is possible that they may not be allocated land there (Bossen, 2011; Yang and Xi, 2006). Thus, it is not surprising that women farmers also look to wage-labor opportunities as migrants rather than rely solely on farming.

The more open economy gives rural women more occupational choice and control over money. Ellen Judd (1994a:204) outlined two strategies pursued by rural women in response to China's policies toward economic development: household commodity production and employment in village industry. Those in villages with good commercial locations (near towns and cities or good transportation) can grow and sell commercial crops. Other villages and townships have established rural industries that employ women from their own and outside villages. Generally, they hire women at low wages and offer few benefits. In addition, younger women increasingly migrate long distances to reach urban and township enterprise zones that produce for export and pay higher wages. There, they work in sweatshops and on assembly lines producing items such as clothing or electronic products in a more competitive, capitalist fashion. These industries often pay their casual women workers higher wages than money-losing state industries, but the women have few protections in terms of safe working conditions, benefits, or job security (Chang, 2008; Ngai, 2005; Hessler, 2010:282–424). See Chapters 8 and 10 for more on this.

Unlike the former collective system that paid women's work points to the household head, the market economy allows women to receive individual

Robert E. Gamer

Tea pickers bringing their leaves to town from the fields.

wages (Bossen, 1994a, 2002; Woon, 1990:153, 159). This often lets them accumulate their own personal savings and gain more economic independence—especially when they migrate or when male migration leaves them with greater control over household income. Yet in Beijing, Li Zhang reports that many young migrant girls work for urban migrant bosses in family-run cottage industries for very low pay, living in their employer's house under strict control with little freedom to go out (2001:126–129). In other areas, such as the Pearl River Delta, where a large proportion of males have migrated overseas, wives who collect remittances from abroad have enjoyed prosperity by withdrawing from agriculture and other local production and investing in higher education for their sons and daughters (Woon, 1990:163).

The reform period has brought liberalizing policies to the rural economy, but it has also tightened government controls on reproduction (Greenhalgh and Winckler, 2005). The controversial family planning policy, discussed in Chapter 8, has meant that rural families have less choice over the number of children they raise than in the past. This policy limits urban families to one child but is more permissive in rural areas, favoring what Kay Ann Johnson calls a "one-son-or-two-child policy" (1996:81). Whether local governments enforce the limit as a two-child policy or let rural families have children until they produce a son (different rules apply in different places), the policy has a profound effect on women. First, it is largely implemented through direct bodily controls on women, including intrauterine devices (IUDs), abortion, and sterilization, with

X-rays and ultrasound tests for pregnancy (Greenhalgh, Zhu, and Li, 1994; Gifford, 2007:129–183). Second, the policy accentuates the importance of sons by forcing families to confront the risk of having no son at all if their first and second children are girls. This is believed to have increased China's unbalanced sex ratio by provoking families to get rid of daughters, whether through infanticide, abandonment, or sale, in order to try again for a son. In the past, such desperate measures were associated with extreme poverty, but under the growing prosperity of the post-Mao era they seem to result from both the excesses and the failures of government policy (Bossen, 2006, 2011; Banister, 2004; Greenhalgh and Winckler, 2005; Croll, 2001; Johnson, 1996; Sen, 1994). The increasingly imbalanced sex ratios shown by China's census data are a sign that government has not established the foundations for gender equality. By 2010, the birth sex ratio had reached 118.06 male live births for every 100 females ("China's Mainland," 2011), an alarming ratio demonstrating that strong discrimination against girls and women continues. On the positive side, the government has finally publicly recognized imbalanced sex ratios as a social problem and has begun to adopt measures to encourage parents to value and raise daughters (Li and Zhu, 2001). This shift appears to arise largely out of fears that a future surplus of unmarried males will result in social instability.

The birth control procedures employed by the state are highly invasive of women's privacy, yet women do not perceive them as entirely bad (Greenhalgh and Winckler, 2005). Withdrawal of state control of births would not necessarily leave women with the right to make their own decisions about reproduction. Rather, the patriarchal family, the traditional institution vested with social control over women's sexuality, could force women to bear more children than they want. Most rural women in China clearly do wish to bear children until, as required by custom, they produce a son, who secures their position within their husband's family and who legally owes them economic support in old age. But women may also welcome the power of the state against a family that wants them to produce an expanding labor force. Research on women's attitudes toward birth control suggests that they do not want to return to high fertility levels.

While the reforms of the economy and of family planning head in opposite directions toward lesser and greater state intervention, respectively, women's legal rights in rural areas are still largely unprotected by effective mechanisms of law enforcement. Outside personnel do not have the capacity or motivation to challenge the control of villages by local men linked by patrilineal descent. Village cadres entrusted with law enforcement ignore laws that, in theory, should protect women. Women who are abducted or coerced into marriages with village men get little support from village cadres. Newspaper accounts of efforts by women's families or the All-China Women's Federation to retrieve women who have been abducted to serve as wives in distant villages generally report a wall of silence, concealment, and noncooperation from villages where the women are held (Wong, 1996:293, 326–329). Yet in the 1990s, urban and rural women increased their ability to communicate their concerns to the media using letters, telephones, and radio (Xue, 2003) and to organize and mobilize themselves for a variety of purposes (Hsiung, Jaschok, and Milwertz, 2001; Jacka, 2005).

The increased prosperity associated with the economic reforms, the greater access to market commodities, and the relaxation of communist moral doctrines surrounding marriage have permitted the revival of marriage transactions involving both bridewealth (usually in the form of funds given by the groom's family to the bride's family) and dowry (usually in the form of goods provided by the bride's family)—both of which were common prior to the revolution. Such marriage transactions were suppressed during the collective period but have escalated dramatically in the past decade (Yan, 1996, 2003, 2009:155–183). Although the payment of bridewealth does not mean that a bride has been purchased, the escalating demands for bridewealth make it difficult for men from poor villages to attract wives. These men are then tempted to resort to marriage brokers who use deceit or abduction to supply brides (Yan, 1996; Han, 2001). On the other side, in marriage negotiations where women have a choice, brides are increasingly demanding and getting a new house and earlier separation from the husband's parents as well as greater control over material goods as conditions for marriage (Yan, 2003).

In urban China, the effects of the economic reforms on women have been varied. The relatively small proportion of women workers who were once privileged to have access to state jobs found that initially in the more competitive reform economy, state industries were more likely to discharge their female employees and to demand male employees when hiring new workers or university graduates. However, recent reports of a preference for hiring women suggest that the pampered only-sons born in the 1980s are deficient employees in comparison to their sisters (*Economist,* 2007:60). Although the constitution of 1982 and the Women's Rights Protection Law of 1992 pledge to protect women, some observers argue that protective regulations requiring women to retire five years earlier than men and clauses prohibiting them from doing certain kinds of work (such as night shifts, work in harsh conditions, work that results in exposure to industrial poisons, or work that is physically strenuous) during menstruation, pregnancy, the postpartum period, and while nursing have the effect of fostering biologically-based discrimination. Margaret Woo observed that "when faced with providing protective benefits, some factory managers simply chose not to hire women workers, or to dismiss them. Thus, in the city of Nantong, women constituted 70 percent of the total number of workers fired from their jobs in 1988" (1994:281–282). However, she argued that "the conclusion that women's interests have been subordinated to the state's goal of economic development is best supported by the conditions in the 'special economic zones,' which the government has set up to promote economic development. In these special economic zones, where female labor is needed, the 'return home' policy is not promoted, and protective regulations are non-existent" (1994:287). In these areas, women form a high proportion of the workforce but are primarily temporary workers lacking the benefits and guarantees of state-sector workers.

Reports of a foreign manufacturer's preference for hiring women staff from all over China suggest that men are less desirable as employees in comparison to daughters. "The managers believe that women are generally harder-working and tend to stay longer. But schools and universities have cottoned on to this now and set quotas on the number of women that firms can recruit. The company says that for every group of women it selects, it now has to hire a share of men too" (*Economist,* 2007:60).

In Chapter 10, Zang Xiaowei discusses the lives of the millions of migrant women working for the private entrepreneurs and reformed state enterprises. And the expansion of commercial activities and services in urban centers has offered women alternatives to state and private factory employment. Many of the new businesses in the informal sector have been established by women independently or as family enterprises (Bruun, 1993; Von Eschen, 2000; Chang, 2008). Often these businesses sell labor-saving products and services that were unavailable in the days of revolutionary austerity, when manual labor was considered noble.

Improvements in household appliances came first to the urban sector, but the revival of free markets responding to supply and demand has rapidly brought industrial commodities even to farm families. They, too, have invested in electric washing machines, rice cookers, microwave ovens, and other items that allow women to spend less time in drudgery. Increased disposable income in women's hands has also led to an explosion in the fashion industry that stimulates and caters to women's desires to be attractive, selling a profusion of beauty products and services. Purveyors of hair treatments, skin creams, shampoos, perfumes, jewelry, plastic surgery, and designer fashions in clothes and shoes increasingly beckon the daughters of a post-Mao generation, whose mothers uniformly grew up wearing drab blues and grays that were mandated by the Maoist unisex, antifashion ideology. Especially for urban women enjoying disposable income for the first time, these commodities bring excitement and a feeling of participation in the modern world. For rural migrants, they bring possibilities for purchasing some of the symbols of sophisticated urban lifestyles formerly denied them. After years of material sacrifice for the revolution and politically mandated denial of gender difference, Chinese women are now seeking different routes to social and economic success. Indeed, the frenzied consumer choices Chinese women are now making have caused Western feminists to gasp at how they mirror Western women's insecurities, joining in the never-ending quest for beauty and the latest designer labels (Evans, 2000; Honig and Hershatter, 1988; Wong, 1996).

Robert E. Gamer

Saleswomen in a women's clothing store in Kaili, Guizhou.

All major cities now have gleaming new shopping centers boasting international stores (Walmart, Carrefour, Ikea), fast-food chains, and comparable new Chinese businesses affordable to large numbers of Chinese consumers. Women of the growing, status-conscious middle class feel increased pressure not only to beautify themselves, but also to beautify their homes, which, in the reform period, have been transformed into private property.

Women and Politics

The Communist Party, as part of its commitment to sexual equality, initiated policies designed to bring women into the political process. It did so in part by creating affirmative action programs, by setting quotas or targets for the minimum participation of women in political bodies, and by establishing the All-China Women's Federation, a national body to oversee women's interests. Critics have argued that the political bodies to which women were appointed are largely powerless. They also point out that the women's federation is not an organization arising in response to women's own initiatives; rather it is a government bureaucracy controlled by the party to transmit and implement party policies directed at women (Barlow, 1994:341–344). Women in the federation are state employees. Nonetheless, the All-China Women's Federation is a large and diverse national organization with branches in each province, county, and town. The rise of a more independent women's movement in the reform period has stimulated staff within the official organization to mobilize women not only for general societal interests, but also for their own interests as women facing an emergent market economy (Hershatter, 2007; Hsiung, Jaschok, and Milwertz, 2001; Judd, 2002).

What have Chinese women gained in the political sphere? Is their position in the formal political structure simply a pitch for "symbolic capital"—a way to enhance China's reputation among nations? Have communist policies generally improved women's possibilities for formal political influence? Have state policies imposing quotas and requiring female participation been effective?

China is governed by the Communist Party and the State Council. The highest body within the party is the Politburo, a group of twenty-five full members and their alternates and led by a core group of nine men, called the Standing Committee. Since the Communist Party was founded, only five women (three of them wives of powerful men) have served as full members of the Politburo, but none of them have been on the Standing Committee. In 2012, one was serving. Female membership in the party's Central Committee, the body from which the Politburo derives, with a membership of about 200, averaged about 12 percent between 1956 and 1992. Women's participation in these bodies peaked during the Cultural Revolution and, since the reforms, has been sliding back down toward earlier levels. In 2002 it was 8 percent; in 2011 6 percent. The thirty-five-member State Council has four women members (Rosen, 1995:317; NBS, 2004:84; Wale, 2011).

The National People's Congress (the national legislature) is similarly divided between its Standing Committee, which has greater decisionmaking powers, and the whole congress, which meets for policy discussion. Women's participation on the Standing Committee, a group ranging from fifty-five to eighty members, averaged only 5 or 6 percent in the 1950s, increased to over 20 percent in the 1970s, dropped back down to 12 or 13 percent in the late 1980s, and remains there. The proportion of female representatives to the National People's Congress, a body of nearly 3,000 members, is higher and increased from 12 percent in the 1950s to just over 20 percent in the 1970s, where it has remained fairly constant to the present (Rosen, 1995:320; NBS, 2004:87). The UN *Human Development Report* bases its evaluation of China's position in its gender empowerment index on the proportion of women in the National People's Congress, which many consider to be a body too large for actual decisionmaking. National People's Congress meetings discuss and ratify decisions already made in other bodies (Ogden, 1995:256). *New York Times* journalist Fox Butterfield recalls Chinese friends joking that "delegates to the National People's Congress had only two rights: to raise their hands to vote yes and to applaud the speeches of Communist leaders" (1982:421).

When moving down the hierarchy to lower, regional levels of the political structure, government reports on female participation tend to combine "head and deputy head" and "chief and deputy chief" positions. In this way, the proportions of females represented hover around 4 to 6 percent for city mayors, township heads, county chiefs, and prefectural and provincial governors. However, the vast majority of women are at the "deputy" or "vice mayor" level, with no women holding the highest position in party or government at provincial, autonomous region, or administered cities levels. This suggests strong reluctance to place women in positions of authority over men. At the lower levels of city, county, township, and small town, women hold only 1 to 2 percent of the top positions (Rosen, 1995:325). Most of the small proportion of women who reach higher office at these levels of government hold "vice" or "deputy" positions where they are usually one of several, and not to be promoted. Another consideration is that women in Chinese politics are often confined to the less influential spheres of responsibility, concentrating on issues concerning women, children, health, and education. In recent years, the Communist Party has raised the percentage of female members from only 14.5 percent in 1990 to 17.8 percent in 2002 (NBS, 2004:88), possibly in response to the United Nations conferences on women. In sum, although state quotas and priorities brought women into political bodies where they might otherwise be completely absent, the proportions tend to be so low and their positions so secondary and marginal that the state commitment to equality loses credibility.

In rural China, women rarely hold positions of political leadership. Apart from the sole position of director of women's affairs, local village councils are in almost all cases composed only of men. The director of women's affairs is typically designated the local representative of the national women's federation and has responsibility for women's work or family planning (Rosen, 1995:325–327; Bossen, 1994b, 2002; Croll, 1995; Huang Shu-min, 1989; Judd, 1994b, 2002; Potter and Potter, 1990). During the Cultural Revolution, Rosen (1995) and the Chinese sources he cites claim that women broke out of the mold and went beyond the typical women's slots. One reason for this may have been the policy of sending educated youths, including young women, to the countryside, where their literacy and knowledge of bureaucracy could be useful to village governments negotiating with outside officials. Urban, educated young women sent to rural areas had a chance to assume political positions at the lower levels of the political hierarchy. In the reform period this ended; educated urban youth were no longer being sent to the countryside, and those who had gone returned to the cities. Now that the pool of leadership is once again confined to native villagers, few women are selected. The common pattern today is similar to that found by Norma Diamond (1975) early in the revolutionary period. The few women active in village leadership usually come from among a small, atypical group of women who did not marry outside the village into which they were born.

In urban China, the increasing exposure to international standards not only in material goods but also in education and culture has stimulated efforts to revive an autonomous feminist movement within China (Hsiung, Jaschok, and Milwertz, 2001). New forms of women's writing have begun to explore different ways of looking at Chinese women's experiences (Zhu Hong, 1994; Yuan 2005), and women intellectuals have begun to establish women's studies programs in universities (Du Fangqin, 2001). A growing number of young Chinese women have received university educations abroad and have returned with new views on feminism and human rights. The Marxist conception of women's liberation is gradually being displaced by debates about the nature and future of an autonomous women's movement and of more diverse ways of organizing women (Li, 1995; Hershatter, 2007; Hsiung, Jaschok, and Milwertz, 2001; Barlow 2004). The tension between state control and autonomous women's groups was evident at the 1995 UN World Conference on Women, where the Chinese government did its best to restrain such groups, both among Chinese women and among their international counterparts.

Conclusion

China's revolutionary leaders sought to include women in development by emphasizing education, labor force participation, and marriage reform. Compared to the constraints women faced in the nineteenth and early twentieth centuries, when neither the state nor the family was obliged to treat them as individual citizens, Chinese women from all walks of life have benefited. More women than ever are educated and work outside the home. These are very positive signs. On the negative side, persisting patriarchal institutions allow men to retain control of village politics and resources, while male-dominated party politics at the national level have favored male leadership. One of the greatest weaknesses in China's legal system is that it still has neither granted women effective individual rights to land (whether as daughters, wives, or widows) nor permitted land to escape from the traditional control of patrilineal village corporations in which women's influence is virtually nil (Bossen, 2006; Li and Bruce, 2005). Even when village land in periurban areas is expropriated for urban development, it remains exceedingly difficult for women to exercise their right to compensation for property and job losses due to "gender inequalities in village citizenship" (Sargeson and Song, 2011).

In comparing the reform period to the earlier revolutionary period, it is clear that the state has abandoned many of its earlier efforts to command greater female participation in the labor force, politics, and education. This has resulted in stagnation in some areas but also some gains. Few women hold meaningful political posts. Women's access to education has improved greatly when compared to the nineteenth and early twentieth centuries, but there is a gender gap in higher education. Most women still work outside the home, but gender differences in type of occupation and level of remuneration remain significant. Women remain culturally constrained by traditional obligations to perform child care and housework (Entwisle and Henderson, 2000).

Despite the weakened state support for equality, women in the reform period have undeniably benefited, as have men, from greater opportunities for occupational and residential choice. The marketplace has opened up new opportunities for women to engage in commercial activities on their own account and to earn cash incomes that are paid directly to women employees rather than to household heads. Although women are disproportionately responsible for unskilled farmwork, young women increasingly draw on their education and greater exposure to the outside world to take risks in seeking urban and nonfarm employment. These trends tend to undermine China's resistant patriarchal family institutions by giving women alternatives. However, women who attempt to act independently in the labor market and in the marriage and sexual market, where there is growing demand for their services, need effective legal protection against the resurgence of coercive practices (Yan, 2009:25–154). Between 10 and 20 million women work in karaoke bars and massage parlors (see Chapter 10). Particularly in rural areas, women need better protection against violence, abduction, forced marriage, and forced labor. They also need protection of their property rights in cases of divorce. Improved systems of communication and the increasing levels of female education that enable them to use public communication (letters, the Internet, newspapers, the broadcast media, and telephones) to inform others when their rights are violated may help women to obtain greater legal protection.

The government's family planning program uses heavy-handed methods of enforcement aimed primarily at women that deprive them of choice, but it also acts as a buffer against patriarchal demands for large families. Withdrawal of the state program would not necessarily empower women to make their own reproductive choices or to limit childbearing. The state policies bring about results that, for the majority of rural women fortunate enough to bear a son, are probably close to what they would choose for themselves. The minority who fail to bear a son desperately desire to do so and many have broken the rules. China's highly skewed sex ratios are evidence of systematic discrimination against girls in order to have a son. Despite its illegality, the practice of sex-selective abortion has become very widespread (Nie, 2005; BBC, 2007).

Finally, if we evaluate the role of women in China's development from a global perspective, there is reason for optimism. The efforts of the state to extend education and health care to its female population have improved women's life expectancies and given them more skills with which to participate in society than they had in the past. Women have held their ground in the market economy of the reform period and gained some economic independence. China is performing significantly better than India, its most obvious Asian analogy in terms of its size, agrarian population, and patriarchal traditions. India's maternal mortality rate is roughly ten times higher, and its mortality rate among children under age five is over three times higher than China's (see Table 5.2). In China, women have longer life expectancy, later age at marriage, and higher literacy and educational levels than women in India (UNDP, 1994:144–156; UNDP, 2006). Chinese women still have major battles to fight if they are to achieve economic and political equality, but now that the majority of women are educated and less encumbered by reproduction, they are better positioned to organize themselves and make their own demands in the future. In this respect, Chinese women have an interest in the development of more democratic institutions and an effective legal system that respects civil and human rights for all its citizens.

Bibliography

All-China Women's Federation Research Institute. 1991. *Zhongguo funu tongji ziliao (1949–1989)* (Statistics on Chinese Women). Beijing: Zhongguo Tongji Chubanshe (China Statistical Publishing House).

Andors, Phyllis. 1983. *The Unfinished Liberation of Chinese Women, 1969–1980.* Bloomington: Indiana University Press.

Attané, Isabelle. 2005. *Une Chine Sans Femmes?* Paris: Editions Perrin. www.editions-perrin.fr.

Banister, Judith. 2004. "Shortage of Girls in China Today." *Journal of Population Research* 21(1): 19–45.

Barlow, Tani. 1994. "Politics and Protocols of Funu." In *Engendering China: Women, Culture, and the State,* edited by Christina Gilmartin, Gail Hershatter, Lisa Rofel, and Tyrene White, 339–359. Cambridge, MA: Harvard University Press.

———. 2004. *The Question of Women in Chinese Feminism.* Durham, NC: Duke University Press.

BBC (British Broadcasting Company). 2007. "China to Act on Gender Imbalance," August 25. http://news.bbc.co.uk.

Bernhardt, Kathryn. 1996. "Chinese Women's History." In *Remapping China: Fissures in Historical Terrain,* edited by Gail Hershatter, Emily Honig, Jonathan Lipman, and Randal Stross, 42–58. Stanford, CA: Stanford University Press.

———. 1999. *Women and Property in China, 960–1949.* Stanford, CA: Stanford University Press.

Bossen, Laurel. 1991. "Changing Land Tenure Systems in China: Common Problem, Uncommon Solution." *Sociological Bulletin: Journal of the Indian Sociological Society* 40(1–2): 47–67.

———. 1994a. "Gender and Economic Reform in Southwest China." In *Femmes, féminisme, et développement* (Women, feminism, and development), edited by Huguette Dagenais and Denise Piché, 223–240. Montreal: McGill-Queens University Press.

———. 1994b. "The Household Economy in Rural China: Is the Involution Over?" In *Anthropology and Institutional Economics,* edited by James Acheson, 167–191. Monographs in Economic Anthropology no. 12. Lanham, MD: University Press of America.

———. 1994c. "Zhongguo nongcun funu: shenma yuanyin shi tamen liu zai nong tian li?" (Chinese rural women: What keeps them down on the farm?). In *Xingbie yu Zhongguo* (Gender and China), edited by Li Xiaojiang, Zhu Hong, and Dong Xiuyu, 128–154. Beijing: Shenghuo-Dushu-Xinhe Sanlian Shudian (SDX Joint Publishing Company).

———. 2002. *Chinese Women and Rural Development: Sixty Years of Change in Lu Village, Yunnan.* Lanham, MD: Rowman and Littlefield. Chinese translation by Yukun Hu. *Zhongguo Funu yu Nongcun Fazhan: Lucun liushi nian de bianqian.* 2005. Jiangsu Peoples Publishing House.

———. 2006. "Land and Population Controls in Rural China." *Bulletin of the National Musuem of Ethnology* (Osaka, Japan) 30(3): 421–449.

———. 2011. "Reproduction and Real Property in Rural China: Three Decades of Development and Discrimination." In *Women, Gender, and Rural Development in China,* edited by Sally Sargeson and Tamara Jacka, 97–123. Cheltenham, UK: Edward Elgar.

Bossen, Laurel, Wang Xurui, Melissa Brown, and Hill Gates. 2011. "Feet and Fabrication: Footbinding and Early 20th Century Rural Women's Labor in Shaanxi. *Modern China* 37(4): 347–383.

Bruun, Ole. 1993. *Business and Bureaucracy in a Chinese City: An Ethnography of Private Business Households in Contemporary China.* Berkeley: University of California, Institute for East Asian Studies.

Buck, John L. 1937. *Land Utilization in China.* Nanking: University of Nanking Press.

Butterfield, Fox. 1982. *China: Alive in the Bitter Sea.* Toronto: Bantam.

Cass, Victoria B. 1999. *Dangerous Women: Warriors, Grannies, and Geishas of the Ming.* Lanham, MD: Rowman and Littlefield.

Chaffee, John W. 1991. "The Marriage of Sung Imperial Clanswomen." In *Marriage and Inequality in Chinese Society,* edited by Rubie Watson and Patricia B. Ebrey, 133–169. Berkeley: University of California Press.

Chang, Leslie T. 2008. *Factory Girls: From Village to City in a Changing China.* New York: Spiegel and Grau.

"China's Mainland Population Grows to 1.3397 Billion in 2010: Census Data." 2011. *English News,* April 28. http://news.xinhuanet.com/english2010.

Croll, Elizabeth. 1983. *Chinese Women Since Mao.* London: Zed Books.

———. 1995. *Changing Identities of Chinese Women.* Hong Kong: Hong Kong University Press.

———. 2001. *Endangered Daughters: Discrimination and Development in Asia.* London: Routledge.

Davin, Delia. 1975. "Women in the Countryside of China." In *Women in Chinese Society,* edited by Margery Wolf and Roxane Witke, 243–273. Stanford, CA: Stanford University Press.

———. 1999. *Internal Migration in Contemporary China.* New York: St. Martin's.

Diamant, Neil. 2000. *Revolutionizing the Family: Politics, Love, and Divorce in Urban and Rural China, 1949–1968.* Berkeley: University of California Press.

Diamond, Norma. 1975. "Collectivization, Kinship, and the Status of Women in Rural China." In *Toward an Anthropology of Women,* edited by Rayna Reiter, 372–395. New York: Monthly Review Press.

Du Fangqin. 2001. "'Manoeuvering Fate' and 'Following the Call': Development and

Prospects of Women's Studies." In *Chinese Women Organizing: Cadres, Feminists, Muslims, Queers,* edited by Ping-Chun Hsiung, Maria Jaschok, and Cecilia Milwertz, with Red Chan, 237–249. Oxford: Berg.

Ebrey, Patricia Buckley. 1993. *The Inner Quarters: Marriage and the Lives of Chinese Women in the Sung Period.* Berkeley: University of California Press.

Economist, The. 2007. "Capturing Talent." August 18, 59–61.

Entwisle, Barbara, and Gail E. Henderson (eds.). 2000. *Re-drawing Boundaries: Work, Households, and Gender in China.* Berkeley: University of California Press.

Evans, Harriet. 2000. "Marketing Femininity: Images of the Modern Chinese Woman." In *China Beyond the Headlines,* edited by Timothy Weston and Lionel Jensen, 217–244. Lanham, MD: Rowman and Littlefield.

Fei, Hsiao-Tung. 1949 [1939]. *Peasant Life in China: A Field Study of Country Life.* London: Kegan Paul, Trench, and Trubner.

Fei, Hsiao-Tung, and C. I. Chang. 1948. *Earthbound China: A Study of Rural Economy in Yunnan.* London: Routledge and Kegan Paul.

Gaetano, Arianne M. and Tamara Jacka. 2004. *On the Move: Women and Rural-to-Urban Migration in Contemporary China.* New York: Columbia University Press.

Gamble, Sidney. 1968 [1954]. *Ting Hsien: A North China Rural Community.* Stanford, CA: Stanford University Press.

Gates, Hill. 1989. "The Commoditization of Chinese Women." *Signs* 14(4): 799–832.

———. 1996. *China's Motor: A Thousand Years of Petty Capitalism.* Ithaca, NY: Cornell University Press.

———. 1997. "Footbinding and Handspinning in Sichuan: Capitalism's Ambiguous Gifts to Petty Capitalism." In *Constructing China: The Interaction of Culture and Economics,* edited by Kenneth G. Lieberthal, Shuen-fu Lin, and Ernest P. Young, 177–194. Ann Arbor: University of Michigan Press.

———. 2001. "Footloose in Fujian: Economic Correlates of Footbinding." *Comparative Studies in Society and History* 43(1): 130–148.

———. 2005. "Girls' Work in China and North-Western Europe: Of *Guniang* and *Meisjes*." In *Marriage and the Family in Eurasia: Perspectives on the Hajnal Hypothesis,* edited by Theo Engelen and Arthur Wolf, 319–341. Amsterdam: Aksant.

Gifford, Rob. 2007. *China Road: A Journey into the Future of a Rising Power.* New York: Random House.

Gilmartin, Christina, Gail Hershatter, Lisa Rofel, and Tyrene White (eds.). 1994. *Engendering China: Women, Culture, and the State.* Cambridge, MA: Harvard University Press.

Greenhalgh, Susan, and Edwin A. Winckler. 2005. *Governing China's Population: From Leninist to Neoliberal Biopolitics.* Stanford, CA: Stanford University Press.

Greenhalgh, Susan, Zhu Chuzhu, and Nan Li. 1994. "Restraining Population Growth in Three Chinese Villages." *Population and Development Review* 20(2): 365–395.

Han, Min. 2001. *Social Change and Continuity in a Village in Northern Anhui, China.* Osaka: National Museum of Ethnology.

Hanley, Susan, and Arthur Wolf (eds.). 1985. *History and Population in East Asia.* Stanford, CA: Stanford University Press.

Hershatter, Gail. 1986. *The Workers of Tianjin, 1900–1949.* Stanford, CA: Stanford University Press.

———. 1991. "Prostitution and the Market in Women in Early Twentieth-Century Shanghai." In *Marriage and Inequality in Chinese Society,* edited by Rubie Watson and Patricia B. Ebrey, 256–285. Berkeley: University of California Press.

———. 2007. *Women in China's Long Twentieth Century.* Berkeley: University of California Press.

Hessler, Peter. 2010. *Country Driving: A Journey Through China from Farm to Factory.* New York: Harper.

Hinsch, Bret. 2002. *Women in Early Imperial China.* Lanham, MD: Rowman and Littlefield.

Honig, Emily. 1986. *Sisters and Strangers: Women in the Shanghai Cotton Mills, 1919–1949.* Stanford, CA: Stanford University Press.

Honig, Emily, and Gail Hershatter (eds.). 1988. *Personal Voices: Chinese Women in the 1980s.* Stanford, CA: Stanford University Press.

Hsiung, Ping-Chun, Maria Jaschok, and Cecilia Milwertz, with Red Chan (eds.). 2001. *Chinese Women Organizing: Cadres, Feminists, Muslims, Queers.* Oxford: Berg.

Huang, Philip. 1990. *The Peasant Family and Rural Development in the Yangzi Delta, 1350–1980.* Stanford, CA: Stanford University Press.

Huang Shu-min. 1989. *The Spiral Road: Change in a Chinese Village Through the Eyes of a Communist Party Leader.* Boulder: Westview.

Jacka, Tamara. 1997. *Women's Work in Rural China: Change and Continuity in an Era of Reform.* Cambridge: Cambridge University Press.

———. 2005. *Rural Women in Urban China: Gender, Migration, and Social Change.* Armonk, NY: M. E. Sharpe.

Jaschok, Maria. 1988. *Concubines and Bondservants: A Social History.* London: Zed Books.

Jaschok, Maria, and Suzanne Miers (eds.). 1994. *Women and Chinese Patriarchy: Submission, Servitude, and Escape.* London: Zed Books.

Johnson, Kay Ann. 1983. *Women, the Family, and Peasant Revolution in China.* Chicago: University of Chicago Press.

———. 1996. "The Politics of the Revival of Infant Abandonment in China, with Special Reference to Hunan." *Population and Development Review* 22(1): 77–98.

Judd, Ellen. 1994a. "Alternative Development Strategies for Women in Rural China." In *Femmes, féminisme, et développement* (Women, feminism, and development), edited by Huguette Dagenais and Denise Piché, 204–222. Montreal: McGill-Queens University Press.

———. 1994b. *Gender and Power in Rural North China.* Cambridge: Cambridge University Press.

———. 2002. *The Chinese Women's Movement: Between State and Market.* Stanford, CA: Stanford University Press.

Judge, Joan. 2008. *The Precious Raft of History: The Past, the West, and the Woman Question in China.* Stanford, CA: Stanford University Press.

Ko, Dorothy. 1994. *Teachers of the Inner Chambers: Women and Culture in Seventeenth-Century China.* Stanford, CA: Stanford University Press.

———. 2005. *Cinderella's Sisters: A Revisionist History of Footbinding.* Berkeley: University of California Press.

Ladany, Laszlo. 1992. *Law and Legality in China: The Testament of a China-Watcher.* London: Hurst.

Lee, Hui-shi. 2010. *Empresses, Art, and Agency in Song Dynasty China.* Seattle: University of Washington Press.

Li, Danke. 2010. *Echoes of Chongqing: Women in Wartime China.* Champaign: University of Illinois Press.

Li Shuzhuo, and Zhu Chuzu. 2001. *Research and Community Practice on Gender Difference in Child Survival in China.* Beijing: China Population Publishing House.

Li Shuzhuo, Jin Xiaoyi, Marcus Feldman, Li Nan, and Zhu Chuzhu. 2006. "Research Summary" (in English) in *Dangdai Zhongguo Nongcun de Zhaohui Nuxu* (Uxorilocal Marriage in Contemporary Rural China). Beijing: Social Sciences Academic Press.

Li, Xiaojiang. 1995. "Economic Reform and the Awakening of Chinese Women's Collective Consciousness." In *Engendering China: Women, Culture, and the State,* edited by Christina Gilmartin, Gail Hershatter, Lisa Rofel, and Tyrene White, 360–382. Cambridge, MA: Harvard University Press.

Li, Zongmin, and John Bruce. 2005. "Gender, Landlessness, and Equity in Rural China." In *Developmental Dilemmas: Land Reform and Institutional Change in China,* edited by Peter Ho, 270–295. London: Routledge

Mann, Susan. 1991. "Grooming a Daughter for Marriage: Brides and Wives in the Mid-Ch'ing Period." In *Marriage and Inequality in Chinese Society,* edited by Rubie Watson and Patricia Buckley Ebrey, 204–230. Berkeley: University of California Press.

———. 1994. "Learned Women in the Eighteenth Century." In *Engendering China: Women, Culture, and the State,* edited by Christina Gilmartin, Gail Hershatter, Lisa Rofel, and Tyrene White, 27–46. Cambridge, MA: Harvard University Press.

———. 1997. *Precious Records: Women in China's Long Eighteenth Century.* Stanford, CA: Stanford University Press.

———. 2007. *The Talented Women of the Zhang Family.* Berkeley: University of California Press.

Mao Zedong. 1990. *Report from Xunwu.* Trans. and Intro. by Roger Thompson. Stanford, CA: Stanford University Press.

Mexico, Zachary. 2009. *China Underground.* New York: Soft Skull Press.

Momsen, Janet Henshall. 1991. *Women and Development in the Third World.* London; New York: Routledge.

NBS (National Bureau of Statistics). 2004. *Women and Men in China: Facts and Figures.* Department of Science, Social Science, and Technology. www.stats.gov.cn/english/statisticaldata/otherdata/men&women_en.pdf.

Ngai, Pun. 2005. *Made in China: Women Factory Workers in a Global Workplace.* Chapel Hill, NC: Duke University Press.

Nie, Jing-Bao. 2005. *Behind the Silence: Chinese Voices on Abortion.* Lanham, MD: Rowman and Littlefield.

Ogden, Susan. 1995. *China's Unresolved Issues: Politics, Development, and Culture.* 3rd ed. Englewood Cliffs, NJ: Prentice Hall.

Ono, Kazuko. 1989. *Chinese Women in a Century of Revolution, 1850–1950.* Stanford, CA: Stanford University Press.

Pasternak, Burton. 1985. "On the Causes and Demographic Consequences of Uxorilocal Marriage in China." In *History and Population in East Asia,* edited by Susan Hanley and Arthur Wolf, 309–334. Stanford, CA: Stanford University Press.

Perry, Elizabeth J. 1980. *Rebels and Revolutionaries in North China, 1845–1945.* Stanford, CA: Stanford University Press.

Potter, Sulamith, and Jack Potter. 1990. *China's Peasants: The Anthropology of a Revolution.* Cambridge: Cambridge University Press.

Pruitt, Ida. 1967 [1945]. *A Daughter of Han: The Autobiography of a Chinese Working Woman.* Stanford, CA: Stanford University Press.

Rosen, Stanley. 1995. "Women and Political Participation in China." *Pacific Affairs* 63(3): 315–341.

Sankar, Andrea. 1984. "Spinster Sisterhoods." In *Lives: Chinese Working Women,* edited by Mary Sheridan and Janet Salaff, 52–70. Bloomington: Indiana University Press.

Sargeson, Sally, and Tamara Jacka (eds.). 2011. *Women, Gender, and Rural Development in China*, Cheltenham, UK: Edward Elgar.

Sargeson, Sally, and Song Yu. 2011. "Gender, Citizenship and Agency in Land Development." In *Women, Gender, and Rural Development in China*, edited by Sally Sargeson and Tamara Jacka. Cheltenham: UK: Edward Elgar.

Sen, Amartya. 1994. "Population, Delusion, and Reality." *New York Review of Books*, September 22, 62–71.

Shih, James. 1992. *Chinese Rural Society in Transition: A Case Study of the Lake Tai Area, 1368–1800*. Berkeley, CA: Institute of East Asian Studies.

Silbur, Cathy. 1994. "From Daughter to Daughter-in-Law in the Women's Script of Southern Hunan." In *Engendering China: Women, Culture, and the State*, edited by Christine Gilmartin, Gail Hershatter, Lisa Rofel, and Tyrene White, 47–68. Cambridge, MA: Harvard University Press.

Smith, Christopher. 1990. *China: People and Places in the Land of One Billion*. Boulder: Westview.

Spence, Jonathan. 1999. *The Search for Modern China*. New York: W. W. Norton.

Stacey, Judith. 1983. *Patriarchy and Socialist Revolution in China*. Berkeley: University of California Press.

Stockard, Janice. 1989. *Daughters of the Canton Delta: Marriage Patterns and Economic Strategies in South China, 1860–1930*. Stanford, CA: Stanford University Press.

Theiss, Janet M. 2005. *Disgraceful Matters: The Politics of Chastity in Eighteenth Century China*. Berkeley: University of California Press.

T'ien, Ju-kang. 1988. *Male Anxiety and Female Chastity: A Comparative Study of Chinese Ethical Values in Ming-Ch'ing Times*. Leiden: E. J. Brill.

Topley, Marjorie. 1975. "Marriage Resistance in Rural Kwangtung." In *Women in Chinese Society*, edited by Margery Wolf and Roxanne Witke, 247–268. Stanford, CA: Stanford University Press.

Tung, Jowen R. 2000. *Fables of the Patriarchs: Gender Politics in Tang Discourse*. Lanham, MD: Rowman and Littlefield.

UNDP (UN Development Programme). 1994. *Human Development Report 1994*. New York: Oxford University Press.

———. 2006. *Human Development Report 2006*. New York: Oxford University Press. http://hdr.undp.org/en/media/hdr06_complete.pdf, p. 364, table 24.

Von Eschen, Kristin. 2000. "A Green Light for the Geti: The Divergent Experiences of Reform-Era China's Male and Female Private Entrepreneurs." MA thesis, Department of Anthropology, McGill University.

Wale, Samuel. 2011. "On State Council, Women Hold Up 11.43% of the Sky." *China Digital Times*, June 24. http://chinadigitaltimes.net.

Wang, Zheng. 1993. "Three Interviews: Wang Anyi, Zhu Lin, Dai Qing." In *Gender Politics in Modern China*, edited by Tani Barlow, 159–208. Durham, NC: Duke University Press.

Watson, James. 1976. "Chattel Slavery in Chinese Peasant Society: A Comparative Analysis." *Ethnology* 15: 361–375.

Watson, Rubie. 1994. "Girls' Houses and Working Women: Expressive Culture in the Pearl River Delta, 1900–1941." In *Women and Chinese Patriarchy: Submission, Servitude, and Escape*, edited by Maria Jaschok and Suzanne Miers, 25–44. London: Zed Books.

Watson, Rubie, and Patricia B. Ebrey (eds.). 1993. *Marriage and Inequality in Chinese Society*. Berkeley: University of California Press.

Whyte, Martin King, and William L. Parish. 1984. *Urban Life in Contemporary China*. Chicago: University of Chicago Press.

Wolf, Arthur, and Huang Chieh-shan. 1980. *Marriage and Adoption in China, 1845–1945*. Stanford, CA: Stanford University Press.
Wolf, Margery. 1985. *Revolution Postponed: Women in Contemporary China*. Stanford, CA: Stanford University Press.
Wong, Jan. 1996. *Red China Blues: My Long March from Mao to Now*. Toronto: Doubleday.
Woo, Margaret Y. 1994. "Chinese Women Workers: The Delicate Balance Between Protection and Equality." In *Engendering China: Women, Culture, and State*, edited by Cristina Gilmartin, Gail Hershatter, Lisa Rofel, and Tyrene White, 279–295. Cambridge, MA: Harvard University Press.
Woon, Yuen-fong. 1990. "From Mao to Deng: Life Satisfaction Among Rural Women in an Emigrant Community in South China." *Australian Journal of Chinese Affairs* 25: 139–169.
Xinran, Xinran. 2010. *Message from an Unknown Chinese Mother: Stories of Loss and Love*. New York: Chatto and Windus.
Xue, Xinran. 2003. *The Good Women of China: Hidden Voices*. New York: Anchor.
Yan, Yunxiang. 1996. *The Flow of Gifts: Reciprocity and Social Networks in a Chinese Village*. Stanford, CA: Stanford University Press.
———. 2003. *Private Life Under Socialism: Love, Intimacy, and Family Change in a Chinese Village, 1949–1999*. Stanford, CA: Stanford University Press.
———. 2009. *The Individualization of Chinese Society*. New York: Berg.
Yang Li, and Xi Yin-sheng. 2006. "Married Women's Rights to Land in China's Traditional Farming Areas." *Journal of Contemporary China* 15(49): 621–636.
Yang Yue-qing. 1999. "Nushu: A Hidden Language of Women in China" (video). Vancouver: East-West Film Enterprise.
Yuan, Lijun. 2005. *Reconceiving Women's Equality in China: A Critical Examination of Models of Sex Equality*. Lanham, MD: Lexington Books.
Zhang, Li. 2001. *Strangers in the City: Reconfigurations of Space, Power, and Social Networks Within China's Floating Population*. Stanford, CA: Stanford University Press.
Zhang, Lijia. 2009. *"Socialism in Great!" A Worker's Memoir of the New China*. New York: Anchor.
Zhang, Naihua, with Xu Wu. 1995. "Discovering the Positive Within the Negative: The Women's Movement in a Changing China." In *The Challenge of Local Feminisms: Women's Movements in Global Perspective*, edited by Amrita Basu, 25–57. Boulder: Westview.
Zhou, Kate Xiao. 1996. *How the Farmers Changed China: Power of the People*. Boulder: Westview.
Zhu Hong. 1994. "Women, Illness, and Hospitalization: Images of Women in Contemporary Chinese Fiction." In *Engendering China: Women, Culture, and the State*, edited by Christina Gilmartin, Gail Hershatter, Lisa Rofel, and Tyrene White, 318–338. Cambridge, MA: Harvard University Press.

12

Religion

Chan Hoiman and Ambrose Y. C. King

Chinese religion is not a subject that can be approached in any straightforward or uncontroversial manner. Chinese society and culture were rarely if at all dominated by any state religion or an associated order of church and priesthood worshiping a supreme godhead; yet its religious orders have generally been dominated by the state, and the state has been operated in accordance with religious precepts. The social order of the Chinese people has long been permeated by ritual practices with clear supernatural overtones, giving propitiatory ritual offerings to ancestors or idols; yet Chinese have seldom belonged to organized religious bodies. Scholars can therefore alternatively maintain that the Chinese are not a very religious people at all and that they are permeated with superstition of a magical, "prereligious" kind. Chinese scholars of a "New Confucian" bent retort that Chinese culture is verily "beyond belief," with spiritual reaches and depths that cannot be contained within the usual institutional or intellectual frameworks of religions. Even at the end of the nineteenth century, the missionary scholar Arthur Smith would still characterize the religious life of the Chinese people as simultaneously "pantheistic, polytheistic, and atheistic" (1894:chap. 26).

Scholars have taken many approaches to the study of China's religions. In the late nineteenth century, the great German sociologist Max Weber (1864–1920), undertook his famous study of China's religion (1964 [1922]) as part of his much broader examination of capitalism and comparative civilizations, approaching Chinese civilization from the perspective of two major "homegrown" religions, Confucianism and Daoism. He sought to demonstrate that the social structure of China contained components that can contribute to the growth of capitalism. But Confucian orthodoxy emphasized above all a "rational adaptation" to secular life, generating in the people a traditionalist and conservative propensity that became the decisive obstacle to the growth of aggressive modern capitalism. Daoism gave people some outlet from this conformity by promoting personal values, which also did not support capitalism. The so-called Weber thesis on Confucianism and the underdevelopment of capitalism in China has since become the subject of heated scholarly debates.

The Dutch sinologist Jan de Groot (1854–1921) conceived the ambitious vision of a comprehensive and detailed study of Chinese religion, which was published three decades earlier (1972 [1892]) than Weber's work. He was interested in Chinese religion as laid out in textual canons and as actually practiced in the religious life of the people. He richly detailed such topics as "the burial of the dead," "ancestor worship," and other ritual practices and advocated China's religion as a field of scientific study (Freedman, 1979).

Coming to the field a generation later than either Weber or de Groot and following Emile Durkheim's quest to unravel the "collective consciousness," Marcel Granet's seminal work (1975 [1922]) suggested that in China "peasant religion" was the foundation of the religion of the literary class—a point Charles Laughlin makes about China's whole literary tradition in Chapter 13. Granet (1884–1940) looked at archaic history for the "essence" of Chinese religion. Later an urban populace would develop a "feudal religion," and kings created an "official religion" to support their sovereignty. All this subsequently diversified into specific religious currents or doctrines.

More recently, a US sociologist of Chinese descent, C. K. Yang, noted the contrast between institutional and diffused religions: "Institutional religion functions independently as a separate system, while diffused religion functions as a part of the secular social institutions" (1991:295). This basic distinction may be employed in addressing some of the alternative explanations we mentioned in the opening paragraph. Confucianism, by and large a diffused religion, functions through such secular institutions as the state, the family, and the education system. Only in the cases of Buddhism (imported from India) and, to a lesser extent, Daoism, can one speak of proper institutional religion with its monastic order and specialized priesthood. Diffused religion is inevitably a less powerful form of religiosity, merely providing spiritual rationale to secular institutions. Yang concluded that although Chinese religions were rich and dynamic on the surface, they were at heart restricted.

In this chapter, we want to give you an overview of how China's religions evolved and how they cover both the spiritual and the secular realms of life. We shall examine the development of China's religions in terms of the interplay between diversity and syncretism—how religious streams alternatively diversified and converged in China's history. At each stage in the unfolding of the Chinese religious universe, new impetus and horizons were opened up and then reconciled with existing beliefs (Yao and Zhao, 2010). From this perspective, the development of Chinese religion remains an ongoing story, an ebb and flow between diversity and syncretism. We are suggesting that China has experienced three great historical periods or configuratic syncretism, when competing rites and doctrines (some i diffused, in Yang's terminology) were juxtaposed and r ing syncretism, in time, would be broken up by the intr beliefs. Those three historical configurations are summar you can see, the table leaves us with a question. The fir diverse religious streams began to take place in the twel second began in the third century BCE, and the third in the tenth century CE. Is a fourth syncretism emerging in the twenty-first century?

Table 12.1 Development of Chinese Religions

First configuration (to 256 BCE)	Ancient cults (2000–1123 BCE): totemism, animism, occultism. Zhou syncretism (1122–256 BCE): The rise of humanistic religion.
Second configuration (to 220 BCE)	Axial diversification (772–481 BCE): Confucianism, Daoism, the Yin-Yang school. Han syncretism (206 BCE –220 CE): The canonization of Confucianism.
Third configuration (to 1279)	Foreign impetus (1): Indian Buddhism, Near Eastern Nestorianism, Manichaeanism. Song syncretism (906–1279): The rise of neo-Confucianism.
Fourth configuration (to 2008)	Foreign impetus (2): Christianity. Marxism-Maoism as antireligion. Toward a new syncretism?

First Configuration: The Rise of Humanistic Religion

We begin with the legendary, Neolithic origins of Chinese religion. Marcel Granet would readily point out that much that is unique about the orientation of China's religion can be traced to that era. Julia Ching (1993) and Richard von Glahn (2004) maintain that elements of those ancient beliefs and cults persist even to this date, still retaining their archaic, primitive mode.

As Table 12.1 indicates, ancient Chinese religious beliefs go back at least to the Neolithic and Bronze Ages and were widely practiced during the first, archaic dynasties in classical China (Eliade, 1985:3–6; Wang, 2000). During the Zhou dynasty, between 1122 and 256 BCE, they merged with some new ideas in a syncretic reconciliation of beliefs (Sommer, 1995). The archaic gestation period of Chinese religion shared traits of primitive religions elsewhere. People became aware of and curious about nature and made crude, halting mpts to justify human social life on the basis of larger-than-life forces and deas; especially relevant for China were aspects of totemism, animism, and occultism.

Totemism

Totemism is a familiar elementary form of religious belief, identifying human groups with species of animals, birds, or even plants from which they presumably descended. A group sharing the same totemic ancestor bonded together for community and warfare against groups sharing other totems. Scholars like Emile Durkheim and Claude Lévi-Strauss point out that this classificatory system based on common descent of a group from the same mythic animal, bird, or imaginary monster helped set people apart in their own minds from other groups sharing a different totem, providing them with a rich sense of prehistoric genesis based on legend. The proliferation of totemic groups generated dynamics of war and alliance. The first step toward a unified Chinese culture was allegedly achieved when the mythical Huang Di (the Yellow Emperor) fostered a federation of totemic groups powerful enough to sustain control over what became the heartland of China (Chang, Yu, and Ch'un, 1998). Down to the times of the Xia, Shang, and Zhou (see Table 3.1), the ruling dynasties and the kings were mainly the great chiefs who held the totemic alliances together. The passage into history took place at the point when totemic alliances were formalized into government and totemic groups became clans. Even today, Chinese often designate themselves "descendants of dragons," if not because they actually believe in it, at least because they still want to.

Animism

Animism forms the other major strand of ancient Chinese beliefs (von Glahn, 2004:18–44). Again, it is a mentality widely shared among peoples of the ancient world. Animism is belief in the omnipresence of spirits, that other living creatures and even inanimate objects or phenomena also possess spiritual essences that can impact the lives of humans. It is usually regarded by anthropologists as the most basic form of religious belief, based on the inability to distinguish between objective reality and the fantasy world of spirits. Yet as the case of China demonstrates, animism can far outlive its ancient origins. Animism is well documented in the archaeological finds of the Shang dynasty, mainly in sacrificial inscriptions on tortoise shells and animal bones (Keightley, 1978). These inscriptions indicate that people believed in and made offerings to spirits of natural phenomena like thunder and rain, of natural objects like mountains and rivers, of beasts and birds, and especially of deceased humans (Lewis, 2006). Many of these practices were to continue in the folk religions of China in later times (Kieschnick, 2003).

Occultism

Occultism is closely connected with animism and concerns how the supernatural influence of spirits can be detected or even changed for human purposes. In the mind of believers, spirits were usually given form and character closely resembling human beings and shared our temperaments as well. It is therefore logical to assume that human beings can communicate with these spirits and in the process perhaps take advantage of their power. This may be achieved by specialized religious personnel obtaining blessings from these spirits and foretelling the future through their power. And in archaic China, these religious personnel often held political roles as well, serving as the foundation of kingship (Ching, 1997). The Shang dynasty indulged extensively in occultist practice and also embraced the notion of the supreme lord (*di*), the personified supernatural overlord of all beings, toward whom acts of offerings and divination were ultimately directed (Eliade, 1985:7–9). The worship of *di* can be interpreted in a polytheistic mode, where the all-powerful *di* presided over the spiritual pantheon of the animistic world and answered to the pleadings and inquiries of the people.

The three themes of totemism, animism, and occultism formed the religious scaffolding of remote, archaic China. In the passage from the Xia and Shang dynasties into the Zhou dynasty—and from prehistory into documented history—two important strands of prehistoric beliefs would be assimilated into and continued in the religion of Zhou. These beliefs were the worship of heaven (*tian*) on the one hand and ancestral worship on the other. Both of these motifs were to exert heavy influences on the religious life of China to come. The worship of *tian* is essentially the depersonalized version of the former worship of *di*. In the transition from Shang into Zhou, the personified supreme deity of *di* was to be gradually metamorphosed into an impersonal, transcendental force. Although this ultimate force was no longer cast in a humanized mode, it nonetheless had purpose and direction. Comprehending and abiding by the will and Mandate of Heaven (*tianming*) would be among the key religious principles in Chinese culture—the belief that earthquakes, drought and hunger, and rising poverty are signs that heaven has withdrawn its approval of the ruler and he can be overthrown, as discussed in Chapter 4 (Loewe, 1986; Shahar and Weller, 1996). And the worship of *tian* would in later days converge with the imperatives of the *dao* (the way), whether defined in Confucian, Daoist, or yin-yang terms. As for ancestral worship, this is a heritage from totemism for which China has become particularly famous. It makes little difference that the early totemic ancestors were mainly legendary animals or even hybrids; they kindled a religious sentiment that constantly beckoned to the ancestral fountainhead, which would continue to oversee the conduct and welfare of the latter-day descendants. The impersonal, immutable *tian* and the highly personal, affectionate ancestors (*zu*) would form the two essential axes of supernatural beliefs, handed down as they were from the prehistoric past first to the Zhou civilization and in turn to Chinese culture as a whole.

Zhou Syncretism and Humanistic Religion

During the Zhou dynasty, these beliefs were assimilated and consolidated, especially in the Western Zhou. The individual traditions did not disappear; but society and scholars drew together important elements from all of them to bolster secular institutions along with religious ideas and practices (Eliade, 1985:9–13; Fung, 1997). Divination and other animistic, magical practices continued (also discussed in Chapter 13); but at the same time, thinkers and religious practitioners combined them with other religious traditions, picking what seemed best from each to form a new body of doctrines and rituals. It was truly a syncretism—a generally contrived, strained sense of integration that would last for a few centuries and finally begin to fall apart under that strain. Then new diverse religious strands would unravel, to be brought back together in a second syncretism, discussed below. This is how China's religious traditions have evolved amid the diversity and immensity of the Chinese religious universe—an interplay of unity and difference.

The Zhou syncretism emerged because, after a long prehistoric childhood, Chinese society had reached a stocktaking threshold requiring a more stable and "rational" framework of social life. As explained in Chapter 3, the Zhou people of the west toppled the Shang dynasty, which had grown corrupt and obsolete. They sought to create the underpinnings of a new social order. Although construction of the Zhou order was generally accredited to the Duke of Zhou, the younger brother of the founding emperor, it must also be seen as a product of its time.

The Duke of Zhou presided over construction of a strong program of humanism, centering primarily on humanistic interests and ideals, that was to permeate all subsequent evolution of the Chinese religious world. The personified godhead of *di*—the closest that China ever came to professing a supreme, monotheistic deity—became the abstract, ramified force of *tian* and of nature, no longer intervening directly in the mundane details of social life. *Tian* was a "hidden god." Although *tian* and nature had purpose and will, they were part of bigger cosmic dynamics that had no use for divine design or intervention. And if human affairs must nonetheless abide by heavenly principles, they do so mainly for the sake of harmony and felicity in social life. In this way, then, the rise of Zhou humanism signified an essential new twist in the religious consciousness of the Chinese, in which both the sacred and the profane derived their meanings from within the concrete operation of the secular, human world (Nakamura, 1964:chap. 15). This would be the all-important leitmotiv that both Confucianism and Daoism took up in later times.

Starting with this basic propensity toward a humanistic religion, Zhou syncretism placed dual emphasis on rites and ethics that (in the absence of divine decrees) together set the standard of proper behavior. The notion of, and the word for, "rite" (*li*) had its origin in the archaic ritual of making offerings to the gods. People were instructed to participate in rites with sincerity and care, just as their ancestors had done when worshiping their pantheon of animistic spirits and *di,* the mandate of gods and heaven. In addition, practice of rite evolved into social institutions and ideological doctrines. Rite as social institution defined proper behavior in different social occasions—celebrations, initiations, mourning, interaction, and so on (Armstrong, 1998). Rites would shape the elementary social structure of the community, visually demonstrating the sovereignty and power of the rulers and the rights and responsibilities of different social roles. Philosophical and ideological frameworks justified and codified the practice of rites, ensuring their continuity even beyond the reign of Zhou. That codification was partly recorded in the canonical *Book of Rites,* the compilations of ancient documents broadly related to this movement.

In lieu of divine decrees, the intellectual foundation of *li*—and of Zhou humanism in general—was primarily ethical in character. At the heart of this ethic was the use of blood ties and kinship dynamics as the foundation of values and standards of social relationship. In the absence of divine ordinance, blood ties were to become the most sacred organizing principle of society. The Zhou dynasty presided over a feudal social order, with peasants bonded to the estates of noblemen. Feudalism was founded upon the lineage rule (*zhongfa*) system, which determined rights and duties on the basis of blood ties. This *zhongfa* system also prescribed the distribution and inheritance of family resources from one generation to another. It raised familial and filial values into "social absolutes," serving as the ethical-sacred foundation of Zhou humanism.

Instead of following a more familiar pattern of religious movement from animism into polytheism and then into monotheistic religion, Zhou syncretism generally sought to break with theistic religion altogether. Henceforth, the "great tradition" of Chinese religion would be characterized above all by what Max Weber called "this-worldly religion"—religious beliefs having little to do with transcendental order and divine godheads (Weber, 1964 [1922]:1–3). Already in the time of Zhou, an "enlightened" outlook had developed, affirming the primacy and autonomy of humanity as the sole source of both existential enigma and fulfillment and asserting that humanity remains truly autonomous only when ritually bonded to the community and its rulers (Lewis, 2006). Thus the rise of Zhou syncretism set the distinct temperament of Chinese religious beliefs, marking the master trend that later stages continued to deepen and enrich but never did abandon or supersede.

Second Configuration: The Axial Age and the Rise of Confucianism

During later centuries, the Zhou syncretism broke down and contending schools of thought emerged. This lively stage of development, when such prominent schools as Confucianism and Daoism came into existence, is by far the most celebrated among observers. Beginning around 1000 BCE, India, Greece, Mesopotamia, and China all experienced major advances in their civilizations, independently of one another; scholars think of these civilizations as occupying several parallel lines or planes, each serving as axis to subsequent progress of their civilizations, and call this period the "axial" age (see Chang, 1990; Roetz, 1993). In China, these advances occurred during the so-called Spring and Autumn Period and Warring States Period and extended into the short-lived Qin dynasty (see Table 3.1). The Han dynasty would then seek a synthesis among these contending schools (Loewe, 2005). This second syncretism, building upon but moving beyond the first syncretism created earlier in the Zhou dynasty, stands unmistakably at the heart of cultural China. Even to this day, Chinese culture is identified as Han.

First we will focus on three schools among the many contending during the axial age: Confucianism, Daoism, and yin-yang. Then we will examine how the yin-yang cosmological framework was deployed as the scaffolding upon which Confucianism and Daoism acquired tenuous syncretic unity during the Han dynasty.

Confucianism

Confucius lived from 551 to 479 BCE (see Table 3.1). He sought a return to the humanist emphasis on rites and ethics found in the earlier Zhou syncretism (Strathern, 1999; Yao, 2000; Nylan, 2001; Nylan and Wilson, 2010; Goldin, 2011; Chin, 2007; Littlejohn, 2011). His, too, is essentially a "secular religion," founded upon beliefs about proprieties of human conduct: social values, social practice, and the image of the ideal person. In society and the individual, the ultimate ends of life coincide with the worldliness of the mundane here and now (see Fingarette, 1998; Strathern, 1999; Yao, 2000; Poceski, 2009).

The social values associated with Confucianism center on the cardinal notion of *ren,* rendered variously by sinologists as "benevolence," "humaneness," and "compassion." In the *Analects*—the record of Confucius's teachings—*ren* is made the foundation of social life (Brooks and Brooks, 1998; Bo, 2003:99–204; Adler, 2002; Plaks and Yao, 2004). Divine authority should be respected but is generally irrelevant. *Ren* literally means "two persons"; it is not just a set of ethical rules but an inalienable inner necessity, a moral imperative for human personal and social existence. It cannot be approached as an individualistic ethic, because human nature itself is inherently social; social interaction and relations between humans will take priority over personal interest and experience. We have an innate moral mandate to show affection, sympathy, compassion, and benevolence toward our fellow humans by conforming to specific conventions of social behavior. Instinctive consciousness of that mandate sets humanity apart from other living beings. The value and goodness of *ren* is not something that should be validated by reason or logic. *Ren* is both higher and deeper than the mere exercise of intellect. In the end, mutual affection and sympathy—emotional bonds—best validate and vindicate its primacy. The individuals who exemplify these ideals by properly performing rites and social conventions are literally defining who they are, demonstrating their humanity.

The celebrated Confucian obsession with *li* (ritual and propriety) can be properly appreciated against this backdrop (Eliade, 1985:22–25; Ivanhoe, 2000; Kern, 2005; Lai, 2006; Yao, 2006). The elaborate and meticulous rituals governing social interaction are the practical articulation of the cherished ideal of *ren*—personal actors defining their own worth by the collective sentiment they show toward social solidarity (Eno, 1990). Art, literature, and moral discourse must help individuals cultivate these social proprieties.

The Confucian distinction between gentleman (*junzi*) and commoner (*xiaoren*) also becomes clear in this context. Although achieving the remote ideal of becoming a Confucian sage is beyond the reach of most mortals, true followers of Confucianism can hope to become *junzi*—someone who desires and is far advanced in the attainment and practical pursuit of *ren*. A gentleman is not merely someone generally righteous, honest, and knowledgeable. These well-accepted virtues must be assessed and related in terms of the core value of *ren;* a true Confucian gentleman is not motivated to attain individual success or precious assets but rather shows his benevolence to others by practicing the social rituals with propriety (Tu, 1993). In contrast, the *xiaoren* (literally, "small-minded men") are imperfect in attaining *ren,* or humanity. The *xiaoren* is the direct opposite of the *junzi* not because he is perhaps evil-minded or dishonest, but mainly because he is only concerned with his own interest and private desire. At their worst, such individuals ignore the cardinal value of *ren* by expressing frustration and social discontent; at their best, they show their respect for it by giving special deference to *junzi.* (See Chapter 4 for more on the concrete interplay of these principles.) Confucianism intertwines ethics and religion to regulate social behavior (Wilson, 2003). But it lacks a religious hierarchy to mandate its authority and is not inspired by divine authority from above, but rather by the inner benevolence of human nature itself (Hall and Ames, 1987). Mo Tzu and Mencius, who lived shortly after Confucius, touch upon these ideas (de Bary, Bloom, and Adler, 2000; Hansen, 2000:153–196; Huang, 2001; Ivanhoe, 2002; Shun, 2000; Mozi, 2003; Xunzi, 2003).

Daoism

The other major indigenous religious tradition in China is Daoism, which (as indicated in Chapter 3) originated during the same period of axial diversification. The relation between Confucianism and Daoism is a contrast between orthodoxy and heterodoxy—a distinction made famous by Weber in his study of Chinese religion. Although Confucianism pertains overwhelmingly to the social aspects of human life, Daoism pertains more to nature and the individual (Kirkland, 2004; Bo, 2003:205–296; Pas, 2006; Wang, 2004; Yu, 2000; Adler, 2002). Although Confucianism gives primacy to asserting and striving for social values, Daoism gives primacy to tactically avoiding these allegedly superficial pursuits. Daoism rose as a contrasting parameter to assert the values that Confucianism neglected. It was permissible and common for people to take on both Confucian and Daoist outlooks, letting each fill the void left by the other. The two together broadly demarcate the field of diversification in the axial age.

Standing at the heart of Daoism is the concept of *dao,* which can variously be understood as "the principle," "the way," and "the word" (Waley, 1988; Ames, Hall, and Bernstein, 2003). Thus, *dao* can be regarded as a mode of behavioral tactics, specifying the principles that are most closely compatible with the dynamics of human and natural affairs (Clarke, 2000; Roth, 2004). Or *dao* is perceived in more philosophical rubrics as "the way," postulating the presence of a universal pattern or law that underlies the conduct of social and natural phenomena. And if *dao* is seen as "the word," it denotes the need for doctrines and codes to be formulated and espoused in words or utterances, for the articulation of the *dao.* These three aspects of the *dao* all revolve around the concept of virtue (*de*), suggesting that *dao* is by nature virtuous (Eliade, 1985:25–33; Moeller, 2004). These multiple meanings explain why *dao* remains so much an enigma in Chinese thought, readily associated both with the crudest kind of magical practices and with philosophical enlightenment of a lofty order (Birrell, 2000; Pregadio, 2006; Wong, 1997; Yang, 2007; Yu and Fortin, 2000). As a metaphor or concept of truth, *dao* was commonly evoked even in doctrines outside Daoism. For example, the Confucian classics were replete with the use of the concept when discussing truth and its method, albeit with specific Confucian reference.

Whether according to Laozi (Anthony, 1998; Balkin, 2002; Cook, 2003; Marshall, 2001; Roth, 2004; Wagner, 2000; Wang, 2004) or Zhuangzi (Ames, 1998; Chuang Tzu, 1997; Cook, 2003; Zhuangzi, 2003; Henricks, 2005; Kjellberg and Ivanhoe, 1996; Mair, 1983, 1998), the two legendary founders of Daoism, the gist of *dao* lies not in human endeavor but rather in evading the futility of human endeavor. The universe is the totality of all being, generated from an unimaginable cosmic void, the omnipresent *dao. Dao* is emptiness, mystical and all-pervasive. The world derives from that emptiness. Humans can achieve a linkage with that emptiness by refraining from individual ambition and social activity and seeking oneness with *dao.*

The belief in *dao* naturally reinforces a passive attitude of retreat. Extreme Daoists preached a social doctrine calling for small social units, with minimal government structure, and as little social interaction as possible (Schipper, 1993). They saw the numerous moral values and ethical codes cherished by the Confucians as unwanted baggage; if social ties and interaction were avoided or minimized to begin with, most problems the Confucians set out to confront would not even exist. Submitting oneself to the *dao* can create a very different kind of individual and social order.

Other Daoist schools believe that moving in accordance with the propensity and force of the *dao* would make the individual much more compatible and effective in the world, rather than in retreat from it. Correctly perceiving and abiding by the movement of *dao* actually strengthens one's potential and power. By this ironic twist, the passivity of Daoist tenets is transformed into tactical endeavor. This tempts one to channel the force of *dao*—by magical or physical means—to become a source of religious fulfillment. The tremendous hidden power of the *dao* can be manipulated to fulfill other personal needs as well. Practices such as macrobiotic diets and divination can be used to achieve such utilitarian ends. This utilitarian dimension receives prominence in the later development of Daoism. Its canonical doctrines emphasize a detached, spontaneous life attitude commensurate with the natural unfolding of the *dao,* even as one carries out social responsibilities. The institutional religion that came to surround these doctrines could point to utilitarian personal benefits to be gained from adhering to the religion—an effective way of persuading worldly believers (Anthony Yu, 2005:53–89).

The Yin-Yang School

The axial age in China boasted the blossoming of "nine currents and ten schools" (*jiuliu sijia*). Among them, the yin-yang school is another current standing at the heart of religious formation in China, with important practical implications for both Confucianism and Daoism. The yin-yang school systematized some of the magical practices from earlier primitive religion. It is generally deemed less important than Confucianism and Daoism because it is less sophisticated, but it helped reconcile these more elaborate doctrines and became responsible for many of the more speculative, magical tenets of both Confucianism and Daoism.

Yin and yang in harmony.

Yin-yang is represented graphically as the opposition and complementarity of light and darkness—expressing their inherent difference while suggesting that the essence of each is somehow related to that of the other (Fung, 1983b:7–131). The polarity of yin-yang also underlined part of Confucianism and Daoism. In addition, this polarity may be viewed as an ancient articulation of what later came to be known as binary thinking. The yin-yang dichotomy is the primordial impulse of classification—the very first act of intellectual classification that preceded all subsequent acts of intellectual operation (Bo, 2003:33–98). Other contrasts such as weak-strong, low-high, feminine-masculine, cold-hot, absorbing-penetrating, passive-active, darkness-light, earth-heaven, and so on, can be defined by their juxtaposition as opposites—the master framework of yin-yang—irrespective of their actual substance or referents.

Yet the yin-yang school took this to much greater extremes. The manifestation and transformation in any phenomenon can be charted and even foretold in accordance with the interplay of yin-yang dynamics. The entire universe can become unified and understood under sets of yin-yang–related principles or pseudotheories. There are, for instance, the five elements (*wuxin*), which referred to the constitutive elements of the material world—fire, water, wood, metal, and earth. Each of these elements has different associations along the spectrum of the yin-yang principle, forming a unique system of checks and balances, harmony and conflict, diversity and unity. In addition, the four directions, four seasons, stellar configurations, aspects of human virtues, and so forth, all attain similar cosmological and magical attributes that resonate above and beyond their natural and human forms. By weaving together a closed cosmology that attributes order to the world and a teleology that shows its design and ultimate ends, the yin-yang school developed immense appeal. The yin-yang dynamics became, in effect, the articulation, perhaps even actualization, of both the elusive *tian* and *dao*—of heaven on high and the way of life on earth.

Han Syncretism: The Canonization of Confucianism

The Spring and Autumn Period (771–476 BCE), when Confucius, Laozi, and Zhuangzi lived, was the last phase of axial diversification before the breakdown of the Zhou dynasty. The nine currents and ten schools of thought flourishing during that era shared some common traits with roots in the earlier Zhou syncretism (Smith and Kwok, 1993). Such continuities led to the famous hypothesis that the diverse schools of the axial age all originated from the former imperial officials of the Zhou government. Like the preceding Zhou syncretism, none of these schools looked to a single divine being as the ultimate source of religious spirit. Magic, spirit, hybrids, and a metaphorical heaven were still regarded as normal parts of the world where humans live. And the cornerstone of Zhou humanism stayed in place, whether in the Confucian values of *ren* and *li,* the Daoist postulate of the all-pervasive *dao,* or the yin-yang resonance (*ganyin*) among humans, world, and cosmos.

In this light, the founding of the Han dynasty in 206 BCE following the Qin unification of China acquired different levels of meaning. In terms of intellectual and religious development, the Han period became the second major movement of syncretism in Chinese religious thought. Unlike the epochal breakthrough in Zhou humanism, however, Han syncretism can boast of no similar fundamental innovation, at least not in intellectual terms. Han syncretism is significant mainly in its practical consequence for Chinese religion. It was during the consolidation of Han syncretism that Confucianism was first favored above all other competing doctrines, that the writings of classical Confucianism were canonized as the supreme source of authority. But this process brought into Confucianism important strands from those competing doctrines and provided ways for other religions to coexist with it (Csikscentmihalyi, 2006; Kramers, 1986; Loewe, 2005).

Han syncretism elected an orthodoxy only subsequent to the consolidation of a variety of thought currents. The dynasty opened on a Daoist note when the second emperor of Han, Wendi, chose to adopt a more withdrawn, noninterventionist approach to state administration, so that the country could recover from the protracted war of unification under the first Han emperor, Gaozu. Yet he did not attempt to privilege Daoism above other doctrines. It was the great Wudi (reigning from 140 to 87 BCE) who instituted the Five Confucian Classics as the official syllabus of education. Dong Zhongshu (179–104 BCE), the intellectual architect of this movement, advocated "dismissing the hundred other schools in respect of Confucianism alone." Dong was simultaneously the great advocate of Confucianism and its formidable revisionist, drawing into it Daoist and yin-yang themes and traditions of folk religion and magical practices.

Dong sought to reconcile heaven (*tian*) and humanity (*ren*). His formulation for this is *tianren ganyin*—resonance between heaven and humans. From this perspective, human and transcendental realities are intrinsically linked. A primarily humanistic approach such as classical Confucianism, which focuses solely on humanity, is too simplistic. The yin-yang school saw *tian* as essentially unchangeable, overpowering forces. Dong sought to revise that passive view by reintroducing the notion of supernatural forces that would oversee the conduct of men. This element, while not entirely absent in classical Confucianism, was greatly amplified by the hand of Dong. Confucius's humanism was too abstract and impalpable for common individuals. By making *tian* once again a supreme will accessible to human supplications through the intervention of supernatural forces, Dong gave Confucianism greater popular appeal. Heaven does not intervene directly into human affairs, yet heaven is responsive to human conduct. Misdemeanors and crime, beyond a certain threshold of seriousness and scale, would trigger signs from heaven, usually in the form of natural disasters and mystical omens. So humanity can decipher the way of heaven and build a moral social order on its basis. The purpose of life is not just to attain harmony and well-being, but ultimately to attain a state of unity with heaven (*tianren heyi*); this ideal would make orthodox Confucianism more explicitly religious (Loewe, 2005).

The emperor Wudi accepted not only Dong's version of Confucianism but also the proposal that Confucianism should be honored above all other schools of thought and beliefs. In subsequent ages, the Han syncretism came to be known as *Hanxue* (Han learning). *Hanxue* represented the first major reworking of Confucianism, not only by Dong but also through extensive exegetical works on the Confucian canon by other Han scholars. The Han syncretism, however, proved problematic for later Confucians; it was revisionist in spirit yet meticulously preserved the classical heritage. The Han dynasty collapsed at the end of the second century CE, but it left behind an established Confucian tradition.

Third Configuration: Foreign Impetus and Neo-Confucianism

The two syncretic stages configuring Chinese religion up to this point involved ideas and doctrines that may seem somewhat removed from the modern conception of religion. There was little by way of established religious institutions, worship of a specific deity, or the use of sacred texts for transcendental communication. Even magical practice and beliefs were found only among marginalized Daoist and yin-yang cults. Orthodox Confucianism never set up a priesthood or houses of worship. In contrast to other major world religions, Chinese religion did not seek immortality, inner ecstasy, or salvation for its adherents. Chinese religious development was to remain heavily intellectual, secular, and humanistic. The purest form of belief was ultimately in humanity as such, for all its virtues, follies, and possibilities. But the adherents of this belief could attain the same fervor, commitment, and faith common to all religious traditions.

The next two configurations of religious development in China would be more complicated and colorful. Though the humanism persisted, it was subjected to searching challenges, the latest episode of which is still happening today. These challenges came largely from outside, in the form of foreign religious traditions that either sought to take root in China on their own or sought to trigger transformations of the Chinese religions from within (Demieville, 1986). The religions involved are Buddhism from India, the three religions of Abraham from Europe and the Near East, and finally Marxism-Maoism, which figured as yet another thought system of heavy humanistic-religious bent.

Indian Buddhism

The great religious event dominating China's cultural landscape while Europe was experiencing its "Dark Ages" and medieval period was the introduction and expansion of Buddhism (Adler, 2002; Liu, 2006; Ling, 2004; Lopez, 1996; Williams, 2008; Poceski, 2009). From that time forward, the tripartite epithet of Confucianism-Buddhism-Daoism (*ru-xi-dao*) would become the standard litany describing Chinese religion. In other words, Buddhism was the only foreign religion that has successfully taken root in China and exerted sweeping cultural and intellectual influence on mainstream religious belief. Buddhism is a highly institutionalized religion, with its own elaborate miscellany of sects and monastic orders, specialized personnel, institutional discipline, and theological doctrines. In contrast, Confucianism maintained a much more secular, moralistic outlook, precisely in its attempt not to separate social and sacred lives. And Daoism was largely split between its intellectual and institutional facades, with the Daoist institutions catering above all to the more magical, witchcraft-inclined aspects of religious life, whereas the loftier side of Daoist philosophy remained in the domain of intellectuals (Robinet, 1997). Buddhism was the only "all-round" religion in traditional China, encompassing the full range of religious sentiment, forms, and levels of thought.

Buddhism seeks to "take flight" from the world, which allegedly only brings human suffering. It adopts a passive posture not unlike that of Daoism but seeks to extend this to its logical extreme, renouncing individual consciousness and cravings so as to better perceive the ontological abyss of nothingness (*sunya* in Sanskrit, *kung* in Chinese). Buddhism added new dimensions to indigenous Chinese religions.

Historically, Buddhism is another product of the world axial breakthrough, established in India around 600 BCE by Siddhartha Gautama of the Sakya clan, who became Sakyamuni—"the sage of the sakyas" (Armstrong, 2004; Sakyamuni, 1993). Modern scholarship has come to the broad consensus that the earliest documented arrival in China of Buddhists and their canon was during the early Han dynasty (see Table 3.1). Although Buddhism had practically no role to play in Han syncretism, it was during the Han dynasty that institutional support for Buddhism was first secured—royal sponsorship, monasteries in the capital city, the beginning of scriptural translation, and so forth (Tsai, 1994; Watson, 2000). And into the late Han and the subsequent era of political instability, Buddhism would greatly expand its influence, taking on first Daoism and then Confucianism to become a major religio-cultural force by the time of the Song dynasty (960–1279 CE), the other great era of syncretism in traditional China (Gernet, 1998 [1956]; Tsai, 1994; Anthony Yu, 2005:90–134; Mollier, 2009). Buddhism became assimilated as an indigenous part of Chinese religious traditions via a twofold process: the translation of concepts and the search for original texts and developments of sects.

The initial assimilation of Buddhism was greatly facilitated by emphasizing facile similarity and overlap between Buddhism and the indigenous Daoist doctrine. This strategy was formally known as "matching of meanings" (*keyi*). The broad application of *keyi* served two purposes. On the one hand, it secured

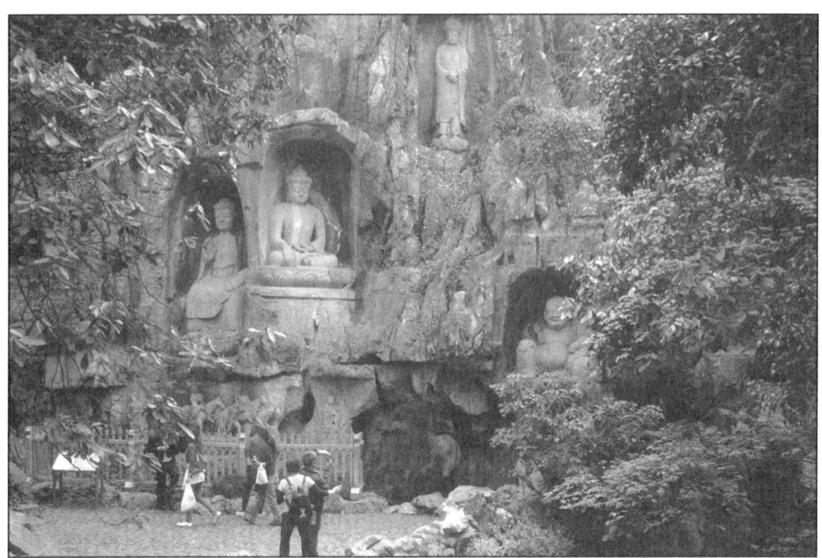

Some of the Buddhas carved into Feilai Feng ("the peak that flew over from India") on a hill outside Hangzhou, Zhejiang.

acceptance and even popularity for Buddhism without significant resistance from the Chinese populace. On the other hand, and more important, the method also ensured that Buddhism would soon shed its Indian outlook and become assimilated into the Chinese religious world—truly achieving *keyi* as a method of cross-cultural communication (Fung, 1983b:407–532).

Keyi refers to the practice of translating Indian Buddhist concepts into Daoist categories, a method pioneered by Faya, a fourth-century Chinese monk. *Keyi* could range from translating particular concepts, like the Sanskrit *sunya* (emptiness) into the Daoist *wu* (nothingness) or Buddha into the Daoist *shensen* (deities), all the way to systematically rendering entire sutras (Buddhist classics) into Daoist idiom and analogy, even annotating sutras with Daoist classics. The worth of Buddhism was measured by its ability to hold its own in debates on Chinese culture and scholarship. During the four divisive centuries of post-Han China, many of the well-known Buddhist monks and masters earned their celebrity by demonstrating unexpected depths and insights in Daoist learning. In outsmarting the Daoist-leaning Confucian scholar-officials of the time—during sessions of idle talk *(qingtan)*—famous monks like Daoan and Huiyuan gained respect and footing for Buddhism. *Keyi* would go a long way in transforming the foreign outlook of Buddhism into what would soon be regarded as properly Chinese.

The height of Buddhist influence came during the influential, unified Tang dynasty (618–907 CE). An imperial census of Buddhist communities counted 260,000 monks and nuns, 4,600 temples, and some 40,000 shrines altogether. Each temple and shrine owned land and other properties donated by believers, giving them great social and economic prominence (Foltz, 2010; Fraser, 2003; McNair, 2007; Qiang, 2004). Clashes with local authorities and indigenous beliefs resulted in repression. This census, in fact, was compiled as a database for the short-lived official suppression of Buddhism in 845 CE. During episodes of official repression, most temples and shrines were destroyed, their land confiscated, and their monks secularized.

During the Tang dynasty, Chinese Buddhism developed along two fronts—the accelerated assimilation of Indian Buddhism and the growth of native Buddhist sects (Fung, 1983b:293–406; Weinstein, 1987). Famous Buddhist pilgrims went to India to systematically study Buddhist sutras and treatises (*lun*). Moving beyond *keyi,* they felt compelled to explore these works at their source, taking on Indian Buddhism in its own terms. The most famous pilgrims were Yijing, Faxian, and especially the towering figure of Xuan Zang, who has become a rich source of inspiration and contribution not only to Buddhism but to Chinese culture in general (Wriggins, 2003). Xuan Zang left China for India in 629 CE and did not return until 645. During that time, he also visited Sri Lanka. He brought back a great number of original Sanskrit texts and spent the rest of his life rendering them into Chinese, a task continued by his disciples after his death. His is the best-known example of a Chinese pilgrimage seeking a more authentic understanding of religion in the outside world; Chapter 13 discusses Xuan Zang further. This enterprise of scriptural translation would be among the most significant, catalytic events in the growth of Chinese Buddhism (Tung, 2000).

Formation of Chinese Buddhism in the Tang dynasty divided into two streams: "the three sects under the creed" (*jiaoxia sanzong*) and the "alternative teaching outside the creed" (*jiaowai biequan*). The three sects were the more mainstream Tiantai, Huayen, and Faxian (Cleary, 1983; Gimello and Gregory, 1983). The alternative teaching refers to the highly unique and controversial development of Zen Buddhism (Adamek, 2007; Cleary, 2005; Dumoulin, 2005; Faure, 1995, 1997; Ferguson, 2005; Kieschnick, 2003; Welter, 2006). Both streams sought to reconcile Indian Buddhism with Chinese sociocultural conditions and, in the process, contributed significant progress to Buddhism at large. The three sects focused especially on doctrines that implored people to treat their fellow humans properly and embark on various stages of enlightenment, by way of compassionate deeds to help others lead a better earthly life and to start their own paths toward enlightenment (Bocking, 1995). Zen Buddhism, both in its moderate (*jian*) or radical (*dun*) version, sought spiritual liberation and enlightenment (*wu*) not through understanding doctrines and carrying out deeds, but by uncovering and acknowledging one's innate self (*jue*), one's Buddhist nature (*foxing*), trying to remove all thoughts and desires and connect with the universal mind during meditation.

In thus breaking free from the constraints of culture or even of Buddhist doctrines themselves, this endeavor was the more extreme attempt to abandon the Indian roots of Buddhism altogether. This alternative stream of Buddhism and popular beliefs like the pure land (*jingtu*) sect, which proposed down-to-earth doctrines and ritual practices for different social occasions, would survive the suppression of Buddhism in the ninth century to become a part of Chinese culture. There was no perceived fundamental schism between such forms of Buddhism and Confucianism or Daoism. It was not unusual, in fact, for intellectuals or the lay public to adhere to parts of all these creeds (Li, 1999). In essence and fundamental philosophy, all defied the notions of any ruling supreme deity or heavenly salvation for individual souls.

Near Eastern Manichaeanism and Nestorianism

During the Tang dynasty, Manichaeanism (*molijiao*) and Nestorianism (*jingjiao*) came to China from the Near East (Foltz, 2010). Manichaeanism was associated with the Zoroastrianism of ancient Persia, whereas Nestorianism was a heretical sect of early Christianity. The Tang dynasty maintained close contact with many of the adjacent regions and cultures, and the imperial capital, Ch'angan (Xi'an), housed a sizable community of foreigners, known generally as *hu*. This general milieu greatly facilitated the introduction of these religions, and their initial spread was somewhat sheltered by the success of Buddhism. Yet being much smaller in scale, they suffered heavily during the occasional crackdowns on Buddhism and other foreign religions during the Tang dynasty and after. The Nestorians were heavily subdued whenever nativism surged in China; they were also persecuted and denounced as heretical by the Christian church in the West. The Manichaeans went underground to associate with Chinese popular cults seeking "millennial" uprisings against the state, inducing further suppressions in subsequent dynasties. These intensely theistic and otherworldly religions never commanded the same respect and attention as Buddhism. And yet they completed the spectrum of foreign religious impetus that entered China during the medieval time and may be seen as preparatory moments for the next major stage of Chinese religious development, when Christianity and the Christian civilization would clash with the Chinese world in the most ruthless manner possible.

Song Syncretisim

By the time of the Tang dynasty, Confucianism, whether as state belief or moral philosophy, was by and large already part of the invisible, taken-for-granted ground rules of everyday life (Chiu-Duke, 2000). Daoism was somewhat in the middle, straddling the gap between superstition and high philosophy (Katz, 2000). Buddhism, too, catered to more down-to-earth religious needs while standing its ground in intellectual terms. Like Daoism, the schism between its role as folk religion and as moral pillar for society rendered its

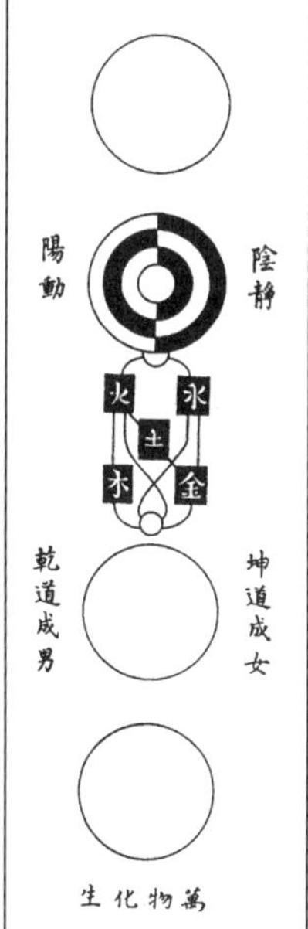

A diagram of the Supreme Ultimate, depicting the neo-Confucian image of the division and unity of the yin-yang poles.

reception among both literati and commoner often eclectic and superficial. Once again, there was a need to draw together strains of thought and belief.

The dynamic of this development set the backdrop for the new syncretism of the Song (Hymes, 2002; Miller, 2007). This would be a syncretism operating at two levels of sophisticated religious ideas, and of folk beliefs and practice. Song syncretism reconciled both contending thought systems and the eclectic mosaic of folk beliefs and superstition. The Song dynasty saw the maturation of Chinese religious consciousness and its split into contrasting levels and aspirations.

At the heart of the new syncretism was neo-Confucianism. This is often referred to as the "second phase" in the development of Confucianism, the "first phase" being Confucianism in the time of Confucius himself. Neo-Confucianism accommodated the doctrinal challenge from Daoism and Buddhism in Confucian terms, but not without cost. By focusing more on inner religious experience and less on human relations, it may even have weakened the Song dynasty's defense against encroaching nomadic invaders and hence hastened its demise (Liu, 1988).

There were, broadly, four celebrated schools of neo-Confucianism: the Lian, Lo, Guan, and Min, named after the home territories of their respective founders (Kramers, 1986). These schools were not so much different sects of neo-Confucianism as different steps of development. They developed chronologically in nearly the order given above, and their founders were often intellectual (and actual) kinsmen. The neo-Confucian schools all sought to strengthen, if not actually rebuild, the foundation that underlined the Confucian faith in morality, benevolence, and humanity (Wyatt, 1996; Bol, 2010). The rise of Buddhism (Gregory and Getz, 2002; Halperin, 2006; Jia, 2007; Poceski, 2007; Hymes, 2002) and increasing popularity of Daoism rendered the emphasis on compassion or moral goodness no longer the prerogative of Confucianism alone. The same urge for virtuous conduct and mutual compassion figured prominently in Buddhism and even populist Daoism. The point was then both to reinforce and to rebuild the foundation of the Confucian faith, so that the Confucian way could be demonstrated to be distinctive from and superior to other alleged champions of virtue and humanity. For this purpose, two general agendas emerged.

The first agenda, undertaken mainly by the Guan school, sought to reaffirm the necessity of morality and benevolence by a familial analogy binding humanity with the universe. This position was pronounced with great persuasiveness and clarity in the manifesto of the Guan school—the Western Inscription (*ximing*) by Zhang Zhai (Kasoff, 1984). As presented in the *ximing*, heaven (*tian*) and earth (*kun*) were but the benevolent universal parents of humans. Within this ultimate parenthood, every relationship—social, material, and natural—must accord with prescribed ethical (filial) standards. The recognition of universal parenthood would render an ethical, benevolent worldview necessary and inviolable.

The second and eventually the more influential agenda was represented by Chu Hsi and the Min school. Instead of developing yet another set of beliefs like universal parenthood, Chu Hsi sought to create a more systematic metaphysical foundation for Confucianism (Chan, 1986, 1989; Tillman, 1992). His elaborate intellectual construction explored the dichotomy between *li* (principle) and *qi* (expression) in order to demonstrate the unity and universality of principle as opposed to the multifariousness of expression. He deepened the rationale and assumptions behind the Confucian world of belief. Influenced by Buddhist and Daoist practices, he sought to relate human needs and feelings to doctrine and ritual behavior, sidestepping Confucian ethics in favor of seeking "higher" and ultimate metaphysical reality by incessant probing of inner experience. Chu's approach brought a convergence in form and spirit (if not in doctrine) of the three religions but risked the danger of retreating into speculative musing and self-diagnosis. The subsequent development of neo-Confucianism into the Ming dynasty would be heavily tainted by the transcendental mood of a "Confucian Zen" (de Bary, 1975:141–217).

A traditional representation of a Daoist deity.

At the other end of Song syncretism was the growing popularity of folk beliefs and magical practices borrowing indiscriminately from the systematic religions, whose insight and fine points often eluded the ability and concern of the general public. These folk beliefs were characterized by an abundance of gods, worshiped either as local deities or as more universal idols. The figures popular among folk worship included historical figures, deceased local celebrities, animals, and even Confucian sages, all of whom were turned into idols that, after proper sacrificial offerings, might bestow blessings and grant requests (Kang, 2006). They might simultaneously worship other deities like the Amitabe Buddha (*milafo*), Kanon (*guanyin,* a Buddhist bodhisattva), the Jade Emperor (*yuhuang dadi*), Gods of the Five Mountains (*wu yue dijun*), and the Immaculate Lady of the Ninth Heaven (*jiutian xuannu*). Confucianism, Buddhism, Daoism, and popular legends all contributed to this pantheon (Gregory and Getz, 2002). These deities and idols could be worshiped selectively or collectively, depending on the needs of the worshipers (Yu, 2000). They were also worshiped regardless of their religious origins. This is syncretism in the strong sense of the term, with an easy sense of unity gained by simply ignoring gaps and incoherence.

Syncretic folk creeds formed as well. Manichaeanism dressed itself as a kind of higher-order Buddhism. Its spread within the population was among the main contributing factors to millennial revolts against the dynasty. The well-known White Lotus sect (*bailianjiao*) also preached a form of simplified, eclectic doctrine advocating social reform (ter Haar, 1999). The White Lotus would lead a sustained underground existence into the early twentieth century.

After the Han dynasty, the development of Chinese religion became more complex. Daoism and Confucianism deepened their grasp on Chinese culture and society (Dean, 1998). At the same time, the outside world began to sink in. By the end of the Song dynasty, Chinese religious systems were generally confident of their own value and truthfulness. However, assaults were about to emerge that would call for even more profound and encompassing standards. After the Mongol kingdom overthrew the Song dynasty at the end of the thirteenth century, outside encroachment became broader and deeper; other exotic modes of faith, of religious sentiment and aspiration, asserted powerful new universalist claims.

Fourth Configuration: The Foreign Impetus of Christianity and Communism

The next major movement in the development of Chinese religion was the head-on clash with outside religious precepts, especially Christianity (Wu, 2006) and Marxism-Leninism. Ironically, the Christian faith would take on a strong and relentless political overtone, whereas the political ideology of Marxism-Leninism would be intensified into religiosity of the most fanatical kind. The resulting nexus of cataclysm and innovation looms over Chinese civilization even to this day.

Christianity

As noted above, Christianity was first introduced into China during the Tang dynasty, in the form of Nestorianism (Baum and Winkler, 2007; Moffett,

1998). At that time, however, both Nestorianism and Manichaeanism were broadly lumped together with Buddhism and regarded as variations among exotic Buddhist currents. It was not until the sixteenth century, during the Ming dynasty, that the Roman Catholic Church began the full-fledged process of eastward expansion, first into Japan and then China. Many of the first missionaries were Jesuit priests, like the famous Matteo Ricci (Li Madou), who came to China in 1583, and Niccolo Longobardi (Long Huamin), who arrived in the late sixteenth century (Uhalley and Wu, 2001:117–126; Moffett, 2005; Charbonnier, 2007; Brockey, 2007; Hsia, 2009; Hsia, 2010; Wills, 2011:78–182; Fontana, 2011; Laven, 2011). From the beginning, both the missionaries and the Roman Catholic hierarchy made numerous blunders; the Christian faith had nowhere near the success of Buddhism in converting the Chinese population. But the broader impact of the Christian civilization on China has been immeasurable. China would be forced literally at gunpoint to accept not only the operation of the missionaries in its territory but also many of the values and principles central to Christian civilization. In his chronicle of these momentous developments, Jacques Gernet (1985) characterizes the situation not so much in terms of religious differences but as whole civilizations clashing. We shall approach these dynamics in terms of doctrines, politics, and native reaction.

The question of doctrine was a thorny one right from the beginning. Confucians were simply playing out the religious consequences that follow from their particular conception and understanding of the world. In contrast, Christianity was based on a transcendental leap of faith different from any China had confronted before—the unconditional belief in the reality of the biblical God, the Holy Trinity, and eternal life for individual souls. This voluntary surrender of the autonomy of humans to an abstract and unknowable deity could well be seen by Chinese as a phase of simplistic religious impulse that the Chinese civilization had long since superseded. Although the worship of one god or another was fully permissible, this was usually regarded in China as the less enlightened attitude of the masses. And in any case, none of these deities can claim monopolistic authority. Thus, although Christianity was at first accepted as perhaps one more addition to the pantheon of the people, much as Nestorianism and Manichaeanism were, the idea that this particular god must replace all others would be difficult to accommodate. At risk of oversimplification, one can say that according to the higher humanistic aspiration of the Chinese literati, all deities were equally suspicious, whereas for the Chinese followers of folk religion, all deities were equally real. The Chinese people would be ill-prepared for the kind of "unreasonable" leap of faith adhered to in the West.

Two strategies were adopted by the missionaries to break this bottleneck, both with little effect. One strategy was to camouflage or soften the tough fabric of Christian doctrines, embracing local tenets and precepts and explaining

Robert E. Gamer

Christian churches in Fujian.

away doctrinal differences by pointing out common grounds—assimilating with local mentality as Buddhism had done with the use of *keyi* (Menegon, 2010; Pomplun, 2009; Xi, 2010). This was the strategy of Ricci and his Jesuit colleagues and represented a first effort toward indigenization of Christianity in China. Ricci himself appeared openly to embrace doctrines of Confucianism. He wore Confucian garb, took on a Chinese name (Li Madou), and rendered Christian tenets into Confucian rubrics (Kim, 2005). He stressed his knowledge of science and astronomy in order to gain respect and admiration. This was a strategy to avoid conflict with local beliefs on grounds of doctrinal differences, but it was at best facile. The fundamental opposition in doctrines was put in the background but was far from resolved: true converts, once baptized, must adhere to the core tenets of Christianity in their entirety. The second strategy, adopted largely as the official position of the Roman Catholic Church, was to insist on the hegemonic truth of Christianity right from the start. The church regarded the position of Ricci and other Jesuits as far too liberal. During the Qing dynasty in the eighteenth century, the Vatican officially denounced the Chinese worship of Confucian sages, ancestors, or local deities (Uhalley and Wu, 2001:81–116; Brockey, 2007). This intolerant and impatient stance effectively made the first Chinese Christians into enemies in the eyes of other Chinese. The Qing government answered by expelling Christian missionaries (Laamann, 2006).

From the nineteenth century onward, Christianity would be promoted on more than religious grounds. Together with a wide assortment of other values and institutions of Christian civilization as a whole, it would be forced upon China by military conflict and unequal treaties. The involvement of Christianity in the process provided a higher-minded alibi for what was clearly colonial exploitation. Backed by the full military strength of Christian nations like Britain, Germany, France, and, to a lesser extent, the United States, the increasing importance of Christianity was assured. The missionaries were aware of the human cost of colonial-style exploitation (Turbet, 2002; Luo, 2004). The infamous Opium War of 1839 (discussed in Chapters 6 and 7), for example, had no better excuse than stark imperialist and commercial interests. The reaction of Christian churches and missionaries to the situation was two-pronged. On the one hand, if political sponsorship could ensure the expansion of Christianity in China, so much the better; in fact, many of the Christian missionaries and their colleagues back home were not immune to ideologies of colonialism and racial superiority. Convinced of the prerogative of Christian faith, many missionaries were willing accomplices of politics. On the other hand, whatever the causes—or instigators—of China's social deterioration might be, this was a good opportunity for Christian churches to lend help. In the late nineteenth and early twentieth centuries, Christian churches in China set up welfare organizations of various kinds, running schools, hospitals, and even universities. Ironically, the Christian missionaries were determined to demonstrate their goodwill to a society devastated in its encounter with Christian civilization (Rubinstein, 1996; Sweeten, 2001; Smith, 2005). They gained converts (Bays, 1997). The intertwining of Christianity with colonial politics reached its high point at the turn of the twentieth century, when the alleged protection of Christian churches served as pretext for a number of military interventions into China, most notably the *Tianjin jiaoan,* the religious crime of the Boxers in Tianjin, discussed shortly.

As a result, the Chinese people often accepted or rejected the Christian faith for nonreligious reasons: to receive welfare or an education or to achieve the same earthly power as the imperialist invaders. The native response to Christianity was hence widely divergent and erratic. Two examples can serve to illustrate: the Taiping and Boxer Rebellions. The Taiping Rebellion (also discussed in Chapter 11) took place during the late nineteenth century; it lasted some fifteen years and laid waste to many of the southern provinces. Although it had all the trappings of Chinese peasant "millennial" movements of the past, it was also distinguished by its espoused allegiance to Christianity. The founder of the movement, Hong Xiuquan, actually claimed that he was yet another son of God and that Jesus Christ was his elder brother. Hong, as well as other leaders of the rebellion, also claimed to conduct direct communion with God (Spence, 1996; Chin, 2000). The movement, however, had little connection with or support from Western Christian churches, and the idea that Jesus could have a Chinese brother was not to be taken seriously by Jesus's

Western followers. One can marvel at the extreme significance accorded Christianity, to become the ideological foundation of the *Taiping Tianguo* (Heavenly Kingdom of Eternal Peace). A different perspective is that perhaps Christianity had no special claim to supremacy—it was deployed as an expedient vehicle and pretext for articulating pent-up grievances, much as Manichaeanism and folk cults had been used in past rebellions (Shih, 1967). This mode of Christian fanaticism was clearly not what the Western Christian churches had in mind.

At the other extreme stood what might be seen as anti-Christian fanaticism, represented above all by the Boxer Rebellion (*yihetuan*) of 1900 (Preston, 2001; Sweeten, 2001; Bickers and Tiedemann, 2007; Cohen, 1998). The Boxer Rebellion was characterized by its all-out xenophobia. It was a state-sponsored populist cult, in the same folk-religious order as the White Lotus sect, the Mila sect, and other sects that stood behind historical millennial uprisings (Lutz and Lutz, 1998). Strengthened by support of the empress dowager and her imperial officials, the *yihetuan* appeared ready to confront the Christian religion and civilization head on. Confident that through magical incantation, spells, and other rituals, the true believers could withstand firearms and other forms of attack, the Boxer sect set out to destroy Christian churches and Western embassies, mostly in Beijing. Although the movement was short-lived, at its height it won widespread admiration from common people. The Boxers' destruction was disastrous for China. Eight Western countries formed a military alliance to protect their churches and other interests in China, and the Boxers' magic proved no match against bullets. The Forbidden City soon came under Western control. More unequal treaties (discussed in Chapter 7) would have to be signed before the fiasco of the Boxer Rebellion could be settled. The incident was representative of the nativistic paranoia against Christianity and Christian civilization. The naïveté of the uprising should not hide from view its deep-seated and widely shared objection against the imposition of a foreign faith and the world order that this implied.

The drama of Christian impact continues unabated even now, and the fortune of Chinese Christianity fluctuates with the political climate. It has suffered whenever anti-Western sentiments surge in China. Even under the best of circumstances, Christianity still has a hard time resolving its theological position with the Chinese religious tradition. This major obstacle may have receded somewhat by the late twentieth century, when the Chinese religious traditions themselves were on the wane, after the intrusion of yet another foreign system of thought, Marxism-Leninism.

Marxism-Maoism

In many respects, Marxism and Confucianism are comparable in the positions they occupied in Chinese religious life. Both are doctrines that concern the human order rather than transcendental reality. Both figure as the hegemonic thought system for China as a whole, yet neither can claim to be a religion as such. And both encompass the wide horizon between genuine humanistic sentiment and totalistic authoritarian propensities. These reasons help explain why, although the Christian challenge to Chinese culture was always looked upon with reservation, Marxism was more readily accepted as a viable alternative for China. Their assumptions and tenets may differ, yet at least Confucianism and Marxism operate on the same plane and address the same cluster of concerns. Of course, there are profound differences as well.

In contrast to the tangible humanism of Confucianism, Marxism as introduced to China by Mao Zedong is sweepingly utopian (Kolakowski, 1982:494–523). Confucianism emphasized the here and now, the "rational adaptation" to the world as the route of self-actualization and fulfillment. Utopian thinking was usually associated with folk cults or peasant movements. Marxism-Maoism is, however, forthright in postulating an ideal and inevitable future society, the realization of which is worth present material and human sacrifice. Based on this outlook, since 1949 the development of China has been conducted through a series of social experiments, designed to arrive at the ideal social form. Imitating the Soviet experience during the 1950s proved futile, leaving China to grope for its own way into socialism and thereby the communist utopia. The tremendous havoc and destruction brought on by the Great Leap Forward and the Cultural Revolution were understandable only in relation to their fundamental utopianism, which is very out of character with Confucianism but generally in keeping with the Taiping Rebellion and other millennial movements outside the mainstream of traditional Chinese culture. As in those movements, cultural and literary elites were marginalized. Instead, the society of socialist China would be founded upon the great alliance of the workers-peasants-soldiers (*gongnongbing*).

The Marxian image of society also differs markedly from the Confucian in its emphasis on conflict and contradiction as forces of history. This is totally incompatible with the Confucian vision of a harmonious, benevolent society (Munro, 2001, disagrees). The Marxian conception of social structure is one of change, of differentiation, and of the scramble for social resources. In playing out this dynamic process, individuals join with others of the same social position and interest in a systematic conflict against other social classes. Traditional Chinese culture would have little of this. Conflict and tension were always exceptions to the norm and could be readily redeemed by invoking ethical dogmas. Human nature is, after all, formed of the same benevolent, virtuous essence. To claim as Maoism did that revolution is the highest vehicle for individual and societal purification is to be fundamentally wrongheaded. The Confucian ideal of harmony (*he*), whether between two persons, person and society, or even person and cosmos, instead postulates a society that is intrinsically virtuous and benevolent, that minimizes the occasions of conflict, and comes to resolution should they occur. And Daoism and Buddhism are by and large passive and withdrawn and certainly have not espoused conflict and destruction. One can see the extreme turnabout that took place in China with the holistic embrace of Marxism-Leninism-Maoism (Goosaert and Palmer, 2011:139–166).

Should there still be any doubt regarding the religious—or antireligious—character of Marxism-Maoism, one need only consider that, whatever their substance and tenets, they were articulated above all as fanaticism and cult. The national malaise of the Cultural Revolution and the personality cult of Mao are cases in point. The religious overtone enters because the utopian promises of Maoism can never be sustained or validated by reason and evidence alone; they must be heightened by a state of mass elation.

Toward a New Syncretism?

After Mao's death in 1976, China entered a phase of fundamental reconstruction in all major arenas of society. Socialism is still official ideology, but other competitors are rapidly on the rise—foremost among them, capitalism and nationalism. In the aftermath of disenchantment with Marxism-Leninism-Maoism, China is disoriented. A new mode of faith and belief is being sought to once again provide society with a viable image of social order and with moral and behavioral codes for the social actors. The post-Mao transformation cannot be resolved simply on pragmatic grounds, as Deng Xiaoping suggested. China's leaders have always articulated its ethical standards; after a period during which all prior beliefs were stridently attacked, it needs new guidelines. If the elementary belief system in social reconstruction remains vacuous, much of society would be in limbo and nihilistic or disintegrate into groups with differing belief systems.

The present Chinese government is recognizing the right to religious belief, both traditional and Western, but such freedom has limits. Specific constitutional articles prohibit and even deem treasonous religious beliefs or activities that run counter to national interest. Members of the Communist Party are still officially forbidden to practice religion. For others, religion must stay within the bounds of politics. Churches and temples—in keeping with long tradition—may function only with the approval of the state; they must be registered. Or more metaphorically, the City of God is subordinated to the City of Man (Kindopp and Hamrin, 2004; Xie, 2006; Lazado, 2001). This is the flip side of the separation between church and state. Based on this principle, the Chinese government is deemed justified in its tightened regulation of, for example, Tibetan Buddhism (see Chapter 6) and unregistered Christian worship. About half of China's 14 million Catholics remain unregistered. For registered Catholics, in 2006, China ordained several Chinese bishops for the local dioceses. This was done through a de facto administrative arm of the Chinese government, the Tianzhujiao Aiguohui (Chinese Catholic Patriotic Association [CCPA]), and against strong protest from the new pope, Benedict XVI, and the Vatican. From the Chinese point of view, the ordination was necessitated by the fact that, of the ninety-seven Catholic dioceses in China, forty had been without a bishop. Most of the bishops in existence were getting old. The Chinese Catholic Patriotic Association hence resorted to its own "democratic election" of bishops, as a way out of this situation (Yan, 2004). In 2007, after years of stalled negotiations, the Vatican consented to the consecration of a bishop by this association. Relations improved, but in 2011, the CCPA announced its intent to ordain forty new bishops. The Vatican proceeded to excommunicate those the CCPA proceeded to ordain. Many of China's 40 to 100 million Protestants refuse to register as well, not wanting to dilute their individual denominational identity within the Three-Self Patriotic Association (Madsen, 1998; Lazado, 2001; Yan, 2004; Kindopp and Hamrin, 2004; Peale, 2005; Xin, 2009; Wielander, 2009; Cao, 2010; Liao, 2011).

As Chapter 6 discusses, the Chinese government is also attempting to choose successors to the Panchen and Dalai Lamas; it is taking a highly political view toward religion. This does not necessarily mean the curtailment of religious freedom, only that the Chinese government will ensure that any such freedom must be enjoyed outside of possible political infiltration and foreign domination. Increasingly, however, the government recognizes that people need beliefs beyond merely acquiring more money and consumer goods as modernization progresses, and that religious institutions can promote social stability (Yang, 2008; Ashiwa and Wank, 2009).

At present, a rough estimate is that 200 to 300 million Chinese embrace religious beliefs of some form, that is, religions with formal institutions—mostly Buddhists, Daoists, Christians, and Muslims, with about 85,000 places of worship (Kindopp and Hamrin, 2004). Beyond this, there has been a strong revival of eclectic religious practices. In rural areas, temple and village associations have revived aspects of popular folk religion for millions of people (Chau, 2005, 2010; Overmyer, 2003; Scott, 2007; Goosaert and Palmer, 2011:201–392). The New Confucians, with encouragement from some top party leaders, seek to revive Confucianism as the belief system most appropriate for China. Of course, this cannot mean merely the reiteration of outdated tenets. Instead, New Confucianism would incorporate other ideological currents that played a part in the shaping of modern China and try to weave these different strands into the new syncretism of a Confucian "Cultural China" (Tu, 1995; de Bary and Tu, 1998; Hall and Ames, 1999; Bell, 2008). The prospect of this drama is still being played out.

Religion and Chinese Society

Standing out in the sets of syncretism charted above is the secular, this-worldly character of Chinese religion. Each of the three great syncretisms in China's history—during the Zhou, Han, and Song dynasties—elevated a humanistic and collectivistic outlook above other competing theistic or pantheistic currents. In the final analysis, it is this strongly practical, societal, and moral commitment to the here and now that distinguishes the spirit of Chinese religion. The answers to ultimate questions of existence and meaning are neither unknowable nor hiding in the transcendental beyond. They can be answered only by imputing the secular here and now with sacred authority and authenticity—by the clear-minded sacralization of the secular and mundane. The secret of Chinese religion does not lie in the quest for immortality, salvation, or ecstatic liberation. Rather, it is only in renouncing all these perhaps mystical ideals that the worldly reality would emerge as the only reality there is, and hence the only source of meaning and value to questions both profane and sacred. In brief, the Chinese religious tradition renders the human order (*renlun*) itself sacred. If the social world is all that there is, then striving for social order and harmony would be the highest ideal that can be hoped for and the most sacred quest that human beings can conduct. Religious sentiment and commitment are defined above all by their focus on the primacy of social relations, as the actual dynamics of the human order. Hence the celebrated Chinese emphasis on *guanxi* (relation) as the stuff that human order is made of (King, 1995). In the present context, this relationship may be taking on added importance.

There are two fundamental categories of *guanxi:* ascribed and achieved. In Confucian terms, ascribed relationships are the cornerstone of human order and more often than not have primacy over achieved relations. Ascribed relationships are part of the *wulun* (five orders), denoting the fundamental ties based on a priori principles like Mandate of Heaven and blood ties that the individual has no choice but to honor. These five orders include relations between emperor and ministers, father and son, husband and wife, one brother and another, and also between kin and friends. One is born or placed into the first four of these relationships, which are therefore ascribed. They help ensure that one's family and the country's leaders will command supreme loyalty. As to the fifth relationship, which is achieved, the relationship between kin and between friends must also be conducted according to predetermined, proper principles and codes. These five relationships are the stable building blocks of human society and are the main obligations of every individual. In upholding these relationships, definite values and principles apply. The medium being exchanged in these relations must rise above the mundane concerns of economic or material benefit. It is essentially an exchange of goodwill, of human compassion (*renqing*). In thus exchanging acts of goodwill—in the form of gifts, help, favor, understanding, kind words, and so forth—mutual compassion among individuals and toward society as a whole can be better consolidated. In this way, Confucian ideals such as loyalty, filial piety, honesty, and agnatic ties are articulated into concrete social dynamics.

In addition to ascribed relationships, into which one enters without choice, one can also achieve *guanxi* with people of one's own choosing. These are usually classmates, fellow villagers, associates at work, or other people close enough to decide they will exchange *renqing* favors. In addition to a genuine sense of compassion, strategic calculation can come into play in the give-and-take of these achieved relationships. For example, one might use these exchanges to help get oneself out of debt or to incur debt from others. Such subtle strategies evolve into elaborate power games in Chinese social life. Many of the techniques invoked are Daoist in origin, as clever adoption of cherished moral values or propensities of the situation to favor oneself.

The emphasis on *guanxi* and *renqing* is by no means a thing of the past, as Chapters 4, 5, and 13 also attest (Kipnis, 1997; Gold, Guthrie, and Wank, 2002; Yan, 1996). Belief systems may displace one another, yet the same stress on human order persists. During the modern socialist era, the ascribed ethical ties have become weakened. Yet conversely, the obsession with achieved social relationships is on the rise as new market opportunities appear. It is well known that, nowadays in China, nothing much can be accomplished—regardless of the sphere of activities concerned—without getting in touch with the right person and setting up the right kind of ties. This network of social ties has in many respects replaced the open, institutional channels of social organization. That private network is an adaptation of Confucian ethics that has remained alive in spirit and practice today. Hence it is not surprising that in 1995 the National People's Congress announced a new national initiative (also discussed in Chapters 1, 4, 9 and 14)—the achievement of a "harmonious society" bonding man and nature, people and government, law and justice, urban and rural, rich and poor. Once again, China is attempting to synthesize a moral commitment that focuses overwhelmingly on the personal affective side of social and cultural dynamics.

Chinese religion is essentially of this world, and it has withstood many of the forces that pull in other directions. Its emphasis on maintaining social order helps restore stability after periods of turmoil but also generally resists social change. Its emphasis on personal social relations also encourages people to tend to their own social circle at the expense of others to whom they do not owe direct obligations. This streak of conservatism can be both a blessing and a curse for China's enigmatic transition into the modern world and for its search for a new spiritual syncretism.

In this new millennium, China is still searching for a new spiritual direction. Hu Jintao and Wen Jiabao, reviving a term used by Deng Xiaoping, called for a basically well-off *xiaokang* society, based on the Confucian "Records of Rites," with a large middle class seeking social and natural order. In this quest, it faces new challenges. One aspect of the picture applies to the separatist movements of Tibet and Xinjiang; both nativistic movements are founded to a large extent upon their respective religious traditions, namely Tibetan Buddhism (see Chapter 6; Schmidt-Leukel, 2006:127–138; Thurman, 1996;

Powers, 2008; Williams, 2008; Elverskog, 2010) and Islam (Dillon, 1999; Foltz, 2010; You, 2004; Murata, 2000). The dramatic intertwining of religion and politics in these two regions is a much-publicized development that challenges the sovereignty and integration of the Chinese state. The harshly suppressed demonstrations by the Tibetan monks in 2008 show the resilience of that challenge. Another aspect of the picture is the confrontation between the government and the populist *qigong* movement (Palmer, 2007; Ashiwa and Wank, 2009). *Qigong* is a form of yoga that emphasizes a variety of breathing exercises, bodily postures, and even meditation (Chen, 2003; Palmer, 2007). Much of the *qigong* movement is suppressed in the new era, after it overstepped the simple pursuit of health and stamina to become a stand-in for spiritual guidance and an active opponent of Chinese government policies. The term *xie jiao* (evil cult) is in particular invoked by the Chinese government against Falun Gong (Chang, 2004; Ownby, 2003), the most influential among the *qigong* currents, since 10,000 members of that organization—including a number of high-level members of the party and government—successfully staged a peaceful demonstration outside the Communist Party headquarters at Tiananmen Square in 1999. The intriguing trajectory whereby the quest for personal health can become transformed into a vehicle of "evil" goes a long way in underscoring the spiritual void of the majority of the Chinese population as the new millennium progresses (Metzger, 2006).

Bibliography

Adamek, Wendi. 2007. *The Mystique of Transmission: On an Early Chan History and Its Contexts.* New York: Columbia University Press.

Adler, Joseph A. 2002. *Chinese Religious Traditions.* Upper Saddle River, NJ: Prentice Hall.

Ames, Roger T. 1998. *Wandering at Ease in the Zhuangzi.* Albany: State University of New York Press.

———. 1999. *The Analects of Confucius: A Philosophical Translation.* New York: Ballantine.

Ames, Roger T., David L. Hall, and Tracy Bernstein. 2003. *Dao de Jing: A Philosophical Translation.* New York: Ballantine.

Anthony, Carol K. 1998. *The Philosophy of the I Ching.* 2nd ed. New York: Anthony Publishing.

Armstrong, David E. 1998. *Alcohol and Altered States in Ancestor Veneration Rituals of Zhou Dynasty China and Iron Age Palestine.* Lewiston, NY: Edwin Mellen.

Armstrong, Karen. 2004. *Buddha.* New York: Penguin.

Ashiwa, Yoshiko, and David Wank (eds.). 2009. *Making Religion, Making the State: The Politics of Religion in Modern China.* Stanford, CA: Stanford University Press.

Balkin, Jack M. 2002. *The Laws of Change: I Ching and the Philosophy of Life.* New York: Pantheon.

Baum, Wilhelm, and Dietmar Winkler. 2007. *The Church of the East: A Concise History.* London: Taylor and Francis.

Bays, Daniel H. (ed.). 1997. *Christianity in China: From the Eighteenth Century to the Present*. Stanford, CA: Stanford University Press.
Bell, Daniel A. 2008. *China's New Confucianism: Politics and Everyday Life in a Changing Society*. Princeton, NJ: Princeton University Press.
Berger, Patricia Ann. 2003. *Empire of Emptiness: Buddhist Art and Political Authority in Qing China*. Honolulu: University of Hawaii.
Bickers, Robert, and R. G. Tiedemann (eds.). 2007. *The Boxers, China, and the World*. Lanham, MD: Rowman and Littlefield.
Birrell, Anne (trans.). 2000. *The Classic of Mountains and Seas*. New York: Penguin.
Bo, Mou (ed.). 2003. *Comparative Approaches to Chinese Philosophy*. Burlington, VT: Ashgate.
Bocking, Brian. 1995. *Nagarjuna in China: A Translation of the Middle Treatise*. Lewiston, NY: Edwin Mellen Press.
Bol, Peter K. 2010. *Neo-Confucianism in History*. Cambridge, MA: Harvard East Asian Monographs.
Brockey, Liam Matthew. 2007. *Journey to the East: The Jesuit Mission to China*. Cambridge, MA: Belknap Press of Harvard University Press.
Brooks, E. Bruce, and A. Taeko Brooks. 1998. *The Original Analects: Sayings of Confucius and His Successors*. New York: Columbia University Press.
Cao, Nanlai. 2010. *Constructing China's Jerusalem: Christians, Power, and Place in Contemporary Wenzhou*. Stanford, CA: Stanford University Press.
Chan, Wing-tsit. 1986. *Chu Hsi and Neo-Confucianism*. Honolulu: University of Hawaii Press.
———. 1989. *Chu Hsi*. Honolulu: University of Hawaii Press.
Chang, H. 1990. "Some Reflections on the Problems of the Axial Age Breakthrough in Relation to Classical Confucianism." In *Ideas Across Cultures: Essays on Chinese Thought in Honor of Benjamin I. Schwartz*, edited by Paul A. Cohen and Merle Goldman. Cambridge, MA: Harvard University Press.
Chang, Leo S., Yu Feng, and Ch'un Chang. 1998. *The Four Political Treatises of the Yellow Emperor: Original Mawangdui Texts with Complete English Translations and an Introduction*. Honolulu: University of Hawaii Press.
Chang, Maria Hsia. 2004. *Falun Gong: The End of Days*. New Haven, CT: Yale University Press.
Charbonnier, Jean. 2007. *Christians in China* A.D. *600 to 2000*. Trans. M. F. L. Couve de Murville. San Francisco: Ignatius Press.
Chau, Adam Yuet. 2005. *Miraculous Response: Doing Popular Religion in Contemporary China*. Stanford, CA: Stanford University Press.
——— (ed.). 2010. *Religion in Contemporary China: Revitalization and Innovation*. London: Routledge.
Chen, Nancy N. 2003. *Breathing Spaces: Qigong, Psychiatry, and Healing in China*. New York: Columbia University Press.
Chin, Aanping. 2007. *The Authentic Confucius: A Life of Thought and Politics*. New York: Scribners.
Chin, Shunshin. 2000. *The Taiping Rebellion*. Trans. Joshua A. Fogel. Armonk, NY: M. E. Sharpe.
China Quarterly. 2003. Special issue on religion in China (March).
Ching, Julia. 1993. *Chinese Religions*. Maryknoll, NY: Orbis Books.
———. 1997. *Mysticism and Kingship in China: The Heart of Chinese Wisdom*. Cambridge: Cambridge University Press.
Chiu-Duke, Josephine. 2000. *To Rebuild the Empire: Lu Chih's Confucian Pragmatist*

Approach to the Mid-T'ang Predicament. Ithaca: State University of New York Press.

Chuang Tzu [see also Zhuangzi]. 1997. *Wandering on the Way: Early Taoist Tales and Parables of Chuang Tzu.* Trans. Victor H. Mair. Honolulu: University of Hawaii Press.

Clarke, J. J. 2000. *The Tao of the West: Western Transformations of Taoist Thought.* London: Routledge.

Cleary, Thomas. 1983. *Entry into the Inconceivable: An Introduction to Hua-yen Buddhism.* Honolulu: University of Hawaii Press.

———. 2005. *Classics of Buddhism and Zen: The Collected Translations of Thomas Cleary.* 5 vols. Boston: Shambhala.

Cohen, Paul A. 1998. *History in Three Keys: The Boxers as Event, Experience, and Myth.* New York: Columbia University Press.

Confucius. 1992. *The Analects.* 2nd ed. Trans. D. C. Lau. Hong Kong: Chinese University Press.

Cook, Scott. 2003. *Hiding the World in the World: Uneven Discourses on the Zhuangzi.* Albany: State University of New York Press.

Csikscentmihalyi, Mark (ed.). 2006. *Readings in Han Chinese Thought.* Indianapolis: Hackett.

Dean, Kenneth. 1998. *Lord of the Three in One: The Spread of a Cult in Southeast China.* Princeton, NJ: Princeton University Press.

de Bary, William Theodore. 1972. *The Buddhist Tradition: In India, China, and Japan.* New York: Vintage.

———. 1975. *The Unfolding of Neo-Confucianism.* New York: Columbia University Press.

———. 1981. *Neo-Confucian Orthodoxy and the Learning of the Mind-and-Heart.* New York: Columbia University Press.

———. 2007. *Confucian Tradition and Global Education.* New York: Columbia University Press.

de Bary, William Theodore, Irene Bloom, and Joseph Adler (eds.). 2000. *Sources of Chinese Tradition: From Earliest Times to 1600.* 2nd ed., Vol. 1. New York: Columbia University Press.

de Bary, William Theodore, and Tu Weiming. 1998. *Confucianism and Human Rights.* New York: Columbia University Press.

de Groot, Jan Jakob Maria. 1972 [1892]. *The Religious Systems of China: The Ancient Forms, Evolution, History, and Present.* 6 vols. Leiden: E. J. Brill.

Demieville, P. 1986. "Philosophy and Religion from Han to Sui." In *The Cambridge History of China,* Vol. 1, edited by Denis Twitchett and John K. Fairbank. Cambridge: Cambridge University Press.

Dillon, Michael. 1999. *China's Muslim Hui Community: Migration, Settlement, and Sects.* London: Curzon Press.

Dumoulin, Heinrich. 2005. *Zen Buddhism: A History, India and China.* Bloomington, IN: World Wisdom.

Dunch, Ryan. 2001. *Fuzhou Protestants and the Making of a Modern China, 1857–1927.* New Haven, CT: Yale University Press.

Ebry, Patricia Buckley, and Peter N. Gregory (eds.). 1993. *Religion and Society in T'ang and Sung China.* Honolulu: University of Hawaii Press.

Eliade, Mircea. 1985. *A History of Religious Ideas: From Gautama Buddhas to the Triumph of Christianity.* Vol. 2. Chicago: University of Chicago Press.

Elverskog, Johan. 2010. *Buddhism and Islam on the Silk Road.* Philadelphia: University of Pennsylvania Press.

Eno, Robert. 1990. *The Confucian Creation of Heaven: Philosophy and the Defense of Ritual Mastery.* Albany: State University of New York Press.

Faure, Bernard. 1995. *The Rhetoric of Immediacy: A Cultural Critique of Chan/Zen Buddhism.* Princeton, NJ: Princeton University Press.

———. 1997. *Chan Insights and Oversights: An Epistemological Critique of the Chan Tradition.* Princeton, NJ: Princeton University Press.

Ferguson, Andrew. 2005. *Zen's Chinese Heritage: The Masters and Their Teachings.* Bloomington, IN: World Wisdom

Fingarette, Herbert. 1998. *Confucius: The Secular as Sacred.* Long Grove, IL: Waveland Press.

Foltz, Richard C. 2010. *Religions of the Silk Road: Premodern Patterns of Globalization.* New York: Palgrave Macmillan.

Fontana, Michele. 2011. *Matteo Ricci: A Jesuit in the Ming Court.* Lanham, MD: Rowman and Littlefield.

Fraser, Sarah. 2003. *Performing the Visual: The Practice of Buddhist Wall Painting in China and Central Asia, 618–960.* Stanford, CA: Stanford University Press.

Freedman, Maurice. 1979. "On the Sociological Study of Chinese Religion." In *The Study of Chinese Society,* edited by Maurice Freedman. Stanford, CA: Stanford University Press.

Fung, Yu-lan. 1983a. *A History of Chinese Philosophy, Vol 1: The Period of the Philosophers (from the Beginnings to Circa 100 B.C.).* Trans. Derk Bodde. Princeton, NJ: Princeton University Press.

———. 1983b. *A History of Chinese Philosophy, Vol 2: The Period of Classical Learning (from the Second Century B.C. to the Twentieth Century A.D.).* Trans. Derk Bodde. Princeton, NJ: Princeton University Press.

———. 1997. *A Short History of Chinese Philosophy.* Trans. Derk Bodde. New York: Free Press.

Gernet, Jacques. 1985. *China and the Christian Impact.* Cambridge: Cambridge University Press.

———. 1998 [1956]. *Buddhism in Chinese Society: An Economic History from the Fifth to the Tenth Centuries.* Trans. Franciscus Verellen. New York: Columbia University Press.

Gimello, Robert M., and Peter N. Gregory (eds.). 1983. *Studies in Ch'an and Hua-Yen.* Honolulu: University of Hawaii Press.

Gold, Thomas, Doug Guthrie, and David Wank (eds.). 2002. *Social Connections in China: Institutions, Culture, and the Changing Nature of Guanxi.* Cambridge: Cambridge University Press.

Goldin, Paul R. 2011. *Confucianism.* Berkeley: University of California Press.

Goosaert, Vincent, and David A. Palmer. 2011. *The Religious Question in Modern China.* Chicago: University of Chicago Press.

Granet, Marcel. 1975 [1922]. *The Religion of the Chinese People.* Trans. Maurice Freedman. New York: Harper and Row.

Gregory, Peter N., and Daniel A. Getz (eds.). 2002. *Buddhism in the Sung.* Rev. ed. Honolulu: University of Hawaii Press.

Hall, David L., and Roger T. Ames. 1987. *Thinking Through Confucius.* Albany: State University of New York Press.

———. 1999. *The Democracy of the Dead: Dewey, Confucius, and the Hope for Democracy in China.* New York: Open Court.

Halperin, Mark. 2006. *Out of the Cloister: Literati Perspectives on Buddhism in Sung China, 960–1279.* Cambridge, MA: Harvard University Asia Center.

Hansen, Chad. 2000. *A Daoist Theory of Chinese Thought: A Philosophical Interpretation.* New York: Oxford University Press.

Henricks, Robert G. 2005. *Lao Tzu's Tao de Ching: A Translation of the Startling New Documents Found at Guodian.* New York: Columbia University Press.

Hsia, Florence C. 2009. *Sojourners in a Strange Land: Jesuits and Their Scientific Missions in Late Imperial China.* Chicago: University of Chicago Press.

Hsia, R. Po-Chia. 2010. *A Jesuit in the Forbidden City: Matteo Ricci, 1552–1610.* New York: Oxford University Press.

Huang, Chun-Chieh. 2001. *Mencian Hermeneutics: A History of Interpretations in China.* New Brunswick, NJ: Transaction Publications.

Hymes, Robert. 2002. *Way and Byway: Taoism, Local Religion, and Models of Divinity in Sung and Modern China.* Berkeley: University of California Press.

Ivanhoe, Philip J. 2000. *Confucian Moral Self-Cultivation.* Indianapolis: Hackett.

———. 2002. *Ethics in the Confucian Tradition: The Thought of Mengzi and Wang Yangming.* Indianapolis: Hackett.

Jia, Jinhua. 2007. *The Hongzhou School of Chan Buddhism in Eighth Through Tenth Century China.* Binghamton: State University of New York Press.

Jones, Charles Brewer (ed.). 1999. *Buddhism in Taiwan: Religion and the State, 1660–1990.* Honolulu: University of Hawaii Press.

Kang, Xiaofei. 2006. *The Cult of the Fox: Power, Gender, and Popular Religion in Late Imperial and Modern China.* New York: Columbia University Press.

Kasoff, Ira E. 1984. *The Thought of Chang Tsai (1020–1077).* Cambridge: Cambridge University Press.

Katz, Paul R. 2000. *Images of the Immortal: The Cult of Lu Dongbin at the Palace of Eternal Joy.* Honolulu: University of Hawaii Press.

Keightley, David N. 1978. *Sources of Shang History: The Oracle-Bone Inscriptions of Bronze Age China.* Berkeley: University of California Press.

Kern, Martin (ed.). 2005. *Text and Ritual in Early China.* Seattle: University of Washington Press.

Kieschnick, John. 2003. *The Impact of Buddhism on Chinese Material Culture.* Princeton, NJ: Princeton University Press.

Kim, Sangkeun. 2005. *Strange Names of God: The Missionary Translation of the Divine Name and Chinese Responses to Matteo Ricci's "Shangti" in Late Ming China, 1583–1644.* Bern: Peter Lang.

Kindopp, Jason, and Carol Lee Hamrin. 2004. *God and Caesar in China: Policy Implications of Church-State Tensions.* Washington, DC: Brookings Institution.

King, Ambrose. 1995. "Kuan-hsi and Network Building: A Sociological Interpretation." In *The Living Tree: The Changing Meaning of Being Chinese,* edited by Wei-ming Tu, 109–126. Stanford, CA: Stanford University Press.

Kipnis, Andrew B. 1997. *Producing Guanxi: Sentiment, Self, and Subculture in a North China Village.* Durham, NC: Duke University Press.

Kirkland, Russell. 2004. *Taoism: The Enduring Tradition.* London: Routledge.

Kjellberg, Paul, and Philip J. Ivanhoe (eds.). 1996. *Essays on Skepticism, Relativism, and Ethics in the Zhuangzi.* Albany: State University of New York Press.

Kohn, Livia (ed.). 1993. *The Taoist Experience: An Anthology.* Albany: State University of New York Press.

Kolakowski, Leszek. 1978. *Main Currents of Marxism: Its Rise, Growth, and Dissolution.* Vol. 3. Trans. P. S. Falla. Oxford: Clarendon Press.

———. 1982. *Religion.* New York: Oxford University Press.

Kramers, R. 1986. "The Development of the Confucian Schools." In *The Cambridge*

History of China, vol. 1, edited by Denis Twitchett and John K. Fairbank. Cambridge: Cambridge University Press.

Laamann, Lars Peter. 2006. *Christian Heretics in Late Imperial China: The Inculturation of Christianity in Eighteenth and Early Nineteenth Century China.* London: Routledge.

Lai, Karyn. 2006. *Learning from Chinese Philosophies: Ethics of Interdependent and Contextualized Self.* Burlington, VT: Ashgate.

Laven, Mary. 2011. *Mission to China: Matteo Ricci and the Jesuit Encounter with the East.* London: Faber and Faber.

Lazado, Eriberto P. Jr. 2001. *God Aboveground: Catholic Church, Postsocialist State, and Transnational Processes in a Chinese Village.* Stanford, CA: Stanford University Press.

Lewis, Mark Edward. 2006. *The Flood Myths of Early China.* Albany: State University of New York Press.

Li, Chenyang. 1999. *The Tao Encounters the West: Explorations in Comparative Philosophy.* Albany: State University of New York Press.

Liao, Yiwu. 2011. *God Is Red: The Secret Story of How Christianity Survived and Flourished in Communist China.* Trans. Wenguang Huang. New York: HarperOne.

Ling, Haicheng. 2004. *Buddhism in China.* Shanghai: China International Press.

Liu, James T. C. 1988. *China Turning Inward: Intellectual-Political Changes in the Early Twelfth Century.* Cambridge, MA: Council on East Asian Studies, Harvard University.

Littlejohn, Ronnie. 2011. *Confucianism: An Introduction.* New York: Tauris.

Liu, JeeLoo. 2006. *An Introduction to Chinese Philosophy: From Ancient Philosophy to Chinese Buddhism.* London: Blackwell.

Loewe, Michael. 1986. "The Concept of Sovereignty." In *The Cambridge History of China,* vol. 1, edited by Denis Twitchett and John K. Fairbank. Cambridge: Cambridge University Press.

———. 2005. *Faith, Myth, and Reason in Han China.* Indianapolis: Hackett.

Lopez, Donald S., Jr. (ed.). 1996. *Religions of China in Practice.* Princeton, NJ: Princeton University Press.

Lowe, Scott. 1992. *Mo Tzu's Religious Blueprint for a Chinese Utopia: The Will and the Way.* Lewiston, NY: Edwin Mellen.

Luo, Weihong. 2004. *Christianity in China.* Shanghai: Chinese Intercontinental Press.

Lutz, Jessie G., and Rolland Ray Lutz. 1998. *Hakka Chinese Confront Protestant Christianity, 1850–1900, with the Autobiographies of Eight Hakka Christians and Commentary.* Armonk, NY: M. E. Sharpe.

Madsen, Richard. 1998. *China's Catholics: Tragedy and Hope in Emerging Civil Society.* Berkeley: University of California Press.

———. 2007. *Democracy Dharma: Religious Renaissance and Political Development in Taiwan.* Berkeley: University of California Press.

Mair, Victor H. 1983 (ed.). *Experimental Essays on Chuang-tzu.* Honolulu: University of Hawaii Press.

———. 1998. *Wandering in the Way: Early Taist Tales and Parables of Chuang Tzu.* Honolulu: University of Hawaii Press.

Marshall, S. J. 2001. *The New Mandate of Heaven: Hidden History of the I Ching.* New York: Columbia University Press.

McNair, Amy. 2007. *Donors of Longmen: Faith, Politics, and Patronage in Medieval Buddhist Sculpture.* Honolulu: University of Hawaii Press.

Menegon, Eugenio. 2010. *Ancestors, Virgins, and Friars: Christianity as a Local Religion in Late Imperial China.* Cambridge, MA: Harvard University Asia Center.

Metzger, Thomas A. 2006. *A Cloud Across the Pacific: Essays on the Clash Between Chinese and Western Political Theories Today.* Hong Kong: Chinese University Press.

Miller, Tracy. 2007. *The Divine Nature of Power: Chinese Rural Architecture at the Sacred Site of Jinchi.* Cambridge, MA: Harvard University Asia Center.

Moeller, Hans-Georg. 2004. *Daoism Explained: From the Dream of the Butterfly to Fishnet Allegory.* Peru, IL: Open Court.

Moffett, Samuel Hugh. 1998. *A History of Christianity in Asia: Beginnnings to 1500.* Vol 1. Maryknoll, NY: Orbis Books.

———. 2005. *A History of Christianity in Asia: 1500 to 1900.* Vol. 2. Maryknoll, NY: Orbis Books.

Mollier, Christine. 2009. *Buddhism and Taoism Face to Face: Scripture, Ritual, and Iconographic Exchange in Medieval China.* Honolulu: University of Hawaii Press.

Mozi. 2003. *Basic Writings.* Trans. Burton Watson. New York: Columbia University Press.

Munro, Donald J. 2001. *The Concept of Man in Early China.* Ann Arbor: Center for Chinese Studies, University of Michigan.

Murata, Sachiko. 2000. *Chinese Gleams of Sufi Light: Wang Tai-yu's Great Learning of the Pure and Real and Liu Chih's Displaying the Concealment of the Real Realm.* Ithaca: State University of New York Press.

Nakamura, H. 1964. *Ways of Thinking of Eastern Peoples.* Honolulu: University of Hawaii Press.

Nylan, Michael. 2001. *The Five "Confucian" Classics.* New Haven, CT: Yale University Press.

Nylan, Michael, and Thomas Wilson. 2010. *Lives of Confucius: Civilization's Greatest Sage Through the Ages.* New York: Doubleday.

Overmyer, Daniel L. 2003. *Religion in China Today.* Cambridge: Cambridge University Press.

Ownby, David. 2003. *Falungong and China's Future.* Lanham, MD: Rowman and Littlefield.

Palmer, David A. 2007. *Qigong Fever: Body, Science, and Utopia in China.* New York: Columbia University Press.

Pas, Julian F. 2006. *The A to Z of Taoism.* Lanham, MD: Scarecrow.

Peale, John. 2005. *The Love of God in China: Can One Be Both Chinese and Christian?* Lincoln, NE: iVerse.

Plaks, Andrew, and Xinzhong Yao (eds. and trans.). 2004. *Ta Hsueh and Chung Yung (The Highest Order of Cultivation and On the Practice of the Mean).* New York: Penguin.

Poceski, Mario. 2007. *Ordinary Minds as the Way: The Hongzhou School and the Growth of Chan Buddhism.* New York: Oxford University Press.

———. 2009. *Introducing Chinese Religions.* New York: Routledge.

Pomplun, Trent. 2009. *Jesuit on the Roof of the World: Ippolito Desiteri's Mission to Tibet.* New York: Oxford University Press.

Powers, John. 2008. *A Concise Introduction to Tibetan Buddhism.* Ithaca, NY: Snow Lion.

Pregadio, Fabrizio. 2006. *Great Clarity: Daoism and Alchemy in Early Medieval China.* Stanford, CA: Stanford University Press.

Preston, Diana. 2001. *The Boxer Rebellion: The Dramatic Story of China's War on Foreigners That Shook the World in the Summer of 1900.* Berkeley: University of California Press.

Qiang, Ning. 2004. *Art, Religion, and Politics in Medieval China: The Dunhuang Cave of the Zhai Family.* Honolulu: University of Hawaii Press.

Robinet, Isabelle. 1997. *Taoism: Growth of a Religion.* Stanford, CA: Stanford University Press.

Roetz, Heiner. 1993. *Confucian Ethics of the Axial Age: A Reconstruction Under the Aspect of the Breakthrough Toward Postconventional Thinking.* Albany: State University of New York Press.

Roth, Harold (ed.). 2004. *Original Tao: Inward Training (Nei-yeh) and the Foundations of Taoist Mysticism.* New York: Columbia University Press.

Rubinstein, Murray A. 1996. *The Origins of the Anglo-American Missionary Enterprise in China, 1807–1840.* Lanham, MD: Scarecrow.

Sakyamuni. 1993. *The Lotus Sutra.* Trans. Burton Watson. New York: Columbia University Press.

Schipper, Kristofer. 1993. *The Taoist Body.* Trans. Karen C. Duval. Berkeley: University of California Press.

Schmidt-Leukel, Perry (ed.). 2006. *Buddhism, Christianity, and the Question of Creation.* Burlington, VT: Ashgate.

Scott, Janet Lee. 2007. *For Gods, Ghosts, and Ancestors: The Chinese Tradition of Paper Offerings.* Seattle: University of Washington Press.

Shahar, Meir, and Robert P. Weller (eds.). 1996. *Unruly Gods: Divinity and Society in China.* Honolulu: University of Hawaii Press.

Shih, Vincent. 1967. *The Tai Ping Ideology.* Seattle: University of Washington Press.

Shun, Kwong-Loi. 2000. *Mencius and Early Chinese Thought.* Stanford, CA: Stanford University Press.

Smith, Arthur Henderson. 1894. *Chinese Characteristics.* New York: Revell.

Smith, Carl T. 2005. *Chinese Christians: Elites, Middlemen, and the Church in Hong Kong.* Hong Kong: University of Hong Kong.

Smith, Richard J., and D. W. Y. Kwok (eds.). 1993. *Cosmology, Ontology, and Human Efficacy: Essays in Chinese Thought.* Honolulu: University of Hawaii Press.

Sommer, Deborah (ed.). 1995. *Chinese Religion: An Anthology of Sources.* New York: Oxford University Press.

Spence, Jonathan. 1996. *God's Chinese Son.* London: HarperCollins.

Strathern, Paul. 1999. *Confucius in Ninety Minutes.* Chicago: Ivan R. Dee.

Sweeten, Alan R. 2001. *Christianity in Rural China: Conflict and Accommodation in Jiangxi Province, 1860–1900.* Ann Arbor: Center for Chinese Studies, University of Michigan.

ter Haar, B. J. 1999. *The White Lotus: Teachings in Chinese Religious History.* Honolulu: University of Hawaii Press.

Thurman, Robert A. F. 1996. *Essential Tibetan Buddhism.* New York: HarperCollins.

Tillman, Hoyt Cleveland. 1992. *Confucian Discourse and Chu Hsi's Ascendancy.* Honolulu: University of Hawaii Press.

Tsai, Kathryn Ann. 1994. *Lives of the Nuns: Biographies of Chinese Buddhist Nuns from the Fourth to Sixth Centuries.* Honolulu: University of Hawaii Press.

Tu, Wei-ming. 1993. *Way, Learning, and Politics: Essays on the Confucian Intellectual.* Albany: State University of New York Press.

———. 1995. "Cultural China: The Periphery as the Center." In *The Living Tree: The Changing Meaning of Being Chinese,* edited by Wei-ming Tu, 1–34. Stanford, CA: Stanford University Press.

Tung Yueh. 2000. *The Tower of Myriad Mirrors: A Supplement to Journey to the West.* Trans. Shuen-fu Lin and Larry J. Schulz. Ann Arbor: Center for Chinese Studies, University of Michigan.
Turbet, Richard. 2002. *The Bible and the Gun: Christianity in South China, 1860–1900.* London: Routledge.
Uhalley, Stephen, Jr., and Xiaoxin Wu. 2001. *China and Christianity: Burdened Past, Hopeful Future.* Armonk, NY: M. E. Sharpe.
von Glahn, Richard. 2004. *The Sinister Way: The Divine and the Demonic in Chinese Religious Culture.* Berkeley: University of California Press.
Wagner, Rudolph G. 2000. *The Craft of a Chinese Commentator: Wang Bi on the Laozi.* Albany: State University of New York Press.
Waley, Arthur. 1988. *The Way and Its Power: A Study of the Tao te Ching and Its Place in Chinese Thought.* New York: Grove Press.
Wang, Aihe. 2000. *Cosmology and Political Culture in Early China.* Cambridge: Cambridge University Press.
Wang, Yie. 2004. *Daoism in China.* Shanghai: China International Press.
Watson, Burton (trans.). 2000. *The Vimalakirti Sutra.* New York: Columbia University Press.
Weber, Max. 1964 [1922]. *The Religions of China: Confucianism and Taoism.* Trans. Hans H. Gerth. New York: Free Press.
Weinstein, Stanley. 1987. *Buddhism Under the T'ang.* Cambridge: Cambridge University Press.
Welter, Albert. 2006. *Monks, Rulers, and Literati: The Political Ascendancy of Chan Buddhism.* New York: Oxford University Press.
Wielander, Gerda. 2009. "Bridging the Gap? An Investigation of Beijing Intellectual House Church Activities and Their Implications for China's Democratization." *Journal of Contemporary China* 18(62): 849–864.
Williams, Paul. 2008. *Mahayana Buddhism: The Doctrinal Foundations.* 2nd ed. New York: Routledge.
Wills, John E. (ed.). 2011. *China and Maritime Europe, 1500–1800: Trade, Settlement, Diplomacy, and Missions.* Cambridge: Cambridge University Press.
Wilson, Thomas A. (ed.). 2003. *On Sacred Grounds: Culture, Society, Politics, and the Formation of the Cult of Confucius.* Cambridge: Harvard University Asia Center.
Wong, Eva. 1997. *Harmonizing Yin and Yang.* Boston: Shambhala.
Wriggins, Sally Hovey. 2003. *The Silk Road Journey with Xuanzang.* Boulder: Westview.
Wu, Xiaoxin (ed.). 2006. *Christianity in China: A Scholar's Guide to Resources in the Libraries and Archives of the United States.* 2nd ed. Armonk, NY: M. E. Sharpe.
Wyatt, Don J. 1996. *The Recluse of Loyang: Shao Yung and the Moral Evolution of Early Sung Thought.* Honolulu: University of Hawaii Press.
Xi, Lian. 2010. *Redeemed by Fire: The Rise of Popular Christianity in Modern China.* New Haven, CT: Yale University Press.
Xie, Zhibin. 2006. *Religious Diversity and Public Religion in China.* Burlington, VT: Ashgate.
Xin, Yalin. 2009. *Inside China's House Church Network.* Lexington, KY: Emeth.
Xunzi. 2003. *Basic Writings.* Trans. Burton Watson. New York: Columbia University Press.
Yan, Kejia. 2004. *Catholic Church in China.* Shanghai: China International Press.
Yan, Yunxiang. 1996. *The Flow of Gifts: Reciprocity and Social Networks in a Chinese Village.* Stanford, CA: Stanford University Press.
Yang, C. K. 1991. *Religion in Chinese Society: A Study of Contemporary Social*

Functions of Religion and Some of Their Historical Factors. Prospect Heights, IL: Waveland Press.

Yang, Erzeng. 2007. *The Story of Han Xiangzi: The Alchemical Adventures of a Daoist Immortal*. Trans. Philip Clark. Seattle: University of Washington Press.

Yang, Mayfair Mei-hui. 1994. *Gifts, Favors, and Banquets: The Art of Social Relations in China*. Ithaca, NY: Cornell University Press.

——— (ed.). 2008. *Chinese Religiosities: Afflictions of Modernity and State Formation*. Berkeley: University of California Press.

Yao, Xinzhong. 2000. *An Introduction to Confucianism*. Cambridge: Cambridge University Press.

———. 2006. *Wisdom in Early Confucian and Israelite Traditions*. Burlington, VT: Ashgate.

Yao, Xinzhong, and Yanxia Zhao. 2010. *Chinese Religion: A Contextual Approach*. New York: Continuum International.

You, Jia. 2004. *Islam in China*. Shanghai: Chinese Intercontinental Press.

Yu, Anthony C. 2005. *State and Religion in China: Historical and Textual Perspectives*. Peterborough, NH: Open Court.

Yu, Chun-fang. 2000. *Kuan-yin: The Chinese Transformation of Avalokitesvara*. New York: Columbia University Press.

Yu, David C., and Genevieve M. Fortin. 2000. *History of Chinese Daoism*. Vol. 1. Lanham, MD: University Press of America.

Yu, Xue. 2005. *Buddhism, War and Nationalism: Monks in the Struggle Against Japanese Aggressions, 1931–1945*. London: Routledge.

Zhuangzi [see also Chuang Tzu]. 2003. *Basic Writings*. Trans. Burton Watson. New York: Columbia University Press.

13

Literature and Popular Culture

Charles A. Laughlin

As we approach the end of this book, I want to encourage you to include China in the poetry, short stories, and novels you read, the movies you see, the sports you enjoy, and other aspects of your entertainment. If you've read this far, you have enough knowledge about people, places, events, and traditions to enjoy both current and classic literature and popular forms of entertainment from China. The themes are universal—love, bravery, murder and intrigue, drunken revelry, jealousy, adultery, war, heroic men and women, moral uprightness, physical prowess. They also provide a lively and entertaining way to learn more about China, now that you have begun. Today we have evidence that Chinese classics derived from popular culture; contemporary Chinese thinkers and writers often challenge an age-old distinction between elite and popular culture, between the civilized and the "vulgar." Some of China's most exciting new writers—like the Beijing novelist and screenwriter Wang Shou, or the magic-realist novelist Mo Yan, who wrote the novel behind the epoch-making film *Red Sorghum*—attract attention precisely because they blur or even demolish this distinction, mixing the sublime with the ridiculous until they become almost impossible to distinguish. This challenge to stuffy elitism is not a modern invention.

Today we associate popular culture with mass media, advertising, and high technology. To bring Chinese popular culture into focus, though, we must highlight the ways tradition lives and breathes in the contemporary imagination. Popular culture has always been the driving force, stimulus for change, and source of variety for Chinese literature. Fathoming just how much writing has been produced in China over the past 3,000 years is somewhat like imagining the distance to the nearest galaxy. That literature embodies seething, wrangling cultural diversity. Confucianism dominated, but as discussed in

Chapter 12, many other traditions came into play as well. Over the long course of Chinese cultural history, writers and artists distilled into writing, visual arts, and drama a vast multiplicity of recreational, religious, and everyday social practices.

I recommend Chen Shou-yi's *Chinese Literature: A Historical Introduction* (1961) and Liu Wu-chi's *An Introduction to Chinese Literature* (1966) as standard histories of Chinese literature. But the story is told from the point of view of the "literati"—the elite class of intellectuals who mastered the difficult Chinese written language. It is true that almost all we know about popular culture in ancient and early modern China comes through the prism of the writings and art of the literate elite, who capture only part of the richness of creative popular expression in their times. Nevertheless, looking through this prism, we can reconstruct the rich and diverse cultural panorama lying behind it.

Writing: The Human Pattern

It is often thought that the Chinese language is totally different from other languages because of its tonality (often misunderstood as "musicality") and its pictorial elements. Such notions, though inaccurate, were an important inspiration for modernism (particularly imagism) in English and French poetry. The Chinese writing system lends itself to such theories because its characters look a bit like pictures, but by the time the earliest Chinese texts were written, the pictures in Chinese characters had long since ceased to be the primary means through which meaning was conveyed.

Still, the fact that written Chinese did not develop into a phonetic system like the Greek and Roman alphabets had far-reaching implications for literacy and literary expression. Because written Chinese involved learning thousands of distinct characters, it was very hard to learn to read and write even in the earliest times—so hard, in fact, that the few who were able to manage it remained a small and closely knit group throughout the centuries. Indeed, the "literati" can almost be equated with the ruling class, as literacy was the sole avenue to power. The written language was their stock-in-trade, and it made them socially indispensable.

The practice of divination, or fortune-telling, in the royal courts of the Shang and Zhou dynasties (see Table 3.1) was the foundation for the use of images in the Chinese language. As an official ritual with great political significance (see Chapter 12), divination was one of the activities that first required developing and preserving common symbols. Divination, by putting interpretation (and thus symbolic ambiguity) at the center of reading in a sense produced some of China's earliest literary texts. In Shang times, divination often involved applying a heated metal pin to a hole drilled in a tortoise shell or the shoulder blade of a sheep, and the cracking pattern determined the cosmic response to the question. The diviner's task, then, in addition to ensuring the correct technique, was to interpret the cracks. The earliest examples of Chinese writing available to us today are the inscriptions on these "oracle bones" indicating the question asked and the significance of the response. The later (Zhou dynasty) technique of fortune-telling with milfoil or yarrow stalks relied on a standard manual of interpretation; human situations were divided into a finite number of possibilities. A random toss of the stalks indicated the appropriate situation, which the manual associates with a vivid image. The diviner would then use the image to answer the question. The *Classic of Change* (*Yijing*) is the most famous such manual. In it, language provides indirect access to truth and cosmic forces through the ambiguity of literary images.

To the literate class of officials and diviners, language lay at the heart of relations between humanity and the natural world, the universe as a whole. In an early commentary on the *Classic of Change,* for example, the origin of human culture is associated with observation of natural patterns:

> When in ancient times Lord Bao Xi ruled the world as sovereign, he looked upward and observed the images in heaven and looked downward and observed the models that the earth provided. He observed the patterns on birds and beasts and what things were suitable for the land. . . . Nearby, adopting them from his own person, and afar, adopting them from other things, he thereupon made the eight trigrams in order to become thoroughly conversant with the virtues inherent in the numinous and the bright and to classify the myriad things in terms of their true, innate natures. (Lynn, 1994:77–80)

Later, the literary theorist Liu Xie expanded on this by conceiving of *wen* as "human markings," or the "pattern of humanity" in an organic world where everything has its own pattern:

> Dragon and phoenix show auspicious events in the brilliance of their design; the tiger by his brightness, the leopard by the tended lushness of his spots ever indicate a magnificence of manner. . . . If such things, unaware, possess the radiance of many colors swelling within, how can this human vessel of mind lack its own aesthetic pattern [*wen*]? (Owen, 1985:19)

Explanations like these show important assumptions that underlie use of language in early China. Writing preserves a symbolic connection between humanity and the universe, revealed through concrete literary images that bring us closer to particular events and situations. Among ancient Chinese philosophers (see Chapter 12), the Daoists exploit literary techniques and images the most, but early Daoists were both imaginative and skeptical about the role of language. Daoist classics like Laozi's *Dao de jing* and *Zhuangzi* question the ability of human language to transmit truths. The seemingly paradoxical opening line of *Dao de jing* (*The Classic of the Way and Its Power*), for instance, states that "the way that can be spoken of is not the constant Way"

(Laozi, 1963:57). *Zhuangzi,* one of the earliest repositories of narrative literature in Chinese, compares language to a "fish trap": once you have caught the fish (meaning), the trap can be disposed of. The narrator, Zhuangzi, yearns for a companion who, like him, has transcended the limitations of language to discuss the undiscussable (Zhuangzi, 1981:140; Knight, 2012:1–24).

Confucius and his followers, though they had a very different worldview, shared with the Daoists a fondness for using analogy and metaphor. In contrast with Daoists, however, the Confucians' faith in language (and anxiety to apply it properly) made them careful editors, compilers, and interpreters of texts, with huge consequences for the subsequent development of literature. They used writing to connect humanity with universal truths. Their compilation of the *Classic of Poetry* (*Shi jing*), the earliest existing collection of Chinese poetry, gave political and moral interpretations of even the most ordinary-sounding folk songs, whether or not such interpretation was justifiable, creating a tradition of reading and writing that took such interpretive leaps for granted. Similarly, the earliest historical records and descriptions of archaic rituals and court music became centerpieces of Confucian classical tradition; Confucius declared that their value lay in embodying the morally superior ways of ancient kings. In the Confucian tradition, reading and commenting on these texts centered on identifying and abstracting these moral principles and, through teaching and governing, putting them into practice in the contemporary world. The symbolic and interpretive functions of language come through also in Chinese philosophy of Confucius's time and the centuries immediately following. In the next section, we can see how Confucian attitudes toward literature and writing helped set the pattern for the relationship between elite and popular cultures.

Singers and Poets

Singing has been the most widespread and lasting medium for expressing personal and collective emotions: love, social grievance, the joys and suffering of labor. These experiences, activities, and emotions are the constant subjects of song, from ancient millet fields and orchards to royal palaces, aristocratic residences, urban taverns, merchants' pleasure gardens, and even today's dance halls and karaoke clubs, and are the source from which all forms of Chinese poetry emerges. Confucians' obsessive interest in the moral powers of literature conditioned the selection, preservation, and interpretation of historical, literary, and philosophical texts from the earliest times. For the moral edification of future literate generations, they preserved texts embodying the virtues and moral principles they held most sacred: humanity, decorum, righteousness, and respect for superiors. Poetry was no exception (Owen, 2006). The literati observed truth and feeling in the songs of the common people and committed some of these songs to writing. But the Confucian filter could never hide the fact that singing, chanting, and telling stories is not always motivated by Confucian virtues. It is said that Confucius compiled the 305 poems of the *Classic of Poetry* from a pool of over 3,000 folk songs chosen to assess the morale of each state, yet even those 305 rarely extol Confucian virtues explicitly. The first of the collection's four sections, the "Airs of the States" (*Guo feng*), makes up about half of the entire collection yet consists largely of love songs, harvest chants, and complaints about government harshness and corruption.

Literati poetry, though, largely moved away from popular themes, immersing itself in the exquisite extravagance of palace life or indulging in obscure metaphysical speculation, using complicated formal techniques of rhyme, assonance, alliteration, meter, and tone. After centuries of evolution, poetry was brought to its highest level of artistry in the Tang dynasty by vastly expanding subject matter and themes. Tang poetry was fresh in that it expressed profound insights and powerful emotions from an engaging, familiar perspective. The poetry of Wang Wei (699–759), for instance, embodies the Buddhist transcendence of the individual self through an impersonal immersion into peaceful natural landscapes; the poet literally loses himself in the environment:

> Empty hills, no one in sight,
> only the sound of someone talking;
> late sunlight enters the deep wood,
> shining over the green moss again.
> (Watson, 1984:200)

In this quatrain, the senses of vision and hearing indicate consciousness, but there is no self, no "I." There is also no sermonizing about the spiritual dangers of attachment to the self and the world.

Li Bai (701–762), whose extravagant, romantic poetic personality has made him a favorite among Western readers, blends the expansive imagination of the *Songs of the South* (*Chu ci*), a Han dynasty work rich with botanical images and cosmic journeys derived from liturgical shaman chants (Qu Yuan, 1985), the paradoxical Daoist wit of *Zhuangzi*, and the reclusive, wine-soaked nature love of the fourth-century poet Tao Yuanming, with an almost effortless command of existing poetic forms and techniques. In "A Night with a Friend," Li exploits the comfortable roominess of the ancient style to subtly bring together the classic themes of friendship, moonlight, landscape, and wine:

> Dousing clean a thousand cares,
> sticking it out through a hundred pots of wine,
> a good night needing the best of conversation,

a brilliant moon that will not let us sleep—
drunk we lie down in empty hills,
heaven and earth our quilt and pillow.
(Watson, 1984:212)

Li Bai's major competitor in the popular imagination for the title of "China's greatest poet" is the slightly younger Du Fu (712–770), who has quite a different poetic voice. People generally first notice Du Fu's gloomy, severe themes and subject matter. But he is also one of the boldest technical innovators, accompanying this progressiveness with a highly traditional (Confucian) attitude about the mission of poetry. From sad narratives of abandoned women to critiques of official neglect of the people's suffering to expression of his personal woes, Du Fu's poetic vision was deeply committed to social justice. Du's "Dreaming of Li Bai" provides an alternative image of the latter poet, down to earth and entangled in the tribulations of society and politics:

Parting from the dead,
I've stifled my sobs,
but this parting from the living brings me constant pain.
South of the Yangtze is a land of plague and fever;
no word comes from the exile.
Yet my old friend has entered my dreams,
proof of how long I've pined for him.
He didn't look the way he used to,
the road so far—farther than I can guess.
His spirit came from where the maple groves are green,
then went back, leaving me in borderland blackness.
Now you're caught in the meshes of the law—
how could you have wings to fly with?
The sinking moon floods the rafters of my room
and still I seem to see it lighting your face.
Where you go, waters are deep, the waves so wide—
don't let the dragons, the horned dragons harm you!
(Watson, 1984:231)

Though their approaches differ considerably, the greatest Tang dynasty poets expanded the thematic scope of poetry, making it more emotional and personal. There are no Chinese, whether literate or not, who do not at least know who Li Bai and Du Fu are, and few who have never heard of Wang Wei. Though these poets were basically refining a difficult, elite cultural form, their resulting renown also made them almost heroic figures, even in the eyes of ordinary people.

In Tang poetry and fiction, it is hard to confidently draw a distinction between popular and elite culture (Owen, 2007). Some poems of famous Tang poets circulated on all levels of society, even (orally) among illiterates. Especially popular was Bai Juyi (772–846), another teller of sad stories but with less of the moral burden found in Du Fu's work; Bai was interested in the emotional effect of a tragic story, particularly of a woman. The simplicity of his language, the ease of its rhythms, and his sensitivity to emotional suffering made him a medieval prototype of the modern singer-songwriter. By his own observation as well as that of his admirers (and detractors), Bai Juyi's poetry had penetrated the breadth of China at all social levels. In Bai Juyi's own words:

> In my travels from Changan to Jiangxi, over a distance of three to four thousand li, I have seen my poems written on the walls of village schools, Buddhist monasteries, and wayside inns, as well as on the boards of passenger boats. And I have heard my songs sung by students, monks, widows, maidens, and men in the streets. (Ch'en, 1961:314)

More interesting evidence of the popular attitude toward elite literature is provided by the huge collection of books and scrolls that were sealed up in the famous Dunhuang grottoes around the tenth century. Rediscovered by European explorers in 1908, the Dunhuang manuscripts are a repository of Tang Buddhist and secular literature, much of it copied by common people not of the elite literati class. The manuscripts provide an alternative perspective on official literary history. There are texts in many non-Chinese languages and foreign narrative materials and forms even in the Chinese texts, and the collection gives physical evidence of a thriving, popular culture of writing and performance. Alongside copies of works by famous writers were found popularized tales from the Buddha's life or the lives of Buddhist saints that incorporate Chinese folklore and history and oral storytelling, as well as semiliterate attempts to imitate or parody elite forms. This is the beginning of a little-recognized trend of Chinese cultural history. From the Tang dynasty on, as the ability to read and write slowly seeped out of the literati's exclusive control, popular, folk, and foreign forms fed back into elite culture. The line dividing "elite" from "common" was blurring.

By now it should be evident that I am using the term "popular culture" to refer to the full range of activities from folk singing to religious ritual to secular performing arts, involving performers and spectators from all social classes. From the late Tang dynasty on, different forms of entertainment for city dwellers (including merchants, laborers, and artisans) as well as for literati began to influence elite writing. Storytelling in the marketplace and at temple fairs, with its roots in Buddhist popular evangelism, influenced the emergence of written vernacular tales about ordinary people. And the literate class (including semiliterate merchants with highly cultivated tastes) began to develop its own distinctive forms of culture.

Much of this leisure culture of the literate centered on collecting and appreciating exquisite objects (vases, tea bowls, ancient bronzes), fashioning carefully landscaped gardens within private estates, and enjoying various entertainments provided by sophisticated courtesans. Many poems of the major Tang poets praise famous singing and dancing ladies who are no longer always the royal palace courtesans of previous dynasties but often "freelance" talents who might move from palaces to the entourages of rich merchants or officials and back again. Tang poets such as Du Fu, Yuan Zhen (779–831), and Bai Juyi were struck by the sadness of their unstable, transient lives in contrast to the joys and opulence of which they sang. It was in this later part of the Tang that the radically new form of poetry called *ci* began to evolve.

The term *ci* refers to lyrics of popular songs. The art of *ci* consisted of writing new lyrics to familiar songs, usually love songs of Central Asian origin that were part of the courtesan's repertoire and widely known at all levels of society. Because we know poems about professional entertainers began to appear in the high Tang, even though *ci* itself was not commonly used until a century or so later, it appears that literati officials of the highest rank were enjoying these performances for some time before becoming artistically interested in the songs being sung. The practice of providing new words was probably widespread long before *ci* were written and included in the corpus of major poets. The original lyrics of these songs relating to the song's title are often forgotten. Some of the most famous *ci* written to a given tune have nothing to do with the song's title.

Although in the late Tang *ci* poems were something of a novelty, by the time of the Northern Song dynasty (960–1126), the *ci* form dominated poetic expression. The *shi* forms of regulated verse and quatrain, which began during the Han and reached their peak in the high Tang, though still widely used (people still write *shi* today), were already then looked upon as stodgy, old-fashioned, and lifeless. At this point, popular forms successfully invaded the culture of writing, affirming their own style and content; they tolerated less elite distortion, and elite literary forms would never again monopolize writing. Elite writers shifted their emphasis from poetry to fiction and drama.

Storytellers and Novelists

Classical Tales

The roots of Chinese fiction are numerous and complex; although vernacular fiction can be confidently traced to oral storytellers manipulating an originally Buddhist tradition of popular evangelism (see Chapter 12), written fictional narrative had already existed in various forms in all kinds of early texts, including poetry, philosophy, and historical and geographical records.

History provided the most powerful narrative models for fiction; ancient works like the Zhou dynasty "Zuo Commentary" on the Spring and Autumn Annals (*Zuo Zhuan*) and the Han dynasty "Records of the Historian" (*Shi Ji*) by Sima Qian were revered throughout Chinese history as models of beautiful writing as well as sources of historical and moral knowledge. Interestingly, though people doubted the existence of ghosts and other supernatural beings as early as the Han dynasty, fictional and factual narrative were not separate categories, and so stories of the superhuman and supernatural were viewed as a special type of history. In ancient times, whether a story was true was much less important than whom and what it was about. Such unofficial chronicles included legendary stories about historical figures as well as tales of visitations by ghosts and deities. However, the good stories were not limited to historical records; some of the most charming and fantastical early stories are retold in the works of Warring States Period philosophers, especially the Daoists (Zhuangzi, 1981; Liezi, 1990). Though travel narratives are unusual in poetry, Qu Yuan's "Encountering Sorrow" from *Songs of the South* in the Han dynasty is another extended narrative of a cosmic journey (Qu Yuan, 1985).

Another narrative genre that stressed creativity was imaginative geography. The best-known and perhaps oldest of this category is the *Classic of Mountains and Seas* (*Shanhai jing*, ca. fourth century BCE). This work preserves ancient lore about foreign lands organized into a kind of schematic map around the outskirts of the known world (China). The *Classic of Mountains and Seas* and similar works are more descriptive than narrative, but their vocabulary and imagination set the tone for later narrative treatments of fantastical events and journeys. The worldview that underlies the *Classic of Mountains and Seas* clearly reflects China's self-perception as a core of civilization surrounded by frightening, inscrutable, and barbaric peoples and also projects other fears and anxieties suggested by, for example, the frequent mention of fireproof materials and elixirs of immortality in exotic lands.

Within the written traditions, then, the origins of imaginative narrative can be identified with the ancient practice of chronicling the strange and wonderful (*zhiguai*). *Zhiguai* emerged during and after the Han dynasty as generally biographical material based on popular accounts considered unsuitable for official histories. Such material included fantastical stories of historical figures, biographies of superhuman beings (especially Daoist immortals), and records of miraculous or astonishing events (Campany, 1996). In the context of popular culture, the *zhiguai* can be viewed along with the *Classic of Poetry* as being one of the earliest existing adoptions of popular or folk materials in the form of writing. But *zhiguai* were often ignored and suppressed by historians concerned with the purity of the textual legacy, and it was not until centuries later that collections like these were actively unearthed and reintroduced into the literary corpus.

An interest in the wondrous mixed with a fascination with love themes and legendary beauties led Tang dynasty literati to experiment with writing more self-consciously crafted tales in classical Chinese modeled on Han dynasty prose. This trend arose not only because of increasing interest in fictional narrative as a form of creative expression, but also as a reaction against the stilted, artificial form of "balanced prose" writing (*pianwen*) that prevailed until the late Tang in the civil service examinations discussed in Chapter 4 (Ch'en, 1961:285–317). This can be compared with the attraction to *ci* as a new form of poetry after centuries of overdevelopment of the *shi*. The classical prose movement provided a better medium for the naturalistic expression of emotions and narration of events than the ornate, symmetrical *pianwen*. Literate gentlemen who converged on cosmopolitan Chang'an (Map 3.1), whether successful in official careers or not, brought with them from their hometowns or from the streets of the capital itself personal experiences and popular tales that helped them produce eerie, moving stories. Despite the formal classicism and political conservatism of the classical prose movement, many of the stories created or passed along by Tang writers like Yuan Zhen and Bai Xingjian (Bai Juyi's brother) became staples of popular literature and performing arts for centuries to come.

Like the *zhiguai,* these "romance tales" (*chuanqi*) included elements of the supernatural and the fantastical; more importantly, they embodied the more personal and realistic emphasis of the Tang dynasty poet-officials (Nienhauser, 2010). The exploration of emotional and moral dilemmas—represented perhaps best by Yuan Zhen's masterpiece, "The Story of Yingying" (*Yingying zhuan*) (Ma and Lau, 1978:139–145)—guaranteed that the *chuanqi* would continue to be a major resource for both elite and popular literature in centuries to come. "The Story of Yingying" narrates a chance love affair between the ambitious student Zhang and Yingying, a talented and beautiful young woman languishing in her widowed mother's house. Zhang, however, resolves to leave her and forget about her forever when he goes to the capital for the civil service examinations. The indignant Yingying resigns herself to bitterness and eventually marries someone else but never forgives Zhang for his faithlessness, refusing to see him when he visits her after he has married. "The Story of Yingying" is a classical and emotionally raw rendition of the conflict between the demands of social convention and emotional power that ends tragically, with social convention winning—a far cry from the amusing allegorical fables of the Warring States philosophers, or the strange supernatural chronicles and far-ranging adventures that were the earliest foundations of Chinese fiction.

Yuan Zhen and other writers of *chuanqi* accomplished in fiction what writers had been doing with poetry: exploring values that were based not on rigid or abstract moral principles but on emotional sensitivity and integrity, values that hold their own claim to truth but that sometimes come into dramatic conflict with conventional Confucian moral duties. The artistic exploration of an emotion-based value system is central to the Tang dynasty's contribution to Chinese literature, and it owed as much for material and themes to the thriving cultures of professional entertainment—singing courtesans, professional dancers—as to poets' and writers' own experiences and imagination.

Vernacular Fiction

This new fashion in the Tang dynasty of telling strange, moving, and wondrous stories in terse, classical Chinese is only one strand of the development of Chinese narrative. Even more crucial to the later development of Chinese fiction and drama was the vehicle of oral storytelling with its roots in Buddhist popular evangelism dating back to the pre-Tang period. The contributions of Buddhism to Chinese literature were not limited to philosophical and spiritual themes like karma and the value of compassion, but included new horizons of fantasy and imagination as well as new techniques and conventions of vernacular storytelling (the inclusion of a moral at the end of a tale, a mixture of poetry and prose, and an emphasis on stories about anonymous, ordinary peo-

Depiction of a crowd gathered around a storyteller.

ple). For example, Buddhist source texts like the Sanskrit *Lotus Sutra* (406 CE) already possessed all these features (Watson, 1993:ix).

The venue of such storytelling, widespread by the Tang dynasty, was the urban or suburban marketplace. This was the focal point of the Chinese community, the hub of often multicultural commercial transactions, the meeting point of all walks of life—from travelers to merchants, farmers, public officials, prostitutes, and entertainers. The entire cross section of Chinese society converged on the marketplace or square, from the county seat to the large mercantile centers and the capital. The square is crowded, and the crowd is as diverse as can be—everyone drawn by the center, the marketplace itself, where everything happens, or where at least one can hear of everything. This is where the stories are told, of great sages or heroes real and imaginary, remote in history or just around the corner, full of ordinary people fighting for or running from the law, of great generals annihilating their enemies or entangled in political intrigue, and of ghosts, fox-spirits, gods, talking animals, sniveling cowards, and heroic prostitutes. All of this is the stock-in-trade for storytellers competing for his or her street audience with acrobats, magicians, theatrical troupes, blind balladeers with three-stringed guitars, and other storytellers keeping rhythm with bamboo or metal clappers or drums.

The telling of stories as such was not alien to Chinese elite culture; because of the Confucians' obsession with significance and cultural value, some of the earliest historical texts preserved are also some of China's most compelling narratives, and Chinese history was one of the vernacular storyteller's richest resources of material. But the official histories as well as the more exotic materials already discussed could be read only by the literate minority, which was extremely small in ancient and medieval times, and it is difficult to tell whether the same stories were being told among illiterate people at the time. What Buddhist and Buddhist-influenced storytelling had to offer Chinese narrative, then, was a form that lent itself to public performance, thus providing a bridge between literati art and a much broader, often illiterate audience. Chinese legends, mythology, and historical records provided the storytellers with material and themes. One of the most attractive aspects of Chinese historical narrative to the storytelling, theatrical, and ultimately film and television audiences is the combination of moral character (loyalty in particular) and the ingenuity and fighting prowess of the knight-errant. Stories of such exploits abounded in the official histories, legendary biographies, and oral tales in the marketplace. As they multiplied in the repertoire of storytellers, many such legends were grouped together in long series of tales, often loosely based on historical events.

One such repository for narrative and lore in Song and Ming dynasty storytelling was the famous story of the Tang dynasty monk Xuan Zang (596–664), whose pilgrimage to India to fetch the complete set of Mahayana Buddhist scriptures is described in Chapter 12. As in the past, the exotic foreign journey

Robert E. Gamer

Storytellers and musicians perform nearly every day in this Hangzhou park.

was a favorite subject of tale spinners with a taste for the bizarre and supernatural. The Xuan Zang story was gradually embellished by adding various pilgrim assistants to protect the priest from earthly and otherworldly dangers on the road. Somewhere along the line, this set of stories came into contact with the ancient Indian legends of a Monkey King of overweening ambition, and such a monkey became Xuan Zang's chief disciple.

The resulting story, *Journey to the West* (*Xi you ji,* 1592), then, links dozens of existing tales of the fantastical, of overcoming and outwitting animal spirits and supernatural beasts, under the premise of this sacred pilgrimage (Wu, 1977). This chain of episodes is cemented by a common set of characters centering on the monk and the monkey and other pilgrim-guardians, a gluttonous talking pig, and a dragonlike water spirit. The adventures are placed, in turn, into a cosmic context in which the monkey's mission to assist Xuan Zang is understood as penance for his past outrageous acts of mischievous hubris (he tried to overthrow heaven) narrated in the novel's opening chapters. Although the novel maintains a folksy irreverence toward traditional hierarchy, orthodoxy, and morality, the Buddha and his pantheon come out essentially invincible, and the sacred necessity of Xuan Zang's mission is never questioned.

Similar to *Journey to the West*'s snowballing of popular legends, stories of gallantry and heroism, particularly ones featuring rebellious, unorthodox figures, tended to attach themselves to the Song dynasty rebel uprising of Song

Jiang (Hsia, 1996:76). Stories based on these events began to solidify during Southern Song rule, gaining a wide audience for their patriotic appeal because of the Southern Song regime's status as almost a government in exile as northern China was overrun by foreign people. These legends associated martial prowess, superhuman physical strength, and a brutally straightforward loyalty with China's integrity and Han race.

These swashbuckling stories coalesced in a sixteenth-century (Ming dynasty) vernacular novel, *Outlaws of the Marsh* (*Shuihu zhuan*), which narrates the gathering of 108 colorful, Robin Hood–like heroic outlaws through a variety of adventures, in which they ultimately lead a series of successful battles against the Song imperial troops and then surrender out of patriotism and turn their energies toward assisting the Song in suppressing the evil rebel Fang La (Luo, 1981). *Outlaws,* particularly through its contribution of heroic figures like the leader Song Jiang and the colorful heroes Wu Song and Li Kui, is seminal in its contribution to the tradition of martial arts fiction (*wuxia xiaoshuo*), part of the lifeblood of Chinese popular culture to this day.

For the purposes of the *reading* audience of vernacular fiction, mere transcriptions and clever rearrangements of popular oral stories were ultimately limited in their appeal. The Qing dynasty novel *Dream of the Red Chamber* (*Hong lou meng,* 1791), however, is by all accounts the masterpiece of the full-length, vernacular Chinese novel (Wang, 1992). What people cannot agree on is what makes it so, and an entire scholarly tradition has been devoted to this one novel's study and interpretation. Although *Journey to the West* and *Outlaws of the Marsh* string together a vast number of almost unrelated episodes drawn from history, myth, and traditional storytelling material, *Dream* is completely original, with a series of interlocking plots revolving around the declining fortunes of the wealthy Jia, Xue, Shi, and Wang families, who have ties to the imperial court. The novel is said to be largely based on the personal experiences of its author, Cao Xueqin (1715?–1763). The setting is during the eighteenth century in the final glow of China's last dynasty, the Qing. A grandfather clock in the Jia family's mansion hints at China's contact with European powers, whose missionary efforts by late Qing times were a conspicuous aspect of the Chinese countryside and port cities.

Dream of the Red Chamber is remarkable in its time for its lack of physical action, the narrative's almost complete confinement to the Jia mansion and the surrounding capital suburbs, and its concentration on the relationships among a core group of young men and women, at the center of whom are Baoyu, second son of the Jia family's youngest generation; Xue Baochai, the charming, practical girl to whom he is eventually betrothed; and Daiyu, an ill-starred, frail, and gloomy beauty to whom Baoyu is more strongly attracted (though the two seem able only to make each other unhappy).

This triangle is nestled in countless other relationships and conflicts among these and other families, amid armies of servants, dozens of vividly realized, colorful characters, and lavish descriptions of costume, decorations, and genteel entertainments ranging from tea appreciation to poetry games and theatrical performances. The epic family saga is further placed within a cosmic frame constructed of equal parts of Buddhism and Daoism, in which Baoyu is cast not only in his earthly form of the effeminate, hypersensitive, and eccentric boy with no scholarly (social, political) ambitions who only likes to be among women, but ultimately as a superfluous stone left over from the mythical goddess Nü Wa's restoration of the damaged masonry of the heavens. This stone is cursed by the gift of consciousness with the desire to experience life in the human world, a wish granted to him by a Buddhist monk and a Daoist priest. Once his fate is sealed, a further adventure on the stone's part forms the supernatural basis of Baoyu's relationship with Daiyu: as a Divine Stone Page in the otherworldly Garden of the Goddess of Disillusionment, he is moved by kindness to water a parched fairy plant with dew, which thus incurs a "debt of tears" that Daiyu (the human incarnation of the fairy plant) must repay in the human world. Most of the other major young women characters are also spirits burdened with debts in heaven or former lives, whereas all the male characters except Baoyu himself represent the human world, the constricting influences of society, politics, money, and power.

Despite the development of the novel in late imperial China into increasingly unified and complex forms, the vitality of the oral short story was not exhausted by its absorption into novels like *Journey to the West* and *Outlaws of the Marsh.* As late as the end of the Ming and through the Qing dynasties, prominent connoisseurs of popular literature like Feng Menglong (1574–1646), Ling Mengchu (1580–1644), and Pu Songling (1640–1715) preserved in written form oral storytellers' (*huaben*) tales that were by then as many as several hundred years old. They also offered many original stories. More than any of the forms of fiction discussed so far, these stories feature characters of illiterate classes: merchants, farmers, artisans, entertainers, and prostitutes, always placed in unlikely and awkward situations and often in compelling moral predicaments (Birch, 1958; Ma and Lau, 1978). The plots of such stories rely on multiple coincidences, often also using physical objects to string events together and dramatic, even shocking, scenes.

Pu Songling's somewhat later creations, written in classical Chinese rather than the vernacular, are much more homogeneous than the late Ming *huaben* stories edited by Feng and Ling. They more generally reflect the experience and imagination of the young scholar on his way to the city or capital to take part in the civil service examinations, revealing a similarity to the Tang *chuanqi.* In *huaben* tales, scholars encounter beautiful courtesans or other women who make them forget their wives, harm their reputations, or do poorly on the examinations. Pu Songling's scholars, however, are beset by all manner of supernatural beings—ghosts, demons, and fox and snake spirits—who materialize as beautiful women but also somehow get in the way of or complicate the scholar's career or family life (P'u, 1989).

This consistency of plot and narrative perspective speaks to the combination of elements in the character of the Chinese novelist that caused him to fail the civil service examinations and yet become a fertile cultural resource in his own right. It also suggests the commonality of experience among writers and readers of this sort of writing, who were almost exclusively young examination candidates themselves. These elements are equally conspicuous in the Chinese drama, which is heavily reliant on the fictional tradition for narrative material; but this brings us to another strand of the story.

Priests and Playwrights

Until recent years, discussions of Chinese drama in English invariably stress the "belatedness" of its appearance in comparison with other literary genres and other cultures. However, recent research on Chinese folk ritual and drama shows that this view uncritically privileges the written literary canon and disregards folk culture. We now know that the performance practices, modes of representation, and stage conventions on which Chinese theatrical performance is based can be traced far back into shamanistic rituals and exorcisms of evil spirits, which continue to be practiced in their primitive form in many parts of China to the present day.

In addition to ritual and folk practices, the performing arts also drew on medieval palace entertainment and urban storytelling. As early as the Song dynasty, both Kaifeng and Hangzhou had bustling theater districts nicknamed "tiles" after their jam-packed audiences (Liu, 1966:162–163). Song "variety plays" opened with a medley followed by a number of short pieces that may not have been linked together by a single story or group of characters. Some of the differences between the northern and southern theater of the Yuan and Ming dynasties were already established by this time.

The link between oral performance and full-fledged operatic drama is substantiated by the Jin dynasty work *Romance of the Western Chamber* (*Xi xiang ji zhugong diao*) in which Yuan Zhen's above-mentioned "Story of Yingying" is presented in "medley" (*zhugong diao*) format (Ch'en, 1994). That is, the story is told in the framework of a musical composition in which successive sections have different musical modes (*diao*), and each section is made up of poems that share a single mode interspersed with prose narrative passages. The reputed author, Master Dong, gave Yuan Zhen's story a happy ending.

Later in the thirteenth century, the *Western Chamber* story was adapted again, this time by Wang Shifu, to become perhaps the most famous work of Chinese drama, *Xi xiang ji* (*Romance of the Western Chamber*), a northern *zaju*. *Zaju* (also called "northern drama") inherited from earlier forms like the previously mentioned medley the alternation of prose and verse passages, the latter of which were sung to musical accompaniment. The sung parts were limited to a single actor, providing a unity to northern drama further enhanced by its tight, four-act structure. The other major contribution of the Yuan dynasty *zaju* to operatic theater and Chinese literature in general is its unique new form of verse, called *sanqu*. Like the Song dynasty *ci, sanqu* represented a further innovation in the coordination of verse with music, allowing for a certain amount of variation and the addition of grammatical particles and colloquial expressions (Liu, 1966:186; West and Idema, 2010).

Although the Yuan *zaju* was associated with the capital of Dadu (modern Beijing), the southern drama that had been in existence at least since Song times was associated with the opulent and culturally sophisticated southern cities of Hangzhou and Suzhou. These southern dramas, also called *chuanqi* like the Tang tales upon which they were often based, were extraordinarily long (running to thirty or forty scenes). They did not rise to central prominence in the history of Chinese theater until the Ming dynasty. There are hundreds of *chuanqi* plays from the Ming and Qing dynasties, but the best known are *The Lute* (*Pipa ji*) by Gao Ming (ca. 1305–ca. 1370) and especially *Peony Pavilion* (*Mudan ting*) by Tang Xianzu (1550–1617).

Gao Ming's *The Lute* is based on an old story of a brilliant scholar who, after achieving glory in the civil service examinations, is induced to marry the daughter of the prime minister, though he had left a wife at home, and forgets about his ailing parents. After his parents pass away, the scholar is finally reminded of his neglect by his first wife, who slowly works her way to the capital by performing with her lute on the road. Tang Xianzu's *Peony Pavilion,* also known as *Return of the Soul* (*Huan hun ji*), is based on a vernacular story and incorporates a supernatural theme of love beyond death (Tang, 1980). It features the popular formula of a well-born young lady coming across a talented scholar, but with the twist that they only meet in their dreams. Before they can get together, the heroine Du Liniang's passion overcomes her and she dies. However, when the scholar encounters Liniang's buried portrait, the power of his love brings her soul back from the underworld. Now united, they are confronted with the wrath of Du Liniang's incredulous father, but she persuades him the scholar is innocent, emphasizing the importance of feelings over reason. Music and stirring poetry enhance the potency of a whole series of climactic moments and confrontations. The play is a storehouse of lyrical allusions scouring the length of Chinese literary history, as well as a showcase for Tang Xianzu's gift for wordplay and symbolism.

Although later forms of theater, notably the well-known Beijing opera (Goldstein, 2007), are of less literary interest than these earlier masterpieces, they do give us valuable hints as to the unique stagecraft and dramaturgy of Chinese drama, of which the texts of the earlier plays give us little idea. For example, although we know that by the Yuan dynasty, dramatic roles had

Robert E. Garner

A Beijing acrobatic performance.

already been reduced into certain stock types—the “old scholar,” the “clown,” the “painted lady”—it is only by watching the Beijing opera that we can get an idea of how costume and makeup are manipulated to signal these roles (for example, a white spot or spots on the face to indicate a clown). We do not know for sure, but it seems safe to assume that, like Beijing opera, earlier forms of theater used few of the props or scenic backdrops of Western theater, relying instead on descriptive dialogue, stock gestures, and symbolic objects to suggest location and movement. Finally, the figure of the devoted opera fan, still in existence today, indicates the challenge posed by Chinese theater to the traditional literati’s monopoly on literary culture. The visual spectacle of opera along with its acrobatics and musical accompaniment came together to form entertainment of great sophistication that was now accessible to the illiterate. Oral storytelling, vernacular fiction, and the theater all represent the slippage over the centuries of elite culture from the hands of the literate minority. Modern technological advances were about to create the potential for even greater cultural engagement on the part of the population at large, but new forms of cultural elitism would still maintain a stubborn division between the educated and the "masses."

Resisting Modern Orthodoxies

The May Fourth Movement: Modern Cultural Orthodoxy

May 4, 1919: the last traditional dynasty, the Qing, had ended eight years before and China was now a modern republic, or trying to be. But at the Versailles Peace Conference after World War I, when the victorious powers transferred German holdings in the Chinese province of Shandong to Japan, the Republic of China's representatives did not or could not resist the agreement. As a result, a history-making demonstration of students, professors, and other patriots took place at Tiananmen Square (the Gate of Heavenly Peace in front of the Forbidden City in Beijing), passionately opposing the weakness of the Chinese government (references to this treaty and movement in Chapters 4, 7, and 11 give a sense of the importance of this date). For students and writers, the demonstration represented the culmination of a groundswell of youthful antitraditionalism represented by Chen Duxiu's popular magazine *New Youth* (*Xin qingnian*) and the literary revolution sponsored by Hu Shi, signified by his promotion of writing forcefully and directly in the modern vernacular. China was a republic, but its culture was not yet modern.

As in ancient times, cultural progress was still being measured in terms of writing. However, there was a decidedly modern, nationalistic side to the May Fourth Movement as well. After decades of humiliating military and diplomatic defeats at the hands of European countries, the United States, and Japan, both popular and elite culture in modern times were saturated with a feeling that these indignities were suffered in large part because China's political and military leaders were too effeminate, lacking in the essential qualities of the *nanzi Han* (loosely translatable as "the virile Chinese man"), the decisive, physically powerful, and charismatic leader for which Chinese history and literature provide numerous models (Tsu, 2005).

May Fourth intellectuals, equipped with Western learning, knowledge of foreign languages, and an acute sense of historical crisis, were making a revolution from above by writing in a new vernacular much closer to everyday speech, using quite different techniques borrowed in part from European novelists and thinkers. They were also writing fiery essays about what the new literature was for—the destruction of old thinking and the construction of a clean, healthy, and fair new China (Schwarcz, 1990)

The cultural agenda of the May Fourth Movement is well represented by the work of Lu Xun (1881–1936). Lu Xun's short stories represented a break from the past, for the most part because they were written in the modern vernacular, a mode of expression until then alien to writing (Laughlin, 2008b).

The stories often tell of a young intellectual returning to his home in the countryside after receiving a foreign education and having been exposed to Western ideas, only to find that he can no longer fit in with the people and landscapes of his youth (Lu Xun, 1990). Unlike most writers that followed him, however, Lu Xun was a master of irony and distortion, and his vision of the world, though stridently politicized, was nightmarish and often bordered on the absurd and sinister.

But instead of signaling a triumph for popular literature, the May Fourth Movement set up a New Culture in opposition to traditional orthodox culture. Thus by the 1920s, a clearly defined cultural triangle appeared: (1) traditional Chinese culture, the educational foundation of even the most radical cultural revolutionaries and the target of almost universal and incessant attack by modern writers; (2) the modern New Culture orthodoxy, based on humanism, science, and democracy—all murkily defined—and foreign (largely European) behavior, dress, and thought; and (3) mass media popular culture embodied in newspapers and magazines, radio, and film that began to emerge in the nineteenth century (Laughlin, 2002, 2005, 2008a, 2011). This third leg of the triangle, like the first, has been neglected and disdained by historians who identify with the May Fourth Movement.

The issue is further complicated by the fact that both theorists and practitioners of the modern "progressive" or "revolutionary" art and literature, particularly in the first half of the twentieth century, consciously aligned and identified themselves with "the masses," "popular culture," or "folk culture" even as they transformed and distorted it for their own artistic and ideological ends. Apart from this explicit lip service being paid to the "popular," elites appropriating and distorting some of the same popular forms they criticize should by now seem familiar; it is very much the traditional stance of the custodians of the written word in China.

Not that the May Fourth generation and their leftist successors did not innovate a great deal. The "serious" side of modern Chinese literature, including poetry and drama, ushered in phenomena rare or nonexistent elsewhere, including a universally adopted rhetoric of "cultural hygiene" (a 1983 government-led rectification campaign attacked "spiritual pollution" from abroad); the merging of individual subjectivity with national identity; and the idea of art as a dangerous weapon. This last idea not only fueled artists' and writers' sense of self-importance but also got them censored, jailed, and even killed at a higher rate than in most other parts of the world.

The importance attributed by historians to the May Fourth Movement tends to obscure the even more profound changes in China's cultural activity brought about by the emergence of mass media in the mid-nineteenth century; the literary revolution itself was to a certain extent indebted to these changes. Newspapers, telegraph, telephone, radio, and even the railroad made it possible for a much broader swath of the population to engage in the same cultural activities. Reading news and illustrated fiction in newspapers and magazines and watching motion pictures made available in Shanghai almost as early as in New York, Paris, and London drastically changed the cultural and social life of even the most conservative (Yue, 2006; Yeh, 2006, 2008; Des Forges, 2007; Laughlin, 2005). Before elite New Culture authors, editors, and their student readers began to dominate mass media, the commercial print media's audience consisted largely of urban sophisticates similar to the opera buffs discussed in the previous section. Printed advertisements in mass-circulation newspapers, often exploiting graphic images—even accessible to illiterates—as much as text, brought larger audiences to theatrical performances and larger markets to books and magazines. These eye-catching pictures (particularly in commercial print media, but also on billboards, shingles, and flyers) broadened the affected market substantially beyond the literate (Yeh, 2006; Lee and Nathan, 1985).

In the meantime, the higher-technology mass media provided more of what a broader audience demanded: not the epoch-making, brooding short stories of writers like Lu Xun, but traditional-style vernacular fiction about love, detectives, fantastic journeys, and the exploits of superhuman martial arts heroes, mixed with accounts of real journeys to Europe and the United States (Liu, 1984; Zhang, 1997; Wong, 2003).

May Fourth thinkers associated mass media popular culture with traditional China; they were largely indifferent to or unaware of what was modern (i.e., nontraditional) about it, and so the rejection of popular fiction became one of the cornerstones of the movement. They could not see, for instance, the Western influences on Zeng Pu's *Flower in a Sinful Sea* (*Niehai hua,* 1905), on Xu Zhenya's *Jade Pearl Spirit* (*Yuli hun,* 1912), or on Zhang Henshui's *Fate of Tears and Laughter* (*Tixiao yinyuan,* 1930)—the latter being one of the most popular Chinese novels of the twentieth century—because they were presented in the form and language of traditional vernacular fiction. However, just like the vernacular novel and oral storytelling in previous centuries, the very popularity of what Perry Link calls the "literature of comfort" (1981:196–235) worked against the self-important authority of the New Culture and thus took on a progressive value.

This is borne out by the mixed feelings modern writers and critics had about popular literature. Although they called for something radically different to blow away the cobwebs of a morally bankrupt culture, they were at the same time some of its most avid readers and promoters. Lu Xun was one of popular fiction's most strident critics, yet by assigning grudging praise to late Qing dynasty satirical works like Li Boyuan's *Brief History of Enlightenment* (*Wenming xiaoshi,* 1903) and Wu Woyao's *Strange Events Witnessed over Twenty Years* (*Ershinian mudu zhi guai xianzhuang,* 1907) in his *Brief History of Chinese Fiction* (*Zhongguo xiaoshuo shilüe,* 1959), he actually guaranteed the continued recognition of these works and others long after the cultural supremacy of the May Fourth Movement had given way to more radical visions. Zheng Zhenduo and Ah Ying (Qian Xingcun), two of modern China's most prominent leftist cultural activists, were also foremost scholars and enthusiasts of premodern popular culture.

The New Culture movement's attitude toward popular literature was based in part on an unfortunate identification of seriousness with progressiveness: the more fun a work of literature or art, the more politically incorrect it was thought to be. Underlying this was the prejudice that the practitioners and audience of popular literature were inferior in character and intelligence to the cultural revolutionaries of the May Fourth Movement. Moreover, existing mass media culture was incorrectly identified with an ill-defined idea of "traditional China," which was overwhelmingly viewed as an evil order to be thoroughly uprooted and eradicated.

Lao She (1899–1966), one of modern China's most uncommon and prolific novelists, at least implicitly defied the May Fourth generation's disdain for humor and frivolity. In works like *The Two Mas* (*Er ma,* 1931) and *Rickshaw Boy* (*Luotuo ziangzi,* 1938), Lao She creates a humorous, satirical vision of modern Chinese society that nevertheless expresses a yearning for something better. Influenced by Charles Dickens among others, Lao She had a mastery of humor unusual for a modern Chinese writer, making readers laugh without trivializing his subject matter or his characters. He exploits the fine line between comedy and tragedy so that one is constantly aware of the tragic implications of the comic situations he creates. In *The Two Mas,* he accomplishes this through the cultural and generational misunderstandings created between a Chinese father and son residing in London in the 1920s when the son falls in love with a British woman. In *Rickshaw Boy* he does so in the story of a simple, forthright laborer in Beijing who wants nothing more than to make enough money to buy his own rickshaw but is constantly thwarted by the dishonesty of those around him, the sheer scarcity of wealth, and the military instability of 1930s China.

Leftist Mass Culture

Once the May Fourth Movement had passed its prime and the literary revolution gave way to revolutionary literature, leftism and communism in China inherited the movement's awkward relationship with popular culture (Laughlin, 2008b, 2008c, 2009). By the 1930s, leftist writers and critics occupied important, arguably mainstream positions in the New Culture industry. Old-style popular novels and magazines continued to sell and be written, but their audience was dwindling due to a new generation of readers with Western-style educations; their teachers had often been May Fourth activists like Lu Xun and so inherited the May Fourth hatred for old China.

Ding Ling (1904–1985) is representative of the shift from self to society that characterized the 1930s. Her *Diary of Miss Sophie* (*Shafei nüshi de riji,* 1927; Ding, 1989:49–81), one of the best-known works of modern Chinese literature, narrates through the protagonist's diary entries of an ailing young Westernized woman's struggle between desire and reason as she alternately tortures, manipulates, and pursues different male friends. The work can be viewed as taking the innovations of May Fourth literature, already colored by self-obsession, sexuality, and despair, to (or beyond) their logical extremes. But only three or four years after writing this and several similar stories, Ding Ling's narrative personalities were dissolving into the masses, her febrile self-obsession transforming into enthusiastic engagement in social and historical change; she was attempting to align herself with, indeed lose herself among, workers and peasants.

This shift need not be viewed as paradoxical. The writer's attempt to become one with the people saturates the fiction, poetry, drama and reportage, and even films of the 1930s. Chinese leftists were much more keenly aware than the May Fourth generation of the power of mass media and better acquainted with its mechanics as well, and this is particularly evident in 1930s Chinese cinema. In *Street Angels* (*Malu tianshi,* 1937), for example, the familiar entertainment, fun, romance, and sensationalism of Hollywood are all exploited to advance themes of social injustice, class friction, and economic crisis, calling to mind the efforts of Charlie Chaplin. But although leftists seemed at home in the modern mass media, like their predecessors and teachers from the May Fourth Movement, they were ambivalent about traditional popular and folk culture.

Leftists, particularly in rural base areas like Mao Zedong's Jiangxi Soviet (1931–1934), in a desire to unleash the revolutionary potential of the masses, went beyond the limits of literacy and explored traditional performing arts forms as potential vehicles for political propaganda. Viewing Western-style spoken dramas, the legacy of May Fourth, as boring, they turned toward traditional dramatic forms like the *yangge,* a New Year's variety show (largely song and dance) with roots in ritual performance. But in their efforts to remold these forms and inject them with new moralistic content, communists failed to observe many of the features that made them work, from their coordination with the lunar calendar and characteristic bawdiness and irreverence to the formal aspects of performance and relationship between form and content. The "new *yangge*," by displacing the old and having little appeal in itself (being an incongruous patchwork quilt of the traditional and the modern), effectively wiped out *yangge* from the areas in which it was promoted (Holm, 1991). This is characteristic of the Communist Party's kiss of death to all kinds of traditional forms clear through the Cultural Revolution (1966–1976): from storytelling to comedic dialogue, from music to drum singing to dance, the Communist Party had a tendency to ruin popular, traditional art forms in the attempt to make them "modern" and useful. Fortunately, popular performing arts are experiencing a revival in recent years due to a trend toward regionalism in contemporary culture.

Alternative Voices

There were at the same time modern Chinese writers not so committed to the social functions of literature as such. Shen Congwen and Xiao Hong, for example, brought to modern literature a lyrical vision of the rural countryside in which the familiar questions of national identity, ethnic outrage, and indignation at the Japanese invasions took a back seat to the vivid, subjective re-creation of the rhythms and emotional structure of rural life. Both of these writers discovered and constructed a new aesthetic in the life of the Chinese countryside that had never existed in Chinese narrative literature before but that also bore no close resemblance or debt to Western literary forms.

Meanwhile, particularly during World War II, popular fiction was making a comeback and achieved unprecedented success in the novels of Eileen Chang (Zhang Ailing). In a way, Eileen Chang was the first truly modern writer in her open defiance of one of the most sacred credos of Chinese literary culture, that literature must have a positive social function. Chang's "modern *chuanqi*" take the mood of traditional romantic tales—conflicts between emotional fulfillment, social obligations, and material gain; the jealousy, manipulation, and open struggle among wives and concubines; love triangles; and so forth—and bring them into the cultural soup of modern China, expanding them into a psychological dimension replete with dark and unpredictable personalities and even insanity (Chang, 2006, 2007a, 2007b). One of Chang's most innovative contributions to modern literature is dispassionate narration of the experience of revolution and agricultural reform (an unthinkable sacrilege for a leftist writer) in such works as *Love in a Barren Land* (*Chidi zhi lian,* 1954) and *Rice-Sprout Song* (*Yangge,* 1953). Eileen Chang's importance, ignored by communist literary historians, has been vindicated not only through the influential assessment of C. T. Hsia (1996; see also Gunn, 1980; Huang, 2005), but also through her inspiration of a whole generation of contemporary writers in all of the Chinas, from Wang Anyi in Shanghai and Lillian Lee in Hong Kong to Li Ang and Zhu Tianwen in Taiwan. The 2007 Ang Lee film "Lust, Caution," though only based on a short story by Chang, can also be seen as a tribute to her entire fictional world.

Contemporary Literature and Culture in the Three Chinas

Eileen Chang's predicament in 1949—whether to stay in China after the communist takeover and years of bitter civil war or go abroad and continue her career free of pressure from political persecution—was probably difficult only for personal reasons, but it was emblematic of the path of modern Chinese elite and popular cultures. Many gifted writers decided to stay; some, like Shen Congwen, sadly never wrote again, whereas others, like Lao She, adopted, willingly or not, a rhetoric and mentality vastly different from those of the works that established their reputations. In the 1950s and 1960s, writers were largely compelled to extol the new society, and even courageous criticisms were deeply entangled in the ideology of literature in the service of politics alone. Eileen Chang's vision would have been even less tenable than Shen Congwen's.

Modern Chinese literary history is generally marked out in terms of cataclysmic political or historical events. The importance of the May Fourth Movement to modern Chinese literature has already been noted, but there were to be many more such dates, including the anticommunist purge of 1927, the Japanese invasion of Manchuria on September 18, 1931, the outbreak of war with Japan in December 1937, the rape of Nanjing in January 1938, and the communist victory in 1949. When we get to 1949, we tend to think of things in more geographical terms, imagining completely separate cultures in contemporary mainland China, Taiwan, and Hong Kong.

This view, however, is becoming problematic. Though still different in many ways from the mainland, Hong Kong reverted to mainland Chinese sovereignty in 1997. Transformation within the cultural scenes on both sides of the Taiwan Strait complicates the issue, as does the give-and-take between both Taiwan and mainland China on the one hand and Hong Kong on the other. Moreover, both mainland China and Taiwan after 1949 had their own cataclysmic political events that are comparable to those in the period before the civil war.

Taiwan's cultural scene throughout the 1950s, though perhaps less oppressive than that of mainland China, was still under tight political control. The Nationalist Party allowed and encouraged literary and artistic visions tied to the conviction that the civil war was not over and that those who fled to Taiwan and other places after 1949 would eventually return home (Lau, 1983:x–xi). But as the Nationalists' position in Taiwan solidified, a new generation of writers too young to remember the war grew up in the 1960s in a society oriented more toward economic development than military goals or political purity, a society much more saturated with mass media and popular culture, including television and a burgeoning film industry. The educational background of the younger generation of Taiwan writers (many of whom studied at the University of Washington or the International Writing Program at the University of Iowa) also led to a remarkable upsurge in the late 1950s through the early 1970s of modernist poetry and fiction in Taiwan.

The works of Ch'en Ying-chen, Huang Ch'un-ming, and Wang Chen-ho, all writers who in one way or another resisted the current of pro-US sentiment and feverish economic development, best represent this period in Taiwanese literature. These writers, whether consciously or not, preserve the modern Chinese tradition of literature as the voice of opposition to authority established by Lu Xun. They were against the status quo in Taiwan without being pro-Beijing—no small achievement under the near-totalitarian political atmosphere of Taiwan in the 1960s.

Li Yongping is often described as a conduit of "native soil literature" (*xiangtu wenxue*), which focused on themes of home, belonging, cultural identity, and the rural Chinese experience; Shen Congwen is in some sense the spiritual ancestor of native soil literature in Taiwan. Native soil writers resisted both the sometimes affected modernism of the previous generation and the more commercialized, movie- and television-drama script phase that many writers went into in Taiwan in the late 1970s and early 1980s. They attempted to create or preserve a culture that belonged to Taiwan above all, as well as the ideal of a socially engaged literature that seemed to be fading from the modern Chinese cultural horizon in the face of feverish economic expansion. However, the lifting of martial law with the death of Chiang Kai-shek in 1975, the deregulation of journalism in 1986, and the gradual implementation of general democratic elections throughout the 1990s have led to a slackening of political intensity in Taiwanese literature and its displacement by the popular literary marketplace as an important factor in literary success.

In mainland China, the deaths of Mao Zedong and Zhou Enlai in 1976, punctuated with particular severity by the devastating Tangshan earthquake, marked the end of an era of apparently blind faith in communism, with profound effects on the cultural scene. In the ensuing years, the rise of Deng Xiaoping and a new vision of the mission of the Communist Party and the trial and imprisonment of the "Gang of Four" for crimes committed during the anarchic Cultural Revolution set the tone for the cultural scene of the 1980s, which ushered in the rehabilitation of cultural figures who had been persecuted since the antirightist campaign of 1958 and had been in and out of prison and labor reform over the ensuing twenty years. Some of the more prominent of these, like Wang Meng, were promoted to important posts, whereas others, like Liu Binyan, were, in part through the good graces of such appointees, enthusiastically promoted in the mainstream literary press and experienced a new surge of creative work (Link, 1983). There was an outpouring of "scar" literature, humanist literature, and literature of historical reflection that reaffirmed the importance of intellectuals and artists after decades of persecution and tried to derive meaning and spiritual comfort from the therapeutic act of *suku* (recounting bitterness).

However, the literature written during this stage (in the early 1980s) did not differ artistically from the familiar conventions of socialist realism. Writers seemed to still accept the premise that literature's highest aim is the realistic depiction of social reality in progressive transformation, as Mao Zedong had himself called for in his 1942 "Talk at the Yan'an Conference on Literature and Art." This was merely a more genuine and honest way of approaching the task than had been common throughout the 1960s and 1970s, in which the bleak truths of contemporary reality were concealed under a false mask of idealism.

Around 1985, a new generation of writers emerged, writers who were too young to have witnessed the turbulent and bewildering persecutions of the older writers since the antirightist campaign. These writers, like Ah Cheng, Zheng Wanlong, and Zhang Chengzhi, were teenagers during the Cultural Revolution. Many had lost a good portion of their education and held a much different view of contemporary Chinese social and cultural reality than the older generation. This view is reflected in their works, which are much less confident in the literary mission of social reform taken for granted until then in mainland China.

One of the most conspicuous trends of these writers' first departures from socialist realism is a variation of native soil literature referred to as "searching-for-roots literature" (*xungen wenxue*). Unlike the more innocently lyrical efforts of Shen Congwen and Xiao Hong, searching for roots involves a more pronounced metaphysical mission derived in part from translations of Western philosophy and literature and in part from the rediscovery of aspects of Chinese culture that had been suppressed in the Chinese communist educational curriculum. These writers also share an interest in rewriting the rural experience without the formulas and heavy hand (with class villains and heroic workers) that were normal within the communist cultural milieu since the Yan'an days of the early 1940s. This cohort of writers inspired the resurgence of films in the mid-1980s, most notably with Zhang Yimou's debut film, *Red Sorghum,* based on the novella of the same title by Mo Yan, and Chen Kaige's adaptation of Ah Cheng's *The King of Children* in 1988.

The kind of critical retrospection represented by searching-for-roots fiction resonated with the concurrent appearance of Bo Yang's *The Ugly Chinaman* and Sun Longkee's *The Deep Structure of Chinese Culture* (Chinese works from Taiwan and the United States, respectively), adding up to a general mood of unstinting and even overwrought cultural self-criticism on the part of Chinese intellectuals. One of the lasting results of this trend was the reemergence of the intellectual as a cultural commentator, even a judge of contemporary cultural phenomena and foreign intellectual and cultural trends, for the first time after decades of Maoist disdain for intellectuals. Today, although the overall influence of intellectuals over the general public is waning, from underpaid university professors to publishing entrepreneurs to up-and-coming voices in North American and European universities, their identity as spokespersons for and interpreters and critics of Chinese culture has become firmly entrenched. Beginning with *The Deep Structure of Chinese Culture* and the *River Elegy* television series, one of the primary tasks of the latest generation of Chinese intellectuals has been to explore recent Western theoretical approaches, from feminism to liberal Marxism to cultural studies, to shed new light on Chinese culture, both traditional and modern.

Another ingredient in the cultural brew that had been fermenting throughout the late 1980s was a confidence or hope that ascendancy of the relatively liberal Deng Xiaoping regime could end totalitarianism in China. This hope kept the literature of the mid-1980s pinned under the continuing moral burden of history inherited from previous generations of modern Chinese writers. The Tiananmen Square massacre of June 1989 put an end to that hope, at least temporarily, and indirectly cast doubt on the necessity of literature's moral burden in mainland China for the first time in the century. Post-1989 writings retained many aspects that had been developing before the suppression of the democracy movement, notably a multifaceted fascination with pre-1949 China, a taste for the exotic, and a burgeoning ethnic nationalism, but now they were scarcely ever concerned with influencing society. Literature became more playful, and clear lines between "serious" literature and art and television, advertising, and entertainment film began to fade.

The shift of box office interest from the films of Chen Kaige (*Yellow Earth, The King of Children, Farewell My Concubine*), whose path-breaking reenvisioning of modern China is nevertheless committed to (at times painfully transparent or banal) historical moral themes, to those of Zhang Yimou (*Red Sorghum, Raise the Red Lantern, Ju Dou, To Live*), wrapped up in engaging stories and extravagantly beautiful images and colors and in which moral concerns become just another ingredient in his fragrant cinematic soup, is emblematic of parallel transformations within the realm of literature (Su, 1993). Like Chen Kaige, Zhang Yimou makes a special point of adapting the fictional works of contemporary writers, and his choices reflect changes in literary priorities after 1989, even when the works in question were from before that time (Xudong Zhang, 1997, 2008; Berry, 2005; Chow, 2007; Kuoshu, 2002; Ni, 2002; Clark, 2005).

It seems likely that the pop culture rediscovery of traditional and interwar China will continue for some time; there may even be a more genuine resurgence (rather than freeze-dried preservation) of traditional performing arts. However, the temptation to fall into ruts has already proven irresistible to some filmmakers. Take, for example, the formula of building a movie around a family or village who depend for their survival on a traditional craft. The late 1980s and early 1990s were filled with films about liquor brewers, cloth dyers, rice-tofu makers, ginseng growers, sesame oil squeezers, and even firecracker makers, not to mention Beijing opera actors. There is also a tendency like that of the traditional theater to consolidate characters into stock roles, particularly in films with rural settings: the ancient village elder, the often mute and always male village idiot, the sexually awakening young woman and her two or three virile suitors. It is not surprising, then, that a village has been constructed in barren northern Shaanxi province for the sole purpose of shooting these so-called Chinese westerns. Few people have caught the irony that this locale was the crucible in which the Chinese Communist Party established its political and social order in the 1930s and 1940s.

These developments in mainland Chinese film owe much to the formulas of Taiwan and, especially, Hong Kong entertainment film, which in turn descended from the lively Shanghai film industry of the 1920s–1940s (Davis and Ru-Shou, 2007; Haili Kong, 2005; Lu, 2005; Morris, 2006). In keeping with the pulse of traditional Chinese popular culture, film in Hong Kong draws heavily upon traditional sources like martial arts fiction or vernacular tales of love and the supernatural. Even when the setting is contemporary, plots often center on fighting prowess, chivalric virtues and values, and outlaws and police work. Much short vernacular fiction since the Yuan dynasty consisted of detective stories, with wise magistrates like Judge Pao or Judge Dee as their heroes. This trend came into its own after Ang Lee's epic *Crouching Tiger, Hidden Dragon* won the Oscar for best foreign-language film in 2001, and mainland directors such as Chen Kaige and Zhang Yimou vied with each other to make their own blockbuster martial arts classics (Hunt, 2003; Xu, 2007; Lu, 2004; Curtin, 2007).

These tendencies also strongly influence television in the three Chinas, where long serial dramas reenact or completely rewrite familiar fictional or historical stories. However, contemporary domestic drama commands a much more conspicuous presence on television than in the cinema. In mainland China, such melodramas as *Yearning* (*Kewang*, 1991) and *Tales from the Editorial Department* (*Bianjibu de gushi*, 1991), though refreshingly free from the contrived moral teaching of earlier programming, often serve as barometers of sensitive social and cultural issues (Zhong, 2010). Even more so was the ambitious 1986 documentary *River Elegy* (*He shang*, 1986), which portrays the Chinese people's futile attempts across millennia to come to terms with the cruel whims of the Yangtze River as suggestive of the people's helplessness under communist rule.

In contrast, Wang Shuo, one of the chief architects of the contemporary Chinese soap opera, reintroduces humor and irreverence with no moral strings attached. Starting out as a screenwriter of television series gave Wang insight into mechanisms of melodrama that let him create outrageously humorous situations by thwarting audience expectations and embedding inconceivable surprises. But he is best known for his characters: cynical, lackadaisical Beijingers whose moral blankness and black humor are strangely refreshing (Barmé and Jaivin, 1992:217–247).

Closer to the streets, screenplays and novels by Wang Shuo, lurid detective fiction, film magazines, martial arts novels, sex manuals, tales of the paranormal or the superhuman feats by masters of *qigong* (the art of vital force), and English-language textbooks and cassettes all clutter the most reliable indicator of mainland Chinese consumers' cultural tastes—streetside bookstalls. Whether just a tarp laid out on the sidewalk, a folding table, or a full-fledged shop with yards of shelving in a subway station or underground bazaar, bookstalls have in the post-Mao period been the backbone and richest source of information on contemporary popular literature. State-run bookstores, whose inventory is determined by the government's cultural policies, tell one very little about what Chinese people want to read, but the bookstall's very survival depends on its knowledge of the market. More recently, massive book supermarkets (often called "Book Cities") have largely displaced the state-run Xinhua operation, and their display arrangements and inventory dramatically demonstrate the triumph of the market in contemporary Chinese publishing.

Even before it was legal to do so, independent book peddlers sold banned books like the anonymous Ming dynasty novel *Plum in the Golden Vase,* collections of literary works like the 1930s essays of Liang Shiqiu and Lin Yutang, or books smuggled from Taiwan and Hong Kong. Biographies of famous historical figures sell very well, whether written by Chinese authors or translated from foreign languages. Certain books by Western authors about China, like Robert van Gulik's *Sexual Life in Ancient China* and Ross Terrill's biographies of Mao Zedong and Jiang Qing, appear in usually unauthorized translations, selling many times better than the most popular books distributed through normal channels. Western literature, previously represented in Chinese almost exclusively by nineteenth-century classics and a handful of award-winning twentieth-century works, took on a more popular guise in the 1980s with the appearance of books by authors like Sidney Sheldon at about the same time that series like *Dynasty* and *Falcon Crest* appeared on television. This, of course, strongly influenced Chinese people's perception of the United States (Shuyu Kong, 2005).

Teahouses are still fixtures in the cities and towns of southwestern China, set up with bamboo furniture in old pavilions or makeshift bamboo shacks with thatched roofs. In such places in the past, one would have enjoyed the entertainments of a storyteller or Chinese opera arias while chatting with friends, sipping a bowl of tea, and eating melon seeds and other snacks (Heiss and Heiss, 2007). Now teahouses often play videos of action films with the volume at the highest possible level. Another favorite entertainment is karaoke, a Japanese invention for singing along with music videos of popular recordings in a cocktail lounge setting. Karaoke bars, popular in Hong Kong and Taiwan for years, have now taken mainland China by storm. Although it is tempting to deplore the violent action films blaring in teahouses and the wildfire spread of karaoke, the vitality of Chinese popular culture is unmistakable even in these new high-tech guises. We like to imagine traditional Chinese entertainments as being refined and genteel, but there is no reason to believe that traditional teahouses, theaters, and brothels were any less boisterous and chaotic than modern ones. "Boisterousness" (*renao,* literally, "hot and noisy")—may be one of the defining characteristics and values of Chinese popular culture.

High technology has also helped people pursue concerns peculiar to modern Chinese culture, such as the public discussion of serious social and political issues, national identity, and pride. The rapid spread of Internet access in China, a process that seems irreversible, is undermining the central control of information. While in recent years many Internet "cafés" have become cramped, unsafe dens where preteens and teenagers skip school to indulge in online gaming and dubious Internet surfing, the Internet is also providing an important window to the world as well as an unprecedented means of free communication with people in other places. Most people in medium-to-large cities have broadband access to the Internet from their homes now, and the numbers who take advantage of this access are rapidly growing.

In keeping with the long tradition of Chinese popular culture is the emergence of creative expression and broad parody in the forms of YouTube-like videos, flash animation, and wry commentary on China's Twitter-like Weibo platform, which satirize new mainstream films as well as innumerable social problems and government responses to them (Voci, 2010). This spirit of humor and irreverence has also spilled into television and film in the form of a resurgence in popularity of *xiangsheng* comedic dialogues, embodied in the superstar Guo Degang, and humorous skits called *xiaopin,* which had existed at least since the 1970s but have had new life breathed into them by the emergence of multitalented comedians from northeastern China such as Zhao Benshan and "Xiao Shenyang" ("Little Shenyang"). Like comedic dialogue with its origins in the streets of Beijing and Tianjin, northeastern comedy draws inspiration from its traditional *er ren zhuan* variety shows that mix outrageous comedy with sex (much like the above-mentioned *yangge*) and a vivid sense of the daily life of ordinary people in villages and towns. With these media, it has become possible for the voice and interests of the broader populace to find access to powerful communicative platforms with all their "traditional" humor, irreverence, and exuberance for the first time since before 1949.

Another exciting recent development deriving from technological progress is the rise of amateur documentary filmmaking (Berry, Xinyu, and Rofel, 2010; Pickowicz and Zhang, 2006; Zhang, 2007; Voci, 2010). With the now widespread availability of the digital video camera and sophisticated editing software, a new generation of filmmakers is recording the lives of visual artists and rock musicians as well as, significantly, the traditional performing arts. These films are rarely produced in film studios or publicly released, but information about them is disseminated on the Internet, and cultural communities located in the larger cities screen such documentaries in addition to the more familiar activities of poetry reading, art shows, and theatrical performances. These kinds of artistic salon activities, which used to take place in private homes and officially unavailable spaces, now enjoy a greater variety of public venues in major cities like Beijing, Shanghai, Wuhan, Guangzhou, and Chengdu. Private art galleries, live-music bars, bookstore-cafés/teahouses, and theater-restaurants not only are proving the cultural diversity and vitality of today's China, but are profitable businesses. These new documentaries have created a new language of images; they are a "literature" that takes the visuality and accessibility of modern Chinese culture to a new level.

However, not all popular culture necessarily reflects a politically liberal viewpoint. A case in point is the resurgence of interest and nostalgia over the past ten years in the bygone era of Chinese socialism, which takes a wide variety of forms. The public intellectuals who used to be the liberal vanguard of the 1980s democracy movements are now less conspicuous, being replaced recently by the "new left"—intellectuals who target the evils of globalization and the disappearance of what they perceive as the moral compass of pre-Reform socialist China. On a more popular level, this can also be seen in large groups of city dwellers gathering in parks to joyously sing "Red songs" from the first seventeen years of the People's Republic, and even from the Cultural Revolution. On television, high-budget serial dramas reenact the tumultuous history of the Communist Party and the revolution with young movie stars and singers playing the roles of historical figures they would be too young to remember. Some of these slick productions are loosely based on "Red classics," epic novels written in the 1950s and 1960s that have also been reissued in deluxe editions found not only in bookstores, but in some cases (such as *Red Crag* or *Hong yan*, 1962) even in supermarkets. "Red tourism," one of many forms of socialist-themed consumerism, takes record numbers of travelers along the route of the Long March, to the Jiangxi Soviet and the Yan'an wartime Communist base area in northern Shaanxi, to rekindle reverence for the leaders of the Chinese revolution. This trend has reached a new height in the policies of Chongqing mayor Bo Xilai (see also Chapter 4), who made extraordinary efforts to promote "Red nostalgia" in his city through cultural events, educational policies, and urban planning. Much of this, as can be imagined, finds itself being parodied in the forms of electronic media mentioned above, yet it nevertheless enjoys considerable popular support.

Conclusion

The apparent triumph of popular culture over the elite in contemporary China makes an apt ending to this account of Chinese literature and popular culture. Perhaps the most significant contribution of popular culture to elite (written) literature throughout the ages is its challenge to orthodox moral values and literary forms with an alternative set of values based on sensitivity and emotional response. This is the serious message underlying its comic subversions of or perfunctory nods toward conventional morality—alternative canons that extol not moral excellence (as did the *Classic of Poetry* for the Confucians) or technical artistry, but rather grace, generosity of spirit, a great capacity for love, and emotional integrity.

These values underlie, for instance, the alternate canon of Jin Shengtan, an influential seventeenth-century editor and literary critic who honored as the "Six Works of Genius" the masterpieces of their respective genres: Qu Yuan's "Encountering Sorrow," the *Zhuangzi, Records of the Historian,* the poems of

Du Fu, *Outlaws of the Marsh,* and *Romance of the Western Chamber.* The works in Jin's canon have in common—along with a noticeable self-distancing from the orthodox classics of Confucianism, which were the common denominator of everyone's literacy—values of emotional integrity, intuition, and the immediacy of experience.

Feng Menglong, a late Ming dramatist and editor of vernacular short stories and an avid transcriber of popular tunes and folk songs as well, was perhaps one of the earliest figures in China to offer vocal defense of the unique values of popular cultural forms:

> In this world, the literary minds are few, but the rustic ears are many. Therefore, the short story relies more on the popularizer than on the stylist. Just ask the storyteller to describe a scene on the spot, and it will gladden and startle, sadden and cause you to lament; it will prompt you to draw the sword; at other times to bow deeply in reverence, to break someone's neck, or to contribute money. The timid will be made brave; the lewd chaste; the niggardly liberal; and the stupid and dull, perspiring with shame. Even though you would recite every day the Classic of Filial Piety and the Analects, you would never be moved as swiftly and profoundly as by these storytellers. Alas! Could such results be achieved by anything but popular colloquial writing? (Liu, 1966:216)

By emphasizing the popular underside of traditional Chinese culture on the one hand and the persistent traditional underside of modern Chinese culture on the other, I do not mean to claim that Chinese cultural forms are essentially unchanging, only that a large portion of cultural activity in China tends to flourish quite outside the power of cultural elites to control it. Cultural orthodoxies are always built upon a dazzling profusion of cultural activity, commonly drawing material and techniques from it (Kraus, 2004).

The idea of civil service as the only appropriate goal for the cultivation of literacy and knowledge remains prevalent in the various Chinas (mainland China, Taiwan, Hong Kong, Singapore, and the Chinese diaspora throughout the world), only partially displaced by the modern values of professionalism, science, individualism, and the autonomy of art. This is one reason the tensions between popular and elite, entertainment and edification, common and sophisticated remain at the center of Chinese debates on culture to the present day (Zha, 1995), as they have throughout the ages. The current ascendancy of popular culture is cause for celebration only insofar as it can foster those aspects that made traditional Chinese popular culture both impossible to ignore and yet impossible for the literati to completely assimilate.

Bibliography

Ah Cheng. 1990. *Three Kings: Three Stories from Today's China.* Trans. Bonnie S. McDougall. London: Collins Harvill.

Barmé, Geremie R. 2000. *In the Red: On Contemporary Chinese Culture*. New York: Columbia University Press.
Barmé, Geremie, and Linda Jaivin (eds.). 1992. *New Ghosts, Old Voices: Chinese Rebel Voices*. New York: Random House.
Barmé, Geremie, and John Minford (eds.). 1988. *Seeds of Fire: Chinese Voices of Conscience*. New York: Hill and Wang.
Berninghausen, John, and Ted Huters (eds.). 1976. *Revolutionary Literature in China: An Anthology*. White Plains, NY: M. E. Sharpe.
Berry, Christopher J. 2004. *Chinese Films in Focus: 25 New Takes*. London: British Film Institute.
Berry, Christopher J., Lu Xinyu, and Lisa Rofel (eds.). 2010. *The New Chinese Independent Documentary Film Movement: For the Public Record*. Hong Kong: Hong Kong University Press.
Berry, Christopher J., and Mary Ann Farquhar. 2006. *China on Screen: Cinema and Nation*. New York: Columbia University Press.
Berry, Michael. 2005. *Speaking in Images: Interviews with Contemporary Chinese Filmmakers*. New York: Columbia University Press.
Besio, Kimberley, and Constine Tung (eds.). 2007. *Three Kingdoms and Chinese Culture*. Binghamton: State University of New York Press.
Birch, Cyril (ed.). 1958. *Stories from a Ming Collection: Translations of Chinese Short Stories Published in the Seventeenth Century*. New York: Grove Press.
———. (ed.). 1995. *Scenes for Mandarins: The Elite Theater of the Ming*. New York: Columbia University Press.
Bordwell, David. 2000. *Planet Hong Kong: Popular Cinema and the Art of Entertainment*. Cambridge, MA: Harvard University Press.
Campany, Robert Ford. 1996. *Strange Writing: Anomaly Accounts in Early Medieval China*. Albany: State University of New York Press.
Cao, Xueqin, and E. Gao. 1973–1986. *The Story of the Stone*. Trans. David Hawkes and John Minford. New York: Penguin.
Chang, Eileen. 2006. *Love in a Fallen City*. New York: New York Review of Books Classics.
———. 2007a. *Lust, Caution*. Trans. Julia Lovell. New York: Anchor.
———. 2007b. *Written on Water*. Trans. Andrew Jones. New York: Columbia University Press.
Chang, Yvonne Sung-sheng. 1993. *Modernism and the Nativist Resistance: Contemporary Chinese Fiction from Taiwan*. Durham, NC: Duke University Press.
Ch'en, Li-li. 1994. *Master Tung's Western Chamber Romance*. New York: Columbia University Press.
Ch'en, Shou-yi. 1961. *Chinese Literature: A Historical Introduction*. New York: Ronald Press.
Chen, Xiaomei (ed.). 2010. *The Columbia Anthology of Modern Chinese Drama*. New York: Columbia University Press.
Chi, Pang-yuan, and David Der-wei Wang (eds.). 2000. *Chinese Literature in the Second Half of a Modern Century*. Bloomington: Indiana University Press.
Chow, Rey. 2007. *Sentimental Fabulations, Contemporary Chinese Films: Attachment in the Age of Global Visibility*. New York: Columbia University Press.
Clark, Paul. 2005. *Reinventing China: A Generation and Its Films*. Hong Kong: Chinese University of Hong Kong Press.
Confucius. 1979. *The Analects*. Trans. D. C. Lau. New York: Penguin.
Curtin, Michael. 2007. *Playing to the World's Biggest Audience: The Globalization of Chinese Film and TV*. Berkeley: University of California Press.

Davis, Darrell William, and Ru-shou Robert Chen. 2007. *Cinema Taiwan: Politics, Popularity, and State of the Arts*. London: Routledge.

de Bary, William Theodore, Wing-tsit Chan, and Burton Watson (eds.). 1960. *Sources of Chinese Tradition*. New York: Columbia University Press.

Denton, Kirk A. 1996. *Modern Chinese Literary Thought: Writings on Literature, 1893–1945*. Stanford, CA: Stanford University Press.

Des Forges, Alexander. 2007. *Mediasphere Shanghai: The Aesthetics of Cultural Production*. Honolulu: University of Hawaii Press.

Ding Ling. 1989. *I Myself Am a Woman: Selected Writings of Ding Ling*. Eds. Tani E. Barlow and Gary J. Bjorge. Boston: Beacon Press.

Dirlik, Arif (ed.). 2000. *Postmodernism and China*. Durham, NC: Duke University Press.

Dolezelova-Velingerova, Milena (ed.). 1980. *The Chinese Novel at the Turn of the Century*. Toronto: University of Toronto Press.

Faurot, Jeannette L. (ed.). 1979. *Chinese Fiction from Taiwan: Critical Perspectives*. Bloomington: Indiana University Press.

Feng Zong-Pu. 1998. *The Everlasting Rock: A Novel*. Trans. Aimee Lykes. Boulder: Lynne Rienner.

Forney, Matt. 1998. "People's Theater." *Far Eastern Economic Review* 161(3) (January 15): 48–50.

Fu, Poshek. 2003. *Between Shanghai and Hong Kong: The Politics of Chinese Cinemas*. Stanford, CA: Stanford University Press.

Fu, Poshek, and David Desser. 2002. *The Cinema of Hong Kong: History, Arts, Identity*. Cambridge: Cambridge University Press.

Gao, Ming. 1980. *The Lute: Kao Ming's P'i-p'a chi*. Trans. Jean Mulligan. New York: Columbia University Press.

Gernet, Jacques. 1962. *Daily Life in China on the Eve of the Mongol Invasion, 1250–1276*. Stanford, CA: Stanford University Press.

Goldblatt, Howard (ed.). 1995. *Chairman Mao Would Not Be Amused: Fiction From Today's China*. New York: Grove Press.

Goldman, Merle (ed.). 1977. *Modern Chinese Literature in the May Fourth Era*. Cambridge, MA: Harvard University Press.

Goldstein, Joshua. 2007. *Drama Kings: Players and Publics in the Re-creation of Peking Opera, 1870–1937*. Berkeley: University of California Press.

Gunn, Edward M. 1980. *Unwelcome Muse: Chinese Literature in Shanghai and Peking, 1937–1945*. New York: Columbia University Press.

———. (ed.). 1983. *Twentieth-Century Chinese Drama*. Bloomington: Indiana University Press.

Hanan, Patrick. 1981. *The Chinese Vernacular Story*. Cambridge, MA: Harvard University Press.

Hegel, Robert E. 1981. *The Novel in Seventeenth-Century China*. New York: Columbia University Press.

Heiss, Mary Lou, and Robert J. Heiss. 2007. *The Story of Tea: A Cultural History and Drinking Guide*. Berkeley: Ten Speed Press.

Holm, David. 1991. *Art and Ideology in Revolutionary China*. Oxford: Oxford University Press.

Hsia, C. T. 1996. *The Classic Chinese Novel: A Critical Introduction*. Ithaca, NY: Cornell University East Asia Program.

———. 1999. *A History of Modern Chinese Fiction*. 3rd ed. Bloomington: Indiana University Press.

Hsu, Vivian Ling (ed.). 1981. *Born of the Same Roots: Stories of Modern Chinese Women*. Bloomington: Indiana University Press.

Huang, Nicole. 2005. *Women, War, Domesticity: Shanghai Literature and Popular Culture of the 1940s*. Leiden and Boston: Brill.

Hung, Chang-tai. 1994. *War and Popular Culture: Resistance in Modern China, 1937–1945*. Berkeley: University of California Press.

Hunt, Leon. 2003. *Kung Fu Cult Masters: From Bruce Lee to Crouching Tiger*. London: Wallflower Press.

Huot, Marie Claire. 2000. *China's New Cultural Scene: A Handbook of Changes*. Durham, NC: Duke University Press.

Johnson, David, Andrew J. Nathan, and Evelyn S. Rawski (eds.). 1985. *Popular Culture in Late Imperial China*. Berkeley: University of California Press.

Jones, Andrew F. 2001. *Yellow Music: Media Culture and Colonial Modernity in the Chinese Jazz Age*. Durham, NC: Duke University Press.

Kinkley, Jeffrey C. (ed.). 1985. *After Mao: Chinese Literature and Society, 1978–1981*. Cambridge, MA: Harvard University Press.

Knight, Sabina. 2012. *Chinese Literature: A Very Short Introduction*. Oxford: Oxford University Press.

Kong, Haili. 2005. *One Hundred Years of Chinese Cinema: A Generational Dialogue*. Norwalk, CT: Eastbridge.

Kong, Shuyu. 2005. *Consuming Literature: Best Sellers and the Commercialization of Literary Production in Contemporary China*. Palo Alto, CA: Stanford University Press.

Kraus, Richard Curt. 2004. *The Party and the Arty in China: The New Politics of Culture*. Lanham, MD: Rowman and Littlefield.

Kuoshu, Harry H. 2002. *Celluloid China: Cinematic Encounters with Culture and Society*. Carbondale: Southern Illinois University Press.

Laozi. 1963. *Tao te Ching*. Trans. D. C. Lau. New York: Penguin.

Lau, Joseph S. M. (ed.). 1983. *The Unbroken Chain: An Anthology of Taiwan Fiction Since 1926*. Bloomington: Indiana University Press.

Lau, Joseph S. M., and Howard Goldblatt (eds.). 2007. *The Columbia Anthology of Modern Chinese Literature*. 2nd ed. New York: Columbia University Press.

Lau, Joseph S. M., and Timothy Ross (eds.). 1976. *Chinese Stories from Taiwan, 1960–1970*. New York: Columbia University Press.

Laughlin, Charles A. 2002. *Chinese Reportage: The Aesthetics of Historical Experience*. Durham, NC: Duke University Press.

——— (ed.). 2005. *Contested Modernities in Chinese Literature*. New York: Palgrave.

———. 2007. "*Wenzhang zuofa*: Essay Writing as Education in 1930s China." In *Tradition and Modernity in China: Comparative Perspectives*, edited by Kang-i Sun Chang et al. Beijing: Peking University Press, 2007.

———. 2008a. *The Literature of Leisure and Chinese Modernity*. Honolulu: University of Hawaii Press.

———. 2008b. "The Revolutionary Tradition in Modern Chinese Literature." In *The Cambridge Companion to Modern Chinese Culture*, edited by Kam Louie. Cambridge: Cambridge University Press.

———. 2008c. "The All China Resistance Association of Writers and Artists" and "The Analects Group and the Genre of *xiaopin wen*." In *Literary Societies of Republican China*, edited by Kirk A. Denton and Michel Hockx. Lanham, MD: Lexington Books.

———. 2009. "*The Moon Coming Out from the Clouds*: Jiang Guangci and Early Revolutionary Fiction in China." In *Chinese Revolution and Chinese Literature*, edited by Tao Dongfeng et al. Newcastle upon Tyne: Cambridge Scholars Publishing.

———. 2010. "*Xie zhenshi:* Writing the Actual." In *Words and their Stories*, edited by Ban Wang, 135–148. Amsterdam: Brill.

———. 2011. "Smoking as a Socially Symbolic Act: Essays of the Analects (*Lunyu*) Group in the 1930s." *Symbolism: An International Journal of Critical Aesthetics* (December).

Lee, Haiyan. 2010. *Revolution of the Heart: A Genealogy of Love in China, 1900–1950*. Stanford, CA: Stanford University Press.

Lee, Leo Ou-fan. 1999. *Shanghai Modern: The Flowering of a New Urban Culture in China, 1930–1945*. Cambridge, MA: Harvard University Press.

Lee, Leo Ou-fan, and Andrew Nathan. 1985. "The Beginnings of Mass Culture: Journalism and Fiction in the Late Ch'ing and Beyond." *Popular Culture in Late Imperial China,* edited by David Johnson, Andrew J. Nathan, and Evelyn S. Rawski, 360–395. Berkeley: University of California Press.

Leyda, Jay. 1972. *Dianying/Electric Shadows: An Account of Films and the Film Audience in China*. Cambridge, MA: MIT Press.

Li, Yu. 1990. *The Carnal Prayer Mat [Rou putuan]*. Trans. Patrick Hanan. New York: Ballantine Books.

Liezi. 1990. *The Book of Lieh-tzu: A Classic of the Tao*. Trans. A. C. Graham. New York: Columbia University Press.

Link, E. Perry, Jr. 1981. *Mandarin Ducks and Butterflies: Popular Fiction in Early Twentieth-Century Chinese Cities*. Berkeley: University of California Press.

——— (ed.). 1983. *People or Monsters? and Other Stories and Reportage from China After Mao*. Bloomington: Indiana University Press.

———. 2000. *The Uses of Literature: Life in the Socialist Chinese Literary System*. Princeton, NJ: Princeton University Press.

Link, E. Perry, Jr., Richard Madsen, and Paul G. Pickowicz (eds.). 1989. *Unofficial China: Popular Culture and Thought in the People's Republic*. Boulder: Westview.

Liu, Jung-en. 1972. *Six Yüan Plays*. Baltimore: Penguin.

Liu Kang. 2004. *Globalization and Cultural Trends in China*. Honolulu: University of Hawaii Press.

Liu, Lydia He. 1995. *Translingual Practice: Literature, National Culture, and Translated Modernity*. Stanford, CA: Stanford University Press.

Liu, Ts'un-yan (ed.). 1984. *Chinese Middlebrow Fiction from the Ch'ing and Early Republican Eras*. Hong Kong: Chinese University Press.

Liu, Wu-chi. 1966. *An Introduction to Chinese Literature*. Bloomington: Indiana University Press.

Lu, Feii. 2005. *Island on the Edge: Taiwan New Cinema and After*. Hong Kong: Hong Kong University Press.

Lu, Sheldon (ed.). 2004. *Chinese-Language Film: Historiography, Poetics, Politics*. Honolulu: University of Hawaii Press.

Lu Xun. 1990. *Diary of a Madman and Other Stories*. Trans. William A. Lyell. Honolulu: University of Hawaii Press.

———. 2010. *The Real Story of Ah-Q and Other Tales of China: The Complete Fiction of Lu Xun*. Trans. Julia Lovell. New York: Penguin.

Luo, Guanzhong. 1981. *Outlaws of the Marsh*. Trans. Sidney Shapiro. Bloomington: Indiana University Press.

———. 1994. *Three Kingdoms: A Historical Novel*. Trans. Moss Roberts. Berkeley: University of California Press.

Lynn, Richard John. 1994. *The Classic of Changes: A New Translation of the I Ching as Interpreted by Wang Bi*. New York: Columbia University Press.

Ma, Y. W., and Joseph S. M. Lau (eds.). 1978. *Traditional Chinese Stories: Themes and Variations.* New York: Columbia University Press.

Mair, Victor H. (ed.). 1996. *The Columbia Anthology of Traditional Chinese Literature.* New York: Columbia University Press.

Morris, Meaghan. 2006. *Hong Kong Connections: Transnational Imagination in Action Cinema.* Durham, NC: Duke University Press.

Ni, Zhen. 2002. *Memoirs from the Beijing Film Academy: The Genesis of China's Fifth Generation.* Durham, NC: Duke University Press.

Nienhauser, William H. 2010. *Tang Dynasty Tales: A Guided Reader.* Singapore: World Scientific.

Owen, Stephen. 1985. *Traditional Chinese Poetry and Poetics: Omen of the World.* Madison: University of Wisconsin Press.

——— (ed.). 1997. *An Anthology of Chinese Literature: Beginnings to 1911.* New York: W. W. Norton.

———. 2006. *The Making of Early Chinese Classical Poetry.* Cambridge, MA: Harvard University Asia Center.

———. 2007. *The Late Tang: Chinese Poetry of the Mid-Ninth Century (827–860).* Cambridge, MA: Harvard University Asia Center.

Pickowicz, Paul G., and Yingjin Zhang (eds.). 2006. *From Underground to Independent: Alternative Film Culture in Contemporary China.* Lanham, MD: Rowman and Littlefield.

Pine, Red (ed. and trans.). 2003. *Poems of the Masters: China's Classic Anthology of T'ang and Sung Dynasty Verse.* Port Townsend, WA: Copper Canyon Press.

Plaks, Andrew H. (ed.). 1977. *Chinese Narrative: Critical and Theoretical Essays.* Princeton, NJ: Princeton University Press.

P'u, Sungling. 1989. *Strange Stories from Make-Do Studio.* Trans. Victor H. Mair and Denis C. Mair. Beijing: Foreign Languages Press.

Qu Yuan. 1985. *The Songs of the South: An Anthology of Ancient Chinese Poems by Qu Yuan and Other Poets.* Trans. David Hawkes. New York: Penguin.

Rolston, David L. 1990. *How to Read the Chinese Novel.* Princeton, NJ: Princeton University Press.

Schwarcz, Vera. 1990. *The Chinese Enlightenment: Intellectuals and the May Fourth Movement of 1919.* Berkeley: University of California Press.

Shen Congwen. 1982. *The Chinese Earth: Stories by Shen Ts'ung-wen.* Trans. Ching Ti and Robert Payne. New York: Columbia University Press.

Shih, Shu-mei. 2001. *The Lure of the Modern: Writing Modernism in Semi Colonial China, 1917–1937.* Berkeley: University of California Press.

———. 2007. *Visuality and Identity: Sinophone Articulations Across the Pacific.* Berkeley: University of California Press.

Silbergeld, Jerome. 2000. *China into Film: Frames of Reference in Contemporary Chinese Cinema.* London: Reaktion Books.

Su Tong. 1993. *Raise the Red Lantern: Three Novellas.* Trans. Michael S. Duke. New York: William Morrow.

———. 1995. *Rice.* Trans. Howard Goldblatt. New York: William Morrow.

Su, Xiaokang, and Wang Luxiang. 1991. *Deathsong of the River: A Reader's Guide to the Chinese TV Series* He Shang. Trans. Richard Bodman and Pin P. Wan. Ithaca, NY: Cornell University Press.

Tam, Vivienne, and Martha Elizabeth Huang. 2000. *China Chic.* New York: Regan Books.

Tang, Xianzu. 1980. *The Peony Pavilion: Mudan ting.* Trans. Cyril Birch. Bloomington: Indiana University Press.

Tang, Xiaobing. 2001. *Chinese Modern: The Heroic and the Quotidian*. Durham, NC: Duke University Press.

Tsu, Jing. 2005. *Failure, Nationalism, and Literature: The Making of Modern Chinese Identity, 1895–1937*. Stanford, CA: Stanford University Press.

Voci, Paola. 2010. *China on Video: Smaller-Screen Realities*. London: Routledge.

Wang, Anyi. 1989. *Baotown*. Trans. Martha Avery. New York: W. W. Norton.

Wang, Ch'iu Kuei. 1995. "Studies in Chinese Ritual and Ritual Theatre: A Bibliographic Report." *CHINOPERL* 18:115–128.

Wang, David Der-wei. 1992. *Fictional Realism in Twentieth-Century China: Mao Dun, Lao She, Shen Congwen*. New York: Columbia University Press.

———. 2004. *The Monster That Is History: History, Violence, and Fictional Writing in Twentieth-Century China*. Berkeley: University of California Press.

Wang, David Der-wei, and Jeanne Tai (eds.). 1994. *Running Wild: New Chinese Writers*. New York: Columbia University Press.

Wang, Jing. 1992. *The Story of Stone: Intertextuality, Ancient Chinese Stone Lore, and the Stone Symbolism in Dream of the Red Chamber, Water Margin, and the Journey to the West*. Durham, NC: Duke University Press.

———. 1996. *High Culture Fever: Politics, Aesthetics, and Ideology in Deng's China*. Berkeley: University of California Press.

Watson, Burton. 1971. *Chinese Lyricism: Shih Poetry from the Second to the Twelfth Century*. New York: Columbia University Press.

——— (ed.). 1984. *The Columbia Book of Chinese Poetry: From Early Times to the Thirteenth Century*. New York: Columbia University Press.

——— (trans. and ed.). 1989. *The Tso Chuan: Selections from China's Earliest Narrative History*. New York: Columbia University Press.

——— (trans. and ed.). 1993. *The Lotus Sutra*. New York: Columbia University Press.

West, Stephen H., and Wilt L. Idema. 2010. *Monks, Lovers, Bandits, and Immortals: Eleven Early Chinese Plays*. Indianapolis: Hackett.

Widmer, Ellen, and David Der-wei Wang (eds.). 1993. *From May Fourth to June Fourth: Fiction and Film in Twentieth-Century China*. Cambridge, MA: Harvard University Press.

Wong, Timothy (trans. and ed.). 2003. *Stories for Saturday: Twentieth Century Chinese Popular Fiction*. Honolulu: University of Hawai'i Press.

Wu, Cheng'en. 1958. *Monkey: Folk Novel of China*. Trans. Arthur Waley. New York: Grove Press.

———. 1977. *The Journey to the West*. Trans. Anthony C. Yu. Chicago: University of Chicago Press.

Wu, Dingbo, and Patrick D. Murphy (eds.). 1989. *Science Fiction from China*. New York: Praeger.

———. 1994. *Handbook of Chinese Popular Culture*. Westport, CT: Greenwood Press.

Xiao, Hong. 1979. *The Field of Life and Death and Tales of Hulan River: Two Novels by Hsiao Hung*. Trans. Howard Goldblatt. Bloomington: Indiana University Press.

Xiaoxiaosheng. 1993–2011. *The Plum in the Golden Vase, or Chin P'ing Mei*. Trans. David Tod Roy. Princeton, NJ: Princeton University Press.

Xu, Gary G. 2007. *Sinascape: Contemporary Chinese Cinema*. Lanham, MD: Rowman and Littlefield.

Yan, Haiping. 1998. *Theater and Society: An Anthology of Contemporary Chinese Drama*. Armonk, NY: M. E. Sharpe.

Yang, Bo. 1992. *The Ugly Chinaman and the Crisis of Chinese Culture*. Trans. Don Cohn. London: Allen and Unwin.

Yau, Esther C. M. (ed.). 2001. *At Full Speed: Hong Kong Cinema in a Borderless World.* St. Paul: University of Minnesota Press.

Yeh, Catherine Vance. 2006. *Courtesans, Intellectuals, and Entertainment Culture, 1850–1910.* Seattle: University of Washington Press.

Yeh, Michelle. 1991. *Modern Chinese Poetry: Theory and Practice Since 1917.* New Haven, CT: Yale University Press.

——— (ed.). 1992. *Anthology of Modern Chinese Poetry.* New Haven, CT: Yale University Press.

Yeh, Michelle, and N. G. D. Malmqvist (eds.). 2001. *Frontier Taiwan: An Anthology of Modern Chinese Poetry.* New York: Columbia University Press.

Yeh, Wen-hsin. 2008. *Shanghai Splendor: A Cultural History, 1843–1949.* Berkeley: University of California Press.

Yeh, Yueh-yu, and Darrell Davis. 2005. *Taiwan Film Directors: A Treasure Island.* New York: Columbia University Press.

Yu, Pauline. 1987. *The Reading of Imagery in the Chinese Poetic Tradition.* Princeton, NJ: Princeton University Press.

Yue, Meng. 2006. *Shanghai and the Edges of Empires.* Minneapolis: University of Minnesota Press.

Zha, Jianying. 1995. *China Pop: How Soap Operas, Tabloids, and Bestsellers Are Transforming a Culture.* New York: New Press.

Zhang, Henshui. 1997. *Shanghai Express: A Thirties Novel.* Trans. William Lyell. Honolulu: University of Hawaii Press.

Zhang, Xudong. 1997. *Chinese Modernism in the Era of Reforms: Cultural Fever, Avant-Garde Fiction, and the New Chinese Cinema.* Durham, NC: Duke University Press.

———. 2008. *Postsocialism and Cultural Politics: China in the Last Decade of the Twentieth Century.* Durham, NC: Duke University Press.

Zhang, Yimou, and Frances Gateward. 2001. *Zhang Yimou: Interviews.* Jackson: University Press of Mississippi.

Zhang, Yingjin (ed.). 1999. *Cinema and Urban Culture in Shanghai, 1922–1943.* Stanford, CA: Stanford University Press.

———. 2004. *Chinese National Cinema.* London: Routledge.

Zhang, Zhen. 2006. *An Amorous History of the Screen: Shanghai Cinema 1896–1937.* Chicago: University of Chicago Press.

———. 2007. *The Urban Generation: Chinese Cinema and Society at the Turn of the Twenty-First Century.* Durham, NC: Duke University Press.

Zhong, Xueping. 2010. *Mainstream Culture Refocused: Television Drama, Society, and the Production of Meaning in Reform-Era China.* Honolulu: University of Hawaii Press.

Zhuangzi. 1981. *Chuang-Tzu: The Seven Inner Chapters and Other Writings from the Book Chuang-tzu.* Trans. A. C. Graham. London and Boston: Allen and Unwin.

14

Trends and Prospects

Robert E. Gamer

At Chinese New Year celebrations, parents deliver little red packets filled with coins to their children, eat noodles and dumplings, hang small wall signs, and shoot off firecrackers to beseech the gods for prosperity and long life as the future unfolds. We too should think about China's future; it is bound to have an enormous impact on the lives of China's populace and on the rest of the world as well. In the United States, discussion about that future tends to center on these questions:

- Will China stay unified?
- Will China's economy continue to boom?
- What will happen to Hong Kong, Taiwan, and Tibet?
- Will China become more democratic?
- Will China and its peoples blend in as responsible members of the world community?

Scholars like Edward Friedman (1995), Baogang He (2007; He and Guo, 2000; Leib and He, 2010), Shaohua Hu (2000), and Bruce Gilley (2005) focus on factors that may transform China and point it in a democratic direction. Others, like Constance Lever-Tracy, David Ip, and Tracy Noel (1996), Daniel Bell and colleagues (1995), Margaret Pearson (2000), Mary Elizabeth Gallagher (2005), Kellee Tsai (2007), Susan Shirk (2007), Pei Minxin (2008), Bruce Dickson (2008), Rob Gifford (2007:165–169, 229–258, 275–285), Randall Peerenboom (2008), and Teresa Wright (2010) focus on the prospects for a more united and less democratic China; they point to factors that promote continuity but may hold back change, slow economic growth, and lead to unrest. The Naisbitts (2010) foresee "vertical democracy" emerging in China, which will keep it united and growing. Sebastian Heilman and Elizabeth Perry (2011) point to the Maoist system's ability to adapt to new challenges. Like all crystal balls, this one can provide differing scenarios depending on where we set our gaze (Li, 2008; Wong and Bo, 2010:13–54, 365–400; Keith, 2009). Although no one can predict China's future with any certainty, we can make some observations that at least indicate what to look for.

First of all, the authors of this book join most other observers of China in their belief that it is inextricably a major part of the world economy in the twenty-first century. All factions of China's leaders—even those most culturally and politically conservative—and its army are deriving extensive benefits from China's economic dealings with the outside world, which began with the 1978 reforms. So are its people. And the rest of the world has come to rely on China for inexpensive manufactured goods, investment in stocks and bonds, investment capital and aid projects, assistance or at least quiet concurrence in settling disputes, and much else. The chapters on family, women, religion, and popular culture all point to tremendous changes in habits and expectations as a result of the economic changes. Mao Zedong's collectivization and Great Leap Forward institutions helped provide a basis for the township and village enterprises and now the small entrepreneurs that are fueling China's phenomenal economic advance; their new companies can be seen as direct outgrowths of Mao—as natural successors rather than renouncers (Wei, 1998; Chan, Madsen, and Unger, 1984:213ff.; Zhou, 1996; Croll, 1994; Yang, 1996; Heilman and Perry, 2011).

In Chapter 1, I point to some "creative tensions" in China's society. Each of those tensions—between Confucianism and capitalism, Confucianism and Christianity and communism, popular culture and formal traditions, regions and the capital city of Beijing, inward and outward reaching—provide China with reasons both to stay unified and to undergo social and political division.

Today, the snapping points on all those tensions are located in the vicinity of Hong Kong and Taiwan. Because Hong Kong and Taiwan are inherent parts of China's economic growth, its prosperity would be very hard to maintain without them; yet the leverage this clout gives them frightens many Beijing leaders and can lead to serious miscalculations. Likewise, calls for greater political openness by Internet bloggers and by Tibetans and minorities in the western provinces among some leaders rouse fears in Beijing that the country could break apart; that has resulted in stern measures against those activists and regions, accompanied by appeals to nationalism, which in turn rouse fears among foreign investors and governments, potentially endangering growth.

Growth will also be endangered if China does not tackle the serious macroeconomic, legal, demographic, social, and environmental problems it confronts—the most serious being the growing disparity between urban and rural and rich and poor, and the melting of glaciers and lowering of water tables. China is developing within itself a new generation of citizens who want these problems solved and their nation to be strong but are skeptical of socialist, capitalist, and democratic ideological solutions. They want to see new approaches but are unsure what they might be. Mette Hansen and Rune Svarverud (2010), James Fallows (2009), Rob Gifford (2007), Zachary Mexico (2009), Lisa Rofel (2007), Xinran Xinran (2010), Peter Hessler (2010), Leslie Chang (2008), Jay Dautcher (2009), Matthew Niederhauser (2009), Leo Ou-fan Lee (2008), Li Zhang and Athwa Ong (2008), Li Zhang (2010), Cheng Li (2010), Michael Dutton and colleagues (2010), Lijia Zhang (2008), Allen Carlson and Mary Gallagher (2010), and Joseph Fewsmith (2010) all offer highly readable introductions to this new mindset. As the old guard retires, this new generation—which is connected to the Internet (over 500 million Chinese, mostly young, are online) and increasingly conversant in English—is taking command of important institutional positions and generating a debate (discussed in Chapter 4) about how China can develop a Chinese-style "civil society" to tackle its problems (Zheng, 2007; Tai, 2006; Zhou, 2005; Yang, 2009). They dislike corruption, greed, mismanagement, the widening gap between rich and poor, and a government run by unelected "princelings" who choose their own successors. Some lean toward greater liberalization, while those in the "new left"—who want a return to the egalitarian values of Mao, but adapted to the new age—have been gaining popularity in intellectual circles, as Charles Laughlin discusses in Chapter 13.

Anyone looking at the books by the authors mentioned above will notice that the attitudes expressed by the people interviewed in them do not lend themselves cleanly to the black-and-white world of the "Orientalists," who write about "the Asian mind" (e.g., organization and control) as being something separate from "the Western mind" (e.g., competition and consumption) or, at the other extreme, as thinking the same way we in the West do. (To introduce yourself to Orientalist approaches, see Said, 1979; Isaacs, 1958; Wittfogel, 1981; Tu, 1995; Hodder, 2000; Jesperson, 1999; Munro, 2001; Vukovich, 2011; and Cohen, 2010.) Samuel P. Huntington's notion that there will be a "clash of civilizations" pitting China and Islamic areas against the West derives from such Orientalism (Huntington, 1998; Gamer, 1994). Bo Yang's *Ugly Chinaman* and the *River Elegy* television series discussed in Chapter 13 also views the two worlds in this way. Richard Madsen (1995) suggests that such attempts to explain the two worlds in simple terms create myths that are often a reflection of what we want to believe about ourselves: the Asians' old communitarian civilization with a respect for authority and concern for social order is becoming more like our new industrial civilization, and hence it will transform into a democratic society dominated by pragmatic technocrats. Occidentalist approaches (see Buruma and Margalit, 2004; Chen and Dai, 2003) adopted by some in Islamic areas and China that view the West as inducing societies to seek only profit and material comfort turn this dichotomous thinking on its head. Madsen points out that thinking like this ignores the reality of what we are (e.g., truly pragmatic and democratic, or selfless and spiritual?), and that this thinking must confront reversals like the 1989 massacre at Tiananmen Square and the attack on the World Trade Center in New York on September 11, 2001, conducted by individuals educated in the modern technocratic tradition. Does modernization inherently move people away from traditional ways of thinking? And Erica Fox Brindley (2010) argues that China's traditional thought has celebrated individualism all along. Madsen suggests that we explore

> new moral visions . . . new American and Chinese dreams, drawing sacred power from the most resonant aspirations of their cultural traditions. These new moral visions would enable Americans, Chinese, and other peoples of the world to recognize the limitations as well as the strengths and insights of their various traditions; they would encourage them not only to tolerate but also to learn from each other and give them a realistic hope that they could see a new way forward to a just and prosperous world community. (1995:227)

The creative tensions that offer hope for China by counseling moderation at the same time make it difficult to solve problems. Hill Gates (1996) captures this dilemma succinctly. She sees part of China's strength deriving from a tension between what she calls China's petty capitalism and its tributary system. China's family-centered Confucian tradition gave families the incentive to set up small capitalist enterprises to support and enrich their members; it also gave state officials the ability to "capture" and exact tribute from those enterprises, but in a form that would keep the enterprises going and the money flowing. This spurred the economy, helped keep China unified, and turned China into the world's greatest economic powerhouse all the way to the nineteenth century (Frank, 1998). The arrival of Western capitalism threatened to upset this delicate balance. Its calls for open markets, contract law, and rewards for people on the basis of ability assaulted the "nepotism," relationships (*guanxi*), layers of bureaucracy, and state controls on which the old system had been based for centuries. As author after author has indicated in this book, those Confucian values are still alive and well (see also Senghaas, 2001; Wong, 2000). Ironically, they are also a strong part of the reason why China's economy is thriving as part of the world capitalist system. In Gates's words:

> East Asia is becoming Number One not because its social formations are becoming more capitalist but because the dynamic of a tributary mode that has captured a petty-capitalist one is geared up yet further by the capture of [world] capitalism. . . . The Chinese petty capitalist mode of production does not generate all the organizations and ideology necessary to extricate the Chinese from their persisting problems. But it contains some of them and is, in any case, the cultural raw material from which their future must,

> inevitably, be forged. The effort to achieve social justice and a human social formation there will not succeed unless and until the Chinese take seriously their own popular traditions. (1996:276, 280)

This is where the dilemma lies: the more seriously Chinese take their traditions, the less likely they are to accept democratic reforms like a fair and impartial judicial system, protection of patents and other intellectual property rights, or the removal of government controls on business or free speech. Yet those traditions are responsible for the thrift, hard work, and entrepreneurial acumen of tightly knit families capable of setting up small businesses that have been powering China's economic resurgence. Gates is pointing directly at the problem. The Chinese must hold on to those values while seeking solutions to problems that can potentially derail economic development and while fostering universities and businesses at the cutting edge of innovation. And the family businesses must be willing to pass decisionmaking into the hands of professional managers who can let them grow beyond their family roots. And they must learn to deal with Hong Kong, Tibet, and Taiwan in new ways. In its long history, China's ideology has absorbed many challenges and will try to do so again. But China will seek its own solutions to such problems; they cannot be imposed from the outside world. The question is whether free markets and safe commercial contracts can be combined with the demands of *guanxi* and devotion to state and family. Gordon Redding (1990) extends this discussion to the entire Chinese diaspora.

In Chapter 3, Rhoads Murphey points to traditions of technology, from irrigated paddy to bamboo carrying poles, that endure even after the technological and industrial revolution has swept in from the West. Likewise, in Chapter 12, Chan Hoiman and Ambrose King point to the resilience of Confucian *guanxi* relationships. They say, "This streak of conservatism can be both a blessing and a curse for China's enigmatic transition into the modern world." It is a selective conservatism, stressing traditions that best suit the moment. These private networks of achieved social relationships may be weakening the open institutional channels of social organization that are also part of the Confucian tradition, resisting social change and ignoring the needs of those to whom they do not owe direct obligations (and thus undermining efforts like those Gates describes to achieve social justice and a human social formation) even as their members rush to acquire the latest designer clothes, electronic gear, fast foods, and blue jeans to wear in trendy karaoke bars. In Chapter 13, Charles Laughlin, noting that "boisterousness" may be one of the defining characteristics and values of Chinese popular culture, points to the current popularity of sex manuals, pornography, martial arts, chivalric mythical heroes, outlaws, police work, and action films—not the sort of fare that focuses on social change or obligations. Laurel Bossen indicates in Chapter 11 that the clearest advances for women have been the chance to earn and spend cash income on "frenzied consumer choices" of cosmetics, clothes, and home appliances. In Chapter 10, Zang Xiaowei points out that having their own incomes gives women greater freedom to choose and divorce their mates. Yet both authors indicate that women remain heavily influenced by their fathers and husbands and are loyal to patriarchal institutions and patrilineages. All the trends surveyed by these authors—the enduring technologies, continuing *guanxi,* consumerism, recreation, and loyalty to patriarchal institutions—keep alive small capitalist enterprises and the ability of officials to exact tribute from them. The question remains whether China also can develop greater adaptation to the outside world and take the steps toward economic openness Sarah Tong and John Wong outline in Chapter 5.

Taiwan, Singapore, South Korea, Malaysia, and other Asian countries have made great strides in democratizing their societies and modernizing their economies (Lim, Siddique, and Feng, 2011). These countries, however, do not face the task of unifying large and diverse populations and territories and defending a large land base against powerful foreign competitors, and they do not contain large numbers of people still largely out of contact with the outside world. The thousands of disputes every year between villagers and their leaders serve as a warning; over the millennia, China's economy, resources, water controls, transportation, and bureaucracies have become heavily intertwined. Increasingly, modern investments cross provincial boundaries.

Part of what has brought modernity to the smaller Asian states also supports solidarity of the larger whole: the role of the overseas Chinese. As explained in Chapter 6, China is the base from which their economic power evolved. Today, many of the *guanxi* connections that hold together their power revolve around China. A turbulent and divided China would disturb not only those connections but also the stability of Asia's business climate. If problems of weak currencies and insolvent businesses and banks (notice Sarah Tong and John Wong's warning about "policy lending"), which have affected neighboring nations to varying degrees, were to bring a vast downturn to China's economy, the effect would be felt throughout the region. Of course, another factor that could disturb peace in Asia would be a militant China challenging Malaysia or Vietnam or the Philippines to control islands and oil under the sea, or confronting India over Tibetan borders, or—most frighteningly—provoking conflict across the Taiwan Strait. Other Asian governments may wish to see China unified but not too militarily powerful, a country devoted to peace and not to war. That, too, depends on the continuance of China's economic growth. If, in fact, this growth continues, China can provide a vast market and investment target for the other countries of Asia and serve as the nucleus of a powerful Asian economy (for speculation on these prospects, see Redding, 1990; Seagrave, 1995; Lever-Tracy, Ip, and Noel, 1996; Brown, 2000; Gambe, 2000; Ash, 2006; Chung, 2006; Meredith, 2007:188–216; Dittmer and Liu, 2006; Li, 2009; and Subramanian, 2011).

In the words of Ma Rong (Chapter 8), "China has never been able to survive with two nations, one rich and one poor." As Rhoads Murphey explains, when dynasties stopped addressing pressing social problems, revolt tended to ensue. As Sarah Tong and John Wong explain, the new economy is widening the gap between rich and poor, urban and rural (Unger, 2002; Whyte, 2010; Davis, 2009; Huang, 2008; Liao, 2009; Xinran, 2010). Considerable civil unrest is already emerging over this. Beijing is addressing that problem with massive development inland combined with repression of dissent. But that development brings land takeovers that remove people from their homes, stagnant incomes, higher costs for food and housing and other essentials, large amounts of corruption, shoddy construction, rising production costs, disruption of culture and communities, and other new problems that anger people and need to be addressed (Oi, Rozelle, and Zhou, 2010).

Nature may provide its own curbs to economic reform. Up to this point, China's growth has depended on cheap credit, land, and energy. China's people must eat, drink, breathe, and retain continued access to natural resources. Degradation resulting from economic development and the continuing rise in population endanger China's ability to sustain adequate supplies of food, water, fresh air, and other staples—not to mention electricity, petroleum, timber, and other requisites of modern economic development (Elvin, 2006; Economy, 2005). Rhoads Murphey explains in Chapter 3 that degradation of the environment has always been a problem when population grows. With the unprecedented growth of population Ma Rong (Chapter 8) discusses, will the new measures to protect the environment that I (Chapter 4), Sarah Tong and John Wong (Chapter 5), and Richard Edmonds (Chapter 9) discuss be adequate to bring that degradation under control—especially the decline in water resources (Ma, 2004)? If not, agricultural yields may decline and even world markets may not be able to supply adequate food for China's people. This possibility could result in starving children, reduced food consumption, lower resistance to disease (which can spread around the world during flu and pneumonia season, as was demonstrated by the 2003 SARS outbreak), and the diversion of economic resources away from growth activities. This makes it imperative that China continue to work at home and with international organizations to find solutions to these pressing problems. They are unlikely to be solved without cooperation at a worldwide level and without expansion of the rights of Chinese citizens to discuss all these problems.

China's prospects for unity, continued economic boom, movement toward democracy, and peaceful absorption into the world community therefore depend on the policies the country's leaders will be willing to craft, and on good fortune in carrying them out. A source of China's strength lies in the interdependence of its regions. Rhoads Murphey points to the extensive cultural advances that emanated from the seagoing south while the inward-centered north imposed order; as Ma Rong says, the market economy those coastal people supply has been at its liveliest when effective rulers unify great portions of the country. The longer-term prospects for Tibet and the western provinces are more murky. Ma Rong, referring to the regions Stanley Toops introduces in Chapter 2 as China Proper and the Frontier, points to the "tie and tension between the interior and the coast"; although many in those regions have reasons to desire greater cultural autonomy, it would be hard for them to advance economically on their own. And with the extensive urbanization and economic development discussed in Chapters 4, 5, 6, and 8, compounded by Han immigration, they are no longer entirely culturally separate. Yet as Chapter 6 indicates, Tibet's religious traditions stand in contrast to those of China. Islam, the religion of many inhabitants of the vast western provinces, is even further removed from Chinese culture; it does not even share any common Buddhist themes. Like Christianity, it allows for belief in immortality, ecstasy, and salvation in heaven for individuals by an omnipotent supreme God, with punishment in hell for those who reject the appeal of his prophet on earth. In the words of Chan and King in Chapter 12, such religions can be "tolerated as perhaps harmless pastimes for a worn-out nation" but not accepted if they "run counter to national interest." The suicide bomber seeking immortality through ecstatic detonation certainly runs counter to national interest and to Han experience; milder forms of such ecstasy might easily be misconstrued as running counter to those values as well. Yet, if China is to develop a secular syncretism between its values and those of the outside, it must develop a spiritual syncretism as well.

It is unlikely that China will adopt Western-style democracy in any kind of foreseeable future. But it is also unlikely that China can again withdraw from the world; China and overseas Chinese have become too absorbed into the world economy, and the world economy has become too dependent on China, to allow for retreat. Long-time China watcher James Fallows notes that "so many people have so much to lose from any radical change, that the country's own buffering forces would contain a disruption even if the government weren't cracking down so hard. . . . An uneasy status quo might go on indefinitely" (2011:58). China has the resources, human and natural, to sustain economic growth and political unity. And behind its diversity of interests and beliefs lies a widespread reservoir of commitment to sustain that growth and unity.

Still, China's government has much cause for worry. It has relied on massive building of infrastructure and housing, high domestic savings, and a heavy stream of exports bolstered by low labor costs and an undervalued yuan, to fuel its dynamic economic growth. That leaves it vulnerable to uncertainties of fluctuating global markets and overextended bank loans. Its growth is slowing, and some capital is fleeing. Now it needs to create more domestic consumers to buy all these vacant new housing flats, cars, and other products from its millions of factories and stores (World Bank, 2012). To do that, it must deal with some problem solving for which it is ill equipped. The many Chinese citizens who face rising unemployment, low wages, poor welfare services, and rapidly rising prices cannot make big purchases or save a lot, and they are prone to be unhappy about that, especially when they watch their richest neighbors driving around in BMWs and Masaratis. Meanwhile, environmental degradation threatens water supplies, public health, and the quality of life. Yet, if individuals cannot organize and exercise free speech, if the national government cannot control the excesses of provincial and local officials and enterprises, and if entrepreneurs cannot adapt to new knowledge-based innovation, it is increasingly difficult to raise wages, provide adequate unemployment compensation and health insurance and pensions (for aging couples with only one child to help support them), improve access to quality education, curb inflation, slow the rising gap between rich and poor, and protect the environment. The process of passing along power to party princelings isolates the top leadership from experiencing these realities and makes them wary of trying new policies. And the new generation of tweeters and bloggers, who do experience these realities, are not experienced at organizing and thinking through how to combat them.

If China is to achieve a civil society that can hold on to its strengths as its role in the global economy grows, education may be the biggest challenge of all. Can it develop a responsible commitment to seeking the truth, to solving problems, and to confronting officials with forewarnings that their policies may be at variance with both? That will not be easy.

Bibliography

Angle, Stephen C. 2002. *Human Rights and Chinese Thought: A Cross-Cultural Inquiry.* Cambridge: Cambridge University Press.

Ash, Robert, David Shambaugh, and Seichiro Takagi (eds.). 2006. *China Watching: Perspectives from Europe, Japan, and the United States.* London: Routledge.

Baken, Borge. 2000. *The Exemplary Society: Human Improvement, Social Control, and the Dangers of Modernity in China.* Oxford: Oxford University Press.

Bell, Daniel, David Brown, Kanishka Jayasuriya, and David Martin Jones. 1995. *Towards Illiberal Democracy in Pacific Asia.* New York: St. Martin's.

Blum, Susan D., and Lionel M. Jensen (eds.). 2002. *China Off Center: Mapping the Margins of the Middle Kingdom.* Honolulu: University of Hawaii Press.

Brindley, Erica Fox. 2010. *Individualism in Early China: Human Agency and the Self in Thought and Politics.* Honolulu: University of Hawaii Press.

Brown, Rajeswary Ampalavanar. 2000. *Chinese Big Business and the Wealth of Asian Nations.* New York: Palgrave.

Buruma, Ian. 2002. *Bad Elements: Chinese Rebels from Los Angeles to Beijing.* New York: Vintage.

Buruma, Ian, and Avishai Margalit. 2004. *Occidentalism: The West in the Eyes of Its Enemies.* New York: Penguin.

Carlson, Allen, and Mary E. Gallagher (eds.). 2010. *Contemporary Chinese Politics: New Sources, Methods, and Field Strategies.* New York: Cambridge University Press.

Chan, Anita, Richard Madsen, and Jonathan Unger. 1984. *Chen Village: The Recent*

History of a Peasant Community in Mao's China. Berkeley: University of California Press.

Chang, Leslie T. 2008. *Factory Girls: From Village to City in a Changing China.* New York: Spiegel and Grau.

Chen, Xiaomei, and Dai Jinhua. 2003. *Occidentalism: A Theory of Counter-Discourse in Post-Mao China.* 2nd ed. Lanham, MD: Rowman and Littlefield.

Chung, Jae Ho (ed.). 2006. *Charting China's Future: Political, Social, and International Dimensions.* Lanham, MD: Rowman and Littlefield.

Cohen, Paul A. 2010. *Discovering History in China: American Historical Writing on the Recent Chinese Past.* New York: Columbia University Press.

Croll, Elizabeth. 1994. *From Heaven to Earth: Images and Experiences of Development in China.* London: Routledge.

Dautcher, Jay. 2009. *Down a Narrow Road: Masculinity and Identity in a Uyghur Community in Xinjiang China.* Cambridge, MA: Harvard University Asia Center.

Davis, Deborah. 2009. *Creating Wealth and Poverty in Post-Socialist China.* Stanford, CA: Stanford University Press.

Dickson, Bruce J. 2008. *Wealth into Power: The Communist Party's Embrace of China's Private Sector.* Cambridge: Cambridge University Press.

Dittmer, Lowell, and Guoli Liu (eds.). 2006. *China's Deep Reform: Domestic Politics in Transition.* Lanham, MD: Rowman and Littlefield.

Dutton, Michael, Hsiu-Ju Stacy Lo, and Dong Dong Wu. 2010. *Beijing Time.* Cambridge, MA: Harvard University Press.

Economy, Elizabeth. 2005. *The River Runs Black: The Environmental Challenge to China's Future.* Ithaca, NY: Cornell University Press.

Elvin, Mark. 2006. *The Retreat of the Elephants: An Environmental History of China.* New Haven, CT: Yale University Press.

Fallows, James. 2009. *Postcards from Tomorrow Square: Reports from China.* New York: Vintage.

———. 2011. "Arab Spring, Chinese Winter." *The Atlantic,* September.

Fewsmith, Joseph (ed.). 2010. *China Today, China Tomorrow: Domestic Politics, Economy, and Society.* Lanham, MD: Rowman and Littlefield.

Frank, Andre Gunder. 1998. *REORIENT: Global Economy in the Asian Age.* Berkeley: University of California Press.

Friedman, Edward. 1995. *National Identity and Democratic Prospects in Socialist China.* Armonk, NY: M. E. Sharpe.

Gallagher, Mary Elizabeth. 2005. *Contagious Capitalism: Globalization and the Politics of Labor in China.* Princeton, NJ: Princeton University Press.

Gambe, Annabelle. 2000. *Overseas Chinese Entrepreneurship and Capitalist Development in Southeast Asia.* New York: Palgrave.

Gamer, Robert E. 1994. "Modernization and Democracy in China: Samuel P. Huntington and the 'Neo-Authoritarian' Debate." *Asian Journal of Political Science* 2(1): 32–63.

Garnaut, Ross, Guo Shutian, and Ma Guonan (eds.). 1996. *The Third Revolution in the Chinese Countryside.* Cambridge: Cambridge University Press.

Gates, Hill. 1996. *China's Motor: A Thousand Years of Petty Capitalism.* Ithaca, NY: Cornell University Press.

Gerth, Karl. 2004. *China Made: Consumer Culture and the Creation of the Nation.* Cambridge, MA: Harvard University Asia Center.

Gifford, Rob. 2007. *China Road: A Journey into the Future of a Rising Power.* New York: Random House.

Gilley, Bruce. 2005. *China's Democratic Future: How It Will Happen and Where It Will Lead.* New York: Columbia University Press.

Hansen, Mette Halskov, and Rune Svarverud (eds.). 2010. *iChina: The Rise of the Individual in Modern Chinese Society.* Honolulu: University of Hawaii Press.

He, Baogang. 2007. *Rural Democracy in China: The Role of Village Elections.* New York: Palgrave Macmillan.

He, Baogang, and Yingji Guo. 2000. *Nationalism, National Identity, and Democratization in China.* Burlington, VT: Ashgate.

Heilman, Sebastian, and Elizabeth J. Perry. 2011. *Mao's Invisible Hand: The Political Foundations of Adaptive Governance in China.* Cambridge, MA: Harvard University Asia Center.

Hessler, Peter. 2010. *Country Driving: A Journey Through China from Farm to Factory.* New York: Harper.

Hodder, Rupert. 2000. *In China's Image: Chinese Self-Perception in Western Thought.* New York: Palgrave.

Hu, Shaohua. 2000. *Explaining Chinese Democratization.* Westport, CT: Praeger.

Huang, Yasheng. 2008. *Capitalism with Chinese Characteristics: Entrepreneurship and the State.* Cambridge: Cambridge University Press.

Huntington, Samuel P. 1998. *The Clash of Civilizations and the Remaking of World Order.* New York: Touchstone.

Isaacs, Harold R. 1958. *Scratches on Our Minds: American Views of China and India.* New York: John Day.

Jenner, W. J. F. 1994. *The Tyranny of History: The Roots of China's Crisis.* London: Penguin.

Jesperson, T. Christopher. 1999. *American Images of China, 1931–1949.* Stanford, CA: Stanford University Press.

Keith, Roland C. 2009. *China From the Inside Out: Fitting the People's Republic Into the World.* New York: Pluto Press.

Lee, Leo Ou-fan. 2008. *City Between Worlds: My Hong Kong.* Cambridge, MA: Belknap Press of Harvard University.

Leib, Ethan J., and Baogang He (eds.). 2010. *The Search for Deliberative Democracy in China.* New York: Palgrave.

Lever-Tracy, Constance, David Ip, and Tracy Noel. 1996. *The Chinese Diaspora and Mainland China: An Emerging Economic Synergy.* New York: St. Martin's.

Li, Cheng (ed.). 2008. *China's Changing Political Landscape: Prospects for Democracy.* Washington, DC: Brookings Institution.

——— (ed.). 2010. *China's Emerging Middle Class: Beyond Economic Transformation.* Washington, DC: Brookings Institution.

Li, Minqi. 2009. *The Rise of China and the Demise of the Capitalist World Economy.* New York: Monthly Review Press.

Liao, Yiwu. 2009. *The Corpse Walker: Real Life Stories, China From the Bottom Up.* Trans. Wen Huang. New York: Anchor.

Lim, William S. W., Sharon Siddique, and Tan Dan Feng (eds.). 2011. *Singapore Shifting Boundaries: Social Change in the Early 21st Century.* Singapore: Asian Urban Lab and Select Books.

Ma, Jun. 2004. *China's Water Crisis.* Norwalk, CT: Eastbridge.

Madsen, Richard. 1984. *Morality and Power in a Chinese Village.* Berkeley: University of California Press.

———. 1995. *China and the American Dream: A Moral Inquiry.* Berkeley: University of California Press.

Meredith, Robyn. 2007. *The Elephant and the Dragon: The Rise of India and China.* New York: W. W. Norton.

Mexico, Zachary. 2009. *China Underground.* New York: Soft Skull Press.

Munro, Donald J. 2001. *The Concept of Man in Contemporary China.* Ann Arbor: University of Michigan Press.

Naisbitt, John, and Doris Naisbitt. 2010. *China's Megatrends: The 8 Pillars of a New Society.* New York: Harper.

Niederhauser, Matthew. 2009. *Sound Kapital: Beijing's Music Underground.* Brooklyn, NY: Powerhouse Cultural Entertainment.

Oi, Jean C., Scott Rozelle, and Xueguang Zhou (eds.). 2010. *Growing Pains: Tensions and Opportunity in China's Transformation.* Stanford, CA: Asia-Pacific Research Center.

Pearson, Margaret M. 2000. *China's New Business Elite: The Political Consequences of Economic Reform.* Berkeley: University of California Press.

Peerenboom, Randall. 2008. *China Modernizes: The Threat to the West or Model for the Rest?* New York: Oxford University Press.

Pei, Minxin. 2008. *China's Trapped Transition: The Limits of Developmental Autocracy.* Cambridge, MA: Harvard University Press.

Redding, S. Gordon. 1990. *The Spirit of Chinese Capitalism.* Berlin: Walter de Gruyter.

Rofel, Lisa. 2007. *Desiring China: Experiments in Neoliberalism, Sexuality, and Public Culture.* Durham, NC: Duke University Press.

Said, Edward W. 1979. *Orientalism.* New York: Pantheon.

Seagrave, Sterling. 1995. *Lords of the Rim.* New York: G. P. Putnam.

Senghaas, Dieter. 2001. *The Clash Within Civilizations: Coming to Terms with Cultural Conflicts.* London: Routledge.

Shirk, Susan. 2007. *China: Fragile Superpower.* Oxford: Oxford University Press.

Spence, Jonathan. 1999. *The Chan's Great Continent: China in Western Minds.* New York: W. W. Norton.

Subramanian, Arvind. 2011. *Eclipse: Living in the Shadow of China's Economic Dominance.* Washington, DC: Institute for International Economics.

Tai, Zixue. 2006. *The Internet in China: Cyberspace and Civil Society.* London: Routledge.

Tsai, Kellee S. 2007. *Capitalism Without Democracy: The Private Sector in Contemporary China.* Ithaca, NY: Cornell University Press.

Tu, Wei-ming. 1995. "Cultural China: The Periphery as the Center." In *The Living Tree: The Changing Meaning of Being Chinese,* edited by Wei-ming Tu, 1–34. Stanford, CA: Stanford University Press.

Unger, Jonathan. 2002. *The Transformation of Rural China.* Armonk, NY: M. E. Sharpe.

Vukovich, Daniel. 2011. *China and Orientalism: Western Knowledge Production and the PRC.* London: Routledge.

Wei, Pan. 1998. *The Politics of Marketization in Rural China.* Lanham, MD: Rowman and Littlefield.

Weston, Timothy B., and Lionel M. Jensen. 2000. *China Beyond the Headlines.* Lanham, MD: Rowman and Littlefield.

Whyte, Martin King (ed.). 2010. *One Country, Two Societies: Rural-Urban Inequality in Contemporary China.* Cambridge, MA: Harvard University Press.

Wittfogel, Karl August. 1981. *Oriental Despotism: A Comparative Study of Total Power.* New York: Random House.

Wong, John, and Zhiyu Bo. 2010. *China's Reform in Global Perspective.* Singapore: World Scientific.

Wong, R. Bin. 2000. *China Transformed: Historical Change and the Limits of European Experience*. Ithaca, NY: Cornell University Press.
World Bank and Development Research Center. 2012. *China 2030: Building a Modern, Harmonious, and Creative High-Income Society*. http://www.worldbank.org.
Wright, Teresa. 2010. *Accepting Authoritarianism: State-Society Relations in China's Reform Era*. Stanford, CA: Stanford University Press.
Xinran, Xinran. 2010. *China Witness: Voices from a Silent Generation*. New York: Anchor.
Yang, Dali L. 1996. *Calamity and Reform in China: Rural Society and Institutional Change Since the Great Leap Famine*. Stanford, CA: Stanford University Press.
Yang, Guobin. 2009. *The Power of the Internet in China: Citizen Activism Online*. New York: Columbia University Press.
Zhang, Li. 2010. *In Search of Paradise: Middle Class Living in a Chinese Metropolis*. Ithaca, NY: Cornell University Press.
Zhang, Li, and Athwa Ong (eds.). 2008. *Privatizing China: Socialism from Afar*. Ithaca, NY: Cornell University Press.
Zhang, Lijia. 2008. *"Socialism Is Great!" A Worker's Memoir of the New China*. New York: Atlas.
Zheng, Yongnian. 2007. *Technological Empowerment: The Internet, State, and Society in China*. Stanford, CA: Stanford University Press.
Zhou, Kate Xiao. 1996. *How the Farmers Changed China: Power of the People*. Boulder: Westview.
Zhou, Yongming. 2005. *Historicizing Online Politics: Telegraphy, the Internet, and Political Participation in China*. Stanford, CA: Stanford University Press.

The Contributors

Laurel Bossen is professor emerita of anthropology at McGill University, Monteal, Quebec, and a Radcliffe Institute for Advanced Study Fellow.

Chan Hoiman is associate professor of sociology at the Chinese University of Hong Kong.

Richard Louis Edmonds is visiting professor in geographical studies at the University of Chicago, lecturer in the Hopkins-in-Nanjing Study Abroad Program, and former editor of the *China Quarterly.*

Robert E. Gamer is professor emeritus of political science at the University of Missouri, Kansas City.

Ambrose Y. C. King is professor emeritus of sociology at the Chinese University of Hong Kong.

Charles A. Laughlin is professor of Chinese literature and Weedon Chair in East Asian Studies at the University of Virginia.

Ma Rong is associate director of the Institute of Sociology and Anthropology, Beijing University.

Rhoads Murphey is professor emeritus of history at the University of Michigan, Ann Arbor.

Sarah Y. Tong, an economist, is a researcher with the East Asian Institute at the National University of Singapore.

Stanley W. Toops is associate professor of geography and international studies at Miami University in Oxford, Ohio.

John Wong is professor of economics and research director at the East Asian Institute at the National University of Singapore.

Zang Xiaowei is professor of sociology and head of the School of East Asian Studies at the University of Sheffield, UK.

Index

About the Book

The new edition of Understanding Contemporary China has been thoroughly revised to reflect a half-decade of significant events and trends, both domestically and in the international arena. The result is an accessible, well-grounded exploration of the most crucial issues affecting China today.

The authors assume no prior knowledge on the part of the reader, making the book a perfect choice for interdisciplinary "Introduction to China" courses, as well as for courses in political science and sociology. Numerous maps and photographs enhance the text.

Robert E. Gamer is professor emeritus of political science at the University of Missouri, Kansas City. His publications include *Governments and Politics in a Changing World, The Politics of Urban Development in Singapore,* and *The Developing Nations: A Comparative Perspective.*